McDougal Littell Middle School

COURSE 1 Math

Larson   Boswell   Kanold   Stiff

McDougal Littell
A HOUGHTON MIFFLIN COMPANY

Evanston, Illinois   •   Boston   •   Dallas

From the Authors...

Ron Larson

"My goal is to write books that are mathematically correct, instructionally sound, and student friendly."

I think of myself as a facilitator of teaching and learning — writing instructional materials that teachers have told me they need. Over the years, my greatest input has come from the thousands of teachers who have used our books in real classes with real students. Based on this input, we have written books that meet a variety of teaching and learning needs.

Ron Larson is a professor of mathematics at Penn State University at Erie, where he has taught since receiving his Ph.D. in mathematics from the University of Colorado. Dr. Larson is well known as the author of a comprehensive program for mathematics that spans middle school, high school, and college courses. Dr. Larson's numerous professional activities keep him in constant touch with the needs of teachers and supervisors. He closely follows developments in mathematics standards and assessment.

Laurie Boswell

"To reach all students, you need to address different learning styles."

As a mathematics teacher, I quickly learned that to engage all students, I needed to provide for different learning styles. I also learned the importance of designing lessons that would challenge and motivate students. Using a balance of direct instruction, student-engaged activities, and meaningful communication has enabled me to help all students learn.

Laurie Boswell is the mathematics department chair at Profile Junior-Senior High School in Bethlehem, New Hampshire. A recipient of the Presidential Award for Excellence in Mathematics Teaching, she has also been a Tandy Technology Scholar. She serves on the National Council of Teachers of Mathematics Board of Directors. She speaks frequently on topics related to instructional strategies and course content.

ISBN: 0-618-50814-7   X23456789–DWO–09 08 07 06 05 04   Internet Web Site: http://www.classzone.com

Timothy Kanold

"Balance is the key to successful learning."

The key to creating a middle school math program that will help students be successful is balance — balance between skill development, conceptual understanding, and problem solving strategies; between instruction by the teacher and student discovery; between paper-and-pencil methods and appropriate use of technology.

Timothy Kanold is the superintendent of Adlai E. Stevenson High School District 125, where he served as a teacher and the Director of Mathematics for 16 years. He recently received his Ph.D. from Loyola University Chicago. Dr. Kanold is a recipient of the Presidential Award for Excellence in Mathematics and Science Teaching and served on The Academy Services Committee for NCTM. He is a frequent speaker at mathematics meetings where he shares his in-depth knowledge of mathematics teaching and curriculum.

Lee Stiff

"All students must have opportunities to make continuing progress."

I am proud to be part of an author team that shares my goals and commitment to setting high mathematics standards for all students. Our focus in writing this program has been to help all students acquire the knowledge, skills, and problem-solving abilities they need in order to become successful adults.

Lee Stiff is a professor of mathematics education in the College of Education of North Carolina State University at Raleigh. His extensive experience in mathematics education includes teaching at the middle school and high school levels. He has received the W. W. Rankin Award for Excellence in Mathematics Education, and was Fulbright Scholar to the Department of Mathematics of the University of Ghana. He served as President of the National Council of Teachers of Mathematics (2000–2002).

Advisers and Reviewers

Curriculum Advisers and Reviewers

Donna Foley
Curriculum Specialist for Math
Chelmsford Middle School
Chelmsford, MA

Barbara Nunn
Secondary Mathematics Specialist
Broward County Schools
Fort Lauderdale, FL

Wendy Loeb
Mathematics Teacher
Twin Groves Junior High School
Buffalo Grove, IL

Tom Scott
Resource Teacher
Duval County Public Schools
Jacksonville, FL

Teacher Panels

Florida Panel

Kathy Adams
Mathematics Teacher
Allapattah Middle School
Miami, FL

Micki Hawn
Mathematics Teacher
Pompano Beach Middle School
Pompano Beach, FL

Barbara Schober
Mathematics Department Chair
Okeeheelee Middle School
West Palm Beach, FL

Sue Carrico-Beddow
Mathematics Teacher
Bayonet Point Middle School
New Port Richey, FL

Pat Powell
Mathematics Department Chair
Stewart Middle School
Tampa, FL

Laurie St. Julien
Mathematics Teacher
Oak Grove Middle School
Clearwater, FL

Melissa Grabowski
Mathematics Teacher
Stone Middle School
Melbourne, FL

Kansas and Missouri Panel

Linda Cordes
Department Chair
Paul Robeson Middle School
Kansas City, MO

Rhonda Foote
Mathematics Department Chair
Maple Park Middle School
North Kansas City, MO

Jan Rase
Mathematics Teacher
Moreland Ridge Middle School
Blue Springs, MO

Linda Dodd
Mathematics Department Chair
Argentine Middle School
Kansas City, KS

Cas Kyle
District Math Curriculum Coordinator
Richard A. Warren Middle School
Leavenworth, KS

Dan Schoenemann
Mathematics Teacher
Raytown Middle School
Kansas City, MO

Melanie Dowell
Mathematics Teacher
Raytown South Middle School
Raytown, MO

Texas Panel

Judy Carlin
Mathematics Teacher
Brown Middle School
McAllen, TX

Judith Cody
Mathematics Teacher
Deady Middle School
Houston, TX

Lisa Hiracheta
Mathematics Teacher
Irons Junior High School
Lubbock, TX

Kay Neuse
Mathematics Teacher
Wilson Middle School
Plano, TX

Louise Nutzman
Mathematics Teacher
Sugar Land Middle School
Sugar Land, TX

Clarice Orise
Mathematics Teacher
Tafolla Middle School
San Antonio, TX

Wonda Webb
Mathematics Teacher
William H. Atwell Middle School
and Law Academy
Dallas, TX

Karen Young
Mathematics Teacher
Murchison Elementary School
Pflugerville, TX

Field Test Teachers

Kathryn Chamberlain
McCarthy Middle School
Chelmsford, MA

Sheree Daily
Canal Winchester Middle School
Canal Winchester, OH

Deborah Kebe
Canal Winchester Middle School
Canal Winchester, OH

Jill Leone
Twin Groves Junior High School
Buffalo Grove, IL

Wendy Loeb
Twin Groves Junior High School
Buffalo Grove, IL

Melissa McCarty
Canal Winchester Middle School
Canal Winchester, OH

Deb Mueth
St. Aloysius School
Springfield, IL

Gail Sigmund
Charles A. Mooney Middle School
Cleveland, OH

Teacher Reviewers

Susanne Artiñano
Bryn Mawr School
Baltimore, MD

Lisa Barnes
Bishop Spaugh Academy
Charlotte, NC

Beth Bryan
Sequoyah Middle School
Oklahoma City, OK

Jennifer Clark
Mayfield Middle School
Oklahoma City, OK

Lois Cole
Pickering Middle School
Lynn, MA

Louis Corbosiero
Pollard Middle School
Needham, MA

James Cussen
Candlewood Middle School
Dix Hills, NY

Kristen Dailey
Boardman Center Middle School
Boardman, OH

Shannon Galamore
Clay-Chalkville Middle School
Pinson, AL

Tricia Highland
Moon Area Middle School
Moon Township, PA

Myrna McNaboe
Immaculate Conception
East Aurora, NY

Angela Richardson
Sedgefield Middle School
Charlotte, NC

James Richardson
Booker T. Washington Middle School
Mobile, AL

Dianne Walker
Traverse City Central High School
Traverse City, MI

Stacey Wood
Cochrane Middle School
Charlotte, NC

Course 1 Overview Selected Examples

Algebra Preparation Throughout

Problem Solving in Each Lesson

Unique Test-Taking Features for Each Unit

UNIT 1 Algebraic Thinking, Measurement, and Decimals

CHAPTER 1 Number Sense and Algebraic Thinking

Chapter 1 Highlights

xy ALGEBRA	PS PROBLEM SOLVING	STANDARDIZED TEST PREP
· Patterns, 7–9, 19 · Exponents, 16–20, 25, 45 · Order of Operations, 21–25, 33 · Variables and Expressions, 29–33, 40 · Solving Equations, 36–40, 45	· Guided Problem Solving, 14, 23, 44 · Extended Problem Solving, 32 · Choose a Strategy, 33, 35 · Brain Game, 2, 3, 25, 47	· Multiple Choice, 9, 15, 19, 25, 33, 40, 51 · Short Response, 15, 33, 51 · Extended Response, 45, 51

UNIT 1 Algebraic Thinking, Measurement, and Decimals

CHAPTER 2 Measurement and Statistics

Chapter 2 Highlights

CHAPTER 3 Decimal Addition and Subtraction

Chapter 3 Highlights

XY ALGEBRA	PS PROBLEM SOLVING	STANDARDIZED TEST PREP
· Solving Inequalities, 121 · Variables and Expressions, 133, 137, 139 · Properties, 136–140 · Order of Operations, 140	· Guided Problem Solving, 115, 132, 138 · Extended Problem Solving, 133 · Choose a Strategy, 111, 117, 135 · Brain Game, 104, 105, 123, 143	· Multiple Choice, 111, 117, 121, 128, 140, 147 · Short Response, 128, 140, 147 · Extended Response, 133, 147

UNIT 1　Algebraic Thinking, Measurement, and Decimals

CHAPTER 4　Decimal Multiplication and Division

Chapter 4 Highlights

XY ALGEBRA	PS PROBLEM SOLVING	STANDARDIZED TEST PREP
· Properties, 155, 156, 159–162 · Order of Operations, 157, 184 · Variables and Expressions, 157, 162, 172, 178, 183 · Formulas, 160, 162, 166, 167 · Coordinate Graph, 168 · Solving Equations, 173, 195 · Exponents, 173, 195	· Guided Problem Solving, 171, 182, 193 · Extended Problem Solving, 190, 194 · Choose a Strategy, 157, 186 · Brain Game, 173, 195	· Multiple Choice, 157, 162, 168, 173, 179, 184, 190, 201 · Short Response, 157, 168, 184, 201 · Extended Response, 195, 201

CHAPTER

5 Number Patterns and Fractions

Chapter 5 Highlights

XY ALGEBRA	**PS PROBLEM SOLVING**	**STANDARDIZED TEST PREP**
· Properties, 219 · Solving Equations, 229, 231, 246, 251 · Variables and Expressions, 248 · Formulas, 231	· Guided Problem Solving, 224, 237 · Extended Problem Solving, 218 · Choose a Strategy, 221, 232, 252 · Brain Game, 210, 211, 219, 248	· Multiple Choice, 219, 225, 232, 238, 248, 252, 256 · Short Response, 219, 225, 238 · Extended Response, 242

CHAPTER 6 Addition and Subtraction of Fractions

Chapter 6 Highlights

xy ALGEBRA	PS PROBLEM SOLVING	STANDARDIZED TEST PREP
· Variables and Expressions, 271, 274, 280, 287, 293 · Solving Equations, 274	· Guided Problem Solving, 273, 279 · Extended Problem Solving, 280 · Choose a Strategy, 281, 294, 297 · Brain Game, 275, 303	· Multiple Choice, 270, 275, 281, 288, 294, 307 · Short Response, 270, 281, 307 · Extended Response, 301, 307

UNIT 2 Fraction Concepts, Expressions, and Operations

CHAPTER 7 Multiplication and Division of Fractions

Chapter 7 Highlights

UNIT 3 Proportions, Percent, and Geometry

CHAPTER 8 Ratio, Proportion, and Percent

Chapter 8 Highlights

xy ALGEBRA	PS PROBLEM SOLVING	STANDARDIZED TEST PREP
· Solving Equations, 382–387, 388–391 · Patterns, 378 · Properties, 383 · Variables and Expressions, 383 · Formulas, 389, 391, 408, 409, 411	· Guided Problem Solving, 381 · Extended Problem Solving, 377, 410 · Choose a Strategy, 378, 403, 405 · Brain Game, 378, 413	· Multiple Choice, 378, 382, 387, 391, 398, 410, 417 · Short Response, 387, 398, 410, 417 · Extended Response, 403, 417

UNIT 3 Proportions, Percent, and Geometry

9 Geometric Figures

Chapter 9 Highlights

XY ALGEBRA	PS PROBLEM SOLVING	STANDARDIZED TEST PREP
· Solving Equations, 429, 432, 433, 438–441, 448, 452, 456, 463 · Properties, 434 · Patterns, 452	· Extended Problem Solving, 434, 452 · Choose a Strategy, 453, 459 · Brain Game, 418, 419, 429, 453	· Multiple Choice, 429, 434, 440, 448, 453, 457, 463, 469 · Short Response, 424, 448, 453, 469 · Extended Response, 469

UNIT 3 Proportions, Percent, and Geometry

CHAPTER 10 Geometry and Measurement

Chapter 10 Highlights

XY ALGEBRA	*PS* PROBLEM SOLVING	STANDARDIZED TEST PREP
· Formulas, 475–479, 480–483, 485–490, 491–495, 510–513 · Solving Equations, 477–479, 481–483, 509, 511–513 · Exponents, 489 · Order of Operations, 503	· Guided Problem Solving, 502, 508, 512 · Extended Problem Solving, 513 · Choose a Strategy, 489, 505 · Brain Game, 489, 517	· Multiple Choice, 479, 483, 489, 503, 509, 513, 521 · Short Response, 483, 503, 509, 521 · Extended Response, 495, 521

UNIT 4 Integers, Algebra, and Probability

11 Integers

Chapter 11 Highlights

xy ALGEBRA	PS PROBLEM SOLVING	STANDARDIZED TEST PREP
• Variables and Expressions, 536, 541, 545, 547, 551, 553, 557, 566 • Order of Operations, 547 • Formulas, 553 • Patterns, 553 • Coordinate Graphs, 558, 562–566, 570, 571	• Guided Problem Solving, 564 • Extended Problem Solving, 557 • Choose a Strategy, 558, 561, 571 • Brain Game, 530, 531, 549, 558	• Multiple Choice, 536, 541, 547, 553, 558, 566, 579 • Short Response, 541, 547, 579 • Extended Response, 571, 579

UNIT 4 Integers, Algebra, and Probability

CHAPTER 12 Equations and Functions

Chapter 12 Highlights

XY ALGEBRA	*PS* PROBLEM SOLVING	STANDARDIZED TEST PREP
· Variables and Expressions, 583–586, 601 · Solving Equations, 586, 587–591, 592–595, 596, 597, 598–601, 609, 616 · Graphs, 586, 595, 609, 612–617 · Solving Inequalities, 602, 603 · Functions, 604–609, 612–617	· Guided Problem Solving, 590, 594 · Extended Problem Solving, 591, 616 · Choose a Strategy, 609, 611 · Brain Game, 597, 609	· Multiple Choice, 586, 591, 595, 601, 616, 623 · Short Response, 591, 616, 623 · Extended Response, 609, 623

UNIT 4 Integers, Algebra, and Probability

CHAPTER 13 Probability and Statistics

Chapter 13 Highlights

Contents of Student Resources

Pre-Course Skills and Problem Solving

PRE-COURSE SKILLS

Ongoing Review of Basic Skills

The Mixed Review exercises at the ends of lessons include Basic Skills exercises that provide ongoing practice of pre-course skills. Students also practice basic skills in the Warm-Up Games and the Getting Ready to Learn exercises.

 ## PRE-COURSE PROBLEM SOLVING

Ongoing Practice with Problem Solving Strategies

Opportunities to practice problem solving occur throughout the book:

- A four-step problem solving plan in Lesson 1.7
- Problem Solving in every exercise set
- Guided Problem Solving exercises

- A problem solving strategy featured in every chapter
- Choose a Strategy exercises
- Extended Problem Solving exercises

Diagnostic Test of Skills

 Number Sense and Operations

Whole Numbers *(Skills Review, pp. 684–687)*

Write the number in expanded form and in words.

1. 4586   **2.** 50,423   **3.** 918,437   **4.** 3,540,692

Use a number line to order the numbers from least to greatest.

5. 3, 11, 14, 7, 6, 15   **6.** 17, 11, 6, 0, 3, 5   **7.** 6, 12, 17, 9, 3, 10, 13

Round the number to the place value of the red digit.

8. 18   **9.** 289   **10.** 945   **11.** 2575

Operations with Whole Numbers *(Skills Review, pp. 688–691)*

Find the sum, difference, product, or quotient.

12. 655 + 348   **13.** 3369 + 241   **14.** 965 − 38   **15.** 4580 − 362

16. 46 × 27   **17.** 568 × 73   **18.** 6327 ÷ 9   **19.** 878 ÷ 22

Estimating with Whole Numbers *(Skills Review, pp. 692–695)*

Estimate the sum, difference, product, or quotient.

20. 441 + 333 + 789   **21.** 67 + 72 + 69   **22.** 946 − 487   **23.** 5589 − 1377

24. 246 × 318   **25.** 9333 × 65   **26.** 955 ÷ 89   **27.** 2521 ÷ 32

Find a low and high estimate for the product or quotient.

28. 858 × 29   **29.** 9723 × 44   **30.** 258 ÷ 7   **31.** 95,661 ÷ 5

Operations with Decimals and Fractions *(Skills Review, pp. 698–700)*

Find the sum or difference.

32. 19.6 + 34.7   **33.** 4.67 + 8.53   **34.** 12.55 − 9.39   **35.** 13.88 − 6.32

36. Alex has $12.38, Megan has $14.15, and Katherine has $28.55. How much do they have all together?

Write a fraction to represent the shaded region or part of a set.

37.

38.

Measurement

Units of Time *(Skills Review, p. 701)*

Copy and complete.

39. 6 hours 45 min = _?_ min

40. 4 days 6 hours = _?_ hours

41. 25 days = _?_ weeks _?_ days

42. 32 days = _?_ weeks _?_ days

Geometry

Perimeter and Area *(Skills Review, p. 702)*

Find the perimeter and area.

43.

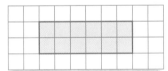

44.

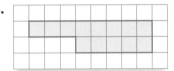

Data Analysis

Reading Bar Graphs and Line Graphs
(Skills Review, pp. 704–705)

In Exercises 45–47, use the bar graph.

45. Which fruit was the least favorite?

46. Which fruit did 10 people vote for?

47. Which fruit got 4 fewer votes than apples did?

In Exercises 48 and 49, use the line graph.

48. In what year were the most books checked out?

49. In what year were 2000 books checked out?

Pictographs *(Skills Review, pp. 706–707)*

50. Make a pictograph of the data in the table.

Grade	3rd	4th	5th	6th
Bottles collected	13	26	36	28

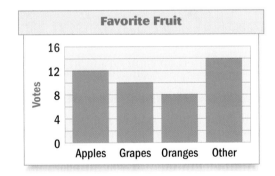

Favorite Fruit

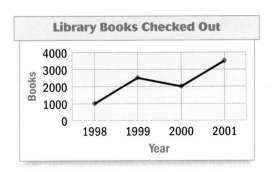

Library Books Checked Out

Skill Practice

Number Sense and Operations

Whole Numbers *(Skills Review, pp. 684–687)*

Write the number in expanded form and in words.

1. 6981   **2.** 60,309   **3.** 817,549   **4.** 2,340,702

Write the number in standard form.

5. $(2 \times 100,000) + (6 \times 1000) + (4 \times 10)$ **6.** seven hundred sixty-one thousand, twelve

Use a number line to order the numbers from least to greatest.

7. 9, 2, 12, 8, 16   **8.** 7, 0, 4, 6, 13   **9.** 7, 5, 16, 8, 12

Compare the numbers.

10. 12 and 17   **11.** 10 and 0   **12.** 17 and 1   **13.** 3 and 9

Round the number to the place value of the red digit.

14. 186   **15.** 2567   **16.** 34,457   **17.** 49,598

In Exercises 18–19, copy and complete the number fact family.

18. $15 - 8 = 7$ $15 - \underline{?} = 8$ $\underline{?} + 7 = 15$ $7 + \underline{?} = \underline{?}$

19. $27 \div 3 = 9$ $9 \times \underline{?} = 27$ $27 \div \underline{?} = 3$ $3 \times \underline{?} = 27$

20. Write a related division equation for $4 \times 8 = 32$.

Operations with Whole Numbers *(Skills Review, pp. 688–691)*

Use a number line to add or subtract the numbers.

21. $9 + 7$ **22.** $7 + 9$ **23.** $6 - 4$ **24.** $11 - 6$

Find the sum or difference.

25. $39 + 17$ **26.** $81 - 58$ **27.** $172 - 45$ **28.** $241 + 63$

29. $446 + 278$ **30.** $2298 + 197$ **31.** $878 - 199$ **32.** $5430 - 186$

Find the product or quotient.

33. 294×64 **34.** 7694×58 **35.** $873 \times 1,000$ **36.** $8753 \times 100,000$

37. $4864 \div 8$ **38.** $892 \div 13$ **39.** $2958 \div 34$ **40.** $7675 \div 25$

Estimating with Whole Numbers *(Skills Review, pp. 692–695)*

Estimate the sum.

41. $321 + 538 + 689$ **42.** $845 + 311 + 196$ **43.** $83 + 78 + 81 + 77$ **44.** $46 + 49 + 52 + 54$

Find a low and high estimate for the difference.

45. $835 - 324$ **46.** $662 - 178$ **47.** $7654 - 2848$ **48.** $3879 - 1428$

Find a low and high estimate for the product.

49. 18×45 **50.** 783×42 **51.** 671×562 **52.** 8912×77

Use compatible numbers to estimate the product.

53. 26×32 **54.** 499×33 **55.** 187×211 **56.** 1109×89

Find a low and high estimate for the quotient.

57. $243 \div 6$ **58.** $754 \div 7$ **59.** $3286 \div 5$ **60.** $5878 \div 6$

Use compatible numbers to estimate the quotient.

61. $864 \div 88$ **62.** $399 \div 27$ **63.** $3806 \div 83$ **64.** $6033 \div 21$

Solving Problems Using Whole Numbers *(Skills Review, pp. 696–698)*

65. Anna collected 245 cans for recycling and Jim collected 382. How many cans did they collect in all?

66. Last week a family spent $145 on groceries. This week they spent $183. How much more did they spend on groceries this week than last week?

67. There are 24 cans of soda in a case. You need 600 cans of soda for a school dance. How many cases do you need to buy?

68. You buy a book for $8.95. How much change should you receive from a $10.00 bill?

Operations with Decimals and Fractions *(Skills Review, pp. 699–700)*

Find the sum or difference.

69. $3.87 + 9.63$ **70.** $11.66 + 8.49$ **71.** $19.1 - 11.7$ **72.** $55.76 - 7.98$

Write a fraction to represent the shaded region or part of a set.

73.    **74.**    **75.**

Measurement

Units of Time *(Skills Review, p. 701)*

Copy and complete.

76. 5 hours 15 min = _?_ min

77. 18 days = _?_ weeks _?_ days

78. 50 hours = _?_ days _?_ hours

79. 310 sec = _?_ min _?_ sec

Geometry

Perimeter and Area *(Skills Review, p. 702)*

Find the perimeter.

80.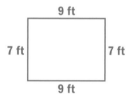

81.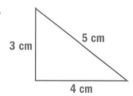

82.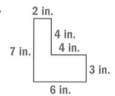

Find the area.

83.

84.

85.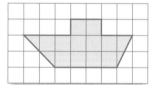

Data Analysis

Venn Diagrams and Logical Reasoning *(Skills Review, p. 703)*

86. Draw a Venn diagram of the set of whole numbers less than 18 where set *A* consists of multiples of 4 and set *B* consists of multiples of 6.

87. Use the Venn diagram in Exercise 86. If a number is in set *A*, is it *always, sometimes,* or *never* in set *B*?

88. Use the Venn diagram in Exercise 86. If a number is prime, is it *always, sometimes,* or *never* in set *A*?

Reading Bar Graphs and Line Graphs *(Skills Review, pp. 704–705)*

In Exercises 89–92, use the bar graph. It shows the number of students in a class who bought, rather than brought, lunch each day.

89. On what day did the fewest number of students buy lunch?

90. On what day did 10 students buy lunch?

91. On what day did 12 more students buy lunch than on Tuesday?

92. Between what two days was there the least change in the number of students buying lunch?

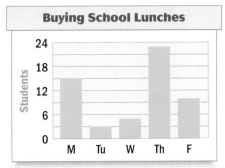

Buying School Lunches

In Exercises 93–96, use the line graph. It shows the temperature at different times of the day.

93. When was the temperature the highest? the lowest?

94. When were the recorded temperatures the same?

95. Over what two-hour period did the temperature decrease the most?

96. What is the difference between the highest and lowest temperature on the graph?

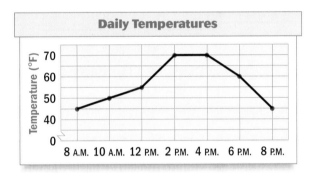

Daily Temperatures

Pictographs *(Skills Review, pp. 706–707)*

In Exercises 97–99, use the pictograph. It shows an ice cream stand's cone sales for one day.

97. How many strawberry cones were sold?

98. How many more chocolate than vanilla cones were sold?

99. Which cone was ordered twice as often as mint?

Monday's Cone Sales

100. Students at a school named their favorite place to study. Use the data in the table below to make a pictograph.

Where Students Like to Study				
At a table	At a desk	On a couch	On the floor	Other
36	22	16	20	10

Solve the problem and show your work.

1. **Make a Model** You are making a birthday card out of a large piece of paper. You are going to fold the paper in half and then in half again, as shown, but you first want to draw a picture for the cover of the card. On what side and in what corner of the large piece of paper should you draw? *(Strategy Review, p. xxxiv)*

2. **Draw a Diagram** A line dance starts with the moves listed below.

> **Line Dance Steps**
> 2 steps forward
> 5 steps to the right
> 3 steps to the left
> 4 steps backward
> 2 steps to the left

What steps would a person have to take to get back to his or her original position? *(Strategy Review, p. xxxv)*

3. **Draw a Diagram** A ladder has 7 steps. The bottom of each step is 16 inches above the bottom of the previous step. The distance from the bottom of the ladder to the bottom of the first step is 4 inches. The distance from the bottom of the last step to the top of ladder is 8 inches. How many feet long is the ladder? *(Strategy Review, p. xxxv)*

4. **Guess, Check, and Revise** In yesterday's basketball game, Christy scored all of her points by making two-point and three-point shots. Christy made 5 more two-point shots than she did three-point shots. If she scored a total of 30 points, how many of each shot did she make? *(Strategy Review, p. xxxvi)*

5. **Guess, Check, and Revise** A patio furniture store sells chairs and chaise longues. You can buy 2 chairs and 2 chaise longues for a total of $160. You can buy 4 chairs and 1 chaise longue for a total of $170. How much does one chair cost? How much does one chaise longue cost? *(Strategy Review, p. xxxvi)*

6. **Work Backward** You have $100 to spend on concert tickets at a theater. The theater has three sections of seating. The first section costs twice as much as the third section. The second section costs $20 more than the third section. One ticket in the second section costs $50. Do you have enough money to buy two tickets in the first section? *(Strategy Review, p. xxxvii)*

7. **Make a List or Table** You have $5 to spend at a concession stand. How many pairs of two different snacks can you buy? *(Strategy Review, p. xxxviii)*

> **Concession Stand Snacks**
> Hot dogs $3.50
> Slice of pizza $2.00
> Popcorn $2.50
> Pretzel $1.50

8. **Make a List or Table** Blake Middle School is hosting a pancake breakfast to raise money for the school's athletic teams. The ticket prices are given below. Bryn sold 4 tickets to the pancake breakfast. What are all the possible dollar amounts that Bryn's ticket sales could equal? *(Strategy Review, p. xxxviii)*

```
Pancake Breakfast
Tickets

Adults        $8
Children      $5
```

9. **Look for a Pattern** Robert is cooking rice in a microwave oven. The directions on the box give the cooking times below. The entire box of rice contains 9 servings. If Robert wants to cook the entire box of rice, for how many minutes should he cook it? *(Strategy Review, p. xxxix)*

Servings	2	4	6
Minutes	6	8	10

10. **Look for a Pattern** At Pinewood Middle School, a bell rings at regular intervals to signal the end of each period within a school day. In her notebook, Susan records the times at which the first four bells ring.

```
First bell      9:00 A.M.
Second bell     9:55 A.M.
Third bell     10:50 A.M.
Fourth bell    11:45 A.M.
```

If there are 7 periods in a day, at what time does the last bell ring? *(Strategy Review, p. xxxix)*

11. **Break into Parts** Your telephone bill is calculated using the rates below.

```
Unlimited local calls    $20
Regional calls           5¢ per minute
Long distance calls      10¢ per minute
```

This month you have made 35 local calls, 100 minutes of regional calls, and 80 minutes of long distance calls. What is the amount of your phone bill this month? *(Strategy Review, p. xl)*

12. **Solve a Simpler Problem** At the beginning of one year, Shawn decides to save his money according to a schedule. In week 1, Shawn puts 1 penny a jar. In week 2, Shawn puts 2 pennies in the jar. In week 3, Shawn puts 3 pennies in the jar. Shawn continues saving in this manner for the 52 weeks of the year. How many pennies are in the jar at the end of the year? *(Strategy Review, p. xli)*

13. **Use a Venn Diagram** At the end of the school year, the sixth graders at Langley Middle School took a trip to an amusement park. There were 22 sixth graders who went on the log flume and the water slide, but not on the rollercoaster. There were 18 sixth graders who went on the rollercoaster and the water slide, but not on the log flume. There were 37 sixth graders who went on all three rides. There were 15 sixth graders who rode the rollercoaster but not the log flume or the water slide. If 82 sixth graders went on the rollercoaster, how many sixth graders went on the rollercoaster and the log flume? *(Strategy Review, p. xlii)*

Problem Solving Practice

Solve the problem and show your work.

Make a Model

1. A rectangular tablecloth is folded in half lengthwise and then in half widthwise, as shown below. This process is repeated one more time. The folded tablecloth is a rectangle that is 18 inches by 12 inches. What are the original dimensions of the tablecloth? *(Strategy Review, p. xxxiv)*

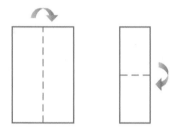

2. Chris has three railroad ties that measure 10 feet, 18 feet, and 7 feet. Can Chris make a triangular garden with these dimensions? *(Strategy Review, p. xxxiv)*

3. A rectangular raft is 5 feet long and 2 feet wide. How many of these rafts can fit (without gaps or overlaps) in a rectangular pool that is 20 feet long and 8 feet wide? *(Strategy Review, p. xxxiv)*

Draw a Diagram

4. On rainy days, a custodian at a school rolls out mats to prevent students from slipping on wet floors. Each mat is the same length. The main hallway in the school is 39 feet long. If a mat is unrolled at either end of the hall and there is 3 feet of overlap where the two mats meet, how long is each mat? *(Strategy Review, p. xxxv)*

5. Your little brother thought it would be fun to hide your birthday present outside. He wrote instructions for finding the present, using your front door as the starting point. How far from the front door is your birthday present? *(Strategy Review, p. xxxv)*

> Go 15 steps north.
>
> Go 8 steps east.
>
> Go 10 steps north.
>
> Go 17 steps west.
>
> Go 25 steps south. You will see your present.

6. Mike and Sal are canoeing in opposite directions on a river. Every hour, Mike canoes 2 miles north. Every hour, Sal canoes 1 mile south. If Mike and Sal start canoeing at the same time and leave from the same place, in how many hours will they be 12 miles apart? *(Strategy Review, p. xxxv)*

7. In lacrosse, one type of passing drill involves having 5 groups of players stand in a circle, as shown below. Group A always passes to group C, group B always passes to group D, group C always passes to group E, group D always passes to group A, and group E always passes to group B. The drill is named after the shape that the path of the ball forms. What is the shape? *(Strategy Review, p. xxxv)*

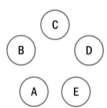

Solve the problem and show your work.

Guess, Check, and Revise

8. The sum of two numbers is 21. The difference of the two numbers is 3. What are the numbers? *(Strategy Review, p. xxxvi)*

9. A store sells $1, $2, and $3 birthday cards. Rick spends $11 on the purchase of 5 cards. If Rick bought at least one of each kind of card, how many of each kind of card did he buy? *(Strategy Review, p. xxxvi)*

10. In track and field, the triple jump involves taking a hop, a step, and a jump. Kylie always hops 2 more feet than she jumps, and jumps 2 more feet than she steps. If Kylie does a triple jump of 42 feet, how far did she hop, step, and jump? *(Strategy Review, p. xxxvi)*

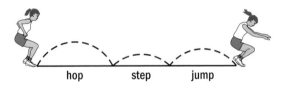

hop   step   jump

11. Shandi has $1.20 worth of nickels and dimes in her pocket. If Shandi knows that she has twice as many nickels as dimes, how many of each does she have? *(Strategy Review, p. xxxvi)*

12. How can each circle in the triangle below be filled with one of the digits 1, 2, 3, 4, 5, and 6 so that the sum of the numbers on each side of the triangle is 12? Each digit must be used exactly one time. *(Strategy Review, p. xxxvi)*

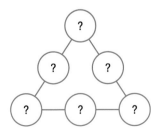

Work Backward

13. Henry ran twice as far on Tuesday as he did on Monday. He ran three times as far on Wednesday as he did on Tuesday. If Henry ran 18 miles on Wednesday, how far did he run on Monday? *(Strategy Review, p. xxxvii)*

14. Kathleen wants to watch her favorite TV show at 8:00 P.M. Before she can watch the show, she has to do 50 minutes of homework, take 15 minutes to clean her room, and allow 12 minutes for taking a shower. What is the latest time that Kathleen can start these activities and still finish in time to watch her favorite TV show? *(Strategy Review, p. xxxvii)*

15. Colin is 4 times as old as Fiona. Fiona is 5 years younger than Brad. If Colin is 20 years old, how many years older is he than Brad? *(Strategy Review, p. xxxvii)*

16. You keep only $1 bills and $5 bills in your wallet. At the end of the day, you find that you have triple the number of $1 bills and double the number of $5 bills that you had in your wallet at the start of the day. If you have nine $1 bills and four $5 bills in your wallet, how much money did you have at the start of the day? *(Strategy Review, p. xxxvii)*

Make a List or Table

17. You have sixteen 1-foot by 1-foot square patio bricks. If the bricks are arranged to form a rectangle, what is the greatest the perimeter of the rectangle can be? What is the least the perimeter of the rectangle can be? *(Strategy Review, p. xxxviii)*

Problem Solving Practice *Continued*

Solve the problem and show your work.

18. Binary code is a system in which data is represented using only 0's and 1's. How many different three-digit codes can be formed using 0 or 1 for each of the digits? For example, 001 is one possible code. *(Strategy Review, p. xxxviii)*

?	?	?

19. Roberto, Amy, and Paul go to a movie theater together. How many different ways can the three friends sit in a row? *(Strategy Review, p. xxxviii)*

20. You and a group of your friends are putting on a puppet show to raise money for your town's library. Tickets cost $3 for children and $5 for adults. You are responsible for selling 6 tickets. What are all the possible dollar amounts that your ticket sales could total? *(Strategy Review, p. xxxviii)*

Look for a Pattern

21. Describe the pattern shown below. Then draw the next figure in the pattern. *(Strategy Review, p. xxxix)*

22. Mara teaches swimming lessons during the summer. The cost of one lesson for various numbers of students is given in the table. How much would each student have to pay for a swimming lesson in a group of 6 students? *(Strategy Review, p. xxxix)*

Number of students	1	2	3	4
Total cost	$40	$50	$60	$70

23. A radio station plays the number one pop song according to the schedule shown. When is the next time that you would expect the radio station to play the number one pop song? *(Strategy Review, p. xxxix)*

Number one song	12:10 P.M.
Commercial break	12:15 P.M.
Commercial break	12:35 P.M.
Number one song	12:50 P.M.
Commercial break	12:55 P.M.
Commercial break	1:15 P.M.
Number one song	1:30 P.M.
Commercial break	1:35 P.M.
Commercial break	1:55 P.M.
Number one song	2:10 P.M.

24. The bar graph shows the prices for 3 sizes of the same drink at a movie theater. The manager of the movie theater is considering adding a 22 fluid ounce drink size. What would you expect the price to be for a drink that size? *(Strategy Review, p. xxxix)*

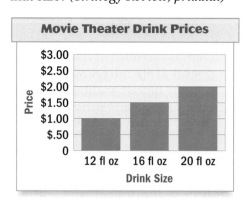

25. Colin plants a square garden that has a side length of 1 yard. Each year, he plans to increase the length of each side of the square garden by 1 yard. In his tenth year of planting, how many yards of fencing will Colin need to enclose his garden? *(Strategy Review, p. xxxix)*

Solve the problem and show your work.

Break Into Parts

26. Mrs. Smith's class is taking a field trip to a science museum. The costs are given below. If 35 people are going on the field trip, using one bus, what is the total cost? What should each person pay to go on the field trip? *(Strategy Review, p. xl)*

Bus rental	$70
Museum admission	$6 per person
Lunch	$4 per person

27. Paul earns $12 per hour for working 40 hours a week in a cafeteria. For every hour over 40 hours that Paul works in one week, he earns $18 per hour. How much does Paul earn if he works 46 hours in one week? *(Strategy Review, p. xl)*

28. Coach Roberts is running a summer basketball league. The costs are given below. If the basketball league will have 80 players and is going to run for 8 weeks, how much will running the league cost? *(Strategy Review, p. xl)*

T-shirts	$6 per player
Referees	$200 per week
Court time	$80 per week

Solve a Simpler Problem

29. A *palindromic number* is a number that is the same when written forward or backward. For example, 101 is a palindromic number. How many 3-digit palindromic numbers are there? *(Strategy Review, p. xli)*

30. A manager at a banquet hall has a total of 8 small rectangular tables that can be pushed together to make one large table. Individually, each small table can seat 6 people as shown. What is the maximum number of people that can be seated at one large table? *(Strategy Review, p. xli)*

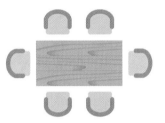

Use a Venn Diagram

31. On a beach there are 13 people wearing hats, but not sunglasses. There are 17 people wearing sunglasses, but not hats. There are 19 people wearing both a hat and sunglasses. How many people are wearing sunglasses? *(Strategy Review, p. xlii)*

32. A party of 12 people is having dinner at a restaurant. Two of the people order both a salad and a dessert. Four of the people order a salad, but not a dessert. Five of the people order a dessert. How many people ordered neither a salad nor a dessert? *(Strategy Review, p. xlii)*

33. Three of the households on Maple Street subscribe to a movie channel, but don't have a VCR or a DVD player. Eight of the households have both a VCR and a DVD player, but do not subscribe to a movie channel. Ten of the households have a DVD player, but not a VCR or a movie channel. Two of the households have all three. If 25 of the households have a DVD player, how many households on Maple Street subscribe to a movie channel and have a DVD player but no VCR? *(Strategy Review, p. xlii)*

Problem Solving Strategy Review

Make a Model

PROBLEM You are making a quilted pillow using scrap pieces of cloth from other projects. You have a rectangular piece of cloth that measures 9 inches by 4 inches. Using as few cuts as possible, how can you cut and then sew the cloth so that it forms a square?

| Make a Model |
| Draw a Diagram |
| Guess, Check, and Revise |
| Work Backward |
| Make a List or Table |
| Look for a Pattern |
| Break into Parts |
| Solve a Simpler Problem |
| Use a Venn Diagram |

 Read and Understand

Using the least number of cuts as possible, you need to turn a 9 inch by 4 inch rectangle into a square that has the same area.

 Make a Plan

It is hard to tell how the cloth should be cut without actually seeing the shape of the cloth and trying out different cuts. Making a model of the cloth can help.

 Solve the Problem

Make a model to represent the piece of cloth. Draw and cut out a 9 unit by 4 unit rectangle on a piece of graph paper. Count the number of grid squares in the rectangle. There are 36 squares, so the rectangle has an area of 36 square units.

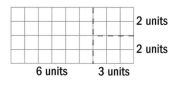

To form a square, the grid squares would have to be arranged in 6 rows of 6 grid squares. Cut 3 units off the length of the original rectangle so that the remaining length is 6 units. Then cut the new rectangle in half as shown.

The three pieces can now be arranged as shown to form a square. The 9 inch by 4 inch piece of cloth can be cut and sewn in a similar fashion to form a square.

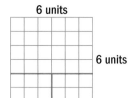

 Look Back

Make sure that it is impossible to form a square using fewer than two cuts. The first cut results in a 6 unit by 4 unit rectangle and a 4 unit by 3 unit rectangle. Since these rectangles cannot be put together to form a square, there must be more than one cut.

Practice the Strategy

A construction worker wants to fit a piece of plywood through a window opening that is 35 inches by 30 inches. If the piece of plywood is a square with a side length of 40 inches, will the construction worker be able to fit the plywood through the window opening?

Draw a Diagram

Make a Model
Draw a Diagram
Guess, Check, and Revise
Work Backward
Make a List or Table
Look for a Pattern
Break into Parts
Solve a Simpler Problem
Use a Venn Diagram

PROBLEM In the town of Springfield, the library is 3 miles north of the grocery store. The video store is 9 miles south of the library. How far and in what direction would you have to travel to get from the video store to the grocery store?

1 Read and Understand

You need to find the distance between the video store and the grocery store. You also need to find what direction the grocery store is from the video store.

2 Make a Plan

The given information involves both distances and directions. Drawing a diagram would make it easier to see how to use this information to find the answer to the problem.

3 Solve the Problem

The library is 3 miles north of the grocery store. First draw a point to represent the grocery store. Since the library is north of the grocery store, draw a point for the library directly above the point for the grocery store. Label the distance between the grocery store and the library as 3 miles.

The video store is 9 miles south of the library. Notice that the grocery store is 3 miles south of the library. Draw a point for the video store directly below the point for grocery store. Label the distance between the library and video store as 9 miles.

From the diagram you can see that the distance between the video store and the grocery store is $9 - 3 = 6$ miles. You would have to travel 6 miles north to get from the video store to the grocery store.

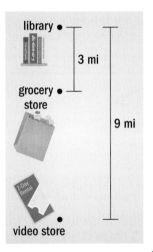

4 Look Back

Reread the problem and check that your diagram is consistent with each piece of the given information.

Practice the Strategy

From left to right, the order in which four friends stand for a photo is Jan, Henry, Pete, and Sri. Jan switches places with Pete. Then the first and last people switch places. Finally, the first and second people switch places. What is the final order, from left to right, of the four friends?

Problem Solving Strategy Review

Guess, Check, and Revise

Make a Model
Draw a Diagram
Guess, Check, and Revise
Work Backward
Make a List or Table
Look for a Pattern
Break into Parts
Solve a Simpler Problem
Use a Venn Diagram

PROBLEM The 24 players on the Dale High School football team voted for next year's team captain. Players could vote for one of the seniors on the team: John or Bill. John received three times as many votes as Bill. How many more votes did John receive than Bill?

 Read and Understand

You need to find the difference in the number of votes received by John and by Bill. To find the difference, you first need to find the number of votes each senior received.

 Make a Plan

You are given two pieces of information: there are a total of 24 votes, and John received three times as many votes as Bill. Each piece of information says something about both numbers of votes, but not the individual numbers of votes. This suggests the strategy of guessing, checking, and then revising an answer.

 Solve the Problem

Because there are 24 players on the team, there are a total of 24 votes. The number of votes received by each of the two seniors must be between 0 and 24.

Try guessing 20 votes for John. That leaves 4 votes for Bill. But since 20 is 5 times 4, this guess is incorrect.

Try guessing 18 votes for John. That leaves 6 votes for Bill. Since 18 is 3 times 6, this guess is correct. John received 18 votes and Bill received 6 votes. Since $18 - 6 = 12$, John received 12 more votes than Bill.

 Look Back

Reread the problem to make sure that you answered the question being asked. Notice that the question asks for the difference in the numbers of votes, not the number of votes received by each senior.

Practice the Strategy

The sum of two numbers is 56. The difference of the same two numbers is 14. What is the product of the two numbers?

Work Backward

PROBLEM Liz is filling 14 backpacks with school supplies for kids in an after-school program. There are 86 pencils and 21 rulers available. Liz wants to place the same number of pencils in each backpack. If there are 16 pencils left over, how many pencils did Liz put in each of the backpacks?

Make a Model
Draw a Diagram
Guess, Check, and Revise
Work Backward
Make a List or Table
Look for a Pattern
Break into Parts
Solve a Simpler Problem
Use a Venn Diagram

1 Read and Understand

You need to find the number of pencils in each of the backpacks.

2 Make a Plan

You know that when the number of pencils in each backpack is multiplied by 14 and then 16 pencils are added to the result, you have 86 pencils. You can work backward from 86 pencils, undoing each operation, to find the number of pencils in each backpack.

3 Solve the Problem

The total number of pencils placed in the backpacks plus 16 pencils equals 86 pencils. To find the total number of pencils placed in the backpacks, work backward by subtracting 16 from 86:

86 pencils − 16 pencils = 70 pencils

Since the number of pencils in each backpack times 14 equals 70 pencils, work backward by dividing 70 by 14 to find the number of pencils in each backpack:

70 pencils ÷ 14 = 5 pencils

Liz put 5 pencils in each of the backpacks.

4 Look Back

Work forward to check that your answer is correct. Liz put a total of 5 × 14 = 70 pencils in the backpacks. There are 16 pencils left over, so the total number of available pencils is 70 + 16 = 86 pencils. The answer is correct.

Practice the Strategy

A youth group is selling rolls of wrapping paper. This year, the youth group sold 55 more rolls than they did last year. Last year, the youth group sold twice as many rolls as they did the year before. If the youth group sold 295 rolls this year, how many rolls did they sell two years ago?

Problem Solving Strategy Review

Make a List or Table

Make a Model
Draw a Diagram
Guess, Check, and Revise
Work Backward
Make a List or Table
Look for a Pattern
Break into Parts
Solve a Simpler Problem
Use a Venn Diagram

PROBLEM Kylie is baking oatmeal cookies which take 12 minutes to bake, and sugar cookies which take 9 minutes to bake. Kylie puts one tray of each kind of cookie dough in the oven at 1:20 P.M. As soon as a tray of cookies is baked, Kylie replaces it with a tray of the same kind of cookie dough. At what time will both a tray of oatmeal cookies and a tray of sugar cookies finish baking simultaneously? Show your work.

 Read and Understand

You need to find the time at which both a tray of oatmeal cookies and a tray of sugar cookies finish baking. To do this, you first need to find the number of minutes since the first trays were put in the oven.

 Make a Plan

You need to keep track of the elapsed time as trays of each type of cookie finish baking. Then you can identify when the elapsed time is the same for a tray of each type of cookie. A table is a good way to organize this information.

 Solve the Problem

Record the elapsed time as trays of each type of cookie finish baking.

Tray number	Oatmeal cookies	Sugar cookies
1	12 min	9 min
2	24 min	18 min
3	36 min	27 min
4	48 min	36 min

You can see from the table that after 36 minutes, the third tray of oatmeal cookies and the fourth tray of sugar cookies finish baking. To find the time that this happens, find 36 minutes past 1:20 P.M., which is 1:56 P.M.

 Look Back

Make sure that your answer is reasonable. Since sugar cookies bake faster than oatmeal cookies, it makes sense that 4 trays of sugar cookies are baked in the same time that 3 trays of oatmeal cookies are baked.

Practice the Strategy

Dan is placing four books in a row on a shelf: a dictionary, a thesaurus, a biography, and a novel. Dan wants the dictionary to be on one end of the row. In how many ways can Dan place the books upright on the shelf?

Look for a Pattern

Make a Model
Draw a Diagram
Guess, Check, and Revise
Work Backward
Make a List or Table
Look for a Pattern
Break into Parts
Solve a Simpler Problem
Use a Venn Diagram

PROBLEM A Web site sells jump ropes in packages of six ropes. The costs of packages of six ropes of different lengths are given in the table. How much would you expect a package of six 12-foot ropes to cost?

JUMP ROPE PRICES

Jump rope length	Cost for six
7 ft	$10.80
8 ft	$11.70
9 ft	$12.60
10 ft	$13.50

 1 Read and Understand

You need to predict the cost of a package of six 12-foot jump ropes, based on the given costs of the ropes in the table.

 2 Make a Plan

Since you are not given any information about the cost of a package of 12-foot ropes, you need to look for a pattern in the costs of the ropes that you are given.

 3 Solve the Problem

Notice that as the length of a jump rope increases, the cost of a package of six ropes also increases. Find the amount by which the cost of each package increases.

For each additional 1 foot of length, the cost of a package of jump ropes increases by $.90. So, it can be expected that a package of 11-foot ropes costs $14.40 and a package of 12-foot ropes costs $15.30.

Jump rope length	Cost for 6	
7 ft	$10.80	+ $.90
8 ft	$11.70	+ $.90
9 ft	$12.60	+ $.90
10 ft	$13.50	

 4 Look Back

Make sure that you performed your calculations correctly. To find the cost of a rope 2 feet longer than 10 feet, you add $1.80 to $13.50: $13.50 + $1.80 = $15.30 ✔

Practice the Strategy

A soccer coach has her team sprint a certain distance and then gives the team time to rest. The first four sprinting distances are 10 yards, 20 yards, 40 yards, and 80 yards. If the coach continues to have her team run in this manner, what is the total distance that the team will have run after the fifth sprint?

Problem Solving Strategy Review

Make a Model
Draw a Diagram
Guess, Check, and Revise
Work Backward
Make a List or Table
Look for a Pattern
Break into Parts
Solve a Simpler Problem
Use a Venn Diagram

Break into Parts

PROBLEM Darren wants his birthday party to be held at the local bowling alley. The costs associated with a bowling birthday party are given at the right. How much will a birthday party for 6 people, including Darren, cost?

Bowling
Birthday Party
Costs

Party room rental..$20
Cake $15
Cost of lunch............$4
(per person)
Cost of bowling $5
(per person)

1 Read and Understand

You need to find the cost of a party for 6 people.

2 Make a Plan

Some of the given costs are group costs and apply just one time. Some of the given costs are individual costs and apply to each person at the party. You can break the problem into parts according to the type of cost.

3 Solve the Problem

The cost of the party room rental and the cost of the cake are group costs. The sum of these costs is $20 + $15 = $35.

The cost of lunch and the cost of bowling are individual costs. The sum of these costs is $4 + $5 = $9. For 6 people, this cost is $9 \times 6 = $54.

The total cost is $35 + $54 = $89.

4 Look Back

Estimate to check the reasonableness of your answer. The sum of the individual costs is about $10. Since $10 \times 6 = $60 and $60 + $35 = $95, an answer of $89 is reasonable.

Practice the Strategy

How many different triangles are in the figure shown?

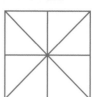

Solve a Simpler Problem

Make a Model
Draw a Diagram
Guess, Check, and Revise
Work Backward
Make a List or Table
Look for a Pattern
Break into Parts
Solve a Simpler Problem
Use a Venn Diagram

PROBLEM An auditorium has seats numbered from 100 through 899. New seat numbers were just placed on each arm rest. By mistake, the letter O was used instead of a zero in the seat numbers. How many of the seats have at least one letter O used in the seat number?

1 Read and Understand

You need to find how many numbers from 100 through 899 contain at least one zero.

2 Make a Plan

To solve the problem, you could write out every single number from 100 through 899 that contains at least one zero, but this would take a long time. Instead, you could look for a simpler problem whose solution can help you find an answer.

3 Solve the Problem

Think of the numbers from 100 through 899 as being in 8 groups. The first group is 100 through 199, the second is 200 through 299, and so on. Solve the simpler problem of finding how many numbers from 100 through 199 contain at least one zero. The numbers are:

| 100 | 101 | 102 | 103 | 104 | 105 | 106 | 107 | 108 | 109 |

| 110 | 120 | 130 | 140 | 150 | 160 | 170 | 180 | 190 |

There are 19 numbers that contain at least one zero in the group of numbers from 100 through 199. Since the only digit that differs from group to group is the digit in the hundreds' place, every group has 19 numbers that contain at least one zero. There are 19 × 8 = 152 numbers from 100 through 899 that contain at least one zero. So, 152 seats have at least one letter O used in the seat number.

4 Look Back

Make sure that you answered the question being asked. Notice that the question does not ask for the total number of zeros contained in the numbers from 100 through 899.

Practice the Strategy

You are collecting rubber bands to make a rubber band ball. The first day you collect 1 rubber band. Each day you collect one more rubber band than the previous day. How many rubber bands will you have collected after 30 days?

Problem Solving Strategy Review

Make a Model
Draw a Diagram
Guess, Check, and Revise
Work Backward
Make a List or Table
Look for a Pattern
Break into Parts
Solve a Simpler Problem
Use a Venn Diagram

Use a Venn Diagram

PROBLEM Your town has organized a trip to a mountain where participants may ski, snowboard, and snowshoe. There are 3 people who have skis, a snowboard, and snowshoes. There are 5 people who have skis and a snowboard, but no snowshoes. There are 2 people who have skis and snowshoes, but no snowboard. If 19 people have skis, how many people have only skis?

1 Read and Understand

You need to find the number of people who have skis but who do not also have snowshoes or a snowboard.

2 Make a Plan

It is not immediately apparent how many people have only skis because some of the people with skis also have snowshoes or a snowboard. A Venn diagram can help organize this type of overlapping information.

3 Solve the Problem

Draw a Venn diagram to represent the given information. You can see that there are $5 + 3 + 2 = 10$ people who have skis and either a snowboard or snowshoes, or both. Since you know that 19 people have skis, you can subtract to find the number of people who have only skis. $19 - 10 = 9$, so 9 people have only skis.

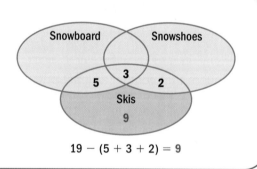

$$19 - (5 + 3 + 2) = 9$$

4 Look Back

Make sure that you placed the numbers in the correct places in the Venn diagram.

Practice the Strategy

A display case has 15 rings with diamonds, 12 rings with rubies, and 10 rings with pearls. 2 rings have all three gems, 3 have only rubies and diamonds, 4 have only pearls and rubies, and 3 have only pearls. How many rings have only diamonds?

UNIT 1

Algebraic Thinking, Measurement, and Decimals

Chapter 1 Number Sense and Algebraic Thinking

- Write and evaluate numerical and variable expressions.
- Use a variety of strategies to predict, find, and check results.

Chapter 2 Measurement and Statistics

- Find lengths, perimeters, and areas in real-world situations.
- Use tables, graphs, and averages to organize and analyze data.

Chapter 3 Decimal Addition and Subtraction

- Name, write, order, and round decimals.
- Estimate and find sums and differences of decimals.
- Estimate and measure length.

From Chapter 4, p. 169

How much do sports cards cost?

Chapter 4 Decimal Multiplication and Division

- Multiply and divide by decimals and powers of ten.
- Use metric units of length, mass, and capacity.

Number Sense and Algebraic Thinking

BEFORE

In previous courses you've...

- Performed whole number operations
- Completed number fact families

Now

In Chapter 1 you'll study...

- Estimating with whole numbers
- Order of operations
- Evaluating variable expressions
- Equations and mental math
- Using a problem solving plan

WHY?

So you can solve real-world problems about...

- cheetahs, p. 9
- biking, p. 12
- weather, p. 31
- volleyball, p. 40

Internet Preview
CLASSZONE.COM

- eEdition Plus Online
- eWorkbook Plus Online
- eTutorial Plus Online
- State Test Practice
- More Examples

Chapter Warm-Up Games

Review skills you need for this chapter in these quick games. Work with a partner.

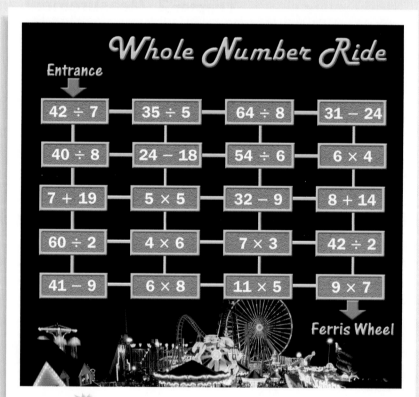

Whole Number Ride

Entrance

42 ÷ 7	35 ÷ 5	64 ÷ 8	31 − 24
40 ÷ 8	24 − 18	54 ÷ 6	6 × 4
7 + 19	5 × 5	32 − 9	8 + 14
60 ÷ 2	4 × 6	7 × 3	42 ÷ 2
41 − 9	6 × 8	11 × 5	9 × 7

Ferris Wheel

BrAiN GAME

Key Skill:
Performing whole number operations

Find your way from the entrance to the Ferris wheel. Begin at the entrance. Find the sum, difference, product, or quotient. Then move one space along a path to a space that has a greater value.

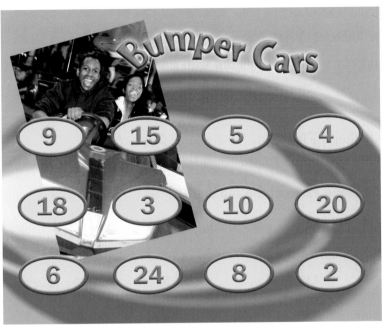

Bumper Cars

9	15	5	4
18	3	10	20
6	24	8	2

BRAIN GAME

Key Skill:
Number facts

Materials:
One paper clip
for each player

Place your paper clips on different numbers. Take turns following the directions below.

- Move one space in any direction to a new number. State one number fact using your old and new numbers. For example, if you move from 9 to 3, you could state these facts: $3 + 9$, $9 - 3$, 3×9, or $9 \div 3$.

- If the value of your number fact matches the number on which the other player is located, you may bump the player to any number except yours. Two players can never be on the same number at the same time. The first player to bump the other player 3 times wins.

Stop and Think

1. **Writing** Suppose you wanted to move from the Ferris wheel to the entrance in *Whole Number Ride*. How would you rewrite the rules of the game?

2. **Critical Thinking** List all the number facts you could make in *Bumper Cars* that would bump a player from the number 9.

Getting Ready to Learn

Review What You Need to Know

Using Vocabulary **Match the word with its correct symbol.**

1. sum   **2.** difference   **3.** product   **4.** quotient

A. ÷   **B.** +   **C.** −   **D.** ×

5. Tell whether the following statement is *true* or *false:* In a division sentence, the divisor is divided by the dividend.

Identify the place value of the red digit. *(p. 684)*

6. 27   **7.** 56   **8.** 197   **9.** 813

Round the number to the place value of the red digit. *(p. 686)*

10. 16   **11.** 31   **12.** 257   **13.** 1909

Find the sum, difference, product, or quotient. *(pp. 689–691)*

14. 7 + 8   **15.** 6 + 5   **16.** 13 − 4   **17.** 11 − 3

18. 7 × 3   **19.** 9 × 5   **20.** 24 ÷ 4   **21.** 16 ÷ 2

Word Watch

Review Words

whole number, p. 684
place value, p. 684
round, p. 686
sum, p. 689
difference, p. 689
product, p. 690
quotient, p. 691
dividend, p. 691
divisor, p. 691

You should include material that appears on a notebook like this in your own notes.

Know How to Take Notes

Keeping a Notebook Some useful items to put in your mathematics notebook include the following:

- vocabulary
- rules and properties
- worked-out examples
- symbols
- formulas

When you copy examples, include reminders about important details.

Lesson 1.1 Whole Number Operations

$$
\begin{array}{r}
\overset{1}{1}34 \\
+\ 49 \\
\hline
183
\end{array}
$$
—— Remember to line up the ones, the tens, and so on.

$$
\begin{array}{r}
\overset{5\ 11\ 14}{6\cancel{2}\cancel{4}} \\
-\ 259 \\
\hline
365
\end{array}
$$
←—— Remember to regroup so you can subtract.

In Lesson 1.5, you will see how a reminder can help you to relate a previous lesson to a new situation.

Whole Number Operations

BEFORE

You learned basic number facts.

▶ **Now**

You'll add, subtract, multiply, and divide whole numbers.

WHY?

So you can find the cost of music lessons, as in Example 3.

📓 **Word Watch**

Review Words

whole number, p. 684
sum, p. 689
difference, p. 689
product, p. 690
quotient, p. 691
divisor, p. 691
dividend, p. 691
remainder, p. 691

Activity **You can use addition skills to complete a magic square.**

In a *magic square*, the numbers in each row, column, and diagonal add up to the same magic number. Follow the steps below to complete the magic square.

1 Add the three numbers in the first row.

2 Add the three numbers in the second column.

3 Add the three numbers along a diagonal.

4 What is the magic number?

5 Copy and complete the magic square.
Explain how you found the missing numbers.

Sums You find the sum of numbers with more than one digit by first lining up the ones. Then you add the ones, then the tens, then the hundreds, and so on. You may need to regroup.

🔵 **with Review**

Need help with place value?
See p. 684.

EXAMPLE 1 **Adding Whole Numbers**

a. To find the sum 49 + 36, first you line up the numbers on the ones' place. Next you add the ones. Then you add the tens.

$$\begin{array}{r} \overset{1}{}49 \\ +\,36 \\ \hline 85 \end{array}$$ 9 + 6 = 15. Regroup the 15 ones as 1 ten and 5 ones.

b. To find the sum 954 + 78, you line up the numbers on the ones' place. Next you add the ones, then the tens, then the hundreds.

$$\begin{array}{r} \overset{11}{}954 \\ +\,78 \\ \hline 1032 \end{array}$$ ← 4 + 8 = 12. Regroup the 12 ones as 1 ten and 2 ones.

    1 + 5 + 7 = 13. Regroup the 13 tens as 1 hundred and 3 tens.

EXAMPLE 2 Subtracting Whole Numbers

To find the difference of 204 and 36, you line up the numbers on the ones' place. Next you subtract the ones, then the tens, and so on.

$$\begin{array}{r} {\scriptstyle 1\,9\,1\,4} \\ 2\cancel{0}\cancel{4} \\ - \quad 36 \\ \hline 168 \end{array}$$

You need more ones to subtract 6, so regroup.
$204 = 100 + 90 + 14.$

Your turn now Find the sum or difference.

1. $95 + 37$ **2.** $406 + 95$ **3.** $82 - 49$ **4.** $500 - 315$

EXAMPLE 3 Multiplying Whole Numbers

Music Lessons Your music lessons cost $25 per week. How much will you pay for 12 weeks of lessons?

Solution You need to find the product 25×12.

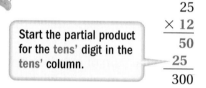

Start the partial product for the tens' digit in the tens' column.

$$\begin{array}{r} 25 \\ \times\ 12 \\ \hline 50 \\ 25 \\ \hline 300 \end{array}$$

First multiply 25 by the ones' digit, 2.
Then multiply 25 by the tens' digit, 1.
Add the partial products.

ANSWER You will pay $300 for 12 weeks of music lessons.

EXAMPLE 4 Dividing Whole Numbers

To find the quotient of 592 and 7, you use long division. The dividend is 592 and the divisor is 7.

Align the 8 in the tens' column.

$$\begin{array}{r} 84\ \text{R}4 \\ 7\overline{)592} \\ 56 \\ \hline 32 \\ 28 \\ \hline 4 \end{array}$$

Divide 59 by 7, because 7 is more than 5.
Multiply: $8 \times 7 = 56$.
Subtract: $59 - 56 = 3$. Bring down the 2.
Repeat the process.
The remainder is 4.

Your turn now Find the product or quotient.

5. 29×31 **6.** 140×15 **7.** $721 \div 6$ **8.** $418 \div 21$

UNITED STATES OF AMERICA

EXAMPLE 5 **Finding Patterns**

Sports The Summer Olympics were held in 1988, 1992, 1996, and 2000. Describe the pattern. Then find the next two years in the pattern.

Solution

Look to see how each number is related to the preceding number. Each year after 1988 is 4 more than the preceding year.

1988   1992   1996   2000   2004   2008
   +4   +4   +4   +4   +4

ANSWER The next two years in the pattern are 2004 and 2008.

Your turn now Describe the pattern. Then find the next two numbers.

9. 1, 4, 7, 10, ? , ?

10. 55, 50, 45, 40, ? , ?

11. 3, 6, 12, 24, ? , ?

12. 320, 160, 80, 40, ? , ?

 **1.1** **Exercises**

More Practice, p. 708

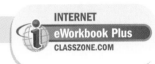

INTERNET
eWorkbook Plus
CLASSZONE.COM

Getting Ready to Practice

Vocabulary **Match the word with its meaning.**

1. difference   **A.** the result of adding two or more numbers

2. quotient   **B.** the result of dividing one number by another

3. sum   **C.** the result of subtracting one number from another

4. product   **D.** the result of multiplying two or more numbers

Find the sum, difference, product, or quotient.

5. $45 + 36$ **6.** $76 - 39$ **7.** 24×18 **8.** $78 \div 5$

9. $802 - 19$ **10.** $305 + 97$ **11.** $607 \div 11$ **12.** 56×34

Describe the pattern. Then find the next two numbers.

13. 60, 50, 40, 30, ? , ?   **14.** 1, 3, 9, 27, ? , ?

15. **Tickets** A ticket to the theater costs $26. If you buy 6 tickets, how much do you pay?

Practice and Problem Solving

HELP with **Homework**

Example	Exercises
1	16–31, 37–47
2	16–31, 37–47
3	16–32, 40–47
4	16–31, 37–47
5	33–36

Online Resources
CLASSZONE.COM

· More Examples
· eTutorial Plus

Find the sum, difference, product, or quotient.

16. $37 + 46$ **17.** $54 - 38$ **18.** 402×5 **19.** $58 \div 3$

20. $281 - 72$ **21.** $164 + 72$ **22.** $725 \div 6$ **23.** 15×40

24. $226 + 175$ **25.** $812 - 125$ **26.** 63×25 **27.** $634 \div 11$

28. $600 - 472$ **29.** $399 + 214$ **30.** $7296 \div 3$ **31.** 249×31

32. Find the Error Describe and correct the error made at the right.

$$\begin{array}{r} 27 \\ \times\ 15 \\ \hline 135 \\ 27 \\ \hline 162 \end{array}$$

Describe the pattern. Then find the next two numbers.

33. 30, 28, 26, 24, __?__ , __?__   **34.** 5, 10, 20, 40, __?__ , __?__

35. 4, 12, 20, 28, __?__ , __?__   **36.** 64, 32, 16, 8, __?__ , __?__

37. Test Scores The scores on your first two math tests were 78 and 91. By how much did your score improve?

38. Shopping A shirt costs $18 and a wallet costs $25. Find the total cost.

39. Road Trip Your family made 3 rest stops each day during a road trip. There was a total of 42 rest stops. How many days did the trip take?

Decide Tell whether the statement is *true* or *false*. If it is false, change the underlined word to make the statement true.

40. The <u>sum</u> of 92 and 13 is 105.   **41.** The <u>difference</u> of 15 and 5 is 75.

42. The <u>product</u> of 26 and 3 is 23.   **43.** The <u>quotient</u> of 64 and 4 is 16.

Mental Math Find the missing digit in the problem.

44.
$$\begin{array}{r} 75 \\ +\ 2\boxed{?} \\ \hline 102 \end{array}$$

45.
$$\begin{array}{r} 8\boxed{?} \\ -\ 36 \\ \hline 45 \end{array}$$

46.
$$\begin{array}{r} 2\boxed{?}5 \\ \times\ \ \ 3 \\ \hline 645 \end{array}$$

47.
$$\boxed{?}\overline{)102} \quad 17$$

48. Look for a Pattern In the magic square shown, the sum of the numbers in each row, column, and four-number diagonal is the same. Copy and complete the magic square.

4	14	?	1
9	?	6	12
5	11	10	?
16	2	3	?

What do you think?
Animals

Cheetahs

A cheetah cub at birth is about 12 inches long from its nose to the end of its tail. An adult cheetah can be about 90 inches long. Is the adult cheetah *less than*, *equal to*, or *greater than* 7 times as long as the cub?

49. **Cheetahs** A litter of cheetah cubs weighs about 3 pounds. One adult cheetah can weigh about 141 pounds. How many litters of cubs taken together would have the same weight as the adult cheetah?

50. **Look for a Pattern** A one-minute phone call costs 13 cents. A two-minute call costs 26 cents. A three-minute call costs 39 cents. Describe the pattern. If this pattern continues, what is the cost of a four-minute call? a five-minute call?

Critical Thinking **You find the product of 67 and 5 to be 335.**

51. How can you use addition to check if you are correct?

52. How can you use division to check if you are correct?

Challenge **You have $7, your cousin has $9, and your two friends each have $11. You use all of this money to buy tickets for carnival rides. Each ticket costs $2.**

53. How many tickets can you buy?

54. Can you split the tickets evenly among all of you? Explain.

55. If the tickets cost $3, how many tickets can you buy? Can you split the tickets evenly?

Mixed Review

Round the number to the place value of the red digit. *(p. 686)*

56. 32
57. 89
58. 951
59. 344
60. 988
61. 1384
62. 7199
63. 4511

Basic Skills **Find the sum, difference, product, or quotient.**

64. 4×8
65. $11 - 7$
66. $14 \div 2$
67. $9 + 2$
68. $6 + 6$
69. 9×3
70. $13 - 8$
71. $30 \div 6$

Test-Taking Practice

INTERNET
State Test Practice
CLASSZONE.COM

72. **Multiple Choice** You have 28 boxes of apples. Each box has 26 apples. Which choice has a value equal to the total number of apples?

A. $28 + 26$ **B.** $28 - 26$ **C.** 28×26 **D.** $28 \div 26$

73. **Multiple Choice** You buy 245 plums. There are 35 plums per bag. How many bags of plums do you buy?

F. 5   **G.** 7   **H.** 31   **I.** 35

Hands-on Activity

GOAL

Use estimation to find a sum, difference, product, or quotient close to a target number.

MATERIALS

· number cube

Hitting the Target

You can use estimation to solve problems where you want to come close to some exact number.

Explore **Form a sum that is close to the target number 100.**

1 Sketch four squares arranged as shown at the right. Roll the number cube and place the result in one of the blank boxes.

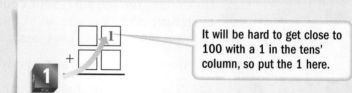

It will be hard to get close to 100 with a 1 in the tens' column, so put the 1 here.

2 Roll again and place the result in another blank box.

Putting the 6 in the tens' column will help you get close to 100.

3 Roll two more times to complete the diagram. Then find the sum. Compare it with the target number 100.

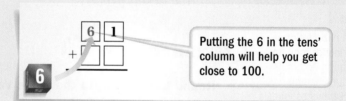

Your turn now **Refer to the target game shown above.**

1. Is it possible to rearrange the digits to get closer to the target sum? If so, how would you rearrange them?

2. Repeat Steps 1–3 above to form another sum that is close to the target. Is it possible to rearrange your digits to get closer to the target sum? If so, how would you rearrange them?

Explore   **Form a product that is close to the target number 200.**

1 Copy the diagram at the right. Think about some possible products that would get you close to 200.

2 Roll the number cube and place the result in one of the blank boxes.

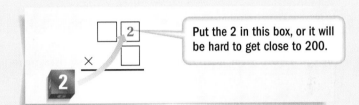

Put the 2 in this box, or it will be hard to get close to 200.

3 Roll two more times to complete the diagram. Then find the product. Compare it with the target number 200.

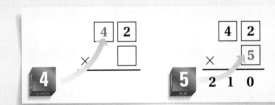

Your turn now   **Refer to the target game shown above.**

3. Is it possible to rearrange the digits to get closer to the target product? If so, how would you rearrange them?

4. Repeat Steps 1–3 above to form another product close to the target. Is it possible to rearrange your digits to get closer to the target product? If so, how would you rearrange them?

Stop and Think

5. **Critical Thinking** Use the diagram at the right to play "target difference." Use a target number of 50. How would you arrange the digits 5, 1, 6, and 3?

6. **Writing** Write instructions telling how to play "target quotient" using the diagram at the right. What would be a good target number? Explain.

Whole Number Estimation

BEFORE	▶ Now	WHY?
You calculated using whole numbers.	You'll round to estimate with whole numbers.	So you can estimate traveling time, as in Example 1.

In the Real World

Word Watch

leading digit, p. 13
compatible numbers, p. 13

Biking The map shows the time it takes to bike from place to place. About how long does it take to bike from the trailhead to the swinging bridge and then to the waterfall?

When you round to estimate a sum or difference, you should round the numbers to the same place value.

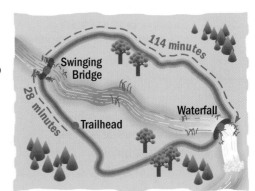

EXAMPLE 1 Estimating Sums

To estimate the answer to the question above about biking, round the time for each part of the ride to the same place value. Then add.

$$
\begin{array}{r} 28 \\ +114 \\ \end{array}
\quad
\begin{array}{l}\textbf{Round each number}\\ \textbf{to the nearest ten.}\end{array}
\quad\Longrightarrow\quad
\begin{array}{r} 30 \\ +110 \\ \hline 140 \end{array}
\quad
\begin{array}{l}\textbf{Round 28 up to 30.}\\ \textbf{Round 114 down to 110.}\end{array}
$$

ANSWER It takes about 140 minutes to bike from the trailhead to the swinging bridge and then to the waterfall.

EXAMPLE 2 Estimating Differences

Use the map shown above. The travel time from the swinging bridge, past the waterfall, to the trailhead is 208 minutes. Estimate how much time it takes to bike from the waterfall to the trailhead.

Solution

$$
\begin{array}{r} 208 \\ -114 \\ \end{array}
\quad
\begin{array}{l}\textbf{Round each number}\\ \textbf{to the nearest hundred.}\end{array}
\quad\Longrightarrow\quad
\begin{array}{r} 200 \\ -100 \\ \hline 100 \end{array}
\quad
\begin{array}{l}\textbf{Round 208 down to 200.}\\ \textbf{Round 114 down to 100.}\end{array}
$$

ANSWER It takes about 100 minutes to bike from the waterfall to the trailhead.

Your turn now Estimate the sum or difference.

1. 27 + 64   **2.** 59 + 623   **3.** 180 + 914

4. 91 − 49   **5.** 612 − 83   **6.** 804 − 623

Using Leading Digits When you round to estimate a product, you should round the numbers to the place value of their *leading digits*. The **leading digit** of a whole number is the first digit at the left.

EXAMPLE 3   **Estimating Products**

HELP with **Solving**

You can estimate an answer if you do not need an exact answer. You can also estimate to check whether a given answer is reasonable.

Estimate to tell whether the given answer is reasonable.

a. $191 \times 11; 2101$

$200 \times 10 = 2000$ Round both numbers to the leading digit.

ANSWER The answer is reasonable because 2000 is close to 2101.

b. $1127 \times 4; 6508$

$1000 \times 4 = 4000$ Round 1127 to its leading digit. Don't round the single digit.

ANSWER The answer is not reasonable because 4000 is not close to 6508.

Quotients When you estimate a quotient, you should look for compatible numbers. **Compatible numbers** are numbers that will make the calculation easier.

EXAMPLE 4   **Estimating Quotients**

HELP with **Reading**

The symbol ≈ can be read "is about equal to."

Estimate the quotient $469 \div 59$.

$469 \div 59 \approx 469 \div 60$ Round the divisor to its leading digit.

$\approx 480 \div 60$ Replace the dividend with a number that is compatible with 60 and close to 469.

$= 8$ Divide. The quotient $469 \div 59$ is about 8.

Your turn now Estimate the product or quotient.

7. 12×79 **8.** 879×31 **9.** 193×4

10. $191 \div 18$ **11.** $213 \div 68$ **12.** $972 \div 4$

Getting Ready to Practice

Vocabulary **Tell whether the numbers are compatible for division. If not, find a dividend compatible with the divisor.**

1. $16 \div 4$

2. $154 \div 20$

3. $7180 \div 90$

Round each number to the given place value. Then estimate the sum or difference.

4. $33 + 87$ (tens)

5. $624 - 139$ (hundreds)

6. $2114 - 872$ (hundreds)

7. $3899 + 5782$ (thousands)

8. **Guided Problem Solving** Hot dogs come in packages of 48. You buy 11 packages for a cookout. Estimate how many hot dogs you buy.

　(**1** What operation do you use to find the number of hot dogs?

　(**2** Round each number to an appropriate place value.

　(**3** Estimate the total number of hot dogs.

Practice and Problem Solving

Estimate the sum or difference.

9. $28 + 74$　**10.** $87 - 19$　**11.** $309 - 188$　**12.** $285 + 307$

13. $914 - 482$　**14.** $682 + 297$　**15.** $78 + 233$　**16.** $427 - 18$

17. $618 - 89$　**18.** $879 + 94$　**19.** $1129 + 403$　**20.** $2015 - 398$

Estimate the product or quotient.

21. 38×2　**22.** $24 \div 5$　**23.** $39 \div 4$　**24.** 59×3

25. $702 \div 7$　**26.** 21×31　**27.** 12×89　**28.** $63 \div 19$

29. 123×41　**30.** $498 \div 11$　**31.** $597 \div 28$　**32.** 287×12

33. **School Carnival** Each student who went to a school carnival received 7 free game tickets. You know that 1337 free tickets were given out to students. About how many students went to the carnival?

34. **Population** Colby has 1811 residents. Arletta has 1227 residents. About how many more people live in Colby than in Arletta?

with **Homework**

Example	Exercises
1	9-20, 41, 42
2	9-20, 34, 41
3	21-32
4	21-32, 33

Online Resources
CLASSZONE.COM

· More Examples
· eTutorial Plus

Estimate to tell whether the given answer is reasonable.

35. $9024 - 7182;\ 1842$ **36.** $1104 + 4018;\ 6122$ **37.** $2912 \div 52;\ 560$

38. $210 \times 391;\ 82{,}110$ **39.** $1982 \times 35;\ 6937$ **40.** $6104 - 3971;\ 3133$

North Carolina The map shows the direct distances in miles between cities in North Carolina.

41. The total distance from Greensboro to Raleigh to Charlotte is 198 miles. Estimate the distance from Raleigh to Charlotte.

42. Is it a longer drive from Greensboro to Raleigh to Charlotte, or from Greensboro to Charlotte to Raleigh?

43. **Painting** You are painting a fence and you don't want to make a second trip to the store for more paint. Should your estimate of the area each can of paint can cover be *high* or *low*? Explain.

44. **Critical Thinking** You want to know whether 5 hours is enough time to read a book for class. To be sure you finish, should your estimate of the number of pages you can read per hour be *high* or *low*? Explain.

45. **Challenge** Explain why you should not round down a single digit number when you estimate a product.

Mixed Review

Find the sum or difference. *(Lesson 1.1)*

46. $429 - 52$ **47.** $3011 - 947$ **48.** $64 + 38$ **49.** $629 + 85$

Basic Skills **Find the product.**

50. 9×7 **51.** 8×8 **52.** 12×6 **53.** 11×11

Test-Taking Practice

54. **Short Response** You are mailing 19 packages. It costs between $9 and $12 to mail each package. Estimate the total cost. Explain your method.

55. **Multiple Choice** There are 8393 people at a football game. There are 5423 people sitting on the home team's side of the stadium. About how many people are sitting on the visiting team's side?

   A. 13,000   **B.** 12,000   **C.** 8000   **D.** 3000

Powers and Exponents

BEFORE   ▶ **Now**   **WHY?**

You multiplied pairs of numbers.   You'll find values of powers.   So you can find the number of friends invited, as in Ex. 28.

In the Real World

Word Watch

factor, p. 16
power, p. 16
base, p. 16
exponent, p. 16

Light-year A light-year is the distance light travels in one year. Astronomers estimate that the distance across the Virgo Spiral Galaxy is about 100,000 light-years. You can write 100,000 as a product.

$$100,000 = 10 \times 10 \times 10 \times 10 \times 10$$

This product has five *factors* of 10. When whole numbers other than zero are multiplied together, each number is a **factor** of the product. To write a product that has a repeated factor, you can use a **power** .

Powers, Bases, and Exponents

The **base** of the power is the repeated factor and the **exponent** is the number of times the factor is repeated.

base   exponent

$$6^3 \quad = \quad 6 \times 6 \times 6$$

power   There are 3 factors.

EXAMPLE 1   **Writing a Power**

Use the distance across the Virgo Spiral Galaxy given above. Write the distance as a power.

$$10 \times 10 \times 10 \times 10 \times 10 = 10^5$$ There are 5 factors.

ANSWER The distance across the galaxy is about 10^5 light-years.

Your turn now   **Write the product as a power.**

1. $8 \times 8 \times 8$ **2.** $6 \times 6 \times 6 \times 6$ **3.** $20 \times 20 \times 20$

Reading Powers When powers have an exponent of 2, the base is "squared." When powers have an exponent of 3, the base is "cubed."

3^2 is read "3 to the **second** power," or "3 **squared**."

4^3 is read "4 to the **third** power," or "4 **cubed**."

2^5 is read "2 to the **fifth** power."

EXAMPLE 2 **Finding the Value of a Power**

a. Find the value of five cubed.

$$5^3 = 5 \times 5 \times 5 \qquad \text{Write 5 as a factor three times.}$$

$$= 125 \qquad \text{Multiply.}$$

b. Find the value of two to the sixth power.

$$2^6 = 2 \times 2 \times 2 \times 2 \times 2 \times 2 \qquad \text{Write 2 as a factor six times.}$$

$$= 64 \qquad \text{Multiply.}$$

EXAMPLE 3 **Powers in Real-World Problems**

Telephone Calls You need to contact members of your softball league. You call 4 members in the morning. Those 4 people each call 4 more people in the afternoon. That night, those additional people each call 4 others. How many people are called that night?

Solution

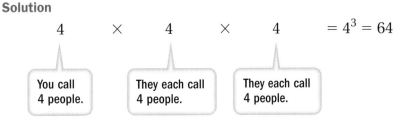

$$4 \qquad \times \qquad 4 \qquad \times \qquad 4 \qquad = 4^3 = 64$$

You call 4 people.   They each call 4 people.   They each call 4 people.

ANSWER That night, 64 people are called.

Your turn now Write the power as a product. Then find the value.

4. 11^2 **5.** 5^4 **6.** 1^7 **7.** 6^2

8. 7 squared **9.** 3 to the fourth power

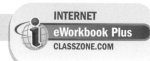

Getting Ready to Practice

Vocabulary Tell whether what is highlighted in red is a *power*, a *base*, or an *exponent*. Then find the value of the power.

1. 3^3 **2.** 9^2 **3.** 1^4

Which power is equal to the given product or power?

4. $2 \times 2 \times 2$ **A.** 2^2 **B.** 2^3 **C.** 3^2 **D.** 3^3

5. 5 squared   **A.** 5^4 **B.** 5^2 **C.** 4^5 **D.** 2^5

6. Classroom Seating A classroom has 6 rows of seats. Each row has 6 seats. How many seats are in the classroom? Write your answer as a power. Then find the value of the power.

Practice and Problem Solving

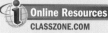
with Homework

Example	Exercises
1	7–12
2	13–27, 29
3	28, 41

Online Resources
CLASSZONE.COM
· More Examples
· eTutorial Plus

Write the product as a power.

7. 8×8 **8.** $12 \times 12 \times 12$ **9.** $9 \times 9 \times 9 \times 9$

10. $4 \times 4 \times 4 \times 4 \times 4$ **11.** $7 \times 7 \times 7 \times 7$ **12.** $3 \times 3 \times 3 \times 3$

13. Find the Error Describe and correct the error in the solution.

$$\times \quad 4^3 = 4 \times 3 = 12$$

Find the value of the power.

14. 7^2 **15.** 12^2 **16.** 6^3 **17.** 100^2

18. 3^5 **19.** 2^5 **20.** 10^4 **21.** 1^6

22. 4 squared   **23.** 8 squared   **24.** 2 cubed   **25.** 10 cubed

26. two to the seventh power   **27.** 10 to the sixth power

28. Invitations On Monday, you invited 2 friends to your party. On Tuesday, each friend invited 2 other friends. On Friday, each of those friends invited 2 more friends. How many people were invited on Friday? Write your answer as a power. Then find the value of the power.

29. Critical Thinking Find the value of 1^8, 1^9, and 1^{10}. What can you say about the value of any power of 1?

Tell which power has a greater value.

30. 2^3 or 3^2 **31.** 4^3 or 6^2 **32.** 1^4 or 3^3 **33.** 10^3 or 13^2

34. 10^2 or 8^3 **35.** 5^3 or 1^5 **36.** 3^4 or 11^2 **37.** 24^5 or 25^5

Tiling You are covering a plant stand with tiles that measure 1 inch by 1 inch. The plant stand measures 6 inches by 6 inches.

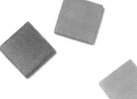

38. How many square tiles do you need? Write your answer as a power. Then find the value.

39. Suppose another stand measures 8 inches by 8 inches. How many tiles will you need to cover it?

40. **Geometry** Draw the next two figures in the pattern shown. Then copy and complete the table.

Number of small squares	1	4	9	?	?
Written as a power	1^2	2^2	?	?	?

41. Find the total number of people called in Example 3 on page 17.

42. **Challenge** Write 256 as a power in three different ways.

Mixed Review

Find the next two numbers in the pattern. *(Lesson 1.1)*

43. 20, 17, 14, 11, _?_, _?_   **44.** 1, 2, 4, 8, _?_, _?_

Estimate the sum, difference, product, or quotient. *(Lesson 1.2)*

45. $157 + 38$ **46.** $672 - 484$ **47.** 72×5 **48.** $179 \div 18$

Basic Skills **Identify the place value of the red digit.**

49. 98   **50.** 1264   **51.** 9035   **52.** 72,406

Test-Taking Practice

53. **Multiple Choice** Which power has a value of 25?

   A. 2^3 **B.** 2^5 **C.** 5^2 **D.** 5^3

54. **Multiple Choice** You stack boxes so that they are 7 high, 7 wide, and 7 long. How many boxes do you stack?

   F. 21   **G.** 49   **H.** 343   **I.** 2401

CALCULATOR

Technology **Activity**

Finding Values of Powers

GOAL Use a calculator to find values of expressions that involve powers.

Example You can use the power key ⌃ to evaluate powers.

A *byte* is a term used to describe a small unit of information stored in a computer's memory. For example, it takes one byte to store one character, such as a number or a letter. A *kilobyte* is defined as 2^{10} bytes. If a computer file is storing one kilobyte of data, how many characters can it be storing?

Solution

To find the value of 2^{10}, use the power key ⌃.

Keystrokes	Display
2 ⌃ 10 =	**1024**

ANSWER One kilobyte is equal to 1024 bytes, so the file can be storing 1024 characters.

with Technology

The keystrokes shown here may not be the same as on your calculator. See your calculator's instruction manual for alternative keystrokes.

Your turn now Use a calculator to find the value of the power.

1. 5^8 **2.** 3^{12} **3.** 4^{10} **4.** 7^7

5. 41^4 **6.** 15^3 **7.** 24^6 **8.** 96^5

9. 348^3 **10.** 832^2 **11.** 145^4 **12.** 627^2

13. twenty-seven cubed   **14.** eighty-four squared

15. nineteen to the fifth power   **16.** twenty-four to the third power

Recall from the example that a computer uses one byte of memory to store one character of data.

17. A megabyte is defined as 2^{20} bytes. If a disk can store one megabyte of data, how many characters can it store?

18. A gigabyte is defined as 2^{30} bytes. If a disk can store one gigabyte of data, how many characters can it store?

Order of Operations

BEFORE	▶ Now	WHY?
You found values with one operation.	You'll evaluate expressions using the order of operations.	So you can calculate the cost of wrapping gifts, as in Ex. 46.

Word Watch

numerical expression, p. 21
grouping symbols, p. 21
evaluate, p. 21
order of operations, p. 21

Expressions A **numerical expression** represents a particular value. It consists of numbers and operations to be performed. An expression can also involve **grouping symbols**, as shown below.

$$7 + (11 - 2)$$

Operations in parentheses are done first.

$$\frac{3 + 7}{9 - 4}$$

A fraction bar groups the numerator separate from the denominator.

You **evaluate** an expression by finding its value. To make sure everyone gets the same result, mathematicians use the **order of operations**.

Order of Operations

1. Evaluate expressions inside grouping symbols.
2. Evaluate powers.
3. Multiply and divide from left to right.
4. Add and subtract from left to right.

Watch Out!

In part (a) of Example 1, multiply *before* subtracting because all multiplication is done first. In part (b), subtract *before* adding because the subtraction is on the left.

EXAMPLE 1 **Using the Order of Operations**

a. $14 - 2 \times 5 = 14 - 10$ First multiply 2 and 5.

            $= 4$ Then subtract 10 from 14.

b. $11 - 8 + 2 = 3 + 2$ First subtract 8 from 11.

            $= 5$ Then add 3 and 2.

c. $16 + 4 \div 2 - 6 = 16 + 2 - 6$ First divide 4 by 2.

                 $= 18 - 6$ Next add 16 and 2.

                 $= 12$ Then subtract 6 from 18.

EXAMPLE 2 Powers and Grouping Symbols

a. $4 + 2^3 = 4 + 8$ First evaluate the power.

$ = 12$ Then add.

b. $(3 + 1) \times 5 = 4 \times 5$ First evaluate inside grouping symbols.

$ = 20$ Then multiply.

c. $\dfrac{8 + 6}{5 - 3} = \dfrac{14}{2}$ Evaluate the numerator and the denominator.

$\phantom{\dfrac{8 + 6}{5 - 3}} = 7$ Then divide.

Your turn now Evaluate the expression.

1. $9 - 7 + 3$ **2.** $8 + 4 \times 3$ **3.** $24 - 8 \times 2 + 9$

4. $21 - 4^2$ **5.** $4 \times (6 - 1)$ **6.** $(24 - 8) \times 2 + 9$

7. $6 + 1 \times 5^2$ **8.** $\dfrac{11 + 19}{3}$ **9.** $\dfrac{2 + 18}{9 - 4}$

EXAMPLE 3 Solving Multi-Step Problems

What do you think?

Science

Aquarium Your class is visiting an aquarium. Admission is $16 per adult and $9 per student. There are 3 adults and 34 students. What is the total cost of admission?

Solution

(**1** Multiply to find the cost of admission for the **adults**.

3 adults $\times$ $16 per adult $=$ **$48**

(**2** Multiply to find the cost of admission for the **students**.

34 students $\times$ $9 per student $=$ **$306**

(**3** Add the **adult** cost and the **student** cost.

$48 + $306 $=$ **$354**

ANSWER The total cost of admission is $354.

■ **Aquarium**

The Florida Aquarium in Tampa offers a tour called DolphinQuest. If the cost is $15 per adult and $10 per person under the age of 13, how much would it cost for you to go with 2 adults and 4 friends who are 11 years old?

Your turn now Use the situation in Example 3.

10. If 4 more adults decide to go on the trip, what will be the new total cost of admission?

Getting Ready to Practice

1. **Vocabulary** Parentheses and fraction bars are examples of _?_.

Evaluate the expression.

2. $9 - 8 + 5$

3. $10 - 4 \div 2$

4. 4×3^2

5. $4 \times (6 \div 3)$

6. $3 \times (7 - 5) + 4$

7. $\dfrac{20}{2 + 8}$

8. **Guided Problem Solving** A compact disc club charges $6 per CD for your first 5 CDs and $10 per CD for your next 4 CDs. If you complete the offer, how much money will you spend?

   (1 What is the total cost for the first 5 CDs?

   (2 What is the total cost for the next 4 CDs?

   (3 How much money will you spend altogether?

Practice and Problem Solving

HELP with **Homework**

Example	Exercises
1	9–14, 28, 29
2	15–26
3	27, 46, 47

Online Resources
CLASSZONE.COM

· More Examples
· eTutorial Plus

Evaluate the expression.

9. $7 - 5 + 1$

10. $6 + 3 - 4$

11. $9 \times 2 \div 3$

12. $4 + 2 \times 3$

13. $9 - 2 \times 4$

14. $7 + 7 \div 7$

15. $8 + 4^2$

16. 5×10^3

17. $12 \div (11 - 5)$

18. $(2 + 8) \times 3$

19. $\dfrac{24}{13 - 5}$

20. $\dfrac{8 + 6}{7}$

21. $10 - 4 \times 1 + 7$

22. $18 \div 3 - 1 \times 4$

23. $6 \times (7 - 5) \div 3$

24. $(8 \div 2) + 2 \times 6$

25. $\dfrac{4^3}{2 + 6}$

26. $\dfrac{40 - 4}{6 + 3}$

27. **Writing** You buy 3 pens for $4 each using your $30 gift card. Find the amount of money you have left to spend on the gift card. Then explain how you solved the problem.

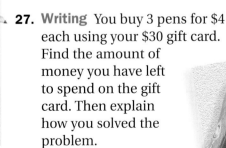

28. Find the Error Describe and correct the error in the solution.

$$\times \quad 6 + 12 \div 3 = 18 \div 3$$
$$= 6$$

29. Critical Thinking If the only operations in an expression are addition and subtraction, in what order do you perform the operations? What if the only operations are multiplication and division?

Tell whether the statement is *true* or *false*. If it is false, find the correct answer.

30. $8 + 3 \times 4 = 44$ **31.** $18 - 15 \div 3 = 1$ **32.** $4 \times (12 + 4) = 64$

33. $15 - 2 + 11 = 24$ **34.** $72 - 6 + 4 = 62$ **35.** $3^2 \times 6 \div 3 = 18$

Estimation **Match the expression with its closest estimate.**

36. $150 - 3 \times 21$ **A.** 100

37. $10 + 3 \times 29$ **B.** 20

38. $5 + 102 \div 4$ **C.** 90

39. $12 \times 8 \div 4$ **D.** 30

 Technology **Use a calculator to evaluate the expression.**

40. $190 - 16 \times 7 + 45$ **41.** $162 \div 18 + 14 \times 12$ **42.** $84 - 78 \div 6 + 5$

43. $378 \div 3^2 - 7 \times 4$ **44.** $11 \times 23 + 5 - 91$ **45.** $5^3 - 39 \div 3 + 2$

46. Gifts You buy 3 rolls of gift wrap for $7 each, 4 rolls of ribbon for $3 each, and 5 packs of gift cards for $4 each. What is the total cost?

47. Seating One side of a movie theater has 20 rows with 4 seats per row. The other side has 18 rows with 6 seats per row. How many seats are there altogether?

Challenge **Insert parentheses to make the statement true.**

48. $12 + 4 \times 4 = 64$ **49.** $8 - 2 \times 6 \div 3^2 = 4$ **50.** $5 + 9 \div 4 - 1 = 8$

51. $2 \times 9 - 4 + 3 = 13$ **52.** $48 \div 8 - 2 + 6 = 4$ **53.** $3 \times 3 + 9 \div 9 = 4$

54. Band Competition Your school band of 50 members is competing in a band competition. Each band member needs $10 for food. The band also rents 2 buses for $225 each. The cost of the buses will be split evenly among the band members. Write an expression for the total cost per student. Then find the total cost per student.

Mixed Review

55. You pay $42 for 6 cases of fruit juice. How much does the juice cost per case? *(Lesson 1.1)*

Write the power as a product. Then find the value. *(Lesson 1.3)*

56. 10^2 **57.** 4^4 **58.** 7^3 **59.** 1^5

Basic Skills **Order the numbers from least to greatest.**

60. 99, 19, 90, 9 **61.** 414, 41, 4, 404 **62.** 555, 50, 510, 505

Test-Taking Practice

63. Multiple Choice What is the first step in evaluating $3 + 5 \times 8 - 7$?

A. $3 + 5$ **B.** 5×8 **C.** $8 - 7$ **D.** $3 + 7$

64. Multiple Choice Evaluate the expression $6 + 18 \div 3^2$.

F. 8 **G.** 31 **H.** 42 **I.** 64

BRAIN GAME

Solve the Riddle

Match each numbered expression in the first column with the letter of the expression in the second column that has the same value. Then replace the number in each box with its matching letter to find the answer to the riddle.

What goes around the world and stays in the corner?

| 3 | 4 | 1 | 3 | 5 | 2 |

1. $3 + 2 \div 1 - 4$

2. $4 - 2 + 9 \div 3$

3. $8 \div (1 \times 2) - 2$

4. $7 + (8 - 4 \times 2)$

5. $1 + 3 \times 4 - 3$

R. $(8 - 4 + 2) \div 2$

S. $0 + (15 - 1) \div 2$

T. $10 - (4 + 3) - 2$

E. $2 \times (12 - 8) + 5$

P. $(10 \div 5) \times 4 - 3$

M. $(7 - 4) \times 3 + 1$

A. $11 - 6 - (12 \div 4)$

Notebook Review

LESSONS 1.1 TO 1.4

Review the vocabulary definitions in your notebook.

Copy the review examples in your notebook. Then complete the exercises.

Check Your Definitions

leading digit, p. 13
compatible numbers, p. 13
factor, p. 16
power, p. 16

base, p. 16
exponent, p. 16
numerical expression, p. 21

grouping symbols, p. 21
evaluate, p. 21
order of operations, p. 21

Use Your Vocabulary

1. Copy and complete: When using the order of operations, you multiply and __?__ from left to right before you add and __?__ from left to right.

2. Identify the base and the exponent in the power 9^5.

1.1–1.2 Can you find exact answers and estimates?

 EXAMPLE Find the exact answer.

a.
$$\begin{array}{r} \overset{1\ 1}{986} \\ +\ 57 \\ \hline 1043 \end{array}$$

b.
$$\begin{array}{r} \overset{2\ 9\ 16}{3\cancel{0}\cancel{6}} \\ -\ 47 \\ \hline 259 \end{array}$$

c.
$$\begin{array}{r} 75 \\ \times\ 42 \\ \hline 150 \\ 300 \\ \hline 3150 \end{array}$$

d.
$$\begin{array}{r} 94\ \text{R1} \\ 8\overline{)753} \\ 72 \\ \hline 33 \\ 32 \\ \hline 1 \end{array}$$

☑ **Find the sum, difference, product, or quotient.**

3. $746 + 389$　　**4.** $921 - 467$　　**5.** 65×23　　**6.** $451 \div 7$

 EXAMPLE Use rounding or compatible numbers to estimate.

a. $431 + 278 \approx 400 + 300 = 700$　　Round to the same place value.

b. $136 - 49 \approx 140 - 50 = 90$　　Round to the same place value.

c. $191 \times 43 \approx 200 \times 40 = 8000$　　Round to the leading digit.

d. $182 \div 21 \approx 180 \div 20 = 9$　　Round the divisor to the leading digit. Find a compatible dividend.

☑ **Estimate the sum, difference, product, or quotient.**

7. $123 + 68$　　**8.** $882 - 407$　　**9.** 87×13　　**10.** $341 \div 5$

1.3–1.4 Can you find values of powers and expressions?

 EXAMPLE

$2^4 = 2 \times 2 \times 2 \times 2 = 16$ Write 2 as a factor four times. Multiply.

☑ **Find the value of the power.**   **11.** 5^2 **12.** 4 cubed

 EXAMPLE

$$28 \div (9 - 5) + 3^2 = 28 \div 4 + 3^2 \quad \text{Evaluate inside grouping symbols.}$$
$$= 28 \div 4 + 9 \quad \text{Evaluate powers.}$$
$$= 7 + 9 \quad \text{Multiply and divide from left to right.}$$
$$= 16 \quad \text{Add and subtract from left to right.}$$

☑ **Evaluate the expression.**   **13.** $4^2 + 18 \div 6$ **14.** $2 \times (3 + 8) - 14$

Stop *and* **Think**   about Lessons 1.1–1.4

15. Estimation Will your estimate of a sum be high or low if you round both numbers up? if you round both numbers down? Explain.

Review Quiz 1

Find the sum, difference, product, or quotient.

1. $29 + 35$ **2.** $90 - 34$ **3.** 32×18 **4.** $124 \div 8$

Estimate the sum, difference, product, or quotient.

5. $284 - 48$ **6.** 147×5 **7.** $1004 + 678$ **8.** $163 \div 4$

Find the value of the power.

9. 10^2 **10.** 7^3 **11.** 2^6 **12.** 10^5

Evaluate the expression.

13. $9 + 7 \times 4$ **14.** $27 \div 3^2 + 5$ **15.** $3 \times (32 - 7)$

16. Phone Card Your phone card has 404 minutes on it. You use 189 minutes. Estimate how many minutes your card has left.

Hands-on Activity

GOAL

Use symbols to represent quantities that may vary.

MATERIALS

• number cube

Representing Quantities

When an unknown quantity might have several different values, you can use a symbol to represent the quantity.

Explore **Roll a number cube to choose values for an unknown quantity.**

		Player 1	Player 2
1	Start with an expression.	$2 \times \boxed{?} - 1$	$4 \times \boxed{?}$
2	Roll the number cube.	**5**	**3**
3	Replace the unknown with the number you roll.	$2 \times 5 - 1$	4×3
4	Evaluate the expression.	9	12

Your turn now **Work with a partner. Use each expression once.**

1. Take turns choosing an expression below and evaluating it following steps 2 through 4 above. Add the values from all your turns to get your score. The player with the highest score is the winner.

 A. $3 \times \boxed{?} - 2$ **B.** $3 + \boxed{?}$ **C.** $17 - 2 \times \boxed{?}$ **D.** $6 \times \boxed{?} \div 3$

 E. $60 \div \boxed{?}$ **F.** $5 \times \boxed{?} - 4$ **G.** $8 \times \boxed{?} - 5$ **H.** $180 \div (3 \times \boxed{?})$

Stop and Think

2. **Critical Thinking** How many different values are possible for each expression when you use a number cube to choose values for the unknown quantity?

3. **Writing** For any given expression, does rolling a high number like 5 always result in a greater value than rolling a low number like 2? Explain.

Variables and Expressions

LESSON 1.5

BEFORE

You evaluated numerical expressions.

▶ **Now**

You'll evaluate expressions that involve variables.

WHY?

So you can find distance traveled while rafting, as in Ex. 45.

In the Real World

Word Watch

variable, p. 29
variable expression, p. 29

Dog's Age The following *rule of thumb* is a useful way to compare the age of an adult dog to the age of a human.

Multiply the dog's age by 4 and then add 15.

Call this the dog's age in "dog years." How many dog years old is a dog that is 4 years old? 6 years old? 10 years old? In Example 2 on page 30 you will use a variable expression to find out.

Variable Expressions A **variable** is a symbol, usually a letter, that represents one or more numbers. A **variable expression** consists of numbers, variables, and the operations to be performed. To evaluate a variable expression, substitute a number for each variable and evaluate the resulting numerical expression.

EXAMPLE 1 Evaluating Expressions

a. Evaluate $4 + t$, when $t = 2$.

$$4 + t = 4 + 2 \qquad \text{Substitute 2 for } t.$$
$$= 6 \qquad \text{Add.}$$

b. Evaluate $x \div 8$, when $x = 16$.

$$x \div 8 = 16 \div 8 \qquad \text{Substitute 16 for } x.$$
$$= 2 \qquad \text{Divide.}$$

Your turn now Evaluate the expression.

1. $s + 9$, when $s = 7$

2. $13 - r$, when $r = 5$

3. $x - 3$, when $x = 8$

4. $m \div 4$, when $m = 32$

Multiplication and Variables To avoid confusion between the multiplication symbol $\times$ and the variable x, you should express multiplication with variables in one of the following ways.

multiplication dot	parentheses	no symbol
$3 \cdot x$	$3(x)$	$3x$

EXAMPLE 2 **Evaluating Multiplication Expressions**

To answer the questions about dog years at the top of page 29, evaluate the expression $4y + 15$ when $y = 4$, $y = 6$, and $y = 10$.

① Choose values for y (age in years).	② Substitute for y in the expression $4y + 15$.	③ Evaluate the expression to find the age in dog years.
4	$4 \cdot 4 + 15$	31
6	$4 \cdot 6 + 15$	39
10	$4 \cdot 10 + 15$	55

ANSWER A 4-year-old dog is 31 dog years old. A 6-year-old dog is 39 dog years old. A 10-year-old dog is 55 dog years old.

EXAMPLE 3 **Expressions with Two Variables**

Evaluate the expression when $x = 8$ and $y = 2$.

a. $x + y = 8 + 2$ Substitute 8 for x and 2 for y.

$\qquad\quad = 10$ Add.

b. $x - y^2 = 8 - 2^2$ Substitute 8 for x and 2 for y.

$\qquad\quad = 8 - 4$ Evaluate the power.

$\qquad\quad = 4$ Subtract.

HELP with Notetaking

You may want to include part (b) of Example 3 in your notebook as a reminder to use the order of operations when evaluating a variable expression.

Your turn now Evaluate the expression when $m = 10$ and $n = 5$.

5. $3m$ **6.** $11n$ **7.** $2n + 4$ **8.** $25 - 2m$

9. $m - n$ **10.** $m + 3n$ **11.** $26 - n^2$ **12.** $n + 9 - m$

Getting Ready to Practice

1. **Vocabulary** Identify the variable in the expression $5a - 2$.

2. What operation is represented by the dot in $10 + 7 \cdot x$?

3. **Find the Error** Describe and correct
   the error in evaluating $3t$ when $t = 2$.

   $$3t = 3(2)$$
   $$= 32$$

Evaluate the expression when $m = 9$ and $n = 3$.

4. $n + 8$ 5. $7m$ 6. $n \div 1$ 7. $14 - n$

8. $m - n$ 9. $m + n$ 10. $m \div n$ 11. $m + 2n$

12. **Boots** Let h represent your height in inches while barefoot. You can
    use the expression $2 + h$ to represent your height while wearing boots
    with 2-inch heels. Use the expression to find how tall you are while
    wearing boots if you are 53 inches tall while barefoot.

Practice and Problem Solving

HELP with **Homework**

Example	Exercises
1	13–18, 27, 29–31
2	19–26, 28
3	32–44

Online Resources
CLASSZONE.COM

· More Examples
· eTutorial Plus

Evaluate the expression.

13. $9 + x$, when $x = 7$

14. $t + 5$, when $t = 8$

15. $y - 7$, when $y = 13$

16. $12 - n$, when $n = 3$

17. $w \div 4$, when $w = 20$

18. $18 \div s$, when $s = 3$

19. $r \cdot 9$, when $r = 5$

20. $6m$, when $m = 10$

21. $16 - a^2$, when $a = 3$

22. $d^2 - 8$, when $d = 5$

23. $5 + 12 \div u$, when $u = 6$

24. $8 \div w + 5$, when $w = 2$

25. $2c - 5$, when $c = 4$

26. $13 + 4z$, when $z = 11$

27. **Weather** You can use the expression
    $n \div 5$ to estimate how far, in miles,
    you are from lightning. The variable
    n represents the number of seconds
    from when you see the lightning to
    when you hear thunder. How far
    away is the lightning when $n = 20$?

28. Dog Years Your dog is five years old. You can estimate a dog's age in dog years by using the expression $4y + 15$, where y represents the dog's age. How old is your dog in dog years?

Geometry **The perimeter of a figure is the sum of the lengths of its sides. Find the perimeter of the triangle when $x = 3$ feet.**

29.

4 ft   5 ft
x

30.

4 ft   4 ft
x

31.

6 ft   5 ft
x

32. Find the Error Describe and correct the error in evaluating $6y + x$, when $x = 3$ and $y = 5$.

$$6y + x = 6 \cdot 3 + 5$$
$$= 18 + 5$$
$$= 23$$

Evaluate the expression when $x = 6$ and $y = 3$.

33. $x + y$ **34.** $x - y$ **35.** $x \div y$ **36.** $x \cdot y$

37. $4x - y$ **38.** $x + 5y$ **39.** $y + 2x$ **40.** $3y - x$

41. $2x \cdot y$ **42.** $y + 18 \div x$ **43.** $x - 18 \div y^2$ **44.** $y - 2 + x^2$

Extended Problem Solving **In Exercises 45–47, use the expression $r \cdot t$ to find how far you travel while rafting. The variable r is your speed, in miles per hour. The variable t is hours traveled.**

45. Explain How far do you travel if you raft at a speed of 6 miles per hour for 3 hours? Explain how you found your answer.

46. Calculate How far does your friend travel if she rafts at a speed of 8 miles per hour for 2 hours?

47. Compare Who travels *faster*, you or your friend? Who travels *farther*?

48. Writing Explain how to evaluate the expression $2u + 5w$ when $u = 7$ and $w = 9$.

Evaluate the expression when $x = 6$, $y = 5$, and $z = 2$.

49. $x - z + y$ **50.** $x \div z + y$ **51.** $y \cdot (x - z)$ **52.** $x + 2y + z$

53. $x^2 + z - y$ **54.** $x + y^2 - z$ **55.** $xy - z$ **56.** $x + yz$

What do you think?

Recreation

■ Rafting

Sections of white water rivers are rated on a scale of 1 to 6. A rating of 1 means the current is slow and it's easy to raft. A rating of 6 means it's too dangerous to raft. What rating would you give to a river section that is rafted only by expert rafters? Explain.

Challenge Use the table to find a rule that relates each number and its result. Write a variable expression to represent the rule for *n*.

57.

Number	Result
1	6
2	7
3	8
4	?
n	?

58.

Number	Result
2	5
3	7
4	9
5	?
n	?

Mixed Review

Evaluate the expression. *(Lesson 1.4)*

59. $8 + 6 \times 3$ **60.** $(24 - 6) \div 3$ **61.** $18 - 3 \times 5$ **62.** $1 + 2^3$

Choose a Strategy Use a strategy from the list to solve the following problem. Explain your choice of strategy.

63. Use the symbols $+$, $-$, $\times$, or $\div$ to make the following statement true. You may use a symbol more than once.

$$8 \underline{\ ?\ } 2 \underline{\ ?\ } 7 \underline{\ ?\ } 4 = 44$$

> **Problem Solving Strategies**
> - Guess, Check, and Revise
> - Make a List
> - Draw a Diagram
> - Work Backward

Basic Skills Tell whether the statement is *true* or *false*. If it is false, find the correct answer.

64. $9 \times 5 = 54$ **65.** $7 + 4 = 11$ **66.** $10 \div 5 = 5$ **67.** $17 - 8 = 9$

68. $8 + 6 = 14$ **69.** $48 \div 8 = 7$ **70.** $13 - 5 = 6$ **71.** $3 \times 7 = 21$

Test-Taking Practice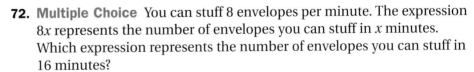

72. Multiple Choice You can stuff 8 envelopes per minute. The expression $8x$ represents the number of envelopes you can stuff in x minutes. Which expression represents the number of envelopes you can stuff in 16 minutes?

A. $8 + 16$ **B.** $16 - 8$ **C.** $8 \cdot 16$ **D.** $16 \div 8$

73. Short Response You have some money saved, and you plan to save an additional $10 per week to pay for a school trip. You can model this situation with the expression $10w + x$, where w is the number of weeks and x is the amount of money you start with. How much money will you have after 14 weeks if you start with $32? Explain how you found your answer.

Draw a Diagram
Make a List
Make a Table
Work Backward
Guess, Check, and Revise
Look for a Pattern
Act It Out

Guess, Check, and Revise

Problem You are selling note cards and calendars to raise money for a class trip. So far, you have sold 18 items worth a total of $159. A box of note cards costs $10, and a calendar costs $7. How many of each item have you sold?

❶ Read and Understand

Read the problem carefully.

You want to know how many of the 18 items you sold were note cards and how many were calendars.

❷ Make a Plan

Decide on a strategy to use.

Guess two whole numbers whose sum is 18. *Check* whether the value of the 18 items is $159. *Revise* your guess as needed.

❸ Solve the Problem

Reread the problem and guess an answer.

Guess: Try 9 boxes of note cards and 9 calendars.

Check: $9 \times \$10 + 9 \times \$7 = \$153$

$153 is less than $159.

Revise: Try more note cards.

Guess: Try 10 boxes of note cards and 8 calendars.

Check: $10 \times \$10 + 8 \times \$7 = \$156$

$156 is less than $159, but closer.

Revise: Try still more note cards.

Guess: Try 11 boxes of note cards and 7 calendars.

Check: $11 \times \$10 + 7 \times \$7 = \$159$

ANSWER You have sold 11 boxes of note cards and 7 calendars.

❹ Look Back

Check that your answer meets all the conditions of the problem. You have sold 18 items, because $11 + 7 = 18$. Their value is $159, because $11 \times \$10 + 7 \times \$7 = \$159$.

Use the strategy *guess, check, and revise*.

1. **Flowers** Your teacher spent $55 on tulips and daffodils. A pot of tulips costs $5, and a pot of daffodils costs $4. If your teacher bought 12 pots, how many pots of each kind of flower did your teacher buy?

2. **Fundraising** You are selling note cards and calendars for a school fundraiser. You have sold 15 items worth a total of $117. A box of note cards costs $10, and a calendar costs $7. How many of each item have you sold?

3. **Quizzes** A math quiz is worth 100 points. There are 13 problems on the quiz. Some problems are worth 5 points, and the rest are worth 12 points. How many of each kind of problem are on the quiz?

4. **Number Sense** The product of two whole numbers is 1122. Their difference is 1. Find both numbers.

5. **Ropes** A rope is 33 feet long. You cut the rope into two pieces so that one piece is 3 feet longer than the other. Find the length of the longer piece.

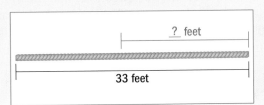

6. **Order of Operations** Use the symbols +, −, ×, or ÷ to make the following statement true. You may use a symbol more than once.

   $$4 \underline{\ ?\ } 5 \underline{\ ?\ } 6 \underline{\ ?\ } 10 = 80$$

Mixed Problem Solving

Use any strategy to solve the problem.

7. **CD Players** You are saving money to buy a CD player that costs $160. So far, you have saved $100. If you save $20 more each month, in how many months will you have exactly $160?

8. **Sweaters** A shop sells sweaters in small, medium, and large. Each size is available in red, blue, black, and white. How many different kinds of sweaters does the shop need to keep in stock?

9. **Rules** Use the table to find one rule that relates each number in Column A with the corresponding number in Column B.

Column A	Column B
11	5
10	4
9	3
8	2
7	1

10. **Computers** Your family plans to buy a computer for $980, plus a sales tax of $49. The first payment will be $150, and the rest of the cost will be paid in 3 equal payments. Find the amount of each equal payment.

Equations and Mental Math

BEFORE	Now	WHY?
You evaluated numerical and variable expressions.	You'll solve equations using mental math.	So you can find how long to save money, as in Ex. 44.

Word Watch

equation, p. 36
solution, p. 36
solve, p. 37

In the Real World

Camping You are going camping with friends. You fill your backpack until it weighs 13 pounds. Your friend adds another item from the list at the right, and your backpack weighs 20 pounds. What item did your friend add?

clothes	3 pounds
food	6 pounds
sleeping bag	4 pounds
tent	7 pounds

EXAMPLE 1 **Guess, Check, and Revise**

To answer the question above about backpacking, you can use the problem solving strategy *guess, check, and revise*.

① Try an item on the list.

$13 + 4 = 17$

This total weight is under 20 pounds.

② Try the food, which is heavier.

$13 + 6 = 19$

This total weight is still one pound low.

③ Try the tent. It weighs 7 pounds.

$13 + 7 = 20$

This total weight equals 20 pounds.

ANSWER Your friend added the tent to your backpack.

Equations You can use *equations* to answer questions like the one above. An **equation** is a mathematical sentence formed by placing an equal sign (=) between two expressions. A **solution** of an equation is a number that, when substituted for a variable, makes the equation true.

EXAMPLE 2 **Checking a Possible Solution**

Tell whether the given number is a solution of the equation.

a. $3y = 21; 6$

$3(6) \stackrel{?}{=} 21$

$18 \neq 21$

↖The symbol $\neq$ can be read "is not equal to."

ANSWER 6 is not a solution.

b. $x - 3 = 7; 10$

$10 - 3 \stackrel{?}{=} 7$

$7 = 7$

ANSWER 10 is a solution.

Solving Equations To **solve** an equation, you find all the solutions of the equation. To solve simple equations using mental math, you can think of the equation as a question.

HELP with Notetaking

In your notes on *Equations and Mental Math*, you may want to include examples showing equations rewritten as questions, like the ones in Example 3.

EXAMPLE 3 Using Mental Math to Solve Equations

Equation	Question	Solution	Check
a. $y - 8 = 4$	What number minus 8 equals 4?	12	$12 - 8 = 4$
b. $10x = 90$	10 times what number equals 90?	9	$10 \cdot 9 = 90$
c. $n \div 4 = 7$	What number divided by 4 equals 7?	28	$28 \div 4 = 7$

Mental Math When you do mental math, keep in mind the following rules that will help you to solve some equations that involve a 0 or a 1.

Operations Involving 0 and 1

Adding 0 The sum of any number and 0 is that number.

Multiplying by 0 The product of any number and 0 is 0.

Multiplying by 1 The product of any number and 1 is that number.

EXAMPLE 4 Mental Math with 0 and 1

Equation	Question	Solution	Check
a. $y + 2 = 2$	What number plus 2 equals 2?	0	$0 + 2 = 2$
b. $6 \cdot x = 6$	6 times what number equals 6?	1	$6 \cdot 1 = 6$

Your turn now Solve the equation using mental math.

1. $x + 10 = 24$ **2.** $13n = 13$ **3.** $35y = 0$

4. $9x = 54$ **5.** $y - 6 = 11$ **6.** $18 \div n = 9$

EXAMPLE 5 Solving Problems Using Mental Math

Salmon Migration You are 100 miles upstream from the sea. Salmon migrating upstream have been spotted 41 miles from the sea. Use mental math to solve the equation $d + 41 = 100$ to find the distance d, in miles, between you and the salmon.

Solution

Think of the equation as a question.

Equation	d	$+$	41	$=$	100
Question	What number	plus	41	equals	100?
Solution	59	plus	41	equals	100.

ANSWER The distance between you and the salmon is 59 miles.

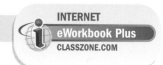

1.6 Exercises

More Practice, p. 708

More Practice, p. 708

INTERNET
eWorkbook Plus
CLASSZONE.COM

Getting Ready to Practice

1. Vocabulary The number 9 is the __?__ of the equation $x - 5 = 4$.

Tell whether 5 is a solution of the equation.

2. $t + 2 = 7$ **3.** $16 - k = 11$ **4.** $15 \div m = 5$ **5.** $4y = 20$

Solve the equation using mental math.

6. $4 + z = 12$ **7.** $x - 2 = 1$ **8.** $6r = 24$ **9.** $w \div 2 = 5$

10. $17 - y = 9$ **11.** $c + 8 = 21$ **12.** $56 \div m = 7$ **13.** $3t = 27$

14. Sports The table shows three major league baseball players and their home run totals as of June 11 of a recent season. Solve the equations in the table to find the number of home runs, x, that each player needed to hit in order to reach 40 home runs.

Player	Home Runs	Equation
Barry Bonds	32	$x + 32 = 40$
Luis Gonzalez	26	$x + 26 = 40$
Manny Ramirez	21	$x + 21 = 40$

Practice and Problem Solving

with Homework

Example	Exercises
1	44
2	15–23
3	24–39
4	40–43
5	54, 55

Online Resources
CLASSZONE.COM

· More Examples
· eTutorial Plus

Tell whether the given number is a solution of the equation.

15. $7 + x = 10$; 3   **16.** $y - 3 = 7$; 4   **17.** $9 - r = 8$; 2

18. $m + 2 = 6$; 4   **19.** $4c = 32$; 9   **20.** $4y = 4$; 1

21. $10s = 77$; 7   **22.** $30 \div x = 10$; 10   **23.** $48 \div r = 6$; 8

Match the equation with the question.

24. $6 - n = 2$ **A.** What number minus 2 equals 6?

25. $n - 2 = 6$ **B.** 2 times what number equals 12?

26. $2n = 12$ **C.** 12 times what number equals 6?

27. $12n = 6$ **D.** 6 minus what number equals 2?

Solve the equation using mental math.

28. $8 + y = 10$ **29.** $s - 5 = 9$ **30.** $14 - z = 1$

31. $d + 3 = 11$ **32.** $2w = 16$ **33.** $27 \div r = 9$

34. $m \div 6 = 7$ **35.** $5w = 45$ **36.** $c + 6 = 13$

37. $23 - t = 10$ **38.** $22 - n = 17$ **39.** $x + 9 = 20$

40. $36h = 36$ **41.** $35 + a = 35$ **42.** $3f = 0$

43. Find the Error Describe and correct the error in solving the equation $5x = 5$.

$$5x = 5$$
$$5(0) = 5$$
So, 0 is the solution.

44. Guess, Check, and Revise You are saving money to buy a camera that costs $195. So far, you have saved $87. If you save $9 more each week, in how many weeks will you have exactly $195?

Choose a Method Tell whether the given number is a solution of the equation. Then tell whether you used *mental math*, *paper and pencil*, or *a calculator* to get each answer.

45. $y - 9 = 2$; 12   **46.** $10 + x = 25$; 15   **47.** $14t = 122$; 8

48. $3x + 2 = 32$; 9   **49.** $16y + 6 = 300$; 18   **50.** $32 - 4r = 8$; 6

51. $9r = 63$; 7   **52.** $110n = 1980$; 19   **53.** $3380 \div w = 13$; 26

54. Computer Games You earned 300 points playing a computer game. Your goal is to reach 500 points. Solve the equation $p + 300 = 500$ to find the number of points, p, you need to reach your goal.

55. Baby-sitting You make $7 an hour baby-sitting. You need to earn $420. Solve the equation $7h = 420$ to find the number of hours, h, you need to baby-sit.

56. Volleyball Your gym class is split up into teams of 6 students for a volleyball tournament. There are 48 students in the class. Choose the equation you can use to find how many teams, t, you have. Then solve the equation using mental math.

A. $t + 6 = 48$ **B.** $6t = 48$

C. $t \div 48 = 6$ **D.** $t - 6 = 48$

Challenge Tell whether the equation has *no solution*, *one solution*, or *many solutions*. Use examples to explain your answer.

57. $0 \cdot x = 0$ **58.** $x \cdot 0 = 8$

59. $1 \cdot x = x$ **60.** $0 + x = 0$

Mixed Review

61. You know that 717 children and 489 adults went to your school fair. Estimate the total number of people who went to the fair. *(Lesson 1.2)*

Evaluate the expression when $y = 3$. *(Lesson 1.5)*

62. $15 - y$ **63.** $8 \cdot y$ **64.** $y + 9$ **65.** $18 \div y$

Basic Skills Tell which expression has the greater value.

66. $8 + 4$ or $20 \div 4$ **67.** $15 - 6$ or $20 \div 2$ **68.** 3×8 or $9 + 9$

Test-Taking Practice

69. Multiple Choice You earn $15 each time you mow your neighbor's lawn. Solve the equation $d \div 4 = 15$ to find the amount of money d, in dollars, you earn by mowing the lawn 4 times.

A. 11   **B.** 19   **C.** 21   **D.** 60

70. Multiple Choice Your friend can read 2 pages per minute in her library book. She read 20 pages last night. Solve the equation $m \cdot 2 = 20$ to find the number of minutes, m, she spent reading.

F. 10   **G.** 20   **H.** 22   **I.** 40

LESSON 1.7

A Problem Solving Plan

BEFORE — **Now** — **WHY?**

You used the strategy *guess, check,* and *revise.*

You'll use a 4-step plan to solve many kinds of problems.

So you can find how many ways to pay a toll, as in Ex. 4.

In the Real World

Word Watch

verbal model, p. 41

Shopping You went to the mall with $29 and came home with $3. Later, you made a list of how much you spent on each item, but you didn't have a receipt for the food. How much did you spend on food?

CD	$8
yo-yo	$3
sunglasses	$5
food	?

EXAMPLE 1 **Understanding and Planning**

To solve the problem about spending money, first make sure you understand the problem. Then make a plan for solving the problem.

Read and Understand

What do you know?

You started with $29. Now you have $3.

You bought a CD for $8, a yo-yo for $3, and sunglasses for $5.

What do you want to find out?

How much did you spend on food?

Make a Plan

How can you relate what you know to what you want to find out?

Write a *verbal model* to describe how the values in this problem are related. A **verbal model** uses words to describe ideas and then uses math symbols to relate the words.

$$\begin{array}{c} \text{Money spent} \\ \text{on food} \end{array} = \begin{array}{c} \text{Money spent} \\ \text{at the mall} \end{array} - \begin{array}{c} \text{Money spent on CD,} \\ \text{yo-yo, and sunglasses} \end{array}$$

Your turn now **Use the information at the top of the page.**

1. How can you figure out how much you spent at the mall?

2. How can you figure out how much you spent for items besides food?

EXAMPLE 2 **Solving and Looking Back**

To solve the problem at the top of page 41 about spending money, you need to carry out the plan from Example 1 and then check the answer.

Solve the Problem

Write a verbal model to relate the amount of money spent on food to the dollar values you are given at the top of page 41.

Money spent on food	=	Money spent at the mall	−	Money spent on CD, yo-yo, and sunglasses
	=	$(29 - 3)$	−	$(8 + 3 + 5)$
	=	26	−	16
	=	10		

ANSWER You spent $10 on food at the mall.

Look Back

Make sure your answer is reasonable. Add the money you spent on each item to what you had left. This should be equal to the amount of money you had when you started.

$$8 + 3 + 5 + 10 + 3 = 29 \checkmark$$

Your turn now **Use Example 2 above.**

3. If you came home with $5 instead of $3, how much did you spend on food at the mall?

Problem Solving Plan

1. **Read and Understand** Read the problem carefully. Identify the question and any important information.

2. **Make a Plan** Decide on a problem solving strategy.

3. **Solve the Problem** Use the problem solving strategy to answer the question.

4. **Look Back** Check that your answer is reasonable.

EXAMPLE 3 **Draw a Diagram**

The mall is 12 miles from your home. Your school is one third of the way from your home to the mall. The library is one fourth of the way from the school to the mall. How far is the library from home?

Solution

Read and Understand Your school and the library are between your home and the mall, which are 12 miles apart. You need to find the distance between your home and the library.

Make a Plan Draw a diagram showing the relationships between the different locations. Use the diagram to solve the problem.

Solve the Problem Draw a number line and mark the locations.

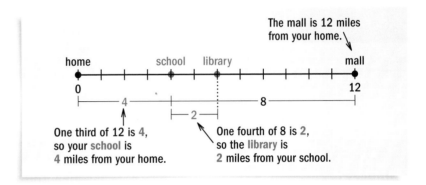

ANSWER From the diagram you can see that the library is $4 + 2 = 6$ miles from your home.

Look Back The mall is 12 miles from your home and the library is between them. Because 6 is less than 12, the answer is reasonable.

Your turn now **The map shows the distances between four cities.**

4. How many different routes are possible from City A to City D without backtracking?

5. What is the longest route from City A to City D?

6. What is the longest route from City C to City B?

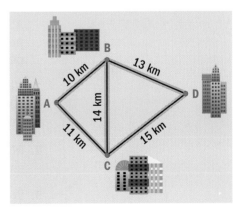

Getting Ready to Practice

1. **Vocabulary** Explain the four steps of the problem solving plan.

2. **Guided Problem Solving** A conductor on a train has run out of quarters and has to make change using only dimes and nickels. What are all the ways that the conductor can make 40 cents in change?

   (1 What are you trying to find?

   (2 How can a table like the one at the right help you to solve the problem?

   (3 Use the table to solve the problem.

   (4 How can you check whether your answer is reasonable?

Number of dimes	Number of nickels	Total value
?	?	?
?	?	?
?	?	?
?	?	?
?	?	?

Practice and Problem Solving

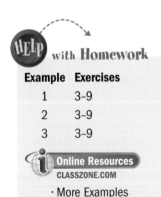

HELP with Homework

Example	Exercises
1	3–9
2	3–9
3	3–9

Online Resources
CLASSZONE.COM
· More Examples
· eTutorial Plus

3. **Fencing** A fence is 30 feet long. You need to place a fence post at both ends of the fence and every 5 feet along the fence. Draw a diagram to find how many posts you need.

4. **Tollbooths** The toll at a tollbooth is 45 cents for each car. Use a table to find all the different ways you can pay the toll exactly if you can use quarters, dimes, and nickels.

5. **Cell Phone** You pay $49 for a cell phone and $19 per month for phone service. Use a verbal model to find your total cost after 12 months.

6. **Video Game** You share the cost of buying a new video game with Alice, Omar, and Celine. You want to decide the order in which each person gets to try the game. Make a list to show all the different possible orders.

7. **Number Sense** The product of two whole numbers is 24. Their sum is 10. Find the two numbers. Begin by making a list of pairs of whole numbers whose product is 24.

8. **Museum** Tickets to a science museum cost $12 per adult and $7 per child. Find the total cost for a group of 6 adults and 4 children.

9. **Writing** Explain how you could find the total cost in Exercise 8 by acting out the problem with a group of people using play money.

10. Find the Error Describe and correct the error in the solution at the right to the problem below.

Your school is sending 177 people on a field trip. Each bus can carry 40 passengers. How many buses are needed?

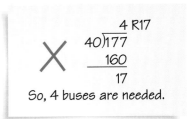

```
      4 R17
   40)177
      160
       17
```
So, 4 buses are needed.

11. Amusement Park You buy 20 tickets. You ride the Ferris wheel for 4 tickets and you visit the house of mirrors for 3 tickets. After you ride the roller coaster, you have 7 tickets left. How many tickets did you use to ride the roller coaster?

12. Basketball You get 1 point for making a free throw, 3 points for making a long 3-point shot, and 2 points for making other shots. What are all the different ways you can score 6 points?

13. Waiting Lines John is second in a line of 11 people. There are 5 people between Lauren and Franco. There are 2 people between Franco and John. How many people are there between Lauren and John? How many people are ahead of Lauren in line?

14. Challenge You forgot the three-digit access code for your garage door. The first digit is 3 and the last two digits are odd numbers. How many different access codes are possible?

Mixed Review

Write the product as a power. *(Lesson 1.3)*

15. 17×17

16. $11 \times 11 \times 11$

17. $8 \times 8 \times 8 \times 8$

Solve the equation using mental math. *(Lesson 1.6)*

18. $x + 9 = 14$

19. $6w = 48$

20. $c \div 2 = 9$

21. $n - 3 = 7$

Basic Skills **Round the number to the red digit.**

22. 2562

23. 17,608

24. 148,563

25. 924,375

Test-Taking Practice

26. Extended Response The balcony section of a theater has 9 rows of seats. Each row has 14 seats. A ticket for a balcony seat costs $23. How many seats are in the balcony section of the theater? If half of the tickets for balcony seats are sold, how much money is raised from tickets for balcony seats? Explain how you found your answer.

LESSONS 1.5 TO 1.7

Notebook Review

Notebook

Review the vocabulary definitions in your notebook.

Copy the review examples in your notebook. Then complete the exercises.

Check Your Definitions

variable, p. 29
variable expression, p. 29

equation, p. 36
solution, p. 36

solve, p. 37
verbal model, p. 41

Use Your Vocabulary

1. Copy and complete: The ? in the expression $x + 2$ is x.

2. Writing Is 5 a solution of the equation $3n = 15$? Why or why not?

1.5 Can you evaluate variable expressions?

 EXAMPLE Evaluate $t + 17$ when $t = 4$.

$t + 17 = 4 + 17 = 21$ Substitute 4 for *t*. Then add.

 Evaluate when $y = 6$. 3. $19 + y$ **4.** $y \div 3$ **5.** $18 - 2 \cdot y$

1.6 Can you solve equations using mental math?

 EXAMPLE To solve $4n = 40$, ask "4 times what number equals 40?"

ANSWER The solution is 10, because $4 \cdot 10 = 40$.

☑ **Solve the equation.** **6.** $r - 1 = 5$ **7.** $7m = 7$ **8.** $40 \div c = 5$

1.7 Can you use a problem solving plan?

EXAMPLE You pay $50 for a gym membership and $3 per visit. What is your total cost for 20 visits?

Understand and Plan Find the total cost by using a verbal model.

Solve Total cost = Membership cost + Cost for visits

$= \$50 + \$3 \cdot 20$

$= \$110$

Look Back $\$50 + \$3 \cdot 20 = \$50 + \$60 = \$110$ ✓

☑ **9.** What is your total cost if you make 30 visits to the gym?

Stop *and* **Think** about Lessons 1.5–1.7

10. Mental Math Is $x \cdot 0 = 12$ true for any value of x? Explain.

11. Writing Explain why *looking back* at your answer is an important part of the problem solving plan.

Review Quiz 2

Evaluate the expression when $a = 12$ and $b = 3$.

1. $15 - a$ **2.** $a \div 6$ **3.** $3 + 5 \cdot b$

4. $9 - 6 \div b$ **5.** $7b$ **6.** $a + b$

Solve the equation using mental math.

7. $r - 1 = 2$ **8.** $5 + z = 25$ **9.** $y \div 3 = 7$ **10.** $12m = 72$

11. Food You are ordering a pizza. You have a choice of three toppings: mushrooms, pepperoni, or peppers. How many different pizzas can you order if you select exactly two different toppings?

To find your way across the river, solve the equations using mental math.

- If the solution is 1 or 6, go to the right.
- If the solution is 2 or 5, go down.
- If the solution is 3, go up.
- If the solution is 4, go to the left.

Write down each equation you solve and its solution.

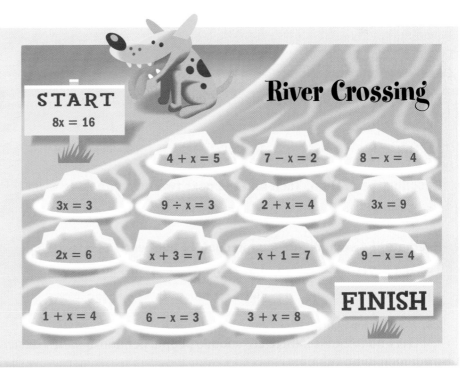

START
$8x = 16$

River Crossing

$4 + x = 5$ $7 - x = 2$ $8 - x = 4$

$3x = 3$ $9 \div x = 3$ $2 + x = 4$ $3x = 9$

$2x = 6$ $x + 3 = 7$ $x + 1 = 7$ $9 - x = 4$

$1 + x = 4$ $6 - x = 3$ $3 + x = 8$ **FINISH**

1 Chapter Review

 **Vocabulary**

leading digit, p. 13
compatible numbers,
  p. 13
factor, p. 16
power, p. 16
base, p. 16
exponent, p. 16

numerical expression,
  p. 21
grouping symbols, p. 21
evaluate, p. 21
order of operations, p. 21
variable, p. 29

variable expression,
  p. 29
equation, p. 36
solution, p. 36
solve, p. 37
verbal model, p. 41

Vocabulary Review

Copy and complete the statement.

1. To make sure that everyone always gets the same result, you evaluate expressions using the _?_ .

2. A _?_ has a base and an exponent.

3. The _?_ of a power is the repeated factor.

4. A _?_ is a symbol, usually a letter, that represents one or more numbers.

5. A mathematical sentence formed by placing an equals sign (=) between two expressions is an _?_ .

6. When a number is substituted for a variable, it is a _?_ of the equation if it makes the equation true.

Review Questions

Find the sum, difference, product, or quotient. *(Lesson 1.1)*

7. $928 + 185$ **8.** $64 - 27$ **9.** 15×35 **10.** $216 \div 9$

11. $471 \div 6$ **12.** 36×12 **13.** $551 - 138$ **14.** $157 + 3094$

Describe the pattern. Then find the next two numbers. *(Lesson 1.1)*

15. $9, 18, 27, 36, \underline{?}, \underline{?}$ **16.** $40, 80, 160, 320, \underline{?}, \underline{?}$ **17.** $67, 57, 47, 37, \underline{?}, \underline{?}$

Estimate the sum, difference, product, or quotient. *(Lesson 1.2)*

18. $149 - 53$ **19.** $286 + 109$ **20.** 39×88 **21.** $411 \div 18$

22. $635 \div 8$ **23.** 592×3 **24.** $2120 + 791$ **25.** $715 - 296$

26. Population About how many people are living in a town with 3411 households if there are about 3 people per household? *(Lesson 1.2)*

Find the value of the power. *(Lesson 1.3)*

27. 7^3 **28.** 10^5 **29.** 5^4 **30.** 1^{100}

31. 13^2 **32.** 9^3 **33.** 50 squared   **34.** 8 cubed

Evaluate the expression. *(Lesson 1.4)*

35. $20 - 3 \times 5$ **36.** $11 - 9 + 2$ **37.** $8 - 6 \div 3$ **38.** $4 \times (9 - 7) + 6$

39. 8×10^4 **40.** $9 + 4 \div 4$ **41.** $\dfrac{9 + 3}{4}$ **42.** 3×5^2

43. $\dfrac{6^2}{5 + 7}$ **44.** $(13 - 6) \times 4$ **45.** $8 \times (4 - 1) \div 6$ **46.** $\dfrac{55 - 6}{1 + 6}$

Evaluate the expression. *(Lesson 1.5)*

47. $x + 4$, when $x = 6$ **48.** $19 - y$, when $y = 12$ **49.** $48 - m$, when $m = 39$

50. $22r$, when $r = 3$ **51.** $s \div 9$, when $s = 63$ **52.** $3n + 7$, when $n = 8$

Evaluate the expression when *x* = 3 and *y* = 5. *(Lesson 1.5)*

53. $5 \cdot x$ **54.** $y + 9$ **55.** $75 \div x$ **56.** $3y - 2$

57. Statues You can represent the total height of a statue standing on an 18 inch platform using the expression $18 + h$, where h is the statue's height in inches. What is the total height of the statue and the platform if the statue is 48 inches tall? *(Lesson 1.5)*

58. Trains The length of a train with an engine and three cars can be represented by the expression $n + 3c$, where n is the length, in feet, of the engine and c is the length, in feet, of a car. What is the train's total length if the engine is 64 feet long and a car is 90 feet long? *(Lesson 1.5)*

Solve the equation using mental math. *(Lesson 1.6)*

59. $9x = 45$ **60.** $n - 3 = 10$ **61.** $8 + y = 8$ **62.** $21 \div n = 3$

63. $x \div 10 = 6$ **64.** $y + 16 = 20$ **65.** $19 - x = 15$ **66.** $3n = 45$

67. Phones To make a phone call, you pay $2 for the first 20 minutes, then 10 cents per minute. What is the total cost of a 32-minute phone call? *(Lesson 1.7)*

68. Highways Exits 1 through 4 are in order on a highway. Exit 4 is 27 miles from Exit 1. Exit 2 is 12 miles from Exit 3 and 16 miles from Exit 4. How many miles is Exit 3 from Exit 1? *(Lesson 1.7)*

1

Chapter Test

Find the sum, difference, product, or quotient.

1. $85 + 47$ **2.** $435 - 18$ **3.** 24×31 **4.** $492 \div 6$

5. $613 - 174$ **6.** $283 + 197$ **7.** $527 \div 11$ **8.** 16×32

Nutrition The table shows the protein content of several foods in a 160-gram serving.

Food	Protein Content
fish sandwich	17 grams
roasted turkey	34 grams
tuna salad	26 grams
fried chicken	27 grams

9. Find the total amount of protein in a fish sandwich and one serving of tuna salad.

10. How many more grams of protein are in one serving of roasted turkey than in one serving of fried chicken?

Estimate the sum, difference, product, or quotient.

11. $86 + 19$ **12.** $91 - 24$ **13.** 19×32 **14.** $272 \div 7$

15. $534 - 18$ **16.** $279 + 316$ **17.** $375 \div 18$ **18.** 4×523

Find the value of the power.

19. 7^2 **20.** 4 cubed   **21.** 2^5 **22.** 3^4

Evaluate the expression.

23. $14 - 8 \div 2$ **24.** $4 + 3 \times 6$ **25.** $36 \div (2 + 7)$

26. $15 - 3^2$ **27.** $(24 \div 4) \times 3$ **28.** $2 + 5 \times 4 - 13$

Evaluate the variable expression when $x = 5$.

29. $9 + x$ **30.** $x - 3$ **31.** $x \cdot 7$

32. $23 - x$ **33.** $x + 16$ **34.** $45 \div x$

Solve the equation using mental math.

35. $9 + x = 15$ **36.** $11 - z = 7$ **37.** $10t = 90$

38. $n - 3 = 12$ **39.** $c + 7 = 21$ **40.** $y \div 5 = 35$

41. **Environment** You are going to plant trees in your neighborhood. You can choose from apple, maple, oak, poplar, and spruce. Make a list to show how many ways you can plant three different trees.

Chapter Standardized Test

Test-Taking Strategy Have a positive attitude during any test so that you can gain confidence and stay focused on each question.

Multiple Choice

1. Find the sum $934 + 357$.

  A. 577   **B.** 1223   **C.** 1291   **D.** 1381

2. Find the difference $623 - 197$.

  F. 426   **G.** 516   **H.** 710   **I.** 820

3. Which expression has a value of 322?

  A. $481 - 129$ **B.** $138 + 194$
  C. 14×23 **D.** $657 \div 3$

4. Estimate the sum $198 + 328$.

  F. 300   **G.** 400   **H.** 500   **I.** 600

5. Estimate the cost per sandwich if you pay $53 for 11 sandwiches.

  A. $3   **B.** $4   **C.** $5   **D.** $6

6. Which power has a value of 9?

  F. 2^3 **G.** 3^2 **H.** 9^2 **I.** 6^3

7. What is the value of 7^3?

  A. 21   **B.** 49   **C.** 283   **D.** 343

8. What is the value of $5 \times 5 \times 5$?

  F. 25   **G.** 125   **H.** 625   **I.** 3125

9. Evaluate the expression $12 - 3 \times 2$.

  A. 3   **B.** 6   **C.** 9   **D.** 18

10. Evaluate the expression $\dfrac{14 + 7}{7 - 4}$.

  F. 1   **G.** 3   **H.** 7   **I.** 11

11. Which expression has a value of 8 when $x = 4$?

  A. $8 - x$ **B.** $2x$ **C.** $36 \div x$ **D.** $x + 6$

12. Evaluate $x \cdot 3 + 7$ when $x = 2$.

  F. 11   **G.** 12   **H.** 13   **I.** 20

13. What is the solution of the equation $7x = 28$?

  A. 2   **B.** 3

  C. 4   **D.** 7

14. Which equation has a solution of 5?

  F. $40 \div x = 8$ **G.** $20 - x = 5$
  H. $x + 8 = 14$ **I.** $5x = 30$

15. You need to deliver 75 plants for a florist. You delivered 25 plants. Solve the equation $x + 25 = 75$ to find how many more plants you need to deliver.

  A. 3   **B.** 45   **C.** 50   **D.** 100

Short Response

16. There are 4 party favors in a package. How many packages do you need to buy if you want to give 2 party favors to everyone in a group of 38 people? Explain.

Extended Response

17. At a restaurant, you can choose from four omelet fillings: cheese, peppers, tomatoes, mushrooms. Use a problem solving plan to find how many different omelets you can choose that use exactly three different fillings. Show your work.

Measurement and Statistics

BEFORE

In previous courses you've...

- Interpreted data displays
- Used measurements in problems

Now

In Chapter 2 you'll study...

- Metric and customary units of length
- Area and perimeter
- Making scale drawings
- Making data displays
- Finding mean, median, and mode

WHY?

So you can solve real-world problems about...

- rock climbing, p. 59
- weather, p. 75
- in-line skating, p. 82
- sea turtles, p. 96

Internet Preview
CLASSZONE.COM

- eEdition Plus Online
- eWorkbook Plus Online
- eTutorial Plus Online
- State Test Practice
- More Examples

Chapter Warm-Up Game

Review skills you need for this chapter in this quick game.

Key Skill: Interpreting data displays

DESERT MATH

HOW TO PLAY

1 **USE** the data displays to answer each question. Then match each answer with a value and a letter from the table.

- What is the average temperature in July in Saguaro National Park?

- Estimate the difference between the average July and January temperatures.

- What is the approximate area of the Sonoran Desert?

- The Chihuahuan Desert is about how many times as large as the Mojave Desert?

2 **FIND** the least and greatest values among your answers. The letters associated with these values spell a two letter abbreviation for a state known for its beautiful deserts.

Match your Answer	
5 A	8 N
180,000 Z	200,000 M
120,000 V	50 U
86 M	36 T
160,000 X	120 C

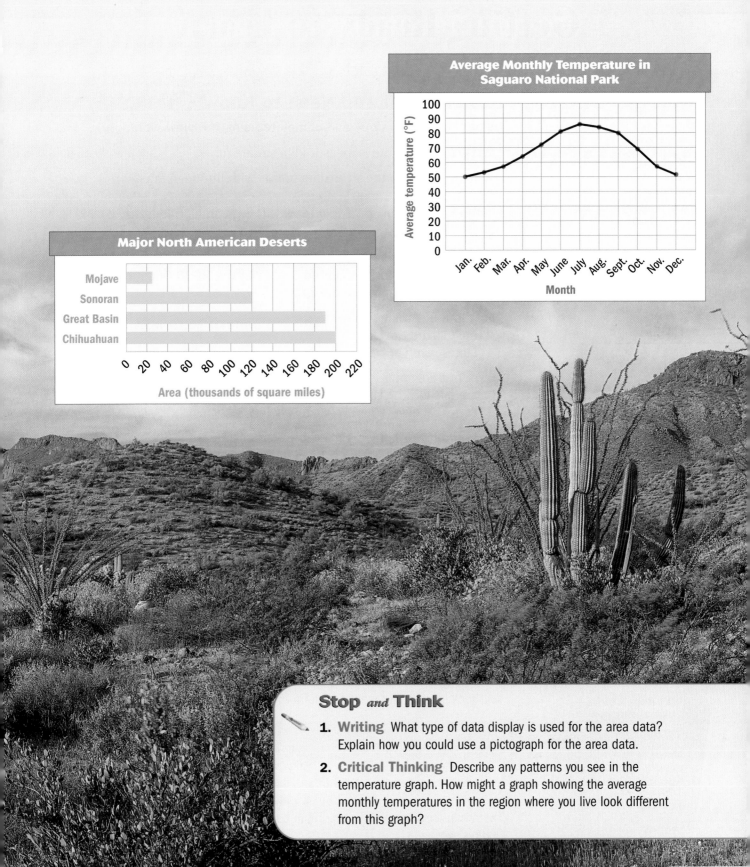

Average Monthly Temperature in Saguaro National Park

Major North American Deserts

Stop and Think

1. **Writing** What type of data display is used for the area data? Explain how you could use a pictograph for the area data.

2. **Critical Thinking** Describe any patterns you see in the temperature graph. How might a graph showing the average monthly temperatures in the region where you live look different from this graph?

Getting Ready to Learn

Review What You Need to Know

Using Vocabulary **Copy and complete using a review word.**

1. The _?_ of a figure is measured in square units.

2. In a _?_, you connect the data points with line segments.

Find the perimeter of a triangle with the given side lengths. *(p. 702)*

3. 5 feet, 2 feet, 6 feet

4. 10 inches, 10 inches, 10 inches

The medal count for the United States in the 2000 Summer Olympics is shown in the bar graph. *(p. 704)*

5. About how many gold medals did the United States receive?

6. About how many silver medals did the United States receive?

7. About how many medals did the United States receive in all?

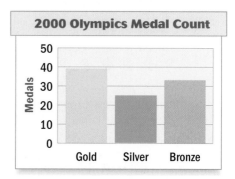

Evaluate the expression when *x* = 8 and *y* = 2. *(p. 29)*

8. $2x$ 9. $4y$ 10. $x + y$ 11. $2x - y$

Word Watch

Review Words

perimeter, p. 702
area, p. 702
data, p. 704
bar graph, p. 704
line graph, p. 705

You should include material that appears on a notebook like this in your own notes.

Know How to Take Notes

Taking Notes While Reading Leave extra space while you take notes in class. Then review the lesson in your textbook to correct or add to your class notes. You may also want to copy the "Help" notes from the textbook in your own words, as shown below.

$m = 3, n = 4$

$m + 2n = 3 + 2 \cdot 4$ ← Follow the order of operations after substituting.
$ = 3 + 8$
$ = 11$

The reminder above will be helpful in Lesson 2.8 when you learn about finding averages.

Measuring Length

LESSON 2.1

BEFORE	▶ Now	WHY?
You used a ruler to draw straight lines.	You'll measure length using customary and metric units.	So you can find lengths, such as lengths of animals in Exs. 9 and 10.

Word Watch

inch, p. 55
foot, p. 55
yard, p. 55
mile, p. 55
millimeter, p. 56
centimeter, p. 56
meter, p. 56
kilometer, p. 56

Activity You can use many different units to measure length.

1 Look at your math book and estimate the length in "paper clips."

2 Using paper clips, measure the length of your book. How does the result compare to your estimate?

3 Look at your math book and estimate the width in "little fingers."

4 Using your little finger, measure the width of your book. How does the result compare to your estimate?

Count the last clip if half or more of it is used.

Customary Units A small paper clip is about one inch long. An **inch** (in.) is a customary unit of length. Three other customary units of length are the **foot** (ft), the **yard** (yd), and the **mile** (mi). Inches, feet, yards, and miles are related to each other.

$$1 \text{ ft} = 12 \text{ in.} \qquad 1 \text{ yd} = 3 \text{ ft} = 36 \text{ in.} \qquad 1 \text{ mi} = 1760 \text{ yd} = 5280 \text{ ft}$$

EXAMPLE 1 **Using Customary Units of Length**

Find the length of the caterpillar to the nearest inch.

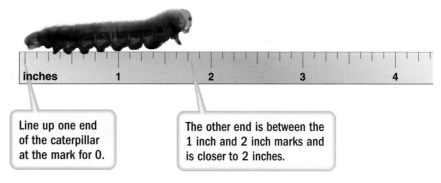

Line up one end of the caterpillar at the mark for 0.

The other end is between the 1 inch and 2 inch marks and is closer to 2 inches.

ANSWER The caterpillar is about 2 inches long.

Metric Units Your little finger is about one centimeter wide. The commonly used metric units of length are the **millimeter** (mm), the **centimeter** (cm), the **meter** (m), and the **kilometer** (km). Here are some common metric unit relationships.

$$1 \text{ cm} = 10 \text{ mm} \qquad 1 \text{ m} = 100 \text{ cm} = 1000 \text{ mm} \qquad 1 \text{ km} = 1000 \text{ m}$$

EXAMPLE 2 **Using Metric Units of Length**

Find the length of the seashell to the nearest millimeter.

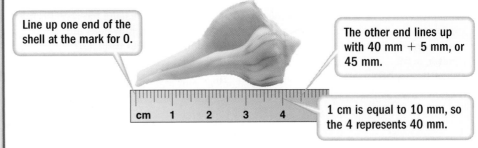

Line up one end of the shell at the mark for 0.

The other end lines up with 40 mm + 5 mm, or 45 mm.

1 cm is equal to 10 mm, so the 4 represents 40 mm.

ANSWER The seashell is about 45 millimeters long.

EXAMPLE 3 **Choosing Appropriate Units**

Choose an appropriate customary unit and metric unit for the length.

  a. distance from Boston to Chicago   **b.** height of a full grown tree

Solution

  a. The distance from Boston to Chicago is much greater than one yard or one meter. So, you should use miles or kilometers.

  b. The height of a full grown tree is much greater than one inch or one centimeter, and much less than one mile or one kilometer. So, you should use feet, yards, or meters.

Your turn now **Measure the object to the nearest whole unit.**

  1. length of your math book (inches)

  2. width of your math book (centimeters)

  3. height of your desk (feet)

Choose an appropriate customary unit and metric unit for the length.

  4. height of a two year old child   **5.** width of a baseball card

Benchmarks for Units of Length

A benchmark approximates the size of a unit.

Customary Units

inch length of a small paper clip

foot distance from elbow to knuckle

yard width of a door

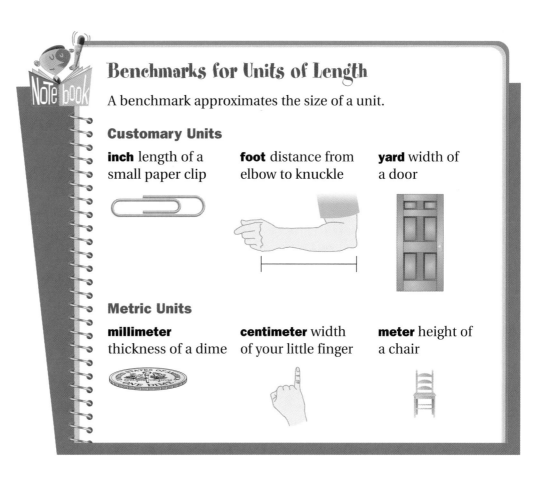

Metric Units

millimeter thickness of a dime

centimeter width of your little finger

meter height of a chair

EXAMPLE 4 **Estimating Length Using Benchmarks**

Estimate the height, in meters, of the door below. Then measure to check your estimate.

1 To estimate, imagine how high the door is in "chairs."

2 To check your estimate, measure the door with a meter stick.

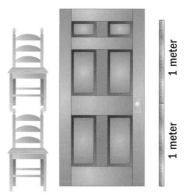

1 meter

1 meter

HELP with Solving

You can use your own height as a benchmark when estimating.

ANSWER The door is about 2 "chairs" high, which is about 2 meters. The height of the door is just over 2 meters.

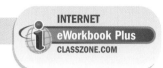

INTERNET
eWorkbook Plus
CLASSZONE.COM

Getting Ready to Practice

Vocabulary **Copy and complete the statement with the appropriate customary unit or metric unit.**

1. 1 yd = 3 _?_   **2.** 1 cm = 10 _?_   **3.** 1 m = 100 _?_   **4.** 1 ft = 12 _?_

5. Measure the length of your math notebook to the nearest millimeter, to the nearest centimeter, and to the nearest inch.

Choose an appropriate customary unit and metric unit for the length.

6. height of a flagpole   **7.** length of a river

8. Use a benchmark to estimate the length of your pencil in inches. Then measure to check your estimate.

Practice and Problem Solving

HELP with Homework

Example	Exercises
1	9–10, 15–16
2	11–14
3	17–24
4	25–30

Online Resources
CLASSZONE.COM
· More Examples
· eTutorial Plus

Find the length of the animal to the nearest inch.

9.    **10.**

Find the length of the line segment to the nearest millimeter and to the nearest centimeter.

11.
```
cm   1   2   3   4
```

12.
```
cm   1   2   3   4
```

Draw a line segment of the given length.

13. 12 centimeters   **14.** 48 millimeters

15. 5 inches   **16.** 8 inches

Choose an appropriate customary unit and metric unit for the length.

17. length of a marathon   **18.** thickness of a CD

19. length of a diving board   **20.** length of a computer screen

21. length of a clarinet   **22.** distance to the moon

23. length of a bike   **24.** height of a building

Estimation Use a benchmark to estimate the length in the given unit. Then measure to check your estimate.

25. height of a stove (feet)

26. length of a bed (feet)

27. width of a television (inches)

28. length of a spoon (inches)

29. height of a lamp (centimeters)

30. length of a shoe (centimeters)

31. **Find the Error** Your friend says that the length of the eraser is about 3 inches. Describe and correct the error.

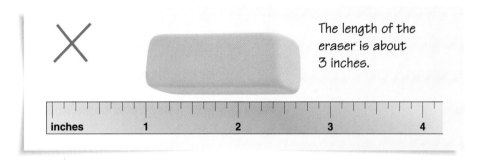

The length of the eraser is about 3 inches.

Tell whether the statement is reasonable. If it is not, change the unit of measure so that it is reasonable.

32. A driveway is 14 *feet* wide.

33. A cat is 12 *inches* long.

34. A bike path is 8 *millimeters* long.

35. A book is 10 *meters* thick.

36. **Rock Climbing** The height of the person in the photo at the left is 6 feet. Estimate the height of the rock that the person is climbing.

Geometry **Without using a ruler, draw a square with the given side length. Then use a ruler to check your drawing.**

37. 6 centimeters

38. 4 inches

39. 7 inches

40. 70 millimeters

41. **Writing** Do you need an actual measurement or an estimate to determine whether a table will fit through a doorway? Explain.

42. **Critical Thinking** A line segment is 6 centimeters long, to the nearest centimeter. Give 5 possible lengths of the line segment in millimeters.

43. **Explain** Choose a benchmark that could be used for a mile. Explain how you would use that benchmark to measure a distance near where you live.

44. **Challenge** You have bought a case that is 15 centimeters tall to protect your electronic game. To the nearest centimeter, your game is also 15 centimeters tall. Assuming that the case is wide enough, can you be sure that your game will fit completely into the case? Why or why not?

Mixed Review

Evaluate the expression when $t = 4$ and $u = 6$. *(Lesson 1.5)*

45. $4t$　　　　　**46.** u^2　　　　　**47.** $2t + u$　　　**48.** $2u - t$

Choose a Strategy Use a strategy from the list to solve the following problem. Explain your choice of strategy.

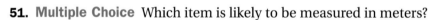

Problem Solving Strategies
- Guess, Check, and Revise
- Draw a Diagram
- Make a List
- Act It Out

49. The *perimeter* of a figure is the distance around the figure. A triangle with two equal sides has a perimeter of 32 inches. The third side is 4 inches shorter than each of the other sides. Find the lengths of the sides.

Basic Skills Copy and complete the number fact family.

50. $\underline{?} \times 2 = 18$　　　$9 \times \underline{?} = 18$　　　$18 \div \underline{?} = 2$　　　$\underline{?} \div 2 = 9$

Test-Taking Practice

INTERNET
State Test Practice
CLASSZONE.COM

51. Multiple Choice Which item is likely to be measured in meters?

A. thimble　　　**B.** leaf　　　**C.** sofa　　　**D.** freeway

52. Multiple Choice Which measure is closest to the length of the item?

F. 5 cm　　　**G.** 53 mm　　　**H.** 58 mm　　　**I.** 6 cm

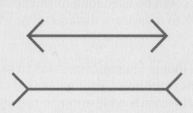

Optical Illusions

Which line segment is longer?

Which person is the tallest?

2.2

Perimeter and Area

BEFORE	▶ Now	WHY?
You found the square of a number.	You'll use formulas to find perimeter and area.	So you can find measurements, such as poster areas in Ex. 28.

In the Real World

Word Watch

perimeter, p. 61
area, p. 62

Carnival A carnival is going to be held in your school's parking lot. How much rope is needed to enclose the carnival? To answer this question, you can find the carnival's *perimeter*.

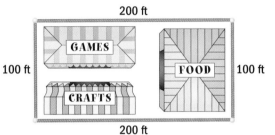

200 ft

GAMES

FOOD

100 ft   100 ft

CRAFTS

200 ft

The **perimeter** of a figure is the distance around the figure. Perimeter is measured in linear units such as feet, inches, or meters.

Perimeter of a Rectangle

Words   Perimeter = 2 · length + 2 · width

Algebra $P = 2l + 2w$

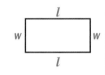

EXAMPLE 1   **Finding the Perimeter of a Rectangle**

To answer the real-world question above, find the perimeter.

$P = 2l + 2w$ Write the formula for perimeter of a rectangle.

$= 2 \cdot 200 + 2 \cdot 100$ Substitute 200 for l and 100 for w.

$= 400 + 200$ Multiply.

$= 600$ Add.

ANSWER The amount of rope needed to enclose the carnival is 600 feet.

Your turn now   **Find the perimeter of the rectangle described.**

1. length = 9 m, width = 5 m   **2.** length = 20 in., width = 12 in.

Area The **area** of a figure is the amount of surface the figure covers. Area is measured in square units such as square feet (ft^2) or square meters (m^2).

Area of a Rectangle

Words   Area = length · width

Algebra $A = lw$

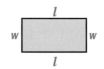

Watch Out!

The units of the answer are square feet, not linear feet. To help you remember this, think of multiplying the units: $lw = \text{ft} \times \text{ft} = \text{ft}^2$.

EXAMPLE 2   **Finding the Area of a Rectangle**

Find the area of the carnival shown at the top of page 61.

$A = lw$ Write the formula for area of a rectangle.

$\quad = 200 \cdot 100$ Substitute 200 for l and 100 for w.

$\quad = 20,000$ Multiply.

ANSWER The area of the carnival is 20,000 square feet.

Squares A square is a rectangle that has four sides with the same length. You can use the following formulas for a square with side length s.

Perimeter of square = 4 · side length   Area of square = (side length)^2

$$P = 4s \qquad\qquad\qquad\qquad A = s^2$$

EXAMPLE 3   **Perimeter and Area of a Square**

Find the perimeter and the area of a 50 yard by 50 yard corral.

Perimeter = $4s$ Area = s^2

$\quad = 4 \cdot 50$ $\quad = 50^2$

$\quad = 200$ $\quad = 2500$

ANSWER The perimeter is 200 yards. The area is 2500 square yards.

Your turn now   Tell whether to find the *perimeter* or the *area* to help you decide how much of the item to buy. Then find the measurement.

3. tiles to cover a 9 ft by 9 ft floor   **4.** fence for a 6 m by 7 m garden

26. Writing Find both the perimeter and area of a 5 inch by 5 inch square using the formulas for a square and for a rectangle. Compare the results.

27. Estimation You are fertilizing a lawn that is 32 feet by 50 feet. Your bag of fertilizer will cover 1500 square feet. Do you have enough? Explain.

28. Movie Posters At one time, 14 inch by 22 inch movie posters were made with a blank rectangle at the top for printing dates and locations. Collectors often find these posters with the blank rectangle trimmed off to form a 14 inch by 17 inch poster. How much area was trimmed off?

29. Describe Describe two different rectangles with a perimeter of 16.

30. Challenge Your rectangular property is 42 yards long and covers 1302 square yards of land. How much fencing is needed to enclose it?

Each figure below is made of rectangles and squares. Find its area.

31.

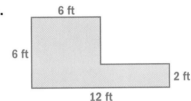

32.

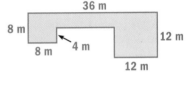

Mixed Review

Find the value of the power. *(Lesson 1.3)*

33. 4^3 **34.** 3^5 **35.** 10^3 **36.** 6^4

Find the length of the segment to the nearest centimeter. *(Lesson 2.1)*

37. ————————   **38.** ————————

Basic Skills **Use front-end estimation to estimate the sum.**

39. $254 + 503 + 739$ **40.** $127 + 182 + 569$

Test-Taking Practice

41. Short Response Use estimation to decide which figure has a greater area, a square that is 87 inches by 87 inches or a rectangle that is 198 inches by 61 inches. Explain your reasoning.

42. Multiple Choice How much trim do you need if you want to sew trim along each edge of a 54 inch by 102 inch tablecloth?

     A. 156 in.   **B.** 312 in.   **C.** 312 in.^{2} **D.** 5508 in.^{2}

Draw a Diagram

Problem You have 18 yards of wire fence to enclose a community garden. What are the different ways you can fence off the area as a rectangle with whole number dimensions?

---

1 Read and Understand

Read the problem at least twice.

You need to find all the rectangles with whole number dimensions and a perimeter of 18 yards.

2 Make a Plan

Decide on a strategy to use.

You can draw diagrams of rectangles that have a perimeter of 18 yards.

---

3 Solve the Problem

Reread the problem and draw diagrams.

Choose a width and draw a rectangle with that width and a length that produces a perimeter of 18 yards.

8 yd
1 yd · · · · · · · · 1 yd
8 yd

$2 \cdot 8 + 2 \cdot 1 = 18$

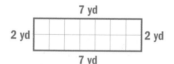

7 yd
2 yd · · · · · · · 2 yd
7 yd

$2 \cdot 7 + 2 \cdot 2 = 18$

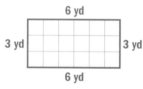

6 yd
3 yd · · · · · · 3 yd
6 yd

$2 \cdot 6 + 2 \cdot 3 = 18$

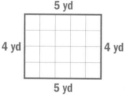

5 yd
4 yd · · · · · 4 yd
5 yd

$2 \cdot 5 + 2 \cdot 4 = 18$

ANSWER The possible dimensions for the community garden are 8 yards by 1 yard, 7 yards by 2 yards, 6 yards by 3 yards, and 5 yards by 4 yards.

---

4 Look Back

Check to make sure that you found all the possibilities. The next width to try would be 5 yards, but this has already been covered by the rectangle that is 5 yards by 4 yards.

Use the strategy *draw a diagram*.

1. **Archaeology** You find an old piece of pottery at a construction site. You have 16 yards of rope to enclose the area around it. Find the different ways you can enclose the area as a rectangle with whole number dimensions.

2. **Lawn Care** You would like to cover your backyard with grass. The backyard is 45 feet by 25 feet. A square patio in one corner that is 15 feet by 15 feet will not be covered by grass. What is the total area that you would like to cover with grass?

3. **Measurement** How can you use the rods shown below to measure a length of 1 centimeter?

|— 5 cm —|

|— 7 cm —|

|— 13 cm —|

4. **Remodeling** You want to cover an area in your kitchen that is 6 feet by 7 feet with blue square tiles that measure 1 foot by 1 foot. Around the tiled area, you would like to arrange a single line of red square tiles of the same size. How many tiles of each color will you need?

5. **Bus Stops** The Youth Center is halfway from your house to the movie theater, which is 8 miles from your house. There is a bus stop three quarters of the way from the theater to the Youth Center. How far is the bus stop from the Youth Center?

Mixed Problem Solving

Use any strategy to solve the problem.

6. **Book Covers** You want to start a business selling textbook covers. You will offer small, medium, and large covers in black, red, and blue. How many different types of covers will you be offering?

7. **Missing Number** What number belongs in the blank?

$$(\underline{\ ?\ } \times 4) \div 2 + 17 = 29$$

8. **Number Pairs** Two numbers have a sum of 45. If you subtract one number from the other, the difference is 7. What are the two numbers?

9. **Riddles** Use the riddle below to name a correct animal that would gain you admission to a dance.

> These animals will
> get you through: elk, yak, dog.
> These animals will
> never do: horse, mouse, frog.

10. **Movie Tickets** A movie theater charges $6 for a matinee and $9 for all other shows. In one day, the movie theater sold 400 matinee tickets and 500 other tickets. How much money did the theater make from ticket sales that day?

Scale Drawings

BEFORE	▶ Now	WHY?
You used rulers to find the actual lengths of objects.	You'll use scale drawings to find actual lengths.	So you can use a map to find distances, as in Exs. 19–21.

Word Watch

scale drawing, p. 68
scale, p. 68

Activity You can use a map to find an actual distance.

Use the map to find the distance you will canoe.

(1) Measure the distance, in centimeters, between the lodge and the dam.

(2) The note in the corner of the map reads 1 cm : 2 km, so a distance of 1 cm on the map represents 2 km on the lake. What distance does your measurement represent?

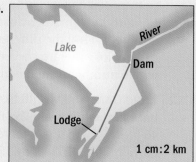

The map in the activity is a *scale drawing*. A **scale drawing** is the same shape as the original object, but not the same size. The **scale** tells how the drawing's dimensions and the actual dimensions are related.

EXAMPLE 1 **Interpreting Scale Drawings**

Canoes Find the actual lengths that correspond to 1 inch, 2 inches, and 3 inches on the scale drawing. How long is the actual canoe?

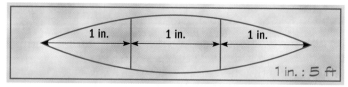

Solution

Make a table. The scale on the drawing is 1 in. : 5 ft. Each inch on the drawing represents 5 feet on the canoe.

Scale drawing length (inches)	Length × 5	Actual canoe length (feet)
1	1 × 5	5
2	2 × 5	10
3	3 × 5	15

ANSWER The actual canoe is 15 feet long.

HELP with Reading

The standard way to write a scale is *scale model : actual object*.

EXAMPLE 2 **Using a Scale to Find Actual Lengths**

Catalogs A catalog pictures a necklace that appears smaller than the actual necklace. The scale is 3 cm : 9 cm. If the length of the necklace in the picture is 18 centimeters, how long is the actual necklace?

Solution

Find the relationship between the known length and the scale.

picture : actual

$\times ?$ ⟨ 3 cm : 9 cm
18 cm : _?_ cm

Ask, "3 times what number equals 18?"

Because $3 \times 6 = 18$, you **multiply by 6** to find the actual length.

3 cm : 9 cm
18 cm : 54 cm ⟩ $\times 6$

ANSWER The actual necklace is 54 centimeters long.

EXAMPLE 3 **Finding Lengths for a Model**

Models You are building a model boat with a scale of 1 in. : 2 ft. The actual boat is 18 feet long. How long do you make your model?

Solution

Find the relationship between the known length and the scale.

model : actual

1 in. : 2 ft
_?_ in. : 18 ft ⟩ $\times ?$ **Ask, "2 times what number equals 18?"**

Because $2 \times 9 = 18$, you **multiply by 9** to find the length of the model: 1 in. $\times 9 = 9$ in.

ANSWER You make your model 9 inches long.

Your turn now **Refer to Examples 1–3.**

1. Find the length of the canoe in Example 1 using the scale 1 in. : 6 ft.

2. Find the actual length of the necklace in Example 2 if the necklace in the picture is 21 centimeters long.

3. Find the length of your model in Example 3 if the scale is 1 in. : 3 ft.

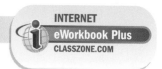

2.3 Exercises

More Practice, p. 709

Getting Ready to Practice

1. Vocabulary Tell what the scale 1 in. : 40 mi means.

The scale on a scale drawing is 1 cm : 12 m. Find the length on the drawing for the given actual length.

2. 24 meters   **3.** 36 meters   **4.** 72 meters   **5.** 120 meters

6. Eiffel Tower A model of the Eiffel Tower is 20 centimeters tall. Use the scale 5 cm : 80 m to approximate the height of the actual Eiffel Tower.

Practice and Problem Solving

HELP with Homework

Example	Exercises
1	7–10
2	7–12
3	13–17

Online Resources
CLASSZONE.COM

· More Examples
· eTutorial Plus

Maps The scale on a map is 1 in. : 150 mi. Find the actual distance, in miles, for the given length on the map.

7. 2 inches   **8.** 4 inches   **9.** 5 inches   **10.** 7 inches

Find the actual length for the length labeled in the photo.

11.

1 cm : 2 cm

3 cm

12.

1 cm : 10 cm

3 cm

Models A model collection uses the scale 1 in. : 16 ft. Find the length of the model, in inches, for the given actual length.

13. 32 feet   **14.** 64 feet   **15.** 112 feet   **16.** 144 feet

17. Find the Error Describe and correct the error in the solution.

The scale is 2 in. : 5 ft. The actual length is 20 feet.

×10 (2 : 5 → 20 : 50) ×10

The length of the model is 50 inches.

18. Draw a Diagram Using the scale 1 in. : 10 ft, make a scale drawing of a dance floor that is 30 ft by 40 ft. Use your drawing to find the distance from one corner of the dance floor to the opposite corner.

What do you think?

History

Lighthouses

The earliest lighthouses were nothing more than bonfires constructed on hillsides so boat pilots could see them. How does the height of a lighthouse influence how effective it is?

Extended Problem Solving The map shows part of Washington, D.C.

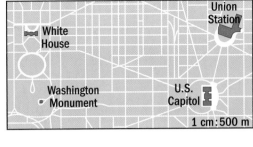

19. **Measurement** How many centimeters apart are the U.S. Capitol and the White House on the map?

20. Find the actual distance for the situation in Exercise 19.

21. **Estimation** Estimate the shortest distance from Union Station to the Washington Monument via the two other red landmarks.

Lighthouses The Port Austin Reef Lighthouse is 60 feet tall. Use the height of the model given to complete the scale. How many times taller than the model is the actual lighthouse?

22. height: 10 inches
    scale: 2 in.: _?_ ft

23. height: 6 inches
    scale: 2 in.: _?_ ft

Mixed Review

Tell whether the statement is reasonable. If it is not, change the unit of measure so that it is reasonable. *(Lesson 2.1)*

24. A bed is 7 *miles* long.

25. A computer keyboard is 18 *inches* long.

26. Find the perimeter and area of a 4 ft by 6 ft rectangle. *(Lesson 2.2)*

Basic Skills Order the numbers from least to greatest.

27. 3, 0, 8, 4, 16, 1

28. 12, 3, 7, 6, 17, 21

29. 22, 25, 14, 11, 23

Test-Taking Practice

INTERNET
State Test Practice
CLASSZONE.COM

30. **Multiple Choice** Find the actual length of the classroom. The scale is 1 cm : 2 m.

    A. 9 m
    B. 6 m
    C. 3 m
    D. 1 m

    Classroom $w = 2$ cm
    $l = 3$ cm

31. **Multiple Choice** An architect constructs a model of a building that will be 120 feet tall. If every 2 inches on the model represents 5 feet on the building, how tall will the architect's model be?

    F. 300 in.
    G. 60 in.
    H. 48 in.
    I. 24 in.

LESSON 2.4

Frequency Tables and Line Plots

In the Real World

Word Watch

data, p. 72
frequency table, p. 72
line plot, p. 73

Art Projects Students in an art class were given the choice of doing a painting, a sculpture, or a drawing as their project this quarter. Which type of project was chosen most often?

One way to organize **data**, or information, is to use a *frequency table*. A **frequency table** lists the number of times each item occurs in a data set.

Student Choices for Art Projects	
painting	sculpture
painting	painting
painting	drawing
sculpture	sculpture
drawing	sculpture
painting	painting

EXAMPLE 1 Making a Frequency Table

To find which type of art project was chosen most often, you can make a frequency table.

Use a tally mark for each time that project was chosen.

The frequency is the number of tally marks.

Art project	Tally	Frequency
painting	⊮Ⅰ	6
sculpture	‖‖	4
drawing	‖	2

ANSWER A painting project was chosen most often.

Your turn now

1. The data at the top of the page could have been recorded in a frequency table as the information was gathered. Explain how this could be done and why this might be a better way to record the data.

2. Make a frequency table of the letters that occur in the word "Mississippi." Which letters occur most often?

Line Plots When the items or categories being tallied are numbers, a *line plot* can be used to visually display the data. A **line plot** uses X marks above a number line to show the frequencies.

EXAMPLE 2 **Making a Line Plot**

Summer Reading The frequency table shows how many books the students in a class read during summer vacation.

Books read	Tally	Frequency
1	JHT	5
2	JHT	5
3	JHT I	6
4	II	2
5		0
6	IIII	4

a. Make a line plot of the data.

b. Use the line plot to find the total number of students.

c. Use the line plot to find how many students read four or more books.

Solution

HELP with **Review**

Need help with number lines? See p. 685.

a.

The number line includes the different numbers of books read.

The X marks above the number line show the frequencies.

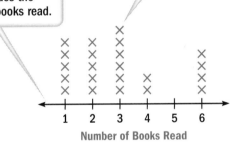

Number of Books Read

b. There are 22 X marks in all, so the total number of students is 22.

c. The total number of X marks above the numbers 4, 5, and 6 is six, so six students read four or more books.

Your turn now **The following data show the numbers of letters in students' names. Use the data in Exercises 3–5.**

6, 5, 4, 4, 5, 3, 9, 8, 6, 4, 3, 4, 7, 5, 4, 3, 8, 4, 9, 3

3. Make a frequency table of the data.

4. Make a line plot of the data.

5. Choose one of the displays and use it to find out whether more students have names with 3 letters or names with 7 or more letters. Which display did you choose and how did you use it to answer the question?

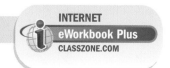

Getting Ready to Practice

1. Vocabulary When creating a frequency table, you count the number of tally marks to find the _?_ for each category.

Bicycles In Exercises 2–4, use the list below showing the numbers of bicycles owned by families of class members.

2, 3, 1, 0, 1, 1, 3, 1, 2, 1, 2, 3, 2, 1, 4, 0, 1, 4, 2, 6, 0

2. Make a frequency table.   **3.** Make a line plot.

4. What number of bicycles is owned by exactly two families? How can you find this answer using the frequency table? using the line plot?

Practice and Problem Solving

Volunteer Fire Department The frequency table shows the calls a small volunteer fire department responded to in one year.

Type of call	Tally	Frequency
building fires	⦀⦀⦀ I	?
other fires	⦀⦀⦀ ⦀⦀⦀ II	?
hazardous materials	⦀⦀⦀ II	?
rescues	III	?
false alarms	⦀⦀⦀ II	?
mutual aid	IIII	?

5. Copy and complete the frequency table.

6. Which type of call occurred most often? least often?

7. How many calls were responded to that year?

8. Music An orchestra has four sections: woodwinds (W), percussion (P), brass (B), and strings (S). The data below show the section each member of one particular orchestra belongs to. Make a frequency table and use it to find which section of the orchestra is the largest.

P, S, B, W, S, S, B, S, W, S, S, W, S, S, B, S, W, S, B, S, W, S, W, S, B, W, S, W, S, S, B, S, B, S, S, S, S, B, S, B, W, B, S, P, S, B, S

Make a frequency table and a line plot of the set of data. Then tell which item(s) occur most often and which item(s) occur least often.

9. Point values of a team's shots during the first half of a basketball game:

2, 2, 1, 3, 2, 2, 1, 3, 2, 2, 1, 2, 3, 2, 2, 1, 2, 1, 2, 1, 1

10. Number of weeks class members attended summer camp:

4, 0, 1, 2, 8, 2, 4, 4, 8, 5, 6, 4, 6, 6, 4, 0, 6, 8, 4, 4, 8, 4, 4, 4, 8, 4

HELP with Homework

Example	Exercises
1	5–12
2	9–11

Online Resources
CLASSZONE.COM

· More Examples
· eTutorial Plus

11. Writing Compare the frequency table and the line plot you created in Exercise 10 on page 74. Describe one way in which each type of display is more helpful or easier to use than the other type.

Weather Use the calendar and codes at the right.

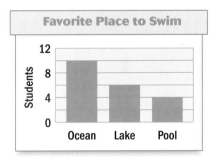

SUNNY   PARTLY CLOUDY   CLOUDY   RAINY

12. Make a frequency table of the types of weather.

13. How many more days were either cloudy or partly cloudy than were sunny?

14. Explain How many days didn't have rain? Give two ways to find the answer.

15. Can you make a line plot of the weather data? Explain.

16. Challenge Use Example 2 on page 73. Find the total number of books read by all the students in the class over the summer.

17. Birthdays Gather data on the birth months of your classmates and of the United States presidents. Make a line plot of each data set and compare the data.

Mixed Review

Use the bar graph. *(p. 704)*

18. How many of the students surveyed chose the ocean?

19. How many more students chose a lake than a pool?

Favorite Place to Swim

Students	Ocean	Lake	Pool
(bar graph showing Ocean ≈ 10, Lake ≈ 6, Pool ≈ 4)			

Basic Skills **Identify the first six numbers if you start with zero and count using the given increment.**

20. count by 4s   **21.** count by 7s   **22.** count by 25s   **23.** count by 20s

Test-Taking Practice

24. Extended Response The list below gives the number of students in each homeroom class in a school. Make a frequency table and a line plot of the data. Use each display to determine which class size is most common and how many classes have fewer than 25 students. Explain your steps.

24, 28, 26, 24, 23, 26, 24, 25, 27, 26, 25, 26

Notebook Review

Review the vocabulary definitions in your notebook.

Copy the review examples in your notebook. Then complete the exercises.

Check Your Definitions

inch, p. 55
foot, p. 55
yard, p. 55
mile, p. 55
millimeter, p. 56

centimeter, p. 56
meter, p. 56
kilometer, p. 56
perimeter, p. 61
area, p. 62

scale drawing, p. 68
scale, p. 68
data, p. 72
frequency table, p. 72
line plot, p. 73

Use Your Vocabulary

1. Writing Define area and perimeter.

2.1–2.2 Can you find perimeter and area?

 EXAMPLE Use a ruler to find the length of the rectangle in centimeters. Then find the perimeter and the area.

$$P = 2l + 2w \qquad A = lw$$

$$= 2 \cdot 3 + 2 \cdot 2 \qquad = 3 \cdot 2$$

$$= 10 \text{ cm} \qquad = 6 \text{ cm}^2$$

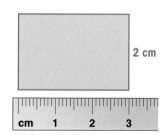

2 cm

cm   1   2   3

☑ **2.** Find the perimeter and the area of a 7 inch by 7 inch square.

3. Estimate then measure the length of this sentence in inches.

2.3 Can you use a scale?

 EXAMPLE The length of a wall on a scale drawing is 192 millimeters. Find the actual length if the scale on the drawing is 8 mm : 2 m.

× 24 ⎧ 8 mm : 2 m
⎩ 192 mm : _?_ m   You multiply by 24, so the actual length is 48 m.

☑ **Find the actual length of the wall in the Example above using the given scale.**

4. 3 mm : 1 m   **5.** 4 mm : 2 m   **6.** 12 mm : 4 m   **7.** 6 mm : 6 m

2.4 Can you make a frequency table and a line plot?

EXAMPLE The list below shows the numbers of pets that students in a class have. Make a frequency table and a line plot of the data.

2, 0, 1, 3, 0, 2, 1, 1, 0, 3, 3, 1, 4, 0, 1, 1, 0, 0, 2, 1, 0

Pets owned	Tally	Frequency
0	JHT II	7
1	JHT II	7
2	III	3
3	III	3
4	I	1

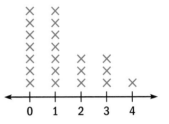

 8. Make a frequency table and a line plot of the data.

12, 11, 10, 15, 14, 12, 13, 10, 11, 13, 15, 15, 13, 11, 12

Stop *and* **Think** about Lessons 2.1–2.4

9. Critical Thinking Describe a situation in which it is okay to estimate a measurement rather than find the actual measurement.

10. Writing Compare a frequency table and a line plot. How are they alike? How are they different?

Review Quiz 1

1. Estimate the length of the line segment in millimeters. Then measure to check. _____

Choose an appropriate customary unit and metric unit for the length.

2. height of a Ferris wheel

3. length of a calculator

Find the perimeter and the area of the rectangle described.

4. length = 4 ft, width = 2 ft

5. length = 7 m, width = 5 m

6. Titanic The scale for a model of the Titanic is 1 cm : 6 m. The model is 45 centimeters long. About how long was the actual Titanic?

7. Make a frequency table and a line plot of the following data showing the heights, in inches, of several teenagers.

52, 53, 52, 50, 54, 54, 53, 52

Hands-on Activity

GOAL
Collect and display data.

MATERIALS
• graph paper

Collecting and Organizing Data

You can make a modified frequency table to display data.

Explore   **Display data you collect from a phone book in a modified frequency table.**

1   Look at the last digit of 25 telephone numbers from a telephone book.

2   List the digits on graph paper. Beside each digit, shade one box for each telephone number that ends with that digit.

Kristine 34 Wrentham	555-0108
Kristine 16 Oakland	555-0198
L J 81 Ten Hills	555-0149
LaNell 515 Coolidge	555-0181
Lodish 64 Stetson	555-0190
Lois 36 Georgia	555-0120
Lucy 6 Lucerne	555-0185
M C 80 Highland	555-0189
M D 85 Melrose	555-0125
Mae 414 Bowdoin	555-0194
Mark 73 Winthrop	555-0191
Martin 7 Norcross	555-0144
Mary J 34 Foster	555-0134
Mary R, Dr 61 Franklin	555-0117
Melissa 652 Shawmut	555-0148
Mervyn 80 Park	555-0114
Mildred 54 Orleans	555-0132
Natalie 28 St Germain	555-0138
P 133 Marlborough	555-0153
Pamela 591 Fisher	555-0164
Pat 77 Moreland	555-0177
Patricia 25 Broadway	555-0173
Patrick 88 Liberty	555-0165
Patrick 84 Central	555-0109
Ruth 22 Haskell	555-0167

Last digit	Tally	Frequency
0		2
1		2
2		1
3		2
4		5
5		3
6		0
7		3
8		4
9		3

3 telephone numbers end in 5.

Your turn now   **Use the data from Steps 1 and 2 above.**

1. Which digit was the last digit most often? least often?

2. Make another modified frequency table using the sixth digit of the telephone number.

Stop and Think

3. Writing Describe how the display you made in Exercise 2 can help you compare frequencies.

Bar Graphs

BEFORE	▶ Now	WHY?
You organized and displayed data using frequency tables.	You'll display data using bar graphs.	So you can visualize data, such as the soccer records in Ex. 8.

In the Real World

Word Watch

bar graph, p. 79
double bar graph, p. 80

Zoo Animals Two hundred sixth and seventh grade students were asked to name their favorite zoo animal. The results are shown in the table. How can you represent this data visually?

A **bar graph** is a type of graph in which the lengths of the bars are used to represent and compare data. A numerical scale is used to determine the lengths of the bars.

Favorite Zoo Animal	
Zoo animal	**Students**
lion	43
giraffe	19
monkey	55
elephant	49
other	34

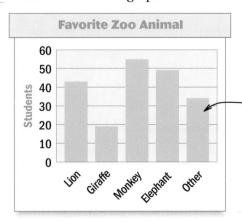

EXAMPLE 1 **Making a Bar Graph**

HELP with **Review**

Need help with reading a bar graph? See page 704.

You can display the data from the table above in a bar graph.

(1 Choose a numerical scale.

Start the scale at 0. The greatest data value is 55, so end the scale at a value greater than 55, such as 60. Use equal increments along the scale, such as increments of 10.

(2 Draw and label the graph.

Favorite Zoo Animal

Use the scale to decide how long to make the bar for each data value.

Double Bar Graphs A **double bar graph** is a bar graph that shows two sets of data on the same graph. The two bars for each category are drawn next to each other.

EXAMPLE 2 **Making a Double Bar Graph**

Zoo Animals Make a double bar graph of the zoo animal data in the table at the right.

Favorite zoo animal	Sixth grade	Seventh grade
lion	19	24
giraffe	13	6
monkey	29	26
elephant	21	28
other	15	19

1. First draw one set of bars using the sixth grade data, as shown below. The greatest data value in the table is 29, so end the scale at 30.

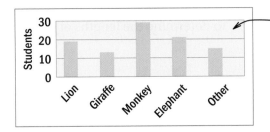

Leave room for the seventh grade bars.

2. Then draw the seventh grade bars next to the sixth grade bars and shade them a different color. Add a title and a key.

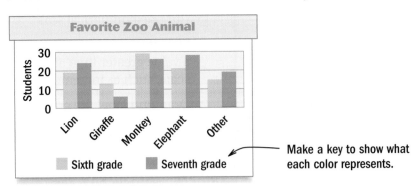

Make a key to show what each color represents.

Your turn now **Make a double bar graph of the data.**

1.

Favorite Sports					
Sport	basketball	swimming	gymnastics	hockey	track
Watching	593	260	370	175	250
Participating	570	319	197	197	209

Exercises
More Practice, p. 709

Getting Ready to Practice

1. Vocabulary Explain how to choose a scale for a bar graph.

A survey asked the question, "What is the most important thing kids can do to protect the environment?" The results are shown in the table.

Activity	Responses
Recycle	834
Buy environmentally friendly products	358
Write your elected representatives	221
Raise money	401
Plant trees	480

2. Choose a scale for a bar graph of the data.

3. Draw and label the bar graph.

4. "Recycle" had about 4 times the number of responses as which other activity?

Practice and Problem Solving

Make a bar graph of the data.

5.

Mountain Ranges of the World	
Range	Peaks (over 6000 m)
Kunlun	228
St. Elias	1
Tien Shan	40
Andes	84

6.

Maximum Life Span of Animals in Captivity	
Animal	Life Span (years)
lion	30
giraffe	36
monkey	37
asian elephant	77

Make a double bar graph of the data.

7.

Cost of Food (cents per pound)		
Food	1990	2000
apples	77	82
chicken	86	108
ice cream	254	366
eggs	100	96
spaghetti	85	88

8.

Major Indoor Soccer League National Conference 2000–2001		
Team	Wins	Losses
Kansas City	14	26
Toronto	21	19
Detroit	13	27
Milwaukee	24	16
Wichita	18	21

9. Use your graph from Exercise 7 to decide which of the foods had the greatest price increase from 1990 to 2000.

with Homework

Example	Exercises
1	5, 6
2	7, 8

Online Resources
CLASSZONE.COM

· More Examples
· eTutorial Plus

10. Movie Ticket Prices Describe how the appearance of the graph will change if the scale goes from 0 to 40 in increments of 10 or from 0 to 200 in increments of 50.

11. Writing How might the scale of a bar graph affect how the bar graph is interpreted?

Movie Ticket Prices

Price (dollars) / Japan, France, Brazil, Switzerland, USA, South Africa

In-line Skating The stacked bar graph shows the results of a survey about how people use in-line skates.

12. Compare and Contrast What are the advantages and disadvantages of a stacked bar graph?

13. Challenge Draw the stacked bar graph as a double bar graph.

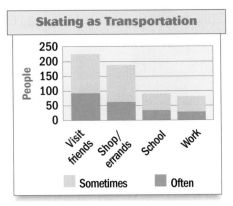

Skating as Transportation

People / Visit friends, Shop/errands, School, Work

Sometimes   Often

Mixed Review

Solve the equation using mental math. *(Lesson 1.6)*

14. $x + 2 = 15$ **15.** $10 - x = 6$ **16.** $3x = 24$ **17.** $72 \div x = 9$

18. Make a frequency table and a line plot of the following scores for a 10 point quiz: 9, 10, 6, 7, 7, 8, 9, 8, 9, 6, 7, 9, 8, 7, 7, 9. *(Lesson 2.4)*

Basic Skills Tell how much change you should receive if you pay for an item of the given price with a $10 bill.

19. $5.25   **20.** $3.75   **21.** $7.75   **22.** $6.50

Test-Taking Practice

INTERNET
State Test Practice
CLASSZONE.COM

23. Multiple Choice Choose the best increment for the numerical scale of a bar graph showing the data values 53, 31, 25, 13, and 46.

A. 1   **B.** 10   **C.** 50   **D.** 100

24. Short Response Explain how to make a double bar graph of favorite school subjects from a graph showing favorites for sixth graders and a graph showing favorites for seventh graders.

Coordinates and Line Graphs

BEFORE	▶ **Now**	**WHY?**
You plotted points on number lines and made bar graphs.	You'll plot points on coordinate grids and make line graphs.	So you can visualize change, as with the Internet data in Ex. 21.

📓 **Word Watch**

ordered pair, p. 83
coordinates, p. 83
line graph, p. 84

Coordinates The graph below shows a point on a coordinate grid. Each point is described by an **ordered pair** of numbers. The numbers are the **coordinates** of the point.

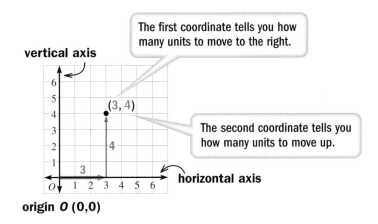

The first coordinate tells you how many units to move to the right.

vertical axis

(3, 4)

The second coordinate tells you how many units to move up.

horizontal axis

origin *O* (0,0)

EXAMPLE 1 **Graphing Points**

a. Graph the point (4, 3) on a coordinate grid.

Start at (0, 0). Move **4** units to the right and **3** units up.

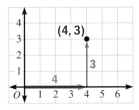

b. Graph the point (0, 2) on a coordinate grid.

Start at (0, 0). Move **0** units to the right and **2** units up.

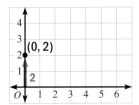

Your turn now Graph the points on the same coordinate grid.

1. (1, 0)   **2.** (2, 1)   **3.** (3, 2)   **4.** (5, 5)

5. In Exercises 1–4, the first coordinate is the number of days after a seed was planted. The second coordinate is the plant's height in centimeters. How high was the plant after 3 days?

Line Graphs A **line graph** represents data using points connected by line segments. Line graphs are often used to show change over time. You can make a break at the beginning of the scale to focus on the interval where the data fall.

■ **Radio Stations**

In 1950 there were 2144 AM radio stations and 691 FM radio stations. How many more total radio stations were there in 1998 than in 1950?

EXAMPLE 2 **Making a Line Graph**

Radio Stations **Make a line graph of the radio station data below. Data were collected at the end of each year.**

AM Radio Stations						
Year	1993	1994	1995	1996	1997	1998
AM stations	4994	4913	4150	4857	4762	4793

Solution

To make a line graph of the data, think of each column in the table as an ordered pair: (**year**, **AM stations**).

1. Choose a scale. Use a break in the scale for AM stations to focus on values from 4000 to 5000.

2. Graph each point.

3. Draw line segments to connect the points.

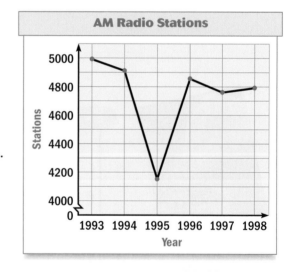

Your turn now **In Exercise 6, use the graph above.**

6. During which year was the increase in the number of AM stations the greatest? How can you tell that from the graph?

7. Make a line graph of the number of FM radio stations.

Year	1993	1994	1995	1996	1997	1998
FM stations	4971	5109	5730	5419	5542	5662

Getting Ready to Practice

Vocabulary **Choose the letter that shows the location of the item on the coordinate grid.**

1. point (2, 1)   **2.** origin

3. point (0, 3)   **4.** vertical axis

Television **Use the data in the table.**

5. Tell which number you would skip to after a break in the minutes scale and where you would end the scale.

6. Make a line graph of the data.

7. Did teenagers watch more television each year? Explain.

Teenager TV Viewing	
Year	**Minutes each day**
1992	190
1994	185
1996	169
1998	178
2000	184

Practice and Problem Solving

Graph the points on the same coordinate grid.

8. (6, 3)   **9.** (2, 7)   **10.** (0, 0)   **11.** (4, 0)

12. (1, 8)   **13.** (0, 6)   **14.** (9, 0)   **15.** (5, 5)

16. Birds Make a line graph of the data. After a break in the scale for species, number the scale from 80 to 94 using increments of 2.

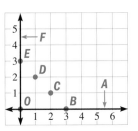

Endangered or Threatened Bird Species in the U.S.									
Year	1992	1993	1994	1995	1996	1997	1998	1999	2000
Species	84	88	90	91	90	93	93	89	93

HELP with Homework

Example	Exercises
1	8–15
2	16–20

Online Resources
CLASSZONE.COM
· More Examples
· eTutorial Plus

Make a line graph of the data.

17.

Hour (A.M.)	7	8	9	10
Cars in lot	1	4	15	17

18.

Hour (P.M.)	1	2	3	4
Tickets sold	81	90	103	120

19.

Year	1998	2000	2002
Students	1253	1425	1310

20.

Day of fair	1	3	5
Dollars raised	105	198	380

21. Internet Make a line graph of the data below. Use it to estimate the number of countries connected to the Internet in 1995.

Year	1988	1990	1992	1994	1996	1998	2000
Countries connected	8	22	43	81	165	200	214

Fitness During exercise, most people's heart rate should be between the minimum and maximum recommended rates shown.

Recommended Heart Rate (beats per minute)		
Age	Minimum	Maximum
20	130	160
30	124	152
40	117	144
50	111	136
60	104	128

22. Make a double line graph. Use a different color for the minimum rates and the maximum rates. Include a key.

23. Estimate the minimum rate for a 25-year-old.

24. Challenge Why is a line graph not appropriate for displaying the data?

Date in January	1	2	3	4	5	6	7	8
Daily snowfall (inches)	6	20	0	3	8	0	1	10

Mixed Review

25. The scale on a map is 2 in. : 15 mi. Explain what this means. *(Lesson 2.3)*

26. You sent 2 postcards on Monday, 13 on Tuesday, 0 on Wednesday, and 1 on Thursday. Make a bar graph of the data. *(Lesson 2.5)*

 **Basic Skills** Find the sum or difference.

27. $3 + 8 + 7$

28. $2 + 13 + 8 + 7$

29. $200 - 125$

Test-Taking Practice

30. Multiple Choice Which measurement is the best estimate of the puppy's weight on Day 6?

A. 11 oz   **B.** 12 oz

C. 13 oz   **D.** 14 oz

Growth of Puppy

31. Multiple Choice Which ordered pair represents point *Z* above?

F. (1, 10)   **G.** (10, 2)   **H.** (2, 10)   **I.** (10, .1)

Creating Data Displays

GOAL Use a spreadsheet to create data displays.

Example You can create bar graphs, line graphs, and other types of data displays using a spreadsheet program.

The table shows the population of the United States from 1996 to 2000. Make a bar graph.

Solution

① Enter the data in the first two columns of the spreadsheet. Use an apostrophe in front of each year ('1996). Highlight the data in cells A2:B6 and insert a chart. Select *column* chart as the chart type.

② Choose chart options, such as the title, gridlines, and a legend (key).

③ Double click on a feature to change its formatting. For example, use a population scale from 0 to 300,000 in increments of 50,000.

	A	B
1	Year	Population (thousands)
2	1996	265,229
3	1997	267,784
4	1998	270,248
5	1999	272,691
6	2000	276,059

> A2:B6 in Step 1 refers to the rectangle of cells whose opposite corners are A2 and B6.

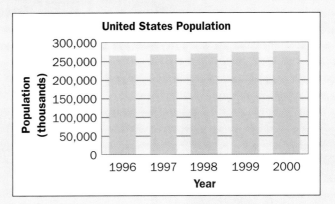

United States Population

Your turn now Use the data below.

1. Make a *double* bar graph of the data. Follow Steps 1–3 above, but highlight three columns of data.

2. Make a double line graph of the data. Follow the steps in the Example, but enter the years without apostrophes, and select a *scatter plot* that connects points with lines as the type of chart. Show *major* gridlines for both axes. The population scale doesn't have to start at 0.

	A	B	C
1	Year	Male population (thousands)	Female population (thousands)
2	1996	129,504	135,724
3	1997	130,783	137,001
4	1998	132,030	138,218
5	1999	133,277	139,414
6	2000	134,979	141,080

Circle Graphs

LESSON 2.7

BEFORE	▶ Now	WHY?
You made and interpreted bar graphs and line graphs.	You'll interpret circle graphs and make predictions.	So you can predict costs, as in Exs. 17–19.

In the Real World

Word Watch

circle graph, p. 88

Roller Coasters A group of teenagers are asked what they think about roller coasters. Their answers are shown in the *circle graph* at the right. How many of them think roller coasters are great?

A **circle graph** is a graph that represents data as parts of a circle. The entire circle represents all of the data. You can make conclusions about the data in a circle graph based on the size of each section.

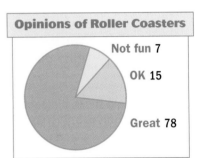

Opinions of Roller Coasters

Not fun 7
OK 15
Great 78

EXAMPLE 1 **Interpreting a Circle Graph**

Use the circle graph above.

a. To find out how many of the teenagers think roller coasters are great, find the data value in the section labeled "Great."

   ANSWER The number who think roller coasters are great is 78.

b. To find out how many of the teenagers do not think roller coasters are great, add the values in the "OK" and the "Not fun" sections: 15 + 7 = 22.

   ANSWER The number who do not think roller coasters are great is 22.

Your turn now The circle graph shows how many people out of 100 prefer each of four types of space materials for a paperweight.

1. Which type of paperweight is least popular?

2. How many of the people do not prefer a meteor?

3. Is it reasonable to say that moon rock is the most popular choice? Explain.

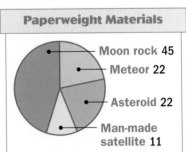

Paperweight Materials

Moon rock 45
Meteor 22
Asteroid 22
Man-made satellite 11

with Reading

Writing down key facts as you read a problem can help you solve it. In Example 2, you know: 100 students were surveyed, 38 of them like vanilla ice cream, and 300 students will be at the party.

EXAMPLE 2 **Using a Graph**

Ice Cream The circle graph shows the favorite ice cream flavors of 100 students. About 300 students will attend an ice cream party. Predict how many students will ask for vanilla ice cream.

Solution

Find the relationship between the number of students surveyed and the number of students who will attend the party: $100 \times 3 = 300$.

Multiply the number of students who prefer vanilla by 3 to predict the number of students who will ask for vanilla at the party: $38 \times 3 = 114$.

ANSWER About 114 students will ask for vanilla ice cream at the party.

Your turn now Use the circle graph in Example 2.

4. Predict the number of students who will ask for strawberry ice cream at an ice cream party for 200 students.

2.7 Exercises

More Practice, p. 709

INTERNET
eWorkbook Plus
CLASSZONE.COM

Getting Ready to Practice

Vocabulary **Which type of graph is best suited for the purpose?**

1. comparing separate categories
2. comparing part of a data set to the entire set
3. showing change over time

A. circle graph
B. line graph
C. bar graph

Population **The circle graph shows the population of the United States, in millions, in 2000.**

4. Which age group was the smallest?

5. How can you tell from the graph that about half the population was under 35 years old?

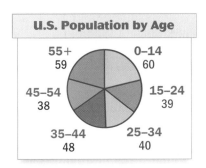

Practice and Problem Solving

with **Homework**

Example	Exercises
1	6–11
2	12–19

Online Resources
CLASSZONE.COM
· More Examples
· eTutorial Plus

Tell which section of the circle graph below fits the description.

6. It represents about half the data.

7. It represents the least data value.

8. It represents the greatest data value.

Geography The circle graph shows the amount of Earth's surface, in millions of square kilometers, that is covered by each ocean.

9. Which ocean covers the least area?

10. Which ocean covers the greatest area?

11. What is the total area of the five oceans?

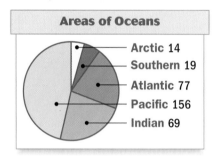

Areas of Oceans
Arctic 14
Southern 19
Atlantic 77
Pacific 156
Indian 69

Predict The circle graph shows the types of hits by Cal Ripken, Jr., in one season. In Exercises 12–15, predict the number of hits he might have gotten in 4 seasons.

12. singles   13. doubles

14. triples   15. home runs

16. Predict the total number of hits Cal Ripken, Jr., might have gotten in 3 seasons.

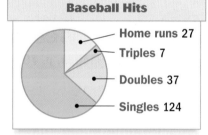

Baseball Hits
Home runs 27
Triples 7
Doubles 37
Singles 124

Marine Mammals The circle graph shows the total amount of money spent to feed the three types of mammals at an aquarium for one year.

17. Predict how much money will be spent to feed the sea otters for four years.

18. There are 4 sea lions. About how much does it cost to feed one sea lion for one year?

19. There are 7 harbor seals. About how much does it cost to feed one harbor seal for one year?

Yearly Food Costs
Sea lions $10,000
Harbor seals $13,300
Sea otters $40,000

Favorite Season **A group of people voted for their favorite season. The results are shown in the circle graph.**

20. Use the data to make a bar graph.

21. Which season got the most votes? Which graph did you use to decide?

22. On which graph can you see that spring and summer combined got slightly more than half the votes?

Favorite Season

Spring 229
Summer 116
Winter 36
Fall 248

Movies **The graph shows the amounts 100 people paid to rent a movie.**

23. How many people out of 300 would you expect to pay $4 or less?

24. **Writing** Explain how a bar graph of the data would be similar to the circle graph.

25. **Challenge** Is a line graph a good choice to represent the data? Why or why not?

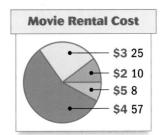

Movie Rental Cost

$3 25
$2 10
$5 8
$4 57

Mixed Review

Evaluate the expression. *(Lesson 1.4)*

26. $\dfrac{2 + 8}{5}$

27. $(8 + 3 + 7) \div 3$

28. $\dfrac{5 + 11 + 8 + 12}{4}$

29. Graph the point $(0, 8)$ on a coordinate grid. *(Lesson 2.6)*

Basic Skills **Find the quotient.**

30. $255 \div 5$

31. $468 \div 3$

32. $1250 \div 25$

33. $4725 \div 21$

Test-Taking Practice

The circle graph shows students' favorite school lunches.

34. **Multiple Choice** How many more students chose hot lunches than homemade lunches?

   A. 10   **B.** 12   **C.** 14   **D.** 18

35. **Multiple Choice** Which is a possible value for the number of students who chose the salad?

   F. 22   **G.** 99   **H.** 250   **I.** 258

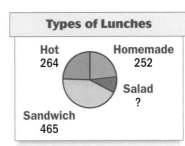

Types of Lunches

Hot 264
Homemade 252
Salad ?
Sandwich 465

Hands-on Activity

GOAL

Use numbers to describe a set of data.

MATERIALS

· counters or coins

Finding Typical Data Values

Explore Use counters to find values to describe a set of data.

1 Create five stacks of counters with the heights 8, 3, 7, 5, and 7. Arrange the stacks in a row from shortest to tallest.

2 Find a typical height of a stack of counters.

> The height of the middle stack is 7 counters.

> The most common stack height is 7 counters.

3 Make the stacks the same height by moving counters.

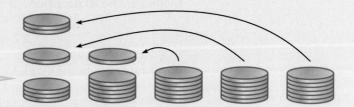

> 6 is also a typical height of a stack of counters.

Your turn now Repeat Steps 1–3 above to find three values to describe the data set.

1. stack heights: 2, 7, 5, 9, 9, 5, 5   **2.** stack heights: 2, 8, 6, 2, 7

Stop and Think

3. Critical Thinking Do you think all three values you found to describe the data could be considered "typical" for the data set in Exercise 1? for the data set in Exercise 2? Why or why not?

Mean, Median, and Mode

BEFORE

You represented data using graphs.

▶ **Now**

You'll describe data using mean, median, mode, and range.

WHY?

So you can find the best average, as in Exs. 13 and 14.

In the Real World

Word Watch

mean, p. 93
median, p. 93
mode, p. 93
range, p. 94

Astronauts In the Apollo space program, each lunar landing mission had one lunar module pilot. The ages of the pilots are listed below. What is the average age?

Apollo mission	11	12	13	14	15	16	17
Pilot's age	39	37	36	40	41	36	37

There are three types of averages used to describe a data set.

Averages

The **mean** of a data set is the sum of the values divided by the number of values.

The **median** of a data set is the middle value when the values are written in numerical order. If a data set has an even number of values, the median is the mean of the two middle values.

The **mode** of a data set is the value that occurs most often. A data set can have one mode, more than one mode, or no mode.

EXAMPLE 1 **Finding a Mean**

To find the mean of the ages for the Apollo pilots given above, add their ages. Then divide by 7, the number of pilots.

$$\text{Mean} = \frac{39 + 37 + 36 + 40 + 41 + 36 + 37}{7} = \frac{266}{7} = 38$$

ANSWER The mean of the Apollo pilots' ages is 38 years.

Range The **range** of a data set is the difference between the greatest value and the least value.

EXAMPLE 2 **Finding Median, Mode, and Range**

Astronauts Find the median, mode(s), and range of the pilots' ages from the top of page 93.

Put the ages in order from least to greatest.

36   36   37   37   39   40   41

Median: The middle number is 37, so the median is 37.

Mode: Both 36 and 37 occur twice. There are two modes, 36 and 37.

Range: Range = Oldest age − Youngest age = 41 − 36 = 5

■ Astronauts

An astronaut's weight on Earth is 139 pounds. The same astronaut weighs about 23 pounds on the moon. How many more pounds does the astronaut weigh on Earth than on the moon?

EXAMPLE 3 **Choosing the Best Average**

Music The minutes that students practice a musical instrument each week are listed below. Choose the best average(s) for the data.

30   30   50   90   100   120   150   630

Solution

Mean: 1200 ÷ 8 = 150

The mean is greater than all but two data values.

Median: (90 + 100) ÷ 2 = 95

Mode: The mode is 30. It is the least data value.

ANSWER The mean and the mode are not typical of the data. The median best represents the data.

HELP with Notetaking

Be sure your notes include an example where there is an even number of data values, as in Example 3. Make note of the fact that the median is the mean of the two middle numbers.

Your turn now Find the mean, median, mode(s), and range.

1. 10, 23, 13, 23, 4, 9, 16   **2.** 27, 23, 30, 26, 19

3. 8, 13, 8, 4, 11, 4, 2, 6   **4.** 91, 150, 80, 71, 74, 81, 80, 77

5. Choose the best average(s) to represent the data in Exercise 4.

Getting Ready to Practice

1. **Vocabulary** The _?_ of a data set is the difference between the greatest and the least values. The _?_ of a data set is the middle value when the values are written in numerical order.

Find the mean, median, mode(s), and range of the data.

2. 2, 3, 1, 1, 3   3. 10, 8, 9, 8, 5   4. 13, 8, 11, 7, 5, 10

5. **Guided Problem Solving** The ages of the counselors at a camp are listed below. What is a typical age?

   21, 49, 23, 25, 23, 21, 21, 25

   ① Find the mean, median, and mode(s) of the ages.

   ② Decide whether each average represents a typical age.

   ③ Choose the average that best represents the data.

Practice and Problem Solving

HELP with Homework

Example	Exercises
1	6–11, 15
2	6–12, 15
3	13, 14, 16

Online Resources
CLASSZONE.COM

· More Examples
· eTutorial Plus

Find the mean, median, mode(s), and range of the data.

6. 7, 9, 12, 5, 12   7. 5, 11, 9, 5, 25

8. 14, 10, 9, 7, 14, 16, 14   9. 42, 37, 25, 33, 25, 18, 37

10. 26, 22, 10, 12, 16, 28   11. 30, 60, 10, 30, 30, 50, 80, 30

12. **Find the Error** Your friend found the median and the mode of a data set. Describe and correct your friend's error(s).

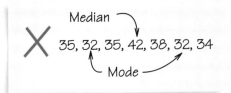

Writing Find the mean, median, and mode(s). Then choose the best average(s) to represent a typical score. Explain your choice.

13. Bowling scores: 180, 170, 190, 200, 130, 30, 180, 160

14. Math test scores: 70, 71, 97, 71, 62, 94, 95

15. **Basketball** The data show the heights, in inches, of the players on the Seattle Storm team at one time. Find the mean, median, mode(s), and range of the data.

    77, 76, 67, 77, 76, 68, 73, 77, 70, 72, 70

16. Sea Turtles Find the mean, median, and mode(s) of the data. What is the best average to use to represent the most typical length?

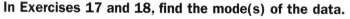

Adult Sea Turtle Lengths			
Type of turtle	Length (inches)	Type of turtle	Length (inches)
Kemps Ridley	30	Loggerhead	48
Olive Ridley	30	Black	39
Leatherback	96	Flatback	39
Green	48	Hawksbill	30

In Exercises 17 and 18, find the mode(s) of the data.

17. green, red, green, blue, blue, green, green, red, red, blue, green, red

18. left, right, straight, right, left, right, straight, left, right, left, straight

19. Explain For Exercises 17 and 18, is there a mean? a median? Explain.

Find the mean of the data.

20. 142, 131, 135, 148, 139

21. 796, 849, 833, 840, 827, 836, 843

Number Sense Tell whether the mean is reasonable. If it is not reasonable, then find the correct mean. Explain your reasoning.

22. 13, 16, 9, 21, 25, 30; Mean: 32

23. 5, 11, 4, 11, 7, 7, 10, 8, 9; Mean: 5

24. 6, 4, 3, 8, 9, 12, 13, 9; Mean: 8

25. 9, 12, 13, 8, 33, 15, 22; Mean: 30

Tell whether the statement is *true* or *false*.

26. The mode is always one of the numbers in a data set.

27. The mean can be one of the numbers in a data set.

28. The median is always one of the numbers in a data set.

29. A data set always has a mode.

30. Writing The average of the temperatures at noon on Inauguration Day from 1957 to 1997 was 36°F. Do you think the temperature was near freezing (32°F) for every inauguration from 1957 to 1997? Explain.

31. Critical Thinking Find a data set for a situation where the best average is the mean. Repeat this exercise for the median and the mode(s).

Challenge Use the given mean or median of the data to find the missing number.

32. 14, 24, _?_, 18, 30; Mean: 23

33. 40, 28, 16, 18, 37, 20, _?_, 35; Median: 26

Mixed Review

The graph shows the results of a survey of 100 people. *(Lesson 2.7)*

Favorite Hot Dog Topping

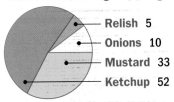

Relish 5
Onions 10
Mustard 33
Ketchup 52

34. How many more people prefer ketchup than mustard?

35. Predict how many people out of 500 would prefer relish.

Choose a Strategy **Use a strategy from the list to solve the following problem. Explain your choice of strategy.**

36. An elevator in a building starts on the ground floor, which is numbered 1. It rises 6 floors, descends 4 floors, rises 15 floors, and descends 12 floors. Which floor is the elevator on?

Problem Solving Strategies

- Guess, Check, and Revise
- Draw a Diagram
- Work Backward
- Make a Model

Basic Skills **Write the number in words.**

37. 35   **38.** 126   **39.** 607   **40.** 1578

Test-Taking Practice

41. **Multiple Choice** Which number is *not* the mean, median, mode, or range of the data set 4, 3, 15, 11, 3, 8, 7, 5?

A. 3   **B.** 5   **C.** 6   **D.** 7

42. **Short Response** Paint for your garage should be applied when the temperature is at or above 60°F. If the average temperature for a week is 65°F, could you have painted every day of that week? Explain.

BRAIN GAME

Lucky Sevens

Each person rolls a number cube seven times and records the result for each roll. After the seventh roll, calculate the median and mode(s) of the results.

The person with the highest median gets one point and the person with the highest mode gets one point. If you tie, play another round.

Play the game three times. Total your scores to see who has the most points.

Notebook Review

LESSONS
2.5 TO 2.8

Review the vocabulary definitions in your notebook.

Copy the review examples in your notebook. Then complete the exercises.

Check Your Definitions

bar graph, p. 79	line graph, p. 84	mode, p. 93
double bar graph, p. 80	circle graph, p. 88	range, p. 94
ordered pair, p. 83	mean, p. 93	
coordinates, p. 83	median, p. 93	

Use Your Vocabulary

1. Copy and complete: The first coordinate in the _?_ (6, 0) tells you how many units to move to the right to graph the point.

2. **Writing** Explain how to find the mean of a set of data.

2.5–2.6 Can you make a bar graph and a line graph?

EXAMPLE Choose appropriate scales and make graphs of the data.

a. Make a bar graph of the data for games won.

b. Make a line graph of the data for male soccer players.

Team	Games won
Bears	14
Cardinals	11
Otters	9
Eagles	13

Year	Male	Female
1995	7691	4285
1996	8626	5251
1997	8303	5348
1998	8232	4935

Games Won

Games: 15, 12, 9, 6, 3, 0
Bears, Cardinals, Otters, Eagles

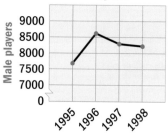

Soccer Players

Male players: 9000, 8500, 8000, 7500, 7000, 0
1995, 1996, 1997, 1998

☑ 3. Describe another appropriate scale for the data in the bar graph.

4. Make a line graph of the data above for female soccer players.

5. Graph the points (2, 4) and (3, 0) on the same coordinate grid.

2.7–2.8 Can you read a circle graph and find averages?

EXAMPLE The graph shows the shoreline lengths, in kilometers, of the Great Lakes and their islands. Find the mean, median, mode(s), and range.

Mean:
$$\frac{6157 + 4385 + 1400 + 2670 + 1168}{5}$$
$$= 3156 \text{ km}$$

Median: The middle number is 2670 km.

Mode: Each number occurs only once, so there is no mode.

Range: $6157 - 1168 = 4989$ km

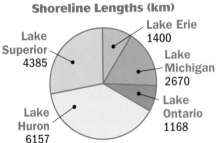

Shoreline Lengths (km)

- Lake Erie 1400
- Lake Superior 4385
- Lake Michigan 2670
- Lake Ontario 1168
- Lake Huron 6157

 6. Use the graph above. Which lake has the least amount of shoreline?

7. Find the mean, median, mode(s), and range: 45, 39, 82, 45, 39, 50.

Stop and Think about Lessons 2.5–2.8

8. Writing Explain how to choose the scale for a bar graph.

9. Critical Thinking Explain why the mean of a data set may not represent the data very well.

Review Quiz 2

1. Make a bar graph of the data in the table at the right.

Monthly Rainfall			
Month	**Jan.**	**Feb.**	**Mar.**
Rainfall (inches)	14	13	11

2. Graph the points (4, 2), (0, 3), and (1, 0) on the same coordinate grid.

3. Find the mean, median, mode(s), and range of the data. Choose the best average(s) to represent the data.

11, 17, 5, 7, 11, 3

Fishing The graph shows the results of a survey of 100 people who like fishing.

4. What type of fishing is the most popular? the least popular?

5. Predict the number of people who would prefer deep-sea fishing in a group of 400 people who like fishing.

Favorite Type of Fishing

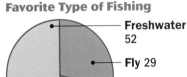

- Freshwater 52
- Fly 29
- Deep-sea 17
- Ice 2

Chapter Review

Vocabulary

inch, p. 55
foot, p. 55
yard, p. 55
mile, p. 55
millimeter, p. 56
centimeter, p. 56
meter, p. 56
kilometer, p. 56
perimeter, p. 61

area, p. 62
scale drawing, p. 68
scale, p. 68
data, p. 72
frequency table, p. 72
line plot, p. 73
bar graph, p. 79
double bar graph, p. 80
ordered pair, p. 83

coordinates, p. 83
line graph, p. 84
circle graph, p. 88
mean, p. 93
median, p. 93
mode, p. 93
range, p. 94

Vocabulary Review

1. Give three examples of customary units of length.

2. Give three examples of metric units of length.

Tell whether the statement is *true* or *false*.

3. The perimeter of a figure is a measure of how much surface the figure covers.

4. A line graph is often used to represent data that changes over time.

Copy and complete the statement.

5. The first ? in the ordered pair (3, 5) is 3.

6. The ? of a data set is the sum of the values divided by the number of values.

7. The ? of a data set is the middle value when the values are written in numerical order. If a data set has an even number of values, the ? is the ? of the two middle values.

8. The ? of a data set is the value that occurs most often.

Review Questions

Choose an appropriate customary unit and metric unit for the length. *(Lesson 2.1)*

9. length of a canoe oar

10. height of a skyscraper

11. length of the Colorado river

Use a benchmark to estimate the length of the object in inches. Then measure to check your estimate. *(Lesson 2.1)*

12.

13.

Use a benchmark to estimate the length of the line segment in centimeters. Then find the length of the line segment to the nearest millimeter and to the nearest centimeter. *(Lesson 2.1)*

14. ——————————— **15.** ———————————

Find the perimeter and the area of the figure described. *(Lesson 2.2)*

16. a rectangle that is 12 cm by 4 cm   **17.** a square that is 9 yd by 9 yd

Models **An airplane model uses the scale 1 in. : 32 in.** *(Lesson 2.3)*

18. If the actual airplane is 512 inches long, how long is the model?   **19.** If a stripe on the model is 8 inches long, how long is the actual stripe?

Marching Band **The data show the scores for a band competition.** *(Lesson 2.4)*
71, 81, 72, 81, 72, 80, 78, 75, 71, 78, 80, 73, 76, 78, 81, 72, 75, 79, 80, 79, 72, 71, 80, 81, 71

20. Make a frequency table of the data.   **21.** Make a line plot of the data.

22. Bike Riding The table below shows how many miles you rode your bike each day of one week. Make a bar graph of the data. *(Lesson 2.5)*

Day	Sun.	Mon.	Tues.	Wed.	Thur.	Fri.	Sat.
Distance (miles)	5	2	0	2	3	0	4

Graph the points on the same coordinate grid. *(Lesson 2.6)*

23. $(7, 1)$ **24.** $(0, 8)$ **25.** $(3, 7)$ **26.** $(4, 0)$

27. Butter Prices The table at the right shows prices of butter, in cents per pound. Make a line graph of the data. *(Lesson 2.6)*

Year	1996	1997	1998	1999
Price	217	246	318	227

The circle graph shows the number of wins, losses, and ties for a hockey team in one season. *(Lesson 2.7)*

28. How many games were played?

29. How many more wins than ties were there?

30. Predict the number of wins for 2 seasons.

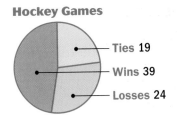
Hockey Games
Ties 19
Wins 39
Losses 24

Find the mean, median, mode(s), and range of the data. *(Lesson 2.8)*

31. Prices of portable CD players (dollars): 70, 180, 110, 100, 200, 100, 80

32. Ages of houses in a neighborhood (years): 28, 20, 28, 26, 20, 63, 23, 24

33. Choose the best average(s) to represent the data in Exercise 32. Explain.

Chapter Test

2

Choose an appropriate customary unit and metric unit for the length.

1. distance between Earth and the sun   **2.** height of a waterfall

3. Use a ruler to draw a line segment that is 4 inches long.

4. Measure to find the length, in centimeters, of one side of the square shown at the right. Then find its perimeter and its area.

5. A scale drawing uses a scale of 1 in. : 3 yd. A distance on the drawing is 12 inches. What is the actual distance?

6. The rolls of a number cube are given. Make a frequency table of the data.

2, 3, 6, 4, 5, 4, 4, 4, 3, 2, 5, 3, 6, 6, 4, 1, 1, 2, 3, 2, 4, 2, 1, 4, 2

7. Astronomy The table at the right shows the number of moons that orbit each of the planets in our solar system. Make a bar graph of the data.

Planet	Number of moons
Mercury	0
Venus	0
Earth	1
Mars	2
Jupiter	28
Saturn	30
Uranus	21
Neptune	8
Pluto	1

Graph the points on the same coordinate grid.

8. (10, 4)   **9.** (4, 5)

10. (0, 7)   **11.** (2, 7)

12. (9, 0)   **13.** (3, 3)

Theater Seats The circle graph shows the number of seats available in a theater.

14. How many seats are in the theater?

15. How many more Orchestra seats than Mezzanine seats are there?

16. How many Mezzanine Box tickets will be sold if a show sells out for 5 performances?

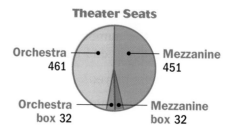

Theater Seats

Orchestra 461 — Mezzanine 451 — Orchestra box 32 — Mezzanine box 32

In Exercises 17 and 18, find the mean, median, mode(s), and range.

17. Monthly allowances: 40, 20, 32, 80, 28, 20, 20, 28, 20

18. Ages of grandchildren: 2, 3, 4, 6, 7, 2, 9, 7

19. In Exercise 17, which is the best average to represent the data?

Chapter Standardized Test

Test-taking Strategy Go through the test and do the easiest questions first. Then go back through the test and do the questions that are more difficult.

Multiple Choice

1. Which of the following ordered pairs corresponds to point L on the coordinate grid?

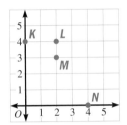

    A. $(2, 4)$ **B.** $(4, 0)$ **C.** $(0, 4)$ **D.** $(2, 3)$

2. Which unit of measure would *not* be used to measure the length of a snake?

    F. millimeters   **G.** centimeters

    H. inches   **I.** kilometers

3. A map uses a scale of 1 in. : 200 mi. The distance between two cities on the map is 4 inches. What is the actual distance in miles?

    A. 50   **B.** 200   **C.** 204   **D.** 800

4. What is the best estimate of the length of the line segment, in inches?

    F. 1   **G.** 2   **H.** 3   **I.** 6

5. A rectangle has an area of 40 square centimeters. The width of the rectangle is 5 centimeters. What is the length of the rectangle, in centimeters?

    A. 8   **B.** 10   **C.** 15   **D.** 200

6. The data below are the siblings in your friends' families. How many X marks would you put above the 2 on a line plot?
    2, 0, 1, 2, 3, 4, 5, 3, 1, 1, 0, 2

    F. 6   **G.** 5   **H.** 4   **I.** 3

7. Which of the scales is the most appropriate for the data set: 16, 31, 82, 105?

    A. 0–100, increments of 10

    B. 0–120, increments of 20

    C. 0–120, increments of 50

    D. 0–200, increments of 200

8. Your scores on six science tests were 95, 84, 82, 90, 93, and 84. What is the range?

    F. 11   **G.** 13   **H.** 84   **I.** 88

Short Response

9. Use the graph below to help you predict how many students walk to school out of a group of 300 students. Show your work.

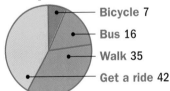

Transportation to School

Bicycle 7
Bus 16
Walk 35
Get a ride 42

Extended Response

10. Find the mean, median, and mode(s) of the weekly grocery bills: $155, $150, $60, $158, and $162. Which is the best average to represent the data? Explain.

3 Decimal Addition and Subtraction

Chapter Warm-Up Games

Review skills you need for this chapter in these quick games.

Key Skill:
Rounding whole numbers

- The numbers above represent distances in centimeters.

- Choose one of the numbers to be your first putt. Choose another number and round it to the nearest 10. The result is your second putt. Round the remaining number to the nearest 100 for your third putt.

- Add your three putts to find your total distance. Then use the same numbers but pick a different order of putts. Try to raise your total distance.

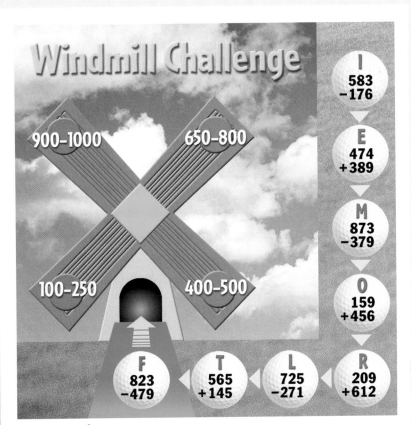

Windmill Challenge

900-1000   650-800

100-250   400-500

I
583
−176

E
474
+389

M
873
−379

O
159
+456

F
823
−479

T
565
+145

L
725
−271

R
209
+612

BRAIN GAME

Key Skill:
Adding and subtracting whole numbers

- Find the sum or difference associated with each golf ball. A golf ball passes through the windmill only if its sum or difference does not fall into any of the ranges on the spokes of the windmill.

- Once you know which golf balls can pass through the windmill, order their sums and differences from least to greatest. The corresponding letters spell out a cry that you might hear on a miniature golf course.

Stop and Think

1. **Writing** What is the greatest distance you can get in *Three-Putt Golf*? What is the least? Explain how you know.

2. **Critical Thinking** In *Windmill Challenge*, are there any sums or differences for which you could use estimation rather than an exact calculation? Explain.

Review What You Need to Know

Using Vocabulary **Copy and complete using a review word.**

1. A ? is a metric unit of length longer than a centimeter.

2. A ? is a metric unit of length shorter than a centimeter.

3. When you ? the number 125 to the nearest ten, the answer is 130.

4. The ? of 17 and 9 is 8.

Graph the numbers on a number line to order them from least to greatest. *(p. 685)*

5. 5, 19, 16, 9, 12, 6, 13

6. 10, 7, 3, 2, 15, 11, 17

Estimate the sum or difference. *(p. 12)*

7. $16 + 27$ **8.** $34 + 79$ **9.** $81 - 42$ **10.** $65 - 17$

Find the length of the line segment to the nearest centimeter. *(p. 56)*

11. ————————   **12.** ———————————   **13.** ———

You should include material that appears on a notebook like this in your own notes.

Know How to Take Notes

Write Questions About Homework As you complete your homework assignments, write down in your notebook any questions you want to ask the teacher. An example is shown below.

Chapter 1 Whole Number Estimation

1. $39 \rightarrow 40$ 2. $345 \rightarrow 350$
    $+ 160 \rightarrow + 160$ $- 171 \rightarrow - 170$
    $\overline{200}$ $\overline{180}$

Am I right to round up? Ask in class tomorrow.

In Lesson 3.4, you may have questions like the one above when you round decimals. Use answers to such questions and corrected homework assignments to study for quizzes and tests.

Decimals and Place Value

LESSON 3.1

BEFORE	Now	WHY?
You learned how to read and write whole numbers.	You'll read and write decimals.	So you can read decimals, such as the race times in Example 3.

Word Watch

decimal, p. 108

Activity You can use base-ten pieces to model numbers.

The diagram below shows the values of the base-ten pieces.

1 one (1 whole)   **1 tenth**   **1 hundredth**

Use base-ten pieces to complete the statement.

1. 1 one = ? tenths

2. 1 one = ? hundredths

3. 1 tenth = ? hundredths

4. 30 tenths = ? ones

5. 40 hundredths = ? tenths

6. 2 ones and 5 tenths = ? tenths

with Notetaking

You might want to record relationships between base-ten pieces in your notebook, such as 1 one = 10 tenths.

EXAMPLE 1 **Expressing a Number in Different Ways**

a. Write 20 hundredths using only tenths.

20 hundredths

2 × 10 hundredths

2 × 1 tenth

2 tenths

Think of **10 hundredths** as **1 tenth**.

b. Write 1 one and 4 tenths using only tenths.

1 one and 4 tenths

10 tenths and 4 tenths

14 tenths

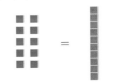

Use the fact that **1 one** equals **10 tenths.**

Your turn now Copy and complete the statement.

1. 500 hundredths = ? tenths

2. 4 ones and 9 tenths = ? tenths

A **decimal** is a number that is written using the base-ten place-value system. Each place value is ten times the place value to its right.

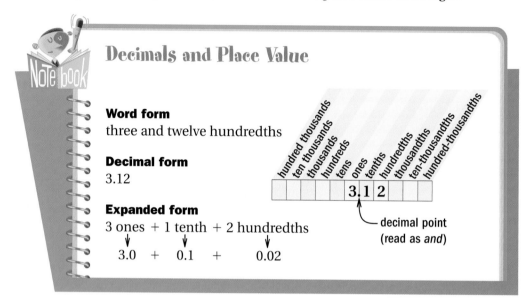

Decimals and Place Value

Word form
three and twelve hundredths

Decimal form
3.12

hundred thousands
ten thousands
thousands
hundreds
tens
ones
tenths
hundredths
thousandths
ten-thousandths
hundred-thousandths

| | | | | | 3. | 1 | 2 | | | |

Expanded form
3 ones + 1 tenth + 2 hundredths
  ↓   ↓   ↓
3.0   +   0.1   +   0.02

decimal point
(read as *and*)

EXAMPLE 2 **Writing Decimals**

Swimming A timer at your swim meet says your time was twenty-eight and six tenths seconds. Write your time as a decimal.

twenty-eight and six tenths

28 . 6 seconds

> The word *and* indicates the decimal point.

EXAMPLE 3 **Reading Decimals**

Auto Racing Helio Castroneves won the 2001 Indianapolis 500. His best lap time was 41.0238 seconds. Write his time in words.

41.0238

> You read a decimal according to the <u>last place value</u>.

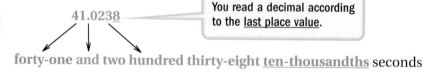

forty-one and two hundred thirty-eight <u>ten-thousandths</u> seconds

---

Your turn now

3. Write *twenty-five and seven hundred-thousandths* as a decimal.

4. Write 5.029 in words.   5. Write 706.25 in words.

Getting Ready to Practice

Vocabulary **Name the place value of the 3 in the decimal.**

1. 1.038   **2.** 16.329   **3.** 4.61093   **4.** 564.0732

5. Find the Error Describe and correct the error in the solution.

 four hundred twelve thousandths = 400.012

Write the number as a decimal.

6. five and eighteen hundredths   **7.** six and nine thousandths

Write the decimal in words.

8. 0.45   **9.** 8.0014   **10.** 7.0009   **11.** 24.006

Practice and Problem Solving

HELP with Homework

Example	Exercises
1	12–15
2	16–25, 33–37
3	20, 26–32

Online Resources
CLASSZONE.COM

· More Examples
· eTutorial Plus

Copy and complete the statement.

12. 4 tenths = ? hundredths

13. 70 tenths = ? ones

14. 200 hundredths = ? tenths = ? ones

15. 1 one and 5 tenths = ? tenths = ? hundredths

Match the number with its decimal form.

16. twenty and four hundred five ten-thousandths   **A.** 20.045

17. twenty and forty-five ten-thousandths   **B.** 20.00045

18. twenty and forty-five hundred-thousandths   **C.** 20.0405

19. twenty and forty-five thousandths   **D.** 20.0045

20. Writing Write the numbers modeled in words and as decimals. Do the models represent the same amount? Explain.

Model A   Model B

Sports

Turbojets

The *Spirit of Australia's* record speed was about 318 kilometers per hour, which is much faster than the maximum speed of some cruise ships, which is about 42 kilometers per hour. About how many times faster can the *Spirit of Australia* go than some cruise ships?

Write the number as a decimal.

21. thirty and fifteen hundredths

22. fifty-eight and twenty-seven thousandths

23. seven hundred five thousandths

24. two hundred seventy-eight ten-thousandths

25. eighty-six and one hundred forty-three ten-thousandths

Write the decimal in words.

26. 0.99   **27.** 4.16   **28.** 0.367

29. 17.022   **30.** 8.0093   **31.** 10.0255

32. Turbojets The *Spirit of Australia* set a record for the fastest water vehicle. This turbojet was timed at 317.58 kilometers per hour. Write this speed in words.

33. Bridges The main section of the Akachi-Kaikyo bridge in Japan is about one and ninety-nine hundredths kilometers long. Write this length as a decimal.

Money Write the amount as a decimal part of a dollar.

34. 1 quarter   **35.** 4 nickels   **36.** 89 pennies   **37.** 7 dimes

Copy and complete the expanded form of the decimal.

38. $8.6 = 8.0 + \underline{?}$ **39.** $5.392 = 5.0 + 0.3 + \underline{?} + \underline{?}$

40. $4.25 = 4.0 + \underline{?} + \underline{?}$ **41.** $0.1472 = 0.1 + 0.04 + \underline{?} + \underline{?}$

Gemstones The table shows the weights of several different gemstones at a jewelry store.

42. Write the weight of the topaz in words.

43. Write the weight of the emerald in words.

44. Which gems weigh less than 1 carat?

45. Sketch a base-ten model to represent the weight of the diamond.

Gemstone	Weight (carats)
amethyst	0.48
diamond	1.29
emerald	1.05
topaz	0.65
sapphire	0.50

Write the decimal described.

46. one tenth more than 20.8   **47.** one hundredth less than 14.77

48. one tenth less than 34.7   **49.** one hundredth more than 85.29

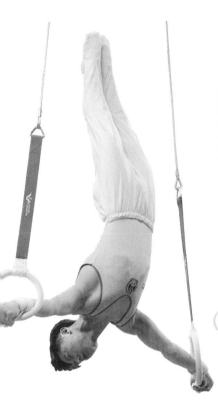

Gymnastics The table shows the scores for men's gymnastics teams at the Olympics.

Team	Score
China	231.919
Ukraine	230.306
Russia	230.019
Japan	229.857
United States	228.983

50. Write China's score in words.

51. Which team's score is between 230 and 230.1?

52. Which team's score is closest to 229?

53. Challenge Sketch a model of 1 ten using ones' pieces. How many ones' pieces did you need? How many tenths' pieces would you need to make the model? How many hundredths' pieces?

Mixed Review

54. Out of 40 students, 4 said they check their e-mail less than once a week, 10 said once a week, 8 said twice a week, 12 said once a day, and 6 said several times a day. Make a bar graph of the data. *(Lesson 2.5)*

Choose a Strategy Use a strategy from the list to solve the problem in Exercise 55. Explain your choice of strategy.

Problem Solving Strategies

- Guess, Check, and Revise
- Draw a Diagram
- Make a List

55. The booths at a carnival are 6 feet wide and spaced 4 feet apart. What is the maximum number of booths you can fit in a row that is 50 feet long?

Basic Skills Write the number in words.

56. 5078   **57.** 4,027,000   **58.** 15,400,000

Test-Taking Practice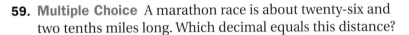

59. Multiple Choice A marathon race is about twenty-six and two tenths miles long. Which decimal equals this distance?

   A. 26.002 mi   **B.** 26.02 mi   **C.** 26.10 mi   **D.** 26.2 mi

60. Multiple Choice The moon revolves around Earth once every 27.3217 days. How do you write this number in words?

   F. twenty-seven and three thousand seven thousandths

   G. twenty-seven and three thousand two hundred seventeen ten-thousandths

   H. two hundred seventy-three and two hundred seventeen thousandths

   I. twenty-seven hundred and three thousand two hundred seventeen ten-thousandths

Hands-on Activity

Using Different Metric Units

You can express the same length using different metric units.

Explore   **Measure the pencil in different units.**

1 Find the length of the pencil in centimeters and millimeters. Write your answer as a sum.

> Line up one end of the pencil with the zero mark on the ruler.

> Look at where the tip of the pencil lines up with the tick marks on the ruler.

The length of the pencil is 9 cm + 4 mm.

2 Find the length of the pencil in millimeters. Use the fact that there are 10 millimeters in 1 centimeter.

9 cm + 4 mm = (10 × 9) mm + 4 mm = 94 mm

Your turn now

1. Copy and complete the table by measuring different objects in your classroom as described above.

Object	Measurement 1	Measurement 2
length of a pencil	9 cm + 4 mm	94 mm
length of a notebook	? cm + ? mm	? mm
height of a desk	? m + ? cm	? cm
width of a door	? m + ? cm	? cm

Stop and Think

2. Writing The length of a pen is 112 millimeters. Explain how you can find the length in centimeters and millimeters without measuring.

3. Critical Thinking For any height given in centimeters, how can you find the height in meters and centimeters without measuring?

Measuring Metric Lengths

BEFORE	▶ Now	WHY?
You measured lengths to the nearest whole metric unit.	You'll use decimals to express metric measurements.	So you can measure lengths precisely, as with the otter in Ex. 17.

In the Real World

Word Watch

Review Words

millimeter (mm), p. 56
centimeter (cm), p. 56
meter (m), p. 56

Fossils Scientists study fossils to learn about plants and animals that lived in prehistoric times. The size of a fossil can help a scientist figure out what type of plant or animal it came from. A scientist finds a dinosaur tooth that is about 3 centimeters long. What is a more precise measurement for the tooth?

EXAMPLE 1 **Writing Measurements as Decimals**

To answer the question above about dinosaur teeth, use a metric ruler and write your answer as a decimal number of centimeters.

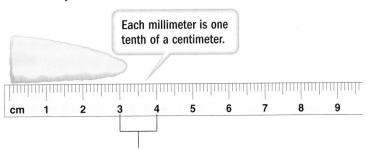

Each millimeter is one tenth of a centimeter.

1 centimeter = 10 millimeters

From the metric ruler you can see that 2 millimeters is 2 tenths of a centimeter. The length is about 3 and 2 tenths centimeters.

ANSWER The length of the dinosaur tooth is about 3.2 centimeters.

Your turn now **Write the length of the line segment as a decimal number of centimeters.**

1.

2.

Metric Units of Length

millimeter (mm)	centimeter (cm)	meter (m)
1 mm = 0.1 cm	1 cm = 10 mm	1 m = 1000 mm
1 mm = 0.001 m	1 cm = 0.01 m	1 m = 100 cm
		1 m = 0.001 km

with Review

Need help with metric units of length? See p. 56.

EXAMPLE 2 Measuring in Centimeters

Find the length of the line segment to the nearest tenth of a centimeter.

6 and 7 tenths centimeters

ANSWER The length of the line segment is about 6.7 centimeters.

with Solving

It takes more of a smaller unit of length to equal a measurement written in a larger unit of length. For example, it takes 300 cm to equal 3 m.

EXAMPLE 3 Measuring in Meters

Dinosaurs Find the length of the triceratops horn to the nearest hundredth of a meter.

The length of the horn is about 25 centimeters. Because 1 centimeter is 1 hundredth of a meter, 25 centimeters is 25 hundredths of a meter.

ANSWER The length of the triceratops horn is about 0.25 meter.

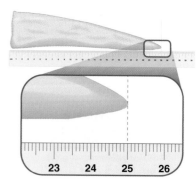

Your turn now Find the length of the line segment to the given unit.

3. to the nearest tenth of a centimeter

4. to the nearest hundredth of a meter

Getting Ready to Practice

Vocabulary **Copy and complete the statement.**

1. 1 centimeter = _?_ meter

2. 1 millimeter = _?_ centimeter

3. 1 meter = _?_ centimeters

4. 1 centimeter = _?_ millimeters

5. **Guided Problem Solving** The wingspan of the Blue Metalmark butterfly is more than 2 centimeters. Write the wingspan as a decimal number of centimeters.

(1 How many millimeters longer than 2 centimeters is the wingspan?

(2 What part of a centimeter is this?

(3 Write the wingspan of the butterfly in centimeters.

Practice and Problem Solving

HELP with Homework

Example	Exercises
1	6–12
2	13–16
3	17–19

Online Resources
CLASSZONE.COM

· More Examples
· eTutorial Plus

Copy and complete the statement.

6. 3 and 8 tenths centimeters = _?_ centimeters

7. 5 and 2 hundredths meters = _?_ meters

8. 1 and 35 hundredths meters = _?_ meters

9. 12 and 4 thousandths meters = _?_ meters

10. **Pancakes** The height of a stack of pancakes is nine and one tenth centimeters. Write this measurement in decimal form.

11. **Desks** The width of a library desk is eighty-eight hundredths of a meter. Write this measurement in decimal form.

12. **Multiple Choice** What is the length of the goldfish?

A. 4.6 meters

B. 4.6 centimeters

C. 4.4 centimeters

D. 44 millimeters

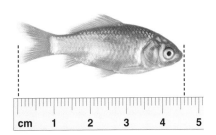

13. Write the measurement for each letter to the nearest tenth of a centimeter.

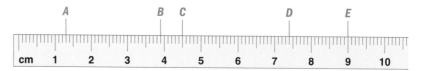

Find the length of the object to the nearest tenth of a centimeter.

14.

15.

16. Find the Error Describe and correct the error in the measurement.

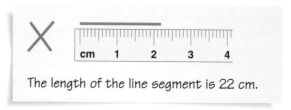

The length of the line segment is 22 cm.

17. Sea Otters Use the meter stick to find the length of the sea otter to the nearest hundredth of a meter.

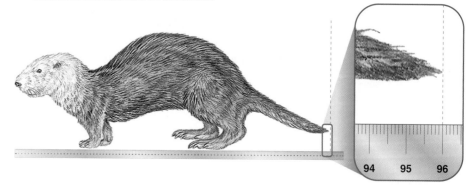

Instruments Write the length to the nearest hundredth of a meter.

18. The length of an electronic keyboard is 85 centimeters.

19. A guitar case is 14 centimeters longer than a meter.

20. Writing Your friend claims that measuring to the nearest tenth of a centimeter is the same as measuring to the nearest thousandth of a meter. Do you agree or disagree? Explain.

Estimation Sketch a line segment of the given length without using a ruler. Then use a ruler to check your estimate. How close was your estimate?

21. 6.5 cm   **22.** 45 mm   **23.** 0.01 m   **24.** 0.15 m

■ Sea Otters

Sea otters will dive 35 meters to find clams, crabs, snails, and starfish to eat! What distance in your school is about 35 meters?

What do you think?

Science

25. Snowboards Use the meter stick to give the measure of the snowboard to the nearest thousandth of a meter.

26. Challenge You measure an object to the nearest centimeter and the result is 4 centimeters. You then measure the same object to the nearest tenth of a centimeter. What results are possible? Explain.

Mixed Review

27. The scale on a scale drawing is 1 cm : 5 m. If your room is 10 meters long, how long is it on the scale drawing? *(Lesson 2.3)*

Choose a Strategy **Use a strategy from the list to solve the problem in Exercise 28. Explain your choice of strategy.**

Problem Solving Strategies
- Guess, Check, and Revise
- Draw a Diagram
- Look for a Pattern
- Solve a Simpler Problem

28. Your friend is thinking of a number between 1 and 10, and this number raised to the fourth power is 81. What is your friend's number?

Basic Skills **Tell whether the number in red is *less than*, *greater than*, or *equal to* the value of the expression.**

29. 3×6; 24   **30.** $48 \div 6$; 7   **31.** $18 - 17$; 1

Test-Taking Practice

32. Multiple Choice In the 1996 Summer Olympics, Joanna Stone threw a javelin 54 centimeters more than 58 meters. Which choice represents the distance she threw the javelin as a decimal number of meters?

A. 5.458 meters
B. 54.58 meters
C. 58.54 meters
D. 585.4 centimeters

33. Multiple Choice What is the length of the line segment to the nearest tenth of a centimeter?

F. 240 mm   **G.** 24 cm   **H.** 2.4 cm   **I.** 2.4 mm

Ordering Decimals

LESSON 3.3

BEFORE	Now	WHY?
You compared and ordered whole numbers.	You'll compare and order decimals.	So you can order data such as ages of volcanoes in Ex. 25.

In the Real World

Word Watch

Review Words
number line, p. 685

Gerbils A Mongolian gerbil's tail is about the same length as its body. A gerbil has a body length of 11 centimeters and a tail length of 10.6 centimeters. Which is longer, the body or the tail?

10.6 cm   **11 cm**

EXAMPLE 1 **Comparing Metric Lengths**

To answer the real-world question above, use a metric ruler. The tail length, 10.6 centimeters, is to the left of the body length, 11 centimeters.

You can say: $10.6 < 11$ or $11 > 10.6$

                      is less than   *is greater than*

HELP with **Reading**

Less than and *greater than* symbols always point to the lesser number.

ANSWER The gerbil's body is longer than its tail.

EXAMPLE 2 **Ordering Decimals on a Number Line**

Order the numbers from least to greatest: 3.1, 3.28, 3.06, 3, 3.15.

Graph each number on a number line. Begin by marking tenths from 3.0 to 3.3. Then mark hundredths by dividing each tenth into ten sections.

ANSWER An ordered list of the numbers is 3, 3.06, 3.1, 3.15, and 3.28.

Your turn now **Use the number line in Example 2.**

1. Order the numbers from least to greatest: 3.2, 3.29, 3.04, and 3.17.

2. Write three numbers that are greater than 3.2 and less than 3.25.

Comparing Decimals When you graph decimals on a number line to compare them, the greater number is farther to the right. You can also compare decimals by looking at their place values.

Steps for Comparing Decimals

1. Write the decimals in a column, lining up the decimal points.

2. If necessary, write zeros to the right of the decimals so that all decimals have the same number of decimal places.

3. Compare place values from left to right.

EXAMPLE 3 Comparing Decimals

Copy and complete the statement with <, >, or =.

a. 5.796 _?_ 5.802

5.796   ⟵ The ones' digits are the same.
5.802

The tenths' digits are different: 7 < 8.

ANSWER 5.796 < 5.802

b. 2.94 _?_ 2.9

2.94   ⟵ The ones' and tenths' digits are the same.
2.90 ⟵ Write a zero.

The hundredths' digits are different: 4 > 0.

ANSWER 2.94 > 2.9

EXAMPLE 4 Ordering Decimals

Order the gerbils from heaviest to lightest.

The digits are the same through the tenths' place. Compare hundredths, then thousandths if necessary: 77.0250, 77.0212, 77.0113, and 77.0033.

ANSWER The gerbils, from heaviest to lightest, are Scruff, Fluff, Edgar, and Scamp.

Gerbil	Weight (grams)
Edgar	77.0113
Fluff	77.0212
Scamp	77.0033
Scruff	77.0250

Your turn now Copy and complete the statement with <, >, or =.

3. 7.54 _?_ 7.45   **4.** 8.5 _?_ 8.50   **5.** 0.409 _?_ 0.411

Getting Ready to Practice

Vocabulary Copy and complete the statement using a decimal that is graphed in red on the number line.

1. 7.41 is less than ? .

2. 7.33 is greater than ? .

3. ? is between 7.33 and 7.41.

4. 7.41 is between 7.33 and ? .

5. Telephone Calls Order the following list of telephone call costs from least to greatest: $3.70, $3.29, $3.07, $3.92, $2.79, and $3.79.

Practice and Problem Solving

Copy and complete the statement with <, >, or =.

6. 2.8 ? 2.6

7. 7.1 ? 6.9

8. 8.5 ? 9.4

9. 1.21 ? 1.12

10. 4.82 ? 4.94

11. 9.50 ? 9.05

12. 8.7 ? 8.70

13. 4.40 ? 4.4

14. 42.1 ? 4.21

15. Explain Will a book that is 27.36 centimeters tall stand upright in a bookcase whose shelves are 27.4 centimeters apart? Explain.

Order the numbers from least to greatest.

16. 5.34, 5.12, 5.43

17. 9.07, 9.06, 9.1

18. 4.3, 4.25, 4.31

19. 0.9, 1.1, 0.1, 1.5

20. 7.4, 7.9, 7, 6.9

21. 1.2, 1.05, 1.15, 0.98

22. 2.94, 2.904, 2.844, 2.899, 2.894

23. 0.055, 0.555, 0.55, 0.065, 0.56

24. Milk Prices The average cost of a gallon of milk in various cities is given below. Order the costs from least to greatest.

Los Angeles	Rio De Janeiro	London	Paris	Hong Kong	Sydney
$3.07	$2.61	$2.08	$2.84	$8.40	$2.62

HELP with **Homework**

Example	Exercises
1	15
2	16–21
3	6–14
4	16–24

Online Resources
CLASSZONE.COM

· More Examples
· eTutorial Plus

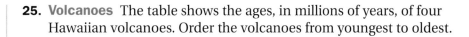

25. Volcanoes The table shows the ages, in millions of years, of four Hawaiian volcanoes. Order the volcanoes from youngest to oldest.

Hawaiian Volcano Ages (millions of years)				
Volcano	Mauna Kea	West Maui	West Molokai	Haleakala
Age	0.375	1.32	1.9	0.75

26. Critical Thinking If the price of every item in a store goes up by the same amount, does the order of least expensive item to most expensive item change? Why or why not?

Algebra **Find a value of *n* that makes the statement true.**

27. $8.3 < n$ and $n < 9$ **28.** $0.5 < n$ and $n < 1$ **29.** $3.6 < n$ and $n < 3.7$

Challenge **In Exercise 30, use only the digits 0 and 1.**

30. Write all the different decimals of the form ⬚ . ⬚ ⬚ .

31. Order the decimals you wrote in Exercise 30 from least to greatest.

■ **Volcanoes**

Lanai is another Hawaiian volcano. It is 1.28 million years old. How does the age of Lanai compare with the ages of the other volcanoes in Exercise 25?

Mixed Review

32. The heights, in feet, of newly planted trees are given below. Find the mean, median, mode, and range of the data. *(Lesson 2.8)*
  4, 5, 7, 5, 3, 4, 6, 5, 4, 5, 6, 4, 7

33. Write the number *twenty-eight and sixteen ten-thousandths* as a decimal. *(Lesson 3.1)*

Basic Skills **Round the number to the place value of the red digit.**

34. 2713   **35.** 106,503   **36.** 1,970,241

Test-Taking Practice

37. Multiple Choice Order the decimals from least to greatest: 0.3454, 0.4345, 0.3354, and 0.3345.

A. 0.4345, 0.3454, 0.3354, 0.3345   **B.** 0.3354, 0.3345, 0.4345, 0.3454

C. 0.3345, 0.3354, 0.3454, 0.4345   **D.** 0.3354, 0.3454, 0.3345, 0.4345

38. Multiple Choice In a competition, four of the participants have completed their performances. Their scores are 9.61, 9.66, 9.64, and 9.60. The highest score wins. Which score will enable the last participant to win the competition?

F. 9.67   **G.** 9.65   **H.** 9.62   **I.** 9.06

Notebook Review

Review the vocabulary definitions in your notebook.

Copy the review examples in your notebook. Then complete the exercises.

Check Your Definitions

decimal, p. 108   centimeter (cm), p. 56   number line, p. 685

millimeter (mm), p. 56   meter (m), p. 56

Use Your Vocabulary

1. Copy and complete: The decimal 2.06 is read "two and six ?."

2. Writing Explain the role of the decimal point in a decimal.

3.1–3.2 Can you measure and write decimal lengths?

 EXAMPLE Write the length of the line segment as a decimal number of centimeters.

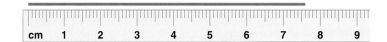

ANSWER The length is 7.6 centimeters.

☑ **Write the length in words and as a decimal.**

3. Find the length of this sentence to the nearest tenth of a centimeter.

4. Find the height of this book to the nearest hundredth of a meter.

3.3 Can you compare and order decimals?

 EXAMPLE Which is greater, 8.4 or 8.42?

8.40
8.42 ——— The first two digits are the same.
The hundredths' digits are different: 2 > 0.

ANSWER 8.42 > 8.4

☑ **Copy and complete the statement with <, >, or =.**

5. 6.54 ? 6.45   **6.** 2.536 ? 2.541   **7.** 9.7 ? 9.70

8. Order the numbers from least to greatest: 0.91, 0.94, 0.09, 0.082, 0.75.

Stop *and* **Think** about Lessons 3.1–3.3

9. Writing Explain the difference between *five hundred ten-thousandths* and *five hundred ten thousandths*.

10. Critical Thinking Explain why 0.50 is equal to 0.5.

Review Quiz 1

Write the decimal in words.

1. 6.52

2. 17.017

3. 0.1234

4. Write the number *eight and seven hundred fifty-two thousandths* as a decimal.

5. Find the length of the line segment to the nearest tenth of a centimeter.

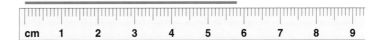

6. Order the numbers from least to greatest: 11.21, 11.02, 11.20, 11, 11.041.

Copy and complete the statement with <, >, or =.

7. 5.02 _?_ 5.21

8. 24.632 _?_ 24.236

9. 38.9 _?_ 38.90

10. Body Temperature If normal body temperature is about 98.6°F, is a temperature of 98.06°F *above* or *below* normal?

What Number Am I?

I have two digits to the left of my decimal point and two digits to the right of my decimal point. My hundredths' digit is two times my tenths' digit. When 1 is subtracted from my tens' digit, the answer is 5. I have a 2 as my tenths' digit. My ones' digit is greater than 0 and less than my tenths' digit. What number am I?

Rounding Decimals

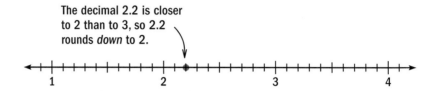

BEFORE	Now	WHY?
You rounded whole numbers.	You'll round decimals.	So you can read large numbers, such as the salaries in Example 4.

Word Watch

Review Words

leading digit, p. 13
round, p. 686

Number Lines A number line can help you picture how to round a decimal.

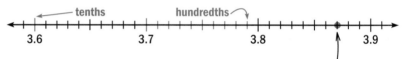

The decimal 2.2 is closer to 2 than to 3, so 2.2 rounds *down* to 2.

EXAMPLE 1 **Using a Number Line to Round**

Use a number line to round 3.87 to the nearest tenth.

tenths   hundredths

3.6   3.7   3.8   3.9

The decimal 3.87 is closer to 3.9 than to 3.8.

ANSWER The decimal 3.87 rounds up to 3.9.

Your turn now Use a number line to round the decimal as specified.

1. 1.3 (nearest one) **2.** 2.8 (nearest one)

3. 3.74 (nearest tenth) **4.** 3.86 (nearest tenth)

Using a Rule On a number line, you round a decimal by deciding which number it is closer to. The same idea applies when you use the rule below.

Rounding Decimals

To round a decimal to a given place value, look at the digit in the place to the right.

• If the digit is 4 or less, round down.

• If the digit is 5 or greater, round up.

EXAMPLE 2 **Rounding Decimals**

Round the decimal to the place value of the red digit.

a. $3.23 \longrightarrow 3.2$ The digit to the right of 2 is 3, so round down.

b. $6.485 \longrightarrow 6.49$ The digit to the right of 8 is 5, so round up.

c. $2.83619 \longrightarrow 2.836$ The digit to the right of 6 is 1, so round down.

d. $5.961 \longrightarrow 6.0$ The digit to the right of 9 is 6, so round up.

Your turn now   Round the decimal as specified.

5. 5.29 (nearest tenth)   **6.** 7.096 (nearest hundredth)

7. 6.48 (nearest one)   **8.** 3.9876 (nearest thousandth)

Rounding Small Numbers You can round a very small number to the place value of its leading digit to help make it easier to understand. In a decimal, the leading digit is the first nonzero digit at the left.

EXAMPLE 3 **Rounding to the Leading Digit**

Music A guitar was created that is 0.0003937 inch long. Round the length of the guitar to the place value of the leading digit.

Solution

The first nonzero digit at the left of 0.0003937 is 3, and it is in the ten-thousandths' place. You should round the length to the nearest ten-thousandth.

    0.0003937   **3 is in the ten-thousandths' place.**

Because 9 is to the right of the ten-thousandths' place, round 3 up to 4.

ANSWER The length of the guitar rounded to the place value of the leading digit is 0.0004 inch.

■ Music

This tiny guitar was created as a fun way to demonstrate technology for making very small objects. If the size of most human cells is 0.00003937 inch, which is larger, the guitar or the cell?

Your turn now   Round the decimal to the leading digit.

9. 0.058   **10.** 0.0091   **11.** 0.0952   **12.** 0.006192

EXAMPLE 4 **Using Decimals for Large Numbers**

Sports The average annual salaries for some positions in major league baseball in a recent year are shown below. Round each salary to the nearest hundred thousand. Then write each rounded salary as a decimal number of millions. Display your results in a bar graph.

Position:	Average Salary:	Round:	Write in millions:
First Base	$4,996,933	$5,000,000	$5.0 million
Outfield	$3,480,792	$3,500,000	$3.5 million
Pitcher	$3,064,021	$3,100,000	$3.1 million
Catcher	$2,767,726	$2,800,000	$2.8 million

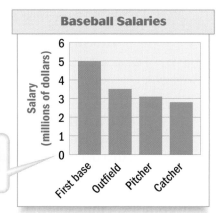

Baseball Salaries

An appropriate scale for the data is 0 to 6 million.

3.4 Exercises

More Practice, p. 710

INTERNET
eWorkbook Plus
CLASSZONE.COM

Getting Ready to Practice

Vocabulary Identify the leading digit of the decimal. Then round to the place value of the leading digit.

1. 0.024   **2.** 0.0078   **3.** 0.00149   **4.** 0.000485

Round the decimal as specified.

5. 8.21 (nearest tenth)   **6.** 1.159 (nearest hundredth)

7. 10.6289 (nearest thousandth)   **8.** 1.498 (nearest one)

9. Round the number 8,438,100 to the nearest hundred thousand. Then write the rounded number as a decimal number of millions.

HELP with Notetaking

As you work on the exercises, remember to write down any questions you want to ask your teacher.

Practice and Problem Solving

HELP with Homework

Example	Exercises
1	10–13
2	14–22, 32
3	23–30
4	33–36

Online Resources
CLASSZONE.COM

· More Examples
· eTutorial Plus

Use a number line to round the decimal as specified.

10. 5.3 (nearest one)　　　　**11.** 9.5 (nearest one)

12. 3.76 (nearest tenth)　　　**13.** 1.41 (nearest tenth)

Round the decimal as specified.

14. 9.41 (nearest one)　　　　　　**15.** 2.59 (nearest one)

16. 8.087 (nearest tenth)　　　　　**17.** 8.981 (nearest tenth)

18. 6.999 (nearest hundredth)　　　**19.** 3.902 (nearest hundredth)

20. 2.5634 (nearest thousandth)　　**21.** 7.2961 (nearest thousandth)

22. Writing After sharing a pizza, you and two friends divide the cost by three. You each owe $2.666666. Explain how to round this to the nearest dime.

Round the decimal to the place value of the leading digit.

23. 0.0263　　**24.** 0.0588　　**25.** 0.0092　　**26.** 0.006178

27. 0.00019　**28.** 0.000231　**29.** 0.00009888　**30.** 0.0000177

31. Skateboarding The table shows the scores of 4 skateboarders after three rounds of a skateboarding competition. Why is it not reasonable to round the scores to the nearest one? Explain.

	Round 1	Round 2	Round 3
Rob	80.7	84.4	80.8
Ruth	83.3	78.6	81.1
Kenny	81.2	83.6	80.6
Jessica	82.7	79.2	80.9

32. Find the Error Describe and correct the error in the form of the answer.

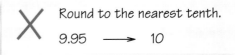

Round to the nearest tenth.

9.95 ⟶ 10

Round the number to the nearest hundred thousand. Then write the rounded number as a decimal number of millions.

33. 15,925,000　**34.** 6,549,000　**35.** 9,987,260　**36.** 14,962,000

Technology A calculator will sometimes give long decimals. Round the number on the calculator display to the nearest hundredth.

37. 1.285714286　　**38.** 1.076923077　　**39.** 1.714285714

What do you think?

Biology

■ Hair

An average person's head typically has 100,000 hairs on it. Suppose the girl in the picture measures a strand of her hair and finds it is 8 inches long. If all of her hair was one continuous strand, about how long would it be?

40. Hair The width of a human hair is about 0.00389763 inch. Explain why it is not reasonable to round the width to the nearest hundredth. Find a reasonable estimate for the width.

Tourism **The table shows the total number of people that visited the state parks of five states in one year.**

State	Visitors
California	76,736,000
Illinois	41,891,000
New York	61,960,000
Ohio	60,220,000
Washington	48,138,000

41. Round each number to the nearest hundred thousand. Then write the rounded number as a decimal number of millions.

42. Display your results in a bar graph.

Number Sense **Find three decimals that round to the number.**

43. 4   **44.** 15   **45.** 3.4   **46.** 8.7

47. Challenge In Exercise 43, you are asked to find three decimals that round to 4. How many answers are possible? Explain.

Mixed Review

Estimate the sum or difference. *(Lesson 1.2)*

48. $136 + 75$ **49.** $418 + 397$ **50.** $572 - 269$ **51.** $343 - 27$

Copy and complete the statement with <, >, or =. *(Lesson 3.3)*

52. $0.79 \underline{?} 0.9$ **53.** $0.05 \underline{?} 0.05000$ **54.** $3.037 \underline{?} 3.073$

Basic Skills **Find the product or quotient.**

55. 214×9 **56.** 125×10 **57.** $345 \div 3$ **58.** $270 \div 10$

Test-Taking Practice

INTERNET

State Test Practice
CLASSZONE.COM

59. Multiple Choice You record the weight of a package weighing 14.57 pounds to the nearest pound. What weight do you record?

    A. 10 pounds   **B.** 14 pounds   **C.** 14.5 pounds   **D.** 15 pounds

60. Short Response The table shows the scores of 5 divers in a school diving competition. Round the scores to the nearest one and order them from greatest to least, to find each diver's rank. Then rank the divers without rounding the scores. Which method is more reasonable to rank the divers? Explain.

Diver	Score
Dionne	136.35
Ashley	137.5
Ellie	136.7
Alina	137.45
Julie	137.35

Hands-on Activity

GOAL
Develop number sense skills for adding decimals.

MATERIALS
· metric ruler
· number cube
· colored pencils or markers

Targeting a Sum of 10

You can use number sense skills to choose values that come close to a target without going over. When these values are ones and tenths, you can use a metric ruler to help you.

Explore Use a metric ruler to come close to 10 centimeters without going over.

1 Draw a line segment that is 10 centimeters long.

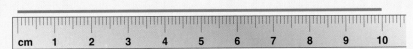

2 Roll a number cube. Decide whether you want the number rolled to represent whole centimeters or tenths of centimeters. Draw a segment of this length below the line segment you drew in Step 1.

 = 6.0 centimeters

3 Repeat Step 2 six more times. Begin each line segment where the last one ended and alternate colors. Try to get as close to 10 centimeters as you can without going over. Measure to see how close you came after seven rolls.

 = 0.3 centimeters

Your turn now Use the steps above.

1. Follow the steps to create a segment that is as close to 10 centimeters long as possible without going over. Record the length you choose for each roll.

Stop and Think

2. **Writing** In Exercise 1, could you choose different lengths for some rolls so that your sum comes closer to 10 centimeters? Explain.

Decimal Estimation

BEFORE	Now	WHY?
You estimated sums and differences of whole numbers.	You'll estimate sums and differences of decimals.	So you can estimate change you'll receive, as in Exs. 18 and 19.

In the Real World

Word Watch

front-end estimation, p. 131

Sports The table shows the number of people, in millions, who participated in five sports in a recent year. About how many people played soccer? About how many more females participated in bicycling than in golf?

Sports Participation (millions)		
Activity	**Males**	**Females**
Bicycling	22.9	20.6
Golf	21.8	5.7
Hiking	14.9	12.3
Soccer	8.2	4.9
Swimming	27.0	31.3

One way to estimate a sum or a difference is to use rounding.

EXAMPLE 1 Estimating Sums and Differences

a. To estimate the answer to the first real-world question above, round each decimal to the nearest whole number. Then add.

$$
\begin{array}{rcl}
8.2 & \longrightarrow & 8 \\
+\,4.9 & \longrightarrow & +\,5 \\
\hline
& & 13
\end{array}
$$

Round 8.2 down to 8.
Round 4.9 up to 5.

ANSWER About 13 million people played soccer.

b. To estimate the answer to the second real-world question above, round each decimal to the nearest whole number. Then subtract.

$$
\begin{array}{rcl}
20.6 & \longrightarrow & 21 \\
-\;\;5.7 & \longrightarrow & -\,6 \\
\hline
& & 15
\end{array}
$$

Round 20.6 up to 21.
Round 5.7 up to 6.

ANSWER About 15 million more females participated in bicycling than in golf.

 **Your turn now** Use the information provided at the top of the page.

1. Estimate the total number of people who participated in hiking.

2. Estimate how many more males participated in swimming than in golf.

EXAMPLE 2 Predicting Results

Shopping You buy a T-shirt that costs $9.21. You give the clerk $20.00. Estimate your change. Is this estimate *high* or *low*?

$$\begin{array}{r} \$20.00 \\ - \ \$9.21 \end{array} \longrightarrow \begin{array}{r} \$20 \\ - \ \$9 \\ \hline \$11 \end{array} \quad \text{Round 9.21 down to 9.}$$

ANSWER Your change is about $11. This estimate is high because you subtracted too little by rounding $9.21 down to $9.

Front-End Estimation You can also estimate sums using **front-end estimation**. You add the front-end digits to get a low estimate. Then you use the remaining digits to adjust the sum and get a closer estimate.

EXAMPLE 3 Using Front-End Estimation

Groceries You have $10 to buy bread, milk, and cereal. If you have enough money, you would like to buy popcorn. The prices of these items are shown. Do you have enough money to buy popcorn?

> Grocery List
> bread $1.79
> milk $2.18
> cereal $3.34
> popcorn $3.65

Solution

Find the sum of all the prices, including the price of the popcorn.

(1 Add the front-end digits: the dollars.

$$\begin{array}{r} \$1.79 \\ \$2.18 \\ \$3.34 \\ + \ \$3.65 \\ \hline \$9 \end{array}$$

(2 Estimate the sum of the remaining digits: the cents.

$$\begin{array}{r} \$1.79 \searrow \\ \$2.18 \rightarrow \$1 \\ \$3.34 \searrow \\ + \ \$3.65 \rightarrow \$1 \\ \hline \$2 \end{array}$$

(3 Add your results.

$$\begin{array}{r} \$9 \\ + \ \$2 \\ \hline \$11 \end{array}$$

ANSWER You do not have enough money to buy popcorn.

Your turn now Use front-end estimation to estimate the sum.

3. 6.42 + 7.64 + 3.94 + 2.21

4. 8.59 + 1.37 + 2 + 6.12

5. How can you estimate the difference in Example 2 so that your answer is a low estimate?

Getting Ready to Practice

1. Vocabulary Identify the front-end digits of $1.12 and $5.86.

Use rounding to estimate the sum or difference.

2. 2.6 + 8.9   **3.** 12.43 + 5.8   **4.** 15.5 − 14.7

5. Guided Problem Solving A table is 73.66 centimeters tall. An iguana cage on the table is 76.2 centimeters tall. Estimate to decide whether they will fit beneath a shelf that is 157.16 centimeters off the floor.

   1 Draw a diagram of the situation.

   2 Estimate the height of the table and the cage combined.

   3 Compare the combined heights to the height of the shelf.

Practice and Problem Solving

Use rounding to estimate the sum or difference.

6. 9.7 + 8.4	**7.** 8.3 + 3.8	**8.** 9.3 − 6.9
9. 7.2 − 4.6	**10.** 10.64 + 7.49	**11.** 2.25 + 0.93
12. 12.81 − 1.92	**13.** 10.72 − 2.85	**14.** 15.99 + 3.4
15. 12.38 + 12.8	**16.** 20.2 − 10.31	**17.** 9.1 − 8.98

Critical Thinking Estimate the change you will receive and tell whether the estimate is *high* or *low*. Explain.

18. You buy several postcards totaling $3.82. You give the clerk $10.00.

19. You buy a bag of pretzels for $1.15. You give the cashier $5.00.

Use front-end estimation to estimate the sum.

20. 4.79 + 5.16 + 8.08   **21.** 6.23 + 4.75 + 3.91   **22.** 4.5 + 8.92 + 9.21

23. 6.46 + 3.22 + 2.58   **24.** 5.55 + 7.19 + 4.49   **25.** 6.31 + 2.5 + 1.93

26. Find the Error Describe and correct the error in the estimate.

$$\times \quad \begin{array}{r} \$4\boxed{.79} \\ + \ \$1\boxed{.22} \\ \hline \$6 \end{array} \rightarrow \$1 \qquad \begin{array}{r} \$6 \\ + \ \$1 \\ \hline \$7 \end{array}$$

with Homework

Example	Exercises
1	6–17
2	18–19
3	20–25

Online Resources
CLASSZONE.COM
· More Examples
· eTutorial Plus

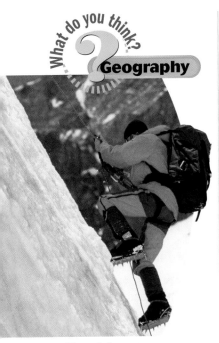

Extended Problem Solving The *Seven Summits* are the highest mountain peaks on each of the seven continents. The heights of the summits are shown in the table. Use the table in Exercises 27–29.

Mountain	Height (miles)
Mount Elbrus (Europe)	3.5
Mount Kosciusko (Australia)	1.38
Mount Aconcagua (South America)	4.33
Mount Everest (Asia)	5.50
Mount Kilimanjaro (Africa)	3.7
Mount McKinley (North America)	3.85
Vinson Massif (Antarctica)	3.04

27. Order the heights of the mountains from least to greatest. Then find the median of the heights.

28. Estimate the mean of the heights. Is your estimate *high* or *low*? Explain.

29. Critical Thinking Which of your answers in Exercises 27 and 28 is more representative of the heights? Explain.

30. Challenge How can you use rounding to overestimate the sum of two numbers? the difference of two numbers? How can you use rounding to underestimate the sum of two numbers? the difference of two numbers? Explain and show examples.

■ **Mountains**

Most climbers of Mount Everest will start from the Everest Base Camp, which is about 3.2 miles high. About how far do they climb from the base camp to the top?

Mixed Review

Evaluate the expression when *x* = 2 and *y* = 3. *(Lesson 1.5)*

31. $x + 14$ **32.** $9y$ **33.** $x + y$ **34.** $y + x \cdot y$

Round the decimal as specified. *(Lesson 3.4)*

35. 17.8023 (nearest thousandth)   **36.** 4.79663 (nearest hundredth)

Basic Skills **Find the sum or difference.**

37. $10.75 + $1.25   **38.** $9.80 + $4.20   **39.** $2.85 − $1.35

Test-Taking Practice

40. Extended Response You have $25 to buy prizes for a game. The table shows the prizes and their prices. Use rounding to estimate the total cost and decide if this estimate is *high* or *low*. Then use front-end estimation to find the total cost. Which method is better when you have a fixed amount of money to spend? Explain.

Prize	Price
yo-yo	$1.48
bear	$9.46
sunglasses	$1.07
magic tricks	$5.91
set of books	$8.00

Problem Solving Strategies

Draw a Diagram
Guess, Check, and Revise
Make a Table
Make a List
Check Reasonableness
Work Backward
Look for a Pattern

Check Reasonableness

Problem You would like to construct wooden photo frames. You need 50 centimeters of wood for each frame. You have a total of 275 centimeters of wood. How many photo frames can you make?

1 Read and Understand

Read the problem carefully.

Your answer should be a whole number of photo frames.

2 Make a Plan

Decide on a strategy to use.

To solve this problem, you need to choose the operation, carry out the operation, and then check the reasonableness of the answer.

3 Solve the Problem

Reread the problem and choose an operation.

You need to divide to find the number of times 50 centimeters goes into 275 centimeters.

$$\begin{array}{r} 5\ \text{R}25 \\ 50\overline{)275} \\ \underline{250} \\ 25 \end{array}$$

Evaluate the reasonableness of 5 R25.

5   R25

5 whole picture frames   25 centimeters left over

You cannot make a complete photo frame with 25 centimeters, so you need to round down to 5.

ANSWER You can make 5 photo frames.

4 Look Back

Check the reasonableness of your solution using estimation. Using compatible numbers, you get $300 \div 50 = 6$. This is an overestimate, because 300 is greater than 275. Your answer is reasonable.

Solve the problems and *check for reasonableness.*

1. **Medals** You are putting ribbons on medals for a sports competition. Each medal needs 25 inches of ribbon. You have 16 feet of ribbon. How many medals can you decorate with ribbon?

2. **Frames** You would like to construct wooden photo frames. You need 40 centimeters of wood for each frame and you have a total of 140 centimeters of wood. How many photo frames can you make?

3. **Buses** You are helping the science teacher plan a field trip to the natural history museum. There are 105 students signed up for the field trip. Each bus can hold 45 students. How many buses do you recommend reserving?

4. **Books** A bookstore needs to mail 225 books. The boxes they will use can hold 12 books each. How many boxes will the bookstore need to mail all of the books?

5. **Gifts** You have $55 to buy three birthday gifts. The prices of three possible gifts and an estimate of the tax are listed below. Will you have enough money?

Mixed Problem Solving

Use any strategy to solve the problem.

6. **Decorating** You are arranging furniture in a 10 foot by 8 foot room. You have a 6 foot by 6 foot rug. You want to place a 4 foot by 3 foot desk against a wall, but not on the rug. Is this possible? Why or why not?

7. **Locks** You can remember the three numbers for a lock, but you can't remember their order. One possibility is shown below. What are the other possibilities?

8. **Supplies** You spent $17 on construction paper and envelopes. If a box of envelopes costs $3 and a package of construction paper costs $4, how many boxes of envelopes and packages of construction paper did you buy?

9. **Shopping** You spend half of your money at the first store in the mall, $5 in the second store, and $7 in the third store. At this point, you have $3 left. How much money did you start with?

Birthday Gifts

CD	$17.99
Book	$12.25
Game	$24.75
Tax	$4.50

LESSON 3.6

Adding and Subtracting Decimals

BEFORE | ▶ **Now** | **WHY?**

You added and subtracted whole numbers. | You'll add and subtract decimals. | So you can find account balances, as in Example 4.

Word Watch

commutative property of addition, p. 137
associative property of addition, p. 137

 Activity You can use base-ten pieces to model decimal addition.

To find the sum of 1.15 and 0.95, combine the pieces.

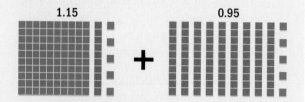

① Model the numbers using base-ten pieces.

1.15   0.95

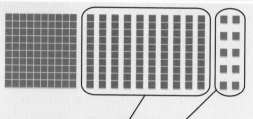

② Combine the pieces.

③ Trade **10 tenths** for **1 one** and **10 hundredths** for **1 tenth**.

$1.15 + 0.95 = 2.1$

2.1

Use base-ten pieces to find the sum.

1. $2.1 + 0.9$ **2.** $1.5 + 0.8$ **3.** $2.23 + 1.89$

To add and subtract decimals, line up the decimal points. Then add or subtract as with whole numbers and bring down the decimal point.

 **with Solving**

You can add zeros following the last digit to the right of the decimal point to help you line up the decimal points.

EXAMPLE 1 Adding and Subtracting Decimals

a. $9.8 + 2.12$

$$\begin{array}{r} 9.80 \\ + 2.12 \\ \hline 11.92 \end{array}$$

b. $8 - 1.65$

$$\begin{array}{r} 8.00 \\ - 1.65 \\ \hline 6.35 \end{array}$$

EXAMPLE 2 **Evaluating Algebraic Expressions**

Evaluate 20 − *x* when *x* = **4.71**.

$$20 - x = 20 - 4.71 \qquad \text{Substitute 4.71 for } x.$$
$$= 15.29$$

Your turn now Evaluate the expression when *x* = **5.82** and *y* = **9.1**.

1. $4.7 + x$ **2.** $12.56 - y$ **3.** $y - x$

EXAMPLE 3 **Using Mental Math to Add Decimals**

Bakery Find the total cost for a sweet roll that costs $1.30, two hard rolls that cost $1.20 each, and a coffee cake that costs $3.70.

List the prices:	Rearrange the prices and group pairs of prices.
$1.30	$1.30
$1.20	$3.70
$1.20	$1.20
$3.70	$1.20

$1.30 and $3.70 → $5
$1.20 and $1.20 → $2.40
$5 and $2.40 → $7.40

ANSWER The bakery goods will cost $7.40.

Mental Math In Example 3, you rearranged numbers and grouped them. The properties that allow you to do this are shown below.

Properties of Addition

Commutative Property You can add numbers in any order.

Numbers $2 + 5 = 5 + 2$ **Algebra** $a + b = b + a$

Associative Property The value of a sum does not depend on how the numbers are grouped.

Numbers $(2 + 5) + 4 = 2 + (5 + 4)$

Algebra $(a + b) + c = a + (b + c)$

Your turn now Tell which property is illustrated. Then find the sum.

4. $9.3 + 2.9 = 2.9 + 9.3$ **5.** $(6.4 + 4.8) + 5.2 = 6.4 + (4.8 + 5.2)$

EXAMPLE **4** **Writing a Model**

Banking You have a balance of $141.82 in an account. You withdraw $30 and then deposit a check for $41.93. What is the new balance?

Solution

Write a verbal model to help you find the new balance.

New balance = Beginning balance − Withdrawal + Deposit

$$= 141.82 - 30 + 41.93 \qquad \text{Substitute.}$$

$$= 111.82 + 41.93 \qquad \text{Subtract.}$$

$$= 153.75 \qquad \text{Add.}$$

ANSWER The new balance is $153.75.

✓ **Check** Use estimation to check that your answer is reasonable. Round $141.82 to $142 and $41.93 to $42. Because 142 − 30 + 42 = 154, the answer is reasonable.

HELP with **Reading**

The *balance* in an account is the amount of money in the account. When you *deposit* money, you add to the balance. When you *withdraw* money, you take away from the balance.

3.6 **Exercises**

More Practice, p. 710

INTERNET
eWorkbook Plus
CLASSZONE.COM

Getting Ready to Practice

1. **Vocabulary** According to the _?_ property, you can add numbers in any order.

Find the sum or difference.

2. 3.6 + 1.89   **3.** 6.54 + 12.1   **4.** 9.8 − 7.96   **5.** 4 − 0.25

Tell which property is illustrated.

6. 3.8 + 4.1 = 4.1 + 3.8   **7.** (3.1 + 2.1) + 9 = 3.1 + (2.1 + 9)

8. **Guided Problem Solving** The Metro heavy rail system in Washington, D.C., has 198.7 miles of track. Cleveland's RTA has 46.7 miles of track. Boston's MBTA has 107.7 miles of track. How many more miles of track does the Metro have than the RTA and the MBTA combined?

    (1 Write a verbal model of the problem.

    (2 Use the model to solve the problem.

    (3 Check your answer using estimation.

Practice and Problem Solving

HELP with Homework

Example	Exercises
1	9–20
2	21–26
3	27–30
4	31–32

Online Resources
CLASSZONE.COM

· More Examples
· eTutorial Plus

Find the sum or difference.

9. $5.56 + 3.7$ **10.** $2.88 + 6.7$ **11.** $16.2 + 8.34$ **12.** $18.4 + 1.6$

13. $4.091 + 5.87$ **14.** $3.781 + 4.19$ **15.** $5.56 - 2.3$ **16.** $7.42 - 3.2$

17. $6.18 - 1.71$ **18.** $9.14 - 6.64$ **19.** $4 - 1.24$ **20.** $8 - 6.68$

Algebra Evaluate the expression when $x = 2.4$ and $y = 8.75$.

21. $4.52 + x$ **22.** $y + 7.5$ **23.** $y - 3.01$

24. $6.48 - x$ **25.** $x + y$ **26.** $y - x$

Mental Math Tell which property is being illustrated. Then use mental math to evaluate the expression in red.

27. $(9.5 + 4.9) + 5.1 = \mathbf{9.5 + (4.9 + 5.1)}$

28. $4.2 + (2.8 + 11.95) = \mathbf{(4.2 + 2.8) + 11.95}$

29. $1.5 + (1.74 + 3.5) = \mathbf{1.5 + (3.5 + 1.74)}$

30. $(3.7 + 8.9) + 6.3 = \mathbf{(8.9 + 3.7) + 6.3}$

Estimation Solve the problem. Use estimation to check that your answer is reasonable.

31. Dining Out Your meal at a restaurant costs $5.29. Your guest's meal costs $4.95. You give the cashier $15 for the two meals. How much change should you get?

32. Banking You have $98 in your savings account. You withdraw $5.50 and deposit $22.75. What is the new balance?

Sports

What do you think?

■ **Orienteering**

On a map an orienteer is using, the scale is 1 cm : 100 m. If the map of the course is 20 cm tall and 30 cm wide, what is the actual area of the course?

Orienteering In Exercises 33 and 34, use the table at the right.

In the sport of orienteering, people use maps and compasses to find their way from point to point along an unfamiliar outdoor course. The table shows the average of the best scores of the top five women orienteers in the world at one time.

Orienteer	Average of Best Scores
Simone Luder	1422.75
Hanne Staff	1394.5
Reeta Kolkkala	1373.75
Vroni Koenig-Salmi	1371.25
Heather Monro	1362.5

33. How much greater was Simone Luder's score than the next best score?

34. Find the range of the scores.

Geometry Find the perimeter of the triangle.

35.
7.5 cm
6 cm
7.5 cm

36. 9.1 mm
6.5 mm
5.85 mm

37.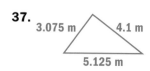
3.075 m   4.1 m
5.125 m

38. Critical Thinking Follow the order of operations to evaluate the expressions $(9.5 - 3.5) - 3.2$ and $9.5 - (3.5 - 3.2)$. Based on your results, decide whether subtraction is associative.

Astronauts On a space shuttle mission, astronauts are allowed 1.5 pounds of personal items. The table shows the weights of some possible items.

39. If an astronaut decides to bring 2 rolls of pennies and a watch on the mission, what other item from the list could the astronaut bring?

Item	Weight (pounds)
2 rolls of pennies	1.12
5 golf balls	0.506
watch	0.09
college sweatshirt	0.75
whistle	0.125
camera	0.625

40. Challenge What is the maximum number of different items an astronaut could bring from the list? What are they? What is their total weight?

Mixed Review

41. Make a frequency table of the data. *(Lesson 2.4)*

2, 3, 5, 9, 4, 1, 0, 2, 3, 4, 5, 6, 7, 8, 1, 3, 5, 9, 1, 3, 5, 6, 4, 5, 1

42. Camping According to the graph, which camping activity was favored by the least number of people surveyed? *(Lesson 2.7)*

Favorite Camping Activities

Canoeing   Campfire
Hiking   Swimming

Basic Skills Find the product.

43. $12 \cdot 14$ **44.** $30 \cdot 15$ **45.** $54 \cdot 16$ **46.** $23 \cdot 74$

Test-Taking Practice

47. Multiple Choice Evaluate the expression $12.4 - 2.35 + 24.6$.

A. 44.65   **B.** 39.35   **C.** 34.65   **D.** 34.75

48. Short Response You buy one video tape for $19.95 and rent one for $4.29. The sales tax is $1.45. How much change should you receive if you give the cashier $30? Explain how you solved the problem.

CALCULATOR

Technology Activity

Adding and Subtracting Decimals

GOAL Use a calculator to add and subtract decimals.

Example You can add and subtract decimals using the ➕ and ➖ keys.

A national collegiate triathlon championship consists of a 0.932 mile swim, a 24.9 mile bike ride, and a 6.21 mile run. What is the total length of the triathlon?

Solution

When using a calculator to add and subtract decimals, you do not have to worry about lining up the decimal points.

Keystrokes

0 ⚫ 932 ➕ 24 ⚫ 9 ➕ 6 ⚫ 21 ═

Display

32.042

ANSWER The triathlon is 32.042 miles long.

✓ **Check** Round 0.932 to 1, 24.9 to 25, and 6.21 to 6. Because 1 + 25 + 6 = 32, the answer is reasonable.

Your turn now Use a calculator to evaluate the expression.

1. 6.705 + 0.68   **2.** 9.83 − 5.846   **3.** 12.753 − 4.1

4. 9.32 − 7.3 − 0.02   **5.** 6.942 + 3.3 − 5.39   **6.** 20.87 − 9.7 + 3.42

7. Geometry A triangle has side lengths of 4.5 inches, 6.2 inches, and 9.4 inches. What is the perimeter of the triangle?

8. Body Temperature To convert a temperature in kelvins (K) to degrees Celsius (°C), you subtract 273.15. Normal body temperature is 310.15K. What is normal body temperature in degrees Celsius?

9. Triathlon A national triathlon championship for athletes who are 11 to 14 years old consists of a 0.114 mile swim, a 6.2 mile bike ride, and a 1.2 mile run. What is the total length of the triathlon?

Review the vocabulary definitions in your notebook.

Copy the review examples in your notebook. Then complete the exercises.

Check Your Definitions

front-end estimation, p. 131

commutative property of addition, p. 137

associative property of addition, p. 137

Use Your Vocabulary

1. When you add front-end digits, is your estimate *high* or *low*?

2. Name the property that allows you to add two numbers in any order.

3.4–3.5 Can you round and estimate answers?

 EXAMPLE

a. Round to estimate the difference.

$$16.7 \rightarrow 17 \quad \text{Round up.}$$
$$-\ 6.2 \rightarrow -\ 6 \quad \text{Round down.}$$
$$\overline{11}$$

b. Use front-end estimation to estimate the sum.

$$
\begin{array}{r}
9.67 \\
8.39 \\
+\ 4.2 \\
\hline
21
\end{array}
\searrow 1
\qquad
\begin{array}{r}
21 \\
+\ 1 \\
\hline
22
\end{array}
$$

☑ **Round the decimal as specified.**

3. 5.643 (nearest tenth)

4. 3.0465 (nearest thousandth)

☑ **Round to estimate the sum or difference.**

5. $3.5 + 6.8$

6. $9.7 - 2.83$

7. $1.42 + 3.59 + 7.98 + 4.06$

3.6 Can you add and subtract decimals?

 EXAMPLE

a. $2.8 + 4.63$

$$
\begin{array}{r}
2.80 \\
+\ 4.63 \\
\hline
7.43
\end{array}
$$
Line up the decimal points.

b. $7.61 - 5.438$

$$
\begin{array}{r}
7.610 \\
-\ 5.438 \\
\hline
2.172
\end{array}
$$
Add a zero.

☑ **Add or subtract.**

8. $6.568 + 9.73$

9. $12.35 - 4.062$

Stop *and* **Think**   about Lessons 3.4–3.6

10. Estimation When estimating a sum of decimals, explain how adjusting the sum of the leading digits alters the estimate.

11. Writing Explain why you line up the decimal points when you add or subtract decimals.

Review Quiz 2

Round the decimal as specified.

1. 5.687 (nearest tenth)

2. 6.7591 (nearest hundredth)

3. 2.1295 (nearest thousandth)

4. 4.987 (nearest one)

Use rounding to estimate the sum or difference.

5. 6.75 + 4.17   **6.** 15.6 + 17.82   **7.** 9.15 − 3.67   **8.** 32.14 − 14.8

9. Buying Music You want to buy 2 CDs and 2 cassette tapes. The CDs cost $16.59 and $17.65. The cassette tapes cost $8.32 and $7.54. Use front-end estimation to estimate the total cost of your purchase.

Find the sum or difference.

10. 3.17 + 9.07   **11.** 5.42 + 8.93   **12.** 4.176 + 7.523   **13.** 1.39 + 14.6

14. 7.65 − 1.982   **15.** 13.657 − 9.4   **16.** 6 − 1.03   **17.** 9 − 7.39

18. Box Office Over a weekend, Movie A earned $14.85 million while Movie B earned $9.6 million. How much more did Movie A earn?

BRAIN GAME

Decimal Challenge

Complete each box with a digit from 0 to 9 and use each digit exactly once. Find the greatest possible sum, the greatest possible difference, the least possible sum, and the least possible difference.

3 Chapter Review

 **Vocabulary**

decimal, p. 108
front-end estimation,
   p. 131

commutative property of
   addition, p. 137

associative property of
   addition, p. 137

Vocabulary Review

1. Write 15.368 in words.

2. Copy and complete: When you add the front-end digits and estimate the sum of the remaining digits, you are using ? .

3. Tell which property is illustrated:
$6.51 + 7.21 = 7.21 + 6.51$.

4. Tell which property is illustrated:
$(4.3 + 6.2) + 9.8 = 4.3 + (6.2 + 9.8)$.

Review Questions

Write the number as a decimal. *(Lesson 3.1)*

5. twelve and two tenths

6. nine and thirty-six hundredths

7. six and eleven thousandths

8. two hundred seven ten-thousandths

Copy and complete the statement. *(Lesson 3.2)*

9. 4 and 4 tenths meters = _?_ meters

10. 7 and 28 hundredths meters = _?_ meters

Measure the line segment to the nearest tenth of a centimeter.
(Lesson 3.2)

11.

12.

Order the numbers from least to greatest. *(Lesson 3.3)*

13. 17.12, 17.02, 17.21, 17.20

14. 1.301, 1.310, 1.133, 3.011, 1.033

Copy and complete the statement with <, >, or =. *(Lesson 3.3)*

15. 8.2 ? 7.3　　**16.** 5.6 ? 5.1　　**17.** 10.2 ? 13.5　　**18.** 23.7 ? 32.7

19. 5.30 ? 5.3　　**20.** 3.401 ? 3.41　　**21.** 6.21 ? 6.215　　**22.** 7.196 ? 7.1960

Round the decimal as specified. *(Lesson 3.4)*

23. 0.0068 (leading digit)　　　　　　**24.** 10.226 (nearest tenth)

25. 1.606 (nearest hundredth)　　　　**26.** 4.8873 (nearest thousandth)

Use rounding to estimate the sum or difference. *(Lesson 3.5)*

27. 7.5 + 3.8　　**28.** 8.4 + 9.9　　**29.** 6.7 − 2.8　　**30.** 7.4 − 3.6

31. 5.38 + 6.65　　**32.** 17.84 + 3.54　　**33.** 12.71 − 3.54　　**34.** 9.2 − 5.81

Use front-end estimation to estimate the sum. *(Lesson 3.5)*

35. 5.6 + 7.2 + 9.3 + 4.8　　　　　**36.** 1.02 + 3.7 + 0.8 + 6.4

37. 3.61 + 1.5 + 7.3 + 5.34　　　　**38.** 3.51 + 6.30 + 9.49 + 4.72

39. Exercise You are exercising on a treadmill. You walk for 1.2 miles, jog for 3.7 miles, then walk for another 0.9 mile. Your goal is to walk and jog for a total of 6 miles. How much farther must you walk or jog? *(Lesson 3.6)*

Food The table shows the costs of a 24 ounce loaf of wheat bread in selected cities. *(Lessons 3.3, 3.4, 3.6)*

City	Cost
Athens	$1.50
Hong Kong	$1.62
London	$0.68
Los Angeles	$1.49
Mexico City	$1.13
Paris	$1.85

40. Round each cost to the nearest dime.

41. Order the costs from least to greatest. In which city is wheat bread most expensive? least expensive?

42. How much more does wheat bread cost in Hong Kong than in Mexico City?

Find the sum or difference. *(Lesson 3.6)*

43. 3.9 + 2.08　　**44.** 4.61 + 1.015　　**45.** 0.8 + 6.47　　**46.** 5.372 + 3.87

47. 9.173 − 1.03　　**48.** 8.32 − 2.161　　**49.** 7 − 2.195　　**50.** 7.62 − 4.7

Evaluate the expression when $x = 9.37$ and $y = 4.16$. *(Lesson 3.6)*

51. $15 - x$　　**52.** $2.8 + x$　　**53.** $y + 3.2$　　**54.** $6.8 - y$

55. $3.287 + x$　　**56.** $y - 3.1$　　**57.** $5.816 - y$　　**58.** $x + y$

3 Chapter Test

1. Write the number *eighteen and six thousandths* as a decimal.

2. Write 0.12 in words.

3. Write 220.0022 in words.

Copy and complete the statement.

4. 6 and 4 tenths centimeters = _?_ centimeters

5. 5 and 28 hundredths meters = _?_ meters

Copy and complete the statement with <, >, or =.

6. 3.07 _?_ 3.009

7. 13.76 _?_ 13.760

8. 25.853 _?_ 25.883

9. 5.5912 _?_ 5.5921

Order the numbers from least to greatest.

10. 6.2, 6.04, 6.16, 6.02, 6.1, 6.056

11. 0.056, 0.49, 0.509, 0.0487, 0.005

Round the decimal as specified.

12. 10.0962 (nearest tenth)

13. 14.925 (nearest hundredth)

14. 0.5691 (nearest thousandth)

15. 0.00291 (leading digit)

16. Astronomy The diameter of the Sun is about 1,392,000 kilometers. Round the diameter to the nearest hundred thousand. Then write the rounded diameter as a decimal number of millions.

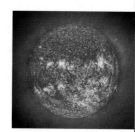

Use rounding to estimate the sum or difference.

17. 6.9 + 0.8

18. 12.4 + 10.7

19. 15.2 − 9.9

20. 5.7 − 2.8

Use front-end estimation to estimate the sum.

21. 4.39 + 1.84 + 5.62 + 9.1

22. 2.07 + 1.74 + 1.24 + 2.88

Find the sum or difference.

23. 18.79 + 3.6

24. 10.29 + 19.71

25. 6.073 − 5.02

26. 7.5 − 1.54

27. Tell which property is illustrated: (10 + 2.9) + 7.1 = 10 + (2.9 + 7.1).

28. Computers Your computer's hard drive has 20 gigabytes of memory, and you are currently using 5.93 gigabytes. How much memory is available on your computer?

Chapter Standardized Test

Test-Taking Strategy Make sure you understand the question before looking for the answer.

Multiple Choice

1. Write *fourteen and fifteen ten-thousandths* as a decimal.

   A. 1.415   **B.** 14.0015   **C.** 14.015   **D.** 14.15

2. Complete the statement with the correct decimal: 2 and 21 hundredths meters equals __?__ meters.

   F. 2.0   **G.** 2.0021   **H.** 2.021   **I.** 2.21

3. 55 centimeters is what decimal part of a meter?

   A. 0.55   **B.** 0.505   **C.** 0.055   **D.** 0.0055

4. Which number is greater than 0.84 and less than 0.845?

   F. 0.8   **G.** 0.82   **H.** 0.843   **I.** 0.847

5. A baseball team manager lists the batting averages of four players on the team. Which list shows their batting averages in order from greatest to least?

   A. 0.298, 0.336, 0.283, 0.332
   B. 0.336, 0.332, 0.283, 0.298
   C. 0.283, 0.298, 0.332, 0.336
   D. 0.336, 0.332, 0.298, 0.283

6. Round 4.658 to the nearest hundredth.

   F. 4.6   **G.** 4.66   **H.** 4.67   **I.** 4.7

7. You buy a new carpet on sale for $829.99. The regular price for the carpet is $1483.99. What is the best estimate of the total amount you save?

   A. $300   **B.** $700   **C.** $1000   **D.** $2200

8. Your friend buys a blouse for $28.95, a pair of sandals for $39.95, and a pair of shorts for $19.90. How much do the three items cost?

   F. $68.90   **G.** $78.80   **H.** $88.80   **I.** $88.85

9. What value of x makes the statement true?

$$5.6 + (0.3 + 4.9) = (5.6 + x) + 4.9$$

   A. 0   **B.** 0.3   **C.** 4.9   **D.** 5.6

10. Evaluate the expression $x + 10.75 - 7.71$ when $x = 2.46$.

   F. 3.04   **G.** 4.5   **H.** 5.5   **I.** 16

Short Response

11. At a department store, you buy a sweater for $29.99, a notebook for $3.79, and a CD for $11.99. You give the cashier $50. About how much change should you expect? Explain your reasoning.

Extended Response

12. The population of Los Angeles has grown rapidly in the last 50 years. The table shows the population

Year	Population
1960	2,479,015
1970	2,816,061
1980	2,966,850
1990	3,485,398
2000	3,694,820

of Los Angeles in several different years. Round the data to the nearest hundred thousand. Write each number as a decimal number of millions. Then display your results in a bar graph. About how much did the population grow, in millions, between the years 1960 and 2000? Explain.

The Grizzlies of Yellowstone

Monitoring the Grizzlies

The grizzly bears of Yellowstone National Park used to feed on garbage dumps in the park. When the dumps were closed in 1967, the amount of food available to the grizzlies was reduced. At first many grizzlies did not survive. For a number of years, scientists have been monitoring the grizzly population of Yellowstone to see how the bears are adjusting to more natural conditions.

The population is hard to count because the bears live in remote places and avoid humans. One way to estimate the total population is to count how many female bears are sighted with a new litter of cubs each year.

Grizzly Bear Counts in Yellowstone National Park					
Year	Females	Cubs	Year	Females	Cubs
1974	15	26	1988	19	41
1976	17	32	1990	25	58
1978	9	19	1992	25	60
1980	12	23	1994	20	47
1982	11	20	1996	33	72
1984	17	31	1998	35	70
1986	25	48	2000	37	72

The table above shows how many female bears with new litters were sighted and the total number of new cubs for even-numbered years from 1974 to 2000. Use the table for Exercises 1–3.

1. Use the data to make a bar graph showing the number of female bears with new litters. Put years on the horizontal axis and put the number of females on the vertical axis.

2. Use the cub data to make a bar graph similar to the one you made in Exercise 1.

3. What patterns do you notice in these two graphs?

Comparing Litter Sizes

Female grizzlies usually have two cubs in a litter but sometimes have as many as four. The table below shows the average litter size for the grizzlies in Yellowstone in different years. Because the numbers are averages, some of them are decimals.

Average Litter Sizes			
Year	Average Litter Size	Year	Average Litter Size
1974	1.7	1988	2.2
1976	1.9	1990	2.3
1978	2.1	1992	2.4
1980	1.9	1994	2.4
1982	1.8	1996	2.2
1984	1.8	1998	2.0
1986	1.9	2000	2.0

4. In what year(s) was the average litter size the greatest? In what year(s) was it the least? What was the difference between the greatest and least average litter sizes?

5. Make a bar graph of the data. What patterns, if any, do you notice about the data? Did the litter size increase over time?

6. **Critical Thinking** Based on the three graphs you have made, do you think the bears in Yellowstone are making a successful recovery after the closing of the garbage dumps? Explain your reasoning.

Project IDEAS

- **Predict** Based on the data given, how many females with new litters do you think were sighted in 2002? How many new cubs?

- **Report** Find out more about Yellowstone Park. What other animals live there? Present your findings to the class.

- **Research** Find out more about the grizzly bear. What kinds of food does it eat? What climates does it live in? Do grizzlies hibernate? Present your findings to the class.

- **Career** The scientists who monitor the grizzlies are called conservation biologists. Find out what other kinds of work conservation biologists do. Present your findings to the class.

INTERNET
Project Support
CLASSZONE.COM

4 Decimal Multiplication and Division

4

BEFORE

In previous chapters you've...

- Multiplied and divided whole numbers
- Added and subtracted decimals

Now

In Chapter 4 you'll study...

- Multiplying and dividing decimals
- Multiplying and dividing by powers of ten
- Measuring mass and capacity

WHY?

So you can solve real-world problems about...

- car washes, p. 159
- sports cards, p. 169
- ice hockey, p. 179
- mountain climbing, p. 189

Internet Preview

CLASSZONE.COM

- eEdition Plus Online
- eWorkbook Plus Online
- eTutorial Plus Online
- State Test Practice
- More Examples

Chapter Warm-Up Game

Review skills you need for this chapter in this game. Work with a partner.

Key Skills:
- Multiplying and dividing whole numbers
- Estimating products and quotients

OPERATION COVER-UP

MATERIALS

- 1 deck of *Operation Cover-up* cards

- 2 *Operation Cover-up* game boards

PREPARE Each player uses his or her own game board. Players share the deck of cards. First shuffle the deck, then place it face down between the two players. On each turn, each player should follow the steps on the next page. Wait until both players are done before beginning the next turn.

...he quotient... numbers is between 5 and 15.

Computation Spaces

The remainder of the quotient is odd.

The sum of the... great...

14 5

81 367

1 **DRAW** 2 cards. Each card has a number.

14 5

HOW TO WIN Be the first player to cover all 6 spaces on your game board, or be the player with the most spaces covered when you run out of cards.

2 **DECIDE** whether the numbers form a product or a quotient that satisfies one of the conditions on a space on your game board.

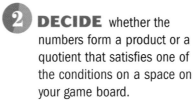

14 5

3 **COVER** the space with your cards. If your numbers do not satisfy any of the conditions that are uncovered, discard them.

14 5

Stop *and* Think

1. **Writing** What strategies do you recommend for someone playing this game? For example, do you recommend that players estimate before computing? Or should players compute before estimating?

2. **Critical Thinking** Explain why you don't need to perform an exact computation to determine that the product of two numbers is between 5000 and 15,000.

151

Getting Ready to Learn

Review What You Need to Know ♻

Using Vocabulary Tell whether the number is the *divisor, quotient,* or *dividend* in the problem shown.

$$\overset{13}{4)\overline{52}}$$

1. 52 **2.** 13 **3.** 4

Find the product or quotient. *(pp. 690–691)*

4. 71×100 **5.** 6×1000 **6.** 95×1000 **7.** 138×100

8. $150 \div 10$ **9.** $1640 \div 10$ **10.** $2300 \div 100$ **11.** $500 \div 100$

Estimate the product or quotient. *(p. 13)*

12. 32×46 **13.** 119×11 **14.** 315×4 **15.** 78×62

16. $25 \div 8$ **17.** $36 \div 5$ **18.** $158 \div 83$ **19.** $211 \div 67$

Round the decimal as specified. *(p. 124)*

20. 1.068 (nearest hundredth) **21.** 28.556 (nearest tenth)

22. 5.21354 (nearest thousandth) **23.** 14.997 (nearest tenth)

Know How to Take Notes

Previewing the Chapter Before you start a lesson or chapter, look at what you are about to learn. Find familiar words and write them down. Then list what you already know about the words and topics you see.

Multiply Whole Numbers

$$\begin{array}{r} 25 \\ \times\ 12 \\ \hline 50 \\ 25 \\ \hline 300 \end{array}$$ ← Line up the partial products correctly.

Decimal

$8\,.\,2\,5\,6$

tenths ⟶ ↑ ⟵ thousandths

hundredths

Commutative Property of Addition

$$3 + 5 = 5 + 3$$

Associative Property of Addition

$$12 + (3 + 5) = (12 + 3) + 5$$

The notes above will help you prepare for Lessons 4.1 – 4.3. You should review other topics, such as division, to prepare for Lessons 4.4 – 4.8.

Multiplying Decimals and Whole Numbers

LESSON 4.1

BEFORE

You multiplied whole numbers by whole numbers.

▶ **Now**

You'll multiply decimals and whole numbers.

WHY?

So you can find the length of a race, as in Example 2.

 Activity **You can use base-ten pieces to multiply.**

With base-ten pieces, *one hundredth* is represented by ■ = 0.01, and
one tenth is represented by ■■■■■■■■■■ = 0.1.

① Model 1 × 0.04.　② Model 2 × 0.04.　③ Model 3 × 0.04.

This is one row of
4 hundredths.

1 × 0.04 = 0.04　　　2 × 0.04 = 0.08　　　3 × 0.04 = 0.12

Use a model to find the product.

1. 3 × 0.02　　　**2.** 3 × 0.2　　　**3.** 4 × 0.03　　　**4.** 4 × 0.3

5. How do the number of decimal places in your answers to Exercises 1–4 compare
to the number of decimal places in the factors?

Multiplying with Decimals When you multiply a decimal and a
whole number, the number of decimal places in the product is the same
as the number of decimal places in the decimal factor.

 **with Solving**

EXAMPLE 1 **Multiplying Decimals by Whole Numbers**

Find the product 7 × 0.006.

Because 0.006 has 3 decimal places, the answer will have 3 decimal places.

$$\begin{array}{r} 0.006 \\ \times \quad 7 \\ \hline 0.042 \end{array}$$ 　Write a zero as a placeholder so that
the answer has 3 decimal places.

Your turn now Find the product. Then write the product in words.

1. 3 × 0.005　　　**2.** 4 × 0.024　　　**3.** 1.2 × 7　　　**4.** 2.36 × 5

Sports

■ **Iditarod Race**

Fourteen teams competed in the 2001 Junior Iditarod race in Alaska. The musher (or driver) for each team of dogs was between the ages of 14 and 17. If each team had 7–10 dogs, estimate how many dogs participated in the race.

Counting Zeros You need to include the zeros at the *end* of a product in order to count the decimal places correctly. Once you place the decimal point, however, you can drop any zeros that occur at the end of the answer, as in Example 2 below.

EXAMPLE 2 Solving a Problem

Junior Iditarod Race In the 2001 Junior Iditarod race, one team completed the race in about 18 hours over two days. The team's average rate was 8.875 miles per hour. About how long was the race? Round to the nearest mile.

Solution

Use the formula *Distance = Rate × Time*.

$$
\begin{array}{r}
8.875 \\
\times \quad 18 \\
\hline
71000 \\
8875 \\
\hline
159.750
\end{array}
$$

Place the decimal point before dropping any zeros.

ANSWER The race was about 160 miles long.

EXAMPLE 3 Checking for Reasonableness

Use estimation to check that the answer to Example 2 is reasonable.

$$
\begin{aligned}
\text{Distance} &= 8.875 \times 18 \\
&\approx 9 \times 18 \qquad \text{Round 8.875 to its leading digit.} \\
&= 162
\end{aligned}
$$

ANSWER Because 160 is close to 162, the distance is reasonable.

Your turn now Find the product.

5. 0.9×50　　**6.** 1.505×8　　**7.** 3.14×75　　**8.** 6.25×22

Use estimation to check that the answer is reasonable.

9. 3.254×18; 58.572　　　　**10.** 12.706×3; 381.18

11. Explain why the answer 84 is *not* reasonable for the product 3×2.8.

12. Explain why the answer 1.06 *is* reasonable for the product 2×0.53.

Properties of Multiplication You used properties of addition in Lesson 3.6. Similar properties for multiplication are shown below.

Properties of Multiplication

Commutative Property In a product, you can multiply numbers in any order.

Numbers $2 \times 6.5 = 6.5 \times 2$ **Algebra** $a \cdot b = b \cdot a$

Associative Property The value of a product does not depend on how the numbers are grouped.

Numbers $(2 \times 6.5) \times 4 = 2 \times (6.5 \times 4)$

Algebra $(a \cdot b) \cdot c = a \cdot (b \cdot c)$

EXAMPLE 4 **Using Properties of Multiplication**

Tell whether the *commutative* or *associative* property of multiplication allows you to rewrite the problem as shown. Explain your choice.

a. $5 \times 3.25 \times 2 = 3.25 \times 5 \times 2$ **b.** $(3.25 \times 5) \times 2 = 3.25 \times (5 \times 2)$

The order of the numbers has changed, so this is an example of the commutative property of multiplication.

The numbers that are grouped have changed, so this is an example of the associative property of multiplication.

Exercises
More Practice, p. 711

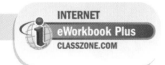

Getting Ready to Practice

1. Vocabulary Which property does $(2 \cdot 8) \cdot 9 = 2 \cdot (8 \cdot 9)$ illustrate?

Copy the answer and place the decimal point in the correct location.

2. $34 \times 1.6 = \mathbf{544}$ **3.** $15 \times 1.04 = \mathbf{1560}$ **4.** $7.841 \times 3 = \mathbf{23523}$

Find the product. Then write the product in words.

5. 3×0.2 **6.** 6×0.9 **7.** 3.164×5 **8.** 2.78×45

Practice and Problem Solving

with Homework

Example	Exercises
1	9–27
2	12–27, 30–33
3	16–27, 34, 35
4	28, 29

Online Resources
CLASSZONE.COM

· More Examples
· eTutorial Plus

Use a model to find the product. Then write the product in words.

9. 4×0.2 **10.** 6×0.03 **11.** 2×0.03

Copy the answer and place the decimal point in the correct location.

12. $27 \times 5.34 = \textbf{14418}$ **13.** $9 \times 0.873 = \textbf{7857}$ **14.** $2.03 \times 5 = \textbf{1015}$

15. Find the Error Describe and correct the error in the solution.

$$\times \quad \begin{array}{r} 0.0028 \\ \times \qquad 4 \\ \hline 00.112 \end{array}$$

Find the product. Use estimation to check your answer.

16. 6×3.5 **17.** 9×2.17 **18.** 0.008×9 **19.** 5.31×18

20. 0.29×82 **21.** 0.32×55 **22.** 7.25×34 **23.** 3.072×8

24. 9.426×3 **25.** 2.125×15 **26.** 52×0.088 **27.** 18×0.005

Copy and complete each statement. Tell whether you used the *commutative* or *associative* property of multiplication.

28. $2 \times 79 \times 0.5 = 79 \times \underline{\ ?\ } \times 0.5$ **29.** $(0.4 \times 83) \times 5 = 0.4 \times (\underline{\ ?\ } \times 5)$

Shopping Find the amount you would spend in the situation.

30. You want to buy balloons for a friend's birthday. The balloons cost $1.50 each. You buy 6 balloons.

31. Each ticket for a rock concert costs $48.35. You buy 7 tickets.

32. It costs $.12 to make a photocopy. You make 84 photocopies.

33. A paintbrush costs $3.79. You buy 11 of them.

Number Sense Use estimation to explain why the statement is false.

34. The product of 5 and 0.85 is more than 5.

35. The product of 24 and 1.107 is less than 24.

36. Bottled Water A beverage company packages spring water in bottles that hold 1.5 liters. How many liters of water are in a case that contains 8 bottles? How many liters are in a case that contains 12 bottles?

37. Writing Explain why you can drop the zero at the end of the products in your answers to Exercise 36. Why might you need to keep the final zero in the product for a situation involving money?

38. Armor The table at the right shows the heights of three suits of armor. Change the heights from centimeters to inches. Use the fact that 1 cm ≈ 0.3937 in.

Type of Armor	Adult	Child	Dog
Height (cm)	185	109	64
Height (in.)	?	?	?

 Algebra **Evaluate the variable expression.**

39. $120x + 3$, when $x = 0.1$ **40.** $7 + 16x$, when $x = 4.2$

41. Challenge Use estimation to find a decimal that when multiplied by 18 gives a product between 24 and 30.

Mixed Review

Evaluate the expression. *(Lesson 1.4)*

42. $104 \times 5 + 2 \times 7$ **43.** $5 \times (36 \div 3)$ **44.** $28 - 2 \times 3^2$

Use front-end estimation to estimate the sum. *(Lesson 3.5)*

45. $3.64 + 8.22 + 2.15$ **46.** $7.1 + 2.83 + 2.15$ **47.** $1.7 + 6.1 + 3.28$

Choose a Strategy **Use a strategy from the list to solve the following problem. Explain your choice of strategy.**

48. You are at an awards dinner and have a choice of 3 dinner entrees, 2 side dishes, and 2 desserts. You can choose only one of each. How many different meals can you select?

> **Problem Solving Strategies**
> - Draw a Diagram
> - Make a List
> - Make a Table
> - Look for a Pattern

Basic Skills **Write the place value of the red digit.**

49. 320,840   **50.** 340,875   **51.** 1,263,920

Test-Taking Practice

52. Multiple Choice Tracy bought 39 basketball tickets that cost $19.25 each. What is the best estimate of the amount Tracy spent?

  A. $600   **B.** $700   **C.** $800   **D.** $900

53. Short Response Kari works five days per week and four hours per day. If she earns $9.75 per hour, how much does she earn per week? Explain how you found your answer.

Multiplying Decimals by Whole Numbers

GOAL Use a spreadsheet to multiply decimals by whole numbers.

Example **You can enter formulas in a spreadsheet to multiply numbers.**

A biologist works 40 hours a week and earns $22.18 an hour. How much does the biologist earn in one week? How much does the biologist earn in one year?

Solution

Create a spreadsheet like the one shown below.

1. Enter the number of hours worked in cell B1.

2. Enter the hourly wage in cell B3.

3. To find the biologist's weekly earnings, use a formula to multiply the number of hours worked by the hourly wage.

	A	B
1	Hours per week:	40
2		
3	Dollars per hour:	$22.18
4		
5	Weekly earnings:	$887.20
6		
7	Yearly earnings:	$46,134.40

In cell B5, enter the formula = B1*B3.

In cell B7, enter the formula = B5*52.

4. To find the biologist's yearly earnings, use a formula to multiply the weekly earnings by the number of weeks in a year.

ANSWER The biologist earns $887.20 a week and $46,134.40 a year.

Your turn now **Use a spreadsheet to find the person's weekly and yearly earnings.**

1. A programmer works 56 hours a week and earns $26.33 an hour.

2. A hairdresser works 50 hours a week and earns $18.89 an hour.

3. A doctor works 40 hours a week and earns $35.21 an hour.

4. A babysitter works 12 hours a week and earns $6.50 an hour.

The Distributive Property

BEFORE

You used order of operations to evaluate expressions.

▶ **Now**

You'll use the distributive property to evaluate expressions.

WHY?

So you can find the cost of a field trip, as in Ex. 6.

Word Watch

distributive property, p. 159

> **In the Real World**

Car Wash Your class held a two-day car wash to raise money. The class washed 40 cars on the first day and 30 cars on the second day. The class charged $5 for each car. How much money did the class raise?

EXAMPLE 1 **Evaluating Expressions**

HELP **with Review**

Remember that 5(70) is another way to write 5 × 70.

Method 1 To answer the question above, first find the total number of cars washed. Then multiply to find the total amount raised.

Charge per car × Total number of cars washed $= 5(40 + 30)$

$$= 5(70)$$
$$= 350$$

Method 2 To answer the question above, first find the amount raised each day. Then add to find the total amount raised.

First day amount + Second day amount $= 5 \times 40 + 5 \times 30$

$$= 200 + 150$$
$$= 350$$

ANSWER Your class raised $350.

The methods used in Example 1 show the **distributive property** .

The Distributive Property

Words You can multiply a number and a sum by multiplying the number by each part of the sum and then adding these products. The same property applies with subtraction.

Numbers $3(4 + 6) = 3(4) + 3(6)$ $2(8 - 5) = 2(8) - 2(5)$

Algebra $a(b + c) = ab + ac$ $a(b - c) = ab - ac$

EXAMPLE **2** **Using the Distributive Property**

a. $2(50 + 6) = 2(50) + 2(6)$

$ = 100 + 12$

$ = 112$

b. $10(8.6 - 2.4) = 10(8.6) - 10(2.4)$

$ = 86 - 24$

$ = 62$

Your turn now **Use the distributive property to evaluate.**

1. $2(17 + 10)$ **2.** $7(20 - 3)$ **3.** $100(6.8 - 4)$ **4.** $0.5(24 + 18)$

EXAMPLE **3** **Evaluating Using Mental Math**

a. To find $6(87)$, rewrite 87.

$6(87) = 6(90 - 3)$

$ = 6(90) - 6(3)$

$ = 540 - 18$

$ = 522$

b. To find $8(6.1)$, rewrite 6.1.

$8(6.1) = 8(6 + 0.1)$

$ = 8(6) + 8(0.1)$

$ = 48 + 0.8$

$ = 48.8$

What do you think?

Science

EXAMPLE **4** **Using a Formula**

Astronomy The Hubble Telescope orbits Earth at a rate of about 4.78 miles per second. How far does the telescope travel in 3 seconds?

Solution

Use the formula *Distance* = *Rate* × *Time*.

Distance $= (4.78)3$	Use 4.78 for the rate and 3 for the time.
$= (5 - 0.22)3$	Rewrite 4.78 as 5 − 0.22.
$= (5)3 - (0.22)3$	Use the distributive property.
$= 15 - 0.66$	Multiply.
$= 14.34$	Subtract.

ANSWER The telescope travels about 14.34 miles in 3 seconds.

■ **Astronomy**

The Hubble Space Telescope is a satellite that takes photographs of outer space and sends them to Earth. The telescope was launched on April 24, 1990. Traveling at about 5 miles per second, how far does the telescope travel in 1 day? in 1 year?

Your turn now **Use mental math to find the product.**

5. $8(53)$ **6.** $4(97)$ **7.** $3(12.8)$ **8.** $7(1.4)$

Getting Ready to Practice

1. **Vocabulary** Rewrite the expression 2(3.1 + 7.4) using the distributive property.

Copy and complete the statement using the distributive property.

2. $3(40 + 5) = 3(\underline{?}) + \underline{?}(5)$

3. $7(50 + 2) = 7(\underline{?}) + \underline{?}(2)$

4. $6(7 + 5.4) = 6(\underline{?}) + \underline{?}(5.4)$

5. $8(3.2 - 9) = 8(\underline{?}) - \underline{?}(9)$

6. **Field Trip** A class of 30 students is taking a field trip to a museum. The cost for each student is $9 for admission plus $5 more for the laser show. How much money is needed to pay for all the students to see the museum and the laser show?

Practice and Problem Solving

Use the distributive property to evaluate the expression.

7. $4(80 + 3)$
8. $6(7 + 50)$
9. $2(39 - 10)$
10. $15(2 + 9)$

11. $6(8.2 + 3)$
12. $8(3.1 + 5.7)$
13. $10(4.8 + 2.7)$
14. $14(8.1 - 6)$

15. $3(90 + 0.6)$
16. $9(7 - 0.11)$
17. $7(13 - 0.02)$
18. $12(3 + 0.4)$

19. **Find the Error** Describe and correct the error in the solution.

$$\begin{aligned} 2(32 + 6) &= 2(32) + 6 \\ &= 64 + 6 \\ &= 70 \end{aligned}$$

with Homework

Example	Exercises
1	7–18, 33
2	7–23
3	22–32
4	33, 37

Online Resources
CLASSZONE.COM

· More Examples
· eTutorial Plus

Copy and complete the statement.

20. $5(30 + 0.2) = 5(30) + \underline{?}(0.2)$

21. $7(40 + 8) = \underline{?}(40) + \underline{?}(8)$

22. $4(7.9) = 4(8 - \underline{?})$

23. $3(67) = 3(\underline{?} + 7)$

Use the distributive property and mental math to find the product.

24. $6(37)$
25. $7(98)$
26. $3(85)$
27. $9(41)$

28. $8(5.7)$
29. $5(9.2)$
30. $9(7.3)$
31. $7(6.9)$

32. Find the product 7(2.006) using the distributive property.

33. **Lunch Costs** For each day of school, you pay $2.50 for lunch and $.45 for milk. How much money do you spend in 5 days?

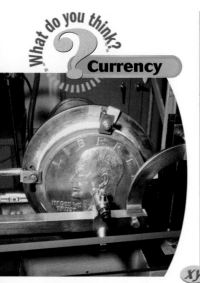

Currency

■ **U.S. Mint**

Coins are minted in Philadelphia and in Denver. Coins minted in Denver have a "D" on the front. Coins minted in Philadelphia have a "P" on the front. Do you think people in your class have coins from Denver or Philadelphia? Why?

U.S. Mint In Exercises 34–36, use the table. It shows what it cost to produce some U.S. coins in two different years.

34. Evaluate the expression $50(2.0 - 1.6)$ to find how much more it cost to produce 50 dimes in 2000 than in 1995.

35. Evaluate the expression $50(0.8 - 0.7)$ to find how much more it cost to produce 50 pennies in 2000 than in 1995.

Coin	1995	2000
Penny	0.7¢	0.8¢
Nickel	2.74¢	3.0¢
Dime	1.6¢	2.0¢
Quarter	3.65¢	5.0¢

36. Write an expression to find how much more it cost to produce 50 nickels in 2000 than in 1995. Then evaluate the expression.

37. **Geometry** Use the formula $P = 2(l + w)$ to find the perimeter of a flower box with length 27 inches and width 6 inches.

 Algebra Use the distributive property to rewrite the expression. For example, $2(x + 4) = 2x + 8$.

38. $3(x + 7)$ **39.** $5(x + 5.2)$ **40.** $6(4 - x)$

Challenge Rewrite the expression as a product using parentheses.

41. $4x + 4y$ **42.** $0.9m - 0.9n$ **43.** $5.5x - 5.5y + 5.5$

Mixed Review

Order the numbers from least to greatest. *(Lesson 3.3)*

44. 2.1, 2.9, 2.8, 2.6   **45.** 7.63, 7.06, 7.61, 7.6   **46.** 0.5, 0.55, 0.05, 0.005

Evaluate the expression when $x = 3.1$ and $y = 5.62$. *(Lesson 3.6)*

47. $x + 2.83$ **48.** $x + y$ **49.** $y - 3.092$

Basic Skills **Round to the place value of the red digit.**

50. 63,498   **51.** 32,921   **52.** 204,238

Test-Taking Practice

53. Multiple Choice Which expression is equal to $4(2 + 6)$?

    A. $2(4 + 6)$ **B.** $4 \times 2 \times 6$

    C. $4 \times 2 + 6$ **D.** $4 \times 2 + 4 \times 6$

54. Multiple Choice Which expression is equal to $2(4.9)$?

    F. $2(4 + 9)$ **G.** $2(4 + 0.9)$ **H.** $2 \times 4 \times 9$ **I.** $2(5 - 1)$

Hands-on Activity

GOAL

Use an area model to find the product of two decimals.

MATERIALS

- graph paper
- colored pencils

Multiplying Decimals Using Models

In this activity, you will use area models to multiply two decimals. The decimals will represent the length and width of a rectangle. The area of the rectangle will represent the product of the decimals.

Explore **Model 0.8 × 0.7 using an area model.**

1 Start with a 10-by-10 square drawn on graph paper.

The whole square represents **1**.

Each of the 100 small squares represents **0.01**.

Each row or column represents **0.1**.

2 Use a colored pencil to shade a rectangle that is 8 rows long by 7 columns wide.

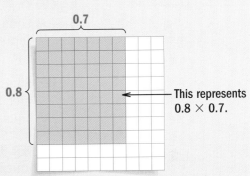

0.7

0.8

This represents 0.8 × 0.7.

3 The area of the rectangle represents the product 0.8 × 0.7. Count the number of squares in the shaded rectangle. Because each small square represents 0.01, 56 of the small squares represent 0.56, or fifty-six hundredths. So, 0.8 × 0.7 = 0.56.

Your turn now **Use a model to find the product.**

1. 0.3 × 0.9 **2.** 0.4 × 0.4 **3.** 0.5 × 0.6 **4.** 0.7 × 0.3

5. In Step 3 above, is the product *greater than* or *less than* each of the numbers being multiplied?

Stop *and* **Think**

6. Critical Thinking Use a model to find the product 0.7 × 0.8. Is the result any different than the result in Step 3 above? Why or why not?

Multiplying Decimals

BEFORE — ▶ **Now** — **WHY?**

You multiplied decimals by whole numbers.

You'll multiply decimals by decimals.

So you can find the distance traveled by a turtle, as in Ex. 30.

Word Watch

Review Words
factor, p. 16

In the Real World

Sloths The sloth is commonly referred to as the "slowest mammal on Earth." Its top speed on the ground is about 0.2 mile per hour. What is the farthest a sloth might go in 0.6 hour?

EXAMPLE 1 **Using a Model to Multiply Decimals**

To find how far a sloth might go in the question above, use a model to find the product 0.2×0.6.

① Draw a 10-by-10 square. The whole square represents 1. Each small square represents 1 hundredth, or 0.01. Each row or column represents 1 tenth, or 0.1.

② Shade a rectangle that is 0.2 by 0.6. The area is 12 hundredths, because 12 small squares are shaded. So, $0.2 \times 0.6 = 0.12$.

ANSWER The farthest a sloth might go in 0.6 hour is 0.12 mile.

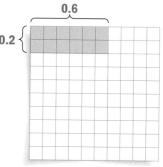

Your turn now **Draw a model to find the product.**

1. 0.1×0.7 **2.** 0.3×0.8 **3.** 0.9×0.7

Multiplying Decimals

Words Multiply decimals as you do whole numbers. Then place the decimal point. The number of decimal places is the total number of decimal places in the factors.

Numbers

$$\underbrace{3.14}_{\text{2 places}} \times \underbrace{15.6}_{\text{1 place}} = \underbrace{48.984}_{\text{3 places}}$$

EXAMPLE 2 **Placing a Decimal Point in a Product**

Place the decimal point in the correct location.

$$252.64 \times 0.842 = 212.72288$$

2 places **3 places** **5 places**

The first factor has 2 decimal places. The second factor has 3 decimal places. Because $2 + 3 = 5$, the answer has 5 decimal places.

ANSWER $252.64 \times 0.842 = 212.72288$

✓ **Check** Estimate: $252.64 \times 0.842 \approx 250 \times 1 = 250$. So, the product 212.72288 is reasonable.

EXAMPLE 3 **Multiplying Decimals**

Find the product.

a. 5.08×2.1 **b.** 1.159×0.03 **c.** 7.215×4.8

Solution

a.
$$
\begin{array}{r}
5.08 \\
\times \quad 2.1 \\
\hline
508 \\
1016 \quad \\
\hline
10.668
\end{array}
$$

2 decimal places
+ 1 decimal place

3 decimal places

b.
$$
\begin{array}{r}
1.159 \\
\times \quad 0.03 \\
\hline
0.03477
\end{array}
$$

3 decimal places
+ 2 decimal places
5 decimal places

c.
$$
\begin{array}{r}
7.215 \\
\times \quad 4.8 \\
\hline
57720 \\
28860 \quad \\
\hline
34.6320
\end{array}
$$

3 decimal places
+ 1 decimal place

4 decimal places

Once you place the decimal point, drop the zero at the end of the final answer. You write the product as 34.632.

Your turn now **Multiply. Use estimation to check your answer.**

4. 2.15×5.4 **5.** 12.7×2.9 **6.** 6.289×0.2 **7.** 0.86×0.04

The American flag hanging from the Hoover Dam is known as Superflag.

EXAMPLE 4 **Finding the Area of a Rectangle**

American Flag One of the largest flags ever made is about 153.9 meters long and 68.6 meters wide. Find the area of the flag to the nearest hundred square meters.

Solution

$A = lw$ Write the formula for the area of a rectangle.

$ = (153.9)(68.6)$ Substitute 153.9 for l and 68.6 for w.

$ = 10{,}557.54$ Multiply.

ANSWER The area of the flag is about 10,600 square meters.

✓ **Check** Round 153.9 to 150 and 68.6 to 70. Because $150 \times 70 = 10{,}500$, the product 10,600 is reasonable.

Your turn now   **Find the area of the rectangle or square.**

8. A square with side length 3.2 meters

9. A rectangle with length 8.1 inches and width 3.25 inches

4.3 Exercises

More Practice, p. 711

INTERNET
eWorkbook Plus
CLASSZONE.COM

Getting Ready to Practice

1. Vocabulary The number of decimal places in a product is equal to the __?__ of the number of decimal places in the factors.

Find the product.

2. 0.4×0.9 **3.** 1.6×0.5 **4.** 1.18×0.02 **5.** 3.74×4.2

Geometry Find the area of the rectangle or square.

6.

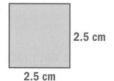

2.5 cm

2.5 cm

7.

2.75 ft

6.3 ft

Practice and Problem Solving

with Homework

Example	Exercises
1	8–10
2	11–14
3	15–26, 29, 30
4	27, 28

Online Resources
CLASSZONE.COM

· More Examples
· eTutorial Plus

Draw a 10-by-10 square to model the product.

8. 0.4×0.5 **9.** 0.3×0.9 **10.** 0.1×0.6

11. Find the Error Describe and correct the error made in the solution.

Copy the answer and place the decimal point in the correct location.

12. $0.17 \times 0.6 = \mathbf{0102}$

13. $16.36 \times 3.7 = \mathbf{60532}$

14. $4.7 \times 6.1 = \mathbf{2867}$

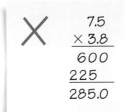

Multiply. Use estimation to check that the product is reasonable.

15. 0.3×0.6 **16.** 1.1×0.4 **17.** 3.72×0.8

18. 4.91×2.3 **19.** 3.052×4.7 **20.** 2.05×5.8

21. 3.25×4.6 **22.** 1.08×0.45 **23.** 1.126×0.08

24. 3.201×0.03 **25.** 9.817×8.6 **26.** 6.87×9.61

Geometry Find the area of the rectangle or square.

27.

1.7 ft

1.7 ft

28.

8.1 cm

10.36 cm

29. Hair Growth Sophia's hair grows at a rate of about 0.5 inch per month. How much does Sophia's hair grow in 4.5 months?

30. Animals A turtle is traveling at a speed of 4.015 meters per minute. How far does the turtle travel in 8.5 minutes? Round your answer to the nearest meter.

Number Sense Copy and complete the statement with <, >, or =.

31. $64.2 \times 1.12 \; \underline{?} \; 64$ **32.** $2.2 \times 0.12 \; \underline{?} \; 2.64$

33. $32.5 \times 0.01 \; \underline{?} \; 3.25$ **34.** $0.505 \times 10.1 \; \underline{?} \; 5.1005$

Estimation Check that the location of the decimal point in the product is reasonable. Correct the answer if necessary.

35. $4.2 \times 0.9; 37.8$ **36.** $32.06 \times 11.94; 3.827964$

37. $109.452 \times 5.7; 623.8764$ **38.** $48.005 \times 17.3; 83{,}0486.5$

Delis In Exercises 39 and 40, use the table. It shows the prices of several foods. You buy 0.75 pound of ham, 0.5 pound of cheese, and 1.25 pounds of turkey.

Food	Price per pound
Ham	$5.49
Cheese	$4.79
Turkey	$4.25

39. Find the price of each item and the total amount you pay for these items. Round your result to the nearest cent.

40. Decide Can you buy 2.5 pounds of turkey if you have only $10?

41. Writing Explain when you need to include a zero as a placeholder in a product. Give an example.

Critical Thinking Choose the correct response and explain your choice.

42. When you multiply two decimals between 0 and 1, is the product *less than* or *greater than* both factors?

43. When you multiply a number greater than 1 by a number between 0 and 1, is the product *less than* or *greater than* the first number?

44. Challenge The simple interest you might earn at a bank is found by the formula $I = Prt$, where I is the simple interest, P is the principal, r is the interest rate, and t is the time. What will the simple interest be when $P = \$200$, $r = 0.03$, and $t = 3.25$?

Mixed Review

Graph the points on the same coordinate grid. *(Lesson 2.6)*

45. (2, 1)   **46.** (1, 4)   **47.** (0, 8)   **48.** (3, 0)

49. Clothesline Length In 1999, a clothesline loaded with clothes set a record at 15.02 miles long. Write the length of the clothesline in words. *(Lesson 3.1)*

Basic Skills Divide.

50. $3\overline{)798}$ **51.** $4\overline{)1340}$ **52.** $13\overline{)208}$ **53.** $21\overline{)315}$

Test-Taking Practice

54. Multiple Choice Find the product 4.769×2.8.

   A. 133,532   **B.** 13,353.2   **C.** 133.532   **D.** 13.3532

55. Short Response Oranges cost $3.29 per pound. You buy 1.8 pounds for yourself and 2.3 pounds for your friend. How much do you spend on oranges to the nearest cent? Explain how you solved the problem.

Dividing by Whole Numbers

LESSON 4.4

BEFORE	Now	WHY?
You multiplied decimals and whole numbers.	You'll divide decimals by whole numbers.	So you can schedule volunteers to work at a school fair, as in Ex. 28.

In the Real World

**Word Watch**

Review Words
dividend, p. 691
divisor, p. 691
quotient, p. 691

Sports Cards Your soccer team orders sports cards for each player. You buy a set of 8 cards for $9.92. How much did you pay for each card?

You can use the rule below to help you find how much you paid for each card.

Dividing a Decimal by a Whole Number

Words When dividing a decimal by a whole number, place the decimal point in the quotient above the point in the dividend.

Numbers

$$6)\overline{32.4} = 5.4$$

Place the decimal point in the quotient above the point in 32.4.

EXAMPLE 1 Dividing a Decimal by a Whole Number

To answer the question above about sports cards, find $9.92 \div 8$.

1 Place the decimal point.

$$8)\overline{9.92}$$

2 Then divide.

$$\begin{array}{r} 1.24 \\ 8)\overline{9.92} \\ \underline{8} \\ 19 \\ \underline{16} \\ 32 \\ \underline{32} \\ 0 \end{array}$$

ANSWER You pay $1.24 for each sports card.

Your turn now Find the quotient.

1. $5)\overline{13.5}$ **2.** $4)\overline{24.8}$ **3.** $7)\overline{4.48}$

Writing Additional Zeros You may need to write additional zeros in the dividend to continue dividing. The zeros do not change the value of the dividend. For example, $14 = 14.0 = 14.00$.

EXAMPLE 2 **Writing Additional Zeros**

Find the quotient 14 ÷ 8.

(1 **Place the decimal point and begin dividing.**

```
      1.
  8)14.
     8
     6
```

→

(2 **Write additional zeros in the dividend as needed.**

```
      1.75
  8)14.00
     8↓↓
     6 0↓
     5 6↓
       40
       40
        0
```

ANSWER $14 \div 8 = 1.75$

EXAMPLE 3 **Using Zeros as Placeholders**

Baseball A batting average is the number of hits divided by the number of times at bat. Find the batting average of a player who made 7 hits in 23 times at bat. Round your answer to the nearest thousandth.

Solution

```
        .3043
  23)7.0000
     6 9↓↓↓
       10↓↓
        0↓↓
       100↓
        92↓
         80
         69
         11
```

Write zeros in the dividend as needed.

> You cannot divide 10 by 23, so put a **zero** in the quotient as a placeholder.

Stop when the quotient reaches the ten-thousandths' place.

ANSWER The player's batting average is 0.304.

 **with Solving**

To round to a given decimal place, divide until the quotient has one more decimal place than needed. Then round back.

Your turn now **Divide. Round to the nearest tenth if necessary.**

4. $4\overline{)26}$ **5.** $8\overline{)10}$ **6.** $8\overline{)49.92}$ **7.** $12\overline{)29.37}$

Getting Ready to Practice

Vocabulary Tell whether the number is the *divisor*, *quotient*, or *dividend* in the problem shown.

$$2)\overline{5.8}^{2.9}$$

1. 2.9   **2.** 5.8   **3.** 2

Divide. Round to the nearest tenth if necessary.

4. $6)\overline{32.4}$ **5.** $5)\overline{22}$ **6.** $7)\overline{51}$ **7.** $6)\overline{7.42}$

8. Guided Problem Solving Use the table at the right.
Speedskater Hiroyasu Shimizu of Japan recorded the times shown for three 500 meter races during the 2000–2001 season. How do these times compare with his time of 34.65 seconds during a 500 meter race at the 2002 Winter Olympic Games?

Time (sec)
34.32
34.83
35.22

(1 Write an expression to find the mean of the times in the table.

(2 Evaluate the expression you wrote in Step 1.

(3 Compare your answer to Step 2 with Hiroyasu's Olympic time of 34.65 seconds.

Practice and Problem Solving

Copy the answer and place the decimal point in the correct location.

9. $49.5 \div 6 = 825$ **10.** $110.16 \div 9 = 1224$ **11.** $7 \div 4 = 175$

Divide. Round to the nearest tenth if necessary.

12. $9.5 \div 5$ **13.** $14.8 \div 2$ **14.** $11 \div 9$ **15.** $2.2 \div 3$

16. $11.6 \div 4$ **17.** $21 \div 6$ **18.** $7.86 \div 6$ **19.** $33.6 \div 7$

20. $43.2 \div 6$ **21.** $31.75 \div 8$ **22.** $44.16 \div 5$ **23.** $20 \div 3$

24. $8 \div 12$ **25.** $28.46 \div 3$ **26.** $34.92 \div 20$ **27.** $24.61 \div 13$

28. School Fair You are organizing volunteers to work at an exhibit at a science fair. You have 6 volunteers to cover a total of 27 hours. How many hours will each volunteer have to work?

29. Compact Discs Your favorite CD has a total running time of 44 minutes. If there are 12 songs on the CD, what is the mean length of a song? Round the answer to the nearest tenth.

HELP with Homework

Example   Exercises
1   9–27
2   12–33
3   24–37

Online Resources
CLASSZONE.COM

· More Examples
· eTutorial Plus

■ **Sky Tram**

In Laon, France, an Automated People Mover (APM) connects the newer part of the city with the historic center. A one-way trip takes about 3 min. If the APM operates 13 hours per day 7 days a week, how many trips does it make in a week?

Restaurant Bills The number of people who eat together at a restaurant and the amount of the bill is given. Find the amount each person pays if the bill is divided equally.

30. 6 people; bill is $47.10

31. 4 people; bill is $39.20

32. 8 people; bill is $102

33. 7 people; bill is $80.50

Batting Averages Find the batting average of the player described. Round the answer to the nearest thousandth.

34. 13 hits in 45 times at bat

35. 8 hits in 26 times at bat

36. 11 hits in 36 times at bat

37. 9 hits in 29 times at bat

Algebra Evaluate the variable expression. Round the answer to the nearest tenth.

38. $5 \div x$, when $x = 3$

39. $6 \div x$, when $x = 14$

40. $23.51 \div x$, when $x = 7$

41. $89.34 \div x$, when $x = 25$

Number Sense Copy and complete the statement using <, >, or =.

42. $1.9 \div 2$? 1

43. $0.36 \div 1$? 0.36

44. $3 \div 9$? 0.3

45. Sky Tram There are 45 students waiting in line to take a tram car to the top of a mountain. Each car can take only 6 people at a time. How many cars will be needed to carry all the students?

46. Shoe Sale An advertisement for a sale at a shoe store says that when you buy 2 pairs of shoes for $24.95 each, you will get a third pair for free. What is the mean cost for a pair of shoes?

47. Explain A chemist is mixing different solutions. If 90 milliliters of a solution need to be divided equally into 8 test tubes, how much should go into each test tube? Does the answer need to be exact or could the chemist use an estimate? Explain your answer.

48. Challenge Sometimes items at a grocery store are priced in groups of items. For lunch, you only want one of each item. Find the total cost for a lunch that includes 1 bagel, 1 apple, 1 box of raisins, and 1 juice package.

Grocery Items	
6 Bagels	$2.88
5 Apples	$1.80
4 Boxes of raisins	$1.10
8 Juice packages	$3.40

Mixed Review

Find the value of the power. *(Lessons 1.3, 4.3)*

49. 10^1 **50.** 10^2 **51.** $(0.1)^2$ **52.** $(0.01)^2$

Solve the equation using mental math. *(Lesson 1.6)*

53. $x - 4 = 5$ **54.** $1 + x = 8$ **55.** $24 \div x = 12$ **56.** $3x = 0$

Find the product. *(Lesson 4.3)*

57. 5.42×6.3 **58.** 1.8×0.04 **59.** 3.107×2.7 **60.** 2.56×4.1

Basic Skills   **Estimate the product.**

61. 11×79 **62.** 2×101 **63.** 53×19 **64.** 187×31

Test-Taking Practice

65. Multiple Choice An industrial arts teacher wants to cut a board that is 8.52 meters long into 4 equal pieces. How long will each piece be?

A. 2 meters   **B.** 2.13 meters   **C.** 2.31 meters   **D.** 23.1 meters

66. Multiple Choice Four people go to a restaurant. The bill is $26.88. If they split the bill equally, how many dollars does each person pay?

F. $.15   **G.** $6.00   **H.** $6.72   **I.** $13.44

BRAIN GAME

Matching Cards

Preparation Write the following quotients and division statements on separate index cards.

Quotients:

0.73	0.0079
0.04	0.3
0.6	0.05
0.52	0.8

Division Statements:

$0.2 \div 4$	$3.65 \div 5$
$1.8 \div 3$	$5.2 \div 10$
$9.6 \div 12$	$0.79 \div 100$
$0.08 \div 2$	$4.8 \div 16$

Game Shuffle and place the cards face down in a 4-by-4 grid.

- Flip over two cards.
- Keep the cards if you match a division statement and its quotient. Otherwise, flip the cards back over.
- The person with the most cards at the end wins the game.

Notebook Review

Review the vocabulary definitions in your notebook.

Copy the review examples in your notebook. Then complete the exercises.

Check Your Definitions

commutative property of multiplication, p. 155
associative property of multiplication, p. 155
distributive property, p. 159

Use Your Vocabulary

1. Copy and complete: The _?_ is illustrated by $a(b + c) = ab + ac$.

4.1 Can you multiply decimals and whole numbers?

 EXAMPLE

$$\begin{array}{r} 3.81 \\ \times \quad 7 \\ \hline 26.67 \end{array}$$

2 decimal places

2 decimal places

✓ **Multiply.**   **2.** 1.742×3 **3.** 0.05×12 **4.** 16×0.78

4.2 Can you use the distributive property?

 EXAMPLE

$4(70 + 9) = 4(70) + 4(9)$ Use the distributive property.

$= 280 + 36$ Multiply.

$= 316$ Add.

✓ **Use the distributive property to evaluate the expression.**

5. $5(50 + 8)$ **6.** $8(30 - 7)$ **7.** $6(70 - 0.5)$ **8.** $10(9.7 + 5.6)$

4.3 Can you multiply decimals?

 EXAMPLE

$$\begin{array}{r} 2.47 \\ \times \quad 0.3 \\ \hline 0.741 \end{array}$$

2 decimal places
+ 1 decimal place
3 decimal places

✓ **Multiply.**   **9.** 1.4×0.3 **10.** 5.61×7.2 **11.** 0.213×0.4

4.4 Can you divide decimals by whole numbers?

 EXAMPLE

$$\begin{array}{r} 2.8 \\ 5{\overline{\smash{\big)}\,14.0}} \\ \underline{10} \\ 4\,0 \\ \underline{4\,0} \\ 0 \end{array}$$

Place the decimal point.

Write and bring down zeros as needed.

 Divide. Round to the nearest tenth if necessary.

12. $3{\overline{\smash{\big)}\,21.9}}$ **13.** $5{\overline{\smash{\big)}\,32.64}}$ **14.** $4{\overline{\smash{\big)}\,13}}$ **15.** $105{\overline{\smash{\big)}\,22}}$

Stop *and* **Think** about Lessons 4.1–4.4

 16. Writing Explain how to use mental math to find the product 7(5.1).

17. Writing Explain how to find the number of decimal places in the product 0.92×2.4.

Review Quiz 1

Multiply. Use estimation to check your answer.

1. 4.7×6 **2.** 0.6512×8 **3.** 4×2.083 **4.** 0.724×12

5. 2.9×2.4 **6.** 1.45×0.03 **7.** 6.08×3.7 **8.** 3.84×2.16

9. Travel A car can travel about 27.5 miles on a gallon of gas. About how far can the car travel on 8 gallons of gas?

Use the distributive property to evaluate the expression.

10. $8(20 + 7)$ **11.** $10(7.6 - 3)$ **12.** $4(9 + 1.5)$

13. Use mental math to find the product 6(9.8).

14. Television One of the largest television sets in the world is in Tokyo, Japan. The screen has a length of 24.3 meters and a width of 45.7 meters. Find the area of the screen.

Divide. Round to the nearest tenth if necessary.

15. $6{\overline{\smash{\big)}\,31.78}}$ **16.** $5{\overline{\smash{\big)}\,44.21}}$ **17.** $9{\overline{\smash{\big)}\,4}}$ **18.** $8{\overline{\smash{\big)}\,15}}$

Multiplying and Dividing by Powers of Ten

BEFORE	▶ Now	WHY?
You multiplied and divided with decimals.	You'll use mental math to help multiply and divide.	So you can find the number of hockey players in Exs. 36–37.

Word Watch

Review Words

power, p. 16
exponent, p. 16

Activity What happens when you multiply by a power of ten?

① Complete the table.

② What do you notice about the movement of the decimal point when you multiply by whole number powers of 10? by decimal powers of 10?

Whole Number Powers of Ten	Decimal Powers of Ten
$10 \times 8.3 = $?	$0.1 \times 8.3 = $?
$100 \times 8.3 = $?	$0.01 \times 8.3 = $?
$1000 \times 8.3 = $?	$0.001 \times 8.3 = $?
$10,000 \times 8.3 = $?	$0.0001 \times 8.3 = $?

Multiplying by Powers of Ten

Multiplying by Whole Number Powers of 10 Move the decimal point one place *to the right* for each zero in the whole number power of 10.

Numbers $3.995 \times 100 = 399.5$

Multiplying by Decimal Powers of 10 Move the decimal point one place *to the left* for each decimal place in the decimal power of 10.

Numbers $399.5 \times 0.001 = 0.3995$

EXAMPLE 1 Multiply Decimals Using Mental Math

a. $0.05 \times 1000 = 0050. = 50$ Move 3 places to the right.

b. $95.38 \times 0.0001 = .009538 = 0.009538$ Move 4 places to the left.

with Solving

When you move a decimal point to the right or left, you may need to write zeros as placeholders.

Your turn now Find the product using mental math.

1. 21.48×10 **2.** 6.07×1000 **3.** 153.6×0.01 **4.** 12×0.001

EXAMPLE 2 Multiply Decimals by Powers of Ten

Bridges The graph shows the number of vehicles that crossed bridges during 2000. How many vehicles crossed the Golden Gate Bridge?

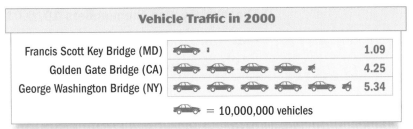

Vehicle Traffic in 2000	
Francis Scott Key Bridge (MD)	1.09
Golden Gate Bridge (CA)	4.25
George Washington Bridge (NY)	5.34

= 10,000,000 vehicles

$4.25 \times 10{,}000{,}000 = 4\,2\,5\,0\,0\,0\,0\,0.$ Move 7 places to the right.

$$= 42{,}500{,}000$$

ANSWER In 2000, 42,500,000 vehicles crossed the Golden Gate Bridge.

Dividing by Powers of Ten

Dividing by Whole Number Powers of 10 Move the decimal point one place *to the left* for each zero in the whole number power of 10.

Numbers $35 \div 100 = 0\,.\,3\,5$

Dividing by Decimal Powers of 10 Move the decimal point one place *to the right* for each decimal place in the decimal power of 10.

Numbers $35 \div 0.001 = 3\,5\,0\,0\,0.$

EXAMPLE 3 Divide Decimals Using Mental Math

a. $508.3 \div 10 = 5\,0\,.\,8\,3 = 50.83$ Move 1 place to the left.

b. $508.3 \div 0.01 = 5\,0\,8\,3\,0. = 50{,}830$ Move 2 places to the right.

Your turn now Find the quotient using mental math.

5. $42.6 \div 100$ **6.** $509 \div 1000$ **7.** $5 \div 0.1$ **8.** $3.2 \div 0.001$

Getting Ready to Practice

Vocabulary Use the numbers 10, 0.01, 100, and 0.1.

1. Which numbers are whole number powers of 10?

2. Which numbers are decimal powers of 10?

Find the product or quotient using mental math.

3. 7.58×10 **4.** 24.831×0.1 **5.** 16.35×0.01 **6.** 0.7×1000

7. $13.4 \div 10$ **8.** $27.65 \div 100$ **9.** $5.21 \div 0.01$ **10.** $3.108 \div 0.1$

11. **Weaving** The width of a tapestry is 56.7 inches. The length of the tapestry is 100 inches. Find the area of the tapestry.

Practice and Problem Solving

with **Homework**

Example	Exercises
1	16–21, 28
2	36, 37
3	12–15, 22–27, 29

Online Resources
CLASSZONE.COM

· More Examples
· eTutorial Plus

Match the expression with its quotient.

12. $320.7 \div 100$ **13.** $320.7 \div 10$ **14.** $320.7 \div 0.01$ **15.** $320.7 \div 0.1$

   A. 32.07   **B.** 3207   **C.** 3.207   **D.** 32,070

Find the product or quotient using mental math.

16. 3.9×10 **17.** 7.434×100 **18.** 459.8×0.001

19. $0.502 \times 10,000$ **20.** 4.9×0.1 **21.** 1000×0.01

22. $726.9 \div 1000$ **23.** $3.457 \div 100$ **24.** $82.93 \div 10$

25. $12.57 \div 0.01$ **26.** $0.9813 \div 0.1$ **27.** $0.31725 \div 0.001$

28. **Alaska** In 1999, the population of Alaska was 0.62 million. Write the population as a whole number.

29. **Microns** A micron is a distance of 0.001 millimeter. An object has a length of 87.2 millimeters. How many microns long is it?

xy **Algebra** **Evaluate the expression.**

30. $8.3x$, when $x = 1000$ **31.** $3.75 \div x$, when $x = 0.01$

32. $5 \div x + 0.02$, when $x = 100$ **33.** $6 \div x + 34$, when $x = 0.01$

34. $50 - 8x$, when $x = 0.001$ **35.** $3.06x - 21.5$, when $x = 10$

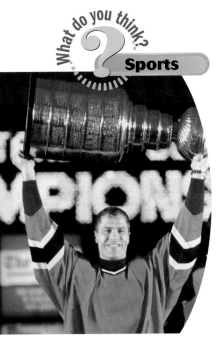

Ice Hockey The graph shows the number of people of different ages who played ice hockey in 2000.

36. Find the number of 12–17 year olds that played ice hockey in 2000.

37. How many more 7–11 year olds played ice hockey in 2000 than 18–24 year olds?

Ice Hockey Players in 2000		
7–11 year olds	🏒 🏒 🏒 🏒	3.74
12–17 year olds	🏒 🏒 🏒 🏒 ◖	4.41
18–24 year olds	🏒 🏒 🏒	2.93
🏒 = 100,000 people		

Number Sense Copy and complete the statement using <, >, or =.

38. 532.4×0.001 __?__ 5.32

39. $12.22 \div 0.01$ __?__ 0.12

Challenge Tell whether the statement is *true* or *false*.

40. When you divide a whole number by a whole number power of 10, the quotient is less than or equal to the dividend.

41. When you divide a whole number by a decimal power of 10, the quotient is less than the dividend.

■ **Ice Hockey**

The Stanley Cup hockey trophy is 35.5 inches tall and weighs 32 pounds. About how many trophies would it take to equal the height of your school? Do you think the trophy weighs more than or less than a bicycle?

Mixed Review

Find the sum or difference. *(Lesson 3.6)*

42. $5.5 + 4.8$ **43.** $18.7 + 2.19$ **44.** $6 - 3.4$ **45.** $7.21 - 5.94$

Find the product. *(Lesson 4.3)*

46. 7.5×6.8 **47.** 2.24×0.04 **48.** 6.02×3.7 **49.** 9.114×5.3

Basic Skills You give a salesclerk $15. Tell how much change you should receive for the given purchase amount.

50. $12   **51.** $14.91   **52.** $11.58   **53.** $6.32

Test-Taking Practice

54. Multiple Choice The price of one nail is $.01. If the price for a whole box of the nails is $36.80, how many nails does the box contain?

A. 37   **B.** 368   **C.** 3680   **D.** 36,800

55. Multiple Choice What is the product 43.64×0.1?

F. 0.4364   **G.** 4.364   **H.** 43.64   **I.** 436.4

Dividing by Decimals

BEFORE	▶ Now	WHY?
You divided by whole numbers.	You'll divide by decimals.	So you can find the gas mileage of a car, as in Ex. 47.

In the Real World

Word Watch

Review Words

dividend, p. 691
divisor, p. 691
quotient, p. 691

Pumpkins At a pumpkin patch you choose a pumpkin weighing 9.5 pounds and pay $4.75. What is the cost per pound of the pumpkin?

You will answer the question above in Example 3. You will need to divide by a decimal.

Dividing by a Decimal

Words When you divide by a decimal, multiply both the divisor and the dividend by a power of ten that will make the divisor a whole number.

Numbers $2.5\overline{)3.75}$ ——Multiply 2.5 and 3.75 by 10.——▶ $\dfrac{1.5}{25\overline{)37.5}}$

EXAMPLE 1 Writing Divisors as Whole Numbers

Rewrite the division problem so that the divisor is a whole number.

a. $1.83 \div 2.5$

$2.5\overline{)1.83}$ ◀— Multiply the divisor and dividend by 10.

ANSWER $18.3 \div 25$

b. $3 \div 0.15$

$0.15\overline{)300}$ ◀— Write zeros as placeholders.

Multiply the divisor and dividend by 100.

ANSWER $300 \div 15$

HELP with Solving

When you divide by a decimal with one decimal place, multiply the divisor and the dividend by 10. For a divisor with two decimal places, multiply by 100, and so on.

Your turn now Rewrite the division problem so that the divisor is a whole number.

1. $0.7\overline{)5.6}$ **2.** $3.8\overline{)4.56}$ **3.** $0.14\overline{)0.84}$ **4.** $0.038\overline{)171}$

EXAMPLE 2 Using Zeros While Dividing

Find the quotient.

a. $0.88 \div 1.6$

$$1.6\overline{)0.88}$$

$$
\begin{array}{r}
.55 \\
16\overline{)8.80} \\
8\ 0 \\
\hline
80 \\
80 \\
\hline
0
\end{array}
$$

ANSWER $0.88 \div 1.6 = 0.55$

b. $30 \div 0.02$

$$0.02\overline{)30.00}$$

$$
\begin{array}{r}
1500 \\
2\overline{)3000} \\
2 \\
\hline
10 \\
10 \\
\hline
0
\end{array}
$$

Sometimes you need to write zeros as placeholders in the quotient.

ANSWER $30 \div 0.02 = 1500$

EXAMPLE 3 Solving Problems Involving Decimals

To find the cost per pound of the pumpkin from page 180, you can divide the total cost of the pumpkin by the number of pounds.

Divide $4.75 by 9.5 pounds.

$$9.5\overline{)4.75}$$

Multiply the divisor and dividend by 10.

$$
\begin{array}{r}
.5 \\
95\overline{)47.5} \\
47\ 5 \\
\hline
0
\end{array}
$$

ANSWER Because money is represented with two decimal places, the pumpkin costs $.50 per pound.

✓ **Check** Estimate: $4.75 \div 9.5 \approx 5 \div 10 = 0.5$. So, the answer of $.50 per pound is reasonable.

What do you think?

Sports

Pumpkin Boat Race

In 1997, New York City hosted the world's first pumpkin boat race. Only 3 pumpkin boats competed in the 0.25 mile race. The boats weighed 814 pounds, 787 pounds, and 752.6 pounds. What was the mean of the weights of the 3 boats?

Your turn now **Divide. Round to the nearest tenth if necessary.**

5. $0.2\overline{)0.99}$

6. $1.3\overline{)7.69}$

7. $0.28\overline{)25.5}$

8. $2.5\overline{)51}$

9. If you paid $10.17 for 3.4 pounds of dried fruit, what was the cost per pound?

4.6 Exercises

More Practice, p. 711

Getting Ready to Practice

1. Vocabulary Identify the dividend and the divisor in the quotient 8.49 ÷ 0.3.

Rewrite the division problem so that the divisor is a whole number.

2. $3.1\overline{)12.8}$ **3.** $0.28\overline{)4.76}$ **4.** $4.6\overline{)9.43}$ **5.** $2.1\overline{)0.04}$

Divide. Round to the nearest tenth if necessary.

6. $0.6\overline{)8.1}$ **7.** $0.03\overline{)15}$ **8.** $0.08\overline{)32.32}$ **9.** $3.2\overline{)6.56}$

10. Guided Problem Solving A stack of books is 1.35 meters tall. Each book is about 0.09 meter thick. How many books are in the stack?

(**1** Do you need to *multiply* or *divide* to solve the problem?

(**2** Write an expression to find the number of books in the stack.

(**3** Evaluate your expression. How many books are in the stack?

Practice and Problem Solving

Rewrite the division problem so that the divisor is a whole number.

11. $9.1 \div 4.3$ **12.** $14.88 \div 0.93$ **13.** $7 \div 0.38$ **14.** $15 \div 0.2$

15. $1.32 \div 0.55$ **16.** $17 \div 0.24$ **17.** $139 \div 3.2$ **18.** $7.67 \div 1.3$

Divide. Round to the nearest tenth if necessary.

19. $48 \div 0.6$ **20.** $45 \div 1.8$ **21.** $7.74 \div 0.9$ **22.** $1.18 \div 0.2$

23. $4.96 \div 1.6$ **24.** $20.3 \div 0.7$ **25.** $3.6 \div 2.4$ **26.** $3.48 \div 2.4$

27. $53 \div 0.7$ **28.** $6.2 \div 0.7$ **29.** $7.9 \div 3.5$ **30.** $199.1 \div 5.5$

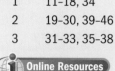 **with Homework**

Example	Exercises
1	11–18, 34
2	19–30, 39–46
3	31–33, 35–38

Online Resources
CLASSZONE.COM
· More Examples
· eTutorial Plus

Choose an Operation Solve. Explain why you chose the operation you used.

31. Photos You have a roll of 24 pictures developed and each picture is 15.24 centimeters long. How long will the pictures be if placed end-to-end?

32. Clothing Costs Your sweatshirt costs $29.99, your jeans cost $34.65, and your sneakers cost $45.50. How much does your outfit cost?

33. Geometry A rectangle has an area of 43.7 square centimeters. The length of the rectangle is 9.5 centimeters. Find the width.

34. Find the Error Describe and correct the error in rewriting the problem.

$$\times \quad 0.38\overline{)17} \longrightarrow 38\overline{)170}$$

Estimation Estimate the cost per pound of the fruit.

35. Apples: 7.1 pounds cost $7.85.

36. Bananas: 4.8 pounds cost $4.93.

37. Pears: 3.2 pounds cost $8.28.

38. Peaches: 4.5 pounds cost $6.75.

Divide. Round to the nearest tenth if necessary.

39. $0.09 \div 3$ **40.** $8.69 \div 4.1$ **41.** $40 \div 0.05$ **42.** $90 \div 0.18$

43. $97.2 \div 0.9$ **44.** $2.16 \div 0.02$ **45.** $21.3 \div 0.07$ **46.** $5.34 \div 1.86$

47. Cars Juan drives his car 470.8 miles and uses 14.5 gallons of gasoline. Find the gas mileage (miles divided by gallons) of Juan's car. Round your answer to the nearest tenth.

48. Critical Thinking Why is it helpful to rewrite a division problem so that the divisor is a whole number?

49. Writing Write an addition, a subtraction, a multiplication, and a division problem with a solution of 3.5.

xy **Algebra Evaluate the expression when *x* = 4.54 and *y* = 7.5. Round to the nearest hundredth if necessary.**

50. $x \div y$ **51.** $y \div x$ **52.** $x + 3.15 \div y$ **53.** $y + x \div 0.8$

World Population Use the table below to answer Exercises 54 and 55. Round to the nearest tenth.

World Population (billions)								
Year	1650	1700	1750	1800	1850	1900	1950	2000
Population	0.51	0.63	0.79	0.97	1.26	1.66	2.56	6.08

54. How many times greater was the population in 2000 than in 1900?

55. How many times greater was the population in 1950 than in 1650?

Number Sense Copy and complete the statement using <, >, or =.

56. $13.42 \div 1.18 \underline{\ ?\ } 134.2 \div 118$ **57.** $6.857 \div 2.56 \underline{\ ?\ } 685.7 \div 256$

58. $43.75 \div 2.28 \underline{\ ?\ } 43.75 \div 22.8$ **59.** $21.74 \div 1.02 \underline{\ ?\ } 21.74 \div 0.102$

60. Amusement Parks The average price to enter an amusement park is $18.50. The park collects about $6.29 million just from entrance fees for the year. About how many people visited the park?

Challenge **Tell whether the statement is *always, sometimes,* or *never* true.**

61. If the divisor is less than the dividend and greater than 0, the quotient is greater than 1.

62. If the divisor is greater than the dividend, and the dividend is greater than 0, the quotient is less than 1.

Mixed Review

Evaluate the expression. *(Lesson 1.4)*

63. $15 \div 5 \times 2$ **64.** $16 \div (2 + 6) \times 4$ **65.** $36 - 2^3$

66. Choose an appropriate customary and metric unit you might use to measure the height of a movie screen. *(Lesson 2.1)*

Find the product. *(Lesson 4.1)*

67. 5×0.6 **68.** 0.02×2 **69.** 8.037×4 **70.** 0.89×21

Basic Skills **The pictograph shows the results of a survey that asked students to choose their favorite fruit. Use the pictograph to answer the following questions.**

71. Which fruit was most popular? How many students chose that fruit?

72. Which two fruits had the same number of responses?

73. Find the total number of students surveyed.

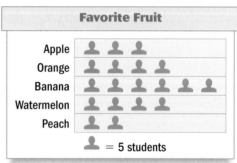

Test-Taking Practice

74. Multiple Choice What is the quotient $6.56 \div 0.4$?

A. 1.64 **B.** 16.4 **C.** 164 **D.** 1640

75. Short Response Write a division problem that has a quotient of 2.6. Explain how you found the divisor and the dividend.

4.7 Problem Solving Strategies

Perform an Experiment

Guess, Check, and Revise
Draw a Diagram
Make a Table
Make a List
Perform an Experiment
Work Backward
Look for a Pattern

Problem You have a 13 cm by 13 cm piece of cardboard. You want to fold it into a box. Which will hold more, a box that is 5 cm by 5 cm by 4 cm or a box that is 10 cm by 10 cm by 1.5 cm?

❶ Read and Understand

Read the problem carefully.

The main idea of the problem is to compare the amounts that two different boxes can hold.

❷ Make a Plan

Decide on a strategy to use.

One way to solve the problem is to perform an experiment. You will need stiff paper or cardboard, a metric ruler, scissors, tape, a metric measuring cup, and 250 milliliters (mL) of rice.

❸ Solve the Problem

Reread the problem and perform an experiment.

First, cut out two squares of paper that measure 13 cm on each side.

Next, cut the corners out of the paper as shown below. Then fold along the dotted lines to form two boxes. Tape the edges.

 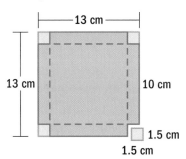

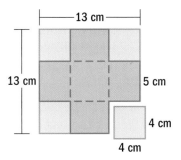

Then, carefully fill each box with rice. Use the metric measuring cup to measure how much rice each box holds.

ANSWER The first box holds 100 mL of rice while the second box holds 150 mL of rice.

❹ Look Back

By performing an experiment, you found that two different sized boxes, created from the same size paper, hold different amounts of material.

Use the strategy *perform an experiment.*

1. Measurement Compare the time it takes to do 10 jumping jacks to the time it takes to jump rope 10 times. Which activity takes you less time to complete?

2. Drawing Use examples to show whether the figure below can be drawn without lifting your pencil off the paper or retracing any segment.

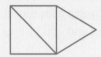

3. Toothpicks There are 18 rectangles of different sizes formed by the toothpicks below. What is the least number of toothpicks that you can remove to have only 3 rectangles?

4. Popcorn You can form a tube by taping together the edges of an $8\frac{1}{2}$ in. by 11 in. piece of paper. Predict which tube will hold more popcorn. Then experiment to test your prediction.

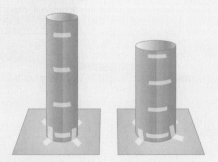

Mixed Problem Solving

Use any strategy to solve the problem.

5. Puppy You need to fence in a part of the backyard for the family puppy. The puppy will need an area of 100 square feet. What are the different ways you can fence off the area as a rectangle with whole number dimensions?

6. Watchbands You are cutting strips of leather for watchbands. Each watchband requires 8 inches of leather. You have 285 inches of leather. How many watchbands can you make?

7. Mystery Numbers Two whole numbers have a product of 575. If you subtract one number from the other, the difference is 2. What are the numbers?

8. Games At a fair, you toss three bean bags at the target below. Each bean bag lands on the target. How many different point totals are possible?

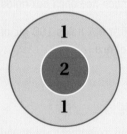

LESSON 4.7

Mass and Capacity

BEFORE	▶ Now	WHY?
You measured length using customary and metric units.	You'll use metric units of mass and capacity.	So you can analyze water usage, as in Exs. 27–29.

Word Watch

mass, p. 187
gram, p. 187
milligram, p. 187
kilogram, p. 187
capacity, p. 188
liter, p. 188
milliliter, p. 188
kiloliter, p. 188

Activity **Perform an experiment to measure *mass*.**

① One person in the group holds a pen in one hand and a paper clip in the other hand.

② Another person adds paper clips until the first person feels that both hands hold the same amount. Record the number of paper clips.

③ Every person in the group takes a turn estimating the pen's mass. Find the mean of the group's results.

④ Based on the mean you found in Step 3, how many paper clips would you have in your hand for 10 pens? for 100 pens?

Units of Mass The **mass** of an object is the amount of matter it has. The **gram** (g) is a metric unit of mass. Two other metric units of mass are the **milligram** (mg) and the **kilogram** (kg).

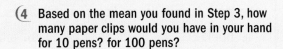

milligram about the mass of a grain of sugar

gram about the mass of a small paper clip

kilogram about the mass of a book

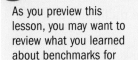

HELP with Notetaking

As you preview this lesson, you may want to review what you learned about benchmarks for metric units of length in Lesson 2.1.

Grams, milligrams, and kilograms are related to each other.

$$1 \text{ g} = 1000 \text{ mg} \qquad 1 \text{ mg} = 0.001 \text{ g} \qquad 1 \text{ kg} = 1000 \text{ g}$$

EXAMPLE 1 **Choosing Units of Mass**

An item has a mass of 10.3 kilograms. Is it a *dog* or a *pencil*? Explain.

The mass of a book is about 1 kg, so 10.3 kg is the mass of about 10 books. The mass of a *dog* is closest to the mass of 10 books, so the item is a dog.

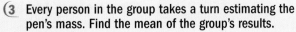

Units of Capacity **Capacity** measures the amount that a container can hold. The **liter** (L) is a metric unit of capacity. Two other metric units of capacity are the **milliliter** (mL) and the **kiloliter** (kL).

milliliter about the capacity of an eyedropper

liter about the capacity of a large bottle of water

kiloliter about the capacity of 5 bathtubs

Liters, milliliters, and kiloliters are related to each other.

$$1 \text{ L} = 1000 \text{ mL} \qquad 1 \text{ mL} = 0.001 \text{ L} \qquad 1 \text{ kL} = 1000 \text{ L}$$

EXAMPLE 2 **Choosing Units of Capacity**

Tell whether the most appropriate unit to measure the capacity of the item is *milliliters*, *liters*, or *kiloliters*.

a. bucket

b. teaspoon

Solution

a. The capacity of a bucket is closest to the capacity of a large bottle of water. You should use liters.

b. The capacity of a teaspoon is closest to the capacity of an eyedropper. You should use milliliters.

EXAMPLE 3 **Choosing Metric Units**

Choose an appropriate metric unit to measure the item.

a. mass of an eraser

b. capacity of a bottle of nail polish

Solution

a. The mass of an eraser is much greater than one milligram and less than one kilogram. So, you should use a gram.

b. The capacity of a bottle of nail polish is much less than one liter or one kiloliter. So, you should use a milliliter.

Your turn now **Choose an appropriate metric unit to measure the item.**

1. mass of a car

2. capacity of a thermos

Getting Ready to Practice

Vocabulary Tell whether the measurement is a *mass*, a *capacity*, or a *length*.

1. 30 mL   **2.** 15 g   **3.** 20 mm

Choose an appropriate metric unit to measure the item.

4. mass of a leaf   **5.** mass of a sofa   **6.** capacity of a pool

7. Ice Tea You want to determine how much ice tea will fit into a pitcher. Do you need to know the mass or the capacity of the pitcher?

Practice and Problem Solving

HELP with Homework

Example	Exercises
1	16, 17, 19, 20
2	18, 27
3	8–15, 21–26

Online Resources
CLASSZONE.COM
· More Examples
· eTutorial Plus

Tell whether the measurement is a *mass*, a *capacity*, or a *length*.

8. 10 L   **9.** 0.68 kg   **10.** 7.5 mm   **11.** 9.2 mL

12. 5.5 g   **13.** 2 m   **14.** 80.4 mg   **15.** 614 cm

16. The mass of an item is 5 kg. Is the item a *shoelace*, a *plate*, or a *bicycle*?

17. Isaac is holding an object that has a mass of 5 grams. Is the object a *book,* a *nickel,* or a *feather?*

18. Gail is describing an object that has a capacity of 1.9 liters. Is she describing a *refrigerator,* a *water pitcher,* or a *cereal bowl?*

Mountain Climbing A mountain climber uses a piece of equipment called a *carabiner*. A carabiner is a small metal ring that attaches to the climber's ropes.

19. Do you think the mass of a carabiner should be measured in *milligrams, grams,* or *kilograms*? Explain your choice.

20. Do you think the mass of the climber should be measured in *milligrams, grams,* or *kilograms*? Explain your choice.

Choose an appropriate metric unit to measure the item.

21. capacity of a sink   **22.** capacity of a lake   **23.** mass of a horse

24. mass of a bubble   **25.** capacity of a glass   **26.** mass of a kick ball

Extended Problem Solving The table shows the amounts of water a person usually uses for certain activities.

Activity	Water used
showering	75.7
brushing teeth	3.8
washing hands	3.2

27. Explain Are the amounts measured in *liters* or *milliliters*? Explain your choice.

28. How much water do 4 people use if each person takes 1 shower, brushes their teeth 3 times, and washes their hands 5 times?

29. How much water is used in a week for 4 people to do the activities in Exercise 28? How would you express this amount in kiloliters?

Copy and complete the statement.

30. 1000 mg = ? g

31. 1 kg = ? g

32. 1 kL = ? L

33. 6 kL = ? L

34. 9 g = ? mg

35. 4 mL = ? L

Challenge Use a benchmark to estimate the mass of a brick. Then estimate the number of bricks you would need to equal the mass of the object. The mass of the object is given.

36. bag of cement; 24 kg

37. sports car; about 1800 kg

Mixed Review

Round the decimal as specified. *(Lesson 3.4)*

38. 5.976 (nearest tenth)

39. 0.0929 (nearest thousandth)

Evaluate the expression. *(Lesson 4.5)*

40. 1.26×1000

41. $5.7 \div 100$

42. $6.3 \div 0.1$

43. 37.4×0.01

Basic Skills **Estimate the quotient.**

44. $10\overline{)98}$

45. $19\overline{)105}$

46. $32\overline{)305}$

47. $102\overline{)9982}$

Test-Taking Practice

48. Multiple Choice Which measurement is most likely the capacity of a fish bowl?

A. 0.5 L   **B.** 3.8 L   **C.** 7.6 L   **D.** 20.5 L

49. Multiple Choice The mass of a piece of paper would most likely be expressed with which unit of measurement?

F. liters   **G.** milligrams   **H.** grams   **I.** kilograms

Changing Metric Units

BEFORE	Now	WHY?
You learned metric units for length, mass, and capacity.	You'll change from one metric unit of measure to another.	So you can find the height of a sunflower in meters, as in Ex. 27.

Word Watch

Review Words

meter, p. 56
gram, p. 187
liter, p. 188

Changing Units You can change from one unit to another in the metric system by multiplying or dividing by a power of 10.

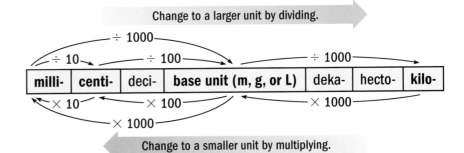

EXAMPLE 1 Changing Units Using Multiplication

Change 0.64 L to milliliters.

1 Decide whether to multiply or divide.

2 Select the power of 10.

Change to a smaller unit by multiplying.

$$mL \longleftarrow \times 1000 \longrightarrow L$$

$$0.64 \times 1000 = 640.$$

ANSWER 0.64 L = 640 mL

EXAMPLE 2 Changing Units Using Division

Change 23.6 g to kilograms.

1 Decide whether to multiply or divide.

2 Select the power of 10.

Change to a larger unit by dividing.

$$g \longrightarrow \div 1000 \longrightarrow kg$$

$$23.6 \div 1000 = 0.0236$$

ANSWER 23.6 g = 0.0236 kg

Your turn now Copy and complete the statement.

1. 230 g = ? kg   **2.** 2.5 mL = ? L   **3.** 0.45 m = ? cm

Comparing Measures To compare measures that have different units, change one of them so that both measures have the *same* units.

HELP with Solving

You can change either unit to the other. In Example 3, you could have changed 1.6 meters to centimeters instead.

EXAMPLE 3 **Comparing Measures**

Which is longer, 170 cm or 1.6 m?

Change 170 cm to meters so the units are the same for both measures.

$\quad$ 170 cm = (170 ÷ 100) m $\quad$ **100 cm = 1 m**

$\qquad\quad$ = 1.7 m

Then compare the measures.

Because 1.7 m > 1.6 m, you know that 170 cm > 1.6 m.

ANSWER 170 cm is longer than 1.6 m.

Your turn now **Copy and complete the statement with <, >, or =.**

$\quad$ **4.** 50 mm ? 3.5 cm $\qquad$ **5.** 450 mL ? 5 L $\qquad$ **6.** 0.01 kg ? 10 g

---

EXAMPLE 4 **Using a Verbal Model**

State Quarters A bank filled with state quarters has a mass of 2.3 kg. The bank's mass is 0.9 kg when empty. Given that a quarter has a mass of about 5.6 g, about how many quarters are in the bank?

Solution

(1 Write a verbal model to find the mass of the quarters in the bank.

$$\begin{array}{ccc} \text{Mass of} \\ \text{quarters} \end{array} = \begin{array}{c} \text{Mass of} \\ \text{full bank} \end{array} - \begin{array}{c} \text{Mass of} \\ \text{empty bank} \end{array}$$

$\qquad\qquad$ = $\quad$ 2.3 kg $\quad$ − $\quad$ 0.9 kg

$\qquad\qquad$ = $\quad$ 1.4 kg

(2 Change the mass of the quarters to grams.

$\qquad$ 1.4 kg = (1.4 × 1000) g

$\qquad\qquad\quad$ = 1400 g

(3 Find the number of quarters by dividing the mass of the quarters by the mass of one quarter.

$$\begin{array}{r} 250. \\ 56\overline{)14000.} \\ 112 \\ \hline 280 \\ 280 \\ \hline 0 \end{array}$$

ANSWER There are about 250 state quarters in the bank.

Getting Ready to Practice

1. **Vocabulary** Name the three base units for length, mass, and capacity in the metric system.

2. To change from a smaller unit to a larger unit, do you *multiply* or *divide?*

Copy and complete the statement.

3. 520 mg = _?_ g

4. 360 cm = _?_ m

5. 0.8 L = _?_ mL

6. **Guided Problem Solving** You are comparing lemonade mixes. Mix A will make four 2 liter pitchers of lemonade. Mix B will make twenty 500 milliliter glasses of lemonade. Which mix will make more lemonade?

   (1 Find the total number of liters of lemonade Mix A makes.

   (2 Find the total number of milliliters of lemonade Mix B makes.

   (3 Change the amount of lemonade Mix B makes to liters.

   (4 Compare the two amounts. Which mix will make more lemonade?

Practice and Problem Solving

Tell whether you would *multiply* or *divide* to change the units.

7. Change milliliters to liters.

8. Change grams to milligrams.

9. Change meters to centimeters.

10. Change grams to kilograms.

Copy and complete the statement.

11. To change from millimeters to centimeters, you divide by _?_ .

12. To change from meters to kilometers, you divide by _?_ .

13. To change from kilograms to grams, you multiply by _?_ .

14. To change from liters to milliliters, you multiply by _?_ .

Copy and complete the statement.

15. 8 mm = _?_ cm

16. 0.04 L = _?_ mL

17. 255 g = _?_ kg

18. 6.25 g = _?_ mg

19. 4 km = _?_ m

20. 468 mL = _?_ L

21. 0.8 kg = _?_ g

22. 7.4 cm = _?_ mm

23. 8.1 kL = _?_ L

HELP with Homework

Example	Exercises
1	7–27
2	7–27
3	28–35
4	36–39

Online Resources
CLASSZONE.COM

· More Examples
· eTutorial Plus

24. How many grams are in 0.49 kilogram?

25. How many liters are in 750 milliliters?

26. **Lions** A grown male lion has a mass of about 180,000 grams. What is the mass of the lion in kilograms?

27. **Flowers** A sunflower has a height of 64 centimeters. What is the sunflower's height in meters?

Copy and complete the statement with <, >, or =.

28. 308 g ? 0.4 kg   **29.** 1.2 km ? 1300 m   **30.** 1.3 kL ? 1300 L

31. 70 mL ? 0.7 L   **32.** 34.8 kg ? 3480 g   **33.** 452 L ? 4600 mL

Animals Tell which dimension is greater.

34. A butterfly has a wingspan of 77 millimeters and a height of 7 centimeters. Which is greater, *wingspan* or *height*?

35. An orangutan has an arm span of 2.1 meters and a height of 140 centimeters. Which is greater, *arm span* or *height*?

Extended Problem Solving In Exercises 36–39, use the chart showing the masses of 6 bowling balls.

36. What common unit of mass could you use so that each mass is in the same unit?

37. **Calculate** Change the masses in the table to the unit you chose in Exercise 36.

38. **Compare** List the masses in order from least to greatest.

Bowling Balls
2.72 kg
7260 g
5,980,000 mg
2,720,000 mg
4.52 kg
6790 g

39. **Decide** Find the mean, median, and mode(s) of the masses. Which averages best represent the data? Explain.

40. **Critical Thinking** Melissa and Jennifer each measure the width of a standard piece of paper. Melissa says the paper is 216 mm wide. Jennifer says the paper is 22 cm wide. Which measurement is more accurate? Explain your reasoning.

Comparing Areas In Exercises 41 and 42, use a square with side length 1.2 kilometers.

41. Find the area of the square in square kilometers.

42. Find the side length of the square in meters and its area in square meters.

43. Based on your answers to Exercises 41 and 42, how do square kilometers compare with square meters?

Algebra Suppose *x* represents a length in meters. Tell whether the expression represents the same length in the given unit.

44. (100*x*) cm

45. (*x* ÷ 1000) km

46. (*x* ÷ 1000) mm

47. Challenge Every centimeter on a map of your town represents an actual distance of 200 meters. If you measure 8.5 centimeters on the map, how many kilometers does it represent?

Mixed Review

Find the value of the power. *(Lesson 1.3)*

48. 3^3

49. 2^6

50. 10 squared

51. 4 cubed

Multiply. Use estimation to check that the product is reasonable. *(Lesson 4.3, 4.5)*

52. 2.8×0.9

53. 0.5×4.8

54. 7.318×5.1

55. 6.94×4.7

56. 1000×3.492

57. 0.01×458.7

58. 0.01×64.76

59. 100×31.6

Basic Skills **Order the numbers from least to greatest.**

60. 64, 78, 29, 32

61. 105, 150, 101, 110

Test-Taking Practice

INTERNET
State Test Practice
CLASSZONE.COM

62. Extended Response A 591 milliliter container of juice costs $1.25. A 1.89 liter container of the same juice costs $3.29. Find the cost per liter for each container of juice. Which container is the better buy? Explain how you found your answer.

Fruit Punch

You want to make some fruit punch, but your little sister has taken the measuring cup you need and she won't tell you where it is. You need to measure out 500 mL of water for the punch.

If you have a pitcher for the fruit punch, an unmarked 300 mL container, and an unmarked 1 L container, how can you measure out the right amount of water for the fruit punch?

Notebook Review

Review the vocabulary definitions in your notebook.

Copy the review examples in your notebook. Then complete the exercises.

Check Your Definitions

mass, p. 187

gram, p. 187

milligram, p. 187

kilogram, p. 187

capacity, p. 188

liter, p. 188

milliliter, p. 188

kiloliter, p. 188

Use Your Vocabulary

1. Copy and complete: The kilogram is a measure of _?_ while the milliliter is a measure of _?_ .

2. **Writing** Explain the first step needed to find the quotient $31.97 \div 2.78$.

4.5 Can you multiply and divide by powers of ten?

 EXAMPLE Evaluate using mental math.

a. $1357.25 \times 0.001 = 1.35725$ **Move decimal point 3 places to the left.**

$= 1.35725$

b. $46.9 \div 0.01 = 4690.$ **Move decimal point 2 places to the right.**

$= 4690$

✓ **Evaluate using mental math.**

3. 38.06×10 **4.** 459.1×0.01 **5.** $621.37 \div 10$ **6.** $97.8 \div 0.001$

4.6 Can you divide by decimals?

 EXAMPLE To divide $24 \div 0.03$, multiply the divisor and dividend by 100.

$24 \div 0.03 \longrightarrow 0.03\overline{)24.00} \longrightarrow \begin{array}{r} 800 \\ 3\overline{)2400} \\ 24 \\ \hline 0 \end{array}$

ANSWER $24 \div 0.03 = 800$

✓ **Divide. Round to the nearest tenth if necessary.**

7. $620 \div 0.58$ **8.** $11.8 \div 0.27$ **9.** $38 \div 1.6$ **10.** $303.2 \div 0.5$

4.7 Can you use metric units of mass and capacity?

EXAMPLE Choose an appropriate metric unit to measure the mass of a laptop computer.

ANSWER A kilogram is about the mass of this book and the mass of a laptop computer would be at least the same as this book. So, kilograms is an appropriate unit of measure for the mass of a laptop computer.

☑ **Choose an appropriate metric unit to measure the item.**

11. mass of a mouse   **12.** capacity of a coffee cup

4.8 Can you change metric units?

EXAMPLE Copy and complete the statement.

a. $52 \text{ g} = \underline{} \text{ mg}$

$52 \times 1000 = 52{,}000$

ANSWER $52 \text{ g} = 52{,}000 \text{ mg}$

b. $36.8 \text{ mL} = \underline{} \text{ L}$

$36.8 \div 1000 = 0.0368$

ANSWER $36.8 \text{ mL} = 0.0368 \text{ L}$

☑ **Copy and complete the statement.**

13. $24.5 \text{ L} = \underline{} \text{ kL}$ **14.** $21.2 \text{ kg} = \underline{} \text{ g}$ **15.** $20 \text{ mm} = \underline{} \text{ cm}$

Stop *and* **Think**   about Lessons 4.5–4.8

16. Writing How do you change from a smaller metric unit to a larger metric unit? How do you change from a larger to a smaller unit?

Review Quiz 2

Find the product or quotient. Use mental math, if possible.

1. 4.56×100 **2.** 9.75×0.01 **3.** $27.9 \div 0.09$ **4.** $135 \div 2.5$

5. $61.4 \div 0.04$ **6.** $36 \div 1.8$ **7.** $50.8 \div 0.5$ **8.** $0.748 \div 0.22$

9. Is the capacity of a backpack measured in *liters* or *milliliters*?

Copy and complete the statement.

10. $10 \text{ L} = \underline{} \text{ mL}$ **11.** $7 \text{ cm} = \underline{} \text{ m}$ **12.** $5.02 \text{ g} = \underline{} \text{ kg}$

Chapter Review

Vocabulary

commutative property of
multiplication, p. 155
associative property of
multiplication, p. 155
distributive property, p. 159

mass, p. 187
gram, p. 187
milligram, p. 187
kilogram, p. 187

capacity, p. 188
liter, p. 188
milliliter, p. 188
kiloliter, p. 188

Vocabulary Review

1. Which property allows you to write
$3(70 + 0.8)$ as $3(70) + 3(0.8)$?

2. Give three examples of metric units used to
measure mass.

3. Give three examples of metric units used to
measure capacity.

Copy and complete the statement.

4. To change from milliliters to liters you
divide by _?_ .

5. To change from kilograms to grams you _?_
by 1000.

Review Questions

Find the product. Use estimation to check your answer. *(Lesson 4.1)*

6. 5.61×7

7. 4.18×5

8. 12×0.324

9. 23×6.284

10. 0.85×6

11. 25.5×4

12. 18×7.89

13. 32×40.78

14. Employment If you earn $8.75 an hour, how much will you be paid
for 15 hours of work? *(Lesson 4.1)*

15. Snow If you charge $14.50 an hour to shovel snow and you worked
9 hours this week, how much did you earn? *(Lesson 4.1)*

Use the distributive property and mental math to find the product. *(Lesson 4.2)*

16. $5(43)$

17. $3(77)$

18. $8(6.1)$

19. $5(3.2)$

20. $3(16.2)$

21. $5(8.9)$

22. $10(1.8 + 2.3)$

23. $100(0.15 + 2.2)$

Multiply. Use estimation to check that the product is reasonable. *(Lesson 4.3)*

24. 1.2×6.4

25. 0.8×3.7

26. 7.04×0.3

27. 8.67×0.06

28. 3.14×1.5

29. 6.1×0.007

30. 3.475×0.08

31. 0.547×4.8

32. 30.08×0.006

33. 28.1×0.45

34. 12.34×0.56

35. 9.63×0.41

36. Fundraising A company will donate $.75 for every dollar raised by the company's employees in a marathon. If the employees raise $250, how much does the company donate? *(Lesson 4.1)*

Divide. Round to the nearest tenth if necessary. *(Lesson 4.4, 4.6)*

37. $21.6 \div 9$

38. $28.2 \div 3$

39. $48.23 \div 7$

40. $18.24 \div 6$

41. $77.36 \div 8$

42. $82.44 \div 12$

43. $45 \div 11$

44. $30 \div 16$

45. $7.9 \div 0.4$

46. $8.5 \div 0.8$

47. $6.2 \div 3.8$

48. $9.9 \div 2.2$

49. $22.5 \div 0.25$

50. $3.35 \div 0.14$

51. $44.82 \div 3.6$

52. $28.49 \div 7.4$

53. Tacos Eight tacos cost $10.80. How much does each taco cost? *(Lesson 4.4)*

54. Muffins Twelve muffins cost $5.49. How much does each muffin cost? *(Lesson 4.4)*

Find the product or quotient using mental math. *(Lesson 4.5)*

55. 2.4×10

56. 6.318×100

57. 656.9×0.001

58. $125 \div 1000$

59. $8.147 \div 100$

60. $0.693 \div 0.1$

61. Geometry A rectangle has an area of 6.72 square millimeters. The width of the rectangle is 2.1 millimeters. Find the length by dividing the area of the rectangle by its width. Check your answer. *(Lesson 4.6)*

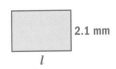
2.1 mm
l

Choose an appropriate metric unit to measure the item. *(Lesson 4.7)*

62. capacity of a tea kettle

63. mass of an ant

64. mass of a train

65. capacity of a raindrop

66. capacity of Lake Michigan

67. mass of a pen

Copy and complete the statement. *(Lesson 4.8)*

68. 647 mm = ? cm

69. 729 mL = ? L

70. 26 kg = ? g

71. 54.9 m = ? mm

72. 0.34 kL = ? L

73. 0.017 g = ? mg

74. 9.5 km = ? m

75. 30 L = ? mL

76. 8 g = ? kg

List the measurements in each table from least to greatest. *(Lesson 4.8)*

77.

Table 1
2.7 mg
270 g
0.027 kg

78.

Table 2
13 mL
1.3 kL
130 L

79.

Table 3
8 cm
8000 mm
0.8 m

Chapter Test

Multiply. Use estimation to check that the answer is reasonable.

1. 5.8×3

2. 9.2×17

3. 2.692×100

4. 3.115×8

5. 7.25×4.6

6. 12.46×3.2

7. 8.51×6.3

8. 13.77×0.04

Use mental math to find the product or quotient.

9. 13.77×1000

10. 12.46×0.01

11. $1.5 \div 100$

12. $6.25 \div 0.1$

13. Auto Racing The distance around the racetrack at Talladega Superspeedway in Alabama is about 2.66 miles. What is the total distance for 16 laps? 100 laps?

Tell whether the *commutative* or *associative* property of multiplication allows you to rewrite the problem as shown.

14. $(3 \times 7.2) \times 2.1 = 3 \times (7.2 \times 2.1)$

15. $2 \times 6.82 \times 25 = 6.82 \times 2 \times 25$

16. Use the distributive property and mental math to find the product 9(4.8).

Divide. Round to the nearest tenth if necessary.

17. $28.95 \div 2$

18. $13.72 \div 4$

19. $9.4 \div 52$

20. $6 \div 16$

21. $10 \div 0.8$

22. $3.24 \div 0.6$

23. $109.2 \div 0.15$

24. $22.54 \div 0.23$

25. Whales Eight whales have been born at an aquarium. Their total mass is 1300 kilograms. Find the mean mass of the whales.

Copy and complete the statement.

26. $0.9 \text{ g} = \underline{\ ?\ } \text{ mg}$

27. $98 \text{ m} = \underline{\ ?\ } \text{ km}$

28. $3200 \text{ L} = \underline{\ ?\ } \text{ kL}$

29. What do you think the mass of a desk lamp might be: 50 mg, 50 g, or 50 kg? Explain.

Copy and complete the statement with <, >, or =.

30. $4300 \text{ L} \underline{\ ?\ } 4.39 \text{ kL}$

31. $215 \text{ kg} \underline{\ ?\ } 2150 \text{ g}$

32. $321 \text{ mm} \underline{\ ?\ } 3.21 \text{ cm}$

33. Soup A can of soup contains 710 milligrams of sodium. How many grams of sodium are in the can?

Chapter Standardized Test

Test-taking Strategy If you have time, check your work. Be sure to use a different method than you originally used. Otherwise, you might make the same mistake twice.

Multiple Choice

1. Estimate the product 4.8×3.2.

   A. 0.15   **B.** 6   **C.** 15   **D.** 25

2. Which answer shows how $5(3 - 0.2)$ can be rewritten using the distributive property?

   F. $5(2.8)$ **G.** $15 - 0.2$

   H. $15 - 0.1$ **I.** $15 - 1$

3. The cheerleaders sold school pennants for $2.50 each. How much money did they raise if they sold 240 pennants?

   A. $60   **B.** $96   **C.** $240   **D.** $600

4. Which answer shows the quotient $14 \div 128$ rounded to the nearest hundredth?

   F. 0.1   **G.** 0.10   **H.** 0.109   **I.** 0.11

5. Four friends divide the cost of a CD equally. The total cost is $17.60. How much does each person pay?

   A. $4.04   **B.** $4.40   **C.** $4.44   **D.** $4.54

6. You pay $14.57 for 2.98 pounds of cheese at a supermarket. Estimate the price per pound.

   F. Less than $2

   G. Between $2 and $3

   H. Between $4 and $5

   I. More than $7

7. What is the value of $0.608 \div 0.1$?

   A. 0.0608 **B.** 6.08   **C.** 60.8   **D.** 608

8. What is the value of 4217.9×0.01?

   F. 4.2179   **G.** 42.179

   H. 42,179   **I.** 421,790

9. Find the quotient $7.248 \div 0.24$.

   A. 0.302 **B.** 3.02   **C.** 3.2   **D.** 30.2

10. Raul describes an object that has a mass of about 145 grams. Which object could he be describing?

   F. a baseball   **G.** a car

   H. a button   **I.** a piano

11. A sports bottle holds 1.63 liters of water. What is the capacity in milliliters?

   A. 0.00163 mL   **B.** 163 mL

   C. 1630 mL   **D.** 16,300 mL

Short Response

12. A rectangle has a length of 8.2 centimeters and an area of 20.5 square centimeters. What is the width of the rectangle? Explain how you found your answer.

13. Tell how you would rewrite $24(9.8)$ using the distributive property. Explain why this may be helpful.

Extended Response

14. You have a choice of two packages of pens to buy. One package contains 8 pens and costs $4.50. The other package has 12 pens and costs $6.25. Which package is the better buy? Explain your reasoning.

Strategies for Answering
Multiple Choice Questions

You can use the problem solving plan on page 42 to solve any problem. If you have difficulty solving a problem involving multiple choice, you may be able to use one of the strategies below to choose the correct answer. You may also be able to use these strategies and others to check whether your answer to a multiple choice question is reasonable.

Strategy: Estimate the Answer

Problem 1

The operation you will use for this problem is multiplication because there are 3.5 times as many cups of sugar in 3.5 pounds of sugar as there are in 1 pound.

There are 2.25 cups of sugar in one pound of sugar. How many cups of sugar are in 3.5 pounds?

A. 1.75

B. 5.75

C. 7.875

D. 78.75

Estimate: $3.5 \times 2.25 \approx 4 \times 2 = 8$, so the correct answer is C.

Strategy: Use Visual Clues

Problem 2

The circle graph shows sales of CDs at a music store. What part of the total sales are pop or rock?

Look at the regions for pop and rock as though they were combined. The combined region is more than half the graph.

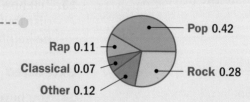

Pop 0.42
Rap 0.11
Classical 0.07
Other 0.12
Rock 0.28

F. 0.14

G. 0.28

H. 0.42

I. 0.7

0.7 is the only one of the given decimals that is greater than 0.5, so the correct answer is I.

Strategy: Use Number Sense

Notice that 0 is a factor in the product $(14.5 \times 3) \times 0$. Use the fact that the product of 0 and any number is 0.

$46.97 + 0 = 46.97$, so the correct answer is A.

Problem 3

Evaluate the expression $46.97 + (14.5 \times 3) \times 0$.

A. 46.97   **B.** 64.47   **C.** 90.47   **D.** 184.41

Eliminating Unreasonable Choices The strategies used to find the correct answers for Problems 1–3 can also be used to eliminate answer choices that are unreasonable or obviously incorrect.

Problem 4

Read the problem carefully. The length of the classroom is $12.2 + 2.6 = 14.8$ meters, not 2.6 meters. To find the area, use the formula $A = lw$.

A middle school classroom is 12.2 meters wide. The length is 2.6 meters more than the width. What is the area?

F. **31.72 square meters**   *Not* the correct answer: $14.8 \times 12.2 \approx 15 \times 12 = 180$.

G. **54 meters**   *Not* the correct answer: area is measured in *square* units.

H. **177.6 square meters**   *Not* the correct answer: the product 14.8×12.2 should end in 6, but it should have two decimal places.

I. **180.56 square meters**   I is the correct answer: $(12.2 + 2.6) \times 12.2 = 180.56$.

Watch Out!

Some answers may appear correct at first glance, but they may be incorrect answers you would find by making common errors.

Your turn now

Explain why the highlighted answer choice is unreasonable.

1. A board that is 2.25 meters long is cut into 5 pieces of equal length. How many meters long is each piece?

     A. 0.25 m   **B.** 0.45 m   ✗**C.** 2.75 m   **D.** 11.5 m

2. Which expression has the greatest value when $x = 10$?

     F. $10x$ ✗**G.** $10 - x$ **H.** $8x + 3$ **I.** $x^2 + 5$

3. A rectangle is twice as long as it is wide. If the rectangle is 3.2 meters wide, what is its perimeter?

     A. 9.6 m   **B.** 19.2 m   **C.** 20.48 m   ✗**D.** 20.48 m^2

Multiple Choice

1. A theater can hold 450 people. During a performance, an usher counted 17 empty seats. How many seats were occupied?

   A. 143 seats   **B.** 433 seats

   C. 443 seats   **D.** 467 seats

2. Marissa puts 52 cards into stacks of 5 cards each. How many cards are left over?

   F. 2 cards   **G.** 5 cards

   H. 8 cards   **I.** 10 cards

3. Eric collected 230 aluminum cans to be recycled. Molly collected 151 cans. Mark collected twice as many cans as Molly. Which expression represents the total number of cans collected for recycling?

   A. $230 + 151 + 2$ **B.** $151 + 2 \times 230$

   C. $230 + 3 \times 151$ **D.** $2(230 + 151)$

4. A family drove 90 miles to attend a family reunion. After the reunion, they drove to a park. When they arrived at the park, they had traveled 110 miles. Solve the equation $90 + d = 110$ to find the distance d, in miles, from the reunion to the park.

   F. 10   **G.** 20   **H.** 79   **I.** 200

5. Gary mows a field that is 120 yards by 75 yards. What is the area he mows?

   A. 195 yards   **B.** 390 yards

   C. 8000 square yards   **D.** 9000 square yards

6. The expression $50x$ represents the distance, in miles, a monarch butterfly can travel in x days during migration. How far can the butterfly travel in 8 days?

   F. 40 mi   **G.** 42 mi   **H.** 400 mi   **I.** 508 mi

7. The circle graph shows how often some students exercise. How many of the students exercise less frequently than once a week?

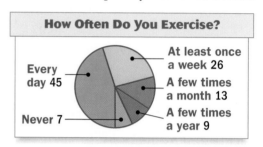

   A. 29   **B.** 45   **C.** 55   **D.** 71

8. Lynann wants to buy a snorkel set for $17.88. She has $9.89. How much more money does Lynann need?

   F. $7.99   **G.** $8.01   **H.** $8.99   **I.** $27.77

9. Sam bought the items shown. What is the best estimate of the total cost of the items?

1 gallon of milk	$2.95
1 dozen eggs	$1.39
bag of bagels	$1.59

   A. $4   **B.** $5   **C.** $6   **D.** $7

10. Kendra bought a box of greeting cards for $12.25. Each card costs $.49. How many cards are in 4 boxes?

    F. 25 cards   **G.** 50 cards

    H. 75 cards   **I.** 100 cards

11. A map of the Nile River has the scale 1 in. : 250 mi. If the length of the river on the map is about 16.5 inches, about how long is the actual river?

    A. 250 miles   **B.** 1515 miles

    C. 4125 miles   **D.** 5175 miles

Short Response

12. An auditorium is divided into two sections. The first section contains 22 rows, and each row has 45 seats. The second section contains 18 rows, and each row has 34 seats. How many seats are in the auditorium? Explain your reasoning.

13. An ant is about 4.2 millimeters long. An enlarged image of the ant is 0.42 meters long. Rewrite the enlarged length in millimeters. Then use a power of 10 to explain how the two sizes are related.

14. Rosa's car can travel 27 miles per gallon of gas. How far can the car travel on 8 gallons of gas? Explain how you can use the distributive property to answer this question.

15. Tennis balls are sold in cans of 3 balls or in cases of 24 cans. Suppose a can of one brand of tennis balls costs $2.58 while a case of the same brand costs $64.48. Which has the lower cost per ball, the *can* or the *case*? Explain how you found your answer.

16. Chang buys 5 liters of punch for a party. Fifteen glasses of punch are poured, with 240 mL in each glass. Is the remaining amount of punch *more than* or *less than* a liter? How many more 240 mL glasses could be poured? Explain your steps.

17. Beth's scores on her math quizzes are 78, 27, 81, 95, 83, and 95. Find the mean, median, and mode of the test scores. What is the best average to use to represent the most typical score? Explain your reasoning.

Extended Response

18. The students in Mr. Hanson's science class planted tree seedlings and are monitoring their growth. The table shows the height of each tree in inches.

Tree	Apple	Maple	Cedar	Oak
Height (inches)	7	15	20	29

Make a bar graph of the heights. Find the difference in height between the tallest and shortest trees. Is it easier to use the *table* or the *bar graph* to answer this question? Which two trees are closest in height? Is it easier to use the *table* or the *bar graph* to answer this question? Explain your answers.

19. A survey was sent to families asking how many times anyone in the family went to an amusement park in the past two years. Completed surveys were returned by 18 families and the results are shown at the right.

Make a frequency table and a line plot of the data. Compare and contrast the displays. Use each display to find the most common response. Use each display to determine how many of the responses were fewer than two times. Explain your steps.

SURVEY

How many trips has your family made to an amusement park in the past two years?

RESULTS

0	4	1	1	2	5	2	2	2
2	4	0	1	1	1	4	2	2

Cumulative Practice for Chapters 1–4

Chapter 1

Multiple Choice In Exercises 1–6, choose the letter of the correct answer.

1. Brian puts 155 pencils in an empty box and Judy puts in 79 pencils. How many pencils are in the box? *(Lesson 1.1)*

   A. 224   **B.** 234   **C.** 334   **D.** 344

2. Andy unloaded 121 bags of rice before lunch and another 286 bags of rice after lunch. About how many bags did he unload in all? *(Lesson 1.2)*

   F. 100   **G.** 200   **H.** 300   **I.** 400

3. How can you write $6 \times 6 \times 6 \times 6$ as a power? *(Lesson 1.3)*

   A. 6×4 **B.** 6^3 **C.** 6^4 **D.** 4^6

4. What is the value of 10^4? *(Lesson 1.3)*

   F. 14   **G.** 40   **H.** 1000   **I.** 10,000

5. What is the value of $60 - (30 \div 5) \times 3$? *(Lesson 1.4)*

   A. 2   **B.** 18   **C.** 42   **D.** 58

6. What is the value of the expression $2m + 8$ when $m = 9$? *(Lesson 1.5)*

   F. 19   **G.** 26   **H.** 34   **I.** 37

7. **Short Response** Sam is the second oldest of 5 friends. Sarah is younger than Sam but she is older than Chris. Maria is the oldest. Scott is older than Sarah. Order the friends from youngest to oldest. *(Lesson 1.7)*

8. **Extended Response** Annabella works at a store and earns $8 an hour. One week she earned $88. *(Lessons 1.2, 1.6)*

   a. Which equation represents the number of hours h that Annabella worked that week: $8h = 88$ or $88h = 8$?

   b. Solve the equation you chose in part (a).

   c. Explain how you can estimate to check whether your answer is reasonable.

Chapter 2

Multiple Choice In Exercises 9–14, choose the letter of the correct answer.

9. Which item is likely to be measured in centimeters? *(Lesson 2.1)*

   A. a grain of rice   **B.** a pencil

   C. a field   **D.** the equator

10. Which expression can be used to find the perimeter of a garden that is 15 feet long and 10 feet wide? *(Lesson 2.2)*

    F. $2(10 \times 15)$ **G.** 10×15

    H. $2(15) + 2(10)$ **I.** $10 + 15$

11. Carmela makes a scale drawing of a room. The room is 33 feet long. She is using the scale 1 in. : 3 ft. How long is the room on the drawing? *(Lesson 2.3)*

    A. 1 in.   **B.** 3 in.   **C.** 11 in.   **D.** 33 in.

12. Which is the best increment for the scale of a bar graph showing the data values 23, 34, 28, 33, 30, and 32? *(Lesson 2.5)*

    F. 1   **G.** 5   **H.** 20   **I.** 30

13. Which point has coordinates (5, 2)? *(Lesson 2.6)*

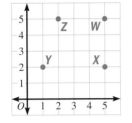

A. W **B.** X

C. Y **D.** Z

14. The graph shows the number of pets in a town. How many more dogs are there than hamsters? *(Lesson 2.7)*

Dogs 283

Cats 331

Rabbits 45

Hamsters 76

F. 76   **G.** 207   **H.** 283   **I.** 359

15. Short Response The table shows the annual amount of snowfall in 7 countries. Explain how to find a reasonable estimate of the mean. How does your estimate compare to the median? *(Lesson 2.8)*

Snow Fall	
Country	**Feet**
Italy	42
Sweden	76
Russia	68
Malaysia	73
Bolivia	45
France	64
Canada	69

16. Extended Response A television show gets the following ratings over a 9 week period. *(Lessons 2.4, 2.5)*

Week	1	2	3	4	5	6	7	8	9
Rating	18	20	19	18	21	22	18	20	18

a. Make a line plot of the data.

b. Make a bar graph of the data.

c. Which one would you use to decide which rating is most common? Why?

Chapter 3

Multiple Choice In Exercises 17–21, choose the letter of the correct answer.

17. One yard is ninety-one and forty-four hundredths centimeters. Which measurement equals one yard? *(Lesson 3.1)*

A. 0.09144 cm   **B.** 91.044 cm

C. 91.44 cm   **D.** 901.44 cm

18. Which measurement represents a length of 35 centimeters written to the nearest hundredth of a meter? *(Lesson 3.2)*

F. 0.35 m   **G.** 3.5 m   **H.** 35 m   **I.** 350 m

19. What is the greatest number in the list below? *(Lesson 3.3)*

5.05, 0.505, 5.5, 5.005, 5.505, 0.0505

A. 0.0505   **B.** 5.005   **C.** 5.5   **D.** 5.505

20. Mark spent $39.90 on sneakers, $19.95 on a basketball, and $7.05 on a new hat. What is a good estimate of how much he spent? *(Lesson 3.5)*

F. less than $40   **G.** $40 to $50

H. $50 to $70   **I.** $70 to $90

21. What is the value of $b - a$ when $a = 3.681$ and $b = 5.04$? *(Lesson 3.6)*

A. 1.359   **B.** 2.469   **C.** 2.641   **D.** 3.177

22. Short Response The recorded times, in seconds, for skiers in a slalom event were 48.37, 49.80, 49.60, 50.16, 49.92, 48.01, 49.61, and 49.34. Order the times from least to greatest and state the winning time. Explain why it does not make sense to round the times to the nearest whole number before ordering them. *(Lessons 3.3, 3.4)*

Cumulative Practice continued

23. Extended Response The Ruiz family wants to spend an average of $200 a week on groceries. The table shows the actual amounts spent for 4 weeks. *(Lessons 3.5, 3.6)*

Week 1	$188.99
Week 2	$202.89
Week 3	$185.66
Week 4	$210.34

a. Estimate the total amount spent.

b. Estimate the average amount spent per week.

c. Did the Ruiz family stay close to their weekly budget? Explain.

Chapter 4

Multiple Choice In Exercises 24–30, choose the letter of the correct answer.

24. What is the cost of a 5 pound bag of peanuts at $3.89 per pound? *(Lesson 4.1)*

A. $8.89 **B.** $15.05

C. $19.45 **D.** $1945

25. Which expression is equivalent to $5(2 + 0.6)$? *(Lesson 4.2)*

F. $5 \times 2 + 0.6$ **G.** $5(2) + 5(0.6)$

H. $10 + 0.30$ **I.** $52 + 0.6$

26. What is the product of 24.5 and 0.07? *(Lesson 4.3)*

A. 0.1715 **B.** 1.715

C. 17.15 **D.** 171.5

27. What is the value of the quotient $0.0456 \div 0.01$? *(Lesson 4.5)*

F. 0.000456 **G.** 0.0456

H. 4.56 **I.** 45.6

28. Pat biked 41.4 miles in 4.5 hours. What was his average rate in miles per hour? *(Lesson 4.6)*

A. 0.092 **B.** 0.92 **C.** 9.2 **D.** 92

29. What unit of measurement would most likely be used to express the mass of a whale? *(Lesson 4.7)*

F. meters **G.** milligrams

H. grams **I.** kilograms

30. A tornado typically moves about 64,000 meters in an hour. How many kilometers is this? *(Lesson 4.8)*

A. 0.064 km **B.** 64 km

C. 640 km **D.** 64,000,000 km

31. Short Response Michelle bought 5 yards of a fabric for $8.45 and 7 yards of another fabric for $10.08. Which fabric is less expensive per yard? Explain. *(Lesson 4.4)*

32. Extended Response A rectangle has a length of 10 centimeters and a width of 8 centimeters. *(Lesson 4.2)*

a. Use the formula for the perimeter of a rectangle to write an expression for the perimeter of this rectangle.

b. Use the distributive property to rewrite the expression.

c. Show that both expressions give the same answer for the perimeter.

Fraction Concepts, Expressions, and Operations

Chapter **5** Number Patterns and Fractions

- Use divisibility rules and find common factors and common multiples.
- Know the relationships between fractions and decimals.
- Use customary units of length.

Chapter **6** Addition and Subtraction of Fractions

- Estimate a sum or difference.
- Add and subtract fractions and mixed numbers to solve problems.
- Add and subtract measures of time.

From Chapter 7, p. 315

How much space do you need for your CDs?

Chapter **7** Multiplication and Division of Fractions

- Use multiplication and division to solve real-world problems.
- Estimate, change, and choose units of capacity and weight.
- Use patterns to predict outcomes and solve problems.

UNIT 2	STANDARDIZED TEST PREP

Strategies and practice directly follow Chapter 7.

5

Number Patterns and Fractions

BEFORE

In previous chapters you've...

- Divided whole numbers
- Ordered decimals

Now

In Chapter 5 you'll study...

- Prime factorization
- Equivalent fractions
- Comparing and ordering fractions and mixed numbers
- Writing decimals as fractions and fractions as decimals

WHY?

So you can solve real-world problems about...

- marching bands, p. 217
- chess, p. 231
- baseball bats, p. 246
- fishing, p. 256

Internet Preview
CLASSZONE.COM

- eEdition Plus Online
- eWorkbook Plus Online
- eTutorial Plus Online
- State Test Practice
- More Examples

Chapter Warm-Up Games

Review skills you need for this chapter in these quick games.

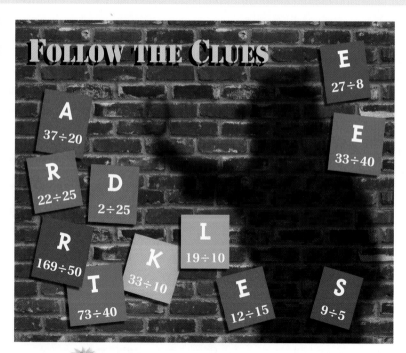

FOLLOW THE CLUES

E 27÷8

A 37÷20

E 33÷40

R 22÷25

D 2÷25

R 169÷50

L 19÷10

K 33÷10

T 73÷40

E 12÷15

S 9÷5

BrAIN GAME

Key Skills:
- Dividing whole numbers
- Ordering decimals

- Each clue shown above contains an expression and a letter. Evaluate the expression on each clue.

- Order your answers from least to greatest. Write the letters associated with the answers in the same order. These letters spell out the name of the type of hat Sherlock Holmes wears.

MYSTERY NUMBERS

A I am a one digit number. I divide evenly into 27 but I do not divide into 30. What number am I?

B I am a two digit number. I can be divided evenly by 5. The sum of my two digits is 12. What number am I?

C I am a two digit number. My tens digit is 7. I can be divided evenly by 12. What number am I?

D I am a two digit number. I can be divided evenly by 7. If you switch my digits, I grow by 18. What number am I?

●●●●●●●●●●●●●●●●●●●●●●●●●●●●●●●●●●●●

A - 8   **B** - 67   **C** ÷ 9   **D** ÷ 5

?   **?**   **?**   **?**

Key Skills:
- Understanding place value
- Dividing whole numbers

- Use the clues to find the mystery numbers.

- Use the mystery numbers to evaluate the expressions above.

- The values of the expressions, written in the order shown, give the year in which Sir Arthur Conan Doyle published the first Sherlock Holmes story.

Stop *and* Think

1. **Critical Thinking** In *Follow the Clues,* could you figure out the hidden word by using estimation rather than exact division? Why or why not?

2. **Writing** Pick a two digit number. Write a few clues about it like the ones in *Mystery Numbers.* Then see if someone else can guess the number.

Getting Ready to Learn

Review What You Need to Know

Using Vocabulary Copy and complete using a review word.

1. 12 inches = 1 _?_   **2.** 3 feet = 1 _?_   **3.** 36 _?_ = 1 yard

4. The numbers 6 and 4 are _?_ of 24.

Write the fraction shown by the model. *(p. 700)*

5.    **6.**

Write the product as a power. *(p. 16)*

7. $5 \times 5 \times 5 \times 5$ **8.** $10 \times 10 \times 10$ **9.** 11×11

10. Estimate the length of the straw to the nearest inch. Then measure to check your estimate. *(p. 55)*

Use a number line to order the decimals from least to greatest. *(p. 118)*

11. 1.4, 1.8, 1.5, 1.6, 1.7, 2   **12.** 2.7, 2.07, 2.77, 2.71, 2.17

13. 3.28, 2.83, 3.82, 8.23, 2.38   **14.** 7.24, 7.31, 7.03, 7.26, 7.17

You should include material that appears on a notebook like this in your own notes.

Know How to Take Notes

Learning Vocabulary You need to learn the complete and accurate meanings of vocabulary words. Copy the words from each lesson's Word Watch in your notebook with a definition and an example.

Vocabulary for Lesson 1.3

Factor - a whole number other than zero that is multiplied by another whole number to give a product.

Example

exponent
base

$6^4 = \underbrace{6 \times 6 \times 6 \times 6}_{\text{There are 4 factors.}} = 1296$

power   product

As you work through Chapter 5, include new vocabulary in your notes.

Hands-on Activity

GOAL

Use number sense to test whether 2, 3, 6, and 9 are factors of a number.

MATERIALS

• paper
• pencil

Divisibility Rules

You can use rules to decide whether certain numbers are factors of another number. For example, 2 is a factor of a number if the number is even.

Explore   **Copy and complete the table to decide if 3 is a factor of each number.**

1 Decide whether 3 is a factor of 18.

Because $18 = 6 \times 3$, you know 3 is a factor of 18.

Number	Is 3 a factor?	Sum of digits	Is 3 a factor of the sum?
18	Yes	9	Yes
60	?	?	?
80	?	?	?
99	?	?	?
315	?	?	?
329	?	?	?

2 Add the digits in the number 18: $1 + 8 = 9$.

3 Decide whether 3 is a factor of the sum from Step 2.

Because $9 = 3 \times 3$, you know 3 is a factor of 9.

4 Repeat Steps 1–3 for all the numbers in the first column of the table.

Your turn now   **Use the table above.**

   1. Decide whether 2 is a factor of each number in the first column.

   2. Follow the steps above to create another table that shows which of the numbers have 9 as a factor.

Stop *and* **Think**

   3. Writing Look back at the tables you made. Write a rule that tells you whether 3 is a factor of a given number. Write a similar rule for 9.

   4. Critical Thinking If 2 and 3 are factors of a number, is 6 always a factor of the number? Explain.

Prime Factorization

You found products of whole numbers.

You'll write whole numbers as the product of prime factors.

So you can form groups, such as the dancers in Example 1.

Word Watch

divisible, p. 214
prime number, p. 215
composite number, p. 215
prime factorization, p. 216
factor tree, p. 216

In the Real World

Dancers A dance teacher is planning a dance for a show. The dancers will be in rows with the same number of dancers in each row. Does a group of 12 dancers or a group of 14 dancers offer more possibilities?

EXAMPLE 1 **Finding Factors**

To answer the question above, list all the factors of 12 and 14 by writing each number as a product of two numbers in as many ways as possible.

12 : 1 × 12   14 : 1 × 14
    2 × 6   Stop when   2 × 7
    3 × 4   a pair of   7 × 2
    4 × 3   factors repeats.

The factors of 12 are 1, 2, 3, 4, 6, and 12.

The factors of 14 are 1, 2, 7, and 14.

ANSWER A group of 12 dancers offers more possibilities than a group of 14 dancers, because 12 has more factors than 14.

Divisibility A number is **divisible** by another number if that other number is a factor of the first. Divisibility rules can help you find factors.

Divisibility Rules for 2, 3, 5, 6, 9, and 10

A whole number is divisible by:

• 2 if the number is even.

• 6 if it is even and divisible by 3.

• 3 if the sum of its digits is divisible by 3.

• 9 if the sum of its digits is divisible by 9.

• 5 if it ends with 5 or 0.

• 10 if it ends with 0.

EXAMPLE 2 Using Divisibility Rules

Test 150 for divisibility by 2, 3, 5, 6, 9, and 10.

150 is even, so it is divisible by 2.

$1 + 5 + 0 = 6$, and 6 is divisible by 3, but not by 9. So, 150 is divisible by 3, but it is not divisible by 9.

150 ends with 0, so it is divisible by 5 and by 10.

150 is even and divisible by 3, so it is divisible by 6.

ANSWER 150 is divisible by 2, 3, 5, 6, and 10, but not by 9.

Your turn now **List all the factors of the number.**

1. 8   **2.** 9   **3.** 15   **4.** 18

Test the number for divisibility by 2, 3, 5, 6, 9, and 10.

5. 100   **6.** 456   **7.** 783   **8.** 1584

Primes and Composites A **prime number** is a whole number greater than 1 whose only factors are 1 and itself. A **composite number** is a whole number greater than 1 that has factors other than 1 and itself. The number 1 is neither prime nor composite.

EXAMPLE 3 Classifying as Prime or Composite

HELP with Solving

Another way to tell if a number is composite is to use divisibility rules. For example, 51 is divisible by 3. So, 3 is a factor of 51 and 51 is composite.

Tell whether the number is *prime* or *composite*.

a. 51   **b.** 59

Solution

a. List the factors of 51: 1, 3, 17, 51.

    ANSWER The number 51 is composite. It has factors other than 1 and itself.

b. List the factors of 59: 1, 59.

    ANSWER The number 59 is prime. Its only factors are 1 and itself.

Your turn now **Tell whether the number is *prime* or *composite*.**

9. 11   **10.** 13   **11.** 14   **12.** 35

Prime Factorization Writing the **prime factorization** of a number means writing the number as the product of prime numbers. You can use a diagram called a **factor tree** to write a factorization of a number. To write the prime factorization, continue factoring until only prime factors appear in the product.

 HELP **with Solving**

Only prime and composite numbers are used in a factor tree. So, the number 1 is not used in a factor tree.

EXAMPLE 4 **Writing a Prime Factorization**

Write the prime factorization of 180.

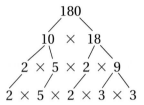

Write the original number.

Factor 180 as 10 times 18.

Factor 10 and 18.

Factor 9.

ANSWER The prime factorization of 180 is $2^2 \times 3^2 \times 5$.

✓**Check** Use multiplication to check your answer.
$2^2 \times 3^2 \times 5 = 4 \times 9 \times 5 = 180$

5.1 **Exercises**
More Practice, p. 712

Getting Ready to Practice

Vocabulary **Write the divisibility rule for the number in your own words.**

1. 2　　　　**2.** 3　　　　**3.** 5　　　　**4.** 6

Vocabulary **Tell whether the number is *prime*, *composite*, or *neither*.**

5. 4　　　　**6.** 9　　　　**7.** 5　　　　**8.** 1

Copy and complete the factor tree. Then write the prime factorization.

9.
$$42$$
$$? \times ?$$
$$2 \times ? \times 7$$

10.
$$68$$
$$2 \times ?$$
$$? \times 2 \times ?$$

11.
$$81$$
$$? \times 9$$
$$? \times 3 \times ? \times 3$$

12. Exercise A fitness instructor needs to arrange 80 people in her class in equal rows. Can she arrange them in rows of 6?

Practice and Problem Solving

with **Homework**

Example	Exercises
1	13-20, 47
2	21-28
3	29-37
4	38-46

Online Resources
CLASSZONE.COM

· More Examples
· eTutorial Plus

List all the factors of the number.

13. 14   **14.** 27   **15.** 19   **16.** 36

17. 100   **18.** 108   **19.** 121   **20.** 91

Test the number for divisibility by 2, 3, 5, 6, 9, and 10.

21. 140   **22.** 144   **23.** 282   **24.** 315

25. 1578   **26.** 4860   **27.** 8745   **28.** 9990

Tell whether the number is *prime* or *composite*.

29. 7   **30.** 19   **31.** 28   **32.** 15

33. 37   **34.** 43   **35.** 49   **36.** 97

37. Summer Camp There are 117 students going to summer camp. Can the campers be divided into small groups of equal size with at least 2 campers in each group? Explain.

38. Find the Error Describe and correct the error in the prime factorization.

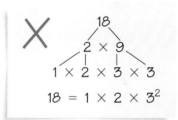

Write the prime factorization of the number.

39. 39   **40.** 55   **41.** 63   **42.** 48

43. 54   **44.** 88   **45.** 150   **46.** 165

47. Marching Band You are planning a half-time show for your school's marching band. There are 75 musicians in the band, and you want to divide them into groups of equal size to make different formations. Which of the following group sizes are possible?

A.   **B.**   **C.**

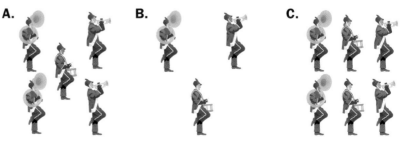

What do you think?

Music

■ Marching Band

At Ohio State University, being the band member that dots the "i" as the band spells "Ohio" on the football field is a big honor. The first time anyone dotted the "i" was October 10, 1936. 46 years earlier, on May 3rd, Ohio State University had played its first football game. What year was that?

48. Writing A student made the factor tree at the right by looking for a prime factor at each step. Make a different factor tree for 140. Compare and contrast the methods and the results.

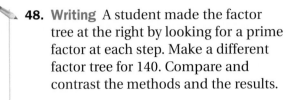

$$140$$
$$2 \times 70$$
$$2 \times 2 \times 35$$
$$2 \times 2 \times 5 \times 7$$

Number Sense **Tell whether the statement is *true* or *false*.**

49. Any number that is divisible by 6 is divisible by 2.

50. Any number that is divisible by 5 is divisible by 10.

51. All prime numbers are odd.

52. All multiples of 3 are composite.

Extended Problem Solving **In Exercises 53–55, you are planning relay races. Information about the races is given at the right.**

53. Mental Math What are the possible team sizes? How many teams would there be for each team size?

54. Decide You want exactly 6 teams in each race. Which team sizes from Exercise 53 are still possible? How many races will be run?

55. Explain You want to have a runoff among the winning teams. What team size from Exercise 54 should you use if you want 4 teams in the runoff? Explain.

Relay Races

48 students participating

Teams of equal size

Maximum team size: 6 students

Find the least number that is divisible by the given numbers.

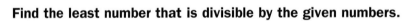

56. 2, 6, and 9

57. 2, 3, and 5

58. 3, 5, and 9

59. 6, 9, and 10

60. Find a number between 30 and 40 that is composite and has prime factors that add up to 12.

61. Cryptography To keep e-mail and other electronic information private, cryptographers use large numbers that are difficult to factor. Use a calculator to find the prime factorization of the number 3551.

62. Critical Thinking Why is a number that is divisible by 3 and 5 always divisible by 15, when a number that is divisible by 2 and 6 isn't necessarily divisible by 12?

63. Challenge Twin primes are pairs of prime numbers whose difference is 2. An example is 3 and 5. Find the next 4 pairs of twin primes.

Mixed Review

Use the distributive property to evaluate the expression.
(Lesson 4.2)

64. $7(40 + 8)$ **65.** $8(30 + 7)$ **66.** $5(50 - 8)$ **67.** $4(60 - 6)$

Divide. Round to the nearest tenth if necessary. *(Lesson 4.4)*

68. $8.6 \div 2$ **69.** $96.3 \div 3$ **70.** $36.8 \div 16$ **71.** $5.9 \div 2$

Basic Skills   **Solve the following problems.**

72. You would like to buy a pair of jeans for $35. You have $23. How much more money do you need?

73. Your sister has 87 stickers. Her friend gives her 16 more. How many stickers does she have?

Test-Taking Practice

74. **Multiple Choice** Which of the following numbers is a composite number?

   A. 11   **B.** 17   **C.** 20   **D.** 23

75. **Short Response** The factor tree at the right is not complete. Copy and complete the factor tree in two different ways. Then write the prime factorization of 450.

$$450$$
$$25 \times 18$$

Which Telephone Number?

Joey has a list of five telephone numbers on a slip of paper, but his hamster ate a part of this paper that had all the names next to the numbers. Now he wants to call Paul, and he does not know which of the five numbers to dial. He does remember the following facts about Paul's number:

1. It is divisible by 9.
2. It is divisible by 2.
3. It is not divisible by 10.
4. It is not divisible by 4.

Ignoring the hyphens, which telephone number could be Paul's?

835-6257
555-6902
903-1248
420-2730
642-3174

Problem Solving Strategies

Draw a Diagram

Guess, Check, and Revise

Look for a Pattern

Work Backward

Make a List or Table

Perform an Experiment

Check Reasonableness

Make a List or Table

Problem You are displaying student art work for a show. You have 30 pieces to display. You will arrange them in alphabetical order across the rows. How many different possibilities for a rectangular display are there if you want no more than 5 rows of posters?

① Read and Understand

Read the problem carefully.

You want to find all of the ways to make a rectangle with 30 art pieces.

② Make a Plan

Decide on a strategy to use.

One way to solve a problem is to make a list or a table of all of the possibilities.

③ Solve the Problem

Reread the problem and make a list or table.

You know that your display will have 30 art pieces. You also know that you will have no more than 5 rows of art pieces. List all of the whole number factors of 30 less than or equal to 5. Column headings help you organize rows and columns for your display.

Rows	Columns	Display
1	30	30
2	15	30
3	10	30
5	6	30

The table allows you to see how many columns you will have for each number of rows.

ANSWER There are 4 different possibilities for a display of 30 pieces of student art.

④ Look Back

Check to make sure that you used all possibilities of whole number factors of 30 less than or equal to 5. You could also draw a diagram of each situation.

Use the strategy *make a list or table*.

1. **Science Fair** You have entered the school science fair with an experiment. The guidelines allocate 40 square feet per participant. How many possibilities for a rectangular space with whole number dimensions are there?

2. **Coins** Copy and extend the table to find all the ways you can combine change to get 25 cents.

Pennies	Nickels	Dimes	Quarters
25	0	0	0
20	1	0	0
15	2	0	0
15	0	1	0

3. **Change** You purchase a magazine and are going to receive a dollar in change. How many different ways can you receive the change if it's given in quarters only, in nickels only, or in quarters and nickels?

4. **Fundraising** You sell $60 worth of merchandise to raise money for a school club. You sell candles for $5 and candleholders for $6. In how many ways could you have earned $60?

5. **Code Words** You and a friend decide to send letters in a secret code. How many different three-letter code words can you make using the letters *A*, *B*, and *C* if repetition of the letters is *not* permitted?

Mixed Problem Solving

Use any strategy to solve the problem.

6. **Find the Number** What number belongs in the blank?

$$(121 \div \underline{\ ?\ }) \times 4 + 8 = 52$$

7. **Photos** You want to display photos of friends on a bulletin board. Assuming adjacent sides of the photos overlap and each corner must be tacked, what is the least number of tacks you need to display six rectangular photos of the same size and shape?

8. **Find the Rule** Use the table to find a rule that relates the number and its result.

Number	Result
4	10
5	12
6	14
7	16
8	18

9. **Trip** You are planning a trip to the beach for seventeen friends. Four parents volunteer to drive and each car will hold four friends. Will four cars be enough? Why or why not?

Greatest Common Factor

BEFORE	▶ Now	WHY?
You found all the factors of a number.	You'll find the greatest common factor of two or more numbers.	So you can divide large groups evenly, as in Ex. 23.

In the Real World

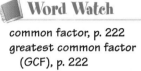

Word Watch

common factor, p. 222
greatest common factor
(GCF), p. 222

Gardening You are dividing a garden into sections. You have 64 marigolds and 120 petunias. You want each section to have the same number of each type of flower, and you want to use all of the flowers. What is the greatest number of sections you can have?

A whole number that is a factor of two or more nonzero whole numbers is a **common factor** of the numbers. The largest of the common factors is the **greatest common factor (GCF)**.

EXAMPLE 1 Finding the GCF of Two Numbers

The greatest number of sections that you can have in the garden described above is the GCF of 64 and 120. Two methods for finding the GCF are shown.

Method 1: List all the factors of 64 and 120.

Factors of 64: 1, 2, 4, 8, 16, 32, 64

Factors of 120: 1, 2, 3, 4, 5, 6, 8, 10, 12, 15, 20, 24, 30, 40, 60, 120

The common factors are 1, 2, 4, and 8. The GCF is 8.

Method 2: Write the prime factorization of 64 and 120. Then find the product of the common prime factors.

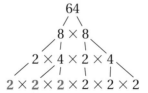
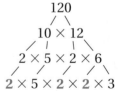

$$64$$
$$8 \times 8$$
$$2 \times 4 \times 2 \times 4$$
$$2 \times 2 \times 2 \times 2 \times 2 \times 2$$

$$120$$
$$10 \times 12$$
$$2 \times 5 \times 2 \times 6$$
$$2 \times 5 \times 2 \times 2 \times 3$$

The common prime factors are 2, 2, and 2. The GCF is 2^3, or 8.

ANSWER The greatest number of sections that you can have is 8.

Finding the Greatest Common Factor (GCF)

Method 1: List all the factors of each number. Then find the greatest factor that is common to all numbers.

Method 2: Write the prime factorization of each number. Then find the product of the prime factors the numbers have in common.

EXAMPLE 2 **Finding the GCF of Three Numbers**

Find the GCF of 12, 21, and 30.

Factors of 12: 1, 2, **3**, 4, 6, 12
Factors of 21: 1, **3**, 7, 21
Factors of 30: 1, 2, **3**, 5, 6, 10, 15, 30

ANSWER The GCF of 12, 21, and 30 is 3.

EXAMPLE 3 **Making a List**

Tours Three groups will take the Cave of the Winds tour of Niagara Falls. The amount they will spend on tickets is given at the right. If each ticket is the same price, what is the most a ticket could cost?

	Amount
Group 1	$27
Group 2	$45
Group 3	$72

Solution

Find the GCF of the amounts spent by listing the factors.

Factors of 27: **1**, **3**, **9**, 27
Factors of 45: **1**, **3**, 5, **9**, 15, 45
Factors of 72: **1**, 2, **3**, 4, 6, 8, **9**,
                12, 18, 24, 36, 72

The common factors are 1, 3, and 9.

ANSWER The most a ticket could cost is $9.

Your turn now Find the GCF of the numbers.

1. 14, 35
2. 16, 36
3. 42, 72
4. 4, 6, 8
5. 12, 24, 30
6. 24, 48, 72

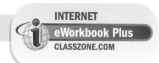

Getting Ready to Practice

Vocabulary **Find the GCF of the numbers using the factors listed.**

1. GCF of 18 and 32
Factors of 18: 1, 2, 3, 6, 9, 18
Factors of 32: 1, 2, 4, 8, 16, 32

2. GCF of 21 and 39
Factors of 21: 1, 3, 7, 21
Factors of 39: 1, 3, 13, 39

3. Use factor trees to find the GCF of 15 and 45.

4. **Guided Problem Solving** For your school's fair, you make 42 magnets and 36 key chains with your school's mascot on them. You want to display them in rows of equal size, but you do not want to mix the items. What is the greatest number of items you can have in a row? How many rows of each item will there be?

⓵ Find the GCF of 42 and 36.

⓶ Divide to find the number of rows of magnets.

⓷ Divide to find the number of rows of key chains.

Practice and Problem Solving

5. **Find the Error** Describe and correct the error in finding the GCF of 28 and 42.

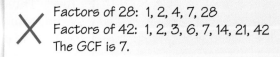

Factors of 28: 1, 2, 4, 7, 28
Factors of 42: 1, 2, 3, 6, 7, 14, 21, 42
The GCF is 7.

Find the GCF of the numbers by listing the factors.

6. 10, 28   **7.** 24, 84   **8.** 16, 48   **9.** 11, 44

Find the GCF of the numbers using factor trees.

10. 12, 54   **11.** 32, 40   **12.** 20, 75   **13.** 36, 90

Find the GCF of the numbers using either method.

14. 9, 42   **15.** 8, 28   **16.** 12, 25   **17.** 15, 52

18. 12, 21, 30   **19.** 16, 40, 88   **20.** 30, 75, 120   **21.** 13, 65, 117

22. **Parades** A group of 45 singers will march behind a group of 30 clowns in a parade. You want to arrange the two groups in rows with the same number of people in each row, but without mixing the groups. What is the greatest number of people you can have in each row?

HELP with **Homework**

Example	Exercises
1	5-17, 22
2	18-21
3	23

Online Resources
CLASSZONE.COM
· More Examples
· eTutorial Plus

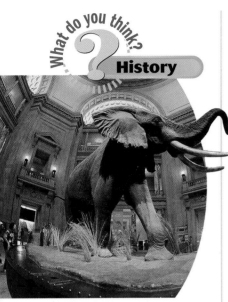

History Museums **In Exercises 23 and 24, use the information below.**
A museum has three groups of people scheduled for tours. The groups
have 48, 112, and 144 people. The tour guides want to divide the groups
into smaller groups of equal size, without mixing any of the groups.

23. What is the greatest number of people each group can have?

24. Explain How many groups of people will there be? Explain.

Tell whether the statement is *always*, *sometimes*, or *never* true.

25. The GCF of two numbers is one of the two numbers.

26. The GCF of two numbers is greater than one of the numbers.

27. The GCF of two prime numbers is 1.

28. Critical Thinking If one number is a factor of another number,
will the GCF always be the lesser number? Explain.

Challenge **Find the GCF of the numbers.**

29. 658, 770   **30.** 279, 414   **31.** 372, 582

Mixed Review

32. Order the numbers 1.26, 1.02, 1.6, 0.96, 1, 0.1, and 1.216 from least to
greatest. *(Lesson 3.3)*

Evaluate the expression using mental math. *(Lesson 4.5)*

33. 0.05 ÷ 100   **34.** 3.46 ÷ 0.01   **35.** 0.9 ÷ 0.001

Basic Skills **What fraction is shown by the model?**

36.   **37.**   **38.**

Test-Taking Practice

39. Multiple Choice What is the greatest common factor of 14 and 26?

   A. 2   **B.** 7   **C.** 14   **D.** 182

40. Short Response Ashley has 27 violet marbles, 54 blue marbles, and
72 white marbles. She wants to divide the marbles into groups so that
each group has the same number of each color marble. What is the
greatest number of groups that Ashley can make? Explain.

■ **History Museums**
An African elephant, such as
the one on display at the
National Museum of Natural
History in Washington, D.C.,
can weigh in the vicinity of
14,000 pounds. The average
mid-size sedan weighs about
3300 pounds. How many
times more does the African
elephant weigh than the
average mid-size sedan?

Hands-on Activity

Modeling Equivalent Fractions

You can use paper models to represent fractions in more than one way.

Explore 1 Model the fraction $\frac{1}{2}$ in different ways.

1 Fold a piece of paper in half. Then unfold the paper and draw a line along the fold. Shade one half as shown.

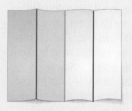

2 Refold the paper. Then fold it in half again in the same direction. Unfold the paper and draw a line along each new fold.

Copy and complete the statement: $\frac{1}{2} = \frac{?}{4}$.

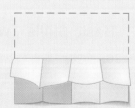
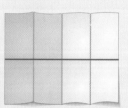

3 Fold the paper in half in the other direction. Then unfold the paper and draw a line along the new fold.

Copy and complete the statement: $\frac{1}{2} = \frac{?}{8}$.

Your turn now Use the fractions in Steps 1–3 above.

1. Describe a pattern in the numerators of the fractions above. Do you see the same pattern in the denominators?

2. Use your answers to Exercise 1 to help you copy and complete the following fractions.

$$\frac{1}{2} = \frac{2}{4} = \frac{4}{8} = \frac{?}{16}$$

Explore 2 **Model the fraction $\frac{1}{3}$ in different ways.**

1 Fold a piece of paper in thirds. Then unfold the paper and draw a line along each fold. Shade one third as shown.

2 Refold the paper. Then fold it in thirds again in the same direction. Unfold the paper and draw a line along each new fold.

Copy and complete the statement: $\frac{1}{3} = \frac{?}{9}$.

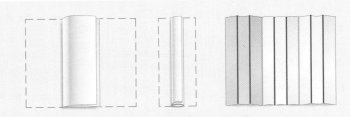

3 Fold the paper in thirds in the other direction. Then unfold the paper and draw a line along each new fold.

Copy and complete the statement: $\frac{1}{3} = \frac{?}{27}$.

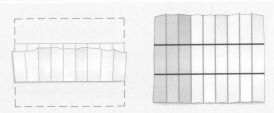

Your turn now **Use the fractions in Steps 1–3 above.**

3. Copy and complete the following fractions.

$$\frac{1}{3} = \frac{3}{9} = \frac{9}{27} = \frac{?}{81}$$

Stop *and* **Think**

4. **Writing** Describe a method you could use to find three fractions with different numerators and denominators that all represent the same fraction.

LESSON
5.3

Equivalent Fractions

BEFORE | ▶ **Now** | **WHY?**

You wrote equivalent decimals. | You'll write equivalent fractions. | So you can simplify fractions, such as the survey responses in Example 3.

Word Watch

fraction, p. 228
equivalent fractions, p. 228
simplest form, p. 229

Fractions Recall that a **fraction** is a number of the form $\frac{a}{b}$, where $b \neq 0$.

$$\frac{a}{b} \quad \longleftarrow \text{ numerator} \\ \longleftarrow \text{ denominator}$$

A fraction can represent part of a whole, as shown below.

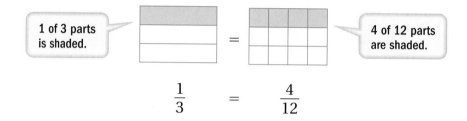

1 of 3 parts is shaded.

4 of 12 parts are shaded.

$$\frac{1}{3} \quad = \quad \frac{4}{12}$$

The fractions above are **equivalent** because they represent the same number. As you may have noticed in the activity, you can write equivalent fractions by multiplying or dividing the numerator and denominator by the *same* number.

HELP with Notetaking

In your notebook, you might want to record models of the equivalent fractions shown in Example 1.

EXAMPLE 1 **Writing Equivalent Fractions**

Write two fractions that are equivalent to $\frac{1}{3}$.

$$\frac{1}{3} = \frac{1 \times 2}{3 \times 2} = \frac{2}{6}$$ Multiply the numerator and denominator by 2.

$$\frac{1}{3} = \frac{1 \times 3}{3 \times 3} = \frac{3}{9}$$ Multiply the numerator and denominator by 3.

ANSWER The fractions $\frac{2}{6}$ and $\frac{3}{9}$ are equivalent to $\frac{1}{3}$.

Your turn now Write two fractions that are equivalent to the given fraction.

1. $\frac{1}{2}$ **2.** $\frac{1}{4}$ **3.** $\frac{3}{5}$ **4.** $\frac{2}{3}$

EXAMPLE 2 **Completing Equivalent Fractions**

Complete the equivalent fraction.

a. $\dfrac{3}{5} = \dfrac{12}{?}$

$$3 \times 4$$
$$\dfrac{3}{5} = \dfrac{12}{20}$$
$$5 \times 4$$

You multiply 3 by 4 to get 12, so multiply the denominator by 4.

b. $\dfrac{16}{24} = \dfrac{?}{12}$

$$16 \div 2$$
$$\dfrac{16}{24} = \dfrac{8}{12}$$
$$24 \div 2$$

You divide 24 by 2 to get 12, so divide the numerator by 2.

Your turn now Copy and complete the statement.

5. $\dfrac{2}{5} = \dfrac{6}{?}$ **6.** $\dfrac{4}{7} = \dfrac{?}{21}$ **7.** $\dfrac{15}{20} = \dfrac{3}{?}$ **8.** $\dfrac{18}{27} = \dfrac{?}{3}$

Simplifying A fraction is in **simplest form** if its numerator and denominator have a greatest common factor of 1. To *simplify* a fraction, divide its numerator and denominator by their greatest common factor.

EXAMPLE 3 **Simplifying Fractions**

Movies In a survey of 16 middle school students, 12 said that comedy was their favorite type of movie. Write this as a fraction in simplest form.

Solution
Write "12 out of 16" as a fraction. Then simplify.

$\dfrac{12}{16} = \dfrac{3 \times 4}{4 \times 4}$ Use the GCF to write the numerator and denominator as products.

$= \dfrac{3 \times \cancel{4}^{\,1}}{4 \times \cancel{4}_{\,1}}$ Divide the numerator and denominator by the GCF.

$= \dfrac{3}{4}$ Simplest form

ANSWER The fraction, in simplest form, of students who said comedy was their favorite type of movie is $\dfrac{3}{4}$.

Your turn now Write the fraction in simplest form.

9. $\dfrac{5}{25}$ **10.** $\dfrac{8}{24}$ **11.** $\dfrac{14}{21}$ **12.** $\dfrac{15}{35}$

> **EXAMPLE 4** **Applying Fractions**

Homework You spent an hour on homework last night. Write a fraction in simplest form to describe the amount of time you spent on each subject.

a. You spent 15 minutes on literature. $\dfrac{15}{60} = \dfrac{1 \times \cancel{15}^{1}}{4 \times \cancel{15}_{1}} = \dfrac{1}{4}$ hour

b. You spent 25 minutes on math. $\dfrac{25}{60} = \dfrac{5 \times \cancel{5}^{1}}{12 \times \cancel{5}_{1}} = \dfrac{5}{12}$ hour

c. You spent 20 minutes on science. $\dfrac{20}{60} = \dfrac{1 \times \cancel{20}^{1}}{3 \times \cancel{20}_{1}} = \dfrac{1}{3}$ hour

5.3 **Exercises**
More Practice, p. 712

Getting Ready to Practice

Vocabulary **Tell whether the fraction is in simplest form. If not, simplify it.**

1. $\dfrac{1}{2}$ **2.** $\dfrac{2}{3}$ **3.** $\dfrac{3}{9}$ **4.** $\dfrac{4}{10}$

Which fraction is not equivalent to the given fraction?

5. $\dfrac{1}{8}$ **A.** $\dfrac{2}{9}$ **B.** $\dfrac{2}{16}$ **C.** $\dfrac{3}{24}$ **D.** $\dfrac{5}{40}$

6. $\dfrac{2}{5}$ **A.** $\dfrac{10}{25}$ **B.** $\dfrac{5}{20}$ **C.** $\dfrac{20}{50}$ **D.** $\dfrac{40}{100}$

7. $\dfrac{16}{40}$ **A.** $\dfrac{8}{20}$ **B.** $\dfrac{4}{10}$ **C.** $\dfrac{2}{5}$ **D.** $\dfrac{1}{4}$

8. $\dfrac{12}{36}$ **A.** $\dfrac{1}{24}$ **B.** $\dfrac{1}{3}$ **C.** $\dfrac{2}{6}$ **D.** $\dfrac{4}{12}$

9. **Beads** You are using the beads below to make a bracelet. Write fractions in simplest form to describe the portion of beads that are each color.

Practice and Problem Solving

with Homework

Example	Exercises
1	10-17
2	18-25
3	26-33
4	34-36

Online Resources
CLASSZONE.COM

· More Examples
· eTutorial Plus

Write two fractions that are equivalent to the given fraction.

10. $\frac{1}{5}$ **11.** $\frac{1}{10}$ **12.** $\frac{3}{7}$ **13.** $\frac{3}{5}$

14. $\frac{3}{11}$ **15.** $\frac{9}{20}$ **16.** $\frac{4}{25}$ **17.** $\frac{3}{100}$

Copy and complete the statement.

18. $\frac{4}{5} = \frac{?}{20}$ **19.** $\frac{7}{9} = \frac{35}{?}$ **20.** $\frac{18}{30} = \frac{6}{?}$ **21.** $\frac{20}{25} = \frac{?}{5}$

22. $\frac{6}{7} = \frac{18}{?}$ **23.** $\frac{9}{11} = \frac{?}{66}$ **24.** $\frac{44}{52} = \frac{?}{13}$ **25.** $\frac{28}{49} = \frac{4}{?}$

Tell whether the fraction is in simplest form. If not, simplify it.

26. $\frac{7}{14}$ **27.** $\frac{9}{27}$ **28.** $\frac{9}{32}$ **29.** $\frac{13}{64}$

30. $\frac{15}{48}$ **31.** $\frac{40}{45}$ **32.** $\frac{24}{77}$ **33.** $\frac{50}{175}$

34. Buying Lunch There are 30 people in a class and 21 of them buy lunch at school. Write the portion of the class that buys lunch at school as a fraction in simplest form.

Chess A chessboard is shown at the right.

35. Write a fraction in simplest form that represents the portion of the squares on the board that are shaded purple.

36. Write a fraction in simplest form that represents the portion of the board covered by one player's chess pieces.

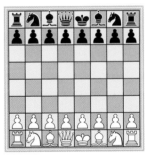

Algebra Find the value of x.

37. $\frac{x}{8} = \frac{25}{40}$ **38.** $\frac{x}{42} = \frac{1}{6}$ **39.** $\frac{12}{x} = \frac{2}{9}$ **40.** $\frac{7}{x} = \frac{49}{70}$

Geometry What fraction of the large rectangle's area is shaded red? Write the answer in simplest form.

41.
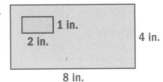

42.
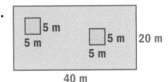

What do you think?

Games

■ **Chess**

In 2000, some historians said that the game of chess had been around for close to 1900 years. If they are correct, when was the game of chess first played?

Critical Thinking Tell whether the statement is *always*, *sometimes*, or *never* true.

43. An equivalent fraction has a smaller denominator than the original fraction.

44. A fraction in simplest form has a smaller denominator than an equivalent fraction that is not in simplest form.

Challenge Write the fraction in simplest form.

45. $\frac{76}{104}$ **46.** $\frac{180}{222}$ **47.** $\frac{95}{245}$ **48.** $\frac{207}{270}$

Mixed Review

Find the GCF of the numbers. *(Lesson 5.2)*

49. 12, 34   **50.** 14, 42   **51.** 36, 40   **52.** 18, 36, 90

Choose a Strategy Use a strategy from the list to solve the following problem. Explain your choice of strategy.

53. The denominator of a fraction is 8 more than the numerator. The denominator is also 3 times the numerator. Find the fraction.

Problem Solving Strategies
- Guess, Check, and Revise
- Make a Table
- Solve a Simpler Problem
- Look for a Pattern

Basic Skills **Find the product.**

54. 10×12 **55.** 100×12 **56.** 1000×12 **57.** $10,000 \times 12$

Test-Taking Practice

58. Multiple Choice Which fraction model does *not* equal $\frac{2}{3}$?

A.   **B.**   **C.**   **D.**

59. Multiple Choice Alaska and Hawaii are not part of the 48 contiguous states in the United States. What fraction of the 50 states are not part of the 48 contiguous states?

F. $\frac{46}{48}$ **G.** $\frac{48}{50}$ **H.** $\frac{2}{48}$ **I.** $\frac{1}{25}$

Notebook Review

Review the vocabulary definitions in your notebook.

Copy the review examples in your notebook. Then complete the exercises.

Check Your Definitions

divisible, p. 214
prime number, p. 215
composite number, p. 215
prime factorization, p. 216

factor tree, p. 216
common factor, p. 222
greatest common factor (GCF), p. 222

fraction, p. 228
equivalent fractions, p. 228
simplest form, p. 229

Use Your Vocabulary

1. Copy and complete: A ? is a whole number greater than 1 whose only factors are 1 and itself.

2. Copy and complete: The factors of 9 are 1, ?, and ?. So, 9 is a ?.

5.1–5.2 Can you use divisibility rules and find factors?

 EXAMPLE Test 574 for divisibility by 2, 3, 5, 6, 9, and 10.

574 is even, so it is divisible by 2.

$5 + 7 + 4 = 16$, which is not divisible by 3 or 9, so 574 is not either.

574 does not end with 0 or 5, so it is not divisible by 5 or 10.

574 is not divisible by 6 because it is not divisible by 3.

 Test the number for divisibility by 2, 3, 5, 6, 9, and 10.

3. 49   **4.** 252   **5.** 396   **6.** 1402

 EXAMPLE Find the greatest common factor (GCF) of 90 and 126.

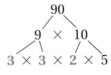

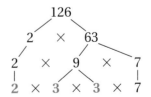

ANSWER The GCF of 90 and 126 is $2 \times 3 \times 3$, or 18.

 Find the GCF.   **7.** 48, 84   **8.** 54, 81

5.3 Can you simplify fractions?

EXAMPLE Use the GCF to write the fraction in simplest form.

a. $\dfrac{6}{24} = \dfrac{1 \times \cancel{6}^{1}}{4 \times \cancel{6}_{1}} = \dfrac{1}{4}$ GCF is 6.   **b.** $\dfrac{15}{33} = \dfrac{5 \times \cancel{3}^{1}}{11 \times \cancel{3}_{1}} = \dfrac{5}{11}$ GCF is 3.

☑ **Write the fraction in simplest form.**

9. $\dfrac{3}{21}$ **10.** $\dfrac{18}{27}$ **11.** $\dfrac{10}{32}$ **12.** $\dfrac{20}{45}$

Stop and Think   about Lessons 5.1–5.3

13. Critical Thinking Why is it helpful to know divisibility rules when finding factors of a number?

14. Writing Write two numbers whose GCF is 8. Explain how you found the answer.

Review Quiz 1

Test the number for divisibility by 2, 3, 5, 6, 9, and 10. Then tell whether the number is *prime* or *composite*.

1. 54   **2.** 77   **3.** 405   **4.** 1270

Write the prime factorization of the number.

5. 34   **6.** 48   **7.** 164   **8.** 840

Find the GCF of the numbers.

9. 7, 56   **10.** 10, 21   **11.** 42, 90   **12.** 8, 40, 54

13. Field Trip Three science classes go on a field trip to an observatory. The classes spend $75, $54, and $96 for student admission. Find the greatest possible student admission price for the observatory.

14. Copy and complete: $\dfrac{6}{11} = \dfrac{?}{55}$.

Write the fraction in simplest form.

15. $\dfrac{6}{45}$ **16.** $\dfrac{10}{110}$ **17.** $\dfrac{14}{50}$ **18.** $\dfrac{39}{130}$

LESSON 5.4

Least Common Multiple

BEFORE

You found greatest common factors.

▶ **Now**

You'll find least common multiples.

WHY?

So you can coordinate schedules, as with the soccer games in Ex. 7.

In the Real World

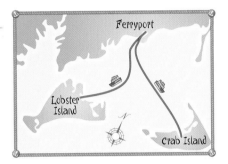

Word Watch

multiple, p. 235
common multiple, p. 235
least common multiple (LCM), p. 236

Ferry Boats Two ferry boats leave a loading platform at the same time. One of the ferry boats returns to the loading platform every 25 minutes. The other returns every 30 minutes. In the next 300 minutes, when will they return at the same time?

You can use *multiples* to answer the question above. A **multiple** of a number is the product of the number and any nonzero whole number.

The three dots show that the pattern continues forever.

Multiples of 2: 2, 4, 6, 8, 10, 12, 14, . . .

A multiple shared by two or more numbers is a **common multiple**.

EXAMPLE 1 **Finding a Common Multiple**

You can use common multiples to answer the question above about ferry boats. Begin by writing the multiples of 25 and 30. Then identify common multiples through 300.

Multiples of 25: 25, 50, 75, 100, 125, **150**, 175, 200, 225, 250, 275, **300**

Multiples of 30: 30, 60, 90, 120, **150**, 180, 210, 240, 270, **300**

The common multiples of 25 and 30 are 150 and 300.

ANSWER The ferry boats will return to the loading platform at the same time in 150 minutes and in 300 minutes.

Your turn now Find two common multiples of the numbers.

1. 2, 3   **2.** 3, 5   **3.** 8, 10   **4.** 6, 18

5. A cuckoo clock has birds that pop out of their nests every 6 minutes and dancers that pop out every 15 minutes. Suppose that the birds and dancers have just popped out at the same time. When will this happen again in the next 60 minutes?

Finding the Least Common Multiple (LCM)

The **least common multiple** of two or more numbers is the smallest of the common multiples. Below are two methods to find the LCM.

Method 1: Start listing the multiples of each number. Then find the smallest of the common multiples.

Method 2: Write the prime factorizations of the numbers. Multiply together the prime factors, using each prime factor the greatest number of times it is a factor of any of the numbers.

with Solving

If the only common factor of two numbers is 1, then their least common multiple is the product of the two numbers.

EXAMPLE 2 Finding the LCM

Find the LCM of 9 and 12.

Multiples of 9: 9, 18, 27, **36**, 45, 54, . . .

Multiples of 12: 12, 24, **36**, 48, . . .

ANSWER The LCM of 9 and 12 is 36.

EXAMPLE 3 Using Prime Factorization

Find the LCM of 42 and 60 using prime factorization.

(1 Write the prime factorizations. Circle any common factors.

$$42 = 2 \times 3 \times 7$$
$$60 = 2 \times 2 \times 3 \times 5$$

(2 Multiply together the prime factors, using each circled factor the greatest number of times it occurs in either factorization.

$$2 \times 2 \times 3 \times 5 \times 7 = 420$$

ANSWER The LCM of 42 and 60 is 420.

Your turn now Find the LCM of the numbers.

6. 8, 12   **7.** 7, 8, 14   **8.** 50, 90

Getting Ready to Practice

Vocabulary **List the first three multiples of the number.**

1. 7   **2.** 8   **3.** 11   **4.** 16

Use the prime factorizations to find the LCM of the numbers.

5. $32 = 2 \times 2 \times 2 \times 2 \times 2$ **6.** $48 = 2 \times 2 \times 2 \times 2 \times 3$

$24 = 2 \times 2 \times 2 \times 3$ $56 = 2 \times 2 \times 2 \times 7$

7. **Guided Problem Solving** You bring the drinks for your soccer team every sixth game. Every third game is a home game. When will you first bring the drinks to a home game? If there are 20 games in a season, how many times will you bring the drinks to a home game this season?

(**1** List the multiples of 6 and 3.

(**2** Find the common multiples of 6 and 3 from 1 to 20.

(**3** Use the results of Step 2 to answer the questions being asked.

Practice and Problem Solving

Find the LCM of the numbers by listing multiples.

8. 3, 7   **9.** 5, 8   **10.** 6, 10   **11.** 10, 12

12. 3, 6, 9   **13.** 4, 8, 16   **14.** 2, 3, 5   **15.** 4, 9, 24

16. **Find the Error** Describe and correct the error in finding the LCM of 24 and 36.

$24 = 2 \times 2 \times 2 \times 3$
$36 = 2 \times 2 \times 3 \times 3$
The LCM of 24 and 36 is $2 \times 2 \times 3 = 12$.

with Homework

Example	Exercises
1	8–15, 25
2	8–15, 25
3	16–25

Online Resources
CLASSZONE.COM
· More Examples
· eTutorial Plus

Find the LCM of the numbers using prime factorization.

17. 21, 28   **18.** 30, 42   **19.** 22, 36   **20.** 32, 40

21. 27, 45   **22.** 56, 64   **23.** 60, 72   **24.** 50, 75

25. **Writing** A store gives every 20th customer a $20 gift certificate. Every 75th customer gets a $75 gift certificate. Which customer will be the first to receive both types of gift certificates? Explain how you found your answer.

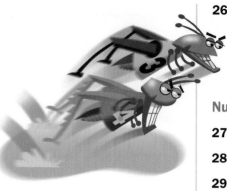

26. Insects A cricket and a grasshopper are in a jumping contest. The cricket jumps three inches every jump and the grasshopper jumps four inches every jump. Name 4 points where the cricket and the grasshopper will both land. How many jumps will it take each of them to land at these points?

Number Sense **Find a pair of numbers that matches the description.**

27. The LCM of two prime numbers is 51.

28. The LCM of two numbers is 48. Their sum is 19.

29. The LCM of two numbers is 16. Their product is 64.

30. Challenge Find the GCF and the LCM of 6 and 12. How does the product of the GCF and the LCM compare to the product of 6 and 12? Try several pairs of numbers. What does this suggest about the product of two whole numbers and the product of their GCF and LCM?

Mixed Review

31. Write *two and fifty-six thousandths* as a decimal. *(Lesson 3.1)*

Find the quotient. *(Lesson 4.6)*

32. $20.44 \div 0.56$ **33.** $13.08 \div 0.24$ **34.** $1.76 \div 5.5$ **35.** $1.8 \div 7.2$

Write two fractions that are equivalent to the given fraction. *(Lesson 5.3)*

36. $\frac{1}{8}$ **37.** $\frac{3}{10}$ **38.** $\frac{5}{12}$ **39.** $\frac{12}{17}$

Basic Skills **Copy and complete the statement with <, >, or =.**

40. $416 \underline{\ ?\ } 419$ **41.** $680 \underline{\ ?\ } 68$ **42.** $32 \underline{\ ?\ } 352$ **43.** $36 \underline{\ ?\ } 390$

Test-Taking Practice

44. Multiple Choice What is the least common multiple of 10 and 3?

   A. 1 **B.** 13 **C.** 30 **D.** 60

45. Short Response Pencils come in packages of 10. Rulers come in packages of 8. Hannah wants exactly one pencil for every ruler. What is the smallest number of packages of each she will need to buy? Explain how you found your answer.

Ordering Fractions

BEFORE	▶ Now	WHY?
You compared and ordered decimals.	You'll compare and order fractions.	So you can compare measures, such as sizes of wrenches in Example 3.

Word Watch

least common denominator (LCD), p. 239

Activity You can use models to compare $\frac{3}{4}$ and $\frac{7}{8}$.

1. Fold one piece of paper into fourths and another piece of paper into eighths as shown.

2. Shade $\frac{3}{4}$ of the first piece and $\frac{7}{8}$ of the second piece.

3. Compare the shaded regions. Because the shaded region for $\frac{3}{4}$ is smaller than the shaded region for $\frac{7}{8}$, you can see that $\frac{3}{4} < \frac{7}{8}$.

Use models to copy and complete the statement with <, >, or =.

1. $\frac{1}{2}$? $\frac{1}{4}$ 2. $\frac{1}{4}$? $\frac{1}{3}$ 3. $\frac{2}{4}$? $\frac{2}{3}$ 4. $\frac{3}{4}$? $\frac{2}{3}$

Least Common Denominator You can use models to compare fractions or you can use the *least common denominator* to write equivalent fractions. The **least common denominator (LCD)** of two or more fractions is the least common multiple of the denominators.

EXAMPLE 1 **Comparing Fractions Using the LCD**

Compare $\frac{5}{6}$ and $\frac{7}{9}$.

1. Find the LCD: Because the LCM of 6 and 9 is 18, the LCD is 18.

2. Use the LCD to write equivalent fractions.

$$\frac{5}{6} = \frac{5 \times 3}{6 \times 3} = \frac{15}{18} \qquad \frac{7}{9} = \frac{7 \times 2}{9 \times 2} = \frac{14}{18}$$

3. Compare: Because 15 > 14, you know that $\frac{15}{18} > \frac{14}{18}$. So, $\frac{5}{6} > \frac{7}{9}$.

HELP with Solving

You can use any common denominator to compare two fractions, but it is usually easiest to use the LCD.

EXAMPLE **2** **Ordering Fractions**

Order the fractions $\frac{3}{10}$, $\frac{2}{5}$, $\frac{1}{4}$ from least to greatest.

① Find the LCD: Because the LCM of 10, 5, and 4 is 20, the LCD is 20.

② Use the LCD to write equivalent fractions.

$$\frac{3}{10} = \frac{3 \times 2}{10 \times 2} = \frac{6}{20} \qquad \frac{2}{5} = \frac{2 \times 4}{5 \times 4} = \frac{8}{20} \qquad \frac{1}{4} = \frac{1 \times 5}{4 \times 5} = \frac{5}{20}$$

③ Compare: Because $\frac{5}{20} < \frac{6}{20}$, you know that $\frac{1}{4} < \frac{3}{10}$.

Because $\frac{6}{20} < \frac{8}{20}$, you know that $\frac{3}{10} < \frac{2}{5}$.

ANSWER The fractions, from least to greatest, are $\frac{1}{4}$, $\frac{3}{10}$, and $\frac{2}{5}$.

Your turn now Order the fractions from least to greatest.

1. $\frac{7}{12}$, $\frac{5}{9}$, $\frac{2}{3}$

2. $\frac{1}{3}$, $\frac{2}{9}$, $\frac{3}{7}$

3. $\frac{1}{5}$, $\frac{3}{10}$, $\frac{7}{15}$

EXAMPLE **3** **Ordering Fractions to Solve a Problem**

Wrench Sizes You are making repairs to your bicycle. You grab a $\frac{1}{2}$ inch wrench from the toolbox, then realize it is too small. Should you try a $\frac{5}{8}$ inch wrench or a $\frac{7}{16}$ inch wrench?

Solution

Order the fractions from least to greatest.

① Find the LCD: Because the LCM of 2, 8, and 16 is 16, the LCD is 16.

② Use the LCD to write equivalent fractions.

$$\frac{1}{2} = \frac{1 \times 8}{2 \times 8} = \frac{8}{16} \qquad \frac{5}{8} = \frac{5 \times 2}{8 \times 2} = \frac{10}{16} \qquad \frac{7}{16}$$

③ Order the fractions: The fractions, from least to greatest, are $\frac{7}{16}$, $\frac{1}{2}$, and $\frac{5}{8}$.

ANSWER You should try the $\frac{5}{8}$ inch wrench.

5.5 Exercises

More Practice, p. 712

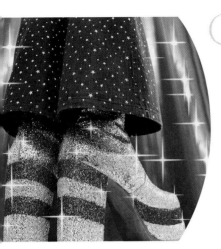

Getting Ready to Practice

1. **Vocabulary** What is a *least common denominator*?

Find the LCD. Then copy and complete the statement with <, >, or =.

2. $\frac{5}{7}$? $\frac{6}{7}$ 3. $\frac{1}{3}$? $\frac{1}{6}$ 4. $\frac{9}{21}$? $\frac{3}{7}$ 5. $\frac{3}{5}$? $\frac{3}{4}$

6. **Shoes** The heights of the heels on three pairs of shoes in a catalog are $\frac{1}{2}$ inch, $\frac{3}{8}$ inch, and $\frac{3}{4}$ inch. Order the heights from least to greatest.

Practice and Problem Solving

Copy and complete the statement with <, >, or =.

7. $\frac{5}{9}$? $\frac{2}{9}$ 8. $\frac{2}{11}$? $\frac{4}{11}$ 9. $\frac{3}{7}$? $\frac{4}{11}$ 10. $\frac{2}{5}$? $\frac{6}{15}$

11. $\frac{1}{6}$? $\frac{1}{8}$ 12. $\frac{2}{3}$? $\frac{5}{7}$ 13. $\frac{5}{8}$? $\frac{2}{3}$ 14. $\frac{5}{6}$? $\frac{3}{4}$

15. $\frac{8}{18}$? $\frac{4}{9}$ 16. $\frac{11}{15}$? $\frac{7}{9}$ 17. $\frac{3}{4}$? $\frac{5}{7}$ 18. $\frac{5}{18}$? $\frac{4}{15}$

19. **Photo Albums** You have two photo albums. One is $\frac{13}{16}$ inch thick, and the other is $\frac{7}{8}$ inch thick. Which one is thicker?

Order the fractions from least to greatest.

20. $\frac{6}{11}, \frac{8}{11}, \frac{5}{11}$ 21. $\frac{3}{4}, \frac{2}{3}, \frac{5}{8}$ 22. $\frac{7}{9}, \frac{5}{6}, \frac{13}{18}$ 23. $\frac{9}{10}, \frac{17}{20}, \frac{4}{5}$

24. $\frac{8}{14}, \frac{11}{28}, \frac{3}{7}$ 25. $\frac{5}{9}, \frac{3}{4}, \frac{7}{12}$ 26. $\frac{7}{10}, \frac{14}{25}, \frac{1}{2}$ 27. $\frac{3}{8}, \frac{11}{24}, \frac{4}{9}$

28. **Writing** Write and solve a real-world problem that involves ordering three fractions. Make one of the denominators a multiple of the others.

29. **Gold** Jewelry made of 14 carat gold is 14 parts gold and 10 parts other metals, or $\frac{14}{24}$ gold. You are looking at three bracelets that are $\frac{1}{2}$, $\frac{5}{12}$, and $\frac{2}{3}$ gold. Which bracelet contains the most gold?

HELP with Homework

Example	Exercises
1	7–19
2	20–27
3	28–29

Online Resources
CLASSZONE.COM

· More Examples
· eTutorial Plus

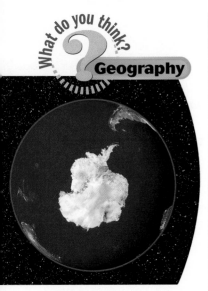
Continents The table shows the fraction of Earth's total land area covered by each continent. Which continent has the greater land area?

Continent	Africa	Antarctica	Asia	Australia	Europe	North America	South America
Fraction of Land Area	$\frac{1}{5}$	$\frac{1}{10}$	$\frac{3}{10}$	$\frac{1}{20}$	$\frac{7}{100}$	$\frac{4}{25}$	$\frac{3}{25}$

30. Asia or Africa

31. North America or Africa

32. Europe or Australia

33. South America or Antarctica

34. Order the continents from smallest to largest.

35. Challenge How could you compare two fractions whose numerators are the same, such as $\frac{2}{7}$ and $\frac{2}{5}$, without changing them to equivalent fractions with the same denominator? Explain your reasoning.

■ **Continents**

The continent of Antarctica, seen here from space, is almost completely covered in ice. If all of Antarctica's ice sheets melted at once, the Earth's oceans would rise about 60 meters everywhere! About how many feet would the oceans rise?

Mixed Review

Copy and complete the statement. *(Lesson 4.8)*

36. $10 \text{ mg} = \underline{\ ?\ } \text{ g}$ **37.** $12 \text{ kg} = \underline{\ ?\ } \text{ g}$ **38.** $15 \text{ L} = \underline{\ ?\ } \text{ kL}$

Write the fraction in simplest form. *(Lesson 5.3)*

39. $\frac{7}{28}$ **40.** $\frac{12}{20}$ **41.** $\frac{16}{40}$ **42.** $\frac{10}{42}$

Basic Skills **Find the difference.**

43. $286 - 149$ **44.** $507 - 376$ **45.** $3200 - 1798$ **46.** $2050 - 1271$

Test-Taking Practice

INTERNET
State Test Practice
CLASSZONE.COM

47. Extended Response Jeff uses a different paintbrush for each color of a painting. For the red paint, he uses a $\frac{7}{16}$ inch paintbrush. For the blue paint, he uses a $\frac{3}{8}$ inch paintbrush. For the green paint, he uses a $\frac{1}{4}$ inch paintbrush. Is the red or green paintbrush larger? Is the blue or green paintbrush larger? Order the paintbrushes from smallest to largest. Show your work.

GOAL

Read fractions of an inch on a ruler and express them numerically.

MATERIALS

• ruler

Measuring Fractions of an Inch

The marks on a ruler represent different fractions of an inch.

Explore **Use a ruler to tell how many fourths are in 1 inch.**

1 Count the number of fourths in 1 inch.

2 Write the result of Step 1 as a fraction:

1 inch $= \dfrac{4}{4}$ inch.

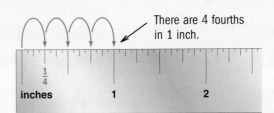

There are 4 fourths in 1 inch.

Your turn now **Follow Steps 1 and 2 above to copy and complete the table.**

1.

Measure	Whole	Halves	Fourths	Eighths	Sixteenths
1 in.	$\dfrac{1}{1}$	$\dfrac{?}{2}$	$\dfrac{4}{4}$	$\dfrac{?}{8}$	$\dfrac{?}{16}$
2 in.	$\dfrac{2}{1}$	$\dfrac{?}{2}$	$\dfrac{?}{4}$	$\dfrac{?}{8}$	$\dfrac{?}{16}$
$2\dfrac{1}{4}$ in.	——	——	$\dfrac{?}{4}$	$\dfrac{?}{8}$	$\dfrac{?}{16}$

Stop and Think

2. Writing How many eighths are in $2\dfrac{5}{8}$ inches? Explain how you can answer this without actually using a ruler.

LESSON 5.6 Mixed Numbers and Improper Fractions

BEFORE	▶ Now	WHY?
You wrote equivalent fractions.	You'll rewrite mixed numbers and improper fractions.	So you can compare lengths, such as the pole vault records in Ex. 36.

Word Watch

mixed number, p. 244
improper fraction, p. 244
proper fraction, p. 245

Measuring Inches You can use a ruler to measure lengths to the nearest half, fourth, eighth, or sixteenth of an inch.

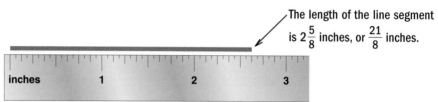

The length of the line segment is $2\frac{5}{8}$ inches, or $\frac{21}{8}$ inches.

The number $2\frac{5}{8}$, read as "two and five eighths," is a *mixed number*. A **mixed number** is the sum of a whole number part and a fraction part. An **improper fraction**, such as $\frac{21}{8}$, is any fraction in which the numerator is greater than or equal to the denominator.

EXAMPLE 1 Measuring to a Fraction of an Inch

Industrial Arts You need to measure a piece of wood for a birdhouse. Write the length as a mixed number and as an improper fraction.

Solution

First write the length as a mixed number: $3\frac{3}{4}$ inches.

Then count fourths to write the length as an improper fraction: $\frac{15}{4}$ inches.

There are 15 fourths in $3\frac{3}{4}$.

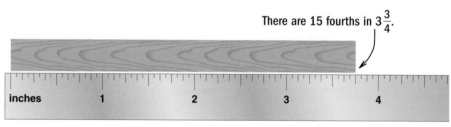

Your turn now Draw a line segment that has the given length.

1. $\frac{15}{2}$ in.

2. $6\frac{1}{4}$ in.

Rewriting Mixed Numbers In the activity on page 243, you may have seen that 1 whole can be written in different forms. You can use these forms of 1 to help you write mixed numbers as improper fractions.

$$1 = \frac{1}{1} \qquad 1 = \frac{2}{2} \qquad 1 = \frac{3}{3} \qquad 1 = \frac{4}{4} \qquad 1 = \frac{5}{5}$$

Watch Out!

In Example 2, don't forget to add the fraction part, $\frac{3}{5}$, after you write the whole part as a fraction.

EXAMPLE 2 Rewriting Mixed Numbers

Write $4\frac{3}{5}$ as an improper fraction.

$$4\frac{3}{5} = \frac{20 + 3}{5} \qquad \text{1 whole} = \frac{5}{5}, \text{ so 4 wholes} = \frac{4 \times 5}{5}, \text{ or } \frac{20}{5}.$$

$$= \frac{23}{5} \qquad \text{Simplify the numerator.}$$

Rewriting Improper Fractions You can also write an improper fraction as a mixed number. First divide the numerator by the denominator, and then put the remainder over the denominator. Make sure that the fraction part is a **proper fraction**, which is a fraction in which the numerator is less than the denominator.

EXAMPLE 3 Rewriting Improper Fractions

Write $\frac{16}{3}$ as a mixed number.

① Divide 16 by 3.

$$\begin{array}{r} 5 \text{ R1} \\ 3)\overline{16} \\ \underline{15} \\ 1 \end{array}$$

After you divide, $\frac{1}{3}$ still remains.

② Write the mixed number. $5 + \frac{1}{3} = 5\frac{1}{3}$

Your turn now Write the mixed number as an improper fraction.

3. $3\frac{2}{3}$ **4.** $2\frac{1}{4}$ **5.** $4\frac{5}{6}$

Write the improper fraction as a mixed number.

6. $\frac{22}{5}$ **7.** $\frac{34}{13}$ **8.** $\frac{41}{12}$

Comparing Numbers To compare and order mixed numbers and improper fractions, begin by writing them all in the same form.

EXAMPLE 4 **Ordering Numbers**

Baseball Bats The widths of three baseball bats are $2\frac{5}{8}$, $2\frac{3}{4}$, and $\frac{9}{4}$ inches. Order the widths from least to greatest.

Solution

(1) Write all of the widths as improper fractions.

$$2\frac{5}{8} = \frac{16+5}{8} = \frac{21}{8} \qquad 2\frac{3}{4} = \frac{8+3}{4} = \frac{11}{4} \qquad \frac{9}{4}$$

(2) Rewrite all of the widths using the LCD, 8.

$$\frac{21}{8} \qquad \frac{11}{4} = \frac{11 \times 2}{4 \times 2} = \frac{22}{8} \qquad \frac{9}{4} = \frac{9 \times 2}{4 \times 2} = \frac{18}{8}$$

(3) Compare the fractions.

Because $\frac{18}{8} < \frac{21}{8}$ and $\frac{21}{8} < \frac{22}{8}$, you know that $\frac{9}{4} < 2\frac{5}{8}$ and $2\frac{5}{8} < 2\frac{3}{4}$.

ANSWER The widths, from least to greatest, are $\frac{9}{4}$, $2\frac{5}{8}$, and $2\frac{3}{4}$ inches.

■ **Baseball bats**

Baseball bats come in many different weights. To find out which bat size is best for you, divide your height, in inches, by 3. Then add 6. This is the weight, in ounces, of a baseball bat that is appropriate for you. What is the best bat weight for you?

5.6 **Exercises**

More Practice, p. 712

Getting Ready to Practice

1. Vocabulary Explain what it means for a fraction to be an improper fraction.

Copy and complete the statement.

2. $6\frac{1}{2} = \frac{?}{2}$ **3.** $3\frac{1}{4} = \frac{?}{4}$ **4.** $\frac{17}{3} = 5\frac{?}{3}$ **5.** $\frac{11}{4} = 2\frac{?}{4}$

Copy and complete the statement with <, >, or =.

6. $\frac{7}{4}$? $1\frac{1}{4}$ **7.** $3\frac{2}{3}$? $\frac{11}{3}$ **8.** $5\frac{2}{5}$? $\frac{28}{5}$ **9.** $2\frac{4}{7}$? $\frac{20}{7}$

Practice and Problem Solving

with Homework

Example	Exercises
1	10–12
2	13–20, 32–35
3	21–28
4	29–31

Online Resources
CLASSZONE.COM
· More Examples
· eTutorial Plus

Measurement **Use a ruler to measure the candle to the end of its wick. Write the answer as a mixed number and as an improper fraction.**

10.

11.

12. Draw a line segment that has a length of $\frac{11}{4}$ inches.

Write the mixed number as an improper fraction.

13. $4\frac{1}{2}$ **14.** $1\frac{5}{8}$ **15.** $3\frac{2}{5}$ **16.** $5\frac{3}{4}$

17. $7\frac{2}{3}$ **18.** $1\frac{9}{10}$ **19.** $10\frac{1}{2}$ **20.** $12\frac{1}{4}$

Write the improper fraction as a mixed number.

21. $\frac{8}{3}$ **22.** $\frac{25}{6}$ **23.** $\frac{18}{5}$ **24.** $\frac{15}{4}$

25. $\frac{13}{2}$ **26.** $\frac{22}{3}$ **27.** $\frac{12}{7}$ **28.** $\frac{33}{4}$

Order the numbers from least to greatest.

29. $\frac{7}{2}, 2\frac{3}{4}, 3$ **30.** $\frac{23}{5}, \frac{19}{4}, 4\frac{1}{2}$ **31.** $5, \frac{41}{8}, \frac{17}{3}, 5\frac{1}{6}$

Write 1 as a fraction using the given denominator.

32. 4   **33.** 6   **34.** 10   **35.** 14

36. **Pole Vaulting** The pole vault records for four different schools are shown in the table. Which school's record is the highest?

School	Oakmont	Chester	Central	Perry
Pole vault height (feet)	$\frac{49}{3}$	$16\frac{3}{8}$	$\frac{33}{2}$	$16\frac{9}{16}$

Critical Thinking **Find a mixed number that is between the numbers.**

37. $1\frac{3}{5}, \frac{11}{5}$ **38.** $\frac{9}{2}, 5$ **39.** $3, \frac{27}{8}$ **40.** $5\frac{4}{9}, \frac{29}{5}$

41. **Challenge** Your friend is thinking of an improper fraction that is more than 2 and less than $2\frac{1}{4}$. The sum of the numerator and the denominator is 19. What is your friend's number?

Mixed Review

Evaluate the expression. *(Lesson 1.5)*

42. $20 \div x$, when $x = 2$

43. $x - 2$, when $x = 21$

44. $15 - x + 4$, when $x = 3$

45. $3x + y$, when $x = 4$ and $y = 6$

Write the decimal in words. *(Lesson 3.1)*

46. 14.1

47. 23.5

48. 64.92

49. 78.15

Basic Skills **Round the number to the place value of the red digit.**

50. 8701

51. 9900

52. 2457

53. 4391

Test-Taking Practice

54. Multiple Choice Which mixed number is equivalent to $\frac{17}{5}$?

A. $1\frac{2}{5}$ 　　 **B.** $2\frac{1}{5}$ 　　 **C.** $3\frac{1}{5}$ 　　 **D.** $3\frac{2}{5}$

55. Multiple Choice A jewelry box is $4\frac{5}{8}$ inches wide. Write this mixed number as an improper fraction.

F. $\frac{20}{8}$ inches 　　 **G.** $\frac{32}{8}$ inches 　　 **H.** $\frac{37}{8}$ inches 　　 **I.** $\frac{37}{5}$ inches

BRAIN GAME

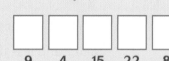

What Does it Say?

To find the saying below, write the improper fractions as mixed numbers. Find the mixed number below the number line and write the corresponding letter in the blank above the improper fraction.

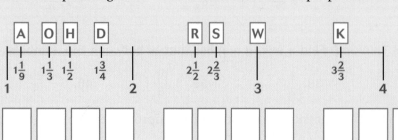

Changing Decimals to Fractions

BEFORE
You wrote decimals and fractions.

▶ **Now**
You'll write a decimal as a fraction.

WHY?
So you can find the miles you've gone on a road trip, as in Ex. 7.

Word Watch

Review Words
simplest form, p. 229
mixed number, p. 244

Activity You can use models to write decimals as fractions.

① Draw a model for 0.25. Each small square represents one hundredth. The shaded part represents twenty-five hundredths.

$$0.25 = \frac{25}{100}$$

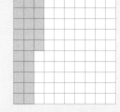

② Draw a model for 0.3. Each column represents one tenth. The shaded part represents three tenths.

$$0.3 = \frac{3}{10}$$

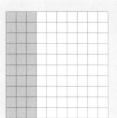

Use a model to write the decimal as a fraction.

1. 0.15   **2.** 0.35   **3.** 0.4   **4.** 0.5

 with **Solving**

With practice, you will learn to recognize the fraction form of several common decimals. Here are some examples.

$0.5 = \frac{1}{2}$ $0.2 = \frac{1}{5}$

$0.25 = \frac{1}{4}$ $0.125 = \frac{1}{8}$

$0.75 = \frac{3}{4}$ $0.4 = \frac{2}{5}$

You can use decimal place value to help you write a decimal as a fraction in simplest form.

one tenth   **one hundredth**   **one thousandth**

$0.1 = \frac{1}{10}$ $0.01 = \frac{1}{100}$ $0.001 = \frac{1}{1000}$

EXAMPLE 1 **Writing Decimals as Fractions**

Write the decimal as a fraction in simplest form.

a. $0.8 = \frac{8}{10}$ Write eight tenths as a fraction.

$= \frac{4}{5}$ Simplify.

b. $0.36 = \frac{36}{100}$ Write thirty-six hundredths as a fraction.

$= \frac{9}{25}$ Simplify.

Lesson 5.7   Changing Decimals to Fractions   **249**

EXAMPLE 2 **Writing Decimals as Mixed Numbers**

Planets The length of a planet's day is the time it takes the planet to rotate once about its axis. Write each length as a mixed number in simplest form.

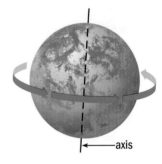

    a. Length of day on Saturn: 10.5 hours

    b. Length of day on Jupiter: 9.92 hours

Solution

   a. $10.5 = 10\frac{5}{10}$ Write ten and five tenths as a mixed number.

        $= 10\frac{1}{2}$ Simplify.

   ANSWER The length of a day on Saturn is $10\frac{1}{2}$ hours.

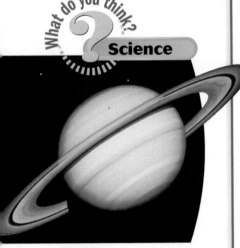

■ **Planets**

The length of a planet's year is the time it takes to revolve once about the Sun. The closer the planet is to the Sun, the shorter its year. The length of Jupiter's year is 4330.6 Earth days. Saturn's year is 10,747 Earth days. Which is closer to the Sun?

   b. $9.92 = 9\frac{92}{100}$ Write nine and ninety-two hundredths as a mixed number.

        $= 9\frac{23}{25}$ Simplify.

   ANSWER The length of a day on Jupiter is $9\frac{23}{25}$ hours.

EXAMPLE 3 **Decimals with Zeros**

Write the decimal as a fraction or mixed number in simplest form.

   a. $2.04 = 2\frac{4}{100}$ Write two and four hundredths as a mixed number.

        $= 2\frac{1}{25}$ Simplify.

   b. $0.608 = \frac{608}{1000}$ Write six hundred eight thousandths as a fraction.

        $= \frac{76}{125}$ Simplify.

Your turn now **Write the decimal as a fraction or mixed number in simplest form.**

   1. 0.4   **2.** 1.82   **3.** 2.005   **4.** 0.405

Getting Ready to Practice

1. Vocabulary Explain how you know a fraction is in simplest form.

2. Find the Error Describe
and correct the error in
the solution.

$$\times \quad 0.7 = \frac{7}{100}$$

Copy and complete the statement.

3. $0.27 = \frac{?}{100}$ **4.** $2.3 = 2\frac{3}{?}$ **5.** $6.2 = 6\frac{?}{10}$ **6.** $5.23 = 5\frac{23}{?}$

7. Road Trip At your first stop during a road trip, you record the distance
you've traveled as 128.4 miles. How could you write this distance as a
mixed number in simplest form?

Practice and Problem Solving

Write the number as a decimal and as a fraction or mixed number.

8. nine tenths

9. fifty-three hundredths

10. two and seven tenths

11. three and eleven hundredths

Write the decimal as a fraction or mixed number in simplest form.

12. 0.16   **13.** 0.72   **14.** 5.9   **15.** 9.3

16. 4.06   **17.** 3.01   **18.** 0.902   **19.** 0.806

20. 0.039   **21.** 0.025   **22.** 6.036   **23.** 9.401

In Exercises 24–26, use the graph.
The graph shows the portion of space in a
mall occupied by different types of stores.
The portions are written as decimals.

24. Which type of store occupies the least
space in the mall? the most?

25. Use the circle graph to order the types
of stores by the portion of space
they occupy.

26. Write the decimals from Exercise 25 as fractions in order from
least to greatest.

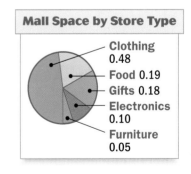

Mall Space by Store Type

Clothing 0.48
Food 0.19
Gifts 0.18
Electronics 0.10
Furniture 0.05

27. Honeybee A bee has a length of approximately 0.4708 inch. Write the bee's length as a fraction in simplest form.

28. Rainfall The normal monthly precipitation for New Orleans is 4.50 inches in April and 3.05 inches in October. Write the difference of these amounts as a mixed number in simplest form.

Challenge **Write the decimal as an improper fraction in simplest form.**

29. 2.37   **30.** 6.95   **31.** 9.86   **32.** 5.34

Mixed Review

Divide. Round your answer to the nearest tenth, if necessary.
(Lesson 4.4)

33. $8 \div 11$ **34.** $6 \div 12$ **35.** $3 \div 5$ **36.** $5 \div 9$

37. Order the fractions $\frac{5}{6}, \frac{1}{2}, \frac{11}{36}$, and $\frac{13}{18}$ from least to greatest. *(Lesson 5.5)*

Choose a Strategy **Use a strategy from the list to solve the following problem. Explain your choice of strategy.**

38. You have 2 photographs that are the same size. How many ways can you arrange them (face up and right-side up) next to each other to form a rectangle with twice the area of one photo?

> **Problem Solving Strategies**
> - Guess, Check, and Revise
> - Draw a Diagram
> - Perform an Experiment
> - Work Backward

Basic Skills **Copy and complete the statement.**

39. 5 hours = ? minutes   **40.** 367 minutes = ? hours ? minutes

Test-Taking Practice

41. Multiple Choice Which fraction is equivalent to the decimal 0.24?

     A. $\frac{1}{24}$ **B.** $\frac{3}{25}$ **C.** $\frac{6}{25}$ **D.** $\frac{12}{25}$

42. Multiple Choice A survey at a middle school said that 0.65 of the sixth grade students named basketball as their favorite sport. Which fraction represents the decimal 0.65?

     F. $\frac{3}{5}$ **G.** $\frac{13}{20}$ **H.** $\frac{7}{10}$ **I.** $\frac{3}{4}$

5.8

Changing Fractions to Decimals

BEFORE	▶ **Now**	**WHY?**
You wrote decimals as fractions.	You'll write fractions as decimals.	So you can order numbers, such as the lengths of the fish in Ex. 34.

In the Real World

terminating decimal, p. 254
repeating decimal, p. 254

Lighthouses At one time, 31 out of the 50 states in the United States had lighthouses. This can be written as the fraction $\frac{31}{50}$. How can you write this fraction as a decimal?

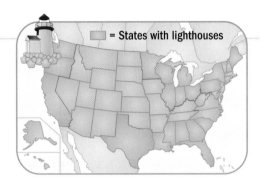

= States with lighthouses

EXAMPLE 1 **Writing a Fraction as a Decimal**

To answer the question above about lighthouses, write the fraction $\frac{31}{50}$ as a decimal by dividing 31 by 50.

$$
\begin{array}{r}
0.62 \\
50\overline{)31.00} \\
\underline{30\ 0} \\
1\ 00 \\
\underline{1\ 00} \\
0 \longleftarrow \text{The remainder is 0.}
\end{array}
$$

ANSWER The quotient is 0.62, so 0.62 of the states had lighthouses.

Writing a Fraction as a Decimal

Words To write a fraction as a decimal, divide the numerator by the denominator.

Numbers $\frac{1}{4}$ means $1 \div 4$ **Algebra** $\frac{a}{b}$ means $a \div b$ $(b \neq 0)$

Your turn now Write the fraction as a decimal.

1. $\frac{1}{2}$ **2.** $\frac{4}{5}$ **3.** $\frac{1}{4}$ **4.** $\frac{3}{8}$

Lesson 5.8 Changing Fractions to Decimals **253**

EXAMPLE 2 **Writing a Mixed Number as a Decimal**

Write $2\frac{1}{8}$ as a decimal.

(1) Divide 1 by 8.

$$\begin{array}{r} 0.125 \\ 8\overline{)1.000} \\ \underline{8} \\ 20 \\ \underline{16} \\ 40 \\ \underline{40} \\ 0 \end{array}$$

The remainder is 0.

(2) Add the whole number and the decimal.

$2 + 0.125 = 2.125$

ANSWER The mixed number $2\frac{1}{8}$, written as a decimal, is 2.125.

with Solving

With practice, you will learn to recognize the decimal form of several common fractions. Here are some examples.

$\frac{1}{2} = 0.5$ $\frac{1}{5} = 0.2$

$\frac{1}{4} = 0.25$ $\frac{1}{3} = 0.\overline{3}$

$\frac{1}{10} = 0.1$ $\frac{1}{8} = 0.125$

Types of Decimals A decimal is called a **terminating decimal** when it has a final digit, such as 0.125 in Example 2. A decimal is called a **repeating decimal** when one or more digits repeat forever. A repeating decimal can be written with a bar over the digits that repeat.

One digit repeats:	Two digits repeat:	Three digits repeat:
$0.3333\ldots = 0.\overline{3}$	$2.010101\ldots = 2.\overline{01}$	$0.4205205\ldots = 0.4\overline{205}$

EXAMPLE 3 **Repeating Decimals**

a. Write $\frac{7}{6}$ as a decimal.

$$\begin{array}{r} 1.166\ldots \\ 6\overline{)7.000} \\ \underline{6} \\ 1\,0 \\ \underline{6} \\ 40 \\ \underline{36} \\ 40 \\ \underline{36} \\ 4 \end{array}$$

The digit 6 repeats.

ANSWER $\frac{7}{6} = 1.1\overline{6}$

b. Write $1\frac{5}{33}$ as a decimal.

$$\begin{array}{r} 0.1515\ldots \\ 33\overline{)5.0000} \\ \underline{3\,3} \\ 1\,70 \\ \underline{1\,65} \\ 50 \\ \underline{33} \\ 170 \\ \underline{165} \\ 5 \end{array}$$

The digits 1 and 5 repeat.

ANSWER $1\frac{5}{33} = 1.\overline{15}$

Your turn now Write the fraction or mixed number as a decimal.

5. $5\frac{2}{5}$ **6.** $3\frac{5}{8}$ **7.** $\frac{2}{3}$ **8.** $3\frac{2}{11}$

5.8 Exercises

More Practice, p. 712

Getting Ready to Practice

Vocabulary Is the decimal *repeating* or *terminating*?

1. 0.875 **2.** 0.2$\overline{3}$ **3.** 4.2$\overline{27}$ **4.** 0.700

Rewrite the repeating decimal using bar notation.

5. 0.111111... **6.** 3.727272... **7.** 8.040404... **8.** 0.466666...

Write the fraction or mixed number as a decimal.

9. $\frac{2}{5}$ **10.** $\frac{9}{20}$ **11.** $2\frac{3}{4}$ **12.** $1\frac{1}{6}$

13. Dog Biscuits You buy $\frac{2}{3}$ pound of dog biscuits at a pet store. If the scale gives a decimal weight to the nearest hundredth, what should the scale read?

Practice and Problem Solving

Write the next four decimal places of the repeating decimal.

14. 0.0$\overline{5}$ **15.** 0.3$\overline{8}$ **16.** 3.4$\overline{12}$ **17.** 0.4$\overline{915}$

Write the fraction or mixed number as a decimal.

18. $\frac{3}{10}$ **19.** $\frac{4}{5}$ **20.** $3\frac{1}{4}$ **21.** $2\frac{21}{25}$

22. $\frac{9}{5}$ **23.** $\frac{15}{4}$ **24.** $\frac{1}{6}$ **25.** $\frac{5}{18}$

26. $\frac{8}{3}$ **27.** $5\frac{8}{9}$ **28.** $1\frac{6}{11}$ **29.** $\frac{7}{12}$

with Homework

Example	Exercises
1	18-19, 22-23
2	20-21, 31-32
3	14-17, 24-30

Online Resources
CLASSZONE.COM

· More Examples
· eTutorial Plus

Gardening Write the number as a fraction or mixed number and as a decimal.

30. A flower petal is two thirds inch long.

31. A carnation's stem is one and three fourths feet long.

32. A plant must be planted in a hole that is two and one half inches deep.

33. Watermelons About $\frac{23}{25}$ of a watermelon is water. Write this fraction as a decimal. Then find what portion of a watermelon is *not* water.

34. Fishing On a fishing trip, you catch five fish. The lengths, in inches, of the fish are given below. Order the lengths from least to greatest.

$$13\frac{3}{16} \qquad 13.25 \qquad \frac{55}{4} \qquad 13\frac{3}{8} \qquad 13.1$$

Critical Thinking *Tell whether the statement is* **true** *or* **false**.

35. If the numerator of a fraction is greater than the denominator, then the decimal is greater than 1.

36. If the denominator of a fraction is a factor of the numerator, then the fraction is not in simplest form.

37. Predict Write $\frac{1}{11}$, $\frac{2}{11}$, and $\frac{3}{11}$ as decimals. Based on your results, what would be the decimal equivalents of $\frac{4}{11}$ and $\frac{5}{11}$?

38. Challenge Write $\frac{1}{7}$ as a decimal. How many digits repeat?

Mixed Review

Round the decimal as specified. *(Lesson 3.4)*

39. 0.45 (nearest tenth)

40. 0.689 (nearest hundredth)

41. 1.9999 (nearest thousandth)

42. 6.9135 (nearest one)

Choose an appropriate metric unit to measure the item. *(Lesson 4.7)*

43. mass of a mouse

44. capacity of a water tank

45. mass of an ant

Write the prime factorization using a factor tree. *(Lesson 5.1)*

46. 38 **47.** 68 **48.** 200 **49.** 504

Basic Skills **Estimate the sum.**

50. 488 + 310 + 845

51. 1987 + 5006 + 2640

Test-Taking Practice

52. Multiple Choice Which decimal is equivalent to the fraction $\frac{21}{40}$?

A. 0.053 **B.** 0.525 **C.** 1.905 **D.** 5.25

53. Multiple Choice Janet got a hit $\frac{7}{27}$ of her times at bat. Write this as a decimal rounded to the nearest thousandth.

F. 0.258 **G.** 0.259 **H.** 0.260 **I.** 0.369

Technology Activity

Decimals and Fractions

GOAL Use a calculator to convert fractions to decimals.

Example **You can write fractions as decimals using a calculator.**

On January 29, 2001, the New York Stock Exchange began reporting all stock prices as decimals instead of fractions and mixed numbers. If the value of a stock was listed as $34\frac{5}{8}$ before the conversion, how would this value be listed after the conversion?

Solution

To convert a mixed number to a decimal, divide the numerator of the fraction by the denominator and add the whole number part.

Keystrokes	Display
5 ÷ 8 + 34 =	**34.625**

Since dollar amounts are given in cents, round your answer to the nearest hundredth.

ANSWER After the conversion, the value of this stock would be listed as $34.63.

 **with Technology**

If your calculator follows the order of operations, you can instead type

 34 + 5 ÷ 8 =

to get the answer.

Your turn now **Write the fraction or mixed number as a decimal. Round to the nearest hundredth if necessary.**

1. $\frac{5}{6}$ 　　2. $\frac{1}{8}$ 　　3. $\frac{5}{16}$ 　　4. $\frac{99}{160}$

5. $5\frac{3}{8}$ 　　6. $4\frac{11}{20}$ 　　7. $13\frac{7}{18}$ 　　8. $18\frac{9}{40}$

9. $29\frac{3}{16}$ 　　10. $45\frac{9}{32}$ 　　11. $50\frac{41}{50}$ 　　12. $67\frac{23}{125}$

13. **Stocks** The value of a stock was listed as $13\frac{3}{8}$ before the conversion to decimals. How was this value listed after the conversion?

Notebook Review

Review the vocabulary definitions in your notebook.

Copy the review examples in your notebook. Then complete the exercises.

Check Your Definitions

multiple, p. 235

common multiple, p. 235

least common multiple (LCM), p. 236

least common denominator (LCD), p. 239

mixed number, p. 244

improper fraction, p. 244

proper fraction, p. 245

terminating or repeating decimal, p. 254

Use Your Vocabulary

1. List the multiples, through 100, of 6 and 8. Is 48 the LCM? Why or why not?

2. Copy and complete: A ? has digits that repeat forever.

5.4–5.5 Can you use the LCM to order fractions?

EXAMPLE Order the fractions $\frac{2}{3}, \frac{2}{9}$, and $\frac{3}{5}$ from least to greatest.

(**1** The LCM of 3, 9, and 5 is 45. Use this to write equivalent fractions.

$$\frac{2}{3} = \frac{30}{45} \qquad \frac{2}{9} = \frac{10}{45} \qquad \frac{3}{5} = \frac{27}{45} \qquad \frac{10}{45} < \frac{27}{45} \text{ and } \frac{27}{45} < \frac{30}{45}$$

(**2** Order: The fractions, from least to greatest, are $\frac{2}{9}, \frac{3}{5}$, and $\frac{2}{3}$.

☑ **3.** Order the fractions $\frac{7}{10}, \frac{7}{25}, \frac{2}{5}$, and $\frac{3}{10}$ from least to greatest.

5.6 Can you rewrite improper fractions and mixed numbers?

EXAMPLE **a.** Write $2\frac{7}{8}$ as an improper fraction.

$$2\frac{7}{8} = \frac{16 + 7}{8} = \frac{23}{8}$$

b. Write $\frac{19}{8}$ as a decimal.

$$19 \div 8 = 2.375$$

☑ **Compare the numbers.**

4. $1\frac{1}{4}$ and $\frac{5}{3}$

5. $\frac{7}{2}$ and $3\frac{1}{8}$

5.7–5.8 Can you rewrite decimals and fractions?

 EXAMPLE

a. Write 2.08 as a mixed number.

$$2.08 = 2\frac{8}{100}$$

$$= 2\frac{2}{25}$$

b. Write $\frac{7}{9}$ as a decimal.

$$\begin{array}{r} 0.77\dots \\ 9)\overline{7.00} \\ \underline{6\ 3} \\ 70 \\ \underline{63} \\ 7 \end{array} \qquad \frac{7}{9} = 0.\overline{7}$$

☑ **6.** Write 0.65 as a fraction.

7. Write $2\frac{13}{20}$ as a decimal.

Stop *and* **Think** about Lessons 5.4–5.8

8. Writing Describe both methods for finding the least common multiple. When would you use each method?

9. Critical Thinking When comparing a mixed number to an improper fraction, is it always necessary to write both numbers in the same form? Explain.

Review Quiz 2

Find the LCM of the numbers.

1. 4, 11   **2.** 4, 14   **3.** 21, 72   **4.** 4, 6, 10

5. Order the fractions $\frac{9}{28}, \frac{3}{14}, \frac{1}{4}$ from least to greatest.

Copy and complete the statement with <, >, or =.

6. $3\frac{2}{5}$? $\frac{16}{5}$ **7.** $1\frac{17}{28}$? $\frac{13}{7}$ **8.** $\frac{28}{15}$? $1\frac{4}{5}$ **9.** $2\frac{1}{11}$? $\frac{45}{22}$

10. Write $\frac{31}{8}$ as a mixed number.   **11.** Write $2\frac{3}{14}$ as an improper fraction.

12. Write $3\frac{4}{15}$ as a decimal. Does it terminate or repeat?

Write the decimal as a fraction or mixed number in simplest form.

13. 0.56   **14.** 0.409   **15.** 1.03   **16.** 1.88

5 Chapter Review

 **Vocabulary**

divisible, p. 214
prime number, p. 215
composite number,
　p. 215
prime factorization,
　p. 216
factor tree, p. 216
common factor, p. 222
greatest common factor
　(GCF), p. 222

fraction, p. 228
equivalent fractions,
　p. 228
simplest form, p. 229
multiple, p. 235
common multiple, p. 235
least common multiple
　(LCM), p. 236

least common
　denominator (LCD),
　p. 239
mixed number, p. 244
improper fraction,
　p. 244
proper fraction, p. 245
terminating or repeating
　decimal, p. 254

Vocabulary Review

1. What is a *common multiple*?

2. What does it mean when one number is divisible by another number?

3. Give three examples of a prime number. What makes them prime?

4. Give three examples of a composite number. What makes them composite?

Copy and complete the statement.

5. Two fractions are _?_ if they represent the same number.

6. A fraction is in _?_ if its numerator and denominator have a GCF of 1.

7. The numerator of a _?_ is less than the denominator.

Review Questions

Test the number for divisibility by 2, 3, 5, 6, 9, and 10. *(Lesson 5.1)*

8. 45　　　　　**9.** 150　　　　　**10.** 522　　　　　**11.** 430

12. 780　　　　**13.** 1464　　　　**14.** 1515　　　　**15.** 2970

Write the prime factorization of the number. *(Lesson 5.1)*

16. 32　　　　　**17.** 80　　　　　**18.** 74　　　　　**19.** 108

20. 250　　　　**21.** 207　　　　**22.** 327　　　　**23.** 441

Find the GCF of the numbers. *(Lesson 5.2)*

24. 6, 45   **25.** 8, 68   **26.** 21, 75   **27.** 25, 70

28. 16, 192   **29.** 18, 405   **30.** 24, 60, 72   **31.** 13, 78, 104

Tell whether the fraction is in simplest form. If not, simplify it. *(Lesson 5.3)*

32. $\frac{7}{35}$ **33.** $\frac{36}{96}$ **34.** $\frac{11}{98}$ **35.** $\frac{22}{62}$

36. Groceries Your friend has a carton of one dozen eggs. The carton falls to the ground and three eggs break. What fraction of the eggs does your friend have left? Write your answer in simplest form. *(Lesson 5.3)*

Find the LCM of the numbers. *(Lesson 5.4)*

37. 4, 10   **38.** 9, 16   **39.** 4, 38   **40.** 35, 45

41. 8, 52   **42.** 10, 100   **43.** 4, 5, 8   **44.** 6, 9, 24

45. Watches Ana sets her watch to beep every 15 minutes. Sam sets his watch to beep every 20 minutes. If they just set their watches, after how many minutes will the watches beep at the same time? *(Lesson 5.4)*

Copy and complete the statement with <, >, or =. *(Lesson 5.5)*

46. $\frac{2}{3}$? $\frac{4}{7}$ **47.** $\frac{5}{6}$? $\frac{7}{9}$ **48.** $\frac{3}{5}$? $\frac{5}{8}$ **49.** $\frac{5}{9}$? $\frac{7}{12}$

Order the fractions from least to greatest. *(Lesson 5.5)*

50. $\frac{1}{7}, \frac{9}{56}, \frac{1}{8}$ **51.** $\frac{5}{28}, \frac{1}{4}, \frac{3}{14}$ **52.** $\frac{1}{6}, \frac{7}{48}, \frac{3}{16}, \frac{1}{8}$ **53.** $\frac{1}{72}, \frac{1}{24}, \frac{1}{18}, \frac{1}{12}$

Rewrite the number as an improper fraction or mixed number. *(Lesson 5.6)*

54. $\frac{15}{7}$ **55.** $4\frac{1}{5}$ **56.** $3\frac{4}{7}$ **57.** $\frac{23}{9}$

Write the decimal as a fraction or mixed number in simplest form. *(Lesson 5.7)*

58. 0.34   **59.** 4.8   **60.** 2.05   **61.** 0.605

Write the fraction or mixed number as a decimal. *(Lesson 5.8)*

62. $\frac{7}{8}$ **63.** $3\frac{2}{5}$ **64.** $5\frac{4}{9}$ **65.** $\frac{17}{8}$

Chapter Test

---

1. Is the number 83 *prime* or *composite*?

2. Test 116 for divisibility by 2, 3, 5, 6, 9, and 10.

Write the prime factorization of the number.

3. 28   **4.** 96   **5.** 125   **6.** 340

Find the GCF of the numbers.

7. 8, 52   **8.** 5, 16   **9.** 7, 56   **10.** 16, 48, 88

11. Write two fractions that are equivalent to $\frac{5}{6}$.

Write the fraction in simplest form.

12. $\frac{4}{20}$ **13.** $\frac{22}{34}$ **14.** $\frac{15}{60}$ **15.** $\frac{14}{42}$

16. Bagels You are buying bagels. You buy 3 blueberry, 6 plain, 5 cinnamon raisin, and 1 honey grain. Find the fraction of the bagels that are cinnamon raisin. Write your answer in simplest form.

Find the LCM of the numbers.

17. 6, 15   **18.** 10, 14   **19.** 5, 18   **20.** 4, 10, 15

21. Sports A baseball player pitches every fifth day. An opposing player pitches every fourth day. The two pitchers just pitched on the same day. After how many days will they pitch on the same day again?

22. Agriculture A farmer plants a variety of crops on his land. He plants $\frac{1}{12}$ of the land with corn, $\frac{1}{4}$ with soybeans, $\frac{3}{8}$ with wheat, and $\frac{3}{16}$ with potatoes. Which crop takes up the most land? the least land?

23. Order the numbers $\frac{17}{5}$, $3\frac{3}{10}$, $\frac{15}{4}$, $3\frac{1}{2}$ from least to greatest.

24. Water About three hundredths of Earth's water is fresh water. Write this number as a decimal and as a fraction.

Rewrite the number as specified.

25. $1\frac{7}{10}$ (fraction)   **26.** 4.3 (fraction)   **27.** $3\frac{5}{9}$ (decimal)   **28.** $\frac{22}{3}$ (mixed number)

Chapter Standardized Test

Test-Taking Strategy Look for choices that are obviously not the right answer and eliminate them first.

Multiple Choice

1. Which number is a prime number?

   A. 62   **B.** 87   **C.** 109   **D.** 129

2. Which number is divisible by 2, 3, 5, 6, 9, and 10?

   F. 120   **G.** 150   **H.** 180   **I.** 600

3. Which number is *not* a multiple of 7?

   A. 98   **B.** 112   **C.** 147   **D.** 163

4. What is the GCF of 20 and 35?

   F. 5   **G.** 7   **H.** 10   **I.** 15

5. What is the LCM of 15 and 45?

   A. 15   **B.** 45   **C.** 90   **D.** 139

6. **Tile Designs** A square tile has a side length of 14 centimeters. A rectangular tile has a length of 20 centimeters. If the tiles are laid out in a line in two separate rows of the same tiles, at what point will the rows be the same length?

   F. at 120 cm   **G.** at 140 cm

   H. at 210 cm   **I.** at 320 cm

7. Which fraction is equivalent to $\frac{7}{15}$?

   A. $\frac{70}{150}$ **B.** $\frac{14}{45}$ **C.** $\frac{28}{80}$ **D.** $\frac{56}{140}$

8. Which fractions are in order from least to greatest?

   F. $\frac{5}{16}, \frac{3}{8}, \frac{1}{4}, \frac{9}{16}$ **G.** $\frac{1}{4}, \frac{5}{16}, \frac{3}{8}, \frac{9}{16}$

   H. $\frac{3}{8}, \frac{9}{16}, \frac{1}{4}, \frac{5}{16}$ **I.** $\frac{9}{16}, \frac{1}{4}, \frac{3}{8}, \frac{5}{16}$

9. Which number is equal to $3\frac{3}{4}$?

   A. $\frac{9}{4}$ **B.** $\frac{10}{4}$ **C.** $\frac{13}{4}$ **D.** $\frac{15}{4}$

10. Which number is equal to 2.08?

    F. $2\frac{2}{25}$ **G.** $2\frac{1}{8}$ **H.** $2\frac{1}{4}$ **I.** $2\frac{8}{25}$

11. Which statement is *false*?

    A. $1\frac{11}{12} > 1.9$ **B.** $\frac{27}{10} < 2\frac{7}{9}$

    C. $\frac{23}{8} > 2.88$ **D.** $3\frac{5}{6} > 3\frac{4}{5}$

Short Response

12. Use the digits 2, 5, and 9 to write a fraction of the greatest possible value. Write this fraction as a mixed number. Is the fraction part in simplest form? Explain.

Extended Response

13. List all the pairs of factors of 60 and write the prime factorization. Describe a relationship between the prime factors and any pair of factors.

Addition and Subtraction of Fractions

BEFORE

In previous chapters you've...

- Compared and ordered fractions
- Changed between mixed numbers and fractions

Now

In Chapter 6 you'll study...

- Estimating sums and differences of fractions and mixed numbers
- Adding and subtracting fractions and mixed numbers
- Measuring time

WHY?

So you can solve real-world problems about...

Internet Preview
CLASSZONE.COM

- eEdition Plus Online
- eWorkbook Plus Online
- eTutorial Plus Online
- State Test Practice
- More Examples

Chapter Warm-Up Game

Review skills you need for this chapter in this game. Work with a partner.

Key Skill:
Comparing fractions and mixed numbers

JUNGLE FRACTIONS

If you want to be amazed, take a walk through the tangled vegetation of a jungle. This matching game involves some amazing facts about jungle animals.

MATERIALS

16 jungle cards

PREPARE The 16 jungle cards consist of 8 fact cards and 8 number cards. Each fact card contains a fraction or mixed number that is equivalent to a fraction on one of the number cards. Shuffle all 16 jungle cards together. Arrange the cards face down in 4 rows.

Some toucans have bills that are about $\frac{1}{3}$ the length of their bodies.

$$\frac{20}{60}$$

1 **REVEAL** 2 cards and read them aloud.

2 **DECIDE** whether the numbers on the 2 cards are equivalent. If they are, you may keep the cards. Otherwise, turn them back over.

3 **REMEMBER** where the cards are so you can find equivalent number pairs on future turns.

HOW TO WIN The player who collects the most cards wins.

Stop *and* Think

1. **Writing** Suppose you get a number card with an improper fraction on it. What can you predict about the numerator and the denominator in the mixed number on the matching fact card? Explain.

2. **Critical Thinking** As you learned in *Jungle Fractions,* a spider monkey's tail is $\frac{7}{12}$ of the monkey's total length. Sketch a visual model to illustrate this fact. Based on your model, would you say that a spider monkey is about twice as long as its tail? Explain your thinking.

Getting Ready to Learn

Review What You Need to Know ↺

Using Vocabulary **Tell whether the number is an *improper fraction*, a *mixed number*, or a *whole number*.**

1. $3\frac{1}{8}$ **2.** $\frac{3}{2}$ **3.** 6   **4.** $\frac{5}{4}$

Copy and complete the statement. *(p. 701)*

5. 2 hours = _?_ min   **6.** 4 min = _?_ sec

7. 400 sec = _?_ min _?_ sec   **8.** 250 min = _?_ hours _?_ min

Find the sum or difference. *(p. 136)*

9. $7.2 + 4.9$ **10.** $2.43 + 16.7$ **11.** $10.8 - 8.9$ **12.** $51.0 - 2.57$

Copy and complete the statement. *(p. 228)*

13. $\frac{3}{6} = \frac{1}{?}$ **14.** $\frac{2}{3} = \frac{?}{12}$ **15.** $\frac{2}{5} = \frac{10}{?}$ **16.** $\frac{6}{16} = \frac{?}{8}$

Find the least common multiple of the numbers. *(p. 235)*

17. 3 and 5   **18.** 8 and 10   **19.** 4 and 12   **20.** 6 and 7

Word Watch

Review Words

fraction, p. 228
equivalent fractions, p. 228
simplest form, p. 229
least common multiple
  (LCM), p. 236
mixed number, p. 244
improper fraction, p. 244
whole number, p. 684

You should include material that appears on a notebook like this in your own notes.

Know How to Take Notes

Writing a Summary To summarize a chapter in your notes, first create an outline of the chapter using the headings from the lesson. Then fill in the outline with concepts and examples from the lesson.

Lesson 5.3 Equivalent Fractions

Write two fractions that are equivalent to $\frac{2}{5}$.

$$\frac{2}{5} = \frac{2 \times 3}{5 \times 3} = \frac{6}{15}$$

$$\frac{2}{5} = \frac{2 \times 4}{5 \times 4} = \frac{8}{20}$$

You can use this tool to summarize each lesson in Chapter 6.

Fraction Estimation

LESSON 6.1

BEFORE	▶ Now	WHY?
You estimated with whole numbers and decimals.	You'll estimate with fractions and mixed numbers.	So you can estimate the length of a rocket, as in Ex. 30.

In the Real World

Word Watch

Review Words
fraction, p. 228
mixed number, p. 244
round, p. 686

Geckos The world's smallest adult reptile is a dwarf gecko that is about $\frac{5}{8}$ inch in body length. From the ruler, you can tell that $\frac{5}{8}$ is closer to $\frac{1}{2}$ than to 1.

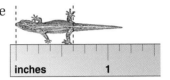

inches   1

One way to round fractions is to compare the numerator and the denominator. Fractions are usually rounded to the nearest half. Mixed numbers are usually rounded to the nearest whole number.

EXAMPLE 1 **Rounding Fractions**

Round the fraction.

a. $\frac{1}{8} \approx 0$ Because 1 is much less than 8, round $\frac{1}{8}$ to 0.

b. $\frac{5}{9} \approx \frac{1}{2}$ Because 5 is about half of 9, round $\frac{5}{9}$ to $\frac{1}{2}$.

c. $\frac{6}{7} \approx 1$ Because 6 is almost as great as 7, round $\frac{6}{7}$ to 1.

EXAMPLE 2 **Rounding Mixed Numbers**

HELP with Solving

If the fraction or mixed number that you are rounding is halfway between two numbers, you usually round to the greater number.

Round the mixed number.

a. $4\frac{1}{3} \approx 4$ Because $\frac{1}{3}$ is less than $\frac{1}{2}$, round $4\frac{1}{3}$ down to 4.

b. $5\frac{3}{4} \approx 6$ Because $\frac{3}{4}$ is greater than $\frac{1}{2}$, round $5\frac{3}{4}$ up to 6.

Your turn now Round the fraction or mixed number.

1. $\frac{1}{4}$ **2.** $\frac{5}{6}$ **3.** $2\frac{9}{16}$ **4.** $5\frac{3}{7}$

EXAMPLE **3** **Estimating a Difference**

Estimate the difference $6\frac{1}{4} - 1\frac{5}{6}$.

$$6\frac{1}{4} - 1\frac{5}{6} \approx 6 - 2 \qquad \text{Round each mixed number.}$$

$$= 4 \qquad \text{Find the difference.}$$

Real-World Estimates In some situations, you may want to round the numbers so that you get an estimate that is high or low.

EXAMPLE **4** **Estimating a Sum**

Visual Arts

Costumes You need $\frac{1}{5}$ yard of ribbon for one costume and $\frac{7}{8}$ yard for another costume. You want to know how much ribbon you need.

    a. Should your estimate of the amount of ribbon be *high* or *low*?

    b. Estimate the amount of ribbon you need.

Solution

    a. Your estimate of the amount of ribbon you need should be high so that you will not run out of ribbon before finishing the costumes.

    b. Estimate the sum $\frac{1}{5} + \frac{7}{8}$.

$$\frac{1}{5} + \frac{7}{8} \approx \frac{1}{2} + 1 \qquad \text{Round each fraction up to get a high estimate.}$$

$$= 1\frac{1}{2} \qquad \text{Find the sum.}$$

ANSWER You will need about $1\frac{1}{2}$ yards of ribbon.

■ **Costumes**

The lead actress in a play needs three costumes. Suppose each costume requires $9\frac{7}{8}$ yards of fabric.

Estimate how many yards will be used to make all 3 costumes.

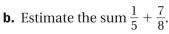

Your turn now **Estimate the sum or difference.**

    5. $\frac{7}{8} + \frac{4}{5}$ **6.** $\frac{9}{16} - \frac{1}{6}$ **7.** $3\frac{1}{5} - 2\frac{7}{10}$ **8.** $1\frac{5}{6} + 2\frac{1}{2}$

    9. An empty ice chest weighs $4\frac{1}{3}$ pounds. You put $3\frac{3}{5}$ pounds of ice into the chest. Estimate how much the ice chest now weighs.

Getting Ready to Practice

1. **Vocabulary** <u>?</u> are usually rounded to the nearest half. Mixed numbers are usually rounded to the nearest <u>?</u>.

Round the fraction or mixed number.

2. $\frac{4}{9}$ 　　　 3. $\frac{1}{6}$ 　　　 4. $1\frac{3}{8}$ 　　　 5. $3\frac{5}{7}$

Estimate the sum or difference.

6. $\frac{11}{12} + \frac{3}{4}$ 　　 7. $2\frac{7}{8} + 4\frac{1}{6}$ 　　 8. $5\frac{3}{10} - 1\frac{1}{8}$ 　　 9. $\frac{4}{7} - \frac{1}{5}$

10. **Long Lines** You wait in line for $1\frac{1}{3}$ hours for a mountain ride and $1\frac{4}{5}$ hours for a water ride. Estimate how many hours you wait in line.

Practice and Problem Solving

Round the fraction or mixed number.

11. $\frac{4}{5}$ 　　 12. $\frac{7}{10}$ 　　 13. $3\frac{1}{2}$ 　　 14. $4\frac{3}{8}$

Estimate the sum or difference.

15. $\frac{1}{6} + \frac{1}{5}$ 　 16. $\frac{6}{7} + \frac{13}{15}$ 　 17. $\frac{2}{7} - \frac{1}{5}$ 　 18. $\frac{9}{10} - \frac{1}{3}$

19. $\frac{9}{16} + \frac{7}{12}$ 　 20. $\frac{4}{9} - \frac{3}{8}$ 　 21. $2\frac{7}{10} + 2\frac{5}{14}$ 　 22. $1\frac{5}{6} + 3\frac{5}{12}$

23. $8\frac{11}{20} - 3\frac{3}{5}$ 　 24. $7\frac{2}{15} - 2\frac{1}{18}$ 　 25. $4\frac{8}{9} - 1\frac{1}{2}$ 　 26. $1\frac{3}{17} + 2\frac{1}{2}$

27. **Muffins** You have $5\frac{5}{8}$ cups of flour. You use $1\frac{1}{3}$ cups of flour to make blueberry muffins. Estimate how much flour you have left.

28. **Paint** You need $4\frac{1}{4}$ gallons of paint for one room and $3\frac{1}{3}$ gallons for another room. Estimate how much paint you need.

29. **Writing** In Exercise 28, tell whether it is better to have a *low* or *high* estimate of the answer. Explain your choice.

with Homework

Example	Exercises
1	11–12
2	13–14
3	15–28
4	15–29

Online Resources
CLASSZONE.COM
· More Examples
· eTutorial Plus

30. Rockets Estimate the total length of the Saturn V rocket shown below.

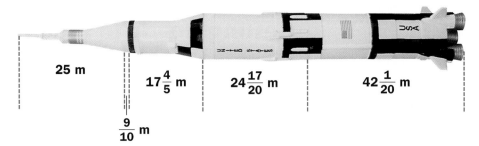

25 m

$17\frac{4}{5}$ m

$24\frac{17}{20}$ m

$42\frac{1}{20}$ m

$\frac{9}{10}$ m

Tell whether the answer is a *high estimate* or a *low estimate*.

31. $3\frac{7}{11} + 8\frac{6}{7} \approx 13$

32. $2\frac{1}{6} + 4\frac{2}{9} \approx 8$

33. $10\frac{4}{5} - 3\frac{1}{8} \approx 6$

34. Explain Suppose you round $\frac{3}{4}$ down to $\frac{1}{2}$, and your friend rounds $\frac{3}{4}$ up to 1. Explain why both answers are reasonable.

35. Challenge Describe a real-world situation in which you would always round two mixed numbers down before estimating the sum.

Mixed Review

Find the GCF of the two numbers. *(Lesson 5.2)*

36. 6 and 14   **37.** 5 and 15   **38.** 7 and 13   **39.** 12 and 18

Write the mixed number as an improper fraction. *(Lesson 5.6)*

40. $7\frac{1}{2}$ **41.** $2\frac{2}{3}$ **42.** $4\frac{9}{10}$ **43.** $8\frac{1}{4}$

Basic Skills **Find the sum or difference.**

44. $178 + 304$ **45.** $627 + 385$ **46.** $375 - 168$ **47.** $926 - 349$

Test-Taking Practice

48. Multiple Choice You run $3\frac{3}{4}$ miles on Friday and $2\frac{1}{3}$ miles on Monday to prepare for a track meet. Estimate the total number of miles you run.

A. 3 miles   **B.** 4 miles   **C.** 6 miles   **D.** 8 miles

49. Short Response You have $2\frac{1}{4}$ yards of fabric and buy $3\frac{7}{8}$ yards more. You use 5 yards to decorate your room. Estimate the total amount of fabric you have left. Show your steps.

LESSON 6.2

Fractions with Common Denominators

BEFORE	**Now**	**WHY?**
You estimated the sums and differences of fractions.	You'll find actual sums and differences of fractions.	So you can analyze a school survey, as in Exs. 35–37.

Word Watch

Review Words

mixed number, p. 244
improper fraction, p. 244

Activity You can use a model to add two fractions.

① Draw a rectangle divided into 5 squares of the same size. Color 1 square red and 3 squares blue.

② Copy and complete the following statement with the correct numbers:

$$\frac{? \text{ red squares}}{? \text{ total squares}} + \frac{? \text{ blue squares}}{? \text{ total squares}} = \frac{? \text{ colored squares}}{? \text{ total squares}}$$

Use a model to find the sum.   **1.** $\frac{2}{9} + \frac{5}{9}$ **2.** $\frac{1}{8} + \frac{3}{8}$

Adding Fractions with Common Denominators

Words To add two fractions with a common denominator, write the sum of the numerators over the denominator.

Numbers $\frac{2}{7} + \frac{4}{7} = \frac{6}{7}$ **Algebra** $\frac{a}{c} + \frac{b}{c} = \frac{a+b}{c}$

 **with Review**

Need help with rewriting improper fractions as mixed numbers? See p. 244.

EXAMPLE 1 Adding Fractions

$$\frac{3}{5} + \frac{4}{5} = \frac{3+4}{5}$$ Add the numerators.

$$= \frac{7}{5}$$ Simplify the numerator.

$$= 1\frac{2}{5}$$ Rewrite the improper fraction as a mixed number.

Your turn now Find the sum. Simplify if possible.

1. $\frac{1}{9} + \frac{7}{9}$ **2.** $\frac{1}{8} + \frac{5}{8}$ **3.** $\frac{5}{7} + \frac{6}{7}$ **4.** $\frac{9}{10} + \frac{3}{10}$

Subtracting with Common Denominators

Words To subtract two fractions with a common denominator, write the difference of the numerators over the denominator.

Numbers $\dfrac{5}{9} - \dfrac{1}{9} = \dfrac{4}{9}$ **Algebra** $\dfrac{a}{c} - \dfrac{b}{c} = \dfrac{a-b}{c}$

 with **Review**

Need help with writing fractions in simplest form? See p. 228.

EXAMPLE 2 Subtracting Fractions

$\dfrac{7}{10} - \dfrac{3}{10} = \dfrac{7-3}{10}$ Subtract the numerators.

$= \dfrac{4}{10}$ Simplify the numerator.

$= \dfrac{2}{5}$ Simplify the fraction.

EXAMPLE 3 Using a Verbal Model

Cookies A recipe for oatmeal cookies uses $\dfrac{5}{8}$ cup of raisins. You have only $\dfrac{3}{8}$ cup of raisins. How many more cups of raisins do you need?

Solution

Amount you need	=	Amount for recipe	−	Amount you have	
	=	$\dfrac{5}{8}$	−	$\dfrac{3}{8}$	Substitute amounts you know.
	=	$\dfrac{2}{8}$			Subtract the fractions.
	=	$\dfrac{1}{4}$			Simplify.

ANSWER You need $\dfrac{1}{4}$ cup of raisins.

Your turn now Find the difference. Simplify if possible.

5. $\dfrac{2}{3} - \dfrac{1}{3}$ **6.** $\dfrac{7}{8} - \dfrac{5}{8}$ **7.** $\dfrac{5}{12} - \dfrac{1}{12}$ **8.** $\dfrac{8}{9} - \dfrac{5}{9}$

Getting Ready to Practice

1. **Vocabulary** To add fractions with a common denominator, add the ? and write the sum over the ? .

Find the sum or difference. Simplify if possible.

2. $\frac{6}{7} - \frac{3}{7}$ **3.** $\frac{4}{5} + \frac{2}{5}$ **4.** $\frac{1}{10} + \frac{3}{10}$ **5.** $\frac{7}{8} - \frac{1}{8}$

6. **Guided Problem Solving** You and two friends are competing in a swim race. Your friends each swim $\frac{1}{5}$ of the race. You swim $\frac{3}{5}$ of the race. How much more of the race do you swim than your friends?

(**1** How much of the race do your two friends swim altogether?

(**2** What fraction of the race do you swim?

(**3** How much more of the race do you swim than your friends?

Practice and Problem Solving

Find the sum or difference.

7. $\frac{1}{3} + \frac{1}{3}$ **8.** $\frac{1}{7} + \frac{4}{7}$ **9.** $\frac{8}{9} - \frac{1}{9}$ **10.** $\frac{4}{5} - \frac{1}{5}$

11. $\frac{1}{4} + \frac{1}{4}$ **12.** $\frac{1}{9} + \frac{2}{9}$ **13.** $\frac{5}{8} - \frac{1}{8}$ **14.** $\frac{7}{10} - \frac{3}{10}$

15. $\frac{3}{7} + \frac{5}{7}$ **16.** $\frac{1}{6} + \frac{5}{6}$ **17.** $\frac{15}{16} - \frac{5}{16}$ **18.** $\frac{7}{9} - \frac{4}{9}$

19. $\frac{9}{14} + \frac{13}{14}$ **20.** $\frac{5}{12} + \frac{11}{12}$ **21.** $\frac{9}{10} - \frac{1}{10}$ **22.** $\frac{3}{4} - \frac{3}{4}$

 with **Homework**

Example	Exercises
1	7–22, 26, 28
2	7–22
3	23–25, 27

 **Online Resources**
CLASSZONE.COM
· More Examples
· eTutorial Plus

23. **Drawing** You finish $\frac{1}{8}$ of a drawing on Friday and $\frac{3}{8}$ more on Tuesday. How much of the drawing do you finish?

24. **Sponges** Your sponge weighs $\frac{1}{16}$ ounce when dry and $\frac{13}{16}$ ounce when you soak part of it in water. How many ounces heavier is the sponge after you soak it?

25. **Snowfall** A weather report states that $\frac{3}{4}$ foot of snow fell on both Sunday and Monday. How many feet of snow fell on the two days?

26. Find the Error Describe and correct the error in the solution.

$$\times \quad \frac{6}{7} + \frac{3}{7} = \frac{9}{14}$$

27. Bobsleds The bobsled track in Winterberg, Germany, is $\frac{14}{17}$ mile. The track in St. Moritz, Switzerland, is $\frac{3}{17}$ mile longer. How long is the track in St. Moritz?

28. Critical Thinking How can you tell whether the sum of two fractions with a common denominator is greater than 1?

XY **Algebra Evaluate the expression.**

29. $x + \frac{1}{8}$, when $x = \frac{1}{8}$ **30.** $y - \frac{2}{5}$, when $y = \frac{3}{5}$

31. $\frac{3}{4} - t$, when $t = \frac{1}{4}$ **32.** $\frac{7}{10} + m$, when $m = \frac{7}{10}$

33. $z + \frac{2}{7}$, when $z = \frac{5}{7}$ **34.** $n - \frac{4}{9}$, when $n = \frac{4}{9}$

Survey The table shows the results of a survey asking 100 students how much of their day is spent online.

35. What fraction of the students spend from 0 to 3 hours per day online?

36. What fraction of the students spend from 2 to 5 hours per day online?

37. What fraction of the students spend more than 5 hours per day online?

Hours per day online	Fraction of students
0–1	$\frac{53}{100}$
2–3	$\frac{31}{100}$
4–5	$\frac{13}{100}$
more than 5	$\frac{?}{100}$

38. Writing Write and solve a real-world addition problem in which the sum of two fractions is 1.

39. Challenge You spend one fifth of a musical rehearsal singing and three fifths dancing. Choose the equation you can use to find how much more of the rehearsal is spent dancing than singing. Then write a related equation and solve it.

A. $\frac{1}{5} + x = \frac{3}{5}$ **B.** $x - \frac{1}{5} = \frac{3}{5}$

Find the LCM of the two numbers. *(Lesson 5.4)*

40. 3 and 4   **41.** 5 and 10   **42.** 6 and 8   **43.** 12 and 18

44. Estimate the sum $\frac{3}{8} + \frac{9}{10}$. *(Lesson 6.1)*

Basic Skills **Find the product.**

45. 13×15 **46.** 26×42 **47.** 135×18 **48.** 271×39

Test-Taking Practice

49. **Multiple Choice** You picked $\frac{1}{5}$ bushel of apples today and $\frac{3}{5}$ bushel yesterday. How many more bushels did you pick yesterday?

A. $\frac{1}{5}$ bushel   **B.** $\frac{2}{5}$ bushel   **C.** $\frac{3}{5}$ bushel   **D.** 2 bushels

50. **Multiple Choice** You make a home movie using $\frac{5}{6}$ hour of family trips and $\frac{5}{6}$ hour of birthday parties. How many hours long is the movie?

F. $1\frac{5}{12}$ hours   **G.** $1\frac{1}{2}$ hours   **H.** $1\frac{2}{3}$ hours   **I.** $2\frac{5}{6}$ hours

BrAIN GAME

Fill in the Digits

- Copy the equations at the right.

- Complete each ? with one of the digits 1 through 9.

- You may use each digit only once, and each fraction you write must be in simplest form.

$$\frac{?}{7} + \frac{?}{7} + \frac{?}{7} = 1$$

$$\frac{?}{11} - \frac{?}{11} = \frac{2}{11}$$

$$\frac{?}{8} - \frac{?}{8} = \frac{1}{4}$$

$$\frac{?}{10} + \frac{?}{10} = 1\frac{1}{5}$$

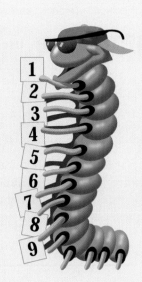

Hands-on Activity

GOAL
Model addition of fractions with different denominators

MATERIALS
· colored pencils

Modeling Addition of Fractions

You can use models to add fractions with different denominators.

Explore Use models to find $\frac{1}{2} + \frac{1}{3}$.

1 Draw a model of $\frac{1}{2}$ by dividing a square vertically.

2 Draw a model of $\frac{1}{3}$ by dividing a square horizontally.

3 Redraw the models so that they are divided in the same way.

4 Combine the models to find the sum.

$$\frac{1}{2} + \frac{1}{3} = \frac{5}{6}$$

Your turn now Use models to find the sum. Simplify if possible.

1. $\frac{1}{4} + \frac{2}{3}$ **2.** $\frac{3}{8} + \frac{1}{2}$ **3.** $\frac{2}{5} + \frac{1}{3}$ **4.** $\frac{3}{4} + \frac{1}{6}$

Stop and Think

5. Writing If you add two fractions whose denominators are 4 and 5, what denominator will their sum have? Write and illustrate an example using models.

6. Critical Thinking Without drawing a model, tell what the denominator will be when you add two fractions whose denominators are 5 and 6.

Fractions with Different Denominators

BEFORE   ▶ **Now**   **WHY?**

You added and subtracted with common denominators.

You'll add and subtract with different denominators.

So you can find how much a plant has grown, as in Ex. 23.

In the Real World

Word Watch

Review Words

least common denominator (LCD), p. 239

Activities The circle graph shows how Kate spent her day. What fraction of her day did she spend playing sports?

You add or subtract fractions with different denominators by finding the least common denominator (LCD).

Kate's School Day
- Studying $\frac{1}{8}$
- Soccer $\frac{1}{12}$
- Softball $\frac{1}{8}$
- Lunch $\frac{1}{15}$
- Classes $\frac{3}{5}$

Adding and Subtracting Fractions

1. Find the LCD of the fractions.

2. Rewrite the fractions using the LCD.

3. Add or subtract the fractions. Simplify if possible.

with Review

Need help with rewriting fractions? See p. 239.

EXAMPLE 1   **Adding Fractions**

Kate spent $\frac{1}{8}$ of her day playing softball and $\frac{1}{12}$ of her day playing soccer.

To answer the real-world question above, find the sum $\frac{1}{8} + \frac{1}{12}$.

$$\frac{1 \times 3}{8 \times 3} \quad = \quad \frac{3}{24}$$

$$+\frac{1 \times 2}{12 \times 2} \quad = \quad +\frac{2}{24}$$ **Rewrite both fractions using the LCD, 24.**

$$\frac{5}{24}$$ **Add the fractions.**

ANSWER Kate spent $\frac{5}{24}$ of her day playing sports.

In your summary of this chapter, you may want to include examples of adding and subtracting fractions with common and different denominators.

EXAMPLE 2 **Rewriting Sums of Fractions**

Find the sum $\dfrac{5}{8} + \dfrac{3}{4}$.

$$\begin{aligned} \dfrac{5}{8} &= \dfrac{5}{8} \\ + \dfrac{3 \times 2}{4 \times 2} &= + \dfrac{6}{8} \qquad && \text{Rewrite } \dfrac{3}{4} \text{ using the LCD, 8.} \\ & \quad\; \dfrac{11}{8}, \text{ or } 1\dfrac{3}{8} && \text{Add the fractions.} \end{aligned}$$

Your turn now Find the sum. Simplify if possible.

1. $\dfrac{1}{3} + \dfrac{1}{9}$ **2.** $\dfrac{2}{3} + \dfrac{1}{2}$ **3.** $\dfrac{4}{5} + \dfrac{3}{4}$ **4.** $\dfrac{5}{6} + \dfrac{7}{10}$

EXAMPLE 3 **Subtracting Fractions**

Rainfall Last week, $\dfrac{2}{3}$ inch of rain fell on Monday and $\dfrac{4}{5}$ inch fell on Tuesday. How much more rain fell on Tuesday than on Monday?

Solution

You need to find the difference $\dfrac{4}{5} - \dfrac{2}{3}$.

$$\begin{aligned} \dfrac{4 \times 3}{5 \times 3} &= \dfrac{12}{15} \qquad && \text{Rewrite both fractions using the LCD, 15.} \\ - \dfrac{2 \times 5}{3 \times 5} &= - \dfrac{10}{15} \\ & \quad\; \dfrac{2}{15} && \text{Subtract the fractions.} \end{aligned}$$

ANSWER On Tuesday, $\dfrac{2}{15}$ inch more rain fell than on Monday.

Your turn now Find the difference. Simplify if possible.

5. $\dfrac{5}{6} - \dfrac{3}{4}$ **6.** $\dfrac{7}{8} - \dfrac{1}{4}$ **7.** $\dfrac{1}{2} - \dfrac{4}{9}$ **8.** $\dfrac{5}{6} - \dfrac{3}{10}$

9. One lap of Speedway A is $\dfrac{2}{5}$ mile. One lap of Speedway B is $\dfrac{3}{4}$ mile. How much longer is one lap of Speedway B?

6.3 Exercises

More Practice, p. 713

Getting Ready to Practice

1. **Vocabulary** To add two fractions with different denominators, first find the ? of the fractions.

Find the sum or difference. Simplify if possible.

2. $\frac{3}{8} + \frac{1}{4}$

3. $\frac{1}{6} + \frac{8}{9}$

4. $\frac{2}{3} - \frac{1}{2}$

5. $\frac{9}{14} - \frac{1}{7}$

6. **Guided Problem Solving** The monkey bars make up $\frac{1}{4}$ of an obstacle course. The tires make up $\frac{1}{3}$ of the course. The tunnel makes up $\frac{5}{12}$ of the course. How much shorter is the tunnel than the monkey bars and tires combined?

   (**1** How much of the course do the monkey bars and tires make up?

   (**2** How much of the course does the tunnel make up?

   (**3** How much shorter is the tunnel than the other two parts combined?

Practice and Problem Solving

Find the sum or difference.

7. $\frac{2}{9} + \frac{1}{3}$

8. $\frac{9}{10} + \frac{1}{2}$

9. $\frac{7}{10} - \frac{1}{3}$

10. $\frac{5}{6} - \frac{2}{5}$

11. $\frac{1}{2} + \frac{6}{7}$

12. $\frac{7}{8} + \frac{2}{3}$

13. $\frac{5}{6} - \frac{5}{12}$

14. $\frac{13}{14} - \frac{1}{2}$

15. $\frac{1}{6} + \frac{3}{4}$

16. $\frac{3}{8} + \frac{5}{6}$

17. $\frac{7}{10} - \frac{1}{8}$

18. $\frac{3}{4} - \frac{1}{6}$

19. $\frac{3}{5} + \frac{1}{15}$

20. $\frac{1}{4} + \frac{11}{16}$

21. $\frac{3}{4} - \frac{2}{7}$

22. $\frac{6}{11} - \frac{1}{2}$

23. **Plants** Your peppermint plant is $\frac{3}{10}$ inch tall. After one week, it is $\frac{1}{2}$ inch tall. How much did the plant grow in one week?

24. **Find the Error** Describe and correct the error in the solution.

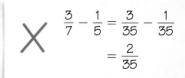

$$\frac{3}{7} - \frac{1}{5} = \frac{3}{35} - \frac{1}{35}$$
$$= \frac{2}{35}$$

 with **Homework**

Example	Exercises
1	7-22
2	7-22
3	7-24

 **Online Resources**
CLASSZONE.COM

· More Examples
· eTutorial Plus

Algebra **Evaluate the expression when** $x = \dfrac{1}{3}$ **and** $y = \dfrac{3}{4}$.

25. $x + \dfrac{1}{2}$ **26.** $\dfrac{5}{6} + y$ **27.** $\dfrac{11}{12} - y$ **28.** $\dfrac{3}{8} - x$

29. $x - \dfrac{2}{9}$ **30.** $y + \dfrac{1}{18}$ **31.** $x + y$ **32.** $y - x$

Geometry **Find the perimeter of the triangle.**

33.

$\dfrac{1}{4}$ in. $\dfrac{3}{4}$ in.

$\dfrac{7}{8}$ in.

34.

$\dfrac{2}{5}$ ft $\dfrac{2}{5}$ ft

$\dfrac{1}{3}$ ft

35.

$\dfrac{3}{7}$ yd

$\dfrac{1}{2}$ yd

$\dfrac{2}{7}$ yd

Evaluate the expression.

36. $\dfrac{1}{2} + \dfrac{1}{8} - \dfrac{1}{4}$ **37.** $\dfrac{1}{4} + \dfrac{1}{6} - \dfrac{1}{3}$ **38.** $\dfrac{7}{10} - \dfrac{1}{6} + \dfrac{3}{5}$

What do you think?

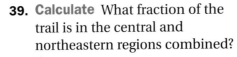

Geography

Extended Problem Solving **In Exercises 39–41, use the map.**
The map shows the fraction of the Appalachian Trail that is in each region.

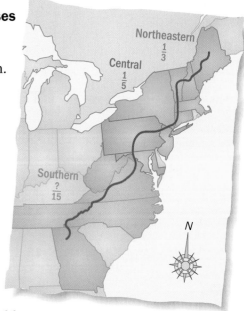

Northeastern $\dfrac{1}{3}$

Central $\dfrac{1}{5}$

Southern $\dfrac{?}{15}$

N

39. Calculate What fraction of the trail is in the central and northeastern regions combined?

40. Explain What fraction of the trail is in the southern region? Explain how you got your answer.

41. Compare Which two regions together make up the longer path, the *northeastern and central regions* or the *central and southern regions*?

■ **Appalachian Trail**

As of 2002, the length of the Appalachian Trail was set at 2168.8 miles. The Appalachian Trail is about how many times as long as the distance across your town?

42. Writing Write and solve a real-world problem in which you would add $\dfrac{2}{3}$ and $\dfrac{1}{2}$.

43. Critical Thinking Your friend finds the sum $\dfrac{3}{4} + \dfrac{1}{2}$ using the common denominator 8. Will your friend get the correct answer? Explain.

Mental Math **Evaluate the expression using mental math.**

44. $\dfrac{2}{3} + \dfrac{1}{3} + \dfrac{3}{7}$ **45.** $\dfrac{5}{9} + \dfrac{4}{9} + \dfrac{5}{12}$ **46.** $\dfrac{2}{5} + \dfrac{3}{5} - 1$

Challenge **Use the information about musical notes given at the right.**

47. What is the combined value of one eighth note, one quarter note, and one half note?

48. What note do you need to add to the notes in Exercise 47 to equal one whole note?

49. What note do you need to add to three eighth notes and two quarter notes to equal one whole note?

Eighth Note
$\frac{1}{8}$

Quarter Note
$\frac{1}{4}$

Half Note
$\frac{1}{2}$

Whole Note
1

Mixed Review

Find the sum. *(Lesson 6.2)*

50. $\frac{1}{8} + \frac{3}{8}$ **51.** $\frac{3}{5} + \frac{3}{5}$ **52.** $\frac{6}{7} + \frac{1}{7}$ **53.** $\frac{11}{12} + \frac{7}{12}$

Choose a Strategy **Use a strategy from the list to solve the following problem. Explain your choice of strategy.**

54. Of all the pairs of whole numbers whose sum is 15, find the pair that has the greatest product.

Problem Solving Strategies
- Guess, Check, and Revise
- Make a List
- Work Backward
- Look for a Pattern

Basic Skills **Order the numbers from least to greatest.**

55. 540, 455, 504, 450, 545   **56.** 1020, 1211, 1002, 1202, 1200

Test-Taking Practice

57. Multiple Choice Two boards are nailed together. One board is $\frac{3}{4}$ inch thick. The other board is $\frac{5}{6}$ inch thick. What is their combined thickness in inches?

A. $\frac{7}{10}$ inch   **B.** $\frac{4}{5}$ inch   **C.** $1\frac{7}{12}$ inches   **D.** $1\frac{3}{4}$ inches

58. Short Response You put $\frac{2}{3}$ ounce of lemon juice in a measuring cup. After you add some water, the cup measures $\frac{7}{8}$ ounce. How much water did you add? Show how you found the answer.

Notebook Review

Review the vocabulary definitions in your notebook.

Copy the review examples in your notebook. Then complete the exercises.

Check Your Definitions

fraction , p. 228

least common denominator (LCD), p. 239

mixed number, p. 244

improper fraction, p. 244

round, p. 686

Use Your Vocabulary

1. Writing Explain how to round $3\frac{1}{2}$ to the nearest whole number.

2. Copy and complete: The LCD of $\frac{3}{8}$ and $\frac{1}{6}$ is __?__.

6.1 Can you estimate with fractions and mixed numbers?

 EXAMPLE Estimate the sum or difference.

a. $\frac{4}{5} + \frac{7}{12} \approx 1 + \frac{1}{2}$

$= 1\frac{1}{2}$

b. $4\frac{5}{6} - 1\frac{1}{4} \approx 5 - 1$

$= 4$

☑ **Estimate the sum or difference.**

3. $\frac{9}{10} + \frac{2}{9}$ **4.** $\frac{7}{8} - \frac{5}{12}$ **5.** $6\frac{1}{5} - 4\frac{5}{8}$ **6.** $3\frac{3}{4} + 2\frac{1}{6}$

6.2 Can you add and subtract fractions with common denominators?

 EXAMPLE Find the sum or difference.

a. $\frac{3}{10} + \frac{1}{10} = \frac{4}{10}$

$= \frac{2}{5}$

b. $\frac{11}{12} - \frac{5}{12} = \frac{6}{12}$

$= \frac{1}{2}$

☑ **Find the sum or difference.**

7. $\frac{2}{9} + \frac{4}{9}$ **8.** $\frac{3}{4} + \frac{3}{4}$ **9.** $\frac{4}{5} - \frac{2}{5}$ **10.** $\frac{11}{16} - \frac{7}{16}$

6.3 Can you add and subtract fractions with different denominators?

 EXAMPLE Find the sum or difference.

a.

$$\frac{2}{7} = \frac{2 \times 2}{7 \times 2} = \frac{4}{14}$$

$$+\frac{1}{14} = +\frac{1}{14} = +\frac{1}{14}$$

$$\frac{5}{14}$$

b.

$$\frac{3}{5} = \frac{3 \times 3}{5 \times 3} = \frac{9}{15}$$

$$-\frac{1}{3} = -\frac{1 \times 5}{3 \times 5} = -\frac{5}{15}$$

$$\frac{4}{15}$$

☑ **Find the sum or difference.**

11. $\frac{1}{10} + \frac{4}{5}$　　**12.** $\frac{5}{8} + \frac{1}{2}$　　**13.** $\frac{3}{4} - \frac{2}{7}$　　**14.** $\frac{8}{9} - \frac{5}{6}$

Stop *and* **Think**　about Lessons 6.1–6.3

15. Estimation Do you get a closer estimate if you round a mixed number to the nearest half or to the nearest whole number? Explain.

16. Critical Thinking When you add or subtract fractions with different denominators, do you have to use the LCD? Explain.

Review Quiz 1

Estimate the sum or difference.

1. $\frac{1}{6} + \frac{9}{10}$　　**2.** $\frac{4}{7} - \frac{2}{11}$　　**3.** $7\frac{11}{16} - 4\frac{2}{15}$　　**4.** $3\frac{5}{8} + 1\frac{7}{9}$

Find the sum or difference.

5. $\frac{7}{8} + \frac{5}{8}$　　**6.** $\frac{7}{10} + \frac{1}{10}$　　**7.** $\frac{8}{13} - \frac{3}{13}$　　**8.** $\frac{11}{15} - \frac{2}{15}$

9. $\frac{5}{18} + \frac{4}{9}$　　**10.** $\frac{2}{3} + \frac{3}{4}$　　**11.** $\frac{1}{2} - \frac{2}{11}$　　**12.** $\frac{3}{4} - \frac{3}{10}$

13. Geometry Estimate the perimeter of the figure at the right.

35 yd

$12\frac{3}{4}$ yd　　$14\frac{5}{6}$ yd

$32\frac{1}{4}$ yd

LESSON 6.4

Adding and Subtracting Mixed Numbers

BEFORE	Now	WHY?
You added and subtracted fractions.	You'll add and subtract mixed numbers.	So you can find the length of skis, as in Ex. 36.

Word Watch

Review Words

simplest form, p. 229
mixed number, p. 244

In the Real World

Sports Korey is training to compete in a race. What is the total distance he will run in the race?

Adding and subtracting mixed numbers is similar to adding and subtracting fractions.

Forest City Race
Prizes awarded to top 3 in each class!

Run $2\frac{1}{3}$ mi
Bike 2 mi
Run $4\frac{1}{3}$ mi

August 2   8:00 A.M.

Adding and Subtracting Mixed Numbers

1. Rewrite the fractions using the LCD.
2. Add or subtract the fractions, then the whole numbers.
3. Simplify if possible.

EXAMPLE 1 **Adding Mixed Numbers**

To solve the real-world problem above, find the sum $2\frac{1}{3} + 4\frac{1}{3}$.

$$
\begin{array}{r}
2\frac{1}{3} \\
+ 4\frac{1}{3} \\
\hline
6\frac{2}{3}
\end{array}
$$ Add the fractions. Then add the whole numbers.

ANSWER Korey will run $6\frac{2}{3}$ miles in the race.

Your turn now Find the sum.

1. $1\frac{4}{9} + 3\frac{1}{9}$ **2.** $3\frac{3}{11} + 2\frac{5}{11}$ **3.** $2\frac{1}{5} + 2\frac{3}{5}$ **4.** $2\frac{1}{7} + 1\frac{3}{7}$

EXAMPLE 2 **Simplifying Mixed Number Sums**

Find the sum $2\frac{1}{12} + 1\frac{3}{4}$.

$$2\frac{1}{12} \quad = \quad 2\frac{1}{12}$$

$$+ 1\frac{3 \times 3}{4 \times 3} \quad = \quad + 1\frac{9}{12} \qquad \text{Rewrite } \frac{3}{4} \text{ using the LCD, 12.}$$

$$3\frac{10}{12}, \text{ or } 3\frac{5}{6} \qquad \text{Add the fractions, then the whole numbers. Simplify.}$$

EXAMPLE 3 **Solving Addition Problems**

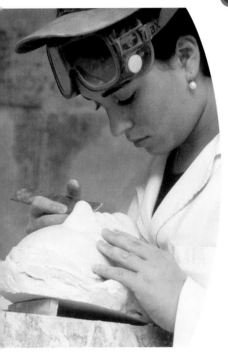

Sculpture The base of a sculpture is $1\frac{1}{2}$ feet tall. The sculpture is $2\frac{2}{3}$ feet tall. How tall is the sculpture with the base?

Solution

You need to find the sum $1\frac{1}{2} + 2\frac{2}{3}$.

$$1\frac{1 \times 3}{2 \times 3} \quad = \quad 1\frac{3}{6}$$

$$+ 2\frac{2 \times 2}{3 \times 2} \quad = \quad + 2\frac{4}{6} \qquad \text{Rewrite both fractions using the LCD, 6.}$$

$$3\frac{7}{6} \qquad \text{Add the fractions, then the whole numbers.}$$

Think of $3\frac{7}{6}$ as $3 + \frac{7}{6}$, or $3 + 1\frac{1}{6}$. To simplify, write the sum as $4\frac{1}{6}$.

ANSWER The sculpture with the base is $4\frac{1}{6}$ feet tall.

Your turn now **Find the sum. Simplify if possible.**

5. $1\frac{4}{9} + 3\frac{1}{3}$ **6.** $6\frac{3}{4} + 3\frac{1}{5}$ **7.** $4\frac{7}{8} + 5\frac{1}{4}$ **8.** $3\frac{3}{5} + 7\frac{9}{10}$

9. A clown is $5\frac{3}{4}$ feet tall while barefoot and $1\frac{1}{3}$ feet taller while wearing stilts. How tall is the clown while wearing stilts?

10. You play two piano pieces at a recital. Each piece is $5\frac{1}{2}$ minutes long. How long are the two piano pieces combined?

Mount St. Helens, after the 1980 eruption

EXAMPLE 4 **Subtracting Mixed Numbers**

Volcanoes Before it erupted in 1980, the height of the Mount St. Helens volcano was about $1\frac{17}{20}$ miles. After the eruption, the height was about $1\frac{3}{5}$ miles. What was the decrease in the height?

Solution

You need to find the difference $1\frac{17}{20} - 1\frac{3}{5}$.

$$
\begin{array}{rcl}
1\frac{17}{20} & = & 1\frac{17}{20} \\
-1\frac{3 \times 4}{5 \times 4} & = & -1\frac{12}{20} \\
\hline
& & \frac{5}{20}, \text{ or } \frac{1}{4}
\end{array}
$$

Rewrite $\frac{3}{5}$ using the LCD, 20.

Subtract the fractions, then the whole numbers. Simplify.

ANSWER The decrease in the height was about $\frac{1}{4}$ mile.

6.4 Exercises

More Practice, p. 713

INTERNET
eWorkbook Plus
CLASSZONE.COM

Getting Ready to Practice

Vocabulary **Write the mixed number in simplest form.**

1. $2\frac{6}{8}$ **2.** $2\frac{4}{3}$ **3.** $3\frac{7}{4}$ **4.** $2\frac{15}{9}$

Find the sum or difference. Simplify if possible.

5. $2\frac{3}{7} + 1\frac{2}{7}$ **6.** $6\frac{5}{6} + 3\frac{1}{10}$ **7.** $2\frac{3}{4} + 3\frac{1}{2}$ **8.** $5\frac{7}{9} + 1\frac{2}{9}$

9. $2\frac{3}{5} - 1\frac{1}{5}$ **10.** $7\frac{7}{8} - 4\frac{1}{8}$ **11.** $4\frac{5}{6} - 1\frac{1}{12}$ **12.** $3\frac{3}{4} - 1\frac{1}{6}$

13. **Frog Jumping** In a jumping contest, your friend's frog jumps $15\frac{1}{4}$ feet. Your frog jumps $16\frac{2}{3}$ feet. How much farther does your frog jump?

Practice and Problem Solving

with **Homework**

Example	Exercises
1	14–21, 28–35
2	14–21, 28–35
3	14–21, 26, 28–36
4	22–25, 27–35

Online Resources
CLASSZONE.COM
· More Examples
· eTutorial Plus

Find the sum or difference.

14. $5\frac{2}{9} + 4\frac{5}{9}$ **15.** $2\frac{1}{6} + 8\frac{1}{6}$ **16.** $9\frac{3}{4} + 3\frac{1}{12}$ **17.** $4\frac{7}{10} + 3\frac{1}{5}$

18. $8\frac{3}{5} + 3\frac{1}{2}$ **19.** $3\frac{2}{3} + 6\frac{3}{4}$ **20.** $2\frac{7}{8} + 7\frac{1}{4}$ **21.** $9\frac{7}{9} + 6\frac{1}{3}$

22. $10\frac{7}{8} - 4\frac{1}{8}$ **23.** $7\frac{11}{12} - 4\frac{1}{3}$ **24.** $8\frac{6}{7} - 5\frac{1}{2}$ **25.** $5\frac{5}{6} - 3\frac{1}{4}$

26. Find the Error Describe and correct the error in the solution.

$$\times \quad 7\frac{2}{5} + 1\frac{4}{5} = 8\frac{6}{5}$$
$$= 8\frac{1}{5}$$

27. Top Hats You use two top hats for a magic show. One hat is $8\frac{3}{4}$ inches tall, and the other is $7\frac{1}{8}$ inches tall. How much taller is the first hat?

Choose a Method **Find the sum or difference. Then tell whether you used *mental math* or *paper and pencil* to find the answer.**

28. $2\frac{5}{8} + 4$ **29.** $8\frac{1}{3} + 3\frac{3}{5}$ **30.** $7\frac{2}{3} - 5\frac{1}{2}$ **31.** $12\frac{5}{6} - 3$

32. $7\frac{3}{4} - \frac{3}{4}$ **33.** $8\frac{7}{10} - \frac{7}{10}$ **34.** $4\frac{5}{7} + \frac{2}{7}$ **35.** $3\frac{8}{9} + \frac{1}{9}$

36. Skis A 6 foot tall ski jumper buys skis that are $2\frac{1}{4}$ feet longer than his height. How long are the skis?

Algebra **Evaluate the expression when $x = 2\frac{1}{3}$ and $y = 1\frac{1}{2}$.**

37. $x + 5$ **38.** $x - 1$ **39.** $y - 1$ **40.** $7 + y$

41. $1\frac{1}{6} + x$ **42.** $3\frac{4}{5} - x$ **43.** $2\frac{3}{4} - y$ **44.** $y + 2\frac{2}{3}$

45. Currency In 1838, bank notes worth $6\frac{1}{4}$ cents and $12\frac{1}{2}$ cents were issued in Pennsylvania. What was the combined value of two $6\frac{1}{4}$-cent notes and two $12\frac{1}{2}$-cent notes?

46. Writing Write and solve a real-world problem in which you would subtract $1\frac{1}{2}$ from $3\frac{2}{3}$.

47. Critical Thinking Find the sum $3\frac{1}{4} + 2\frac{5}{6}$ using the method in Example 3. Then find the sum by first rewriting both mixed numbers as improper fractions. Compare the methods.

Ocean Tides **In Exercises 48 and 49, use the information below.**
A scientist measures the levels of ocean tides from a cliff overlooking the ocean. The high tide is $9\frac{1}{2}$ feet below the edge of the cliff. The low tide is 20 feet below the edge of the cliff.

48. Challenge Choose the equation you can use to find how much higher the high tide is than the low tide.

A. $x - 9\frac{1}{2} = 20$ **B.** $9\frac{1}{2} + x = 20$

49. Solve the equation you chose in Exercise 48 using mental math.

■ **Ocean Tides**

The tidal range is the difference in water level between a high tide and a low tide. In the Hawaiian Islands, tides have a tidal range of about 2 feet. How much less is this tidal range than the one you found in Exercise 49?

Mixed Review

Copy and complete the statement with <, >, or =. *(Lesson 5.5)*

50. $\frac{5}{9} \underline{\ ?\ } \frac{2}{3}$ **51.** $\frac{1}{4} \underline{\ ?\ } \frac{2}{7}$ **52.** $\frac{1}{2} \underline{\ ?\ } \frac{6}{12}$ **53.** $\frac{4}{15} \underline{\ ?\ } \frac{3}{10}$

Find the difference. *(Lesson 6.3)*

54. $\frac{2}{3} - \frac{1}{2}$ **55.** $\frac{4}{5} - \frac{3}{10}$ **56.** $\frac{9}{12} - \frac{1}{4}$ **57.** $\frac{7}{8} - \frac{5}{6}$

Basic Skills **Round the number to the place value of the red digit.**

58. 52,834   **59.** 185,079   **60.** 329,761   **61.** 8,905,794

Test-Taking Practice

62. Multiple Choice You add $17\frac{3}{4}$ pounds of sand to one sandbox and $8\frac{7}{8}$ pounds to another. How many pounds of sand do you use?

A. $8\frac{7}{8}$ pounds   **B.** $9\frac{1}{8}$ pounds   **C.** $25\frac{5}{8}$ pounds   **D.** $26\frac{5}{8}$ pounds

63. Multiple Choice A shoemaker has $1\frac{3}{4}$ yards of leather. After some leather is used, $1\frac{5}{8}$ yards are left over. How many yards are used?

F. $\frac{1}{8}$ yard   **G.** $\frac{3}{8}$ yard   **H.** $1\frac{1}{8}$ yards   **I.** $3\frac{3}{8}$ yards

Hands-on Activity

Using Models to Subtract

Sometimes you need to rename mixed numbers when you subtract.

Explore **Use models to find $3\frac{1}{4} - 1\frac{3}{4}$.**

1 Draw a model of $3\frac{1}{4} - 1\frac{3}{4}$.

2 You can't subtract $\frac{3}{4}$ from $\frac{1}{4}$.
Redraw the model so that
you rename $3\frac{1}{4}$ as $2\frac{5}{4}$.

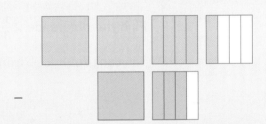

3 Use the model to find the difference.

$3\frac{1}{4} - 1\frac{3}{4} = 1\frac{2}{4}$, or $1\frac{1}{2}$

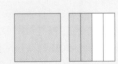

Your turn now **Use models to find the difference. Simplify if possible.**

1. $3\frac{1}{3} - 1\frac{2}{3}$ **2.** $5\frac{1}{5} - 3\frac{4}{5}$ **3.** $6\frac{1}{6} - 4\frac{5}{6}$ **4.** $4\frac{3}{8} - 3\frac{7}{8}$

Stop and Think

5. Writing Explain why you must rename to find $8\frac{2}{5} - 4\frac{3}{5}$.
Then explain how to rename $8\frac{2}{5}$.

Subtracting Mixed Numbers by Renaming

BEFORE	▶ Now	WHY?
You subtracted mixed numbers without renaming.	You'll subtract mixed numbers by renaming.	So you can study the lengths of snakes, as in Exs. 49–51.

📕 **Word Watch**

Review Words

least common denominator (LCD), p. 239
mixed number, p. 244

Renaming When you subtract mixed numbers, as in Example 1, you may need to *rename* the first mixed number.

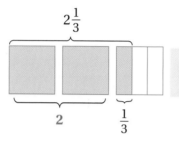

$2\frac{1}{3}$

2 $\frac{1}{3}$

Think of 2 as $1 + \frac{3}{3}$.

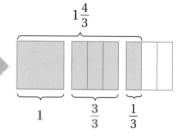

$1\frac{4}{3}$

1 $\frac{3}{3}$ $\frac{1}{3}$

EXAMPLE 1   **Subtracting Mixed Numbers**

Find the difference $2\frac{1}{3} - 1\frac{2}{3}$.

You can't subtract $\frac{2}{3}$ from $\frac{1}{3}$. Think of $2\frac{1}{3}$ as $1 + \frac{3}{3} + \frac{1}{3}$.

$$
\begin{array}{ccl}
2\frac{1}{3} & = & 1\frac{4}{3} \qquad \text{Rename } 2\frac{1}{3} \text{ as } 1\frac{4}{3}. \\[2mm]
-1\frac{2}{3} & = & -1\frac{2}{3} \\[2mm]
\hline
& & \quad\ \frac{2}{3} \qquad \text{Subtract.}
\end{array}
$$

Subtracting Mixed Numbers

1. Rewrite the fractions using the LCD.

2. Rename if necessary.

3. Subtract. Simplify if possible.

Your turn now   **Find the difference. Simplify if possible.**

1. $6\frac{2}{7} - 4\frac{3}{7}$ **2.** $3\frac{1}{4} - 1\frac{3}{4}$ **3.** $6\frac{3}{8} - 3\frac{7}{8}$ **4.** $2\frac{3}{5} - \frac{4}{5}$

Renaming a Whole Number Sometimes you need to rename a whole number as a mixed number. To do this, rename one whole part as a fraction equal to 1.

EXAMPLE 2 **Subtracting from a Whole Number**

Find the difference $5 - 3\frac{1}{7}$.

Think of 5 as $4 + 1$, or $4 + \frac{7}{7}$.

$$
\begin{array}{rcl}
5 & = & 4\frac{7}{7} \qquad \text{Rename 5 as } 4\frac{7}{7}. \\
-3\frac{1}{7} & = & -3\frac{1}{7} \\
\hline
& & 1\frac{6}{7} \qquad \text{Subtract.}
\end{array}
$$

EXAMPLE 3 **Solving Subtraction Problems**

Horses The height of a horse is measured from its shoulders, as shown in the figure. How much taller is the Clydesdale than the Shetland?

$5\frac{1}{3}$ ft

$3\frac{3}{4}$ ft

Solution

You need to find the difference $5\frac{1}{3} - 3\frac{3}{4}$. Use the LCD, 12.

$$
\begin{array}{rcccl}
5\frac{1}{3} & = & 5\frac{4}{12} & = & 4\frac{16}{12} \qquad \text{Rename } 5\frac{4}{12} \text{ as } 4\frac{16}{12}. \\
-3\frac{3}{4} & = & -3\frac{9}{12} & = & -3\frac{9}{12} \\
\hline
& & & & 1\frac{7}{12} \qquad \text{Subtract.}
\end{array}
$$

ANSWER The Clydesdale is $1\frac{7}{12}$ feet taller than the Shetland.

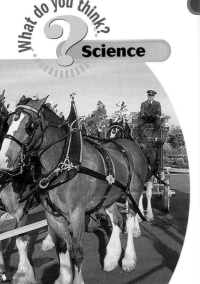

■ **Horses**

Horse heights are measured in hands and inches, where 1 hand = 4 inches. Suppose a horse is 15 hands tall. How tall is the horse in inches?

Your turn now Find the difference. Simplify if possible.

5. $3 - 2\frac{1}{2}$ **6.** $8 - 5\frac{3}{8}$ **7.** $6\frac{1}{4} - 2\frac{3}{5}$ **8.** $10\frac{2}{3} - 7\frac{5}{6}$

6.5 Exercises

More Practice, p. 713

More Practice, p. 713

Getting Ready to Practice

Vocabulary Copy and complete the equivalent mixed number.

1. $2\frac{1}{6} = 1\frac{?}{6}$ **2.** $4\frac{3}{5} = ?\frac{8}{5}$ **3.** $5\frac{1}{3} = ?\frac{4}{3}$ **4.** $3\frac{4}{7} = 2\frac{?}{7}$

Find the difference. Simplify if possible.

5. $4\frac{1}{6} - 2\frac{5}{6}$ **6.** $3\frac{5}{8} - \frac{7}{8}$ **7.** $6 - 4\frac{1}{4}$ **8.** $5 - \frac{2}{7}$

9. Unicycles Members of a unicycle club are taking a two day trip. The trip is a total of $16\frac{1}{4}$ miles. If they travel $6\frac{1}{2}$ miles on the first day, how far will they travel on the second day?

Practice and Problem Solving

10. What renaming do the models represent?

Find the difference.

11. $5\frac{3}{8} - 2\frac{7}{8}$ **12.** $6\frac{1}{4} - 1\frac{3}{4}$ **13.** $5\frac{4}{7} - \frac{6}{7}$ **14.** $9\frac{2}{5} - 7\frac{4}{5}$

15. $4 - 1\frac{7}{8}$ **16.** $9 - 4\frac{3}{10}$ **17.** $10 - \frac{8}{15}$ **18.** $7 - \frac{5}{6}$

19. $3\frac{1}{7} - 1\frac{1}{2}$ **20.** $4\frac{1}{5} - 3\frac{2}{3}$ **21.** $5\frac{1}{2} - 4\frac{3}{4}$ **22.** $8\frac{1}{3} - \frac{7}{9}$

23. Roads A road sign says that you are $1\frac{3}{4}$ miles from Exit 1 and $3\frac{1}{2}$ miles from Exit 2. How far is Exit 2 from Exit 1?

24. Pogo Sticks Your friend can jump 5 inches high on a pogo stick. You can jump $3\frac{2}{3}$ inches high. How much higher can your friend jump?

25. Find the Error Describe and correct the error in the solution.

$$4\frac{2}{5} - 1\frac{4}{5} = 4\frac{7}{5} - 1\frac{4}{5}$$
$$= 3\frac{3}{5}$$

with Homework

Example	Exercises
1	10–14; 25–33, 40
2	15–18, 24, 34–39
3	19–23; 26–33

Online Resources
CLASSZONE.COM

· More Examples
· eTutorial Plus

Number Sense Tell whether you need to rename the whole part and the fraction in the first mixed number to subtract. Explain.

26. $6\frac{1}{4} - 3\frac{1}{2}$ **27.** $7\frac{1}{2} - 2\frac{5}{6}$ **28.** $8\frac{7}{10} - \frac{3}{10}$ **29.** $8\frac{4}{7} - 3\frac{5}{7}$

30. $5 - 2\frac{1}{3}$ **31.** $4\frac{2}{5} - 3$ **32.** $7\frac{5}{8} - 6\frac{1}{6}$ **33.** $9\frac{2}{3} - 4\frac{3}{4}$

34. Blue Crabs A fisherman catches a blue crab that is $2\frac{1}{3}$ inches wide. Blue crabs that are less than 5 inches wide are returned to the water. How much wider must the crab be before it will be 5 inches wide?

Mental Math Find the difference using mental math.

35. $6 - 5\frac{3}{4}$ **36.** $8 - 7\frac{2}{3}$ **37.** $4 - 3\frac{7}{8}$ **38.** $3 - 2\frac{5}{7}$

39. Hockey A professional ice hockey goal is 4 feet tall. You buy a hockey goal that is $3\frac{2}{3}$ feet tall. How much taller is the professional goal?

40. Critical Thinking When subtracting mixed numbers, how do you know whether you need to rename?

 Algebra Evaluate the expression when $x = 3\frac{5}{6}$ and $y = 6\frac{1}{4}$.

41. $5\frac{1}{6} - x$ **42.** $x - 1\frac{7}{8}$ **43.** $8\frac{1}{5} - y$ **44.** $y - 2\frac{3}{4}$

45. $8 - x$ **46.** $4 - x$ **47.** $7 - y$ **48.** $10 - y$

Snakes In Exercises 49–51, use the table at the right. It shows the lengths of four snakes at a zoo exhibit.

49. How much longer is the green water snake than the southern ringneck snake?

50. How much longer is the checkered garter snake than the northern brown snake?

51. The glossy crayfish snake is one half inch shorter than the checkered garter snake. How long is the glossy crayfish snake?

Snake	Length
green water snake	$35\frac{5}{8}$ in.
northern brown snake	$11\frac{5}{6}$ in.
southern ringneck snake	$13\frac{7}{8}$ in.
checkered garter snake	20 in.

52. Writing You are subtracting a mixed number from a whole number. Describe how to find the fraction you should use when you rename the whole number.

Challenge Some of the tallest trees in Massachusetts can be found in the Mohawk Trail State Forest.

53. A White Pine is $47\frac{3}{10}$ feet taller than an American Basswood, which is $7\frac{7}{10}$ feet shorter than a Northern Red Oak. If the Northern Red Oak is 119 feet tall, how tall is the White Pine?

54. Explain A White Ash is $13\frac{4}{5}$ feet shorter than the White Pine in Exercise 53. Is it *taller* or *shorter* than the Northern Red Oak in Exercise 53? How much taller or shorter? Explain your method.

Mixed Review

Find the sum. *(Lesson 6.4)*

55. $3\frac{7}{9} + 1\frac{1}{3}$ **56.** $4\frac{2}{5} + 4\frac{7}{10}$ **57.** $1\frac{7}{12} + 2\frac{1}{6}$ **58.** $7\frac{5}{6} + 5\frac{1}{2}$

Choose a Strategy Use a strategy from the list to solve the following problem. Explain your choice of strategy.

> **Problem Solving Strategies**
> - Guess, Check, and Revise
> - Draw a Diagram
> - Make a Table
> - Solve a Simpler Problem

59. The perimeter of a triangle is 9.8 meters. One side of the triangle is 3.2 meters. The other two sides have the same length. Find the length of the other two sides.

Basic Skills Copy and complete the statement.

60. 8 minutes = $\underline{?}$ seconds

61. 290 min = $\underline{?}$ hours $\underline{?}$ min

62. 343 sec = $\underline{?}$ min $\underline{?}$ sec

63. 11 hours = $\underline{?}$ minutes

Test-Taking Practice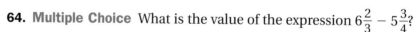

64. Multiple Choice What is the value of the expression $6\frac{2}{3} - 5\frac{3}{4}$?

A. $\frac{1}{12}$ **B.** $\frac{11}{12}$ **C.** $1\frac{1}{12}$ **D.** $1\frac{11}{12}$

65. Multiple Choice A jar contains $2\frac{1}{2}$ cups of honey. You pour $1\frac{3}{5}$ cups into a bowl. How many cups of honey are left in the jar?

F. $\frac{1}{10}$ cup   **G.** $\frac{2}{3}$ cup   **H.** $\frac{3}{5}$ cup   **I.** $\frac{9}{10}$ cup

Technology Activity

Using the Internet

GOAL Use the Internet to find information.

Example | **You can use an Internet search engine to find information about paper sizes.**

Some common paper sizes are U.S. letter (11 in. $\times$ $8\frac{1}{2}$ in.) and European A4. What

are the dimensions of A4 paper? How does this size compare to the U.S. letter size?

HELP with Technology

Your search engine may have special features to help make a search more precise. Read its Help section for alternative search methods.

Solution

Choose a search engine. Type in the key words and phrases that are likely to generate a list of Web sites that give the dimensions of A4 paper, in inches. Then examine the list of sites until you find the information you need.

Find the difference in length and in width of the paper sizes.

| "paper sizes", A4, inches, fraction | Search |

Paper size	Dimensions (length by width)
A4	$11\frac{2}{3}$ in. $\times$ $8\frac{1}{4}$ in.

difference in length

$$11\frac{2}{3} \quad \text{(A4)}$$
$$-11 \quad \text{(U.S. letter)}$$
$$\frac{2}{3}$$

difference in width

$$8\frac{1}{2} = 8\frac{2}{4} \quad \text{(U.S. letter)}$$
$$-8\frac{1}{4} = -8\frac{1}{4} \quad \text{(A4)}$$
$$\frac{1}{4}$$

ANSWER The A4 size is $\frac{2}{3}$ inch longer, and the U.S. letter size is $\frac{1}{4}$ inch wider.

Your turn now | **Use the Internet to find information about the paper sizes. Then find the difference in length and in width.**

1. A5 and A4   **2.** B5 and A5   **3.** legal and letter

Guess, Check, and Revise
Draw a Diagram
Perform an Experiment
Make a List
Work Backward
Make a Table
Look for a Pattern

Work Backward

Problem Your friend is playing a video game and pauses to take a break. After the break, you continue the game and double the current score by crossing a rickety bridge. Next you earn 30 points twice for collecting treasure. Then you lose 15 points for slipping while climbing a mountain. You finish with 155 points. How many points did your friend have right before the break?

① Read and Understand

Read the problem carefully.

- You have 155 points at the end of the game.

- You want to know how many points your friend had before the break.

② Make a Plan

Decide on a strategy to use.

One way to solve the problem is to work backward. To do this, start with the end result and retrace your steps.

③ Solve the Problem

Reread the problem and work backward.

You have 155 points at the end of the video game.

You lost 15 points on a mountain, so add 15 points to 155.

- Total points + Points lost on mountain = 155 + 15 = **170**

You gained 30 points twice for treasure, so subtract 60 points from 170.

- 170 − Points for collecting treasure = **170** − 60 = **110**

You doubled your score at a bridge, so find half of 110 points.

- **110 ÷ 2 = 55**

ANSWER Your friend had 55 points before the break.

④ Look Back

Start with 55 points and check to be sure that your final score is 155.

$155 \stackrel{?}{=} 55 \times 2 + 2 \times 30 - 15$

$155 \stackrel{?}{=} 110 + 60 - 15$

$155 = 155$

Use the strategy *work backward*.

1. **Agility Course** Your dog has a total of 335 points after 4 agility course events. The dog earned 77 points in the last event, 95 points in the third event, and 84 points in the second event. How many points did your dog earn in the first event?

2. **Lunch** You have $4.25 at the end of a school day. You spent $2.75 for lunch. After lunch, a friend gave you $1.50 that he owed you. How much money did you have before lunch?

3. **Number Sense** What number belongs in the blank?

   $(\underline{\;?\;} \div 5) \times 9 + 42 = 150$

4. **Street Maps** To get from the bus stop to the park, you walk 2 blocks north, then 3 blocks west, and then 1 block north. Which point on the map below represents the bus stop?

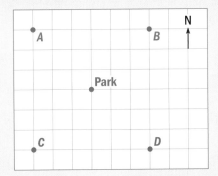

5. **Calendars** Today is Tuesday. You had a track meet 3 days ago. Your friend's party was 8 days before the track meet. Your piano recital was 2 days before the party. On which day of the week was the recital?

Mixed Problem Solving

Use any strategy to solve the problem.

6. **Sandwiches** Your friend can make 3 sandwiches per minute. You can make 2 sandwiches per minute. How many more sandwiches can your friend make than you in 10 minutes?

7. **Number Puzzle** Remove only one number from each row so that the sum of the remaining numbers in each row is the same.

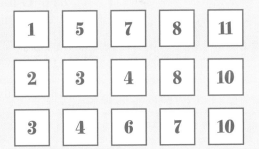

8. **Skateboarding** The mean score for your skateboarding run is 92.5. Three of the four judges gave you scores of 92, 89, and 95. What score did the fourth judge give you?

9. **Patios** The floor area of a patio is 48 square yards. You paint a 2 yard by 2 yard square at each corner of the floor using red paint. You paint the rest of the floor white. What area of the floor is white?

LESSON 6.6

Measures of Time

BEFORE	▶ Now	WHY?
You added and subtracted fractions and mixed numbers.	You'll add and subtract measures of time.	So you can study time zones, as in Exs. 26 and 27.

Word Watch

elapsed time, p. 299

In the Real World

Tour de France Lance Armstrong won the 2001 Tour de France in 86 hours, 17 minutes, and 28 seconds. Jan Ullrich finished 6 minutes and 44 seconds later. What was Jan Ullrich's time?

When you add or subtract measures of time, use the information below.

1 hour (h) = 60 minutes (min)

1 minute (min) = 60 seconds (sec)

EXAMPLE 1 Adding Measures of Time

To answer the real-world question above, add 6 minutes and 44 seconds to 86 hours, 17 minutes, and 28 seconds.

```
    86 h  17 min  28 sec
  +        6 min  44 sec
    86 h  23 min  72 sec   Add the hours, the minutes, and the seconds.
```

Think of 72 sec as 1 min 12 sec. Then add 1 min to 23 min.

ANSWER Jan Ullrich's time was 86 hours, 24 minutes, and 12 seconds.

EXAMPLE 2 Subtracting Measures of Time

```
  11 h  17 min          Think of 11 h 17 min          10 h  77 min    Rename.
 − 8 h  42 min          as 10 h 77 min.             −  8 h  42 min
                                                       2 h  35 min    Subtract.
```

  Add or subtract the measures of time.

1.   5 h 29 min   8 sec
      + 2 h 45 min 33 sec

2.   3 min 26 sec
      − 1 min 40 sec

Elapsed Time The amount of time between a start time and an end time is called **elapsed time** . To find elapsed time, think about the number of hours that pass, then the number of minutes that pass.

EXAMPLE 3 **Finding Elapsed Time**

Winter Solstice The winter solstice occurs on the day with the least amount of daylight. Suppose that on this day, the sun rises at 7:15 A.M. and sets at 4:22 P.M. How long does the daylight last?

Solution

Break the problem into parts.

(1) Find the elapsed time from 7:15 A.M. to 12:00 P.M.

7:15 A.M.   11:15 A.M.   12:00 P.M.
            4 h   45 min

(2) Find the elapsed time from 12:00 P.M. to 4:22 P.M.

12:00 P.M.   4:00 P.M.   4:22 P.M.
            4 h   22 min

(3) Add the two elapsed times.

$$\begin{array}{r} 4\text{ h } 45\text{ min} \\ +\ 4\text{ h } 22\text{ min} \\ \hline 8\text{ h } 67\text{ min} \end{array}$$

Think of 67 min as 1 h 7 min. Then add 1 h to 8 h.

ANSWER The daylight lasts for 9 hours and 7 minutes.

Watch Out!

You can't always subtract two times to find elapsed time. For example, to find the elapsed time from 8:00 A.M. to 4:25 P.M., you can't compute 4 h 25 min − 8 h. You need to break the problem into parts.

Your turn now Find the elapsed time.

3. 6:00 A.M. to 11:00 A.M.

4. 7:30 A.M. to 11:45 A.M.

5. 11:45 A.M. to 2:15 P.M.

6. 8:50 P.M. to 3:30 A.M.

7. Your bus leaves Glenwood Station at 9:23 A.M. and arrives at Park Station at 10:08 A.M. How long is the bus ride?

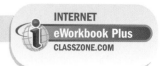

INTERNET
eWorkbook Plus
CLASSZONE.COM

Getting Ready to Practice

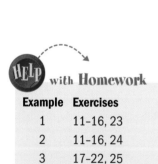

Vocabulary **Copy and complete the statement.**

1. 120 min = _?_ h

2. 3 min = _?_ sec

3. 300 sec = _?_ min

4. 4 h = _?_ min

Add or subtract the measures of time.

5.
```
  4 h 24 min
− 2 h 48 min
```

6.
```
  3 min 35 sec
+ 2 min 50 sec
```

7.
```
  1 h 25 min 52 sec
+ 5 h  5 min 30 sec
```

Find the elapsed time.

8. 7:00 A.M. to 10:00 A.M.

9. 9:30 P.M. to 2:45 A.M.

10. **Snorkeling** You went snorkeling from 9:30 A.M. to 11:15 A.M. How long did you snorkel?

Practice and Problem Solving

Add or subtract the measures of time.

11.
```
  2 h 50 min
+     35 min
```

12.
```
  4 h 38 min
+ 3 h 22 min
```

13.
```
  3 h 12 min 53 sec
+ 2 h 20 min 42 sec
```

14.
```
  4 h 25 min
− 1 h 31 min
```

15.
```
  5 h 10 min
− 2 h 55 min
```

16.
```
  3 h  2 min
−    58 min 12 sec
```

Find the elapsed time.

17. 1:00 P.M. to 3:00 P.M.

18. 2:30 A.M. to 6:35 A.M.

19. 5:10 A.M. to 9:45 A.M.

20. 1:45 P.M. to 10:50 P.M.

21. 9:30 A.M. to 5:20 P.M.

22. 11:20 A.M. to 8:15 P.M.

23. **Baseball** The first game of a baseball double-header lasts 2 hours and 35 minutes. The second game lasts 3 hours and 45 minutes. How long is the double-header?

24. **Trains** The first part of a train ride lasts 3 hours. The second part lasts 1 hour and 8 minutes. How much longer is the first part?

25. **Meteors** You watch a meteor shower from 11:50 P.M. to 1:25 A.M. How long do you watch the meteor shower?

with Homework

Example	Exercises
1	11–16, 23
2	11–16, 24
3	17–22, 25

Online Resources
CLASSZONE.COM

· More Examples
· eTutorial Plus

Time Zones The map shows four standard time zones in the United States. Each time zone differs from the next by one hour.

26. If it is 12:30 P.M. in Chicago, what time is it in Denver?

27. **Decide** Your plane leaves New York at 9:10 A.M., Eastern Standard Time. The flight lasts 5 hours and 30 minutes. Will you land in Los Angeles by 1:00 P.M., Pacific Standard Time?

Los Angeles (Pacific)   Denver (Mountain)   Chicago (Central)   New York (Eastern)

28. **Working Backward** You are playing a role in a school play that begins at 7:30 P.M. It takes you 15 minutes to get into costume, 35 minutes to do your makeup, and 20 minutes to fix your hair. By what time should you start getting ready?

29. **Writing** A movie starts at 7:50 P.M. and runs for 135 minutes. At what time does the movie end? Show how you found your answer.

30. **Challenge** You use your cell phone from 11:57 A.M. to 1:23 P.M. Before the call, you had 941 free minutes left on your calling plan for the month. How much free calling time, in hours, do you have left after the call? Write your answer as a mixed number.

Mixed Review

Test the number for divisibility by 6. *(Lesson 5.1)*

31. 42   **32.** 64   **33.** 261   **34.** 5800

Find the difference. *(Lesson 6.5)*

35. $6\frac{5}{8} - 5\frac{7}{8}$ **36.** $8 - 3\frac{4}{7}$ **37.** $4\frac{1}{6} - 2\frac{5}{9}$ **38.** $6\frac{1}{4} - 1\frac{7}{10}$

Basic Skills Find the product.

39. 4×80 **40.** 9×500 **41.** 6×300 **42.** 7×1000

Test-Taking Practice

43. **Extended Response** The first part of a plane trip lasts 3 hours and 49 minutes. The second part lasts 2 hours and 14 minutes. You have a 50 minute break between flights. How long does the whole trip last? How much longer is the first part than the second part? Explain.

Notebook Review

Review the vocabulary definitions in your notebook.

Copy the review examples in your notebook. Then complete the exercises.

Check Your Definitions

simplest form, p. 229

least common denominator, p. 239

mixed number, p. 244

elapsed time, p. 299

Use Your Vocabulary

1. **Writing** Explain why the mixed number $3\frac{1}{3}$ is equivalent to the mixed number $2\frac{4}{3}$.

2. Copy and complete: The amount of time between a start time and an end time is called __?__.

6.4–6.5 Can you add and subtract mixed numbers?

 EXAMPLE Find the sum.

$$3\frac{7}{8} \quad = \quad 3\frac{7}{8} \quad = \quad 3\frac{7}{8}$$

$$+\,4\frac{3}{4} \quad = \quad +\,4\frac{3\times 2}{4\times 2} \quad = \quad +\,4\frac{6}{8} \qquad \text{Rewrite using the LCD, 8.}$$

$$7\frac{13}{8}, \text{ or } 8\frac{5}{8} \qquad \text{Add. Think of } 7\frac{13}{8} \text{ as } 7 + 1\frac{5}{8}.$$

 EXAMPLE Find the difference.

$$9\frac{2}{9} \quad = \quad 8\frac{11}{9} \qquad \text{Rename } 9\frac{2}{9} \text{ as } 8\frac{11}{9}.$$

$$-\,4\frac{5}{9} \quad = \quad -\,4\frac{5}{9}$$

$$4\frac{6}{9}, \text{ or } 4\frac{2}{3} \qquad \text{Subtract and simplify.}$$

☑ **Find the sum or difference.**

3. $1\frac{4}{7} + 7\frac{1}{7}$ 　　4. $2\frac{5}{12} + 6\frac{7}{8}$ 　　5. $8\frac{17}{28} - 3\frac{1}{4}$ 　　6. $9\frac{8}{9} - 4\frac{2}{9}$

7. $5\frac{1}{4} - 2\frac{2}{3}$ 　　8. $11\frac{1}{5} - 8\frac{1}{3}$ 　　9. $6 - 4\frac{5}{8}$ 　　10. $3 - 1\frac{3}{5}$

6.6 Can you add and subtract measures of time?

 EXAMPLE Find the elapsed time from 9:40 A.M. to 5:35 P.M.

2 h 20 min	Find the elapsed time from 9:40 A.M. to 12:00 P.M.
+ 5 h 35 min	Find the elapsed time from 12:00 P.M. to 5:35 P.M.
7 h 55 min	Add the elapsed times.

☑ **Find the elapsed time.**   **11.** 7:45 A.M. to 2:00 P.M.   **12.** 5:30 P.M. to 1:45 A.M.

Stop and Think about Lessons 6.4–6.6

13. Critical Thinking How is adding and subtracting measures of time similar to adding and subtracting mixed numbers?

Review Quiz 2

Find the sum or difference.

1. $9\frac{3}{5} + 7\frac{1}{5}$ **2.** $3\frac{9}{17} + 11$ **3.** $5\frac{3}{8} + 2\frac{1}{6}$ **4.** $2\frac{3}{10} + 8\frac{3}{4}$

5. $9\frac{5}{7} - 3\frac{2}{7}$ **6.** $10\frac{11}{12} - 4\frac{3}{4}$ **7.** $5\frac{1}{3} - 1\frac{4}{9}$ **8.** $6 - 2\frac{1}{8}$

9. Sleep A baby sleeps from 10:18 A.M. to 12:05 P.M., from 4:10 P.M. to 5:25 P.M., and from 9:36 P.M. to 6:10 A.M. Find the total sleep time.

Magic Square

In the magic square at the right, the sum of each row, column, and diagonal is the same. Copy and complete the magic square.

6 Chapter Review

 **Vocabulary**

fraction, p. 228
simplest form, p. 229

least common
   denominator, p. 239
mixed number, p. 244

improper fraction, p. 244
elapsed time, p. 299
round, p. 686

Vocabulary Review

Copy and complete the statement.

1. You usually round fractions to the nearest __?__ and __?__ to the nearest whole number.

2. If the sum of two fractions is an __?__, you rewrite it as a mixed number.

3. The amount of time between a start time and an end time is called __?__.

4. To add or subtract fractions and mixed numbers with different denominators, you first need to find the __?__.

Review Questions

Estimate the sum or difference. *(Lesson 6.1)*

5. $\frac{8}{9} + \frac{4}{7}$

6. $\frac{1}{6} + \frac{7}{8}$

7. $\frac{11}{12} - \frac{1}{5}$

8. $\frac{9}{10} - \frac{4}{9}$

9. $1\frac{5}{6} + 10\frac{1}{4}$

10. $11\frac{4}{5} + 8\frac{3}{4}$

11. $6\frac{1}{12} - 3\frac{5}{16}$

12. $9\frac{1}{3} - 2\frac{8}{11}$

13. Concert A music concert features two singers. The first singer performs for $1\frac{3}{4}$ hours, and the second singer performs for $2\frac{2}{3}$ hours. Estimate the total number of hours of singing at the concert. *(Lesson 6.1)*

Find the sum or difference. *(Lessons 6.2, 6.3)*

14. $\frac{3}{9} + \frac{5}{9}$

15. $\frac{5}{6} + \frac{5}{6}$

16. $\frac{3}{5} - \frac{1}{5}$

17. $\frac{9}{10} - \frac{3}{10}$

18. $\frac{7}{12} + \frac{3}{4}$

19. $\frac{1}{3} + \frac{4}{15}$

20. $\frac{2}{3} - \frac{1}{4}$

21. $\frac{7}{10} - \frac{3}{5}$

22. **Bike Relay** You and a friend are competing in a two part bike relay. You bike $\frac{4}{5}$ mile in the first part. Your friend bikes $\frac{2}{3}$ mile in the second part. How many miles long is the bike relay? *(Lesson 6.3)*

23. **Candles** You light a candle that is $\frac{5}{6}$ inch tall. The candle melts to $\frac{3}{4}$ inch tall. What is the decrease in height? *(Lesson 6.3)*

Find the sum or difference. *(Lessons 6.4, 6.5)*

24. $9\frac{1}{8} + 4\frac{5}{8}$

25. $6\frac{3}{7} + 1\frac{5}{7}$

26. $8\frac{3}{4} + 1\frac{1}{2}$

27. $3\frac{2}{3} + \frac{1}{7}$

28. $7\frac{3}{8} + 5\frac{5}{6}$

29. $6\frac{4}{5} + 4\frac{7}{10}$

30. $14\frac{3}{4} - 6\frac{1}{4}$

31. $5\frac{3}{5} - 1\frac{1}{6}$

32. $5\frac{1}{3} - 2\frac{5}{12}$

33. $4\frac{7}{9} - 1\frac{8}{9}$

34. $8 - 2\frac{7}{9}$

35. $6 - \frac{3}{10}$

36. **Arm Span** Your cousin's arm span is $3\frac{3}{4}$ feet. Your arm span is $1\frac{1}{8}$ feet wider. How wide is your arm span? *(Lesson 6.4)*

37. **Bass Fishing** The winner of a bass fishing contest caught 14 pounds of bass. The runner-up caught $12\frac{11}{16}$ pounds of bass. How many more pounds did the winner catch than the runner-up? *(Lesson 6.5)*

Add or subtract the measures of time. *(Lesson 6.6)*

38.
$$\begin{array}{r} 6\text{ h }31\text{ min} \\ + 7\text{ h }32\text{ min} \\ \hline \end{array}$$

39.
$$\begin{array}{r} 3\text{ h }14\text{ min }25\text{ sec} \\ + 1\text{ h }25\text{ min }42\text{ sec} \\ \hline \end{array}$$

40.
$$\begin{array}{r} 9\text{ h }10\text{ min} \\ - 4\text{ h }55\text{ min} \\ \hline \end{array}$$

Find the elapsed time. *(Lesson 6.6)*

41. 5:00 A.M. to 7:00 A.M.

42. 1:40 P.M. to 8:00 P.M.

43. 10:30 P.M. to 4:45 A.M.

44. 6:00 A.M. to 3:00 P.M.

45. **Flights** The first part of a flight lasts 2 hours and 38 minutes. The second part lasts 3 hours and 26 minutes. What is the total flight time? *(Lesson 6.6)*

46. **Movies** A movie starts at 9:45 P.M. and ends at 12:20 A.M. How long is the movie? *(Lesson 6.6)*

Chapter Test

Estimate the sum or difference.

1. $\frac{1}{8} + \frac{17}{20}$

2. $\frac{7}{12} - \frac{2}{11}$

3. $6\frac{3}{10} - 3\frac{9}{16}$

4. $3\frac{1}{6} + 5\frac{3}{8}$

Find the sum or difference.

5. $\frac{5}{7} + \frac{1}{7}$

6. $\frac{3}{5} + \frac{4}{5}$

7. $\frac{7}{10} - \frac{3}{10}$

8. $\frac{7}{12} - \frac{1}{12}$

9. $\frac{5}{6} + \frac{5}{8}$

10. $\frac{7}{16} + \frac{1}{4}$

11. $\frac{2}{3} - \frac{1}{6}$

12. $\frac{4}{5} - \frac{1}{4}$

13. Banquet At a banquet, chicken, vegetarian, and beef dinners are served. The chef knows that $\frac{1}{4}$ of the guests order chicken and $\frac{1}{3}$ order beef. What fraction of the guests order meat dinners?

Find the sum or difference.

14. $2\frac{5}{7} + 8\frac{1}{7}$

15. $7\frac{1}{4} + 2\frac{1}{8}$

16. $6\frac{7}{15} + 3\frac{4}{5}$

17. $4\frac{7}{10} + 5\frac{3}{10}$

18. $7\frac{2}{3} - 4\frac{1}{8}$

19. $12\frac{7}{10} - 8\frac{1}{2}$

20. $8\frac{1}{6} - 4\frac{5}{9}$

21. $5 - 1\frac{3}{5}$

22. Helmets Your friend's bicycle helmet weighs $23\frac{1}{2}$ ounces. Your helmet weighs $43\frac{1}{5}$ ounces. Estimate how much more your helmet weighs. Then find the exact answer.

Add or subtract the measures of time.

23. $\quad$ 4 h 35 min
$\quad +\quad$ 45 min

24. $\quad$ 9 h 20 min 52 sec
$\quad - \;$ 2 h 42 min 4 sec

Find the elapsed time.

25. 1:50 P.M. to 3:35 P.M.

26. 6:38 A.M. to 10:05 A.M.

27. 4:45 A.M. to 2:15 P.M.

28. 7:25 P.M. to 12:30 A.M.

29. Video You use 2 hours and 48 minutes of a 6 hour videotape to record your sister's school play. How much time is left on the tape?

Chapter Standardized Test

Test-Taking Strategy During a test, make notes, sketches, or graphs on a separate piece of paper. Remember to keep your answer sheet neat.

Multiple Choice

1. Estimate the sum $\frac{9}{10} + \frac{4}{7}$.

    A. $\frac{1}{2}$ **B.** 1   **C.** $1\frac{1}{2}$ **D.** 2

2. Estimate the difference $7\frac{1}{6} - 3\frac{7}{8}$.

    F. 3   **G.** 6   **H.** 10   **I.** 11

3. To find the sum $\frac{1}{6} + \frac{3}{4}$, use the LCD, _?_.

    A. $\frac{3}{4}$ **B.** $\frac{11}{12}$ **C.** 6   **D.** 12

4. Find the difference $\frac{9}{10} - \frac{3}{10}$.

    F. $\frac{3}{10}$ **G.** $\frac{1}{2}$ **H.** $\frac{3}{5}$ **I.** $\frac{7}{10}$

5. Find the sum $\frac{7}{9} + 2\frac{1}{4}$.

    A. $3\frac{1}{36}$ **B.** $2\frac{35}{36}$ **C.** $3\frac{1}{12}$ **D.** $3\frac{1}{6}$

6. The sum $2\frac{5}{8} + 4\frac{3}{4}$ is between which numbers?

    F. 5 and 6   **G.** 6 and 7

    H. 7 and 8   **I.** 8 and 9

7. Which expression has the least value?

    A. $3\frac{1}{4} + 2\frac{1}{4}$ **B.** $8\frac{1}{3} - 1\frac{1}{2}$

    C. $6\frac{1}{4} + 1$ **D.** $12\frac{2}{5} - 5$

8. Find the difference $10 - 4\frac{1}{7}$.

    F. $5\frac{1}{7}$ **G.** $5\frac{6}{7}$ **H.** $6\frac{1}{7}$ **I.** $6\frac{6}{7}$

9. Which expression do you need to rename?

    A. $3\frac{1}{6} - 1\frac{1}{6}$ **B.** $9\frac{5}{7} - 2\frac{2}{7}$

    C. $8\frac{1}{4} - 4\frac{3}{4}$ **D.** $7\frac{5}{12} - 5$

10. Which has the shortest elapsed time?

    F. 9:30 A.M. to 1:00 P.M.

    G. 7:00 A.M. to 11:45 A.M.

    H. 5:15 P.M. to 9:00 P.M.

    I. 11:30 P.M. to 2:45 A.M.

11. A train leaves Carline at 11:45 A.M. and arrives in Trenton 3 hours and 50 minutes later. At what time does the train arrive?

    A. 2:35 P.M.   **B.** 3:30 P.M.

    C. 3:35 P.M.   **D.** 3:50 P.M.

Short Response

12. A baseball game begins at 6:00 P.M. It takes you 15 minutes to get to the bus stop and another 50 minutes to get to the stadium. What time should you leave home? Explain.

Extended Response

13. The perimeter of a triangle is $17\frac{1}{6}$ feet. The lengths of two of the sides are $6\frac{2}{3}$ feet and $4\frac{3}{4}$ feet. Estimate the length of the third side, then find the exact length. Show your steps.

Measuring the Day

Monthly Variation

Have you ever noticed that the sun rises and sets at different times each day? Using the data given below and on page 309, you will determine how much the number of daylight hours varies through the year in two different cities in the United States.

The table below gives the time of the sunrise and the time of the sunset in Miami, Florida. The data are for the twenty-first of each month during 2002. The times given are Eastern Standard Time.

Sunrise and Sunset in Miami, Florida						
	Jan.	**Feb.**	**Mar.**	**Apr.**	**May**	**June**
Sunrise	7:08 A.M.	6:51 A.M.	6:24 A.M.	5:53 A.M.	5:33 A.M.	5:30 A.M.
Sunset	5:56 P.M.	6:18 P.M.	6:33 P.M.	6:47 P.M.	7:03 P.M.	8:15 P.M.
	July	**Aug.**	**Sept.**	**Oct.**	**Nov.**	**Dec.**
Sunrise	5:42 A.M.	5:57 A.M.	6:09 A.M.	6:23 A.M.	6:43 A.M.	7:03 A.M.
Sunset	7:13 P.M.	6:51 P.M.	6:18 P.M.	5:48 P.M.	5:30 P.M.	5:35 P.M.

1. Find the elapsed time from sunrise to sunset for each month. Record your results in a table. The elapsed time describes the number of daylight hours during the day.

2. Use your table from Exercise 1 to make a line graph. Put the months on the horizontal axis. Put number of daylight hours on the vertical axis. Use a scale from 5 hours to 20 hours in half hour increments.

3. **Interpret** What patterns do you see in your line graph? During which month or months does Miami have the greatest number of daylight hours? the least number of daylight hours?

4. The summer solstice occurs on the day with the greatest number of daylight hours. The winter solstice occurs on the day with the least number of daylight hours. Find the difference between the number of daylight hours on the summer solstice and the number of daylight hours on the winter solstice. This difference describes Miami's seasonal variation in daylight hours.

Regional Variation

The length of time between sunrise and sunset varies not only due to the time of the year, but also due to location on the globe.

Anchorage, Alaska, is much closer to the North Pole than Miami, Florida. The table below gives the sunrise and sunset times for Anchorage for the twenty-first of each month in 2002. The times given are Alaska Standard Time.

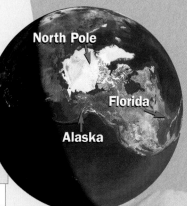

Sunrise and Sunset in Anchorage, Alaska						
	Jan.	**Feb.**	**Mar.**	**Apr.**	**May**	**June**
Sunrise	9:45 A.M.	8:24 A.M.	6:57 A.M.	5:20 A.M.	3:58 A.M.	3:20 A.M.
Sunset	4:37 P.M.	6:03 P.M.	7:17 P.M.	8:38 P.M.	9:56 P.M.	10:42 P.M.
	July	**Aug.**	**Sept.**	**Oct.**	**Nov.**	**Dec.**
Sunrise	4:05 A.M.	5:24 A.M.	6:41 A.M.	7:58 A.M.	9:22 A.M.	10:14 A.M.
Sunset	10:05 P.M.	8:40 P.M.	7:02 P.M.	5:29 P.M.	4:09 P.M.	3:41 P.M.

5. Find the elapsed time from sunrise to sunset for each month. Record your results in a table. Then plot these data on the graph you made in Exercise 2.

6. **Interpret** Compare the graphs for the two cities. How are they alike? How are they different? When do the summer and winter solstices occur for each city? How does Anchorage's seasonal variation in daylight hours compare with Miami's?

Project IDEAS

- **Report** Find information about the daylight patterns at the North Pole and at the equator. Present your findings to the class.

- **Research** Find information about daylight-saving time. Why do people use daylight-saving time? How does its use affect sunrise and sunset times? Present your findings.

- **Predict** Make a prediction about how the number of daylight hours where you live changes over the year. Describe how you might check your prediction.

- **Career** Meteorologists study weather and other natural occurrences, such as the sunrise and sunset. Find out what kinds of work meteorologists do. Present your findings to the class.

INTERNET
Project Support
CLASSZONE.COM

Multiplication and Division of Fractions

BEFORE

In previous chapters you've...

• Modeled and written fractions
• Compared and ordered fractions and mixed numbers
• Added and subtracted fractions

Now

In Chapter 7 you'll study...

• Multiplying and dividing fractions and mixed numbers
• Using customary units

WHY?

So you can solve real-world problems about...

• national parks, p. 316
• glaciers, p. 324
• soccer, p. 328
• caves, p. 335
• camels, p. 351

Internet Preview
CLASSZONE.COM

• eEdition Plus Online
• eWorkbook Plus Online
• eTutorial Plus Online
• State Test Practice
• More Examples

Chapter Warm-Up Games

Review skills you need for this chapter in these quick games.

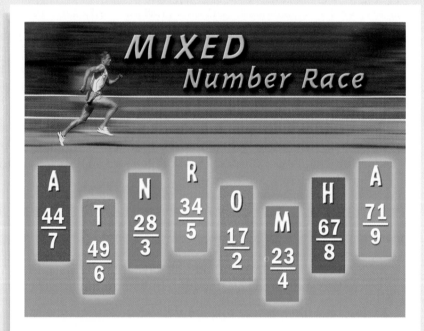

MIXED Number Race

A $\frac{44}{7}$ T $\frac{49}{6}$ N $\frac{28}{3}$ R $\frac{34}{5}$ O $\frac{17}{2}$ M $\frac{23}{4}$ H $\frac{67}{8}$ A $\frac{71}{9}$

BRAIN GAME

Key Skills:
• Writing fractions as mixed numbers
• Ordering mixed numbers

• Write the improper fractions as mixed numbers. Then order the mixed numbers from least to greatest.

• The letters associated with the numbers will spell out the name of a town in ancient Greece whose name is used for a modern track and field event.

Triple Jump

$\frac{1}{6}$ of a Hop ✛ $\frac{1}{4}$ of a Step ✛ $\frac{1}{3}$ of a Jump = Total Distance

BrAIN GAME

Key Skill:
Finding parts of
whole numbers

In the triple jump, athletes perform a hop, a step, and a jump. In this game you will complete a mathematical triple jump.

• Choose one of the following numbers to be your hop, one to be your step, and one to be your jump: 24, 36, 48. Use each number once.

• Use the fractions in the formula above. Find the given parts of the hop, step, and jump numbers you chose. Then add these results to find your total distance. Your goal is to get the greatest distance possible.

Stop *and* Think

1. **Writing** In *Mixed Number Race,* a student thinks that $\frac{71}{9}$ is greater than $\frac{67}{8}$ because 71 is greater than 67 and 9 is greater than 8. What is wrong with the student's reasoning?

2. **Critical Thinking** What is the greatest total distance you can get in *Triple Jump?* What is the least total distance? Explain how you know.

Getting Ready to Learn

Review What You Need to Know

Using Vocabulary **Copy and complete using a review word.**

1. _?_ measures the amount that a container can hold.

2. Two numbers that go together nicely to make a calculation easier are called _?_.

Word Watch

Review Words

compatible numbers, p. 13
capacity, p. 188
mixed number, p. 244
improper fraction, p. 244

Estimate the quotient. *(p. 12)*

3. $47 \div 8$ **4.** $186 \div 22$ **5.** $342 \div 48$

Copy and complete the statement. *(p. 191)*

6. $16 \, \text{kg} = \underline{?} \, \text{g}$ **7.** $25 \, \text{L} = \underline{?} \, \text{mL}$ **8.** $150 \, \text{cm} = \underline{?} \, \text{m}$

Write the mixed number as an improper fraction. *(p. 244)*

9. $4\frac{1}{6}$ **10.** $6\frac{2}{3}$ **11.** $2\frac{5}{6}$ **12.** $1\frac{3}{4}$

Round to the nearest whole number. *(p. 267)*

13. $\frac{7}{8}$ **14.** $1\frac{2}{9}$ **15.** $7\frac{1}{4}$ **16.** $2\frac{8}{11}$

You should include material that appears on a notebook like this in your own notes.

Know How to Take Notes

Drawing a Model When you take notes, include the visual models that are used in the lesson. Seeing the models can help you to understand and remember what you have learned. Below are some fraction models.

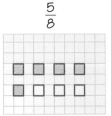

$\frac{5}{8}$

5 out of 8 objects

$\frac{9}{20}$

9 out of 20 parts

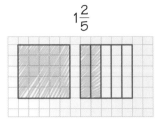

$1\frac{2}{5}$

1 whole and $\frac{2}{5}$ of 1 whole

In Lessons 7.1 and 7.2, you will use models to multiply by a fraction.

Multiplying Fractions and Whole Numbers

BEFORE	▶ Now	WHY?
You multiplied decimals and whole numbers.	You'll multiply fractions and whole numbers.	So you can interpret data shown in a circle graph, as in Ex. 35.

Word Watch

Review Words

compatible numbers, p. 13
whole number, p. 684

Activity You can use repeated addition to multiply a fraction by a whole number.

1. The product $6 \times \frac{2}{3}$ can be written as the sum $\frac{2}{3} + \frac{2}{3} + \frac{2}{3} + \frac{2}{3} + \frac{2}{3} + \frac{2}{3}$.

Show that the sum is equal to $\frac{6 \times 2}{3}$.

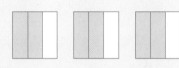

2. Write a rule for multiplying a fraction by a whole number. Then try another product to check your rule.

In the activity, you may have become aware of the following rule by thinking about multiplication as repeated addition.

Multiplying Fractions by Whole Numbers

Words To multiply a fraction by a whole number, multiply the numerator of the fraction by the whole number and write the product over the original denominator. Simplify if possible.

Numbers $2 \times \frac{3}{7} = \frac{6}{7}$ **Algebra** $a \cdot \frac{b}{c} = \frac{a \cdot b}{c}$

with Notetaking

When you write the rule for multiplying fractions by whole numbers in your notebook, you may want to include a model like the one in the activity.

EXAMPLE 1 Multiply Fractions by Whole Numbers

$$6 \times \frac{3}{4} = \frac{6 \times 3}{4} \qquad \text{Multiply the numerator by the whole number.}$$

$$= \frac{18}{4}$$

$$= \frac{9}{2}, \text{ or } 4\frac{1}{2} \qquad \text{Simplify.}$$

EXAMPLE 2 **Multiply Whole Numbers by Fractions**

a. $\frac{3}{8} \times 2 = \frac{6}{8}$

$= \frac{3}{4}$

b. $\frac{4}{3} \times 2 = \frac{8}{3}$

$= 2\frac{2}{3}$

Your turn now **Find the product. Simplify if possible.**

1. $3 \times \frac{3}{10}$ **2.** $9 \times \frac{3}{8}$ **3.** $\frac{6}{5} \times 7$ **4.** $\frac{5}{6} \times 3$

5. Look at the results in Example 2. Then predict whether the product will be *greater than 2* or *less than 2* when 2 is multiplied by $\frac{13}{8}$.

Using Mental Math You can sometimes find the product of a whole number and a fraction using mental math or a model, as in Example 3.

EXAMPLE 3 **Using Mental Math or a Model**

Party Music You are choosing 18 CDs to bring to a party. You want $\frac{2}{3}$ of the CDs to have dance music. How many dance music CDs should you choose?

Solution

The number of dance music CDs you should choose is $\frac{2}{3}$ *of* 18, or $\frac{2}{3} \times 18$. You can use a model or mental math to find this product.

Method 1 Use a model. Draw 18 circles. Divide them into three equal parts. Circle two of the three parts.

Method 2 Use mental math. Think: $\frac{1}{3}$ of 18 is 6, because $18 \div 3 = 6$. So, $\frac{2}{3}$ of 18 is 12, because $2 \times 6 = 12$.

ANSWER You should choose 12 dance music CDs to bring to the party.

EXAMPLE 4 **Estimating a Product**

CD Rack You have 15 CDs and each CD case is $\frac{3}{8}$ inch wide. Estimate how wide a space you need on your CD rack to fit your 15 CDs.

$$\text{Space} = \frac{3}{8} \times 15 \qquad \text{Multiply width of a CD case by number of cases.}$$

$$\approx \frac{3}{8} \times 16 \qquad \text{Replace 15 with a number compatible with 8.}$$

$$= 6 \qquad \text{Think: } \frac{1}{8} \text{ of 16 is 2, so } \frac{3}{8} \text{ of 16 is 6.}$$

ANSWER You need a space that is about 6 inches wide.

Your turn now Use mental math.

6. Find $\frac{3}{4}$ of 28. **7.** Find $36 \times \frac{2}{9}$. **8.** Estimate $\frac{3}{4} \times 25$.

7.1 Exercises

More Practice, p. 714

INTERNET
eWorkbook Plus
CLASSZONE.COM

Getting Ready to Practice

1. Vocabulary Is 9 compatible with 36 in the product $\frac{7}{9} \times 36$?

Find the product. Simplify if possible.

2. $5 \times \frac{2}{7}$ **3.** $\frac{7}{4} \times 2$ **4.** $\frac{1}{2} \times 8$ **5.** $24 \times \frac{5}{8}$

Use compatible numbers to estimate the product.

6. $\frac{5}{6} \times 23$ **7.** $\frac{2}{7} \times 15$ **8.** $39 \times \frac{3}{4}$ **9.** $18 \times \frac{3}{10}$

10. Guided Problem Solving Each student needs $\frac{3}{4}$ pound of sand for an experiment. About how much sand is needed for 21 students?

(**1** Write an expression for what you need to find.

(**2** Choose a compatible number to substitute for 21.

(**3** Use mental math to estimate the answer.

Practice and Problem Solving

HELP with **Homework**

Example	Exercises
1	11-26
2	11-26
3	19-24
4	27-34

Online Resources
CLASSZONE.COM
· More Examples
· eTutorial Plus

Find the product.

11. $6 \times \frac{3}{7}$ **12.** $3 \times \frac{3}{10}$ **13.** $\frac{3}{2} \times 5$ **14.** $\frac{4}{3} \times 4$

15. $2 \times \frac{5}{12}$ **16.** $6 \times \frac{2}{9}$ **17.** $\frac{1}{6} \times 15$ **18.** $\frac{5}{8} \times 6$

19. $\frac{1}{5} \times 30$ **20.** $\frac{5}{6} \times 12$ **21.** $70 \times \frac{4}{7}$ **22.** $40 \times \frac{9}{10}$

Find the amount.

23. Number of minutes in $\frac{2}{3}$ of an hour

24. Cost of $\frac{3}{4}$ pound of nuts at \$8 per pound

25. Distance run if you run 10 times around a $\frac{1}{4}$ mile track

26. Distance walked in a week if you walk $\frac{1}{2}$ mile each day

Estimation **Identify the closest whole number that is compatible with the denominator of the fraction. Then estimate the answer.**

27. $\frac{1}{4}$ of 19   **28.** $\frac{1}{7}$ of 47   **29.** $\frac{2}{5}$ of 28   **30.** $\frac{5}{8}$ of 43

31. $\frac{7}{8} \times 46$ **32.** $\frac{8}{9} \times 83$ **33.** $32 \times \frac{2}{3}$ **34.** $53 \times \frac{2}{11}$

35. **National Parks** The total land area in the National Park system is about 78 million acres. Estimate the land area for each category shown in the circle graph.

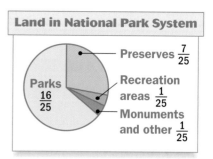

Land in National Park System

Preserves $\frac{7}{25}$

Recreation areas $\frac{1}{25}$

Parks $\frac{16}{25}$

Monuments and other $\frac{1}{25}$

36. **Predict** Predict whether the product of 24 and each of the following fractions is *less than 24* or *greater than 24*: $\frac{2}{3}, \frac{5}{3}, \frac{1}{2}, \frac{3}{2}, \frac{3}{8}, \frac{9}{8}$. Then find the product to check your answer.

37. **Critical Thinking** Is the estimate in Example 4 on page 315 *high* or *low*? Is that appropriate for the situation? Explain.

What do you think?

History

■ **National Parks**

The Statue of Liberty National Monument has a total area of 58.38 acres. Its land consists of Liberty Island and Ellis Island. The official area of Liberty Island is 10.38 acres and of Ellis Island is 27.5 acres. About how many acres of the park are under water?

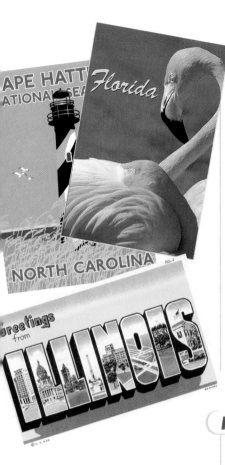

38. Postcard Collections You and a friend exchanged travel postcards. You gave your friend $\frac{1}{6}$ of a collection of 54 cards. Your friend gave you $\frac{2}{9}$ of a collection of 63 cards. How many cards do you each have now?

Use the commutative and associative properties to find the product.

39. $\left(4 \times \frac{5}{7}\right) \times 35$ **40.** $15 \times 8 \times \frac{2}{3}$ **41.** $\frac{2}{9} \times 11 \times 18$

Measurement Use the formula $F = \frac{9}{5}C + 32$, where F is the temperature in degrees Fahrenheit (°F) and C is the temperature in degrees Celsius (°C). Write the temperature in degrees Fahrenheit.

42. 0°C   **43.** 35°C   **44.** 100°C

Challenge Use the part of a set to find the size of the whole set.

45. $\frac{1}{3}$ of a set is 8.   **46.** $\frac{3}{4}$ of a set is 9.   **47.** $\frac{5}{6}$ of a set is 10.

Mixed Review

Multiply. Use estimation to check your answer. *(Lesson 4.3)*

48. 18.7×4.2 **49.** 2.63×0.51 **50.** 0.034×6.8 **51.** 0.74×0.059

Round the fraction to the nearest half. *(Lesson 6.1)*

52. $\frac{9}{10}$ **53.** $\frac{5}{12}$ **54.** $\frac{4}{7}$ **55.** $\frac{1}{9}$

Basic Skills Write a fraction to represent the shaded region.

56.    **57.**   **58.**

Test-Taking Practice

59. Extended Response You plan to make 6 times a chili recipe and 6 times a guacamole recipe. The chili recipe calls for $\frac{2}{3}$ cup of chopped tomatoes and the guacamole recipe calls for $\frac{3}{4}$ cup. One small tomato makes about $\frac{1}{2}$ cup of chopped tomatoes. Will 12 small tomatoes be enough? Explain your reasoning.

GOAL

Understand how to model the product of two fractions.

MATERIALS

· tiles (plastic counters, pennies, squares of paper)
· graph paper

Modeling Products of Fractions

In this activity, you will model products of fractions in two ways. To create a model for the product $\frac{1}{3} \times \frac{1}{2}$, you need to find $\frac{1}{3}$ of $\frac{1}{2}$ of a whole.

Explore 1 Model $\frac{1}{3} \times \frac{1}{2}$ using a rectangle of tiles.

1 Make a 2 by 3 rectangle of tiles to model halves and thirds.

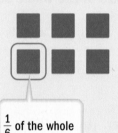

$\frac{1}{6}$ of the whole

2 Each row is $\frac{1}{2}$ of the tiles.

Each column is $\frac{1}{3}$ of the tiles.

$\frac{1}{2}$ $\frac{1}{3}$

3 Now, select $\frac{1}{2}$ of the tiles.

$\frac{1}{2}$

4 Next, find $\frac{1}{3}$ of $\frac{1}{2}$ of the tiles.

$\frac{1}{3} \times \frac{1}{2} = \frac{1}{6}$

Your turn now **Model the product using the given size rectangle of tiles.**

1. $\frac{1}{4} \times \frac{3}{4}$, 4 by 4 rectangle   **2.** $\frac{1}{2} \times \frac{3}{4}$, 2 by 4 rectangle   **3.** $\frac{3}{5} \times \frac{4}{7}$, 5 by 7 rectangle

4. Writing Explain how you can decide what size rectangle of tiles to use to create a model for the product $\frac{1}{3} \times \frac{5}{6}$.

Explore 2 Model $\frac{1}{3} \times \frac{1}{2}$ on graph paper.

1 Draw a 2 by 3 rectangle on graph paper to model halves and thirds. There are 6 small squares, so each square is $\frac{1}{6}$ of the rectangle.

2 Shade $\frac{1}{2}$ of the rectangle.

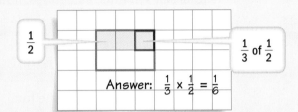

$\frac{1}{2}$ $\frac{1}{3}$ of $\frac{1}{2}$

Answer: $\frac{1}{3} \times \frac{1}{2} = \frac{1}{6}$

3 Then select $\frac{1}{3}$ of the $\frac{1}{2}$.

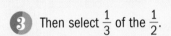 **Model the product on graph paper.**

5. $\frac{1}{4} \times \frac{3}{4}$ **6.** $\frac{1}{2} \times \frac{3}{4}$ **7.** $\frac{3}{5} \times \frac{4}{7}$

8. Copy and complete the table. Use the model shown above and the ones you drew in Exercises 5–7.

Product	$\frac{1}{3} \times \frac{1}{2} = \frac{?}{?}$	$\frac{1}{4} \times \frac{3}{4} = \frac{?}{?}$	$\frac{1}{2} \times \frac{3}{4} = \frac{?}{?}$	$\frac{3}{5} \times \frac{4}{7} = \frac{?}{?}$
Number of squares in large rectangle you drew	6	?	?	?
Product of denominators	?	?	?	?
Number of squares in small rectangle you selected	1	?	?	?
Product of numerators	?	?	?	?

Stop *and* **Think**

9. Critical Thinking Use the information in your table to suggest a method for finding the product of two fractions without using a model.

10. Number Sense For each product in the table, compare the answer to each of the fractions being multiplied. Is the answer *greater than* or *less than* the first fraction? the second fraction? Explain why this happens.

Multiplying Fractions

BEFORE	▶ Now	WHY?
You multiplied a fraction by a whole number.	You'll multiply fractions.	So you can find distances in a relay race, as in Exercise 35.

In the Real World

Word Watch

Review Words

factor, p. 16
common factor, p. 222
simplest form, p. 229

Scooter Sales The table shows the fraction of a sporting goods store's total sales in three categories. John, a salesperson at the store, made $\frac{2}{3}$ of the push scooter sales. What fraction of the total sales is this?

Fraction of Total Sales	
push scooters	$\frac{1}{5}$
in-line skates	$\frac{1}{10}$
bicycles	$\frac{3}{5}$

John's sales are $\frac{2}{3}$ of $\frac{1}{5}$ of the total. When you find part *of* a part, you are multiplying two fractions.

EXAMPLE 1 Using a Model to Multiply Fractions

To answer the question above about John's sales, you can use a model to find $\frac{2}{3}$ *of* $\frac{1}{5}$, or $\frac{2}{3} \times \frac{1}{5}$.

(1) Draw a 3 by 5 rectangle to model thirds and fifths. Each small square is $\frac{1}{15}$ of the whole.

(2) Shade $\frac{1}{5}$ of the rectangle.

(3) Select $\frac{2}{3}$ of the shaded rectangle.

ANSWER Two of the 15 squares are selected, so $\frac{2}{3} \times \frac{1}{5} = \frac{2}{15}$.

John's push scooter sales are $\frac{2}{15}$ of the store's total sales.

Your turn now Draw a model to find the product.

1. $\frac{1}{2} \times \frac{1}{5}$ **2.** $\frac{2}{3} \times \frac{2}{5}$ **3.** $\frac{3}{4} \times \frac{5}{7}$

---

320 Chapter 7 Multiplication and Division of Fractions

Using a Rule Look back at the model of the product $\frac{2}{3} \times \frac{1}{5}$ in Example 1 to see how the model is related to the rule below.

$$\frac{\text{area of selected rectangle}}{\text{area of whole rectangle}} = \frac{2 \times 1}{3 \times 5} = \frac{\text{product of the numerators}}{\text{product of the denominators}}$$

Multiplying Fractions

Words product of fractions $= \dfrac{\text{product of the numerators}}{\text{product of the denominators}}$

Numbers $\dfrac{3}{4} \times \dfrac{5}{8} = \dfrac{15}{32}$ **Algebra** $\dfrac{a}{b} \cdot \dfrac{c}{d} = \dfrac{a \cdot c}{b \cdot d}$

EXAMPLE 2 **Multiplying Two Fractions**

$\dfrac{2}{5} \times \dfrac{4}{3} = \dfrac{2 \times 4}{5 \times 3}$ Use the rule for multiplying fractions.

$\phantom{\dfrac{2}{5} \times \dfrac{4}{3}} = \dfrac{8}{15}$ Multiply. The product is in simplest form.

EXAMPLE 3 **Evaluating an Algebraic Expression**

HELP with **Solving**

Notice in Example 3 that the product of $\frac{1}{3}$ and $\frac{2}{7}$ is less than either fraction.

xy **Algebra** **Evaluate the expression $\frac{1}{3}n$ when $n = \frac{2}{7}$.**

$\dfrac{1}{3}n = \dfrac{1}{3} \times \dfrac{2}{7}$ Substitute $\frac{2}{7}$ for n.

$\phantom{\dfrac{1}{3}n} = \dfrac{1 \times 2}{3 \times 7}$ Use the rule for multiplying fractions.

$\phantom{\dfrac{1}{3}n} = \dfrac{2}{21}$ Multiply. The product is in simplest form.

Your turn now **In Exercises 4–7, find the value.**

4. Find the product $\dfrac{1}{3} \times \dfrac{1}{6}$. **5.** Find the product $\dfrac{3}{7} \times \dfrac{1}{4}$.

6. Evaluate $\dfrac{3}{4}n$ when $n = \dfrac{3}{5}$. **7.** Evaluate $\dfrac{2}{3}x$ when $x = \dfrac{4}{9}$.

8. Is the product in Example 2 less than both fractions?

Simplifying First When you multiply fractions, it is sometimes easier to simplify before carrying out the multiplication.

EXAMPLE 4 Simplifying Before Multiplying

with Solving

To simplify in Example 4, find the greatest factor of 8 that is also a factor of 12 or 15.

$$\frac{1}{12} \times \frac{8}{15} = \frac{1 \times 8}{12 \times 15}$$ Use the rule for multiplying fractions.

$$= \frac{1 \times \overset{2}{\cancel{8}}}{\underset{3}{\cancel{12}} \times 15}$$ 4 is a factor of 8 and 12. Divide 8 and 12 by 4.

$$= \frac{1 \times 2}{3 \times 15}$$ Rewrite.

$$= \frac{2}{45}$$ Multiply.

You can use the rule for multiplying fractions to find the product of three or more fractions. You may be able to divide by more than one common factor when you simplify.

EXAMPLE 5 Multiplying Three Fractions

Watch Out!

Rewrite the fraction after dividing out common factors. You will be less likely to make an error when you multiply.

$$\frac{1}{6} \times \frac{3}{4} \times \frac{2}{5} = \frac{1 \times 3 \times 2}{6 \times 4 \times 5}$$ Use the rule for multiplying fractions.

$$= \frac{1 \times \overset{1}{\cancel{3}} \times \overset{1}{\cancel{2}}}{\underset{2}{\cancel{6}} \times \underset{2}{\cancel{4}} \times 5}$$ 3 is a factor of 3 and 6. Divide 3 and 6 by 3.
2 is a factor of 2 and 4. Divide 2 and 4 by 2.

$$= \frac{1 \times 1 \times 1}{2 \times 2 \times 5}$$ Rewrite.

$$= \frac{1}{20}$$ Multiply.

Your turn now Multiply. Write the answer in simplest form.

9. $\frac{3}{8} \times \frac{5}{9}$ **10.** $\frac{6}{7} \times \frac{2}{3}$ **11.** $\frac{5}{16} \times \frac{8}{15}$

12. $\frac{1}{2} \times \frac{3}{5} \times \frac{1}{6}$ **13.** $\frac{3}{7} \times \frac{5}{9} \times \frac{7}{10}$ **14.** $\frac{2}{5} \times \frac{1}{4} \times \frac{10}{11}$

15. Look at the rule for multiplying fractions on page 321. Use algebraic symbols to write a rule for multiplying three fractions.

Getting Ready to Practice

1. **Vocabulary** How can you tell whether a fraction is in simplest form?

2. Draw a model to find the product $\frac{2}{3} \times \frac{4}{5}$.

3. Find $\frac{3}{5}$ of $\frac{1}{2}$.   4. Find $\frac{1}{6}$ of $\frac{6}{11}$.   5. Find $\frac{7}{8}$ of $\frac{4}{5}$.

 Algebra **Evaluate the expression when $x = \dfrac{3}{4}$.**

6. $\frac{1}{5}x$ 7. $\frac{8}{9}x$ 8. $\frac{3}{4}x$

9. **Find the Error** Describe and correct the error in the solution.

$$\times \quad \frac{3}{4} \times \frac{5}{9} = \frac{\overset{1}{\cancel{3}} \times 5}{4 \times \underset{2}{\cancel{9}}} = \frac{5}{8}$$

Practice and Problem Solving

 **with Homework**

Example	Exercises
1	10
2	11-18, 22, 35
3	19-21
4	23-30, 36
5	31-34

Online Resources
CLASSZONE.COM
· More Examples
· eTutorial Plus

10. Draw a model to find the product $\frac{3}{5} \times \frac{1}{4}$. Use the model to explain why the product is less than 1.

Find the product.

11. $\frac{1}{3} \times \frac{4}{7}$ 12. $\frac{1}{3} \times \frac{1}{3}$ 13. $\frac{3}{4} \times \frac{1}{4}$ 14. $\frac{7}{8} \times \frac{1}{2}$

15. $\frac{1}{2} \times \frac{3}{10}$ 16. $\frac{4}{5} \times \frac{6}{7}$ 17. $\frac{2}{5} \times \frac{2}{9}$ 18. $\frac{6}{5} \times \frac{3}{7}$

Algebra **Evaluate the expression when $x = \dfrac{1}{5}$.**

19. $\frac{1}{7}x$ 20. $\frac{7}{10}x$ 21. $\frac{6}{11}x$

22. **Soap Bubbles** You and a friend want to make one half of a batch of soap bubble solution. How much dishwashing liquid do you need?

SOAP BUBBLE SOLUTION
1 cup warm water
$\frac{1}{4}$ cup dishwashing liquid
1 teaspoon salt
Combine all ingredients.
Mix well until salt dissolves.

Find the product.

23. $\frac{1}{4} \times \frac{8}{15}$

24. $\frac{1}{2} \times \frac{4}{7}$

25. $\frac{2}{3} \times \frac{3}{8}$

26. $\frac{6}{1} \times \frac{1}{6}$

27. $\frac{7}{9} \times \frac{9}{14}$

28. $\frac{3}{7} \times \frac{7}{9}$

29. $\frac{5}{8} \times \frac{24}{25}$

30. $\frac{11}{10} \times \frac{5}{22}$

31. $\frac{3}{4} \times \frac{5}{6} \times \frac{1}{2}$

32. $\frac{2}{3} \times \frac{3}{5} \times \frac{7}{10}$

33. $\frac{5}{8} \times \frac{3}{10} \times \frac{16}{21}$

34. $\frac{7}{8} \times \frac{4}{15} \times \frac{3}{14}$

35. Sports Two teams of four students are running a relay race. The total distance of the race is $\frac{1}{2}$ mile. The teams are tied $\frac{3}{4}$ of the way through the race. At this point, how far have the teams run?

36. Fingernails Healthy fingernails grow about $\frac{4}{5}$ inch per year. A month is what fraction of a year? Use that result to find how much healthy fingernails grow per month. Is your answer reasonable? Explain.

Number Sense Copy and complete the statement using <, >, or =.

37. $\frac{3}{8} \times \frac{4}{5} \underline{\ ?\ } 1$

38. $1 \times \frac{2}{3} \underline{\ ?\ } \frac{2}{3}$

39. $\frac{3}{8} \times \frac{5}{5} \underline{\ ?\ } \frac{3}{8}$

40. $\frac{1}{3} \times \frac{4}{3} \underline{\ ?\ } \frac{1}{3}$

41. $\frac{1}{3} \times \frac{4}{3} \underline{\ ?\ } \frac{4}{3}$

42. $\frac{1}{3} \times \frac{3}{4} \underline{\ ?\ } \frac{1}{3}$

Evaluate the expression.

43. $\frac{2}{3} + \frac{1}{3} \times \frac{3}{4}$

44. $\frac{5}{6} - \frac{1}{6} \times \frac{1}{2}$

45. $\frac{1}{2} \times \left(\frac{3}{5}\right)^2$

46. Glaciers The World Glacier Inventory contains data from over 67,000 glaciers around the world. About $\frac{1}{50}$ of the glaciers are in North America. About $\frac{5}{8}$ of these are in the Queen Elizabeth Islands in Northern Canada. What fraction of the glaciers are in the Queen Elizabeth Islands? Estimate the number of glaciers in the Queen Elizabeth Islands to the nearest hundred. Explain your steps.

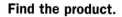

Science

■ **Glaciers**

A glacier is a large mass of ice that flows over land. Glaciers are often between 300 and 10,000 feet thick. Is a glacier thicker than your school is tall?

Find the product.

47. $\frac{7}{24} \times \frac{18}{13} \times \frac{16}{21}$ **48.** $\frac{48}{77} \times \frac{33}{52} \times \frac{7}{18}$ **49.** $\frac{36}{49} \times \frac{25}{54} \times \frac{21}{40}$

50. Basketball This season the school basketball team played $\frac{3}{7}$ of their games at night and $\frac{4}{7}$ of their games during the day. They won $\frac{3}{4}$ of their night games and $\frac{1}{2}$ of their day games. What fraction of their games did they win during the season? Explain how you found your answer.

51. Challenge Use number sense to order the expressions from least to greatest without finding the products. Explain how you decided.

$\frac{17}{32} \times \frac{7}{12}$ $\qquad$ $\frac{7}{12} \times \frac{13}{27}$ $\qquad$ $\frac{18}{19} \times \frac{7}{12}$ $\qquad$ $\frac{7}{12} \times \frac{1}{2}$ $\qquad$ $\frac{7}{12} \times \frac{2}{21}$

Mixed Review

Copy and complete the statement. *(Lesson 5.6)*

52. $4\frac{2}{5} = \frac{?}{5}$ $\qquad$ **53.** $5\frac{1}{3} = \frac{16}{?}$ $\qquad$ **54.** $\frac{17}{6} = ?\frac{5}{6}$ $\qquad$ **55.** $\frac{25}{7} = 3\frac{?}{7}$

Use compatible numbers to estimate the product. *(Lesson 7.1)*

56. $\frac{2}{5} \times 31$ $\qquad$ **57.** $\frac{5}{8} \times 18$ $\qquad$ **58.** $40 \times \frac{5}{6}$ $\qquad$ **59.** $28 \times \frac{2}{3}$

Basic Skills **Use clustering to estimate the sum.**

60. $28 + 33 + 31 + 27 + 30 + 32$ $\qquad$ **61.** $209 + 195 + 211 + 193 + 198$

Test-Taking Practice

62. Multiple Choice Which product is equal to $\frac{3}{5}$?

A. $\frac{1}{5} \times \frac{2}{5}$ $\qquad$ **B.** $\frac{3}{7} \times \frac{7}{10}$ $\qquad$ **C.** $\frac{5}{6} \times \frac{9}{25}$ $\qquad$ **D.** $\frac{5}{6} \times \frac{18}{25}$

63. Short Response A town is building a new school that will be about $\frac{1}{2}$ of a block wide and about $\frac{2}{3}$ of a block long. Draw a rectangle to represent one block and model the area of the school on the rectangle. Then give the area of the school in square blocks.

Multiplying Mixed Numbers

BEFORE ▸ **Now** **WHY?**

You multiplied fractions. You'll multiply mixed numbers. So you can find areas, such as the area of a trampoline in Example 3.

Word Watch

Review Words

mixed number, p. 244
improper fraction, p. 244

Activity You can use a picture of measuring cups to find $\frac{1}{2} \times 1\frac{1}{3}$.

① Draw a picture of $1\frac{1}{3}$ cups.

1 cup $\frac{1}{3}$-cup

② Replace 1 cup with three $\frac{1}{3}$ cups.

There are now four $\frac{1}{3}$ cups, or $\frac{4}{3}$ cups.

$\frac{1}{3}$-cup $\frac{1}{3}$-cup
$\frac{1}{3}$-cup $\frac{1}{3}$-cup

③ Circle $\frac{1}{2}$ of $\frac{4}{3}$. There are $\frac{2}{3}$ selected,

so $\frac{1}{2} \times 1\frac{1}{3} = \frac{2}{3}$.

$\frac{1}{3}$-cup $\frac{1}{3}$-cup
$\frac{1}{3}$-cup $\frac{1}{3}$-cup

Draw a picture to find the product. **1.** $\frac{2}{3} \times 1\frac{1}{2}$ **2.** $\frac{1}{2} \times 2\frac{2}{3}$

In the activity, $1\frac{1}{3}$ is shown as $\frac{4}{3}$. When finding a product involving a mixed number, it is helpful to first write all the numbers in fraction form.

EXAMPLE 1 **Multiplying with Mixed Numbers**

a. $\dfrac{5}{8} \times 1\dfrac{2}{3} = \dfrac{5}{8} \times \dfrac{5}{3}$ Write $1\frac{2}{3}$ as an improper fraction.

$= \dfrac{5 \times 5}{8 \times 3}$ Use the rule for multiplying fractions.

$= \dfrac{25}{24}$, or $1\dfrac{1}{24}$ Multiply. The answer is in simplest form.

b. $1\dfrac{3}{4} \times 3 = \dfrac{7}{4} \times \dfrac{3}{1}$ Write $1\frac{3}{4}$ and 3 as improper fractions.

$= \dfrac{7 \times 3}{4 \times 1}$ Use the rule for multiplying fractions.

$= \dfrac{21}{4}$, or $5\dfrac{1}{4}$ Multiply. The answer is in simplest form.

HELP with **Solving**

In part (b) of Example 1, the whole number 3 was rewritten as the fraction $\frac{3}{1}$ (read "3 wholes"). You could instead have left the 3 in whole number form and multiplied as in Lesson 7.1.

$\dfrac{7}{4} \times 3 = \dfrac{21}{4}$

EXAMPLE **2** **Simplifying Before Multiplying**

$$2\frac{2}{9} \times 4\frac{4}{5} = \frac{20}{9} \times \frac{24}{5}$$ Write $2\frac{2}{9}$ and $4\frac{4}{5}$ as improper fractions.

$$= \frac{\overset{4}{\cancel{20}} \times \overset{8}{\cancel{24}}}{\underset{3}{\cancel{9}} \times \underset{1}{\cancel{5}}}$$ Use the rule for multiplying fractions.
Divide out common factors.

$$= \frac{4 \times 8}{3 \times 1}$$ Rewrite.

$$= \frac{32}{3}, \text{ or } 10\frac{2}{3}$$ Multiply. The answer is in simplest form.

✓**Check** Round $2\frac{2}{9}$ to 2 and $4\frac{4}{5}$ to 5. Because $2 \times 5 = 10$, the product $10\frac{2}{3}$ is reasonable.

Your turn now **Multiply. Write the answer in simplest form.**

1. $2\frac{1}{3} \times \frac{5}{6}$ **2.** $5 \times 2\frac{2}{5}$ **3.** $3\frac{1}{3} \times 2\frac{1}{4}$ **4.** $3\frac{1}{4} \times 2\frac{3}{5}$

Sports

■ **Trampoline**

Trampoline became an Olympic sport in 2000. A trampoliner jumps to heights of up to 30 feet. If a trampoliner is 5 feet 6 inches tall, about how many times her height could she jump?

EXAMPLE **3** **Multiplying to Solve Problems**

Trampoline Olympic trampoliners get points deducted from their scores if they land outside a rectangle called the *jump zone*. The jump zone measures $7\frac{1}{21}$ feet by $3\frac{1}{2}$ feet. What is the area of the jump zone?

Solution

$$\text{Area} = \text{Length} \times \text{Width}$$ Write formula for area of a rectangle.

$$= 7\frac{1}{21} \times 3\frac{1}{2}$$ Substitute for length and width.

$$= \frac{148}{21} \times \frac{7}{2}$$ Write $7\frac{1}{21}$ and $3\frac{1}{2}$ as improper fractions.

$$= \frac{\overset{74}{\cancel{148}} \times \overset{1}{\cancel{7}}}{\underset{3}{\cancel{21}} \times \underset{1}{\cancel{2}}}$$ Use the rule for multiplying fractions.
Divide out common factors.

$$= \frac{74}{3}, \text{ or } 24\frac{2}{3}$$ Multiply. The answer is in simplest form.

ANSWER The area of the jump zone is $24\frac{2}{3}$ square feet.

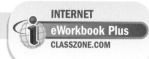
INTERNET
eWorkbook Plus
CLASSZONE.COM

Getting Ready to Practice

1. **Vocabulary** Give an example of a mixed number and an example of an improper fraction.

Tell whether you can simplify before multiplying. If so, tell how.

2. $\frac{7}{3} \times \frac{3}{2}$ 3. $\frac{5}{2} \times \frac{5}{3}$ 4. $\frac{3}{2} \times \frac{15}{13}$ 5. $\frac{18}{25} \times \frac{10}{9}$

Multiply. Write the answer in simplest form.

6. $\frac{5}{8} \times 2\frac{1}{4}$ 7. $3\frac{2}{5} \times 10$ 8. $3\frac{4}{7} \times 2\frac{1}{3}$ 9. $1\frac{5}{6} \times 1\frac{13}{22}$

10. **Soccer** An indoor soccer goal is $6\frac{1}{2}$ feet high. An outdoor soccer goal is $1\frac{3}{13}$ times as high as an indoor goal. How high is an outdoor goal? Estimate to check that your answer is reasonable.

Practice and Problem Solving

Find the product.

11. $1\frac{5}{6} \times \frac{1}{2}$ 12. $\frac{3}{4} \times 2\frac{1}{4}$ 13. $2 \times 5\frac{2}{3}$ 14. $1\frac{2}{5} \times 4$

15. $1\frac{1}{6} \times 2\frac{1}{2}$ 16. $3\frac{2}{3} \times 3\frac{1}{2}$ 17. $1\frac{2}{5} \times 2\frac{1}{3}$ 18. $7 \times \frac{4}{9}$

19. $1\frac{1}{6} \times 8$ 20. $2\frac{1}{3} \times \frac{3}{5}$ 21. $1\frac{1}{2} \times 1\frac{1}{3}$ 22. $1\frac{4}{5} \times 2\frac{1}{3}$

23. $\frac{1}{6} \times 6\frac{3}{4}$ 24. $2\frac{2}{3} \times 5\frac{2}{5}$ 25. $\frac{5}{8} \times 36$ 26. $6 \times 2\frac{2}{9}$

Estimation **Use rounding to estimate the product.**

27. $4\frac{5}{8} \times 3\frac{1}{3}$ 28. $6 \times 5\frac{7}{8}$ 29. $3\frac{2}{3} \times 3\frac{4}{5}$ 30. $2\frac{1}{8} \times 1\frac{2}{9}$

Geometry **Find the area of the rectangle.**

31.
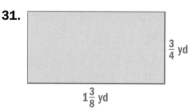
$\frac{3}{4}$ yd
$1\frac{3}{8}$ yd

32.
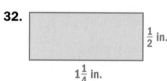
$\frac{1}{2}$ in.
$1\frac{1}{4}$ in.

HELP **with Homework**

Example	Exercises
1	11–26, 35
2	11–30, 35
3	31–34

Online Resources
CLASSZONE.COM
· More Examples
· eTutorial Plus

Projects In Exercises 33 and 34, the students in a class are presenting their research projects. There are 20 students in the class. Each student will give an oral report that lasts about $3\frac{1}{2}$ minutes.

33. How much time will it take for all 20 reports to be presented?

34. A 15 minute presentation by the teacher was recorded on a $1\frac{1}{2}$ hour videotape. Can all the oral reports be recorded on that same videotape?

35. Find the Error Describe and correct the error in the solution.

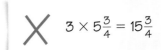

$$\times \quad 3 \times 5\frac{3}{4} = 15\frac{3}{4}$$

Find the product.

36. $3\frac{5}{7} \times 8\frac{4}{5}$ **37.** $4\frac{3}{8} \times 2\frac{1}{15}$ **38.** $6\frac{5}{7} \times 1\frac{5}{9}$ **39.** $1\frac{1}{9} \times 13\frac{1}{8}$

40. Writing Look back at Example 4 on page 315 of Lesson 7.1. Explain how you can use this approach to estimate the product of a fraction and a mixed number. Describe the steps you would use to estimate $\frac{5}{8} \times 42\frac{2}{5}$.

41. Critical Thinking Jason is estimating $5\frac{1}{2} \times 2\frac{1}{2}$. Would he get a better estimate if he calculated 6×3 or 5×3? Explain your answer.

42. Number Sense Denise found the product $3 \times 6\frac{1}{4}$ mentally by calculating $(3 \times 6) + \left(3 \times \frac{1}{4}\right)$. Use the distributive property to show why Denise's method works.

43. Miniature Books The Morgan Library in New York City owns a miniature book *Book of Hours* that dates back to around 1535. The front cover measures $2\frac{4}{5}$ inches by $1\frac{9}{10}$ inches. What is the area of the front cover?

Measuring in Smoots

In 1958, Massachusetts Institute of Technology student Oliver Reed Smoot, Jr., was used as a unit of measure to determine the length of the Harvard Bridge in Boston.
(See Brain Game, p. 330.)

Measurement In Exercises 44–46, one "Smoot" equals $5\frac{7}{12}$ feet. The length of the Harvard Bridge is $364\frac{2}{5}$ Smoots plus one ear.

44. Find the number of feet in 360 Smoots.

45. Use rounding to estimate the number of feet in $4\frac{2}{5}$ Smoots.

46. Use Exercises 44 and 45 to estimate the length of the bridge in feet.

47. Challenge Find the product $3\frac{12}{17} \times \frac{34}{45} \times 18 \times 1\frac{1}{24}$.

Mixed Review

Find the elapsed time. *(Lesson 6.6)*

48. 6:20 P.M. to 1:35 A.M.

49. 9:15 A.M. to 3:42 P.M.

Choose a Strategy Use a strategy from the list to solve Exercise 50. Explain your choice of strategy.

> **Problem Solving Strategies**
> - Guess, Check, and Revise
> - Draw a Diagram
> - Work Backward
> - Look for a Pattern

50. After spending $1 for bus fare and $4 for lunch and then earning $3, you have $6. How much money did you start with?

Basic Skills Use the division equation $48 \div 6 = 8$. The 48 tells you the total number of people who are being split into groups.

51. If the 6 tells you the size of each group, what does the 8 tell you?

52. If the 6 tells you the number of equal groups, what does the 8 tell you?

Test-Taking Practice

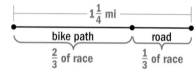

53. Multiple Choice In the race shown, how many miles are on the road?

A. $\frac{1}{4}$ mi   **B.** $\frac{5}{12}$ mi   **C.** $1\frac{1}{4}$ mi   **D.** $1\frac{5}{12}$ mi

54. Short Response A recipe makes 12 muffins. Your pan will hold a total of 18 muffins. Will your pan hold $1\frac{1}{2}$ times the recipe? Explain.

BrAIN GAME

Making Up Your Own Unit of Measure

That's about $7\frac{1}{16}$ Amandas long.

1. Choose a student in your group to be a unit of measure. Then decide on a name for the unit.

2. Use your unit to measure the length and the width of your classroom. Describe your method of measuring. If the length and width were not a whole number of units, how did you measure the fractional parts?

3. Calculate the area of your classroom in your units.

4. Compare the area you calculated to the areas calculated by other groups. How do you account for any differences?

Notebook Review

Review the vocabulary definitions in your notebook.

Copy the review examples in your notebook. Then complete the exercises.

Check Your Definitions

compatible numbers, p. 13

factor, p. 16

common factor, p. 222

simplest form, p. 229

mixed number, p. 244

improper fraction, p. 244

whole number, p. 684

Use Your Vocabulary

1. Copy and complete: to multiply mixed numbers, rewrite them as _?_ .

7.1 Can you multiply a fraction and a whole number?

 EXAMPLE   **a.** Find $4 \times \frac{2}{9}$.   **b.** Estimate $\frac{3}{5} \times 31$.

a. $4 \times \frac{2}{9} = \frac{4 \times 2}{9} = \frac{8}{9}$ Multiply the numerator by the whole number.

b. $\frac{3}{5} \times 31 \approx \frac{3}{5} \times 30$ Replace 31 with a number compatible with 5.

$= 18$ Think: $\frac{1}{5}$ of 30 is 6, so $\frac{3}{5}$ of 30 is 18.

☑ **Estimate. Then find the product.**

2. $\frac{1}{6} \times 19$ **3.** $\frac{3}{4} \times 11$ **4.** $15 \times \frac{3}{8}$ **5.** $30 \times \frac{2}{7}$

7.2–7.3 Can you multiply fractions and mixed numbers?

 EXAMPLE $3\frac{1}{8} \times 3\frac{3}{5} = \frac{25}{8} \times \frac{18}{5}$ Write $3\frac{1}{8}$ and $3\frac{3}{5}$ as fractions.

$$= \frac{\overset{5}{\cancel{25}} \times \overset{9}{\cancel{18}}}{\underset{4}{\cancel{8}} \times \underset{1}{\cancel{5}}}$$ Use rule for multiplying fractions. Divide out common factors.

$= \frac{45}{4}$, or $11\frac{1}{4}$ Multiply.

✓ **Check** Estimate: $3\frac{1}{8} \times 3\frac{3}{5} \approx 3 \times 4 = 12$. So, $11\frac{1}{4}$ is reasonable.

☑ **Find the product.**

6. $\frac{2}{5} \times \frac{5}{7}$ **7.** $\frac{2}{3} \times 7$ **8.** $3 \times 1\frac{3}{4}$ **9.** $7\frac{1}{5} \times 3\frac{1}{8}$

Stop *and* Think about Lessons 7.1–7.3

10. Number Sense When you multiply a nonzero whole number by a fraction, how can you tell if the product will be less than or greater than the whole number?

Review Quiz 1

Find the product.

1. $5 \times \frac{3}{4}$

2. $\frac{5}{6} \times 42$

3. $\frac{1}{8} \times \frac{2}{9}$

4. $\frac{3}{5} \times \frac{7}{10}$

5. $\frac{3}{4} \times \frac{2}{7} \times \frac{4}{5}$

6. $7 \times 2\frac{3}{7}$

7. $2\frac{2}{3} \times \frac{3}{4}$

8. $2\frac{6}{7} \times 4\frac{1}{12}$

Estimate the product.

9. $19 \times \frac{2}{9}$

10. $26 \times \frac{5}{9}$

11. $1\frac{7}{8} \times 7$

12. $4\frac{1}{4} \times 6\frac{7}{8}$

13. Paperback Books The front cover of a paperback book measures $5\frac{5}{16}$ inches by 8 inches. What is the area of the front cover?

Fill in the Fractions

Copy the equations. To read a secret message, find pairs of numbers that make the equations true and fill in their letters. Use each number once.

| ? × ? = $\frac{3}{8}$ |
| ? × ? = $1\frac{3}{5}$ |
| ? × ? = $\frac{1}{2}$ |
| ? × ? = $7\frac{1}{2}$ |

First Column

$C = \frac{5}{6}$

$E = 2\frac{1}{4}$

$I = 2\frac{2}{5}$

$N = \frac{3}{4}$

Second Column

$K = 3\frac{1}{3}$

$O = \frac{2}{3}$

$R = \frac{3}{5}$

$W = \frac{1}{2}$

Hands-on Activity

GOAL
Understand how to divide by a fraction.

MATERIALS
- ruler

Modeling Fraction Division

In this activity, you will use a ruler and patterns to explore fraction division.

Explore Model dividing by $\frac{3}{8}$. Use a table to look for a pattern.

1 Use a ruler to find the quotient $3 \div \frac{3}{8}$.

$\frac{3}{8}$ inch fits into 3 inches 8 times, so $3 \div \frac{3}{8} = 8$.

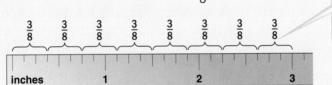

2 Copy the table below. Use a ruler to complete the left side. Then complete the right side.

Dividend	Divisor		Quotient	Dividend	Multiplier		Product
3	$\div$ $\frac{3}{8}$	=	8	3	$\times$ $\frac{8}{3}$	=	8
$\frac{3}{4}$	$\div$ $\frac{3}{8}$	=	?	$\frac{3}{4}$	$\times$ $\frac{8}{3}$	=	?
$\frac{3}{8}$	$\div$ $\frac{3}{8}$	=	?	$\frac{3}{8}$	$\times$ $\frac{8}{3}$	=	?

3 For each dividend, compare the product to the quotient. $3 \div \frac{3}{8} = 8$ and $3 \times \frac{8}{3} = 8$.

Your turn now Use a ruler to find the quotient. Then find the product.

1. $3 \div \frac{3}{4}$; $3 \times \frac{4}{3}$

2. $\frac{3}{4} \div \frac{1}{8}$; $\frac{3}{4} \times 8$

3. $\frac{3}{8} \div \frac{3}{16}$; $\frac{3}{8} \times \frac{16}{3}$

Stop and Think

4. Critical Thinking Describe how the divisor and the multiplier are related in the table shown above and in Exercises 1–3.

5. Writing Explain how you could use multiplication to find the quotient $\frac{3}{4} \div \frac{3}{16}$. Try your method. Use a ruler to check your result.

Dividing Fractions

BEFORE	Now	WHY?
You multiplied fractions.	You'll use reciprocals to divide fractions.	So you can solve problems involving rates, as in Example 2.

Word Watch

reciprocal, p. 334

Reciprocals For each pair of fractions being multiplied, the numerator and denominator of the product are equal, so the product is 1. Notice the relationship between the two fractions in each pair.

$$\frac{5}{3} \times \frac{3}{5} = \frac{15}{15} = 1 \qquad\qquad \frac{1}{12} \times \frac{12}{1} = \frac{12}{12} = 1$$

Two numbers, such as $\frac{5}{3}$ and $\frac{3}{5}$, whose product is 1 are **reciprocals** .

Every number except 0 has a reciprocal. To find it, write the number as a fraction, and then switch the numerator and the denominator.

EXAMPLE 1 Writing Reciprocals

	Original number	Fraction	Reciprocal	Check
a.	$\frac{4}{7}$	$\frac{4}{7}$	$\frac{7}{4}$	$\frac{4}{7} \times \frac{7}{4} = \frac{28}{28} = 1$
b.	10	$\frac{10}{1}$	$\frac{1}{10}$	$10 \times \frac{1}{10} = \frac{10}{10} = 1$
c.	$1\frac{3}{8}$	$\frac{11}{8}$	$\frac{8}{11}$	$1\frac{3}{8} \times \frac{8}{11} = \frac{88}{88} = 1$

Your turn now Write the reciprocal of the number.

1. $\frac{1}{2}$ **2.** 6   **3.** 1   **4.** $1\frac{2}{5}$

In the activity on page 333, you may have become aware of the following rule for dividing by a fraction.

Dividing Fractions

Words To divide by a fraction, multiply by its reciprocal.

Numbers $\frac{2}{3} \div \frac{3}{4} = \frac{2}{3} \times \frac{4}{3}$ **Algebra** $\frac{a}{b} \div \frac{c}{d} = \frac{a}{b} \cdot \frac{d}{c}$

EXAMPLE 2 Dividing Two Fractions

Caves An underground boat ride at Howe Caverns in New York is $\frac{1}{4}$ mile long. Find the average rate of travel when the ride takes $\frac{1}{3}$ hour.

$$\text{Rate} = \text{Distance} \div \text{Time}$$ Write the formula.

$$= \frac{1}{4} \div \frac{1}{3}$$ Use $\frac{1}{4}$ for the distance and $\frac{1}{3}$ for the time.

$$= \frac{1}{4} \times \frac{3}{1}$$ Multiply by the reciprocal of the divisor.

$$= \frac{1 \times 3}{4 \times 1}$$ Use the rule for multiplying fractions.

$$= \frac{3}{4}$$ Multiply.

ANSWER The boat's average rate of travel is $\frac{3}{4}$ mile per hour.

Howe Caverns, New York

EXAMPLE 3 Dividing a Fraction and a Whole Number

a. How can you share $\frac{3}{4}$ pound of a food equally among 6 people?

b. How many people does 6 cups serve, if $\frac{3}{4}$ cup serves one person?

Solution

a. Divide $\frac{3}{4}$ by 6.

$$\frac{3}{4} \div 6 = \frac{3}{4} \div \frac{6}{1}$$ Write 6 as a fraction.

$$= \frac{3}{4} \times \frac{1}{6}$$

$$= \frac{\overset{1}{\cancel{3}} \times 1}{4 \times \cancel{6}_2}$$

$$= \frac{1}{8}$$

ANSWER Each person gets $\frac{1}{8}$ pound.

b. Divide 6 by $\frac{3}{4}$.

$$6 \div \frac{3}{4} = \frac{6}{1} \div \frac{3}{4}$$

$$= \frac{6}{1} \times \frac{4}{3}$$

$$= \frac{\overset{2}{\cancel{6}} \times 4}{1 \times \cancel{3}_1}$$

$$= 8$$

ANSWER 6 cups serve 8 people.

Watch Out!

When dividing, be sure to take the reciprocal of the divisor, not the dividend. You can multiply to check your work. In Example 3, $\frac{1}{8} \times 6 = \frac{3}{4}$ and $8 \times \frac{3}{4} = 6$, so the divisions are correct.

Your turn now Divide. Write the answer in simplest form.

5. $\frac{5}{8} \div \frac{4}{3}$ **6.** $\frac{7}{10} \div \frac{1}{2}$ **7.** $\frac{9}{10} \div 3$ **8.** $12 \div \frac{2}{3}$

7.4 Exercises

More Practice, p. 714

Getting Ready to Practice

Vocabulary Tell whether the two numbers are reciprocals.

1. $\frac{3}{10}$ and $\frac{5}{3}$ **2.** $1\frac{1}{2}$ and $\frac{2}{3}$ **3.** 8 and $\frac{1}{8}$ **4.** 1 and 1

Rewrite the division expression as an equivalent multiplication expression. Then evaluate the expression.

5. $\frac{9}{2} \div \frac{3}{4}$ **6.** $\frac{5}{8} \div \frac{1}{3}$ **7.** $\frac{2}{3} \div 4$ **8.** $3 \div \frac{6}{5}$

9. Guided Problem Solving How many decorative magnets can you make with 12 inches of magnetic tape if each magnet uses $\frac{5}{8}$ inch of tape?

  (1 Write a division expression.

  (2 Use multiplication by the reciprocal to find the quotient.

  (3 Explain how to interpret the quotient to answer the question.

Practice and Problem Solving

Write the reciprocal of the number.

10. $\frac{4}{5}$ **11.** $\frac{3}{7}$ **12.** $\frac{9}{4}$ **13.** $\frac{1}{3}$

14. 12   **15.** 10   **16.** $2\frac{1}{7}$ **17.** $3\frac{1}{2}$

18. Explain How can you check whether two numbers are reciprocals?

Mental Math Copy and complete the statement.

19. $\frac{8}{5} \times \underline{?} = 1$ **20.** $\underline{?} \times 7 = 1$ **21.** $3 \times \frac{1}{3} = \underline{?}$ **22.** $\frac{7}{6} \times \frac{6}{7} = \underline{?}$

23. $6 \div \frac{1}{5} = 6 \times \underline{?} = \underline{?}$ **24.** $4 \div \frac{1}{6} = \underline{?} \times \underline{?} = \underline{?}$

25. Find the Error
Describe and correct the error in the solution.

$$\times \quad \frac{3}{4} \div \frac{1}{8} = \frac{4}{3} \times \frac{1}{8} = \frac{4}{24} = \frac{1}{6}$$

HELP with **Homework**

Example	Exercises
1	10–22
2	25–31, 38
3	23–24, 32–37, 39–41

Online Resources
CLASSZONE.COM

· More Examples
· eTutorial Plus

Find the quotient.

26. $\frac{1}{3} \div \frac{2}{3}$ **27.** $\frac{7}{8} \div \frac{3}{5}$ **28.** $\frac{5}{2} \div \frac{3}{4}$ **29.** $\frac{7}{5} \div \frac{1}{10}$

30. $\frac{2}{9} \div \frac{1}{4}$ **31.** $\frac{1}{12} \div \frac{5}{24}$ **32.** $8 \div \frac{4}{5}$ **33.** $\frac{25}{9} \div 5$

34. $\frac{1}{8} \div 4$ **35.** $\frac{3}{10} \div 6$ **36.** $5 \div \frac{20}{7}$ **37.** $3 \div \frac{10}{9}$

38. How many $\frac{1}{4}$ cup scoops can you get from $\frac{7}{8}$ cup of tuna salad?

39. **Travel Rate** You drive 15 miles in $\frac{1}{3}$ hour. Find your average rate of travel in miles per hour.

40. **Writing** Write and solve a problem that can be represented by $\frac{3}{8} \div 6$.

Extended Problem Solving It takes you $\frac{9}{16}$ pound of clay to make a teacup and $\frac{7}{8}$ pound of clay to make a mug.

41. **Calculate** How many teacups can you make with 5 pounds of clay? How many mugs can you make with 5 pounds of clay?

42. **Compare** Which uses more clay, a teacup or a mug?

43. **Decide** If you have a certain amount of clay, would you be able to make more teacups or more mugs? Explain how you know.

Number Sense Copy and complete the statement using <, >, or =. Explain how you can tell without actually finding the quotient.

44. $\frac{4}{9} \div 1 \ \underline{?} \ \frac{4}{9}$ **45.** $\frac{3}{5} \div 4 \ \underline{?} \ \frac{3}{5}$ **46.** $4 \div \frac{2}{3} \ \underline{?} \ 4$ **47.** $6 \div \frac{3}{2} \ \underline{?} \ 6$

 **Algebra** Evaluate the expression when $p = \frac{1}{3}$, $q = \frac{5}{9}$, and $r = 3$.

48. $p \div q$ **49.** $q \div p$ **50.** $(p \div q) \div r$ **51.** $p \div (q \div r)$

52. **Interpret** Use your results from Exercises 48–51. Can you conclude that fraction division is commutative? associative? Explain.

53. You earn $8 for $\frac{2}{3}$ hour of work. Find your hourly rate of pay.

54. **Critical Thinking** Use the diagram. Explain why you can find $3 \div \frac{1}{4}$ by multiplying 3×4.

55. Construction Nine acres of land are being divided into $\frac{3}{4}$ acre lots to build new houses. How many lots are there? What happens to the number of lots if the number of acres of land needed per lot is doubled?

56. Writing Copy and complete the statements. Then explain how dividing by a power of 10 follows the rule for dividing by a fraction.

Dividing by the decimal 0.1 has the same effect as multiplying by __?__.
Dividing by 10 has the same effect as multiplying by the decimal __?__.

57. Challenge In Exercise 54, a model is used to show why $3 \div \frac{1}{4} = 3 \times 4$.
Use models to find $3 \div \frac{2}{4}$ and $3 \div \frac{3}{4}$.
Copy and complete the chart. Use the results to explain why you can divide by multiplying by the reciprocal.

$$3 \div \frac{1}{4} = 12 = 3 \times 4$$
$$3 \div \frac{2}{4} = \underline{\ ?\ } = 3 \times 4 \times \frac{1}{?}$$
$$3 \div \frac{3}{4} = \underline{\ ?\ } = 3 \times 4 \times \frac{1}{?}$$

Mixed Review

Estimate the quotient. *(Lesson 1.2)*

58. $569 \div 8$ **59.** $145 \div 18$ **60.** $253 \div 42$ **61.** $308 \div 59$

Find the product. *(Lessons 7.2, 7.3)*

62. $\frac{3}{5} \times \frac{1}{9}$ **63.** $\frac{7}{2} \times \frac{6}{7}$ **64.** $8 \times 2\frac{1}{2}$ **65.** $2\frac{2}{3} \times 1\frac{5}{6}$

Basic Skills **You are given the price of an item. Determine the amount of change you will receive if you give the clerk a $20 bill.**

66. $7.50   **67.** $14.78   **68.** $.97   **69.** $12.39

Test-Taking Practice

INTERNET
State Test Practice
CLASSZONE.COM

70. Multiple Choice You have 4 pounds of trail mix. You put it in bags so that there is $\frac{2}{3}$ pound in each bag. How many bags do you fill?

    A. 2   **B.** $2\frac{2}{3}$ **C.** 3   **D.** 6

71. Multiple Choice Three gold prospectors pan $\frac{7}{8}$ ounce of gold from a stream. They split their gold into equal shares. Which choice shows each prospector's share?

    F. $\frac{1}{8}$ ounce   **G.** $\frac{7}{24}$ ounce   **H.** $\frac{1}{3}$ ounce   **I.** $\frac{7}{12}$ ounce

Dividing Mixed Numbers

LESSON 7.5

BEFORE ▶ **Now** **WHY?**

You divided fractions. You'll divide mixed numbers. So you can plan schedules, such as audition times in Exs. 43–45.

Word Watch

Review Words

compatible numbers, p. 13
mixed number, p. 244
improper fraction, p. 244

Modeling Division You can use a model to find the quotient $3\frac{1}{3} \div \frac{2}{3}$. Begin by drawing a model for $3\frac{1}{3}$. Then divide the model into groups of $\frac{2}{3}$.

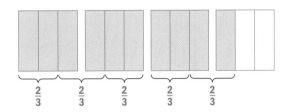

There are 5 groups of $\frac{2}{3}$. So, $3\frac{1}{3} \div \frac{2}{3} = 5$.

You can also find the quotient $3\frac{1}{3} \div \frac{2}{3}$ using paper and pencil, as in part (a) of Example 1. First you have to rewrite the mixed number as an improper fraction. In the model above, you can see that $3\frac{1}{3} = \frac{10}{3}$.

EXAMPLE 1 **Dividing a Mixed Number**

a. $3\frac{1}{3} \div \frac{2}{3} = \frac{10}{3} \div \frac{2}{3}$ Write $3\frac{1}{3}$ as an improper fraction.

$= \frac{10}{3} \times \frac{3}{2}$ Multiply by the reciprocal of the divisor.

$= \frac{\overset{5}{\cancel{10}} \times \overset{1}{\cancel{3}}}{\underset{1}{\cancel{3}} \times \underset{1}{\cancel{2}}}$ Use the rule for multiplying fractions. Divide out common factors.

$= 5$ Multiply.

b. $2\frac{5}{8} \div 6 = \frac{21}{8} \div \frac{6}{1}$ Write $2\frac{5}{8}$ and 6 as improper fractions.

$= \frac{21}{8} \times \frac{1}{6}$ Multiply by the reciprocal of the divisor.

$= \frac{\overset{7}{\cancel{21}} \times 1}{8 \times \underset{2}{\cancel{6}}}$ Use the rule for multiplying fractions. Divide out common factors.

$= \frac{7}{16}$ Multiply.

EXAMPLE 2 Dividing by a Mixed Number

$$6\frac{3}{5} \div 2\frac{1}{4} = \frac{33}{5} \div \frac{9}{4}$$ Write $6\frac{3}{5}$ and $2\frac{1}{4}$ as improper fractions.

$$= \frac{33}{5} \times \frac{4}{9}$$ Multiply by the reciprocal of the divisor.

$$= \frac{\overset{11}{\cancel{33}} \times 4}{5 \times \underset{3}{\cancel{9}}}$$ Use the rule for multiplying fractions. Divide out common factors.

$$= \frac{44}{15}, \text{ or } 2\frac{14}{15}$$ Multiply.

✓ **Check** Round $2\frac{1}{4}$ to 2 and replace $6\frac{3}{5}$ with the compatible number 6. The answer is reasonable because it is close to the estimate $6 \div 2 = 3$.

Your turn now Divide. Use estimation to check your answer.

1. $9\frac{1}{6} \div 5$ **2.** $6\frac{2}{3} \div \frac{8}{9}$ **3.** $\frac{7}{8} \div 3\frac{1}{4}$ **4.** $12\frac{1}{2} \div 3\frac{3}{4}$

5. Which quotient in Exercises 1–4 is less than 1?

EXAMPLE 3 Choosing an Operation

Cider Forty pounds of apples make about $3\frac{1}{2}$ gallons of cider. About how many pounds of apples are needed to make 1 gallon of cider?

Solution

① Choose the operation by thinking about a similar whole number problem: If 40 pounds of apples made 4 gallons of cider, you would *divide* 40 by 4. So, *divide* 40 by $3\frac{1}{2}$.

② Divide. $40 \div 3\frac{1}{2} = \frac{40}{1} \div \frac{7}{2}$

$$= \frac{40}{1} \times \frac{2}{7}$$

$$= \frac{40 \times 2}{1 \times 7}$$

$$= \frac{80}{7}, \text{ or } 11\frac{3}{7}$$

ANSWER You need about $11\frac{3}{7}$ pounds of apples to make 1 gallon of cider.

Getting Ready to Practice

1. **Vocabulary** Find the reciprocal of the mixed number $2\frac{3}{8}$.

Write the reciprocal of the divisor. Then find the quotient. Use estimation to check your answer.

2. $5\frac{1}{4} \div \frac{7}{8}$

3. $\frac{5}{6} \div 4\frac{2}{7}$

4. $8\frac{1}{2} \div 3\frac{3}{4}$

5. $14 \div 2\frac{2}{3}$

6. **Volunteer Work** If you split $5\frac{1}{2}$ hours of volunteer work equally over the next three weeks, how much time will you volunteer each week?

Practice and Problem Solving

HELP with Homework

Example	Exercises
1	7–8, 10–14, 22
2	9, 15–21, 23–27
3	28–31

Online Resources
CLASSZONE.COM
· More Examples
· eTutorial Plus

7. What division problem involving a mixed number is represented by the model? What is the quotient?

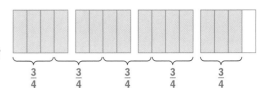

8. Sketch a model similar to Exercise 7 for $2\frac{4}{5} \div \frac{2}{5}$. Find the quotient.

9. **Decide** Are $3\frac{2}{5}$ and $3\frac{5}{2}$ reciprocals? Why or why not?

Find the quotient.

10. $7\frac{1}{5} \div \frac{2}{5}$

11. $8\frac{2}{3} \div \frac{2}{9}$

12. $4\frac{7}{8} \div \frac{13}{16}$

13. $2\frac{1}{10} \div 3$

14. $3\frac{4}{7} \div 5$

15. $\frac{5}{9} \div 4\frac{1}{6}$

16. $\frac{3}{8} \div 2\frac{1}{4}$

17. $5 \div 3\frac{1}{8}$

18. $11 \div 2\frac{4}{9}$

19. $15 \div 2\frac{1}{7}$

20. $4\frac{1}{4} \div 2\frac{1}{2}$

21. $2\frac{5}{6} \div 5\frac{1}{6}$

22. **Recipes** You have only a $\frac{1}{4}$ cup measure. How many times must you fill the $\frac{1}{4}$ cup measure for a recipe that uses $2\frac{1}{4}$ cups of milk?

23. **Packaging** You are stacking books in a box that is 12 inches high. Each book is $1\frac{1}{4}$ inches thick. How many books can you fit in the box in a single stack?

Estimation **Estimate the quotient.**

24. $15\frac{1}{3} \div 2\frac{2}{3}$ **25.** $28\frac{9}{10} \div 5\frac{1}{4}$ **26.** $18\frac{3}{5} \div 1\frac{11}{12}$ **27.** $20 \div 3\frac{1}{7}$

Choose the Operation **Solve. Explain why you chose the operation you used.**

28. Books One book is $2\frac{11}{16}$ inches thick. Another book is $1\frac{3}{8}$ inches thick. Will the books fit beside each other on a shelf that has a 4 inch space?

29. Twins Twin babies weigh $7\frac{1}{2}$ and $6\frac{5}{16}$ pounds. How much more does the heavier baby weigh than the lighter baby?

30. Dog Food If a bag contains 20 cups of dog food and you feed your dog $2\frac{2}{3}$ cups per day, how many days can you feed your dog from this bag?

31. Alligators An alligator has a total length of $11\frac{3}{4}$ feet. The length of the alligator's tail is one half of its total length. How long is the tail?

Describe the pattern. Then find the next two numbers in the pattern.

32. $25, 5, 1, \frac{1}{5}, \underline{\ ?\ }, \underline{\ ?\ }$

33. $\frac{1}{2}, \frac{1}{4}, \frac{1}{8}, \frac{1}{16}, \underline{\ ?\ }, \underline{\ ?\ }$

Critical Thinking **Predict whether the value of the expression** $4\frac{4}{5} \div x$ **will be *greater than 1* or *less than 1* for the given value of *x*. Then evaluate the expression.**

34. $x = 4\frac{2}{5}$ **35.** $x = \frac{3}{5}$ **36.** $x = 6$ **37.** $x = 5\frac{1}{3}$

38. Find the Error A recipe calls for $2\frac{1}{3}$ cups of broth. A cook is making $\frac{3}{4}$ of the recipe. Describe and correct any errors in finding the amount of broth needed.

$$2\frac{1}{3} \div \frac{3}{4} = \frac{7}{3} \div \frac{3}{4}$$
$$= \frac{3}{7} \times \frac{3}{4}$$
$$= \frac{9}{28} \ cup$$

39. Football Your football team gains $3\frac{1}{2}, 5, 4\frac{1}{2}, 8,$ and $6\frac{1}{2}$ yards on five consecutive plays. Find the mean number of yards gained for the plays.

Evaluate the expression.

40. $\left(6\frac{3}{4} \div \frac{3}{8}\right) \times 1\frac{1}{2}$ **41.** $4\frac{3}{8} \div 5 + 1\frac{3}{10}$ **42.** $7\frac{1}{6} - 2\frac{1}{4} \div 3\frac{6}{7}$

Extended Problem Solving Talent show auditions are scheduled to last about $3\frac{3}{4}$ hours. There are 31 acts to be viewed.

43. **Represent** Write an expression that represents the amount of time, in hours, for one act if each act is allowed the same amount of time.

44. **Estimate** Use a pair of compatible numbers to estimate the value of the expression you wrote in Exercise 43.

45. **Interpret** How many whole minutes should be allowed for each act?

 Algebra **Evaluate the expression for** $x = \frac{5}{8}$ **and** $y = 2\frac{1}{2}$.

46. $\dfrac{2x}{y}$ **47.** $y + \dfrac{2}{x}$ **48.** $\dfrac{x}{4 - y}$

49. **Challenge** A movie theater is open from 12:30 P.M. to 1:00 A.M. The length of each movie being shown at the theater is $2\frac{1}{4}$ hours. How many movies can be shown on each screen during one day? Does your answer change if there is a 15 minute break between movies? Explain.

Mixed Review

50. Use a benchmark to estimate the length of a fork in inches. Then measure to check your estimate. *(Lesson 2.1)*

Find the sum or difference. *(Lessons 6.4, 6.5)*

51. $6\frac{4}{7} + 2\frac{5}{7}$ **52.** $3\frac{2}{3} + 4\frac{3}{4}$ **53.** $7 - 3\frac{4}{9}$ **54.** $5\frac{1}{4} - 2\frac{7}{10}$

Basic Skills **Copy and complete the statement.**

55. 5 weeks 3 days = _?_ days   **56.** 265 min = _?_ hours _?_ min

Test-Taking Practice

57. **Multiple Choice** If it takes you $\frac{3}{4}$ hour to read one chapter of your book, how many chapters can you read in $5\frac{1}{4}$ hours?

A. $3\frac{15}{16}$ **B.** $4\frac{1}{2}$ **C.** 6   **D.** 7

58. **Short Response** How many shelves that are $1\frac{1}{2}$ feet long can you cut from a board that is $4\frac{3}{4}$ feet long? Is there wood left over? Explain.

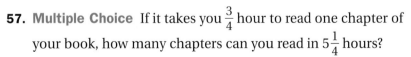

LESSON 7.6

Weight and Capacity in Customary Units

BEFORE You used metric units of mass and capacity.

▶ **Now** You'll use customary units of weight and capacity.

WHY? So you can estimate weights, such as that of a hang glider in Ex. 24.

In the Real World

Word Watch

ounce (oz), p. 344
pound (lb), p. 344
ton (T), p. 344
fluid ounce (fl oz), p. 345
cup (c), p. 345
pint (pt), p. 345
quart (qt), p. 345
gallon (gal), p. 345

Bakery If a baker slices a 1 pound loaf of bread into 16 slices, each slice weighs 1 ounce. Knowing the weight of familiar objects, such as a slice of bread, can help you to choose appropriate units.

Three customary units of weight are the **ounce** (oz), the **pound** (lb), and the **ton** (T).

1 ounce
about the weight
of a slice of bread

1 pound
about the weight
of a soccer ball

1 ton
about the weight
of a compact car

Ounces, pounds, and tons are related to each other.

1 lb = 16 oz   1 T = 2000 lb

EXAMPLE 1 **Choosing Units of Weight**

Choose an appropriate customary unit to measure the weight.

a. An apple weighs $6\frac{1}{4}$ _?_ .   **b.** A laptop computer weighs $6\frac{1}{4}$ _?_ .

Solution

a. An apple weighs $6\frac{1}{4}$ *ounces*, because it is heavier than a slice of bread and lighter than a soccer ball.

b. A laptop computer weighs $6\frac{1}{4}$ *pounds*, because it is heavier than a soccer ball and much lighter than a compact car.

Your turn now Choose an appropriate customary unit to measure the weight of the item.

1. golf ball   **2.** blue whale   **3.** bicycle

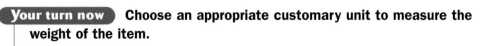

Capacity Five customary units of capacity are the **fluid ounce** (fl oz), the **cup** (c), the **pint** (pt), the **quart** (qt), and the **gallon** (gal).

1 fluid ounce   **1 cup**   **1 pint**   **1 quart**   **1 gallon**

The units of capacity are related to each other.

1 c = 8 fl oz   1 pt = 2 c   1 qt = 2 pt   1 gal = 4 qt

EXAMPLE 2   **Choosing Units of Capacity**

Choose an appropriate customary unit to measure the capacity.

a. large mug   **b.** water cooler

Solution

a. A large mug holds about as much as a pint-sized milk carton does. You can use pints or one of the smaller units, fluid ounces or cups.

b. A water cooler holds much more than a gallon jug does. You can use gallons or quarts, but you wouldn't use the smaller units.

EXAMPLE 3   **Choosing Customary Units**

What does each measure describe about an empty glass aquarium?

a. 55 gal   **b.** 45 lb

Solution

a. A gallon is a measure of capacity, so 55 gallons describes the amount of water the aquarium can hold.

b. A pound is a measure of weight, so 45 pounds describes how much the empty aquarium weighs.

Your turn now   Choose an appropriate customary unit to measure.

4. capacity of
a teakettle

5. capacity of
a juice glass

6. weight of
a toad

Getting Ready to Practice

Vocabulary Order the units from least to greatest.

1. Units of capacity: pints, gallons, cups, quarts, fluid ounces

2. Units of weight: tons, ounces, pounds

Choose an appropriate customary unit to measure the item.

3. weight of a gorilla   **4.** weight of a slipper

5. capacity of a soup bowl   **6.** capacity of a kitchen sink

Practice and Problem Solving

Match the object with its correct weight.

7. wrecking ball   **8.** kitten   **9.** cellular phone

A. $3\frac{1}{2}$ ounces   **B.** $3\frac{1}{2}$ tons   **C.** $3\frac{1}{2}$ pounds

10. Animals Choose an appropriate customary unit to measure the weight of each type of animal in the picture at the left.

Choose an appropriate customary unit to measure the capacity of the item.

11. bathtub   **12.** serving spoon   **13.** cream pitcher

Copy and complete the statement using *fluid ounces*, *pints*, or *gallons*.

14. The capacity of a water bottle is $1\frac{1}{4}$? .

15. The amount of water in a carnival dunking booth is 400 ? .

16. The amount of water you can hold in the palm of your hand is $\frac{3}{4}$? .

17. The capacity of a punch bowl is 24 ? .

Tell whether the measurement is a *weight*, a *capacity*, or a *length*.

18. 7 quarts   **19.** $2\frac{7}{8}$ pounds   **20.** 15 inches

21. $1\frac{1}{2}$ pints   **22.** 4 ounces   **23.** 7 fluid ounces

HELP with Homework

Example	Exercises
1	7–10, 24
2	11–17
3	18–23

Online Resources
CLASSZONE.COM

· More Examples
· eTutorial Plus

24. Hang Glider Choose the best estimate for the weight of a hang glider.

    A. 70 oz   **B.** 70 lb   **C.** 700 lb   **D.** 7 T

Decide **Is the capacity of the given object *less than* a quart, *about equal to* a quart, or *more than* a quart? Explain.**

25. bathroom sink   **26.** bottle of cough syrup   **27.** ice cube tray

28. Compare Order the
empty containers
from smallest to
largest by height,
by capacity, and by
weight. If you can't,
explain why not.

        glass vase   plastic bowl   paper cup

29. Critical Thinking Give a different benchmark than the one pictured for each customary unit of weight and capacity on pages 344 and 345.

30. Challenge Have a family member tape over the weight or capacity measurement on the labels of various containers around your home. Estimate the hidden measurements. Then uncover the labels to see how close each estimate was to the actual measurement.

Mixed Review

Copy and complete the statement. *(Lesson 4.8)*

31. 76 cm = _?_ mm   **32.** 8.5 kg = _?_ g   **33.** 175 mL = _?_ L

Write the fraction as a decimal. *(Lesson 5.8)*

34. $\frac{5}{8}$ **35.** $\frac{3}{40}$ **36.** $\frac{5}{6}$ **37.** $\frac{2}{9}$

Basic Skills **Use multiplication to check if the answer is correct.**

38. 267 ÷ 6 = 41 R1   **39.** 2851 ÷ 9 = 316 R3   **40.** 928 ÷ 23 = 40 R8

Test-Taking Practice

41. Multiple Choice Which object is unlikely to be weighed in ounces?

    A. bagel   **B.** screwdriver   **C.** piano   **D.** ear of corn

42. Short Response One pound of margarine measures 2 cups. You measure 2 cups of breakfast cereal and record its weight. Do you think the breakfast cereal also weighs one pound? Explain your reasoning.

Guess, Check, and Revise

Draw a Diagram

Perform an Experiment

Make a List or Table

Solve a Related Problem

Work Backward

Make a Model

Solve a Related Problem

Problem A friend builds the four shapes below and then challenges you to find the pattern and build the fifth shape.

❶ Read and Understand

Read the problem carefully.

Be sure to pay attention to both the number and the arrangement of small triangles.

❷ Make a Plan

Decide on a strategy to use.

One way to solve the problem is to solve a related problem.

❸ Solve the Problem

Reread the problem and solve a related problem.

Count the number of small triangles in the shapes to form a number pattern. Then solve the related problem of continuing the number pattern.

Shape: 1st   2nd   3rd   4th   5th

Number of small triangles: 1   4   9   16   ?

                          +3   +5   +7   +?

The 5th shape will have $16 + 9 = 25$ small triangles.

ANSWER A row with 2 more triangles is added each time. Add a row of 9 small triangles to the bottom of the 4th shape to create the 5th shape.

  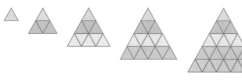

❹ Look Back

To check, you can think about the pattern another way and count small triangle side lengths along each edge.

Practice the Strategy

Use the strategy *solve a related problem*.

1. **Refreshments** You need to decide how many hot dogs to bring for a cookout with 30 students. Based on a party you had, you figure that 10 hot dogs serve 6 students. Describe how this problem is related to the scale drawing problems in Lesson 2.3. Then solve the problem.

2. **Art Project** Your art teacher gives you the pattern below as the beginning for a design. Use a related problem to help describe the pattern. Find the next two figures in the pattern.

3. **Building Shapes** You and a friend take turns adding on tiles as shown. Use a related problem to find the shapes you and your friend will build in the next two turns.

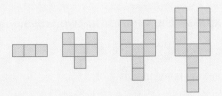

4. **Money** In the old English system of money, 12 pence = 1 shilling and 20 shillings = 1 pound. How is adding money in this system related to adding units of time? Express the sum of the two amounts shown using as few of these coins as possible.

   1 pound, 19 shillings, 10 pence
   2 shillings, 8 pence

Mixed Problem Solving

Use any strategy to solve the problem.

5. **Tests** An 11 question English test is worth 100 points. If vocabulary questions are worth 5 points and short answer questions are worth 20 points, how many of each type are on the test?

6. **Crafts** For a craft project, you have colored straws that measure 5 inches, 9 inches, and 11 inches. How can you use these straws to measure 3 inches?

7. **Find the Number** What number belongs in the blank?

   $(\underline{\ ?\ } \times 9) \div 2 + 6 - 45 = 51$

8. **Spinner** The spinner at the right has 5 equal sections. You spin the spinner two times. How many possible results are there from the two spins?

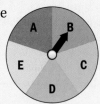

9. **Pictures** You are framing a picture that is $8\frac{1}{2}$ inches by 11 inches. The frame is $\frac{3}{4}$ inch wide and will cover $\frac{1}{4}$ inch along each edge of the picture. What will be the dimensions of the framed picture?

LESSON
7.7

Changing Customary Units

BEFORE	▶ Now	WHY?
You learned the customary units of measure.	You'll change customary units of measure.	So you can interpret measures, such as weight of a submersible in Ex. 39.

📓 Word Watch

Review Words

inch (in.), p. 55
foot (ft), p. 55
yard (yd), p. 55
mi (mi), p. 55

Changing Customary Units You can multiply and divide using the relationships below to change from one customary unit to another.

Length	Weight	Capacity
1 ft = 12 in.	1 lb = 16 oz	1 c = 8 fl oz
1 yd = 3 ft = 36 in.	1 T = 2000 lb	1 pt = 2 c
1 mi = 1760 yd = 5280 ft		1 qt = 2 pt
		1 gal = 4 qt

EXAMPLE 1 **Changing Units Using Multiplication**

Change 3 ft 7 in. to inches.

3 ft 7 in. = 3 ft + 7 in.	Write the measure as a sum.
= (3 × 12) in. + 7 in.	Change the feet to inches.
= 36 in. + 7 in.	Multiply.
= 43 in.	Add.

Watch Out!

There should always be more of the smaller unit and fewer of the larger unit. So, you *multiply* by 12 to change feet to inches and you *divide* by 16 to change ounces to pounds.

EXAMPLE 2 **Changing Units Using Division**

Change 35 oz to pounds. Express the answer in two ways.

There are 16 oz in a pound, so divide 35 by 16.

$$\begin{array}{r} 2 \text{ R}3 \\ 16\overline{)35} \\ \underline{32} \\ 3 \end{array}$$

◀ You can interpret the remainder as 3 oz.

◀ You can also interpret the remainder as $\frac{3}{16}$ lb, because the remaining division $3 \div 16$ can be written as $\frac{3}{16}$.

ANSWER There are 2 lb 3 oz in 35 oz. This can also be written as $2\frac{3}{16}$ lb.

Your turn now Copy and complete the statement.

1. 2 mi 480 yd = _?_ yd   **2.** 26 fl oz = _?_ c   **3.** $7\frac{1}{2}$ T = _?_ lb

---

Multiplying by a Form of 1 You can also change units without deciding whether to multiply or divide. Instead, you always multiply by a fraction that is equal to 1. For example, 1 gal = 4 qt, so $\dfrac{4\text{ qt}}{1\text{ gal}} = 1$.

EXAMPLE 3 Multiplying by a Form of 1

Change $2\dfrac{1}{4}$ ft to yards.

$$2\frac{1}{4}\text{ ft} = \frac{9\text{ ft}}{4}$$ Write the measurement in fraction form.

$$= \frac{9\text{ ft}}{4} \times \frac{1\text{ yd}}{3\text{ ft}}$$ Multiply by a form of 1. Use $\dfrac{1\text{ yd}}{3\text{ ft}}$.

$$= \frac{\overset{3}{\cancel{9\text{ ft}}} \times 1\text{ yd}}{4 \times \underset{1}{\cancel{3\text{ ft}}}}$$ Divide out "ft" so you are left with "yd."

$$= \frac{3}{4}\text{ yd}$$

What do you think? Science

EXAMPLE 4 Finding a Relationship

Camels If a camel is very thirsty, it can drink 30 gallons of water in 10 minutes. How many cups of water is that?

Solution

① Find the relationship between gallons and cups. Use the three relationships 1 gal = 4 qt, 1 qt = 2 pt, and 1 pt = 2 c.

$$\frac{1\text{ gal}}{4\text{ qt}} \times \frac{1\text{ qt}}{2\text{ pt}} \times \frac{1\text{ pt}}{2\text{ c}} = \frac{1\text{ gal} \times 1\cancel{\text{ qt}} \times 1\cancel{\text{ pt}}}{4\cancel{\text{ qt}} \times 2\cancel{\text{ pt}} \times 2\text{ c}} = \frac{1\text{ gal}}{16\text{ c}}$$

So, 1 gallon = 16 cups.

② Multiply 30 gal by a form of 1 that relates gallons and cups.

$$30\text{ gal} \times \frac{16\text{ c}}{1\text{ gal}} = \frac{30\cancel{\text{ gal}} \times 16\text{ c}}{1\cancel{\text{ gal}}} = 480\text{ c}$$

ANSWER A very thirsty camel can drink 480 cups of water in 10 minutes.

■ **Camels**

A camel's foot can be as big as a large plate. About how many inches across is a large plate? How does having such big feet help the camel to travel in the desert?

Your turn now Copy and complete the statement.

4. $\dfrac{5}{8}$ yd = ? in.   **5.** $2\dfrac{3}{8}$ lb = ? oz   **6.** 28 fl oz = ? qt

Solving a Related Problem To add or subtract customary units, think about how you added and subtracted units of time in Lesson 6.6. You will set up the problem and rename units in the same way.

EXAMPLE 5 **Adding and Subtracting Measures**

Model Trains A steam locomotive on a large model train has a length of 3 ft 2 in. The length of a passenger car is 1 ft 11 in.

a. How long is a model train with the locomotive and one passenger car?

b. What is the difference in the lengths of the two cars?

Solution

a. Add. Then rename the sum.

$$
\begin{array}{r}
3 \text{ ft} \quad 2 \text{ in.} \\
+ 1 \text{ ft} \quad 11 \text{ in.} \\
\hline
4 \text{ ft} \quad 13 \text{ in.}
\end{array}
$$

Rename 4 ft 13 in. as 5 ft 1 in.

ANSWER The train is 5 ft 1 in. long.

b. Rename. Then subtract.

Rename one of the feet as 12 in.

$$
\begin{array}{r}
3 \text{ ft} \quad 2 \text{ in.} \\
- 1 \text{ ft} \quad 11 \text{ in.}
\end{array}
\longrightarrow
\begin{array}{r}
2 \text{ ft} \quad 14 \text{ in.} \\
- 1 \text{ ft} \quad 11 \text{ in.} \\
\hline
1 \text{ ft} \quad 3 \text{ in.}
\end{array}
$$

ANSWER The difference is 1 ft 3 in.

The model locomotive shown is $26\frac{3}{8}$ in. long. It is built to a scale of 1 in. : 32 in.

7.7 Exercises

More Practice, p. 714

INTERNET
eWorkbook Plus
CLASSZONE.COM

Getting Ready to Practice

Vocabulary Copy and complete the statement.

1. $1 = \dfrac{8 \text{ fl oz}}{? \text{ c}}$
    2. $1 = \dfrac{? \text{ mi}}{1760 \text{ yd}}$
    3. $1 = \dfrac{1 \text{ lb}}{? \text{ oz}}$
    4. $1 = \dfrac{? \text{ qt}}{1 \text{ gal}}$

Copy and complete the statement.

5. 1 mi 6000 ft = 2 mi $\underline{?}$ ft
    6. 5 qt 1 pt = $\underline{?}$ qt 3 pt

7. 2 T 300 lb = $\underline{?}$ lb
    8. 99 in. = $\underline{?}$ yd $\underline{?}$ in., or $\underline{?}$ yd

In Exercises 9–10, change the measurement to the specified unit.

9. 17 yards to feet
    10. $1\frac{1}{3}$ cups to quarts

11. Find the sum and the difference of 6 lb 3 oz and 4 lb 15 oz.

Practice and Problem Solving

HELP with Homework

Example	Exercises
1	12–28
2	12–28
3	19–28
4	29–31
5	32–38

Online Resources
CLASSZONE.COM

· More Examples
· eTutorial Plus

Copy and complete the statement.

12. 3 lb 7 oz = _?_ oz   **13.** 4 yd 1 ft = _?_ ft   **14.** 5 c 6 fl oz = _?_ fl oz

15. 64 in. = _?_ ft _?_ in.   **16.** 64 in. = _?_ ft   **17.** 30 qt = _?_ gal

18. Amusement Park You must be more than 50 inches tall to go on a certain ride. You are 4 feet 3 inches tall. Are you allowed on the ride?

Change the measurement to the specified unit.

19. 6 T to pounds   **20.** 2 mi to yards   **21.** 10 pt to quarts

22. 24 fl oz to cups   **23.** 45 in. to feet   **24.** 4500 lb to tons

25. $\frac{5}{8}$ lb to ounces   **26.** $40\frac{1}{2}$ in. to yards   **27.** $8\frac{1}{2}$ c to pints

28. Maple Syrup One taphole in a maple tree typically yields enough sap in a year to produce $\frac{1}{3}$ gallon of syrup. How many quarts of syrup is that?

Change the measurement to the specified unit.

29. $1\frac{3}{4}$ qt to cups   **30.** $3\frac{1}{2}$ gal to pints   **31.** 48 fl oz to quarts

32. Find the Error Describe and correct the error in the solution.

$$\times \quad \begin{array}{r} 4 \text{ lb } 3 \text{ oz} \\ -\ 2 \text{ lb } 8 \text{ oz} \end{array} \longrightarrow \begin{array}{r} 3 \text{ lb } 13 \text{ oz} \\ -\ 2 \text{ lb } 8 \text{ oz} \\ \hline 1 \text{ lb } 5 \text{ oz} \end{array}$$

Find the sum or difference.

33. $\begin{array}{r} 6 \text{ ft } 7 \text{ in.} \\ +\ 5 \text{ ft } 8 \text{ in.} \\ \hline \end{array}$ **34.** $\begin{array}{r} 10 \text{ lb } 9 \text{ oz} \\ +\ 11 \text{ lb } 8 \text{ oz} \\ \hline \end{array}$ **35.** $\begin{array}{r} 4 \text{ gal } 1 \text{ qt} \\ +\ 2 \text{ gal } 3 \text{ qt} \\ \hline \end{array}$

36. $\begin{array}{r} 17 \text{ yd } 1 \text{ ft} \\ -\ 14 \text{ yd } 2 \text{ ft} \\ \hline \end{array}$ **37.** $\begin{array}{r} 9 \text{ T } 397 \text{ lb} \\ -\ 2 \text{ T } 478 \text{ lb} \\ \hline \end{array}$ **38.** $\begin{array}{r} 7 \text{ c } 3 \text{ fl oz} \\ -\ 1 \text{ c } 5 \text{ fl oz} \\ \hline \end{array}$

Submersibles ALVIN is an underwater vehicle used for research.

39. ALVIN weighs 35,200 pounds. What is its weight in tons?

40. Technology ALVIN can dive to depths as great as 14,764 feet. What is its depth limit in miles? Round to the nearest tenth of a mile.

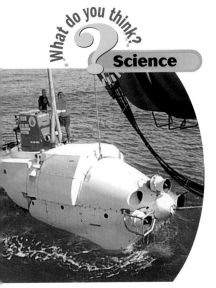

What do you think?
Science

■ **Submersibles**

ALVIN can carry a load of 1500 lb. Certain standard equipment weighs 339 lb. If the three people it carries weigh a total of 480 lb, about how many pounds of load are available for the researchers' equipment and samples? What decimal part of the 1500 lb load is that?

41. Estimation Hank Aaron hit a record 755 home runs in his career. The distance around a baseball diamond is 360 feet. Estimate how many miles Hank Aaron ran after hitting home runs.

Choose a Method Choose *mental math* or *paper and pencil* to copy and complete the statement with <, >, or =. Explain your choice.

42. 3645 lb ___?___ $1\frac{1}{2}$ T

43. $\frac{7}{8}$ mi ___?___ 4875 ft

44. $2\frac{1}{2}$ pt ___?___ $1\frac{1}{4}$ qt

45. $1\frac{2}{3}$ c ___?___ $13\frac{1}{3}$ fl oz

46. $2\frac{5}{12}$ ft ___?___ 30 in.

47. 280 oz ___?___ 17 lb

48. Geometry Find the perimeter of the figure.

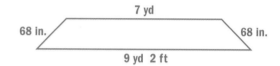

7 yd

68 in. 68 in.

9 yd 2 ft

49. Challenge About 6 gallons of ice cream and related frozen desserts are eaten per person per year in the United States. How many fluid ounces per person per day is that? Round to the nearest whole number.

Mixed Review

Find the next two numbers in the pattern. *(Lesson 1.1)*

50. 94, 87, 80, 73, ___?___ , ___?___

51. 729, 243, 81, 27, ___?___ , ___?___

Find the quotient. *(Lessons 7.4, 7.5)*

52. $\frac{5}{9} \div \frac{10}{27}$

53. $3\frac{1}{9} \div 5$

54. $2\frac{3}{4} \div 2\frac{2}{7}$

55. $\frac{1}{10} \div 7\frac{3}{5}$

Basic Skills Copy and complete the statement.

56. $\frac{4}{5} = \frac{20}{?}$

57. $\frac{3}{11} = \frac{?}{22}$

58. $\frac{42}{18} = \frac{?}{3}$

59. $\frac{16}{36} = \frac{4}{?}$

Test-Taking Practice

60. Multiple Choice Which of the following is *not* equivalent to 64 inches?

A. $1\frac{7}{9}$ yd

B. 5 ft 4 in.

C. $5\frac{1}{3}$ ft

D. $5\frac{1}{4}$ ft

61. Multiple Choice You can buy drinks in three sizes: 12 fluid ounces, $\frac{1}{2}$ pint, 2 cups. Which choice shows these sizes from greatest to least?

F. 12 fl oz, $\frac{1}{2}$ pt, 2 c

G. 2 c, 12 fl oz, $\frac{1}{2}$ pt

H. 12 fl oz, 2 c, $\frac{1}{2}$ pt

I. $\frac{1}{2}$ pt, 2 c, 12 fl oz

Technology Activity

Changing Units

GOAL Use a calculator to change between metric units and customary units.

Example **The calculator memory can help you change units.**

You plan to take the Marine Drive along the coast of Nova Scotia in Canada. The distance is given as 340 kilometers, but you want to know the distance in miles.

Solution

To change metric units to customary units, use the relationships shown in the table.

Length	Capacity	Weight
1 mm ≈ 0.0394 in.	1 mL ≈ 0.0338 fl oz	1 g ≈ 0.0353 oz
1 m ≈ 3.28 ft	1 L ≈ 1.06 qt	1 kg ≈ 2.2 lb
1 km ≈ 0.621 mi	1 kL ≈ 264 gal	

To change between kilometers and miles, use the fact that 1 km ≈ 0.621 mi. You will use 0.621 any time you change between these units, so store this value in memory.

Keystrokes

0.621 [STO ▶] [=]

Display

0.621

To change to miles, you would multiply 340 km × $\frac{0.621 \text{ mi}}{1 \text{ km}}$, so *multiply* by the value in memory. (To change miles to kilometers, you would *divide* by the value in memory.)

Keystrokes

340   [RCL]

Display

211.14

ANSWER The Marine Drive is about 211 miles long.

HELP with Technology

Many calculator keys have two uses. The use shown by the label above the key is called the second function. For this use, press **2nd** before pressing the key. To recall a value, some calculators use [RCL], the second function of **STO ▶**.

Your turn now **Find each value to the nearest whole number.**

1.

Length
127 km = _?_ mi
_?_ km = 34 mi
1388 km = _?_ mi

2.

Capacity
500 mL = _?_ fl oz
_?_ mL = 6 fl oz
1600 mL = _?_ fl oz

3.

Weight
12 kg = _?_ lb
50 kg = _?_ lb
_?_ kg = 77 lb

LESSONS

7.4 TO 7.7

Notebook Review

Review the vocabulary definitions in your notebook.

Copy the review examples in your notebook. Then complete the exercises.

Check Your Definitions

reciprocal, p. 334	ton, p. 344	pint, p. 345
ounce, p. 344	fluid ounce, p. 345	quart, p. 345
pound, p. 344	cup, p. 345	gallon, p. 345

Use Your Vocabulary

1. Copy and complete: A number times its _?_ is equal to 1.

7.4–7.5 Can you divide fractions and mixed numbers?

 EXAMPLE $9 \div 4\frac{2}{3} = \frac{9}{1} \div \frac{14}{3}$ Write 9 and $4\frac{2}{3}$ as improper fractions.

$$= \frac{9}{1} \times \frac{3}{14}$$ Multiply by the reciprocal of the divisor.

$$= \frac{27}{14}, \text{ or } 1\frac{13}{14}$$ Find the product.

✓ **Check** Estimate: $9 \div 4\frac{2}{3} \approx 10 \div 5 = 2.$ So, $1\frac{13}{14}$ is reasonable.

☑ **Find the quotient.**

2. $\frac{5}{6} \div \frac{7}{10}$ **3.** $\frac{4}{7} \div 5$ **4.** $\frac{3}{8} \div 2\frac{2}{5}$ **5.** $6\frac{3}{4} \div 1\frac{3}{4}$

7.6–7.7 Can you use customary units?

 EXAMPLE Copy and complete the statement.

a. 25 oz = _?_ lb _?_ oz = _?_ lb   **b.** 53 fl oz = _?_ pt

    25 ÷ 16 = 1 R9   53 fl oz = 53 fl oz $\times \frac{1 \text{ c}}{8 \text{ fl oz}} \times \frac{1 \text{ pt}}{2 \text{ c}}$

    So, 25 oz = 1 lb 9 oz = $1\frac{9}{16}$ lb. $= \frac{53 \text{ pt}}{16}, \text{ or } 3\frac{5}{16} \text{ pt}$

☑ **In Exercises 6–8, copy and complete the statement.**

6. $\frac{3}{8}$ T = _?_ lb   **7.** $3\frac{1}{2}$ pt = _?_ gal   **8.** 4 ft 10 in. = _?_ in.

9. Find the sum and the difference of 5 yd 1 ft and 2 yd 2 ft.

10. Choose an appropriate customary unit to measure a baby's weight.

Stop *and* Think   about Lessons 7.4–7.7

11. Critical Thinking You can change 30 quarts to gallons by using division or by multiplying by a form of 1. Describe the steps for each method. Then explain how the two methods are similar.

Review Quiz 2

Find the quotient.

1. $\dfrac{2}{15} \div \dfrac{3}{10}$ **2.** $7 \div \dfrac{4}{5}$ **3.** $2\dfrac{5}{8} \div 3$ **4.** $6\dfrac{3}{5} \div 2\dfrac{4}{9}$

Copy and complete the statement using an appropriate customary unit.

5. weight of a bulldozer = 15 ?   **6.** capacity of a thermos = 32 ?

Copy and complete the statement.

7. 5500 lb = ? T ? lb   **8.** $2\dfrac{2}{3}$ yd = ? in.   **9.** 22 c = ? qt

10. Electronics Your television weighs 19 pounds 8 ounces. Your stereo weighs 20 pounds 12 ounces. Can you safely place your television and your stereo on a shelf that holds 40 pounds? Explain.

A Pattern of Measures

For each box in which the measures are equal, list the number shown in red. Work in order across the rows. The numbers you list form a pattern. Look for the pattern and then predict the next two numbers.

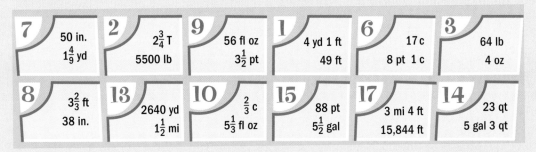

7 Chapter Review

📖 Vocabulary

reciprocal, p. 334
ounce, p. 344
pound, p. 344

ton, p. 344
fluid ounce, p. 345
cup, p. 345

pint, p. 345
quart, p. 345
gallon, p. 345

Vocabulary Review

Tell whether the statement is *true* or *false*.

1. The number 0 has no reciprocal.

2. The number 1 has no reciprocal.

3. The reciprocal of $1\frac{1}{3}$ is $\frac{4}{3}$.

4. The reciprocal of $\frac{1}{5}$ is 5.

5. The unit *pint* is used to measure weight.

6. The unit *ounce* is used to measure capacity.

7. 4 quarts = 1 gallon

8. 1000 pounds = 1 ton

9. 1 yard = 36 inches

10. 1 cup = 2 pints

Review Questions

Use compatible numbers to estimate the product. *(Lesson 7.1)*

11. $\frac{1}{3} \times 20$

12. $35 \times \frac{1}{6}$

13. $42 \times \frac{7}{8}$

14. $\frac{5}{12} \times 35$

15. Basketball You practice dribbling a basketball for $\frac{3}{4}$ hour each day. How much time do you practice dribbling in a week? *(Lesson 7.1)*

Evaluate the expression when $x = \frac{3}{4}$. *(Lesson 7.2)*

16. $\frac{8}{9}x$

17. $\frac{4}{15}x$

18. $\frac{7}{12}x$

19. $\frac{12}{23}x$

Find the product. *(Lessons 7.2, 7.3)*

20. $\frac{4}{7} \times \frac{3}{5}$

21. $\frac{1}{12} \times \frac{2}{3}$

22. $\frac{3}{10} \times \frac{6}{5}$

23. $\frac{7}{9} \times \frac{3}{4} \times \frac{2}{5}$

24. $2 \times 5\frac{1}{6}$

25. $6\frac{2}{5} \times \frac{3}{16}$

26. $2\frac{1}{4} \times 1\frac{2}{3}$

27. $3\frac{2}{7} \times 4\frac{2}{3}$

28. Flying Billboards A flying billboard measures $6\frac{2}{3}$ yards by 15 yards. What is the area of the billboard? *(Lesson 7.3)*

Estimate the product or quotient. *(Lessons 7.3, 7.5)*

29. $3\frac{3}{4} \times 2\frac{2}{7}$ **30.** $6\frac{9}{10} \times 4$ **31.** $11\frac{1}{2} \div 1\frac{7}{8}$ **32.** $26 \div 5\frac{1}{3}$

Find the quotient. *(Lessons 7.4, 7.5)*

33. $\frac{2}{9} \div \frac{2}{3}$ **34.** $\frac{5}{12} \div 10$ **35.** $14 \div \frac{7}{8}$ **36.** $\frac{21}{4} \div \frac{1}{6}$

37. $4\frac{2}{5} \div 4$ **38.** $8\frac{3}{4} \div \frac{5}{8}$ **39.** $\frac{9}{10} \div 2\frac{1}{2}$ **40.** $5\frac{5}{8} \div 3\frac{3}{5}$

41. Sub Sandwiches How many sub sandwiches that are $4\frac{1}{2}$ inches long can be cut from a sub that is 60 inches long? Is any left over? Explain. *(Lesson 7.5)*

Choose an appropriate customary unit of weight. *(Lesson 7.6)*

42. elephant **43.** bowling ball **44.** refrigerator **45.** scoop of ice cream

46. Blender The capacity of the blender shown at the right is $1\frac{1}{2}$ of some unit. Is that unit *fluid ounces*, *quarts*, or *gallons*? *(Lesson 7.6)*

Copy and complete the statement. *(Lesson 7.7)*

47. $2\frac{3}{4}$ lb = ? oz **48.** 86 in. = ? yd ? in.

49. 48 fl oz = ? qt **50.** 8 gal 3 qt = ? qt

51. Trucks A pickup truck weighs about $1\frac{7}{8}$ tons. How many pounds does it weigh? *(Lesson 7.7)*

Add or subtract. *(Lesson 7.7)*

52.
$$\begin{array}{r} 2 \text{ ft} \quad 10 \text{ in.} \\ + 4 \text{ ft} \quad 5 \text{ in.} \\ \hline \end{array}$$

53.
$$\begin{array}{r} 8 \text{ qt} \quad 1 \text{ pt} \\ + 3 \text{ qt} \quad 1 \text{ pt} \\ \hline \end{array}$$

54.
$$\begin{array}{r} 6 \text{ c} \quad 1 \text{ fl oz} \\ - 2 \text{ c} \quad 7 \text{ fl oz} \\ \hline \end{array}$$

55.
$$\begin{array}{r} 14 \text{ lb} \quad 8 \text{ oz} \\ - 9 \text{ lb} \quad 13 \text{ oz} \\ \hline \end{array}$$

Chapter Test

Find the product.

1. $10 \times \frac{4}{15}$

2. $\frac{1}{5} \times \frac{2}{9}$

3. $\frac{5}{12} \times \frac{3}{7}$

4. $\frac{1}{6} \times \frac{3}{8} \times \frac{2}{5}$

5. $3\frac{1}{4} \times 2$

6. $4\frac{5}{8} \times \frac{8}{11}$

7. $5\frac{1}{2} \times 3\frac{1}{3}$

8. $1\frac{2}{9} \times 1\frac{7}{11}$

Estimate the product or quotient.

9. $\frac{1}{7} \times 65$

10. $\frac{5}{8} \times 41$

11. $6 \times 7\frac{2}{3}$

12. $9\frac{1}{2} \div 3\frac{1}{8}$

13. Trains A train has 50 cars. $\frac{3}{5}$ of the cars are carrying grain. How many cars are carrying grain?

14. Evaluate the expression $\frac{3}{8}x$ when $x = \frac{5}{7}$.

Find the quotient.

15. $\frac{5}{6} \div \frac{4}{9}$

16. $\frac{1}{7} \div \frac{7}{12}$

17. $8 \div \frac{2}{5}$

18. $\frac{3}{10} \div 9$

19. $2\frac{5}{8} \div 7$

20. $6\frac{3}{5} \div \frac{3}{4}$

21. $\frac{1}{12} \div 3\frac{1}{4}$

22. $10\frac{1}{2} \div 2\frac{3}{4}$

23. Is the capacity of a teacup measured in *fluid ounces*, *pints*, or *quarts*?

Music Use the instruments shown.

24. An English horn is how many times as long as a flute?

25. Change each length to inches.

26. Copy and complete the statement using *ounces*, *pounds*, or *tons*:

A flute weighs about $15\frac{1}{2}$ _?_ .

$2\frac{5}{8}$ ft

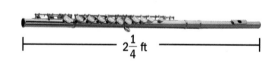

$2\frac{1}{4}$ ft

Copy and complete the statement.

27. $8 \text{ yd} = \underline{\ ?\ } \text{ ft}$

28. $7\frac{1}{2} \text{ gal} = \underline{\ ?\ } \text{ pt}$

29. $19 \text{ fl oz} = \underline{\ ?\ } \text{ c } \underline{\ ?\ } \text{ fl oz}$

30. $5000 \text{ lb} = \underline{\ ?\ } \text{ T}$

31. $5 \text{ lb } 3 \text{ oz} - 3 \text{ lb } 8 \text{ oz} = \underline{\ ?\ } \text{ lb } \underline{\ ?\ } \text{ oz}$

Chapter Standardized Test

Test-Taking Strategy If you are struggling to answer a particular question and find you are becoming very anxious or frustrated, then leave that question and go on.

Multiple Choice

1. A weather update on the news lasts $\frac{2}{15}$ hour. How many minutes does the update last?

A. 2 min **B.** 4 min **C.** 6 min **D.** 8 min

2. What is the value of the expression $\frac{7}{3}n$ when $n = \frac{9}{10}$?

F. $1\frac{7}{10}$ **G.** $\frac{61}{30}$ **H.** $2\frac{1}{10}$ **I.** $2\frac{3}{10}$

3. A lemonade recipe calls for $\frac{2}{3}$ cup of lemon juice. How much lemon juice do you need to make $1\frac{1}{2}$ times the recipe?

A. $\frac{3}{4}$ cup **B.** 1 cup

C. $1\frac{1}{3}$ cups **D.** $\frac{3}{2}$ cups

4. How many pieces of ribbon that are $\frac{1}{8}$ yard long can you cut from $\frac{3}{4}$ yard of ribbon?

F. 2 **G.** 4 **H.** 6 **I.** 8

5. A magic show is scheduled to last $2\frac{3}{4}$ hours. Each of the 6 magicians in the show is given the same amount of time. How long does each magician have?

A. $\frac{5}{12}$ h **B.** $\frac{11}{24}$ h **C.** $\frac{1}{2}$ h **D.** $\frac{3}{4}$ h

6. Which of the following is not a unit of capacity?

F. ounce **G.** cup **H.** pint **I.** gallon

7. Which measurement could be the weight of a bar of soap?

A. $4\frac{3}{4}$ T **B.** $4\frac{3}{4}$ lb **C.** $4\frac{3}{4}$ oz **D.** $4\frac{3}{4}$ fl oz

8. What is the sum of 17 feet 7 inches and 11 feet 9 inches?

F. 5 ft 10 in. **G.** 28 ft 4 in.

H. 29 ft 4 in. **I.** 29 ft 6 in.

9. Which of the following statements is false?

A. $2\frac{1}{2}$ qt > 5 pt **B.** 3 gal < 25 pt

C. 2 pt > 30 fl oz **D.** $5\frac{1}{4}$ c = 42 fl oz

Short Response

10. The diagram shows the dimensions of the pages in a magazine. Estimate the area of each page. Explain your steps.

$10\frac{13}{16}$ in.

$8\frac{1}{4}$ in.

Extended Response

11. A quilt pattern uses squares with sides that are $4\frac{1}{2}$ inches long, not including seams. Sue wants to reduce each side to $\frac{2}{3}$ of the length on the pattern. What are the dimensions of a reduced square? How many reduced squares does she need to sew together to make a 1 foot by 1 foot square? Explain your steps.

Strategies for Answering
Short Response Questions

Problem
There are $3\frac{1}{2}$ cups of flour in one pound of flour. Your recipe for Key Lime cake calls for $1\frac{1}{2}$ cups of flour. How many cakes can you make using a 5 pound bag of flour?

Full credit solution

The number of cakes you can make is the number of cups of flour in a 5 pound bag divided by the number of cups of flour in each cake.

Cups in 5 lb bag = Pounds per bag × Cups per pound

$$= 5 \times 3\frac{1}{2} = \frac{5}{1} \times \frac{7}{2} = \frac{35}{2} = 17\frac{1}{2}$$

Number of cakes = Cups in 5 lb bag ÷ Cups per cake

$$= 17\frac{1}{2} \div 1\frac{1}{2} = \frac{35}{2} \times \frac{2}{3} = \frac{35}{3} = 11\frac{2}{3}$$

You can make 11 cakes.

This reasoning is the key to choosing the operations you need.

The steps of the solution are clearly written.

The question asked is answered correctly.

Partial credit solution

There are $17\frac{1}{2}$ cups of flour in a 5 pound bag.

$$17\frac{1}{2} \div 1\frac{1}{2} = \frac{35}{2} \times \frac{2}{3} = \frac{35}{3} = 11\frac{2}{3}$$

You can make $11\frac{2}{3}$ cakes.

The reasoning and calculations are correct.

The answer makes no sense. You cannot make a fractional number of cakes.

Partial credit solution

$$\frac{35}{2} \times \frac{2}{3} = \frac{35}{3} = 11\frac{2}{3}$$

You can make 11 cakes.

Without explanation, the reasoning behind this calculation is unclear.

The answer is correct.

No credit solution

The wrong operations have been chosen.

$$\left(5 + 3\frac{1}{2}\right) \times 1\frac{1}{2} = 8\frac{1}{2} \times 1\frac{1}{2} = \frac{17}{2} \times \frac{3}{2} = \frac{51}{4} = 12\frac{3}{4}$$

You can make 12 cakes. •- - - - - - - - - - - - - The answer is not correct.

Your turn now

Score each solution to the short response question below as *full credit*, *partial credit*, or *no credit*. Explain your reasoning.

Problem Rina weighed $7\frac{1}{4}$ pounds at birth. She gained an average of $\frac{1}{24}$ pound per day for the first 30 days and an average of $1\frac{1}{4}$ pounds per month for the next 5 months. What was Rina's weight in pounds at six months?

Watch Out!

If a problem involves measurements, don't forget to include units with your solutions.

1. $7\frac{1}{4} + \frac{2}{3} + 1\frac{1}{4} = 9\frac{1}{6}$; Rina's weight at six months was $9\frac{1}{6}$ pounds.

2. Rina gained $30 \times \frac{1}{24} = \frac{30}{24} = \frac{5}{4}$ pounds in her first 30 days and $5 \times 1\frac{1}{4} = \frac{5}{1} \times \frac{5}{4} = \frac{25}{4}$ pounds in the next 5 months. At six months she weighed $7\frac{1}{4} + \frac{5}{4} + \frac{25}{4} = 7\frac{31}{4} = 14\frac{3}{4}$ pounds.

3. Rina's total weight gain was $30 \times \frac{1}{24} + 5 \times 1\frac{1}{4}$, or $7\frac{1}{2}$ pounds, so her weight at six months was $7\frac{1}{4} + 7\frac{1}{2} = 14\frac{3}{4}$ pounds.

Short Response

1. Suppose you earn $4.75 per hour and work 3.5 hours each day, 4 days per week. What is your weekly salary? Explain how you found your answer.

2. A 3.5 pound bag of oranges costs $2.99. Individual oranges are sold at $.89 per pound. Which is the better buy? Explain your reasoning.

3. Sandra has three boards, as shown.

Board	1	2	3
Length (inches)	60	96	120

She needs to cut the boards into short pieces of the same length. What is the greatest possible length that she can use for the short pieces? How many pieces of that length will she have altogether after cutting the boards? Show your steps.

4. Kaylene's score on a quiz was $\frac{23}{25}$. Roger's score was 0.92, and Devon's score was $\frac{9}{10}$. Which two students received the same score? Was the third score *higher* or *lower* than the other two scores? Explain.

5. The sides of a triangular design are $5\frac{1}{2}$ inches, $3\frac{7}{8}$ inches, and $2\frac{1}{4}$ inches long. Is a one foot piece of yarn long enough to fit around the design? Explain.

6. A $3\frac{5}{8}$ inch nail is driven through a wooden door. The nail extends beyond the door by $\frac{7}{8}$ inch. How thick is the door? Explain how you found your answer.

7. Twelve students tried out for speaking parts in the school play. Two thirds of these students will get speaking parts. How many of the students who tried out for a speaking part will *not* get one? Explain how you found your answer.

8. Alice needed $4\frac{5}{6}$ yards of ribbon for a project. She bought 5 yards of ribbon. How many extra inches of ribbon did Alice buy? Show your steps.

9. A bulletin board is 56 inches wide. How many $3\frac{1}{2}$ inch columns can be created if $\frac{1}{4}$ inch is left between columns? Explain how you found your answer.

10. Katie poured 12 fluid ounces of juice from a full 6 quart container. How many cups were left in the container? Explain how you found your answer.

11. Sammy has 4 pounds 8 ounces of trail mix. He wants to make snack bags of the mix that are $\frac{3}{8}$ pound each. How many bags can he make? Show your steps.

12. The circle graph shows the results of a survey that asked people about the amount of sleep they usually get.

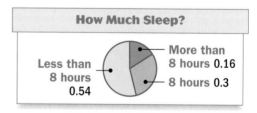

Write each decimal as a fraction and show that the fractions add up to 1. Explain why the fractions must add up to 1.

Multiple Choice

13. Mr. Washington wants to divide his class of 30 students into groups of the same size with none left over. Which number of groups would *not* be possible?

A. 3   **B.** 4   **C.** 5   **D.** 6

14. A mark on the side of a pier shows that the water is $4\frac{7}{8}$ feet deep. When the tide is high, the depth increases by $2\frac{1}{4}$ feet. About how deep is the water when the tide is high?

F. 2 feet   **G.** 3 feet

H. 7 feet   **I.** 8 feet

15. Yesterday, Jerome spent $1\frac{3}{4}$ hours skateboarding, while Alisha played basketball for $\frac{17}{10}$ hours. Yolanda jogged for $1\frac{4}{5}$ hours, while Miguel played soccer for $\frac{3}{2}$ hours. Who devoted the most time to his or her activity?

A. Alisha   **B.** Miguel

C. Jerome   **D.** Yolanda

16. An adult has 206 bones. Of these, 106 are in the feet, ankles, wrists, and hands. What fraction of the bones are in the feet, ankles, wrists, and hands?

F. $\frac{1}{2}$ **G.** $\frac{53}{103}$ **H.** $\frac{6}{11}$ **I.** $\frac{11}{20}$

Extended Response

17. The table below shows the number of minutes of commercials on three stations for a certain number of minutes of viewing time.

Channel	A	B	C
Minutes of commercials	22	29	14
Viewing time (minutes)	90	120	60

Use fractions to decide which channel showed commercials for the greatest portion of the viewing time. Then use decimals to answer this question. Compare and contrast the two methods.

18. Megan left her house at 7:30 A.M. She walked to the bus stop in 14 minutes. The bus ride to the city took 57 minutes. Then she spent 8 minutes walking to her office. Did she arrive at the office before 9 A.M.? Explain.

19. Nick is planning a party. He invites 24 guests. He wants to serve at least 2 cups of fruit punch to each guest. He plans to fill a $3\frac{1}{2}$ gallon punch bowl. Will he have enough punch? Explain your answer.

Cumulative Practice for Chapters 5–7

Chapter 5

Multiple Choice In Exercises 1–11, choose the letter of the correct answer.

1. Which number is prime? *(Lesson 5.1)*

   A. 10   **B.** 41   **C.** 63   **D.** 77

2. What is the prime factorization of 96? *(Lesson 5.1)*

   F. $1 \times 2^5 \times 3$ **G.** $2^5 \times 3$

   H. $4^2 \times 6$ **I.** 2×48

3. You have boards of lengths 80 inches and 128 inches. You divide the boards into pieces of the same length. Find the greatest possible length you can use. *(Lesson 5.2)*

   A. 4 in.   **B.** 8 in.   **C.** 16 in.   **D.** 32 in.

4. Which fraction is *not* equivalent to $\frac{24}{40}$? *(Lesson 5.3)*

   F. $\frac{3}{5}$ **G.** $\frac{6}{10}$ **H.** $\frac{12}{20}$ **I.** $\frac{4}{5}$

5. Which fraction is the simplest form of $\frac{16}{48}$? *(Lesson 5.3)*

   A. $\frac{1}{3}$ **B.** $\frac{2}{6}$ **C.** $\frac{4}{12}$ **D.** $\frac{8}{24}$

6. What is the LCM of 40 and 18? *(Lesson 5.4)*

   F. 24   **G.** 120   **H.** 160   **I.** 360

7. Which list of fractions is arranged in order from least to greatest? *(Lesson 5.5)*

   A. $\frac{1}{3}, \frac{3}{8}, \frac{3}{5}, \frac{5}{6}$ **B.** $\frac{1}{3}, \frac{3}{8}, \frac{5}{6}, \frac{3}{5}$

   C. $\frac{1}{3}, \frac{3}{5}, \frac{3}{8}, \frac{5}{6}$ **D.** $\frac{5}{6}, \frac{3}{5}, \frac{3}{8}, \frac{1}{3}$

8. Which improper fraction is equivalent to $7\frac{5}{8}$? *(Lesson 5.6)*

   F. $\frac{47}{8}$ **G.** $\frac{56}{8}$ **H.** $\frac{61}{8}$ **I.** $\frac{61}{5}$

9. How can $\frac{22}{3}$ be written as a mixed number? *(Lesson 5.6)*

   A. $2\frac{2}{3}$ **B.** $7\frac{1}{3}$ **C.** $7\frac{2}{3}$ **D.** $8\frac{1}{3}$

10. Val has recorded 0.4 of the school concert on a cassette tape. What fraction of the concert has she recorded? *(Lesson 5.7)*

    F. $\frac{1}{4}$ **G.** $\frac{2}{5}$ **H.** $\frac{3}{5}$ **I.** $\frac{3}{4}$

11. Which decimal is equivalent to $\frac{5}{9}$? *(Lesson 5.8)*

    A. $0.\overline{4}$ **B.** 0.5 **C.** $0.\overline{5}$ **D.** 1.8

12. **Short Response** Judy has 126 pencil boxes stacked in piles of equal size. What are all the possible pile sizes? Explain how you found your answer. *(Lesson 5.1)*

13. **Extended Response** Today every eighth customer at a restaurant will get a free sandwich, and every sixth customer will get a free drink. *(Lesson 5.4)*

    a. Which customers will be the first three to get free sandwiches?

    b. Which customers will be the first three to get free drinks?

    c. Which customer will be the first to get both a free drink and a free sandwich?

Chapter 6

Multiple Choice In Exercises 14–21, choose the letter of the correct answer.

14. Which number is the best estimate of the sum $3\frac{6}{7} + 4\frac{1}{8}$? *(Lesson 6.1)*

A. 7   **B.** 8   **C.** 9   **D.** 11

15. Which number is the best estimate of the difference $10\frac{7}{8} - 5\frac{1}{6}$? *(Lesson 6.1)*

F. 3   **G.** 4   **H.** 6   **I.** 7

16. The Tylers canned $\frac{11}{12}$ bushel of peaches yesterday. They canned $\frac{5}{12}$ bushel of peaches today. How much more did they can yesterday than today? *(Lesson 6.2)*

A. $\frac{5}{12}$ bushel   **B.** $\frac{1}{2}$ bushel

C. $\frac{2}{3}$ bushel   **D.** $1\frac{1}{3}$ bushels

17. Find the difference $\frac{13}{14} - \frac{5}{7}$. *(Lesson 6.3)*

F. $\frac{3}{14}$ **G.** $\frac{3}{7}$ **H.** $1\frac{1}{7}$ **I.** $1\frac{9}{14}$

18. Find the sum $4\frac{2}{3} + 1\frac{7}{9}$. *(Lesson 6.4)*

A. $5\frac{4}{9}$ **B.** $5\frac{3}{4}$ **C.** $6\frac{4}{9}$ **D.** $6\frac{5}{9}$

19. One hiking trail is $6\frac{1}{10}$ miles long. Another hiking trail is $3\frac{4}{5}$ miles long. How much longer is the first trail? *(Lesson 6.5)*

F. $2\frac{3}{10}$ miles   **G.** $2\frac{4}{5}$ miles

H. $3\frac{3}{5}$ miles   **I.** $3\frac{7}{10}$ miles

20. On Saturday David spent 1 hour and 30 minutes on homework. On Sunday he spent 1 hour and 45 minutes on homework. How much time did David spend on homework altogether? *(Lesson 6.6)*

A. 1 h 15 min   **B.** 2 h 15 min

C. 3 h 15 min   **D.** 3 h 45 min

21. The Lions plan to arrive at the field at 7:15 A.M. for the baseball playoff. Their game begins at 10:05 A.M. How long will they have to wait until their game starts? *(Lesson 6.6)*

F. 1 h 15 min   **G.** 1 h 20 min

H. 2 h 45 min   **I.** 2 h 50 min

22. Short Response The graph shows the results of a survey about favorite places to visit in a city. What fraction of the people surveyed prefer to go to a museum when they visit the city? Explain how you found your answer. *(Lesson 6.3)*

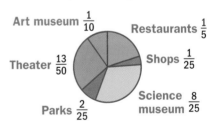

Art museum $\frac{1}{10}$ Restaurants $\frac{1}{5}$

Theater $\frac{13}{50}$ Shops $\frac{1}{25}$

Science museum $\frac{8}{25}$

Parks $\frac{2}{25}$

23. Extended Response A bagel recipe calls for $3\frac{3}{4}$ cups of flour to make 18 bagels. Bob wants to make 36 bagels. *(Lessons 6.4, 6.5)*

a. How much flour does Bob need to make 36 bagels? Explain how you found your answer.

b. Bob has $1\frac{2}{3}$ cups of flour. How much more flour does he need? Explain how you found your answer.

Chapter 7

Multiple Choice In Exercises 24–32, choose the letter of the correct answer.

24. Which number is *not* a reasonable estimate of the product $\frac{5}{6} \times 35$? *(Lesson 7.1)*

    A. 25   **B.** 30   **C.** 35   **D.** 42

25. What is the value of $\frac{3}{4}n$ when $n = \frac{5}{6}$? *(Lesson 7.2)*

    F. $\frac{8}{15}$ **G.** $\frac{5}{8}$ **H.** $\frac{4}{5}$ **I.** $\frac{5}{6}$

26. What is the area of a rectangular pen that is $2\frac{1}{2}$ yards long and $1\frac{2}{3}$ yards wide? *(Lesson 7.3)*

    A. $4\frac{1}{6}$ yd   **B.** $4\frac{1}{6}$ yd^2

    C. $8\frac{1}{3}$ yd   **D.** $8\frac{1}{3}$ yd^2

27. Find the quotient $\frac{4}{5} \div \frac{2}{3}$. *(Lesson 7.4)*

    F. $\frac{2}{15}$ **G.** $\frac{8}{15}$ **H.** $\frac{5}{6}$ **I.** $1\frac{1}{5}$

28. Find the quotient $4 \div \frac{3}{8}$. *(Lesson 7.4)*

    A. $\frac{3}{32}$ **B.** $1\frac{1}{2}$ **C.** $10\frac{2}{3}$ **D.** $11\frac{1}{3}$

29. Sharon uses $11\frac{1}{2}$ cups of flour to make 4 loaves of bread. How many cups of flour does she use for each loaf? *(Lesson 7.5)*

    F. $2\frac{1}{2}$ cups   **G.** $2\frac{7}{8}$ cups

    H. $3\frac{1}{8}$ cups   **I.** $4\frac{1}{8}$ cups

30. Find the quotient $4\frac{1}{5} \div 1\frac{3}{4}$. *(Lesson 7.5)*

    A. $2\frac{14}{37}$ **B.** $2\frac{2}{5}$ **C.** $4\frac{4}{15}$ **D.** $7\frac{7}{20}$

31. Which measurement could be the weight of an apple? *(Lesson 7.6)*

    F. 4 oz   **G.** 4 qt   **H.** 4 lb   **I.** 4 T

32. What is the difference between 12 feet 7 inches and 4 feet 9 inches? *(Lesson 7.7)*

    A. 7 ft 10 in.   **B.** 8 ft 1 in.

    C. 8 ft 2 in.   **D.** 16 ft 16 in.

33. **Short Response** You burn about 450 calories per hour biking. You biked $\frac{3}{4}$ hour on Friday, $1\frac{1}{2}$ hours on Saturday, and $3\frac{1}{4}$ hours on Sunday. How many calories did you burn while biking on those days? Explain. *(Lesson 7.3)*

34. **Extended Response** Use the recipe below. *(Lessons 7.1, 7.7)*

    Onion Dip
    Serves 2

    $\frac{1}{4}$ cup sour cream

    $\frac{1}{2}$ teaspoon lemon juice

    1 tablespoon onion soup mix

    a. Explain how to increase the recipe to serve 14 people.

    b. How many teaspoons of lemon juice will you need if you increase the recipe to serve 14 people?

    c. How many pints of sour cream will you need if you increase the recipe to serve 14 people?

UNIT 3 Proportions, Percent, and Geometry

Chapter 8 Ratio, Proportion, and Percent

- Use ratios, rates, proportions, and percents to solve problems.
- Know the relationships between fractions, decimals, and percents.

Chapter 9 Geometric Figures

- Draw, name, classify, and measure angles.
- Draw, name, and use symbols to represent geometric figures.
- Relate, classify, and know the properties of two-dimensional figures.

From Chapter 8, p. 374

How many cellos are in a school orchestra?

Chapter 10 Geometry and Measurement

- Estimate, find, and relate areas of two-dimensional figures.
- Know the properties of, classify, and draw solid figures.
- Draw circle graphs.

UNIT 3	STANDARDIZED TEST PREP

Strategies and practice directly follow Chapter 10.

8

Ratio, Proportion, and Percent

BEFORE

In previous chapters you've...

- Compared and ordered fractions and decimals
- Found perimeters and areas

Now

In Chapter 8 you'll study...

- Writing ratios and rates
- Solving proportions
- Working with percents
- Changing between percents, decimals, and fractions

WHY?

So you can solve real-world problems about...

- space, p. 379
- kangaroos, p. 387
- school murals, p. 389
- volleyball, p. 399

 Internet Preview
CLASSZONE.COM

- eEdition Plus Online
- eWorkbook Plus Online
- eTutorial Plus Online
- State Test Practice
- More Examples

Chapter Warm-Up Game

Review skills you need for this chapter in this game. Work with a partner.

Key Skill:
Comparing fractions and decimals

NUMBER CHALLENGE

MATERIALS

- 1 deck of *Number Challenge* cards

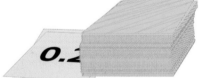

PREPARE Deal half the cards to each player. Place your cards face down in front of you in a pile. On each turn, follow the steps on the next page.

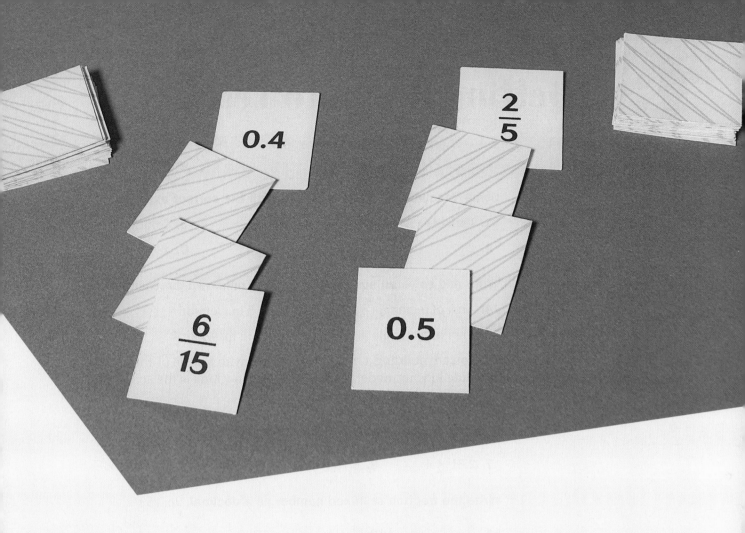

① **COMPARE** Turn over the top cards from your piles. The player with the greater number collects the cards and puts them on the bottom of his or her pile.

② **CHALLENGE** If the two cards have the same value, each player places two new cards face down on the cards played in Step 1. Then repeat Step 1.

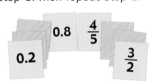

HOW TO WIN Collect all the cards, or collect the greater number of cards after a set period of time.

Stop *and* Think

1. **Critical Thinking** Which cards have the greatest value in this game? If you have all of these cards, is there any way you can lose?

2. **Extension** Design six new cards to add to the deck. The cards may be either decimals or fractions, but make sure that each card has a matching card with an equivalent number on it.

Getting Ready to Learn

Review What You Need to Know

Using Vocabulary **Match the word with the correct example.**

1. variable   **2.** equation   **3.** solution

A. 2   **B.** $x + 3 = 5$ **C.** x

Write and solve an equation to find the unknown dimension. *(p. 61)*

4. Area of rectangle = 12 in.^{2}, width = 3 in., length = ?

5. Area of rectangle = 96 m^2, length = 12 m, width = ?

6. You are building a model playground with a scale of 1 in. : 2 ft. The slide in your model is 6 inches long. How long is the actual slide? *(p. 68)*

Find the product. Simplify if possible. *(pp. 153, 313)*

7. 2.61×4 **8.** 6.78×9 **9.** $\frac{3}{8} \times 24$ **10.** $9 \times \frac{4}{3}$

Write the fraction or mixed number as a decimal. *(p. 253)*

11. $\frac{3}{4}$ **12.** $\frac{8}{9}$ **13.** $3\frac{1}{5}$ **14.** $2\frac{1}{8}$

Word Watch

Review Words

variable, p. 29
equation, p. 36
solution, p. 36
area, p. 62
scale drawing, p. 68
scale, p. 68
decimal, p. 108
fraction, p. 228
simplest form, p. 229

You should include material that appears on a notebook like this in your own notes.

Know How to Take Notes

Drawing a Concept Map You can draw a diagram called a concept map to show connections among key ideas. Here is a concept map showing some forms of numbers.

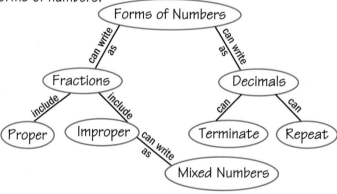

In Lesson 8.5, you will work with percents, fractions, and decimals. Then you will be able to add percents to a concept map showing forms of numbers.

Hands-on *Activity*

Comparing Areas

In this activity, you will use a geoboard to write fractions that compare areas.

Explore **Compare areas of figures using a geoboard.**

Use a geoboard that is 5 pegs long by 5 pegs wide. The smallest square you can make with 4 pegs is called a *unit square.*

1 Use a blue rubber band to make a square around the entire geoboard.

2 Use a red rubber band to make a square that is 3 pegs long by 3 pegs wide.

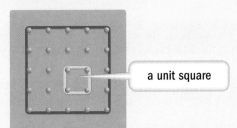

a unit square

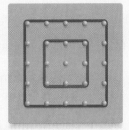

3 Copy and complete the statement at the right to write a fraction that compares the number of unit squares in each figure.

$$\frac{\text{Unit squares in red square}}{\text{Unit squares in blue square}} = \frac{?}{?}$$

Your turn now **Add the given rectangle to your geoboard from Steps 1 and 2 above. Then copy and complete the statement.**

1. green rectangle:
3 pegs long by 2 pegs wide

$$\frac{\text{Unit squares in green rectangle}}{\text{Unit squares in red square}} = \frac{?}{?}$$

2. purple rectangle:
4 pegs long by 3 pegs wide

$$\frac{\text{Unit squares in purple rectangle}}{\text{Unit squares in blue square}} = \frac{?}{?}$$

Stop *and* **Think**

3. Critical Thinking How could you write the fractions you wrote in Step 3 above and in Exercises 1 and 2 in another way? Explain.

Ratios

BEFORE

You wrote fractions and equivalent fractions.

Now

You'll write ratios and equivalent ratios.

WHY?

So you can write a ratio of ingredients in a recipe, as in Ex. 19.

In the Real World

Word Watch

ratio, p. 374
equivalent ratio, p. 375

18 violins   8 violas   6 cellos   3 double basses

School Orchestras In some school orchestras, all of the instruments are stringed: violins, violas, cellos, and double basses. How can you compare the numbers of instruments in the orchestra?

One way to compare the numbers of instruments is to use a *ratio*. The **ratio** of a number a to a nonzero number b is the quotient when a is divided by b. You can write the ratio of a to b as $\frac{a}{b}$, as $a : b$, or as "a to b."

EXAMPLE 1 Writing a Ratio in Different Ways

In the orchestra shown above, 8 of the 35 instruments are violas. The ratio of the number of violas to the total number of instruments, $\frac{\text{Violas}}{\text{Total instruments}}$, can be written as $\frac{8}{35}$, as 8 : 35, or as 8 to 35.

EXAMPLE 2 Writing Ratios in Simplest Form

Use the diagram above. Write the ratio of the number of double basses to the number of cellos in simplest form.

$$\frac{\text{Double basses}}{\text{Cellos}} = \frac{3}{6} = \frac{1 \times \cancel{3}^{1}}{2 \times \cancel{3}_{1}} = \frac{1}{2}$$

ANSWER The ratio is $\frac{1}{2}$, or 1 to 2, so there is 1 double bass for every 2 cellos.

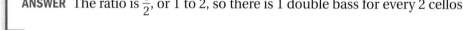

Your turn now In Exercises 1 and 2, write the ratio in three ways.

1. violins to total instruments   2. violas to double basses

3. Write the ratio of the number of cellos to the number of violins in simplest form.

with Review

Need help with equivalent fractions? See p. 228.

Writing Equivalent Ratios You can multiply or divide the numerator and denominator of a ratio by the same number to get an **equivalent ratio** .

EXAMPLE 3 **Writing an Equivalent Ratio**

Complete the statement $\frac{5}{15} = \frac{?}{60}$ to write equivalent ratios.

Solution

Think about the denominators of the two fractions.

$$\overset{5 \times 4}{\overset{\frown}{\underset{\underset{15 \times 4}{\smile}}{\frac{5}{15} = \frac{20}{60}}}}$$

> You multiplied 15 by 4 to get 60, so multiply 5 by 4 also.

ANSWER $\frac{5}{15} = \frac{20}{60}$

Writing Ratios as Decimals Writing ratios as decimals may make it easier to compare the ratios.

EXAMPLE 4 **Comparing Ratios Using Decimals**

Football Allen completes $\frac{3}{4}$ of his pass attempts. Mike completes 7 out of every 10 pass attempts. Who has the better record?

Solution

Write each ratio as a decimal. Then compare the decimals.

Allen: $\frac{3}{4} = 0.75$ Mike: 7 out of 10 $= \frac{7}{10} = 0.7$

ANSWER Because $0.75 > 0.7$, Allen has the better record.

Your turn now Copy and complete the statement.

4. $\frac{2}{3} = \frac{?}{15}$ **5.** $\frac{7}{?} = \frac{35}{50}$ **6.** $\frac{20}{32} = \frac{5}{?}$

Copy and complete the statement using <, >, or =.

7. $\frac{5}{20} \underline{\ ?\ } \frac{4}{10}$ **8.** $\frac{3}{5} \underline{\ ?\ }$ 18 out of 30 **9.** $2:4 \underline{\ ?\ } 7:35$

Getting Ready to Practice

1. Vocabulary Write the ratio $\frac{5}{12}$ in two other ways.

Write the ratio in simplest form.

2. $\frac{6}{15}$ **3.** $\frac{8}{20}$ **4.** $\frac{20}{75}$ **5.** $\frac{12}{3}$

6. Find the Error Describe and correct the error in writing an equivalent ratio.

$$X \quad \frac{7}{9} = \frac{?}{18} \longrightarrow \frac{7}{9} = \frac{16}{18}$$

Copy and complete the statement.

7. $\frac{4}{5} = \frac{?}{10}$ **8.** $\frac{?}{7} = \frac{6}{21}$ **9.** $\frac{5}{6} = \frac{15}{?}$ **10.** $\frac{24}{?} = \frac{8}{9}$

Practice and Problem Solving

HELP with **Homework**

Example	Exercises
1	11, 17
2	12, 18-22
3	13-16
4	23-25

Online Resources
CLASSZONE.COM
· More Examples
· eTutorial Plus

11. Write the ratio 13 to 20 in two other ways.

12. Write the ratio 10 : 15 in simplest form.

Copy and complete the statement.

13. $\frac{3}{8} = \frac{?}{24}$ **14.** $\frac{7}{10} = \frac{14}{?}$ **15.** $\frac{2}{?} = \frac{22}{33}$ **16.** $\frac{?}{2} = \frac{5}{10}$

17. Keyboards On the keyboard shown, 31 of the 76 keys are black. Write this ratio in three different ways.

18. Pets A survey says that 28 out of 42 people have a pet. Write this ratio in simplest form.

19. Party Punch A recipe for party punch suggests mixing 64 fluid ounces of cranberry juice with 128 fluid ounces of orange juice. Write the ratio of cranberry juice to orange juice in the punch in simplest form.

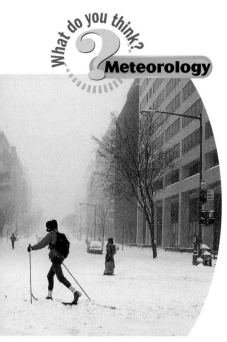

Average Temperatures Use the average December temperatures for the cities shown to write the ratio described in simplest form.

20. $\dfrac{\text{Number of temperatures over }68°\text{F}}{\text{Total number of temperatures}}$

21. $\dfrac{\text{Number of temperatures over }33°\text{F}}{\text{Total number of temperatures}}$

22. $\dfrac{\text{Number of temperatures over }33°\text{F}}{\text{Number of temperatures under }33°\text{F}}$

City	Temperature
Washington, D.C.	39°F
Miami Beach, FL	70°F
Dallas, TX	48°F
Sacramento, CA	45°F
Helena, MT	21°F
Chicago, IL	30°F

■ **Average Temperatures**

Average temperatures can be helpful in predicting future temperatures. Which city in the table above is closest to your city or town? Use the table to predict your city or town's average temperature in December.

Baseball A *batting average* is the ratio of the number of hits to the number of times at bat. Who has the better batting average?

23. Carl: 20 to 50

Joel: $\dfrac{9}{20}$

24. Sara: 0.305

Miranda: $\dfrac{21}{70}$

25. John: 0.258

Mike: $\dfrac{19}{75}$

Extended Problem Solving A chorus has 68 singers. The graph shows that it includes tenors, basses, altos, and sopranos.

26. Find the total number of tenors, basses, and altos in the chorus.

27. **Describe** Find the number of sopranos in the chorus. Describe your method.

28. **Interpret** Write the ratio of the number of sopranos to the number of other singers in simplest form. What does the ratio mean?

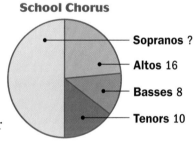

School Chorus
Sopranos ?
Altos 16
Basses 8
Tenors 10

Summer Camp In Exercises 29 and 30, use the table. The ratio of the number of counselors to the number of campers is constant.

29. Write the ratio of counselors to campers in simplest form.

30. Copy and complete the table.

Counselors	2	3	4	5
Campers	16	24	?	?

31. **Critical Thinking** Explain how you could use common denominators to rewrite two ratios in order to compare them.

32. **Geometry** Write the ratio of the perimeter to the area for a square that is 8 meters by 8 meters.

33. **Challenge** Find two numbers that form a ratio equivalent to 2 : 3 that have a sum of 10.

Mixed Review

Copy and complete the statement. *(Lesson 4.8)*

34. 787 mm = _?_ cm   **35.** 16 kL = _?_ L   **36.** 2.6 kg = _?_ g

Choose a Strategy **Use a strategy from the list to solve the following problem. Explain your choice of strategy.**

37. Find the next two figures in the pattern.

> **Problem Solving Strategies**
> ▪ Guess, Check, and Revise
> ▪ Make a List or Table
> ▪ Perform an Experiment
> ▪ Solve a Related Problem

Basic Skills **Divide.**

38. 4.2 ÷ 7   **39.** 60 ÷ 1.2   **40.** 1.36 ÷ 3.4   **41.** 0.497 ÷ 7.1

Test-Taking Practice

42. Multiple Choice A farmer plants corn on 24 acres of a 48 acre field. What is another way to write this ratio?

A. $\frac{1}{3}$ **B.** $\frac{3}{8}$ **C.** $\frac{1}{2}$ **D.** $\frac{2}{3}$

43. Multiple Choice Which ratio is equivalent to 2 : 3?

F. 7 : 9   **G.** 3 : 4   **H.** 6 : 9   **I.** 12 : 27

BRAIN GAME

Ratio Puzzlers

- The number of cats in a neighborhood is 4 more than the number of dogs and the ratio of cats to dogs is 3 : 2. How many cats are there in the neighborhood?

- If the ratio of cats to fish in the neighborhood is 3 : 4, how many fish are there in the neighborhood?

Rates

LESSON 8.2

BEFORE	Now	WHY?
You wrote ratios and equivalent ratios.	You'll write rates, equivalent rates, and unit rates.	So you can find the rate of the water over Niagara Falls in Ex. 19.

In the Real World

Word Watch

rate, p. 379
unit rate, p. 379

Space The International Space Station orbits Earth at an average *rate* of 15 miles every 3 seconds. How long will it take the Station to travel 150 miles?

A **rate** is a ratio of two measures that have different units, such as $\frac{15 \text{ mi}}{3 \text{ sec}}$. A **unit rate** is a rate with a denominator of 1.

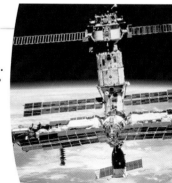

EXAMPLE 1 Writing an Equivalent Rate

To answer the question above, write an *equivalent rate* that has 150 miles in the numerator.

$$\overset{15 \times 10}{\frac{15 \text{ mi}}{3 \text{ sec}} = \frac{150 \text{ mi}}{30 \text{ sec}}}$$
$$3 \times 10$$

> You multiplied 15 mi by 10 to get 150 mi, so multiply 3 sec by 10 also.

ANSWER It will take the Space Station 30 seconds to travel 150 miles.

EXAMPLE 2 Writing a Unit Rate

Write the Space Station's average rate of $\frac{15 \text{ mi}}{3 \text{ sec}}$ as a unit rate.

$$\overset{15 \div 3}{\frac{15 \text{ mi}}{3 \text{ sec}} = \frac{5 \text{ mi}}{1 \text{ sec}}}$$
$$3 \div 3$$

> You divided 3 sec by 3 to get 1 sec, so divide 15 mi by 3 also.

ANSWER The Space Station's average unit rate is 5 miles per second.

HELP with Reading

The word *per* is often used to express division in unit rates, such as miles per second.

Your turn now Copy and complete the statement.

1. $\frac{5 \text{ lb}}{\$10} = \frac{20 \text{ lb}}{?}$

2. $\frac{35 \text{ mi}}{6 \text{ h}} = \frac{?}{12 \text{ h}}$

3. $\frac{32 \text{ oz}}{\$8} = \frac{?}{\$1}$

EXAMPLE 3 **Using a Unit Rate**

Measurement There are 2.54 centimeters in 1 inch. How many centimeters are in 3 inches?

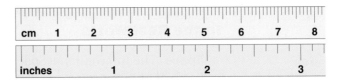

Solution

Write an equivalent rate that has 3 inches in the denominator.

$$\frac{2.54 \text{ cm}}{1 \text{ in.}} = \frac{7.62 \text{ cm}}{3 \text{ in.}}$$

2.54 × 3

1 × 3

You multiplied 1 in. by 3 to get 3 in., so multiply 2.54 cm by 3 also.

ANSWER There are 7.62 centimeters in 3 inches.

EXAMPLE 4 **Comparing Unit Rates**

At the Movies A 12 ounce tub of popcorn costs $3. A 20 ounce tub of popcorn costs $4. Which size is the better buy? Explain.

Solution

The rates for the two sizes are $\frac{\$3}{12 \text{ oz}}$ and $\frac{\$4}{20 \text{ oz}}$. Find the *unit price* for each tub of popcorn by finding the cost for 1 ounce of popcorn.

12 ounce tub

3 ÷ 12

$$\frac{\$3}{12 \text{ oz}} = \frac{\$.25}{1 \text{ oz}}$$

12 ÷ 12

20 ounce tub

4 ÷ 20

$$\frac{\$4}{20 \text{ oz}} = \frac{\$.20}{1 \text{ oz}}$$

20 ÷ 20

Compare the unit prices: $.20 < $.25.

ANSWER Because the unit price for the 20 ounce tub is less than the unit price for the 12 ounce tub, the 20 ounce size is the better buy.

Your turn now **Decide which size is the better buy. Explain.**

4. A 3 pound bag of apples costs $2.25.
A 5 pound bag of apples costs $3.50.

8.2 Exercises

More Practice, p. 715

Getting Ready to Practice

Vocabulary **Tell whether the rate is written as a unit rate.**

1. 2 feet per second

2. 76 words in 2 minutes

Tell whether the rates are *equivalent* or *not equivalent*.

3. $\dfrac{32 \text{ Calories}}{2 \text{ h}}$ and $\dfrac{64 \text{ Calories}}{4 \text{ h}}$

4. $\dfrac{60 \text{ words}}{3 \text{ min}}$ and $\dfrac{25 \text{ words}}{1 \text{ min}}$

5. **Bottled Water** A factory produces an average of 45,000 liters of bottled water per hour. How many liters will the factory produce in 4 hours?

6. **Guided Problem Solving** On average, a Ruby-throated Hummingbird beats its wings about 3000 times in 60 seconds. A Giant Hummingbird beats its wings an average of about 180 times in 15 seconds. Which bird beats its wings faster?

(1 Find the unit rate for the Ruby-throated Hummingbird.

(2 Find the unit rate for the Giant Hummingbird.

(3 Compare the unit rates.

Ruby-throated Hummingbird

Giant Hummingbird

Practice and Problem Solving

Copy and complete the statement.

7. $\dfrac{\$4}{3 \text{ oz}} = \dfrac{\$16}{?}$

8. $\dfrac{40 \text{ gal}}{8 \text{ h}} = \dfrac{20 \text{ gal}}{?}$

9. $\dfrac{54 \text{ mi}}{9 \text{ h}} = \dfrac{?}{3 \text{ h}}$

Write the unit rate.

10. $\dfrac{220 \text{ mi}}{4 \text{ h}}$

11. $\dfrac{81 \text{ m}}{27 \text{ sec}}$

12. $\dfrac{\$15}{12 \text{ muffins}}$

Tell whether the rates are *equivalent* or *not equivalent*.

13. $\dfrac{8 \text{ lb}}{\$4}$ and $\dfrac{12 \text{ lb}}{\$3}$

14. $\dfrac{42 \text{ calls}}{3 \text{ h}}$ and $\dfrac{28 \text{ calls}}{2 \text{ h}}$

Write the rate and unit rate.

15. 20 words in 5 minutes

16. 48 students for 24 computers

17. 160 miles in 4 hours

18. 250 pages in 5 chapters

HELP with Homework

Example	Exercises
1	7–9, 13–14
2	10–12, 15–18
3	19–20
4	25–26

Online Resources
CLASSZONE.COM

· More Examples
· eTutorial Plus

Geography

19. Niagara Falls On average, 700,000 gallons of water flow over the Canadian Falls every second. How many gallons flow over the Canadian Falls in 30 seconds?

20. Gardening You work in a local park removing weeds. You earn $7.50 per hour. How much do you earn for working 6 hours?

Write the unit rate.

21. $\dfrac{6.63 \text{ lb}}{3 \text{ kg}}$ **22.** $\dfrac{56.7 \text{ g}}{2 \text{ oz}}$ **23.** $\dfrac{10.16 \text{ cm}}{4 \text{ in.}}$ **24.** $\dfrac{8.05 \text{ km}}{5 \text{ mi}}$

25. Explain A 12 ounce box of cereal costs $3. An 18 ounce box costs $4. Which box is the better buy? Explain.

26. Decide Your friend purchases 26 bagels for $10.40. You purchase 39 bagels at a price of 3 bagels for $1. Which purchase is the better buy?

27. Critical Thinking Would the result have been different in Example 2 on page 379 if you used the rate $\dfrac{150 \text{ mi}}{30 \text{ sec}}$ to find the unit rate? Explain.

28. Challenge An office has two paper shredders, A and B. On average, shredder A shreds 1100 pounds of paper in 5 hours. On average, shredder B shreds 4.4 pounds of paper per minute. Which machine is faster?

Mixed Review

29. Find the length of a rectangle whose area is 24 square meters and whose width is 4 meters. *(Lesson 2.2)*

30. Find the least common multiple of 21 and 27. *(Lesson 5.4)*

Basic Skills **Find the greatest common factor of the numbers.**

31. 16, 40 **32.** 36, 81 **33.** 18, 72 **34.** 20, 56

Test-Taking Practice

35. Multiple Choice On average, a car gets 20 miles per gallon. At this rate, how many gallons will the car use to travel 80 miles?

A. 2.8 gallons **B.** 3.5 gallons **C.** 4.0 gallons **D.** 4.6 gallons

36. Multiple Choice Denise works for 3 hours and earns $24. At this rate, how much does Denise earn in 1 hour?

F. $16 **G.** $8 **H.** $6 **I.** $4

Solving Proportions

8.3

BEFORE ▶ **Now** **WHY?**

You solved equations.   You'll write and solve proportions.   So you can predict water use, as in Ex. 29.

📓 **Word Watch**

proportion, p. 383
cross products, p. 383

Proportions and Equivalent Ratios A **proportion** is an equation you write to show that two ratios are equivalent. The proportion below shows that the ratios in the pictures are equivalent.

Ratio: 2 out of 3   Ratio: 8 out of 12   Proportion

$$\frac{2}{3} = \frac{8}{12}$$

If you multiply the numerator of each ratio by the denominator of the other ratio, you'll find the *cross products*. For the proportion $\frac{a}{b} = \frac{c}{d}$, where b and d are nonzero, the **cross products** are ad and bc. The cross products for the proportion above are $2 \cdot 12$ and $3 \cdot 8$.

Cross Products Property

Words In a proportion, the cross products are equal.

Algebra

$\frac{a}{b} = \frac{c}{d}$, where b and d are nonzero.

$ad = bc$

Numbers

$\frac{3}{4} = \frac{6}{8}$

$3 \cdot 8 = 4 \cdot 6$

EXAMPLE 1   Checking a Proportion

Use cross products to decide whether the ratios form a proportion.

HELP with **Reading**

The proportion $\frac{3}{5} = \frac{12}{18}$ in part (a) of Example 1 is read "3 is to 5 as 12 is to 18."

a.
$$\frac{3}{5} \stackrel{?}{=} \frac{12}{18}$$
$$3 \cdot 18 \stackrel{?}{=} 5 \cdot 12$$
$$54 \neq 60$$

The cross products are not equal, so the ratios do not form a proportion.

b.
$$\frac{8}{10} \stackrel{?}{=} \frac{20}{25}$$
$$8 \cdot 25 \stackrel{?}{=} 10 \cdot 20$$
$$200 = 200 \checkmark$$

The cross products are equal, so the ratios form a proportion.

Solving Proportions To solve a proportion, you find the value of any missing part. One way to solve a proportion is to use mental math.

EXAMPLE 2 Solving Using Mental Math

Solve the proportion $\dfrac{4}{12} = \dfrac{20}{x}$.

Solution

Method 1 Use equivalent ratios.

$$\overset{4 \times 5}{\underset{12 \times 5}{\dfrac{4}{12} = \dfrac{20}{x}}}$$

> You multiplied 4 by 5 to get 20, so multiply 12 by 5 also.

$12 \times 5 = 60$, so $x = 60$.

Method 2 Use cross products.

$$\dfrac{4}{12} = \dfrac{20}{x}$$

$4x = 240$

$x = 60$

> Ask, "4 times what number equals 240?"

ANSWER The solution is 60.

Your turn now Solve the proportion.

1. $\dfrac{n}{4} = \dfrac{6}{24}$ **2.** $\dfrac{25}{10} = \dfrac{5}{k}$ **3.** $\dfrac{30}{x} = \dfrac{6}{11}$ **4.** $\dfrac{10}{4} = \dfrac{s}{12}$

EXAMPLE 3 Solving Using a Verbal Model

Boating You are on a riverboat trip. You travel 5 miles in 3 hours. At that same rate, how long will it take you to travel 20 miles?

Solution

Use a proportion. Let t represent the total time of the 20 mile trip.

$$\dfrac{\text{Distance traveled}}{\text{Time traveled}} = \dfrac{\text{Total distance}}{\text{Total time}}$$ Write a verbal model.

$$\dfrac{5 \text{ mi}}{3 \text{ h}} = \dfrac{20 \text{ mi}}{t \text{ h}}$$ Substitute values.

$$\dfrac{5}{3} = \dfrac{20}{t}$$ Write the cross products. They are equal.

$$5t = 60$$

$$t = 12$$ Solve using mental math.

ANSWER It will take you 12 hours to travel 20 miles.

■ **Boating**

The tour boat in the photo is traveling on the Moselle River in Germany. The tour boat can carry 250 passengers. About how many classes of students at your school would fit on the boat?

HELP with **Review**

Need help writing a related equation? See p. 687.

EXAMPLE 4 **Solving Using a Related Equation**

Solve the proportion $\frac{30}{12} = \frac{x}{18}$.

Solution

$$\frac{30}{12} = \frac{x}{18}$$ Write the cross products. They are equal.

$$540 = 12x$$

$$540 \div 12 = x$$ Write the related division equation.

$$45 = x$$ Divide.

ANSWER The solution is 45.

Your turn now Solve the proportion.

5. $\frac{x}{15} = \frac{10}{6}$ **6.** $\frac{30}{y} = \frac{50}{60}$ **7.** $\frac{70}{21} = \frac{a}{6}$ **8.** $\frac{32}{20} = \frac{40}{m}$

8.3 **Exercises**

More Practice, p. 715

INTERNET
eWorkbook Plus
CLASSZONE.COM

Getting Ready to Practice

1. Vocabulary The cross products for the proportion $\frac{3}{8} = \frac{9}{x}$ are ? and ? .

Use cross products to decide whether the ratios form a proportion.

2. $\frac{3}{4} \stackrel{?}{=} \frac{9}{12}$ **3.** $\frac{10}{16} \stackrel{?}{=} \frac{5}{8}$ **4.** $\frac{6}{14} \stackrel{?}{=} \frac{8}{20}$ **5.** $\frac{30}{6} \stackrel{?}{=} \frac{20}{15}$

6. Which equation is related to the equation $8x = 112$?

   A. $x = 112 + 8$ **B.** $x = 112 - 8$ **C.** $x = 112 \div 8$

Solve the proportion.

7. $\frac{1}{6} = \frac{5}{x}$ **8.** $\frac{2}{5} = \frac{r}{20}$ **9.** $\frac{n}{28} = \frac{2}{7}$ **10.** $\frac{40}{z} = \frac{15}{3}$

11. Literature In Jonathan Swift's book *Gulliver's Travels*, Gulliver's body height and the height of a Lilliputian are "in the proportion of twelve to one." If a Lilliputian is 6 inches tall, how tall is Gulliver?

Practice and Problem Solving

HELP with Homework

Example	Exercises
1	12–15
2	16–23, 28–30, 33–36
3	31–32
4	24–27, 33–36

Online Resources
CLASSZONE.COM

· More Examples
· eTutorial Plus

Use cross products to decide whether the ratios form a proportion.

12. $\frac{9}{21} \stackrel{?}{=} \frac{3}{7}$ **13.** $\frac{3}{8} \stackrel{?}{=} \frac{15}{40}$ **14.** $\frac{3}{2} \stackrel{?}{=} \frac{12}{10}$ **15.** $\frac{4}{5} \stackrel{?}{=} \frac{16}{21}$

Solve the proportion.

16. $\frac{3}{6} = \frac{x}{2}$ **17.** $\frac{m}{8} = \frac{8}{64}$ **18.** $\frac{5}{z} = \frac{25}{10}$ **19.** $\frac{12}{18} = \frac{2}{p}$

20. $\frac{12}{28} = \frac{3}{c}$ **21.** $\frac{9}{x} = \frac{27}{30}$ **22.** $\frac{a}{5} = \frac{99}{55}$ **23.** $\frac{5}{6} = \frac{n}{120}$

24. $\frac{9}{6} = \frac{h}{14}$ **25.** $\frac{12}{r} = \frac{8}{20}$ **26.** $\frac{24}{36} = \frac{10}{x}$ **27.** $\frac{t}{4} = \frac{45}{18}$

28. Distance You travel about 60 miles on 2 gallons of gasoline. About how far do you travel on 1 gallon of gasoline?

29. Water Use You use about 50 gallons of water per day. About how much water do you use per week?

30. Currency The value of 5 U.S. dollars is about 19 Malaysian ringgits. What is the value in U.S. dollars of 95 ringgits?

Use a verbal model to write a proportion. Then solve the proportion.

31. Quiz Grades You and a friend got the same grade on your quizzes. You got 6 out of 8 questions correct. If your friend's quiz had 12 questions, how many did your friend get correct?

32. E-mail Four out of 10 students surveyed in a class have their own e-mail accounts. If there are 40 students in the class, how many would you expect to have their own e-mail accounts?

Choose a Method Tell whether you would solve the proportion using *mental math* or a *related equation*. Then solve the proportion.

33. $\frac{x}{14} = \frac{3}{7}$ **34.** $\frac{10}{12} = \frac{m}{30}$ **35.** $\frac{6}{y} = \frac{8}{44}$ **36.** $\frac{20}{100} = \frac{5}{w}$

Copy and complete the table using proportions.

37.

Games played	6	9	?	15
Total cost	8	12	16	?

38.

Servings	4	10	16	?
Number of cups	10	?	40	55

39. Kangaroos Hannah and Juan are trying to estimate the distance a kangaroo will cover in 6 hops if it covers 40 feet in 2 hops.

Hannah
$$\frac{2}{40} = \frac{6}{x}$$

Juan
$$\frac{2}{6} = \frac{40}{x}$$

Are both methods correct? Use cross products to check.

40. Writing Six out of 10 students in your school saw a movie last weekend. There are 480 students in your school. Is there enough information to find the number of students in your school who *did not* see a movie last weekend? Explain.

41. Critical Thinking In Example 2 on page 384, you use either equivalent ratios or cross products to solve the proportion. Explain how you can use equivalent ratios to solve Example 4 on page 385.

42. Challenge A flea with a length of 3 millimeters can jump a distance of 33 centimeters. If the jumping ability of a human is proportional to the jumping ability of a flea, how far can a human jump who is 180 centimeters tall?

Mixed Review

43. A puppy's weight is greater than 3.5 pounds and less than 3.55 pounds. Give a possible weight. *(Lesson 3.3)*

44. A boulder has a weight of $8\frac{1}{2}$ tons. How many pounds does it weigh? *(Lesson 7.7)*

Basic Skills **Find the perimeter and the area of the figure described.**

45. a rectangle that is 14 cm by 3 cm   **46.** a square that is 8 ft by 8 ft

Test-Taking Practice

47. Short Response A farmer has 10 hens that produce a total of 7 eggs each day. Use a proportion to find the number of hens it would take to produce 35 eggs each day. Describe the steps you took to solve the problem.

48. Multiple Choice At a health food store, 8 ounces of curry powder cost $8.99. At that rate, find the cost of 12 ounces of curry powder.

A. $4.00   **B.** $12.99   **C.** $13.49   **D.** $20.99

Proportions and Scale Drawings

BEFORE

You used mental math to find the actual length of an object.

▶ **Now**

You'll use proportions to find measures of objects.

WHY?

So you can find the height of the Statue of Liberty in Ex. 3.

In the Real World

Soap Box Derby You are building a car for a Soap Box Derby race. In the *scale drawing* of the Derby car shown below, the car has a length of 2.8 inches. What is the actual length of the Derby car?

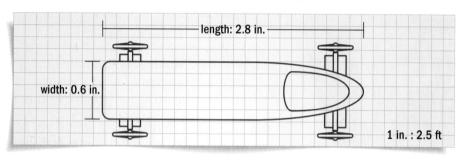

length: 2.8 in.

width: 0.6 in.

1 in. : 2.5 ft

The *scale* of 1 in. : 2.5 ft on the drawing is a ratio that means 1 inch on the drawing represents an actual distance of 2.5 feet on the car.

$$\frac{1 \text{ in.}}{2.5 \text{ ft}} \longleftarrow \text{Measure on drawing} \\ \longleftarrow \text{Actual measure}$$

EXAMPLE 1 **Using a Scale Drawing**

To find the actual length of the car above, write and solve a proportion. Let x represent the Derby car's actual length in feet.

$\dfrac{1 \text{ in.}}{2.5 \text{ ft}} = \dfrac{\text{Length on drawing}}{\text{Actual length}}$ Write a proportion.

$\dfrac{1 \text{ in.}}{2.5 \text{ ft}} = \dfrac{2.8 \text{ in.}}{x \text{ ft}}$ Substitute values.

$1 \cdot x = (2.5)(2.8)$ The cross products are equal.

$x = 7$ Multiply.

ANSWER The actual length of the Derby car is 7 feet.

Your turn now Use the scale drawing shown above.

1. Find the actual width of the Derby car.

2. If the actual wheelbase of the Derby car is 5.5 feet, what is the wheelbase of the car in the scale drawing?

Perimeter and Area The ratio of the perimeter of a scale drawing to the actual perimeter is related to the scale. So is the ratio of the areas.

HELP with **Review**

Need help with finding the perimeter and area of a rectangle? See p. 61.

EXAMPLE 2 **Finding Ratios of Perimeters**

School Murals A finished mural is to be 20 feet by 10 feet. Your scale drawing of the mural is shown below.

a. What is the perimeter of the drawing? of the mural?

b. Find the ratio of the drawing's perimeter to the mural's perimeter. How is this ratio related to the scale?

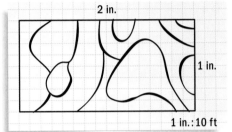

2 in.

1 in.

1 in.: 10 ft

Solution

a. Perimeter of drawing: $P = 2l + 2w = 2(2) + 2(1) = 6$ in.

Perimeter of mural: $P = 2l + 2w = 2(20) + 2(10) = 60$ ft

b. $\dfrac{\text{Perimeter of drawing}}{\text{Perimeter of mural}} = \dfrac{6 \text{ in.}}{60 \text{ ft}} = \dfrac{1 \text{ in.}}{10 \text{ ft}}$

ANSWER The ratio of the perimeters is the same as the scale.

EXAMPLE 3 **Finding Ratios of Areas**

Use the information from Example 2. Find the ratio of the drawing's area to the mural's area. How is this ratio related to the scale?

Solution

Area of drawing: $A = lw = 2 \cdot 1 = 2$ in.^{2}

Area of mural: $A = lw = 20 \cdot 10 = 200$ ft^2

$\dfrac{\text{Area of drawing}}{\text{Area of mural}} = \dfrac{2 \text{ in.}^2}{200 \text{ ft}^2} = \dfrac{1 \text{ in.}^2}{100 \text{ ft}^2} = \dfrac{1 \cdot 1 \text{ in.}^2}{10 \cdot 10 \text{ ft}^2}$

ANSWER The ratio of the areas, 1^2 in.^{2}: 10^2 ft^2, is the square of the scale.

Your turn now A scale drawing of another mural has a length of 5 cm and a width of 3 cm. The scale of the drawing is 1 cm : 2 m.

3. What is the ratio of the perimeters of the drawing and the mural?

4. What is the ratio of the areas of the drawing and the mural?

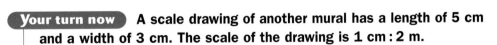

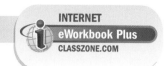

Getting Ready to Practice

1. **Vocabulary** Express the scale 1 in. : 5 ft as a ratio in two other ways.

2. A scale drawing has a scale of 1 in. : 6 ft. The actual length of the object is 48 feet. Choose the proportion you can use to find the length of the drawing. Then find the length.

   A. $\dfrac{1 \text{ in.}}{6 \text{ ft}} = \dfrac{48 \text{ ft}}{\text{Length of drawing}}$ **B.** $\dfrac{1 \text{ in.}}{6 \text{ ft}} = \dfrac{\text{Length of drawing}}{48 \text{ ft}}$

3. **Statue of Liberty** The model shown has a scale of about 1 in. : 20 ft. Copy and complete the proportion below to find the combined height of the actual Statue of Liberty and the pedestal.

   $$\dfrac{1 \text{ in.}}{20 \text{ ft}} = \dfrac{\text{Height of model}}{\text{Height of actual monument}}$$

15 in.

Practice and Problem Solving

with **Homework**

Example	Exercises
1	4–9
2	10–16
3	10–16

Online Resources
CLASSZONE.COM

· More Examples
· eTutorial Plus

A scale drawing of a very small object is larger than the object. The scale of a drawing is 2 cm : 9 mm. Find the unknown measure.

4. length on drawing = 6 cm;
   length of object = __?__

5. width of object = 45 mm;
   width on drawing = __?__

A map uses a scale of 1 in. : 50 mi. Find the actual distance for the given distance on the map.

6. 3 inches   7. 8 inches   8. 0.5 inch   9. 4.5 inches

Geometry In Exercises 10–13, use the table.

10. Choose one of the rectangles. Use a metric ruler to draw the rectangle.

11. **Describe** Enlarge your rectangle so that 2 centimeters on the new rectangle represents 1 centimeter on the original rectangle. Describe your method.

Rectangle 1	4 cm × 2 cm
Rectangle 2	3 cm × 5 cm
Rectangle 3	6 cm × 6 cm

12. Find the perimeters and areas of the original and enlarged rectangles.

13. **Interpret** Write the ratio of the perimeters and the ratio of the areas. Explain how these ratios are related to the scale.

Landscape Architects A landscape architect is designing a garden for a city park. The drawing has a scale of **1 cm : 5 m.** Use the drawing in Exercises 14–16.

14. Find the actual dimensions of the garden.

15. Find the ratio of the drawing's perimeter to the garden's perimeter.

16. Find the ratio of the drawing's area to the garden's area.

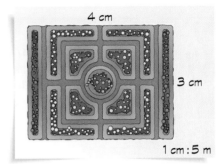
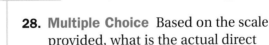

17. **Critical Thinking** Are there 12 square inches in 1 square foot? Are there 3 square feet in 1 square yard? Why or why not? Explain.

18. **Challenge** If a scale drawing has the scale $a : b$, write algebraic expressions for the ratio of the perimeters and for the ratio of the areas.

Mixed Review

19. Choose an appropriate customary unit to measure the weight of a dining table. *(Lesson 7.6)*

Solve the proportion. *(Lesson 8.3)*

20. $\dfrac{5}{4} = \dfrac{x}{16}$ 21. $\dfrac{2}{3} = \dfrac{22}{a}$ 22. $\dfrac{6}{y} = \dfrac{9}{21}$ 23. $\dfrac{10}{n} = \dfrac{25}{40}$

Basic Skills Use mental math to find the quotient.

24. $1.5 \div 10$ 25. $71 \div 10$ 26. $230 \div 100$ 27. $68 \div 100$

Test-Taking Practice

28. **Multiple Choice** Based on the scale provided, what is the actual direct distance from Hamilton to Clinton?

   A. 2 km   **B.** 15 km

   C. 17 km   **D.** 30 km

29. **Multiple Choice** A model airplane uses the scale 2 in. : 15 ft. The model's length is 20 inches. What is the actual length of the airplane?

   F. 30 in.   **G.** 100 in.   **H.** 150 ft   **I.** 400 ft

Notebook Review

Review the vocabulary definitions in your notebook.

Copy the review examples in your notebook. Then complete the exercises.

Check Your Definitions

scale drawing, p. 68

scale, p. 68

ratio, p. 374

equivalent ratio, p. 375

rate, p. 379

unit rate, p. 379

proportion, p. 383

cross products, p. 383

Use Your Vocabulary

1. Copy and complete: A $\underline{\ ?\ }$ is a ratio of two measures that have different units.

2. Copy and complete: A proportion is an equation you write to show that two $\underline{\ ?\ }$ are $\underline{\ ?\ }$.

3. What are the cross products for the proportion $\frac{2}{x} = \frac{4}{6}$?

8.1–8.3 Can you use ratios, rates, and proportions?

 EXAMPLE Solve the proportion.

a. $\frac{3}{4} = \frac{x}{12}$

Use equivalent ratios.

$$3 \times 3$$
$$\frac{3}{4} = \frac{x}{12}$$
$$4 \times 3$$

> You multiplied 4 by 3 to get 12, so multiply 3 by 3 also.

$3 \times 3 = 9$, so $x = 9$.

b. $\frac{10}{4} = \frac{x}{14}$

Use cross products and a related equation.

$$\frac{10}{4} = \frac{x}{14}$$

$$140 = 4x$$

$$140 \div 4 = x$$

$$35 = x$$

4. Copy and complete to write an equivalent rate: $\frac{20 \text{ in.}}{9 \text{ sec}} = \frac{100 \text{ in.}}{?}$.

5. Copy the statement: 8 out of 12 $\underline{\ ?\ }$ $\frac{7}{9}$. Then write the ratios as decimals and use <, >, or = to complete the statement.

6. Four pounds of tomatoes cost $10. Find the unit price.

7. Solve the proportion $\frac{x}{4} = \frac{18}{6}$.

8.4 Can you find measurements with scale drawings?

 EXAMPLE A map uses a scale of 1 in. : 75 mi. On the map, two cities are 2 inches apart. What is the actual distance between the cities?

$$\frac{1 \text{ in.}}{75 \text{ mi}} = \frac{\text{Distance on map}}{\text{Actual distance}}$$ Write a proportion.

$$\frac{1 \text{ in.}}{75 \text{ mi}} = \frac{2 \text{ in.}}{x \text{ mi}}$$ Substitute values.

$$1 \cdot x = 75 \cdot 2$$ The cross products are equal.

$$x = 150$$ Multiply.

ANSWER The actual distance between the cities is 150 miles.

 8. A model uses the scale 2 in. : 5 ft. The length of the model is 50 inches. What is the actual length?

Stop *and* **Think** about Lessons 8.1–8.4

9. Writing Compare a rate with a unit rate. How are they alike? How are they different? Explain.

Review Quiz 1

Match the ratio with an equivalent ratio.

1. 5 to 30   **2.** 12 : 4   **3.** 24 to 18   **4.** 9 : 72

A. 3 to 1   **B.** $\frac{1}{6}$ **C.** 1 : 8   **D.** 4 to 3

5. Shopping A 32 ounce carton of juice costs $3.20. A 16 ounce carton of juice costs $1.92. Which carton is the better buy? Explain.

Solve the proportion.

6. $\frac{4}{21} = \frac{x}{84}$ **7.** $\frac{25}{z} = \frac{100}{84}$ **8.** $\frac{36}{g} = \frac{8}{10}$ **9.** $\frac{n}{30} = \frac{8}{12}$

10. Geometry Use a metric ruler to make a scale drawing of the rectangle shown using the scale 1 cm : 5 cm. Then find the ratio of the area of the original rectangle to the area of the enlarged rectangle.

1 cm

2 cm

GOAL

Use models to represent percents.

MATERIALS

- graph paper
- colored pencils

Modeling Percents

In this activity, you will make models to represent *percents*. A percent is a ratio that compares a number to 100. The symbol for percent is %.

Explore Model 25%.

1 On graph paper, make a border to form a 10 × 10 grid that contains 100 squares.

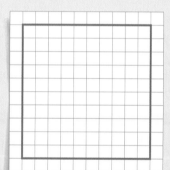

2 Each of the small squares in the grid represents $\frac{1}{100}$ of the grid.

$$\frac{1}{100} = 1\%$$

3 To model 25%, shade 25 squares. The shaded portion represents 25%, the decimal 0.25, and the fraction $\frac{25}{100} = \frac{1}{4}$.

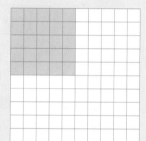

Your turn now Write the percent, decimal, and fraction for the model.

1.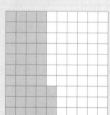

2.

3.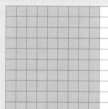

4. Use graph paper to make a model that represents 80%.

Stop and Think

5. Critical Thinking How could you model 100%? 150%? 200%?

Understanding Percent

LESSON 8.5

BEFORE	Now	WHY?
You wrote ratios and rates.	You'll write percents as decimals and fractions.	So you can analyze a survey on computer use, as in Exs. 25–27.

Word Watch

percent, p. 395

Modeling Percents A **percent** is a ratio that compares a number to 100. The word *percent* means "per hundred," or "out of 100." The symbol for percent is %.

There are 100 marbles shown at the right, and 43 out of 100 are blue. You can represent this ratio using a percent, a decimal, or a fraction.

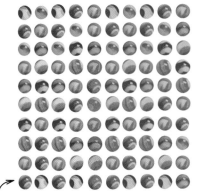

Each marble represents 1% of the group of 100 marbles.

Percent	Decimal	Fraction
43%	0.43	$\frac{43}{100}$

EXAMPLE 1 Writing Ratios in Different Forms

In the diagram above, 7 out of the 100 marbles are red. Write this ratio as a percent, a decimal, and a fraction.

Percent: 7%   **Decimal:** 0.07   **Fraction:** $\frac{7}{100}$

HELP with Notetaking

In your notes, you may want to include percents in a concept map about forms of numbers, like the concept map shown on page 372.

EXAMPLE 2 Writing Percents

Write the number in words and as a percent.

a. $\frac{9}{100}$ **b.** 0.39   **c.** $\frac{32.5}{100}$ **d.** 3, or $\frac{300}{100}$

Solution

a. nine hundredths, or 9%

b. thirty-nine hundredths, or 39%

c. thirty-two and five tenths hundredths, or 32.5%

d. three-hundred hundredths, or 300%

Your turn now Write the number as a percent, decimal, and fraction.

1. 29 hundredths   **2.** 3 hundredths   **3.** 100 hundredths

Writing Percents as Decimals and Fractions

To write a percent as a *decimal*:

Divide the value by 100. $57\% = 57 \div 100 = 0.57$

To write a percent as a *fraction*:

Rewrite the percent using a
denominator of 100. Simplify
if possible. $35\% = \dfrac{35}{100} = \dfrac{7}{20}$

EXAMPLE 3   **Writing Percents in Different Forms**

a. Write 64.5% as a decimal.   **b.** Write 80% as a fraction.

$64.5\% = 64.5 \div 100 = 0.645$ $80\% = \dfrac{80}{100} = \dfrac{4}{5}$

Circle Graphs Circle graphs are often used to represent the results of
a survey. The parts of a circle graph together represent a total of 100%.

EXAMPLE 4   **Circle Graphs with Percents**

Survey In a survey, 100 dog owners
were asked where their dogs sleep.
The results are shown as percents.

a. What percent of the people
responded "Other"?

b. What percent of the people
did *not* respond "Dog bed"?

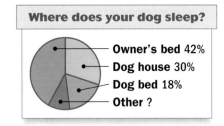

Where does your dog sleep?

- Owner's bed 42%
- Dog house 30%
- Dog bed 18%
- Other ?

Solution

a. The circle graph represents 100%. The sum of the percents given is
$42\% + 30\% + 18\% = 90\%$, so the "Other" part is $100\% - 90\% = 10\%$.

b. The percent of people who did not respond "Dog bed" is
$100\% - 18\% = 82\%$.

Your turn now   Write the percent as a decimal and a fraction.

4. 5%   **5.** 75%   **6.** 20%   **7.** 3.5%

Getting Ready to Practice

1. **Vocabulary** When you write a percent as a fraction, you rewrite the percent using a denominator of _?_.

Write the number in words and as a percent.

2. $\frac{11}{100}$

3. $\frac{81}{100}$

4. 0.04

5. 0.63

6. Write *forty-eight hundredths* as a percent, a decimal, and a fraction.

7. **Walking to School** In one town, 20 out of 100 students walk to school. What percent of students walk to school?

Practice and Problem Solving

Each small square in the model represents 1% $\left(\text{or } \frac{1}{100}\right)$**. Represent the number of shaded squares as a percent, decimal, and fraction.**

8.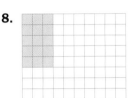

9.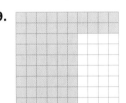

10.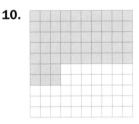

Write the number in words and as a percent.

11. 0.42

12. 0.06

13. 0.57

14. 0.74

15. $\frac{28}{100}$

16. $\frac{19}{100}$

17. $\frac{200}{100}$

18. $\frac{52.8}{100}$

Match the percent with its equivalent decimal or fraction.

19. 34%

20. 40%

21. 85%

22. 17%

A. 0.17

B. $\frac{17}{50}$

C. 0.4

D. $\frac{17}{20}$

23. **Exercise** Of 100 people surveyed, 36 said they exercise daily. Write this result as a percent, a decimal, and a fraction.

24. **Explain** On a necklace of 100 beads, 45 of the beads are round. The rest of the beads are rectangular. What percent of the beads are round? What percent are rectangular? How did you find your answers?

Computer Use The graph shows the results of a survey in which people from 10 to 14 years old were asked how many days a week they use their computer.

25. Critical Thinking What percent of those surveyed use their computers 4 or more days a week? Explain.

26. What percent of those surveyed use their computers 1 day or less?

27. Rewrite the percents for all four sections as decimals and as fractions.

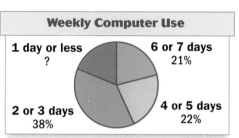

Weekly Computer Use

1 day or less ?

6 or 7 days 21%

2 or 3 days 38%

4 or 5 days 22%

Number Sense Copy and complete the statement using <, >, or =.

28. 50% _?_ 0.05

29. 14% _?_ $\frac{1.4}{100}$

30. 0.4 _?_ 40%

Challenge The ratio of students who play soccer to all students is given. Find the percent of students who do *not* play soccer.

31. 40 out of 100

32. 110 out of 200

33. 60 out of 300

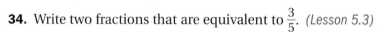

Mixed Review

34. Write two fractions that are equivalent to $\frac{3}{5}$. *(Lesson 5.3)*

35. A basketball game begins at 6:30 P.M. and ends at 8:45 P.M. How long does the game last? *(Lesson 6.6)*

Basic Skills Order the numbers from least to greatest.

36. 2.4, 1.7, 2.9

37. 1.57, 4.1, 3.8

38. 5.3, 3.5, 5.03

39. 9.2, 9, 9.4

Test-Taking Practice

40. Multiple Choice Write 47 out of 100 as a percent.

    A. 4.7%   **B.** 47%   **C.** 470%   **D.** 4700%

41. Short Response Out of 100 students surveyed about the Spring Music Festival, 36 said they will play an instrument, 22 said they will sing, 19 said they will run the equipment, and the rest said they will be in the audience. What percent of the students will *not* be singing or playing an instrument? Show how you found the answer.

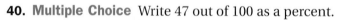

LESSON
8.6

Percents, Decimals, and Fractions

BEFORE	▶ Now	WHY?
You wrote percents as fractions and decimals.	You'll write fractions and decimals as percents.	So you can find the percent of Earth that is desert in Ex. 28.

Review Words
decimal, p. 108
fraction, p. 228
percent, p. 395

In the Real World

Volleyball In a volleyball game, a player's serves must land in a certain region to be playable. What percent of serves did Maria get "in" for today's games? What percent did she get "in" so far this season?

You can use the fraction of Maria's serves that she got "in" to find the percent that she got "in." To do this, you write an equivalent fraction with a denominator of 100.

Serving Record		
Maria	Serves "in"	Total serves
Today	4	10
Season	17	25

EXAMPLE 1 Writing Fractions as Percents

To answer the questions above, first write each record as a fraction. Then write an equivalent fraction with a denominator of 100 to find the percent.

a. $\dfrac{4}{10}$ ← serves "in" today
     ← total serves today

$$4 \times 10$$
$$\dfrac{4}{10} = \dfrac{40}{100}$$
$$10 \times 10$$

$$\dfrac{40}{100} = 40\%$$

ANSWER Maria got 40% of her serves "in" today.

b. $\dfrac{17}{25}$ ← serves "in" this season
      ← total serves this season

$$17 \times 4$$
$$\dfrac{17}{25} = \dfrac{68}{100}$$
$$25 \times 4$$

$$\dfrac{68}{100} = 68\%$$

ANSWER Maria got 68% of her serves "in" so far this season.

Your turn now Write the fraction as a percent.

1. $\dfrac{3}{4}$ **2.** $\dfrac{7}{10}$ **3.** $\dfrac{7}{20}$ **4.** $\dfrac{9}{50}$

EXAMPLE 2 **Writing Decimals as Percents**

Write the decimal as a percent.

a. $0.06 = \dfrac{6}{100}$ 0.06 is six hundredths.

   $= 6\%$

b. $0.6 = \dfrac{6}{10}$ 0.6 is six tenths.

   $= \dfrac{60}{100}$ **Multiply the numerator and denominator by 10 to get a denominator of 100.**

   $= 60\%$

c. $0.025 = \dfrac{25}{1000}$ 0.025 is twenty-five thousandths.

   $= \dfrac{2.5}{100}$ **Divide the numerator and denominator by 10 to get a denominator of 100.**

   $= 2.5\%$

HELP with **Solving**

Remember that you can divide by 10 by moving the decimal point 1 place to the left. In part (c) of Example 2, $25 \div 10 = 2.5$.

Using Decimals If the denominator of a fraction is not a factor of 100, it may be easiest to write the fraction as a decimal first.

EXAMPLE 3 **Using Decimals to Write Percents**

Field Trip You have attended 5 out of 8 Science Club meetings. You must attend at least 60% of the meetings to go on a trip. Can you go?

Solution

$\dfrac{5}{8} = 0.625$ **Divide 5 by 8 to write the fraction as a decimal.**

$= \dfrac{625}{1000}$ **0.625 is 625 thousandths.**

$= \dfrac{62.5}{100}$ **Divide the numerator and denominator by 10 to get a denominator of 100.**

$= 62.5\%$

ANSWER Because 62.5% > 60%, you can go on the field trip.

Your turn now **Write the decimal or fraction as a percent.**

5. 0.3   **6.** 0.105   **7.** $\dfrac{3}{8}$ **8.** $\dfrac{9}{40}$

Common Percents, Decimals, and Fractions

Fifths

$20\% = 0.2 = \frac{1}{5}$

$40\% = 0.4 = \frac{2}{5}$

$60\% = 0.6 = \frac{3}{5}$

$80\% = 0.8 = \frac{4}{5}$

Fourths

$25\% = 0.25 = \frac{1}{4}$

$50\% = 0.5 = \frac{1}{2}$

$75\% = 0.75 = \frac{3}{4}$

Thirds

$33\frac{1}{3}\% = 0.\overline{3} = \frac{1}{3}$

$66\frac{2}{3}\% = 0.\overline{6} = \frac{2}{3}$

EXAMPLE 4 **Using Common Relationships**

Order the numbers $\frac{3}{4}$, 80%, and 0.71 from least to greatest.

Write the numbers as decimals and graph them on a number line.

ANSWER An ordered list of the numbers is 0.71, $\frac{3}{4}$, and 80%.

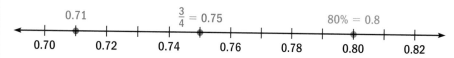

8.6 Exercises

More Practice, p. 715

INTERNET
eWorkbook Plus
CLASSZONE.COM

Getting Ready to Practice

1. Vocabulary What commonly used percent is equal to 0.6?

Match the decimal or fraction with its equivalent percent.

2. 0.17   **3.** 0.05   **4.** $\frac{17}{50}$ **5.** 0.5   **6.** $\frac{3}{5}$

A. 34%   **B.** 50%   **C.** 60%   **D.** 17%   **E.** 5%

7. Sewing A survey asked 50 students if they sew. Eighteen students responded "yes." What percent of the students surveyed do *not* sew?

Practice and Problem Solving

with **Homework**

Example	Exercises
1	8–11, 20–21, 28
2	12–15
3	16–19, 29
4	22–27, 41

Online Resources
CLASSZONE.COM
· More Examples
· eTutorial Plus

Write the fraction or decimal as a percent.

8. $\frac{1}{2}$

9. $\frac{13}{20}$

10. $\frac{3}{50}$

11. $\frac{7}{25}$

12. 0.92

13. 0.2

14. 0.02

15. 0.084

16. $\frac{261}{1000}$

17. $\frac{587}{1000}$

18. $\frac{1}{8}$

19. $\frac{3}{200}$

20. Write two fifths as a percent.

21. Write nine tenths as a percent.

Use a number line to order the numbers from least to greatest.

22. 68%, $\frac{67}{100}$, 0.64

23. $\frac{1}{4}$, 15%, 0.16

24. $\frac{17}{20}$, 82%, 0.88

25. 50%, 0.77, $\frac{7}{10}$, $\frac{2}{3}$

26. $\frac{4}{5}$, 0.72, 79%, $\frac{3}{4}$

27. $\frac{1}{3}$, 33%, 34%, 0.3

28. Deserts Deserts cover about $\frac{1}{5}$ of Earth's land surface. What percent of Earth's land surface is desert?

29. Soccer A survey at the Roosevelt Middle School said $\frac{11}{40}$ of the sixth grade students named soccer as their favorite sport. What percent of the sixth grade students named soccer as their favorite sport?

Geometry **Find the percent of the figure that is shaded. Round to the nearest whole percent.**

30.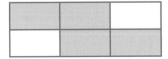

31.

Choose a Method **Tell whether you would use a *calculator, paper and pencil*, or *mental math* to write the fraction as a percent. Round to the nearest whole percent.**

32. $\frac{3}{10}$

33. $\frac{9}{25}$

34. $\frac{2}{7}$

35. $\frac{4}{9}$

Write the decimal as a percent.

36. 1.25

37. 3.5

38. 8.2

39. 0.004

40. Mental Math Copy and complete: If $\frac{3}{20} = 15\%$, then $\frac{6}{20} = \underline{\,?\,}\%$.

41. Quiz Scores On their math quiz papers, John's score is written as "$\frac{22}{25}$ correct," Sam's score is "0.87 correct," and Vince's score is "84.5% correct." Who received the highest score? the lowest score?

 42. Writing What percent of a meter is 5 centimeters? What percent of a meter is 5 millimeters? Explain how you found your answers.

Babies' Names **In Exercises 43 and 44, use the information below.**
In the United States in 2000, Michael and Matthew represented about 2.9% of all the names for newborn males. Madison and Ashley represented about 1.9% of all the names for newborn females.

43. Out of 1000 male babies born in the year 2000, about how many have the name Michael or Matthew?

44. Challenge Out of 1000 female babies born in the year 2000, about how many *do not* have the name Madison or Ashley?

Mixed Review

45. A giant anteater eats 9000 ants in 3 hours. Find the unit rate. *(Lesson 8.2)*

Write the percent as a decimal and a fraction. *(Lesson 8.5)*

46. 2%   **47.** 37%   **48.** 75%   **49.** 96%

Choose a Strategy **Use a strategy from the list to solve the following problem. Explain your choice of strategy.**

50. On a shopping trip, you spend $10.75 at one store. At another store, you spend $16.30. You have $4.35 left. How much did you start with?

> **Problem Solving Strategies**
> ■ Guess, Check, and Revise
> ■ Make a List or Table
> ■ Work Backward
> ■ Solve a Related Problem

Basic Skills **Find the product.**

51. $2 \times 7.5 \times 10$ **52.** $4 \times 50 \times 0.7$ **53.** 0.3×6.25 **54.** 0.005×10

Test-Taking Practice

55. Extended Response A rectangle is 10 meters long and 4 meters wide. You create a new rectangle by multiplying the length and width by 2. Find the area of each rectangle. Write a fraction that compares the area of the small rectangle to the area of the large rectangle. What percent of the large rectangle can be covered by the small rectangle?

Guess, Check, and Revise

Draw a Diagram

Perform an Experiment

Make a List or Table

Solve a Simpler Problem

Work Backward

Solve a Related Problem

Solve a Simpler Problem

Problem Your school is collecting money for a local charity. The first day, 1 dollar bill is placed in a jar. The second day, 2 dollar bills are added to the jar. The third day, 3 dollar bills are added to the jar, and so on. How much money will be in the jar after 100 days?

① Read and Understand

Read the problem carefully.

You need to know the total number of dollar bills in the jar to know the value.

② Make a Plan

Decide on a strategy to use.

Solve a simpler problem using fewer days. Look for a method you can then use with 100 days.

③ Solve the Problem

Reread the problem and solve a simpler problem.

First, find the total amount of money after only 6 days. Pair numbers to help find the total. What do you notice?

$$\underbrace{\$1 + \$2 + \$3 + \$4 + \$5 + \$6}_{} = ?$$

with pairs summing to \$7

The number of pairs is 3, which is half the number of days. The sum of each pair is \$7, which is the sum of the first and last numbers. So, the amount after 6 days is 3(\$7) = \$21.

Now apply this method to find \$1 + \$2 + ⋯ + \$99 + \$100, the amount of money in the jar after 100 days. There will be 50 pairs of numbers, each with a sum of \$101.

ANSWER You will have collected \$5050 after 100 days because 50(\$101) = \$5050.

④ Look Back

To help you find the total or check a method for finding the total, you may want to try a second small number, such as 10 days.

\$1 + \$2 + \$3 + \$4 + \$5 + \$6 + \$7 + \$8 + \$9 + \$10 = 5(\$11) = \$55

Practice the Strategy

Use the strategy *solve a simpler problem*.

1. **Lockers** The lockers at a city pool are numbered from 1 to 150. How many lockers from 1 to 50 will have a 2 in the number? How many lockers from 1 to 150 will have a 2 in the number?

2. **Estimation** You are buying a present for a friend. You spend $15.20 for a gift, $3.75 for a card, $6.90 for wrapping paper, and $2.05 for ribbon. Will $25 be enough money to buy all these items? Explain how you can use estimation to solve the problem. Then solve the problem.

3. **Large Sums** Find the sum of the first 100 odd whole numbers.

$$1 + 3 + 5 + \cdots + 199 = \underline{\ ?\ }$$

4. **Food Drive** Your class has collected 210 cans for a food drive. All the cans are the same size. You want to stack the cans in rows so that each row has 1 more can than the row above it, as shown below. If you put 20 cans in the bottom row, will you have enough cans so that you'll have 1 can in the top row?

5. **Ones' Digits** If you evaluate the power 8^{12}, what will the ones' digit be?

Mixed Problem Solving

Use any strategy to solve the problem.

6. **Stained Glass** You are creating a stained glass border using the pattern below. What will be the shape of the 23rd figure in the pattern? Explain.

7. **School Supplies** You bought pencils and pens for $36. Packages of pencils cost $3. Packages of pens cost $5. How many packages of each type did you buy?

8. **Paper** You have 20 rectangular pieces of colored paper that each measure 1 inch by 2 inches. Is it possible to arrange them to form a 5 inch by 8 inch rectangle with no gaps or overlaps? If so, show one possible arrangement.

9. **Dining Out** At a restaurant, you have a choice of a poultry dish, a vegetable, and a type of potato. How many different meals are possible?

Daily Specials

Your choice of:

POULTRY
• Chicken or Turkey •

VEGETABLE
• Beans, Broccoli, or Zucchini •

POTATOES
• Mashed, Scalloped, or Baked •

Finding a Percent of a Number

BEFORE	▶ Now	WHY?
You multiplied whole numbers by decimals and fractions.	You'll multiply to find a percent of a number.	So you can estimate a tip, as in Ex. 22.

Word Watch

interest, p. 408
principal, p. 408
annual interest rate, p. 408
simple interest, p. 408

Activity You can change a percent to a fraction or a decimal to find a percent of a number.

Recall that "of" means "multiply." To find 50% of 8, find $\frac{1}{2} \times 8$ or 0.5×8.

1. Write the percent as a fraction and multiply to find the percent of the number.

   a. 25% of 72   **b.** 10% of 72   **c.** 62% of 72   **d.** $33\frac{1}{3}\%$ of 72

2. Write the percents in Step 1 as decimals to find the percent of the number.

3. Compare Steps 1 and 2. Which answers were easier to find by changing the percents to fractions? Which answers were easier to find by changing the percents to decimals? Explain.

Finding a Percent of a Number The activity above suggests two ways to find a percent of a number.

- Change the percent to a fraction and multiply by the number.

- Change the percent to a decimal and multiply by the number.

HELP with Notetaking

You may want to include Example 1 in your notes to illustrate when a fraction or when a decimal may be the more convenient form of a percent to use. In part (a), $\frac{3}{4}$ is compatible with 60.

In part (b), you can multiply by 0.1 easily using mental math.

EXAMPLE 1 **Finding a Percent of a Number**

a. Find 75% of 60. Use a fraction.   **b.** Find 10% of 74. Use a decimal.

$$75\% \text{ of } 60 = \frac{3}{4} \times 60$$

$$= \frac{180}{4}$$

$$= 45$$

ANSWER 75% of 60 is 45.

$$10\% \text{ of } 74 = 0.1 \times 74$$

$$= 7.4$$

ANSWER 10% of 74 is 7.4.

Your turn now Find the percent of the number. Explain your method.

1. 50% of 48   **2.** 20% of 45   **3.** 9% of 50   **4.** 10% of 36

EXAMPLE 2 **Finding a Discount**

Sneaker Sale The regular price of a pair of sneakers is $40. The sale price is 25% off the regular price. What is the sale price?

(1 Find the discount.   25% of $40 = $\frac{1}{4} \times$ $40 = **$10**

(2 Subtract the discount $40 − **$10** = $30
from the regular price.

ANSWER The sale price of the sneakers is $30.

EXAMPLE 3 **Finding the Sales Tax**

Feeding Your Dog You are buying dog food that costs $8.50. There is a 6% sales tax. What is the total amount of your purchase?

(1 Find the sales tax.   6% of $8.50 = 0.06 × $8.50 = **$.51**

(2 Add the sales tax to the $8.50 + **$.51** = $9.01
cost of the item.

ANSWER The total amount of your purchase is $9.01.

EXAMPLE 4 **Solving a Simpler Problem**

Leaving a Tip Your bill in a restaurant is $23.78. You want to leave a tip of about 15%. Use simpler percents and mental math to estimate the amount of the tip.

(1 Round the bill to the nearest dollar. $23.78 ≈ $24.00

(2 Find 10% of the bill.   0.1 × $24 = **$2.40**

(3 Find 5% of the bill.
It is half of 10% of the bill. $\frac{1}{2} \times$ **$2.40** = **$1.20**

(4 Add the partial tips.   **$2.40** + **$1.20** = $3.60

ANSWER A 15% tip for a $23.78 bill is about $3.60.

Your turn now **Find the cost described.**

5. A book's regular price is $19.95. Find the cost after a 20% discount.

6. The price of a cat toy is $9.50. Find the cost with a sales tax of 8%.

What do you think?

Animals

■ **Feeding Your Dog**

In 2000, there were about 60,000,000 dogs in United States households. That year, about $7,300,000,000 was spent on dog food. About how much was spent on each dog?

Simple Interest When you save money at a bank, you *earn interest.* When you borrow money, you *pay interest.* **Interest** is the amount paid for the use of money. The amount you save or borrow is the **principal** . The **annual interest rate** is the percent of the principal you earn or pay per year.

Simple Interest Formula

Interest paid only on the principal is **simple interest** .

Words $\dfrac{\text{Simple}}{\text{interest}}$ = Principal · $\dfrac{\text{Annual}}{\text{interest rate}}$ · $\dfrac{\text{Time}}{\text{in years}}$

Algebra $I = Prt$

EXAMPLE 5 Finding Simple Interest

Savings You deposit $75 in an account. The annual interest rate is 4%. How much simple interest will you earn on that money in 1 year?

$I = Prt$	**Write the simple interest formula.**
$= 75\,(0.04)(1)$	**Substitute values. Write 4% as a decimal.**
$= 3$	**Multiply.**

ANSWER You will earn $3 in simple interest in 1 year.

8.7 Exercises

More Practice, p. 715

INTERNET
eWorkbook Plus
CLASSZONE.COM

Getting Ready to Practice

1. Vocabulary What does each variable in the formula $I = Prt$ represent?

Find the percent of the number.

2. 60% of 60   **3.** 45% of 20   **4.** 85% of 12   **5.** 40% of 150

6. Leaving a Tip Your bill in a restaurant is $29.87. Use mental math to estimate a tip of 15%.

Practice and Problem Solving

with Homework

Example	Exercises
1	7–19
2	20, 27–29, 38
3	21, 38
4	22, 36
5	23–26

Online Resources
CLASSZONE.COM

· More Examples
· eTutorial Plus

Find the percent of the number.

7. 50% of 84   **8.** 25% of 80   **9.** 10% of 100   **10.** 11% of 4

11. 75% of 72   **12.** 60% of 15   **13.** 18% of 45   **14.** 83% of 20

15. 31% of 120   **16.** 65% of 150   **17.** $33\frac{1}{3}$% of 63   **18.** $66\frac{2}{3}$% of 9

19. Find the Error Describe and correct the error in the solution.

$$\times \quad 1\% \text{ of } 400 = \frac{1}{10} \times 400 = \frac{400}{10} = 40$$

20. Theater Your class is going to a play. Tickets are usually $20, but because of a group discount, each ticket will be 12% cheaper. How much will each ticket cost?

21. Video Games You are buying a video game that costs $50. There is a 5% sales tax. What is the total amount of your purchase?

22. Pizza You and your friends are eating at a pizza shop after school. The bill is $17.53. You want to leave about 15% for a tip. Estimate the amount of the tip.

Algebra Find the simple interest I = Prt for the given values.

23. $P = \$275$, $r = 4\%$, $t = 5$ years   **24.** $P = \$320$, $r = 3\%$, $t = 4$ years

25. $P = \$84$, $r = 2\%$, $t = 3$ years   **26.** $P = \$112$, $r = 2.5\%$, $t = 2$ years

Mental Math A pair of jeans costs $32. Use mental math to find the discount described.

27. a 10% discount   **28.** a 25% discount   **29.** a 40% discount

Estimation Estimate the percent of the number.

30. 11% of 400   **31.** 75% of 804   **32.** 48% of 7.9

33. 19% of 205   **34.** 6% of 62   **35.** 89% of 80.1

36. Writing Explain how you can use mental math to estimate the amount of a 20% tip on a restaurant bill of $43.72.

37. Critical Thinking If you know that 20% of a number is 16, how can you use this information to find 40% of the number? 60% of the number?

38. Clothing A sweater is on sale for 25% off. There is a 7% sales tax. If the regular price is $56, how much will you pay for the sweater?

Extended Problem Solving **Use this information in Exercises 39–41.**
A sporting goods store offers a package of hockey equipment for
20% less than the cost of the same items sold separately. The costs
of the items are shown in the table. You already have a helmet.

39. Find the total of the costs without the
helmet. Then add 6% sales tax.

40. Find the cost of all the equipment. Then
find the cost of this package after the
20% discount. Then add 6% sales tax.

41. **Compare** Which will cost you less: buying
the package or buying just the equipment
you don't have?

Item	Price
helmet	$46
shoulder pads	$58
shin guards	$46
elbow pads	$30
skates	$110

42. **Challenge** On June 15, you deposited $120 in an account with an
annual interest rate of 4%. It is now December 15 of the same year.
How much simple interest has your money earned in that time?

Mixed Review

Find the mean, median, mode(s), and range. *(Lesson 2.8)*

43. 4, 7, 5, 26, 10, 8, 10

44. 3, 6, 1, 9, 10, 9, 8, 3, 16, 5

45. An engineer looks at a blueprint of a bridge that has a scale of
1 cm : 20 m. On the blueprint, the span of the bridge is 35 centimeters.
What is the actual span of the bridge? *(Lesson 8.4)*

Basic Skills **Find the sum or difference.**

46. 8.8 + 54 **47.** 1.45 + 7.8 **48.** 0.79 − 0.48 **49.** 58 − 45.3

Test-Taking Practice

INTERNET
State Test Practice
CLASSZONE.COM

50. **Multiple Choice** You have a stamp
collection with 120 stamps. The circle
graph shows the percent of stamps
from each country. How many of your
stamps are from Canada?

A. 6 stamps **B.** 18 stamps

C. 24 stamps **D.** 60 stamps

Stamp Collection

United States 50%
Canada 20%
Mexico 15%
France 10%
China 5%

51. **Short Response** You have a coupon for a 15% discount off any item in
a store. You'll pay 5% sales tax on the discounted price. How much will
you pay for a shirt whose regular price is $16.50? Explain how you
found your answer.

CALCULATOR

Finding a Percent of a Number

GOAL Use a calculator to find a percent of a number.

Example **You deposit $100 in an account with an annual interest rate of 5.25%. How much simple interest will you earn on that money in 7 years?**

You can use the percent feature, **2nd** [%], to find a percent of a number. The percent feature can often be found above the left parenthesis key, **(**.

Solution

Use the formula for simple interest $I = Prt$ with $P = \$100$, $r = 5.25\%$, and $t = 7$ years.

Keystrokes	**Display**
100 ☒ 5.25 **2nd** [%] ☒ 7 ▭	**36.75**

ANSWER You will earn $36.75 interest.

✓ **Check** Round 5.25% to 5%. Because $100 \times 5\% \times 7 = 35$, the answer is reasonable.

HELP with **Technology**

The percent key changes a percent to a decimal by dividing by 100 for you. For example,

5.25 **2nd** [%]

is displayed as 0.0525.

Your turn now **Use a calculator to find the answer.**

1. 8% of 90   **2.** 14% of 173   **3.** 57% of 13.7

4. 3.5% of 8   **5.** 24.3% of 99   **6.** 7.28% of 205

7. Simple Interest You deposit $75 in an account with an annual interest rate of 6.5%. How much simple interest will you earn on that money in 4 years?

8. Sales Tax You are buying a CD that costs $14.95. The sales tax is 7%. What is the amount of tax that you owe? What is the total amount of your purchase?

9. Discount A store is having a 35% off sale. If an item was originally priced $49.50, what will you pay for it now, not including sales tax?

LESSONS 8.5 TO 8.7

Notebook Review

Review the vocabulary definitions in your notebook.

Copy the review examples in your notebook. Then complete the exercises.

Check Your Definitions

percent, p. 395	principal, p. 408	simple interest, p. 408
interest, p. 408	annual interest rate, p. 408	

Use Your Vocabulary

1. Copy and complete: Interest paid only on the __?__ is simple interest.

8.5–8.6 Can you use percents?

 EXAMPLE Write the decimal or fraction as a percent.

a. $0.63 = \dfrac{63}{100} = 63\%$

b. $\dfrac{1}{8} = 0.125 = \dfrac{125}{1000} = \dfrac{12.5}{100} = 12.5\%$

 2. Write 16% as a decimal and a fraction.

Write the decimal or fraction as a percent.

3. 0.7   **4.** 0.24   **5.** $\dfrac{6}{25}$ **6.** $\dfrac{7}{8}$

8.7 Can you find a percent of a number?

 EXAMPLE You are buying a pair of in-line skates that cost $48.50. The sales tax is 6%. What is the total amount of your purchase?

(**1** Find the sales tax.   6% of $48.50 = 0.06 × $48.50 = **$2.91**

(**2** Add the tax to the cost. $48.50 + **$2.91** = $51.41

Find the percent of the number.

7. 25% of 400   **8.** 60% of 105   **9.** 10% of 24   **10.** 85% of 130

11. You deposit $150 in a savings account. The annual interest rate is 6%. How much simple interest will you earn on that money in 1 year?

Stop *and* **Think** about Lessons 8.5–8.7

12. Writing Describe the process of finding a percent of a number. What might you consider to make the computation easier?

Review Quiz 2

Write the percent as a decimal and a fraction.

1. 43% **2.** 97% **3.** 2% **4.** 12%

Write the fraction or decimal as a percent.

5. $\frac{27}{100}$ **6.** 0.82 **7.** 0.7 **8.** $\frac{3}{5}$

9. Order the numbers 34%, $\frac{8}{25}$, and 0.37 from least to greatest.

10. Internet Use You spend a total of 15 hours on the Internet during a 2 week period. You research a school project 60% of that time. How many hours do you spend researching the project?

Find the simple interest *I = Prt* **for the given values.**

11. $P = \$375$, $r = 7\%$, $t = 3$ years **12.** $P = \$215$, $r = 3\%$, $t = 5$ years

13. Leaving a Tip Your bill in a restaurant is $28.70. You want to leave about 20% for a tip. Estimate the amount of the tip.

Target 203

Your goal is to find sums of the percents of the given numbers. Is it possible to get a sum as great as 203?

1. Choose any blue percent and any purple number. Find this percent of the number you have selected.

2. Repeat Step 1 until you have selected each number and each percent once. Organize your results.

3. Add your products together. How close are you to 203? What can you do differently to get a sum closer to 203?

Chapter Review

 **Vocabulary**

ratio, p. 374
equivalent ratio, p. 375
rate, p. 379
unit rate, p. 379

proportion, p. 383
cross products, p. 383
percent, p. 395
interest, p. 408

principal, p. 408
annual interest rate,
  p. 408
simple interest, p. 408

Vocabulary Review

Tell whether the statement is *true* or *false*.

1. The ratios $\frac{4}{7}$ and $\frac{16}{21}$ are equivalent.

2. A rate is a ratio of two measures that have different units.

3. A percent is a ratio that compares a number to 100.

Copy and complete the statement.

4. A ? is a rate that has a denominator of 1.

5. In the proportion $\frac{a}{b} = \frac{c}{d}$, *ad* and *bc* are ?.

6. In the proportion $\frac{a}{b} = \frac{c}{d}$, *ad* is equal to ?.

Review Questions

Copy and complete the statement. *(Lesson 8.1)*

7. $\frac{2}{3} = \frac{6}{?}$

8. $\frac{6}{7} = \frac{?}{21}$

9. $\frac{?}{9} = \frac{16}{36}$

10. $\frac{4}{?} = \frac{8}{30}$

Amusement Parks The graph shows the favorite amusement park rides for a group of students. Write the given ratio in simplest form. *(Lesson 8.1)*

11. bumper cars votes to roller coaster votes

12. water slide votes to total students surveyed

13. Ferris wheel votes to water slide votes

14. Auto Racing A racecar travels 110 miles using 22 gallons of fuel. Find the unit rate. *(Lesson 8.2)*

15. Travel You are traveling from New York City to Charlotte, North Carolina, a distance of about 540 miles. Find the unit rate if it takes you 9 hours to make the trip. *(Lesson 8.2)*

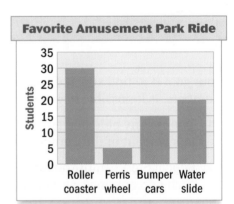

Favorite Amusement Park Ride

Solve the proportion. *(Lesson 8.3)*

16. $\dfrac{x}{4} = \dfrac{21}{12}$ **17.** $\dfrac{8}{g} = \dfrac{24}{27}$ **18.** $\dfrac{6}{10} = \dfrac{9}{y}$ **19.** $\dfrac{12}{10} = \dfrac{b}{25}$

20. Science A desk that weighs 90 pounds on Earth would weigh about 15 pounds on the moon. If a rock weighs 450 pounds on Earth, how much would it weigh on the moon? *(Lesson 8.3)*

In Exercises 21 and 22, use the scale drawing shown. *(Lesson 8.4)*

21. The scale drawing of a parking lot uses the scale 1 in. : 25 ft. What are the actual dimensions of the parking lot?

22. Find the ratio of the scale drawing's area to the parking lot's area.

3 in.

7 in.

Write the number in words and as a percent. *(Lesson 8.5)*

23. $\dfrac{34}{100}$ **24.** $\dfrac{16}{100}$ **25.** 0.05 **26.** 0.65

Write the percent as a decimal and a fraction. *(Lesson 8.5)*

27. 64% **28.** 26% **29.** 90% **30.** 8%

Write the decimal or fraction as a percent. *(Lesson 8.6)*

31. 0.4 **32.** $\dfrac{4}{5}$ **33.** $\dfrac{10}{16}$ **34.** 0.425

35. Order the numbers from least to greatest. *(Lesson 8.6)*

$\dfrac{1}{3}$, 25%, 0.2, 40%, $\dfrac{3}{5}$, 0.35

Find the percent of the number. *(Lesson 8.7)*

36. 80% of 110 **37.** 4% of 300 **38.** 36% of 75 **39.** $66\dfrac{2}{3}$% of 600

40. Taxi Ride You take a taxi ride and your fare comes to $12.80. You want to give the driver a 15% tip. Estimate the amount of the tip. *(Lesson 8.7)*

41. Money You deposit $115 into a savings account with an annual interest rate of 5%. How much simple interest will you earn on that money in 3 years? *(Lesson 8.7)*

42. On Sale What is the cost of a $36 pair of jeans after a 20% discount, not including sales tax? *(Lesson 8.7)*

Chapter Test

Online Shopping **The graph shows the number of people in a survey who chose different reasons for using online shopping. Write the ratios in Exercises 1 and 2 in simplest form.**

Reasons for Online Shopping

Discounts 48
Free gifts 25
Free shipping 27

1. discounts responses to total number of shoppers surveyed

2. free shipping responses to discounts responses

3. Write the ratio $\frac{2}{5}$ in two other ways.

4. **Phones** You pay $3.36 for a 14 minute phone call. Find the unit rate.

Solve the proportion.

5. $\frac{x}{4} = \frac{21}{12}$

6. $\frac{18}{81} = \frac{2}{n}$

7. $\frac{r}{10} = \frac{4}{8}$

8. $\frac{6}{j} = \frac{10}{25}$

9. **Currency** Six U.S. dollars are worth about 804 Japanese yen. How many Japanese yen is one U.S. dollar worth?

10. **Bikes** A model of a bike has a scale of 1 in. : 2 ft. The length of the model is 3.5 inches. What is the actual length of the bike?

Write the decimal or fraction as a percent.

11. 0.36

12. 0.08

13. $\frac{23}{100}$

14. $\frac{2}{25}$

15. Write *fifty-five percent* as a fraction.

16. **Flowers** One sixth of your flower garden is tulips, 0.195 is marigolds, and 18% is roses. Order these numbers from least to greatest.

17. **Geography** In the United States, 23 of the 50 states border an ocean. What percent of the states border an ocean?

18. Find 40% of 85.

19. Find 75% of 60.

20. Find 12% of 150.

21. Find 88% of 1000.

Restaurant Bill **A restaurant bill totals $45.80. Use mental math to estimate the tip described.**

22. 10%

23. 20%

24. 15%

25. 25%

Chapter Standardized Test

Test-Taking Strategy As you take a test, avoid spending too much time on any one question. Go on to another question and come back later if time permits.

Multiple Choice

1. Which ratio is equivalent to $\frac{20}{8}$?

   A. $\frac{10}{5}$ **B.** $\frac{30}{14}$ **C.** $\frac{60}{24}$ **D.** $\frac{14}{4}$

2. Solve the proportion $\frac{7}{3} = \frac{x}{21}$.

   F. 28   **G.** 35   **H.** 42   **I.** 49

3. You deposit $140 in a savings account. The annual interest rate is 4%. How much simple interest will you earn on that money in 2 years?

   A. $5.60   **B.** $7.60   **C.** $11.20   **D.** $16.80

4. You buy a model boat kit for $15 and an extra motor for $5.50. There is a 6% sales tax. What is the total amount of your purchase?

   F. $15.90   **G.** $20.50   **H.** $21.40   **I.** $21.73

5. Your bill in a restaurant is $29.97. You want to leave a tip of about 20%. What is a good estimate for the tip?

   A. $4.50   **B.** $5   **C.** $6   **D.** $8

6. An elephant walks 60 miles in 12 hours. What is the unit rate?

   F. 4 miles per hour

   G. 5 miles per hour

   H. 6 miles per hour

   I. 48 miles per hour

7. Write 0.27 as a percent.

   A. 0.27%   **B.** 2.7%   **C.** 27%   **D.** 270%

8. A school fair raises a total of $24,478. If 25% of this amount goes to a particular charity, how much will the charity receive?

   F. $6119.50   **G.** $6120.50

   H. $18,358.50   **I.** $30,597.50

9. A car is 4 feet tall and 8 feet long. If the scale of a model of the car is 4 in. : 1 ft, how long is the model?

   A. 8 in.   **B.** 32 in.   **C.** 16 ft   **D.** 32 ft

10. The regular price of a pair of hiking boots is $65. If the boots are on sale for 40% off, how much will you save off the regular price?

   F. $25   **G.** $26   **H.** $39   **I.** $45

Short Response

11. Doreen has a collection of 80 baseball caps. Sixteen of the caps are blue. What percent of the caps are blue? Explain how you found your answer.

12. Write a proportion using the numbers 4, 36, 3, and 48. Is there more than one proportion that you can write? Explain.

Extended Response

13. Store A has a jacket that is regularly $36, on sale for 15% off. The same jacket at Store B is regularly $40, on sale for 20% off. You pay 5% sales tax on the discounted price at either store. Find the cost of the jacket at Store A and then at Store B. Which jacket is the better buy? Explain.

Geometric Figures

BEFORE

In previous chapters you've...

- Used ratios and proportions
- Found lengths, perimeters, and areas

Now

In Chapter 9 you'll study...

- Points, lines, and planes
- Angles and angle measures
- Identifying polygons
- Congruent and similar figures
- Line symmetry

WHY?

So you can solve real-world problems about...

- miniature golf, p. 425
- architecture, p. 432
- the Great Pyramid, p. 440
- photography, p. 457

Internet Preview
CLASSZONE.COM

- eEdition Plus Online
- eWorkbook Plus Online
- eTutorial Plus Online
- State Test Practice
- More Examples

Chapter Warm-Up Games

Review skills you need for this chapter in these quick games. Work with a partner.

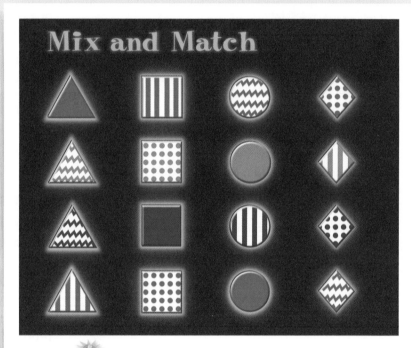

Mix and Match

BRAIN GAME

Key Skill: Classifying objects
Materials: 16 small squares of paper

Computers classify objects by their characteristics. The objects above can be classified based on shape, color, and pattern.

- On your turn, name a characteristic. Use a paper square to cover each object that has that characteristic. For example, you might cover all the green objects, or all the squares, or all the striped objects.

- Take turns, always covering at least one uncovered object. The player who covers the last object wins. Play the game a few times.

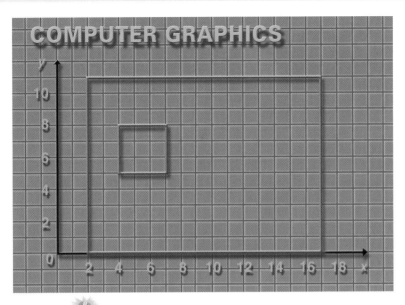

COMPUTER GRAPHICS

Key Skill:
Plotting points on
a coordinate grid

Materials:
graph paper

Computer drawing programs rely on precise instructions. In this game, you'll write instructions for drawing a house on a coordinate grid.

- Follow these instructions to draw a window and the outline of a house:

  Draw a square connecting (4, 5), (4, 8), (7, 8), and (7, 5).

  Draw a rectangle connecting (2, 0), (2, 11), (17, 11), and (17, 0).

- Then write instructions for drawing a door and a roof for the house. Have your partner test your instructions.

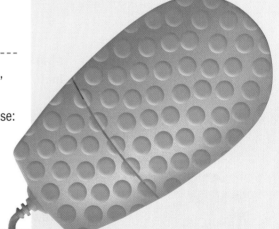

Stop *and* Think

1. **Critical Thinking** Suppose it is your turn in a game of *Mix and Match*. The uncovered shapes are a solid green triangle, a dotted orange square, and a solid purple square. In order to win on your next turn, which characteristic should you name? Explain your thinking.

2. **Writing** Points (8, 8) and (8, 16) are the corners of a square drawn on a coordinate grid. Name two points that could form the other corners of the square. Are these the only points you could use? Explain your thinking.

CHAPTER 9 Getting Ready to Learn

Review What You Need to Know

Using Vocabulary **Copy and complete using a review word.**

Word Watch

Review Words

perimeter, p. 61
ordered pair, p. 83
coordinates, p. 83

1. The first coordinate in an ? tells you how many units to move to the right.

2. The ? of a square can be found using the formula $P = 4s$ where s is the length of each side.

In Exercises 3 and 4, find the perimeter of the rectangle. *(p. 61)*

3. length = 6 in., width = 5 in.   4. length = 10 m, width = 7 m

5. Write and solve an equation to find the length of a side of a square that has a perimeter of 48 centimeters. *(p. 61)*

Find the length of the line segment to the nearest tenth of a centimeter. *(p. 113)*

6. ——————————   7. ————————

Find the length of the line segment to the nearest eighth of an inch. *(p. 244)*

8. ——————————   9. ————————

NoTebook

You should include material that appears on a notebook like this in your own notes.

Know How to Take Notes

Drawing a Venn Diagram Each oval in a Venn diagram represents a group with something in common. The region or regions where the ovals overlap show what the different groups have in common. The Venn diagram below shows that 2 is both even and prime.

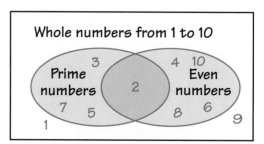

You can use Venn diagrams in your notes for Lesson 9.5 when you learn about different types of quadrilaterals.

Introduction to Geometry

BEFORE	▶ Now	WHY?
You used points and lines to draw diagrams.	You'll identify lines, rays, and segments.	So you can describe maps, as in Exs. 18–21.

📓 Word Watch

point, p. 421
line, p. 421
ray, p. 421
endpoint, p. 421
segment, p. 421
plane, p. 422
intersecting lines, p. 422
parallel lines, p. 422

Geometry In geometry, a **point** is usually labeled with an uppercase letter, such as *A* or *B*. Points are used to name *lines*, *rays*, and *segments*.

Words	Diagram	Symbols
A **line** extends without end in two *opposite* directions.	A ⟷ B	$\overleftrightarrow{AB}$ or $\overleftrightarrow{BA}$
A **ray** has one **endpoint** and extends without end in *one* direction.	A → B	$\overrightarrow{AB}$
A **segment** has two endpoints.	A — B	$\overline{AB}$ or $\overline{BA}$

In the chart, notice that there are two ways to name each line or segment but only one way to name the ray. You can name a line using any two points on the line in any order. You must use the endpoints to name a segment, but they can be listed in any order. When you name a ray, you must list the endpoint first.

EXAMPLE 1 Identifying Lines, Rays, and Segments

Identify and name the *line*, *ray*, or *segment*.

a. M •——• N   b. Q •——• P   c. ←•——•→ R S

Solution

a. The figure is a ray that can be named $\overrightarrow{MN}$.

b. The figure is a segment that can be named $\overline{QP}$ or $\overline{PQ}$.

c. The figure is a line that can be named $\overleftrightarrow{RS}$ or $\overleftrightarrow{SR}$.

Your turn now Identify and name the *line*, *ray*, or *segment*.

1. ←•——• F G   2. ↖•——•→ H J   3. •——• K L

EXAMPLE 2 Naming Lines, Rays, and Segments

Use the aerial photo at the right.

a. Name two rays.

b. Name two segments that have *G* as an endpoint.

c. Name a line.

Solution

a. Two rays are $\vec{JL}$ and $\vec{JK}$.

b. Two segments that have *G* as an endpoint are $\overline{GJ}$ and $\overline{GH}$.

c. One line is $\overleftrightarrow{GH}$.

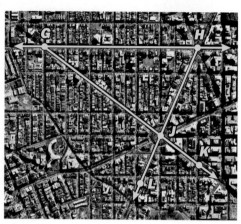

Planes and Lines A **plane** is a flat surface that extends without end in all directions. You can represent a plane by a figure that looks like a floor or a wall. In a plane, two different lines will either *intersect* or be *parallel*. **Intersecting lines** meet at a point. **Parallel lines** never meet.

with Reading

Parallel lines are indicated by special arrows on each line.

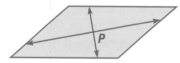

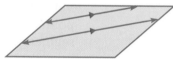

EXAMPLE 3 Intersecting and Parallel Lines

a. Which lines are intersecting?

b. Which lines are parallel?

Solution

a. $\overleftrightarrow{AB}$ and $\overleftrightarrow{BC}$ intersect at point *B*.
$\overleftrightarrow{AD}$ and $\overleftrightarrow{AB}$ intersect at point *A*.

b. $\overleftrightarrow{AD}$ and $\overleftrightarrow{BC}$ are parallel.

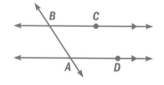

Your turn now **Use the diagram at the right.**

4. What is another way to write $\vec{AD}$? $\overleftrightarrow{EA}$?

5. Which lines are intersecting? parallel?

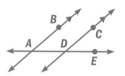

Getting Ready to Practice

Vocabulary **Match the name with the correct figure.**

1. $\overleftrightarrow{XY}$

2. $\overrightarrow{XY}$

3. $\overline{XY}$

A.
X
Y

B.
Y
X

C.
X
Y

Use the diagram at the right.

4. Name a ray.

5. Name a segment that has *Q* as an endpoint.

6. Which lines are intersecting?

7. Which lines are parallel?

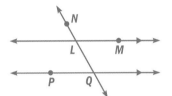
N
L
M
P
Q

Practice and Problem Solving

Identify and name the *line*, *ray*, or *segment*.

8.
H
G

9.
J
K

10.
Y
Z

Use the diagram at the right.

11. Name three points.

12. Name two rays.

13. Name two lines.

14. Name a segment that has *B* as an endpoint.

15. Name $\overline{AE}$ in another way.

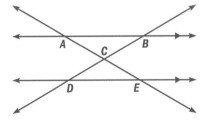
A
C
B
D
E

Decide whether the lines pictured are *parallel* or *intersecting*.

16.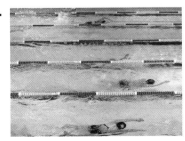

17.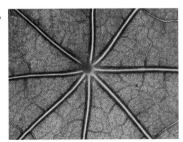

Geography Use the map to give an example of the figure.

18. point

19. ray

20. line

21. segment

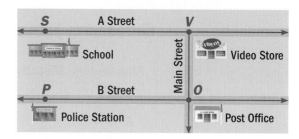

Decide Tell whether the object is best modeled by a *point*, a *ray*, a *segment*, or a *line*.

22. a star in the sky   **23.** a beam of sunlight   **24.** a ruler

Sketch the figure described.

25. $\overrightarrow{WV}$ **26.** $\overleftrightarrow{LK}$ **27.** $\overline{QP}$

Critical Thinking Is the statement *true* or *false*? Explain.

28. $\overrightarrow{AB}$ can be written as $\overrightarrow{BA}$.   **29.** $\overrightarrow{AB}$ can be written as $\overleftrightarrow{AB}$.

30. $\overline{QP}$ can be written as $\overline{PQ}$.   **31.** $\overleftrightarrow{PQ}$ can be written as $\overleftrightarrow{QP}$.

32. Challenge Draw a diagram in which $\overleftrightarrow{LM}$ is parallel to $\overleftrightarrow{NO}$, $\overrightarrow{PQ}$ intersects $\overleftrightarrow{NO}$ at P and $\overleftrightarrow{LM}$ at Q, and $\overline{QR}$ intersects $\overleftrightarrow{NO}$ at a point R between P and O.

Mixed Review

33. Sketch a line segment that is 65 millimeters long without using a ruler. Then use a ruler to check your estimate. How close was your estimate? *(Lesson 3.2)*

34. The regular price of the computer you want is $1100, but the sale price is 25% off the regular price. What is the sale price? *(Lesson 8.7)*

Basic Skills Copy and complete the statement using <, >, or =.

35. 2.9 ?_ 3.1   **36.** 1.8 ?_ 0.99   **37.** 12.5 ?_ 1.25   **38.** 18.7 ?_ 18

Test-Taking Practice

39. Short Response Use the figure at the right to answer the questions. If you drew a line through points M and P, could $\overleftrightarrow{MP}$ be parallel to $\overleftrightarrow{LM}$? to $\overleftrightarrow{LN}$? Explain.

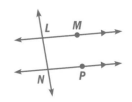

Angles

BEFORE	▶ Now	WHY?
You named lines, rays, and segments.	You'll name, measure, and draw angles.	So you can measure angles formed by a kite string as in Exs. 15–17.

In the Real World

Miniature Golf A miniature golf course has a hole similar to the one shown at the right. You can get a hole-in-one if you hit the ball off of the wall as shown. How can you describe the path of the ball?

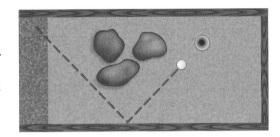

The path of the golf ball forms an *angle*. An **angle** is formed by two rays with the same endpoint. The endpoint is called the **vertex** . The symbol ∠ is used to represent an angle.

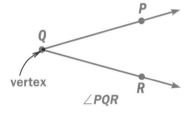

∠*PQR*

EXAMPLE 1 **Naming Angles**

The path of the golf ball above is shown at the right. You can name the angle formed by the path of the golf ball in three ways.

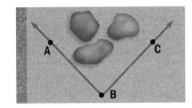

Name the angle by its vertex alone: ∠*B*.

Name the angle by its vertex and two points, with the vertex as the middle point: ∠*ABC*.

Name the angle by its vertex and two points, but switch the order of the two points: ∠*CBA*.

Your turn now **Name the angle in three ways.**

1.

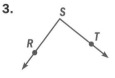

2.

3.

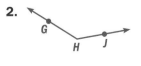

Using a Protractor A protractor is a tool you can use to draw and measure angles. Angles are measured in units called **degrees** (°) . To measure an angle, place the center of the protractor on the vertex of the angle and line up one ray with the 0° line. Then read the measure where the other ray crosses the protractor.

with Reading

Some protractors have an inner scale and an outer scale. You read one scale when measuring clockwise and the other scale when measuring counterclockwise. Make sure you use the same scale for each ray of the angle.

The measure of ∠ABC is 122°. You can write this as m∠ABC = 122°.

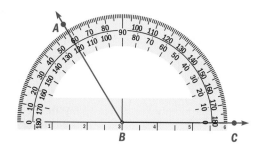

EXAMPLE 2 **Drawing Angles**

Use a protractor to draw an angle that has a measure of 54°.

Solution

① Draw and label a ray.

② Place the center of the protractor at the endpoint of the ray. Line up the ray with the 0° line. Then draw and label a point at the 54° mark on the inner scale.

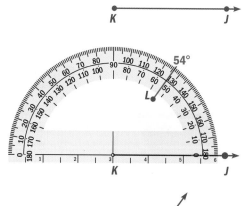

③ Remove the protractor and draw $\overrightarrow{KL}$ to complete the angle.

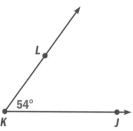

Your turn now Use a protractor to draw an angle that has the given measure.

4. 25°   **5.** 85°   **6.** 145°   **7.** 170°

Estimating Angle Measures You can estimate angle measures by mentally comparing them to 0°, 90°, and 180° on a protractor.

EXAMPLE 3 **Estimating Angle Measures**

Use estimation to name the angle whose measure is closest to the given measure.

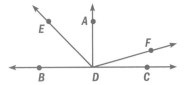

a. 90°   **b.** 15°   **c.** 135°

Solution

Imagine that D is at the center and that $\overrightarrow{DC}$ and $\overrightarrow{DB}$ are on the 0° line.

a. A 90° angle is halfway around a protractor, so $\angle BDA$ and $\angle CDA$ have measures that are equally close to 90°.

b. A 15° angle is close to 0° and less than halfway to 90°, so $\angle CDF$ has the measure that is closest to 15°.

c. A 135° angle is halfway between 90° and 180°, so $\angle CDE$ has the measure that is closest to 135°.

9.2 Exercises

More Practice, p. 716

Getting Ready to Practice

1. Vocabulary Name the vertex of $\angle DEF$ and the rays that form the angle.

Name the angle in three ways.

2.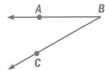

3.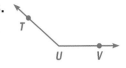

4.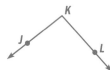

Use a protractor to draw an angle that has the given measure.

5. 30°   **6.** 45°   **7.** 90°   **8.** 130°

Use estimation to name the angle from Exercises 2–4 above whose measure is closest to the given measure.

9. 100°   **10.** 30°   **11.** 135°

Practice and Problem Solving

with Homework

Example	Exercises
1	12, 14
2	13, 15–22
3	23–25

Online Resources
CLASSZONE.COM
· More Examples
· eTutorial Plus

12. Name the angle shown at the right in three ways.

13. Use a protractor to measure the angle in Exercise 12.

14. **Find the Error** Describe and correct the error made in naming the angle.

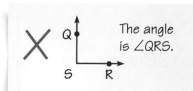

Kites Trace the red angle that the kite string makes with the ground. Then use a protractor to measure the angle.

15. **16.** **17.**

Use a protractor to draw an angle that has the given measure.

18. $33°$ **19.** $72°$ **20.** $165°$ **21.** $180°$

22. Use a protractor to draw and label an angle formed by $\overrightarrow{JK}$ and $\overrightarrow{JL}$ that has a measure of $65°$.

Use estimation to match the angle with its measure. Use a protractor to check your answer.

23. $20°$ **24.** $180°$ **25.** $145°$

A.   **B.**  **C.**

Estimation Tell whether the angle measure is between $0°$ and $45°$, $45°$ and $90°$, $90°$ and $135°$, or $135°$ and $180°$. Then estimate the measure of the angle.

26. 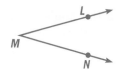 **27.**  **28.**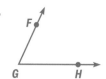

Find the sum or difference. *(Lesson 6.2)*

29. $\frac{4}{11} + \frac{9}{11}$ **30.** $\frac{1}{6} + \frac{4}{6}$ **31.** $\frac{13}{5} - \frac{9}{5}$ **32.** $\frac{7}{10} - \frac{5}{10}$

Solve the proportion. *(Lesson 8.3)*

33. $\frac{4}{x} = \frac{6}{9}$ **34.** $\frac{m}{8} = \frac{10}{5}$ **35.** $\frac{3}{5} = \frac{6}{a}$ **36.** $\frac{9}{12} = \frac{y}{4}$

Basic Skills **Write the decimal in words.**

37. 0.0031 **38.** 1.0325 **39.** 52.141 **40.** 496.85

Test-Taking Practice

41. Multiple Choice The measure of the angle shown at the right is between:

A. $0°$ and $45°$ **B.** $45°$ and $90°$

C. $90°$ and $135°$ **D.** $135°$ and $180°$

42. Multiple Choice Estimate the measure of the angle shown at the right.

F. $35°$ **G.** $90°$

H. $145°$ **I.** $175°$

BRAIN GAME

Flag Team Challenge

Trace the blue angles and extend the rays. Then use a protractor to measure the angles. Find the letter that corresponds to each angle measure. The letters will spell the name of the only state whose flag is not rectangular.

| A = 50° | U = 35° | T = 150° | W = 85° |
| I = 75° | O = 115° | H = 105° | |

Classifying Angles

9.3

BEFORE

You named and measured angles.

▶ **Now**

You'll classify angles and find angle measures.

WHY?

So you can find the angle measure of the Tower of Pisa, as in Example 4.

Word Watch

right angle, p. 430
acute angle, p. 430
obtuse angle, p. 430
straight angle, p. 430
vertical angles, p. 431
complementary angles,
    p. 431
supplementary angles,
    p. 431

Classifying Angles In the photograph at the right, you can see many types of angles. Angles are classified by their measure.

Classifying Angles	
A **right angle** is an angle whose measure is exactly 90°. Indicates a right angle	An **acute angle** is an angle whose measure is less than 90°.
An **obtuse angle** is an angle whose measure is between 90° and 180°.	A **straight angle** is an angle whose measure is exactly 180°.

 **EXAMPLE 1** **Classifying Angles**

Estimate to classify the angles in the figure as *acute*, *right*, or *obtuse*.

∠A is marked as a right angle.

∠B is an acute angle because m∠B is less than 90°.

∠C is an obtuse angle because m∠C is between 90° and 180°.

∠D is an obtuse angle because m∠D is between 90° and 180°.

Your turn now Classify the angle as *acute*, *right*, *obtuse*, or *straight*.

1.   **2.**   **3.**   **4.**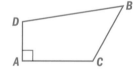

Vertical Angles When two lines intersect, the angles opposite each other are called **vertical angles.** In the diagram at the right, ∠1 and ∠3 are vertical angles, and ∠2 and ∠4 are vertical angles. Vertical angles have equal measures.

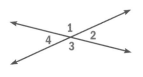

EXAMPLE 2 **Using Vertical Angles**

Find the measure of ∠QRS.

Because ∠QRS and ∠TRU are vertical angles, m∠QRS = m∠TRU = 40°.

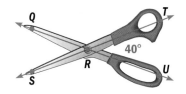

ANSWER The measure of ∠QRS is 40°.

Complementary and Supplementary Angles

Complementary angles Two angles are complementary if the sum of their measures is 90°.

$$m\angle 1 + m\angle 2 = 90°$$

Supplementary angles Two angles are supplementary if the sum of their measures is 180°.

$$m\angle 3 + m\angle 4 = 180°$$

EXAMPLE 3 **Classifying Pairs of Angles**

HELP with **Vocabulary**

To associate complementary angles with 90° and supplementary angles with 180°, remember that "c" is before "s" in the alphabet and 90 is before 180 on a number line.

Decide whether the angles are *complementary* or *supplementary*.

a.

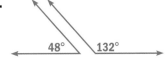

b.

Solution

a. The angles are supplementary because 48° + 132° = 180°.

b. The angles are complementary because 40° + 50° = 90°.

Tower of Pisa
Tuscany, Italy, 1989

EXAMPLE 4 **Solving for an Unknown Measure**

Architecture Before efforts to make the Tower of Pisa more upright began in 1990, the angle between the side of the tower and the ground was about 84.5°. About how many degrees from vertical did the tower lean?

Solution

Start by drawing a diagram. Then find the angle that is complementary to 84.5°.

$$84.5° + x° = 90°$$
$$x = 90 - 84.5$$
$$x = 5.5$$

ANSWER The Tower of Pisa leaned about 5.5° from vertical.

 **9.3** **Exercises**
More Practice, p. 716

INTERNET
eWorkbook Plus
CLASSZONE.COM

Getting Ready to Practice

Vocabulary **Match the type of angle with an appropriate measure.**

1. acute   **2.** obtuse   **3.** right   **4.** straight

A. 180°   **B.** 34°   **C.** 90°   **D.** 112°

Use the diagram at the right.

5. Name a pair of vertical angles.

6. Name a pair of complementary angles.

7. Name a pair of supplementary angles.

Tell whether the angle measures represent angles that are
complementary, *supplementary*, **or** *neither*.

8. 43°, 147°   **9.** 22°, 68°   **10.** 34°, 56°   **11.** 64°, 116°

Use the diagram from Exercises 5–7. Find the angle measure.

12. $m\angle EAF$ **13.** $m\angle EAD$ **14.** $m\angle FAB$

Practice and Problem Solving

with **Homework**

Example	Exercises
1	15–19
2	20–23
3	24–27
4	28–30

Online Resources
CLASSZONE.COM
· More Examples
· eTutorial Plus

Estimate to classify the angle formed by the hands of the clock.

15.
Cairo

16.
Prague

17.
Mexico City

18.
Denver

19. Classify all of the angles in the figure at the right.

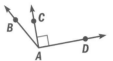

Name the pairs of vertical angles.

20.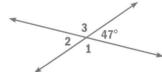

21.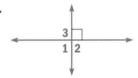

Find the measures of ∠1, ∠2, and ∠3.

22.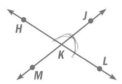

23.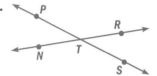

Tell whether the angle measures represent angles that are *complementary,* *supplementary,* **or** *neither.*

24. 105°, 75°   **25.** 51°, 39°   **26.** 15°, 37°   **27.** 108°, 82°

xy **Algebra** **Find the value of x.**

28.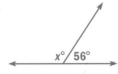

29.

30.

Use a protractor for Exercises 31–34.

31. Draw a right angle.   **32.** Draw an obtuse angle.

33. Draw an angle complementary to an angle measuring 45°.

34. Draw an angle supplementary to an angle measuring 60°.

Lines that meet at a 90° angle are called *perpendicular*. Decide if the lines are *perpendicular, parallel,* or *neither*.

35.    **36.**    **37.**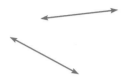

Extended Problem Solving Use the diagram and information below.
When you see an object in a mirror, the light from the object bounces off the mirror to reach your eyes. The measure of the angle that is formed by the ray of light and the mirror is the same before and after the light bounces off the mirror.

38. Find the measure of ∠*YBC*.

39. Find the measure of ∠*ABC*.

40. **Critical Thinking** What is the measure of ∠*ABC* when you are looking at yourself in the mirror?

41. **Challenge** Is there a maximum or minimum angle for seeing something reflected in a mirror? Explain.

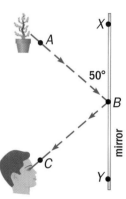

Mixed Review

Use the distributive property to evaluate the expression. *(Lesson 4.2)*

42. 5(70 + 6)   **43.** 7(20 + 4)   **44.** 4(6 + 0.3)

45. Sketch the figures $\overline{AB}$, $\overrightarrow{AB}$, and $\overleftrightarrow{AB}$. *(Lesson 9.1)*

Basic Skills **Find the sum or difference.**

46. 54.2 + 6.12   **47.** 9.49 + 37.8   **48.** 18.02 − 0.45

Test-Taking Practice

49. **Multiple Choice** Estimate to classify the angle shown at the right.

  A. acute   **B.** right

  C. obtuse   **D.** straight

50. **Multiple Choice** Which angle measure represents an angle complementary to a 54° angle?

  F. 36°   **G.** 46°   **H.** 54°   **I.** 126°

GOAL

Investigate the sum of the angles of a triangle.

MATERIALS

• ruler
• scissors
• protractor

Investigating Angles of a Triangle

You can use models to find the sum of the angle measures of a triangle.

Explore **Find the sum of the angle measures of a triangle.**

1 Draw a triangle on a piece of paper. Make each side at least 3 inches long.

2 Cut out your triangle, and tear off the three corners as shown.

3 Arrange the three corners as shown. What type of angle do they appear to form?

4 Repeat Steps 1–3 with a different triangle. What can you conclude about the sum of the angle measures of any triangle?

Your turn now Tell whether the three angle measures could be the angle measures of a triangle. Explain your reasoning.

1. 5°, 80°, 90°   **2.** 30°, 70°, 80°   **3.** 40°, 54°, 86°   **4.** 37°, 42°, 102°

Stop and Think

5. Critical Thinking Choose three angles that you think could form a triangle. Explain how you chose the three angles. Then draw the triangle using a protractor.

Classifying Triangles

BEFORE	▶ Now	WHY?
You classified angles as acute, right, obtuse, or straight.	You'll classify triangles by their angles and by their sides.	So you can classify the triangles of the Great Pyramid, as in Ex. 37.

In the Real World

Word Watch

triangle, p. 436
acute triangle, p. 436
right triangle, p. 436
obtuse triangle, p. 436
equilateral triangle, p. 437
isosceles triangle, p. 437
scalene triangle, p. 437

Carpentry The carpentry work in the photo has many *triangles*. You read △*ABC* as "triangle *ABC.*" A **triangle** is a closed plane figure with three straight sides that connect three points. △*ABC* has sides $\overline{AB}$, $\overline{BC}$, and $\overline{AC}$, and vertices *A*, *B*, and *C*.

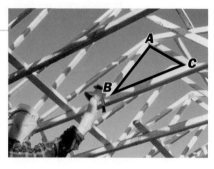

Classifying Triangles by Angles

An **acute triangle** has three acute angles.	A **right triangle** has one right angle.	An **obtuse triangle** has one obtuse angle.

EXAMPLE 1 **Classifying Triangles by Angles**

Classify the triangle by its angles.

a.   b.   c.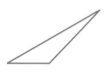

Solution

  a. The triangle is obtuse because it has 1 obtuse angle.

  b. The triangle is acute because it has 3 acute angles.

  c. The triangle is right because it has 1 right angle.

Your turn now **Classify the triangle by its angles.**

1. 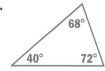   2.   3.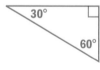

Sides of a Triangle You can use special marks on a drawing to indicate that two sides have the same length as shown at the right.

2 cm

2 cm

Classifying Triangles by Sides		
An **equilateral triangle** has three sides of the same length.	An **isosceles triangle** has at least two sides of the same length.	A **scalene triangle** has three sides of different lengths.

EXAMPLE 2 **Classifying Triangles by Sides**

Classify the triangle by its sides.

a.
4 ft
3 ft
2 ft

b.
5 in.
5 in.
5 in.

c.

Solution

a. The triangle is scalene because all of its sides have different lengths.

b. The triangle is equilateral because all of its sides have the same length.

c. The triangle is isosceles because two of its sides have the same length.

Angles of a Triangle As you may have noticed in the activity on page 435, the measures of the angles of any triangle add up to 180°.

Sum of Angle Measures of a Triangle

Words The sum of the angle measures of a triangle is 180°.

Algebra $m\angle A + m\angle B + m\angle C = 180°$

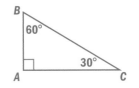

B
60°
30°
A
C

EXAMPLE 3 **Finding Angle Measures of Triangles**

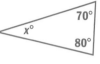

xy **Algebra Find the value of x.**

Use the fact that the measures of the angles of a triangle add up to 180°.

$$70° + 80° + x° = 180°$$ Write the equation.

$$150 + x = 180$$ Simplify.

$$x = 180 - 150$$ Write a related equation.

$$x = 30$$

ANSWER The value of *x* is 30.

9.4 **Exercises**
More Practice, p. 716

Getting Ready to Practice

Match the triangle with its description. Use each description once.

1.
   25°   80°
   75°

2.

3. 100°
   30°   50°

4.

5.

6.

A. acute triangle   **B.** obtuse triangle   **C.** right triangle

D. equilateral triangle   **E.** isosceles triangle   **F.** scalene triangle

7. **Stamps** Classify the stamp shown by its angles and by its sides.

xy **Algebra Find the value of x.**

8.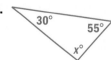
   30°
   55°
   x°

9.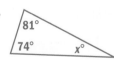
   81°
   74°   *x*°

10.
    x°   50°

Practice and Problem Solving

with Homework

Example	Exercises
1	11–13, 18–19
2	14–17
3	20–22

Online Resources
CLASSZONE.COM
· More Examples
· eTutorial Plus

Classify the triangle by its angles.

11. 138° 22° 20°

12. 90° 25° 65°

13. 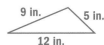 75° 35° 70°

Classify the triangle by its sides.

14. 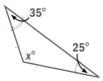 4 ft 4 ft 6 ft

15.

16. 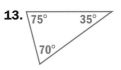 9 in. 5 in. 12 in.

Flags In Exercises 17–19, use the flag of Guyana, a country in South America.

17. Classify the green triangles by their sides.

18. Classify the red triangle by its angles.

19. Trace the flag. Then draw a line segment on the flag to form two obtuse triangles.

xy **Algebra** Find the value of *x*.

20. 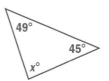 35° 25° x°

21. 49° 45° x°

22. 62° x° 62°

Tell whether the angle measures are those of a triangle. If so, classify the triangle as *acute, right,* or *obtuse*.

23. 35°, 35°, 90°

24. 90°, 52°, 38°

25. 95°, 25°, 60°

26. 56°, 56°, 58°

27. 74°, 55°, 51°

28. 136°, 23°, 32°

Tell whether the statement is *always, sometimes,* or *never* true.

29. A right triangle has one right angle.

30. In a right triangle, the two acute angles are complementary.

31. An obtuse triangle has more than one obtuse angle.

Use a protractor to draw the triangle described.

32. acute isosceles

33. obtuse isosceles

34. obtuse scalene

35. right scalene

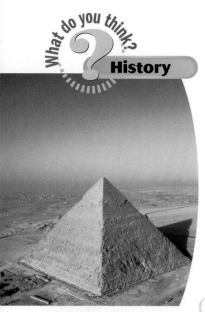
Great Pyramid The triangle at the right shows a view of one of the sides of the Great Pyramid.

36. What is the value of x in the triangle?

37. Classify the triangle by its sides and angles.

38. **Explain** Use what you know about triangles and angles to find the measures of $\angle 2$, $\angle 3$, $\angle 4$, $\angle 6$, and $\angle 7$. Explain how you found your answers.

39. **Challenge** In $\triangle JKL$, the measure of $\angle J$ is 30°. The measure of $\angle K$ is four times the measure of $\angle L$. Find the measure of $\angle K$. What type of triangle is $\triangle JKL$?

Mixed Review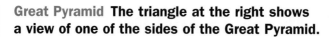

40. A baseball player pitches $\frac{4}{9}$ of a game. The remaining fraction of the game is evenly divided between two relief pitchers. What fraction of the game did each relief pitcher play? *(Lessons 6.5, 7.4)*

Use the figure shown. *(Lesson 9.3)*

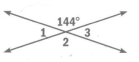

41. Name two pairs of supplementary angles.

42. Find $m\angle 1$, $m\angle 2$, and $m\angle 3$.

Basic Skills Write the decimal as a fraction or mixed number.

43. 0.35   **44.** 0.68   **45.** 6.42   **46.** 12.37

Test-Taking Practice

47. **Multiple Choice** What is the measure of $\angle A$ in $\triangle ABC$?

   A. 115°   **B.** 55°

   C. 30°   **D.** 25°

48. **Multiple Choice** Which triangle is obtuse?

  F.   **G.**   **H.**   **I.**

Technology Activity

Angle Measures of Triangles

GOAL Use a spreadsheet to find unknown angle measures of triangles.

Example **You can use a spreadsheet to calculate angle measures.**

The logo for the Environmental Protection Agency's Research Triangle Park is a triangle that has one 78° angle and one 57° angle. What is the measure of the third angle?

Solution

Create a spreadsheet with the format shown. To calculate the measure of the third angle, you must subtract the sum of the first two angle measures (entered in cells B1 and B2) from 180°. This can be done by entering this formula in cell B3: $= 180 - \text{SUM(B1 : B2)}$.

	A	B
1	1st angle measure (degrees)	78
2	2nd angle measure (degrees)	57
3	3rd angle measure (degrees)	45

$= 180 - \text{SUM(B1 : B2)}$ gives the result $180 - (78 + 57)$, or 45.

ANSWER The measure of the third angle is 45°.

Your turn now **Use a spreadsheet to find the value of x.**

1.
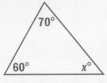

2.

3.
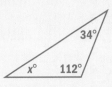

4.
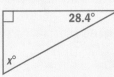

5.

6.
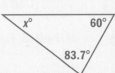

7. Art The logo for the National Tsunami Hazard Mitigation Program is a triangle with two 57.5° angles. What is the measure of the third angle?

8. Science The Nauru99 Triangle is an oceanic and atmospheric research area formed by two research vessels and the island of Nauru. The angle measures at the two research vessels are 80° and 63°. What is the angle measure at the island of Nauru?

Notebook Review

Review the vocabulary definitions in your notebook.

Copy the review examples in your notebook. Then complete the exercises.

Check Your Definitions

point, p. 421
line, p. 421
ray, p. 421
endpoint, p. 421
segment, p. 421
plane, p. 422
intersecting lines, p. 422

parallel lines, p. 422
angle, p. 425
vertex, p. 425
degrees (°), p. 426
angles: straight, right, acute, obtuse, p. 430
vertical angles, p. 431

complementary angles, supplementary angles, p. 431
triangles: acute, right, obtuse, equilateral, isosceles, scalene, pp. 436, 437

Use Your Vocabulary

Copy and complete the statement.

1. An _?_ is formed by two rays with the same endpoint.

2. Two angles are _?_ angles if the sum of their measures is 180°.

9.1 Can you identify lines, rays, and segments?

 Review

EXAMPLE Name a line, a ray, and a segment in the figure at the right.

ANSWER Line: $\overleftrightarrow{AB}$ Ray: $\overrightarrow{CA}$ Segment: $\overline{BC}$

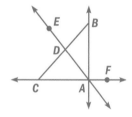

☑ **Use the figure above.**   **3.** Name another ray.   **4.** Name another line.

9.2–9.3 Can you name and classify angles?

 Review

EXAMPLE Name and classify the angle.

a.

R
140°
S   T

∠RST is an obtuse angle.

b.

20°   L
M   N

∠LMN is an acute angle.

☑ **Classify the angle by its measure.**   **5.** $m\angle A = 100°$ **6.** $m\angle B = 180°$

9.4 Can you classify triangles?

Review

EXAMPLE Find the value of x and classify the triangle by its angles.

$48° + 32° + x° = 180°$

$80 + x = 180$

$x = 180 - 80$

$x = 100$

ANSWER The value of x is 100. The triangle is an obtuse triangle.

✓ **Find the value of x. Then classify the triangle by its angles and by its sides.**

7.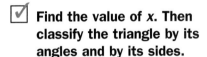

8.

Stop *and* **Think** about Lessons 9.1–9.4

9. Critical Thinking Given the measure of an angle, how do you find the measure of a complementary angle? of a supplementary angle?

10. Writing Explain why a right triangle cannot have two right angles.

Review Quiz 1

Use the figure to name the following.

1. a point   **2.** two rays

3. parallel lines   **4.** a segment

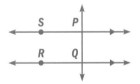

Name the angle in three ways. Then measure it.

5.

6.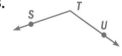

7.

Tell whether the angle is *acute, obtuse, right,* or *straight.*

8. $m\angle A = 180°$ **9.** $m\angle B = 92°$ **10.** $m\angle C = 18°$ **11.** $m\angle D = 90°$

Tell whether the angle measures are those of a triangle.

12. $30°, 60°, 90°$ **13.** $45°, 90°, 45°$ **14.** $35°, 45°, 110°$ **15.** $59°, 43°, 68°$

Hands-on Activity

Angles of Quadrilaterals

You can use a protractor to investigate angles of four-sided figures.

Explore **Investigate the angles of the figures below.**

1 Trace the figures below on a piece of paper.

Figure 1	Figure 2	Figure 3

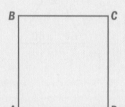 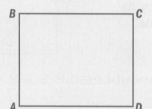 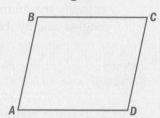

2 Use a protractor to measure the angles. Copy and complete the table.

	$m\angle A$	$m\angle B$	$m\angle C$	$m\angle D$	$m\angle A + m\angle B + m\angle C + m\angle D$
Figure 1	?	?	?	?	?
Figure 2	?	?	?	?	?
Figure 3	?	?	?	?	?

Your turn now

1. Sketch and label a four-sided figure with straight sides. Copy and complete the table in Step 2 for your figure.

Stop and Think

2. Writing Based on the table you completed, write a rule for the sum of the angle measures of a four-sided figure.

3. Critical Thinking What other angle relationships do you notice in your table? Describe these relationships in words.

Classifying Quadrilaterals

BEFORE	▶ Now	WHY?
You classified triangles by their angles and sides.	You'll classify quadrilaterals by their angles and sides.	So you can classify figures in woodwork, as in Exs. 19–21.

📓 **Word Watch**

quadrilateral, p. 445
parallelogram, p. 445
rectangle, p. 445
rhombus, p. 445
square, p. 445

Quadrilaterals A **quadrilateral** is a plane figure formed by 4 segments called *sides*. Each side intersects exactly 2 other sides, one at each endpoint, and no two sides are part of the same line. The chart below shows some types of quadrilaterals.

Special Quadrilateral	Diagram
A **parallelogram** is a quadrilateral with 2 pairs of parallel sides.	
A **rectangle** is a parallelogram with 4 right angles.	
A **rhombus** is a parallelogram with 4 sides of equal length.	
A **square** is a parallelogram with 4 right angles and 4 sides of equal length.	

 **with Notetaking**

Try making a Venn diagram in your notebook to help you organize the different types of quadrilaterals. For help with Venn diagrams, see p. 703.

EXAMPLE 1 Classifying Quadrilaterals

Tell whether the statement is *true* or *false*. Explain your reasoning.

   a. All squares are rectangles.

   b. Some rhombuses do not have 2 pairs of parallel sides.

Solution

   a. True: All squares are parallelograms with 4 right angles, so all squares are rectangles.

   b. False: All rhombuses are parallelograms, so all rhombuses have 2 pairs of parallel sides.

Classify Parallelograms You need to look at all the marks and labels on a parallelogram to decide how to classify it. Some parallelograms can be classified in more than one way.

EXAMPLE 2 Classifying Parallelograms

Classify the parallelogram in as many ways as possible.

a.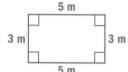

b.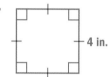

c.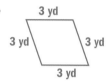

Solution

  a. The parallelogram is a rectangle because it has 4 right angles.

  b. The parallelogram is a rectangle, a rhombus, and a square because it has 4 right angles and 4 sides of equal length.

  c. The parallelogram is a rhombus because it has 4 sides of equal length.

EXAMPLE 3 Drawing a Quadrilateral

Draw a quadrilateral that is a rectangle but not a square.

① Draw one side.

② Draw a right angle. Then draw a side with a different length.

③ Draw two more right angles. Then draw the other two sides and angle.

Your turn now Classify the quadrilateral in as many ways as possible.

1.

2.

3.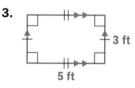

  4. Draw a parallelogram that is neither a rectangle nor a rhombus.

Getting Ready to Practice

Vocabulary **Copy and complete the statement.**

1. A rhombus is a __?__ with 4 sides of equal length.

2. A __?__ is a parallelogram with 4 sides of equal length and 4 right angles.

Tell whether the statement is *true* or *false*. Explain your reasoning.

3. A square is always a rhombus.   4. All squares have 4 right angles.

Quilts **Classify the quadrilateral in as many ways as possible.**

5.
6.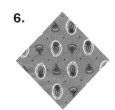
7.

Practice and Problem Solving

Copy and complete the statement using *All* or *Some.*

8. __?__ rectangles are squares.

9. __?__ rhombuses are parallelograms.

10. __?__ squares are rhombuses.

11. __?__ parallelograms are squares.

Classify the parallelogram in as many ways as possible.

12.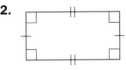
13.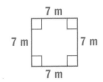
14.

15. Draw a rhombus that is not a square.

Critical Thinking **Identify all quadrilaterals that always fit the description.**

16. 4 equal sides   17. 4 right angles   18. 2 pairs of parallel sides

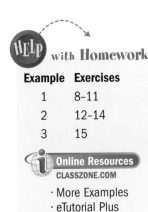

HELP with Homework

Example	Exercises
1	8–11
2	12–14
3	15

Online Resources
CLASSZONE.COM
· More Examples
· eTutorial Plus

Woodworking **Use the woodwork shown.**

19. Classify the numbered quadrilaterals.

20. What type of quadrilateral is the entire woodwork?

21. How many rhombuses that are not squares are shown on the woodwork?

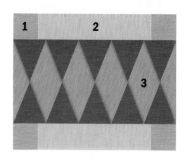

 **Algebra** **The sum of the angle measures of a quadrilateral is 360°. Use this information to find the value of *x*.**

22.

23.

24.

25. Writing Explain why a rhombus that is also a square is always a rectangle.

26. Challenge Is it possible to draw a quadrilateral that has 2 right angles but is not a rectangle? Is this possible with 3 right angles? Explain.

Mixed Review

27. Order the numbers 42%, 0.45, and $\frac{2}{5}$ from least to greatest. *(Lesson 8.6)*

Tell whether the angle measures are those of a triangle. If so, classify the triangle as *acute*, *right*, or *obtuse*. *(Lesson 9.4)*

28. 28°, 38°, 124° **29.** 20°, 80°, 80° **30.** 23°, 55°, 102° **31.** 45°, 45°, 90°

Basic Skills **Find the total amount spent.**

32. 7 light bulbs for $1.50 each

33. 4 bags of pretzels for $2.75 each

Test-Taking Practice

34. Multiple Choice Which figure is *not* a parallelogram?

A.   **B.**   **C.**   **D.**

35. Short Response Explain why a square is a rectangle, a rhombus, a parallelogram, and a quadrilateral.

Polygons

LESSON 9.6

BEFORE

You classified figures by their angles and sides.

▶ **Now**

You'll classify polygons by their sides.

WHY?

So you can classify polygons in street signs, as in Exs. 4–6.

So you can classify polygons in street signs, as in Exs. 4–6.

Word Watch

polygon, p. 449
vertex, p. 449
pentagon, p. 449
hexagon, p. 449
octagon, p. 449
regular polygon, p. 450
diagonal, p. 450

In the Real World

Soccer Many soccer balls are made so that the cover shows two different figures. How can you describe these figures?

A **polygon** is a closed plane figure that is formed by three or more segments called sides. Each side intersects exactly two other sides at a **vertex**.

Classifying Polygons				
Triangle	**Quadrilateral**	**Pentagon**	**Hexagon**	**Octagon**
3 sides	4 sides	5 sides	6 sides	8 sides

HELP with Vocabulary

To help remember how many sides a polygon has, use the following.

"tri" means 3.
"quad" means 4.
"penta" means 5.
"hexa" means 6.
"octa" means 8.

EXAMPLE 1 Classifying Polygons

To describe the figures found on the soccer ball shown above, count the number of sides of each figure.

ANSWER The figures are pentagons and hexagons.

Your turn now Classify the polygon.

1.

2.

3.

Regular Polygons A **regular polygon** is a polygon with equal side lengths and equal angle measures. A stop sign is an example of a regular octagon.

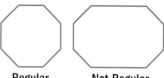

Regular   Not Regular

HELP with Reading

Matching angle marks indicate that the angles have equal measures.

EXAMPLE 2 Classifying Regular Polygons

Classify the polygon and tell whether it is regular.

a.
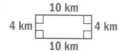
10 km
4 km   4 km
10 km

b.
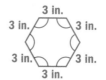
3 in.
3 in.   3 in.
3 in.   3 in.
3 in.

c.
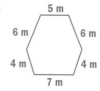
5 m
6 m   6 m
4 m   4 m
7 m

Solution

a. The side lengths of the quadrilateral are not equal, so it is not regular.

b. The side lengths of the hexagon are equal and the angle measures are equal, so it is a regular hexagon.

c. The side lengths of the hexagon are not equal, so it is not regular.

Diagonals A **diagonal** of a polygon is a segment, other than a side, that connects two vertices of the polygon.

EXAMPLE 3 Diagonals of a Regular Polygon

How many diagonals can be drawn from one vertex of a regular pentagon? How many triangles do the diagonals form?

Solution

Sketch a regular pentagon and draw all the possible diagonals from one vertex.

ANSWER There are 2 diagonals and 3 triangles.

Your turn now Tell how many triangles are formed by the diagonals from one vertex of the figure.

4. A regular quadrilateral   **5.** A regular hexagon

Getting Ready to Practice

Vocabulary Match the polygon with its correct classification.

1.

2.

3.

A. hexagon

B. pentagon

C. octagon

Tell whether the figure is a regular polygon.

4.

5.

6.

7. Find the Error Describe and correct the error in finding the number of diagonals that can be drawn from one vertex of an octagon.

There are 7 diagonals.

Practice and Problem Solving

HELP with Homework

Example	Exercises
1	8–10, 16–18
2	8–10, 13
3	11–12

Online Resources
CLASSZONE.COM
· More Examples
· eTutorial Plus

Classify the polygon and tell whether it is regular.

8.

9.

10.

11. How many triangles are formed by the diagonals from one vertex of a rectangle?

12. Repeat Exercise 11 using a regular octagon.

13. Critical Thinking What is another name for a regular quadrilateral?

Algebra Use supplementary angles to find the value of *x*.

14.

15.

HELP with **Review**

For more help with graphing ordered pairs on a coordinate grid, see page 83.

Geometry Graph the points on a coordinate grid and connect them to form a polygon. Then classify the polygon.

16. $A(7, 3)$, $B(3, 3)$, $C(3, 9)$, $D(7, 8)$

17. $A(7, 8)$, $B(7, 3)$, $C(2, 5)$

18. $A(2, 8)$, $B(2, 2)$, $C(8, 2)$, $D(8, 8)$, $E(10, 5)$

Extended Problem Solving Use the table below for Exercises 19–21.

19. Copy and complete the table. You may want to draw the polygon described.

20. **Look for a Pattern** How does the number of diagonals from one vertex change as the number of sides of the polygon increases?

Number of sides of regular polygon	4	5	6
Number of diagonals from one vertex	_?_	_?_	_?_

21. **Predict** Use the pattern you found in Exercise 20 to predict the number of diagonals from one vertex of a regular polygon with 9 sides. Then sketch the polygon to check your answer.

22. **Critical Thinking** What type of polygon has no diagonals?

23. **Stained Glass Windows** Use the expression below to find the measure of each angle of the regular octagon shown in yellow in the stained glass window at the right.

Number of triangles formed by the diagonals from one vertex	× 180 ÷	Number of sides of the polygon

24. The perimeter of a regular pentagon is 45 inches. What is the length of each side?

25. Find the perimeter of a regular octagon that has a side length of 4 meters.

26. Challenge Draw a regular hexagon. Draw two diagonals from different vertices so that you form two triangles and one quadrilateral. Classify the triangles formed by the diagonals.

Mixed Review

Draw a quadrilateral that fits the description. *(Lesson 9.5)*

27. at least 3 right angles

28. 2 pairs of parallel sides

Choose a Strategy **Use a strategy from the list at the right to solve the following problem. Explain your choice of strategy.**

29. Find the sum of the whole numbers from 1 to 500.

Problem Solving Strategies

▪ Draw a Diagram
▪ Solve a Simpler Problem
▪ Work Backward
▪ Guess, Check, and Revise

Basic Skills **Use rounding to estimate the sum or difference.**

30. $4.3 + 6.18$

31. $2.37 + 3.95$

32. $45.15 - 13.8$

Test-Taking Practice

33. Multiple Choice Which figure is a polygon?

A. **B.** **C.** **D.**

34. Short Response Sketch a polygon with ten sides. How many diagonals and triangles can be formed from one vertex of the polygon?

BRAIN GAME

Triangle Teaser

How many triangles are there in the figure?

(Hint: There are more than 16.)

Congruent and Similar Figures

BEFORE	Now	WHY?
You classified polygons by their angles and by their sides.	You'll identify similar and congruent figures.	So you can compare images, such as the photographs in Ex. 13.

Word Watch

congruent, p. 454
similar, p. 454
corresponding parts, p. 455

Activity Use the triangles below to answer the questions.

 2 in.   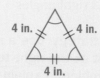 4 in. 4 in.   4 in. 4 in.
                                        4 in.   2 in.   3 in.

(1) Which triangles are the same size and the same shape? Are their angle measures the same? Are their side lengths the same?

(2) Which triangles are the same shape but different sizes? Are their angle measures the same? Are their side lengths the same?

Comparing Figures Two figures are **congruent** if they have the same size and shape. Two figures are **similar** if they have the same shape but not necessarily the same size.

EXAMPLE 1 Congruent and Similar Triangles

Tell whether the triangles are *similar*, *congruent*, or *neither*.

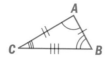  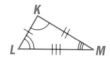

Solution

△ABC, △FGH, and △KLM are similar because they have the same shape. △ABC and △KLM are congruent because they have the same size and shape.

Your turn now Tell whether the triangles are *similar*, *congruent*, or *neither*.

1.   2.

Corresponding Parts When two figures are similar, their *corresponding angles* have the same measure. When two figures are congruent, their *corresponding parts* have the same measure.
Corresponding parts are the matching sides and angles of two figures.

EXAMPLE 2 Listing Corresponding Parts

△**ABC** and △**DEF** are congruent. List the corresponding parts.

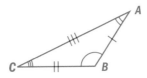 

When listing corresponding parts, list corresponding vertices in the same order.

Corresponding angles: ∠A and ∠D, ∠B and ∠E, ∠C and ∠F

Corresponding sides: $\overline{AB}$ and $\overline{DE}$, $\overline{BC}$ and $\overline{EF}$, $\overline{AC}$ and $\overline{DF}$

EXAMPLE 3 Using Corresponding Parts

Bridges In the photograph, △ABC and △DBC are congruent.

a. If $\overline{AC}$ is about 51 meters long, how long is $\overline{DC}$? Why?

b. If $m\angle A \approx 50°$, what is $m\angle D$? Why?

Solution

a. Corresponding sides of congruent triangles have the same length. So, $\overline{DC}$ has a length of about 51 meters.

b. Corresponding angles of congruent triangles have the same measure. So, $m\angle D \approx 50°$.

The Sunshine Skyway Bridge in Florida

Your turn now △**GHJ** and △**KML** are similar. List the corresponding parts. Then find $m\angle G$ and $m\angle L$.

3.

Getting Ready to Practice

Vocabulary Tell whether the statement is *true* or *false*.

1. △*VUW* is congruent to △*YXZ* because they have the same size and shape.

2. △*VUW* is similar to △*YXZ*.

3. In the figures, $\overline{VW}$ corresponds to $\overline{YX}$.

xy **Algebra** The two figures are congruent. Find the values of *x* and *y*.

4.

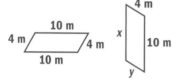

5.

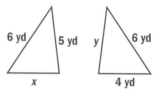

Practice and Problem Solving

Tell whether the triangles are *similar*, *congruent*, **or** *neither*.

6.

7.

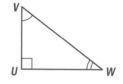

8.

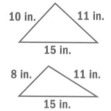

List the corresponding parts of the triangles.

9.

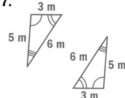

10.

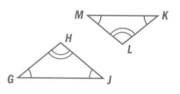

xy **Algebra** The figures are congruent. Find the values of *x* and *y*.

11.

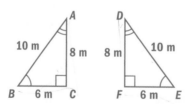

12.

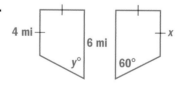

13. Photography You are viewing photographs on a computer screen at a scale of 2 in. : 1 in. Are the images on the screen and the actual photographs similar? congruent? Explain.

Decide if the objects are usually _similar, congruent_, or _neither_. Explain.

14. buttons on your shirt

15. a pair of earrings

16. the drink on the billboard and the actual drink

17. a C battery and a AA battery

18. Draw any triangle. Then draw a triangle with the same angle measures but different side lengths. Are the triangles _similar, congruent_, or _neither_?

19. △XYZ is similar to △ABC. List the corresponding parts.

20. Critical Thinking If two figures are congruent, are they also similar? If two figures are similar, are they also congruent? Explain.

21. Challenge Are all squares similar? Are all rectangles similar? Explain.

Mixed Review

22. Buying CDs A CD that teaches you how to speak Spanish costs $28.75. There is a 6% sales tax and you have $30. Decide whether you can buy the CD. _(Lesson 8.7)_

23. Use a protractor to draw an angle with a measure of 55°. _(Lesson 9.2)_

Basic Skills **Find the product or quotient.**

24. 3.25×5.6 **25.** 9.8×0.62 **26.** $4.85 \div 0.5$

Test-Taking Practice

27. Multiple Choice The triangles shown are congruent. What is the value of x?

A. 2 cm   **B.** 3 cm

C. 5 cm   **D.** 8 cm

28. Multiple Choice The triangles shown are congruent. Find the measure of ∠G.

F. 122°   **G.** 88°

H. 85°   **I.** 65°

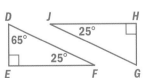

Make a Model

Draw a Diagram

Perform an Experiment

Make a List

Work Backward

Make a Model

Solve a Simpler Problem

Look for a Pattern

Problem If you fold a rectangular piece of paper in half, and then in half again in the other direction, you will form a similar rectangle. If you punch a hole inside the rectangle through all the layers, how many congruent holes will there be when you unfold the paper?

① Read and Understand

Read the problem carefully.

You need to fold a rectangular piece of paper in half, then in half again in the other direction, and punch a hole through all the layers.

② Make a Plan

Decide on a strategy to use.

One way to solve this problem is to make a model. You will need a rectangular piece of paper and a hole punch.

③ Solve the Problem

Reread the problem and make a model.

Begin with a rectangular piece of paper.
Fold the paper in half twice.

Punch a hole inside the rectangle. Unfold the piece of paper and see how many congruent holes you have.

ANSWER There are 4 congruent holes.

④ Look Back

If you make 1 fold, there are 2 layers of paper and 2 holes. If you make 2 folds, there are 4 layers of paper and 4 holes. How many holes would you expect from 3 folds? Try it and see.

Use the strategy *make a model*.

1. **Paper Cutouts** You fold a rectangular piece of paper in half, then in half again in the other direction. Then you cut out a rectangle through all the layers of paper. What is the maximum number of rectangles you can have when you unfold the paper? the minimum number?

2. **Paper Octagons** Describe how to fold a rectangular piece of paper and make a single cut along a line to form an octagon when the paper is unfolded.

3. **Cubes** Which cube cannot be formed by folding the pattern shown?

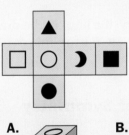

A.   B.

C.   D.

4. **Cube Patterns** Which pattern will form a closed cube when folded?

Mixed Problem Solving

Use any strategy to solve the problem.

5. **Furniture** Your bedroom measures 10 feet by 12 feet and your bed measures 6 feet by 3 feet. Could you fit a desk that is 4.5 feet long and 3 feet wide on the same wall as your bed with the long side against the wall? Why or why not?

6. **Random Drawing** Each student in a school with 635 students is assigned a number from 1 to 635 for a random drawing. How many students will be assigned a number with a 2 in it?

7. **School Supplies** After purchasing 5 pencils, 5 notebooks, 6 folders, and 3 pens at the prices below, you had $12.35.

Price List	
Notebooks	$4.25 each
Folders	3 for $1
Pens	3 for $4
Pencils	$.25 each

Assume there was no sales tax. How much money did you start with?

8. **Home Improvement** You are building a deck that will be 8 feet by 4 feet. You are using boards that are 8 feet by 4 inches. Will 11 boards be enough? Why or why not?

Line Symmetry

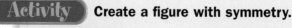

BEFORE

You learned about congruent and similar figures.

▶ **Now**

You'll identify lines of symmetry.

WHY?

So you can find the symmetry of a tennis court, as in Ex. 14.

Word Watch

line symmetry, p. 460
line of symmetry, p. 460

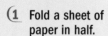 **Activity** Create a figure with symmetry.

① Fold a sheet of paper in half.

② Cut a design out of the folded edge as shown. Unfold the design.

③ Are the figures on the opposite sides of the fold the same size? the same shape?

Line Symmetry A figure has **line symmetry** if a line can be drawn that divides the figure into two congruent parts that are mirror images of each other. The line is called the **line of symmetry**.

EXAMPLE 1 **Identifying Lines of Symmetry**

Tell whether the object has line symmetry. If so, draw the line of symmetry.

a.

Yes, this guitar has line symmetry.

b.

No, this guitar does not have line symmetry.

Your turn now Tell whether the figure has line symmetry. If so, copy the figure and draw the line of symmetry.

1.

2.

3.

Lines of Symmetry

A figure can have zero, one, or multiple lines of symmetry.

no lines of symmetry

1 line of symmetry

2 lines of symmetry

3 lines of symmetry

EXAMPLE 2 **Multiple Lines of Symmetry**

Find the number of lines of symmetry in a square.

Think about how many different ways you can fold a square in half so that the two halves match up perfectly.

vertical fold

horizontal fold

diagonal fold

diagonal fold

ANSWER A square has 4 lines of symmetry.

EXAMPLE 3 **Completing Symmetrical Figures**

 with Solving

To find the mirror image of a point in Example 3, find the distance between the point and the line of symmetry. Place the mirror image point the same distance from the line of symmetry, but on the opposite side.

Complete the polygon so that it has the line of symmetry shown.

1 Draw the mirror image of each vertex that is not on the line of symmetry.

2 Connect the points to complete the mirror image so that the two halves are congruent.

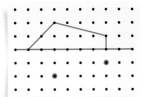

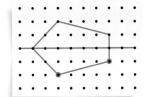

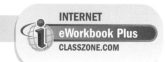

9.8 Exercises

More Practice, p. 716

Getting Ready to Practice

1. **Vocabulary** A figure has _?_ if it can be divided by a line into two congruent parts that are mirror images of each other.

Find the number of lines of symmetry in the object.

2.

3.

4.

Practice and Problem Solving

Tell whether the line shown is a line of symmetry.

5.

6.

7.

Copy the figure and draw all lines of symmetry.

8.

9.

10.

Copy and complete the figure so that it has the line of symmetry shown.

11.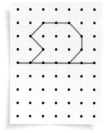

12.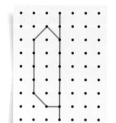

13.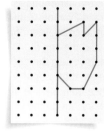

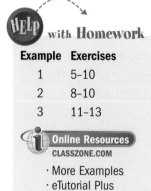

HELP with Homework

Example	Exercises
1	5–10
2	8–10
3	11–13

Online Resources
CLASSZONE.COM

· More Examples
· eTutorial Plus

14. Find the number of lines of symmetry in the tennis court.

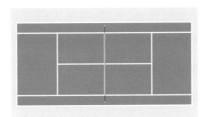

15. Find the number of lines of symmetry in the baseball field.

16. Make a Model Copy the figure at the right. Cut out your copy and use it to find the number of lines of symmetry in the figure.

17. Critical Thinking Is there a type of triangle that has exactly one line of symmetry? If so, identify the type of triangle.

18. Challenge Which quadrilaterals have exactly two lines of symmetry? Sketch the quadrilaterals and show the lines of symmetry.

Mixed Review

Use mental math to solve the equation. (Lesson 1.6)

19. $12 + x = 24$ **20.** $x - 8 = 22$ **21.** $3x = 27$ **22.** $x \div 5 = 4$

Find the product. (Lesson 7.2)

23. $\dfrac{6}{7} \times \dfrac{7}{12}$ **24.** $\dfrac{2}{3} \times \dfrac{1}{2}$ **25.** $\dfrac{3}{2} \times \dfrac{1}{18}$ **26.** $\dfrac{10}{13} \times \dfrac{39}{70}$

Basic Skills   **Estimate the product.**

27. 11×24 **28.** 9×21 **29.** 32×72 **30.** 48×63

Test-Taking Practice

31. Multiple Choice Which letter has no lines of symmetry?

A. E   **B.** F   **C.** T   **D.** W

32. Multiple Choice How many lines of symmetry does the letter H have?

F. none   **G.** one   **H.** two   **I.** four

Notebook Review

Review the vocabulary definitions in your notebook.

Copy the review examples in your notebook. Then complete the exercises.

Check Your Definitions

quadrilateral, p. 445
parallelogram, p. 445
rectangle, p. 445
rhombus, p. 445
square, p. 445

polygons: pentagon, hexagon, octagon, p. 449
regular polygon, p. 450
diagonal, p. 450

congruent, p. 454
similar, p. 454
corresponding parts, p. 455
line symmetry, p. 460

Use Your Vocabulary

1. Copy and complete: A __?__ is a quadrilateral with two pairs of parallel sides.

2. Are all rhombuses regular polygons? Why or why not?

9.5–9.6 Can you classify quadrilaterals and polygons?

Review **EXAMPLE** Classify the polygon shown.

ANSWER The polygon is a quadrilateral, a parallelogram, a rectangle, a rhombus, and a square.

✓ **Classify the polygon.** 3. 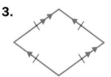 4.

9.7 Can you identify similar and congruent figures?

Review **EXAMPLE** The triangles at the right are similar. List the corresponding parts.

ANSWER Corresponding angles:
∠D and ∠X, ∠E and ∠Y, ∠F and ∠Z
Corresponding sides: $\overline{DE}$ and $\overline{XY}$, $\overline{EF}$ and $\overline{YZ}$, $\overline{FD}$ and $\overline{ZX}$

✓ 5. Tell whether the triangles are *similar* or *congruent*. List the corresponding parts.

9.8 Can you find lines of symmetry?

EXAMPLE Tell whether the figure has line symmetry. If so, draw any lines of symmetry.

ANSWER The figure has one line of symmetry.

☑ **Tell whether the line shown is a line of symmetry.**

6.

7.

8.

Stop *and* **Think** about Lessons 9.5–9.8

9. Writing Your friend says that a regular hexagon is a parallelogram. Is her statement correct? Explain why or why not.

Review Quiz 2

Classify the polygon in as many ways as possible.

1.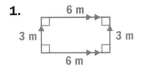

2.

3.

4. A regular pentagon has a perimeter of 15 feet. What is the side length?

Use the congruent quadrilaterals shown.

5. List the corresponding parts.

6. Find the value of *a*.

7. What is $m\angle K$?

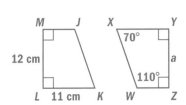

Find the number of lines of symmetry in the figure.

8.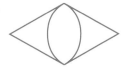

9.

10.

Chapter Review

Vocabulary

point, line, ray, p. 421
endpoint, p. 421
segment, p. 421
plane, p. 422
intersecting lines, p. 422
parallel lines, p. 422
angle, p. 425
vertex, p. 425, 449
degrees(°), p. 426
angles: straight, right,
  acute, obtuse, p. 430

vertical angles, p. 431
complementary, p. 431
supplementary, p. 431
triangles: acute, right,
  obtuse, equilateral,
  isosceles, scalene,
  pp. 436, 437
quadrilaterals:
  parallelogram,
  rectangle, rhombus,
  square, p. 445

polygons: pentagon,
  hexagon, octagon,
  p. 449
regular polygon, p. 450
diagonal, p. 450
congruent and similar
  figures, p. 454
corresponding parts,
  p. 455
line symmetry, p. 460
line of symmetry, p. 460

Vocabulary Review

1. What are vertical angles?

2. Are all rectangles parallelograms?

3. How many acute angles does an acute triangle have?

4. How many obtuse angles does an obtuse triangle have?

5. What is the relationship between two supplementary angles?

Copy and complete the statement.

6. An angle with a measure of 100° is an example of an _?_ angle.

7. A straight angle has a measure of _?_.

8. Two figures are _?_ if they have the same size and shape.

9. A regular polygon has _?_ side lengths and _?_ angle measures.

Review Questions

Use the diagram of a gate to name the following. (Lesson 9.1)

10. three points

11. a horizontal line throught point V

12. a segment that has R as an endpoint

13. a line parallel to the line in Exercise 11

Use the angle at the right. (Lesson 9.2)

14. Name the angle in three ways. What is its vertex?

15. Estimate the measure of the angle. Use a protractor to check your estimate.

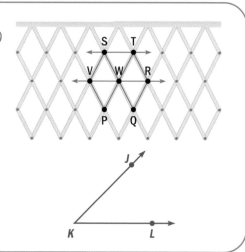

Decide whether the angles are *complementary, supplementary,* or *neither*. *(Lesson 9.3)*

16.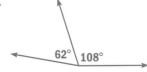

17.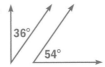

18.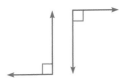

19. Draw an obtuse angle. Measure your angle. *(Lesson 9.3)*

Use the diagram at the right. *(Lesson 9.3)*

20. Are ∠1 and ∠2 vertical angles? Explain why or why not.

21. Find the measures of ∠1, ∠2, and ∠3.

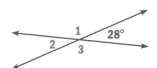

Find the value of *x*. Then classify the triangle by its angles. *(Lesson 9.4)*

22.

23.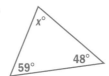

24.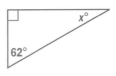

Classify the polygon in as many ways as possible. *(Lessons 9.5, 9.6)*

25.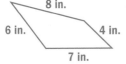

26.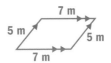

27.

28.

Tell whether the triangles are *similar* or *congruent.* Then list the corresponding parts. *(Lesson 9.7)*

29.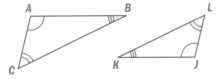

30.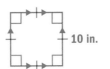

Copy the figure and draw all lines of symmetry. *(Lesson 9.8)*

31.

32.

33.

34.

Chapter Test

Sketch the figure described.

1. $\overline{AB}$ **2.** $\overrightarrow{GF}$ **3.** $\overleftrightarrow{MN}$

4. Television You are adjusting the volume on the television shown. Are the lines that represent the volume *parallel* or *intersecting*? Explain.

Use estimation to name the angle in the diagram whose measure is closest to the given measure.

5. $55°$ **6.** $10°$ **7.** $115°$

8. $170°$ **9.** $180°$ **10.** $80°$

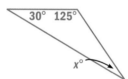

11. Give an example of an acute angle measure and an obtuse angle measure.

12. Find the measure of an angle that is complementary to an angle measuring $25°$.

13. Find the measure of an angle that is supplementary to an angle measuring $80°$.

Find the value of x. Then classify the triangle by its angles.

14.

15.

16.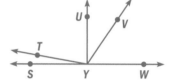

Classify the quadrilateral in as many ways as possible.

17.

18.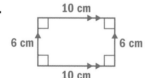

19.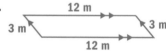

20. The perimeter of a regular hexagon is 48 centimeters. Find the length of each side.

21. $\triangle JKL$ and $\triangle XYZ$ are congruent. List the corresponding parts.

22. Basketball How many lines of symmetry does the basketball court shown at the right have?

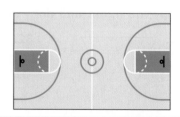

Chapter Standardized Test

Test-Taking Strategy Be careful when choosing an answer. Even though it may seem like the obvious answer, there could be a better choice.

Multiple Choice

1. Which of the following represents a figure that has *M* and *N* as endpoints?

    A. $\overleftrightarrow{MN}$ **B.** $\overrightarrow{MN}$ **C.** $\overrightarrow{NM}$ **D.** $\overline{MN}$

2. Which angle has a measure of 102°?

    F.

    G.

    H.

    I.

3. Which statement is true about the figure?

    A. It has no acute angles.

    B. It has one right angle.

    C. It has more than one obtuse angle.

    D. All statements are true.

4. Which pair of angle measures represent angles that are complementary?

    F. 21°, 59°   **G.** 39°, 61°

    H. 24°, 66°   **I.** 85°, 95°

5. What is the value of *x* in the figure?

    A. 40   **B.** 50

    C. 80   **D.** 90

6. Which angle measures could be those of an acute triangle?

    F. 24°, 63°, 73°   **G.** 30°, 60°, 90°

    H. 36°, 108°, 36°   **I.** 45°, 85°, 50°

7. Which figure is *not* a polygon?

    A.   **B.**

    C.   **D.**

Short Response

8. Use the flag of the Bahamas shown below. How many pairs of congruent figures are in the flag? How many lines of symmetry does the flag have? Explain your answers.

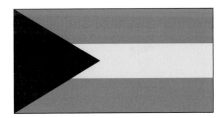

Extended Response

9. Graph the points *A*(2, 4), *B*(4, 4), *C*(4, 8), and *D*(2, 8) and classify the figure they form. Then graph the points *E*(8, 1), *F*(9, 1), *G*(9, 3), and *H*(8, 3) and classify the figure they form. Are the figures *similar*, *congruent*, or *neither*? Explain.

The Geometry of Crystals

Classifying Crystals

Crystals occur when the smallest particles of a mineral are arranged in a structured pattern. This pattern determines the outward appearance of a crystal. The different shaped faces you see result from the pattern. Scientists measure the angles between a crystal's faces to help identify the crystal.

A single mineral may have many different crystal forms. For example, the mineral calcite has over 100 different crystal forms. Three of these forms are shown below.

scalenohedron
(skay-LEE-nuh-HEE-druhn)

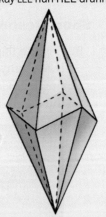

rhombohedron
(RAHM-boh-HEE-druhn)

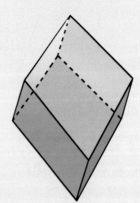

hexagonal prism
(hehk-SAG-uh-nuhl PRIHZ-uhm)

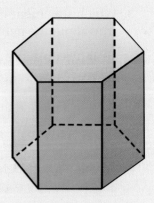

1. The scalenohedron has twelve surfaces, all of which are triangles. Based on the name *scalenohedron*, what kind of triangles do you think the surfaces are?

2. Each surface of the rhombohedron is a rhombus. How many surfaces does the rhombohedron have? Based on what you know about rhombuses, what can you say about the lengths of the edges of the rhombohedron?

3. How many surfaces does the hexagonal prism have? What are the shapes of these surfaces? How many of each type of surface are there?

▶ Measuring Angles in Crystals

Crystals in nature tend to be imperfect and distorted. However, scientists can rely on certain geometric properties of a crystal to help identify it. For a particular type of crystal, the angles between certain faces will always be the same. Scientists often measure these angles as part of the process of identifying a crystal.

4. Note the red and blue faces on the crystal forms on page 470. For each crystal form, tell whether the angle between the colored surfaces appears to be a right angle, an acute angle, or an obtuse angle.

5. Table salt is a crystal. Its crystal form is a cube. What kind of angles are there between the surfaces in a salt crystal?

Project IDEAS

- **Experiment** Scientists use a tool called a goniometer to measure the angles between the faces of a crystal. Find out more about goniometers. Then make your own and use it to measure the angles on an everyday object, such as the roof of a birdhouse.

- **Report** A diamond is one of three crystal forms of carbon. Find out about the other two crystal forms of carbon. Present your findings to the class using a poster or an oral report.

- **Research** Scientists can also use x-ray lasers to directly measure the angles in crystals. Find information about the use of x-ray measurements in identifying crystals.

- **Career** A scientist who studies crystals is called a crystallographer. Find out what kinds of work crystallographers do. What kind of education is required to be a crystallographer? Present your findings to the class.

INTERNET
Project Support
CLASSZONE.COM

Geometry and Measurement

BEFORE

In previous chapters you've...

- Solved measurement problems
- Identified and classified polygons

Now

In Chapter 10 you'll study...

- Area of parallelograms and triangles
- Circumference and area of circles
- Solid figures
- Surface area and volume of rectangular prisms

WHY?

So you can solve real-world problems about...

- geography, p. 477
- hang gliders, p. 483
- basketball, p. 492
- skateboarding, p. 503
- aquariums, p. 511

Internet Preview
CLASSZONE.COM

- eEdition Plus Online
- eWorkbook Plus Online
- eTutorial Plus Online
- State Test Practice
- More Examples

Chapter Warm-Up Game

Review skills you need for this chapter in this game. Work with a partner.

Key Skill:
Identifying and classifying polygons

POLYGON COUNT

HOW TO PLAY

In this game, you'll hunt for polygons in the kite design shown on page 473. In the design, angles that appear to be right angles are right angles. Line segments that appear to be parallel are parallel.

① MAKE a polygon tally sheet like the one shown. Use a separate piece of paper.

② COUNT how many of each type of polygon you find in the kite design. You may count each polygon only once. For example, if you count a polygon as a rectangle, you may not count it as a parallelogram.

③ COMPARE your count with your partner's. Be prepared to justify your thinking.

Polygon Tally Sheet

Triangle	?
Quadrilateral	?
Parallelogram	?
Rectangle	?
Pentagon	?
Hexagon	?

Stop and Think

1. **Writing** Suppose that the words *rectangle* and *parallelogram* were removed from the tally sheet. How would your polygon count change? Explain your thinking.

2. **Critical Thinking** In the game *Polygon Count*, some of the polygons you found in the kite design are part of other, larger polygons. Describe some examples.

Getting Ready to Learn

Review What You Need to Know

Using Vocabulary Copy and complete using a review word.

1. A ? is a quadrilateral with two pairs of parallel sides.

2. A ? is a triangle that has one right angle.

Evaluate the expression when $x = 10$ and $y = 4$. *(p. 29)*

3. x^2 **4.** y^2 **5.** $3x^2$ **6.** $2x^2 - y^2$

Find the area of a rectangle with the given dimensions. *(p. 62)*

7. length = 8 ft, width = 4 ft   **8.** length = 12 in., width = 6 in.

The circle graph at the right shows the ages of the first 42 presidents at the time they took office. *(p. 88)*

9. How many presidents were 61 years old or older?

10. How many presidents were 51 years old or older?

Ages of U.S. Presidents

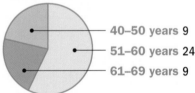

40–50 years 9
51–60 years 24
61–69 years 9

Word Watch

Review Words

area, p. 62
circle graph, p. 88
right triangle, p. 436
parallelogram, p. 445

You should include material that appears on a notebook like this in your own notes.

Know How to Take Notes

Learning to Use Formulas You may want to create a special section in your notebook to write formulas. Be sure to write down the complete formula. Tell what each variable represents, and include an example. You learned the formula for the area of a rectangle in Lesson 2.2.

Area of a Rectangle

A is the area, *l* is the length, and *w* is the width.

$A = lw$
$\quad = 18 \cdot 9$
$\quad = 162$ square yards

9 yd

18 yd

You will write more formulas in your notebook in Chapter 10.

GOAL

Compare the area of a parallelogram and the area of a rectangle.

MATERIALS

• graph paper
• scissors

Investigating Area

In this activity, you will find the area of a parallelogram.

Explore | You can find the area of a parallelogram by finding the area of a rectangle.

1 Draw a parallelogram like the one shown below on graph paper. Cut out the parallelogram.

2 Draw a line to make a right triangle as shown.

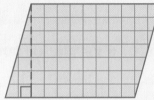

3 Cut out the triangle. Move the triangle to the other side of the parallelogram to form a rectangle.

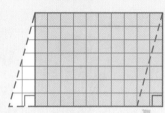

4 You can use the grid squares and the formula $A = lw$ to find the area of the rectangle: $A = 10 \times 7 = 70$. The area of the parallelogram is 70 square units.

Your turn now | Follow the steps above to find the area of the parallelogram.

1.

2.

Stop *and* **Think**

3. Writing Explain how the area of a rectangle compares to the area of a parallelogram with the same length and height.

Area of a Parallelogram

BEFORE	Now	WHY?
You found the area of a rectangle.	You'll find the area of a parallelogram.	So you can estimate the area of Lake Erie, as in Example 3.

Word Watch

base of a parallelogram, p. 476
height of a parallelogram, p. 476
perpendicular, p. 476

Finding Areas The **base of a parallelogram** is the length of any of its sides. The **height of a parallelogram** is the *perpendicular distance* between the side whose length is the base and the opposite side. Two lines are **perpendicular** if they meet at a right angle.

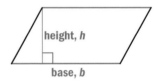

The area of a parallelogram is the product of the base and the height.

Area of a Parallelogram

Words Area = base · height

Algebra $A = bh$

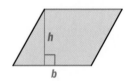

HELP with Notetaking

Include the formula for the area of a parallelogram in your notebook. Include an example like the one shown in Example 1.

EXAMPLE 1 Finding the Area of a Parallelogram

Find the area of the parallelogram shown at the right.

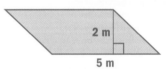

Solution

$A = bh$	Write the formula for the area of a parallelogram.
$= 5 \cdot 2$	Substitute 5 for b and 2 for h.
$= 10$	Simplify.

ANSWER The area of the parallelogram is 10 square meters.

Your turn now Find the area of the parallelogram described.

1. base = 6 in., height = 10 in.   **2.** base = 7 cm, height = 4 cm

EXAMPLE 2 Finding an Unknown Dimension

The area of a parallelogram is 45 square centimeters and the height is 9 centimeters. What is the base?

$A = bh$ Write the formula for the area of a parallelogram.

$45 = b \cdot 9$ Substitute 45 for *A* and 9 for *h*.

$b = 45 \div 9$ Write a related division equation.

$b = 5$ Simplify.

ANSWER The base is 5 centimeters.

What do you think?
Geography

■ Lake Erie

The area of Lake Superior is about 82,100 square kilometers. About how many times as great as the area of Lake Erie is the area of Lake Superior?

EXAMPLE 3 Estimating Area

Geography A parallelogram can be used to approximate the shape of Lake Erie. Use the map and the scale to estimate the area of Lake Erie.

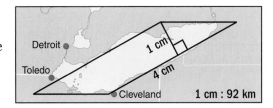

Solution

① Use the scale to find the base, *b*, and the height, *h*, in kilometers.

Base	Height
$\dfrac{1\ \text{cm}}{92\ \text{km}} = \dfrac{4\ \text{cm}}{b\ \text{km}}$	$\dfrac{1\ \text{cm}}{92\ \text{km}} = \dfrac{1\ \text{cm}}{h\ \text{km}}$
$1 \cdot b = 92 \cdot 4$	$1 \cdot h = 92 \cdot 1$
$b = 368$	$h = 92$

② Estimate the area of Lake Erie.

$A = bh$ Write the formula for the area of a parallelogram.

$= 368 \cdot 92$ Substitute 368 for *b* and 92 for *h*.

$= 33{,}856$ Simplify.

ANSWER The area of Lake Erie is about 33,856 square kilometers.

Your turn now Find the unknown length.

3. Area of parallelogram = 72 in.^{2}, base = 12 in., height = _?_

4. Area of parallelogram = 125 mm^2, height = 5 mm, base = _?_

Getting Ready to Practice

1. **Vocabulary** To find the area of a parallelogram, you multiply the ? by the ? .

Find the area of the parallelogram.

2.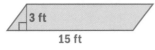
   3 ft
   15 ft

3.
   10 yd
   20 yd

4. **Tennessee** A parallelogram can be used to approximate the shape of Tennessee. Use the scale on the map to estimate the area of Tennessee.

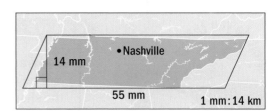
• Nashville
14 mm
55 mm
1 mm : 14 km

Practice and Problem Solving

HELP with **Homework**

Example	Exercises
1	5-9, 12
2	10, 11
3	15

Online Resources
CLASSZONE.COM
· More Examples
· eTutorial Plus

Find the area of the parallelogram.

5.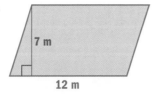
   7 m
   12 m

6.
   10 ft
   7 ft

7.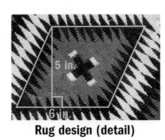
   5 in
   6 in
   Rug design (detail)

8.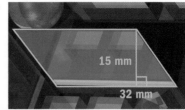
   15 mm
   32 mm
   Digital art (detail)

9. The height of a parallelogram is 9 meters and the base is 7 meters. What is the area of the parallelogram?

10. The area of a parallelogram is 54 square inches and the height is 9 inches. What is the base of the parallelogram?

11. The area of a parallelogram is 120 square yards and the base is 12 yards. What is the height of the parallelogram?

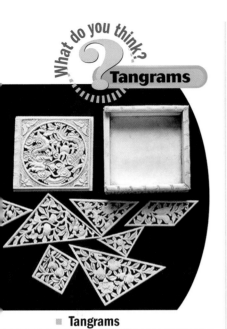
12. Tangrams Tangrams are Chinese puzzle shapes that can be arranged into pictures, like the one shown at the right. Find the area of the parallelogram piece.

13. Draw 2 different parallelograms that each have an area of 12 square centimeters.

14. Quilts The base of one parallelogram in a quilt is 6 inches and the height is 3 inches. About how many of these parallelograms do you need to cover an area of 7500 square inches?

15. Estimation Estimate the area of Puerto Rico. Then tell if your estimate is a *high estimate* or a *low estimate*. Explain your reasoning.

16. Challenge The base of a parallelogram is 3 inches longer than its height. The height is 7 inches. What is the area of the parallelogram?

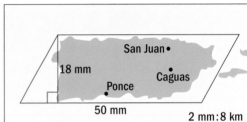

Mixed Review

Solve the equation using mental math. *(Lesson 1.6)*

17. $x + 5 = 12$ **18.** $x - 12 = 30$ **19.** $4x = 32$ **20.** $6x = 72$

21. Sketch 2 different figures that have one line of symmetry. *(Lesson 9.8)*

Basic Skills **Find the product.**

22. $\frac{1}{2} \cdot 4$ **23.** $\frac{1}{2} \cdot 12$ **24.** $\frac{1}{2} \cdot 5 \cdot 6$ **25.** $\frac{1}{2} \cdot 12 \cdot 8$

Test-Taking Practice

26. Multiple Choice The height of a parallelogram is 36 meters and the base is 6 meters. What is the area of the parallelogram?

A. 6 m^2 **B.** 30 m^2 **C.** 42 m^2 **D.** 216 m^2

27. Multiple Choice A parallelogram has an area of 300 square feet and a base of 20 feet. What is the height of the parallelogram?

F. 15 ft **G.** 15 ft^2 **H.** 6000 ft **I.** 6000 ft^2

Area of a Triangle

BEFORE ▶ **Now** **WHY?**

You found the area of a parallelogram.

You'll find the area of a triangle.

So you can find the area of a sail, as in Example 2.

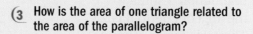
Activity You can use a parallelogram to find the area of a triangle.

(1) Draw the parallelogram shown at the right on graph paper and cut it out. Find its area.

(2) Draw a diagonal like the one shown below. Then cut along the diagonal to form two congruent triangles.

(3) How is the area of one triangle related to the area of the parallelogram?

(4) Use the formula for the area of a parallelogram to write a rule for the area of a triangle.

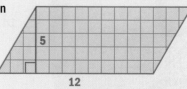

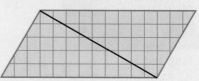

The **base of a triangle** is the length of any of its sides. The **height of a triangle** is the perpendicular distance between the side whose length is the base and the vertex opposite that side.

Area of a Triangle

Words Area of a triangle $= \frac{1}{2} \cdot$ base $\cdot$ height

Algebra $A = \frac{1}{2} bh$

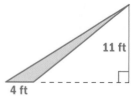

EXAMPLE 1 **Finding the Area of a Triangle**

Find the area of the triangle shown.

$A = \frac{1}{2}bh$ Write the formula for the area of a triangle.

$= \frac{1}{2} \cdot 4 \cdot 11$ Substitute 4 for b and 11 for h.

$= 22$ Simplify.

ANSWER The area of the triangle is 22 square feet.

Your turn now Find the area of the triangle described.

1. base = 12 kilometers, height = 5 kilometers

2. base = 6 inches, height = 4 inches

What do you think?

Recreation

■ **Tall Ships**

The scale on a model of a tall ship is about 2 in. : 12 ft. The length of the model is 46 inches. What is the approximate length of the actual tall ship?

EXAMPLE 2 **Finding the Area of Combined Figures**

Tall Ships A pattern of a sail for a tall ship is shown. How much material, in square feet, is needed to make the sail?

Solution

⟨1 Find the area of each shape.

Area of the triangle:

$$A = \frac{1}{2} \cdot 4 \cdot 3$$

$$= 6$$

Area of the rectangle:

$$A = 4 \cdot 6$$

$$= 24$$

⟨2 Add the areas together to find the total area.

$$6 + 24 = 30$$

ANSWER You will need 30 square feet of material to make the sail.

EXAMPLE 3 **Finding the Height of a Triangle**

The area of a triangle is 36 square inches and the base is 8 inches. What is the height of the triangle?

$$A = \frac{1}{2}bh \qquad \text{Write the formula for the area of a triangle.}$$

$$36 = \frac{1}{2} \cdot 8 \cdot h \qquad \text{Substitute 36 for } A \text{ and 8 for } b.$$

$$36 = 4 \cdot h \qquad \text{Simplify.}$$

$$h = 36 \div 4 \qquad \text{Write a related division equation.}$$

$$h = 9 \qquad \text{Simplify.}$$

ANSWER The height of the triangle is 9 inches.

Your turn now Solve the problems below.

3. Find the area of the figure at the right.

4. The area of a triangle is 45 square feet and the base is 10 feet. Find the height.

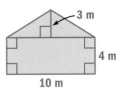

Getting Ready to Practice

Vocabulary Use the triangle at the right.

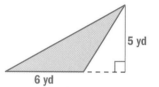

1. The ? of the triangle is 5 yards and the
  ? of the triangle is 6 yards.

2. The ? of the triangle is 15 square yards.

Find the area of the triangle.

3.

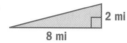

2 mi
8 mi

4.

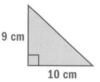

9 cm
10 cm

5.

6 ft
2 ft

6. Pennant A pennant is shown at the right.
How much blue material, in square inches,
was needed to make the pennant?

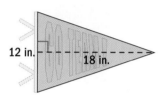

12 in.   18 in.

Practice and Problem Solving

with **Homework**

Example	Exercises
1	7–10
2	11–12
3	13–16

Online Resources
CLASSZONE.COM

· More Examples
· eTutorial Plus

Find the area of the triangle.

7.

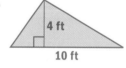

4 ft
10 ft

8.

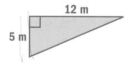

12 m
5 m

9.

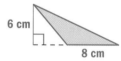

6 cm
8 cm

Find the area of the figure indicated.

10.

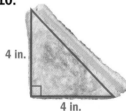

4 in.
4 in.

11.

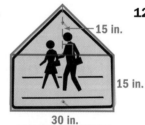

15 in.
15 in.
30 in.

12.

10 cm
23 cm
19 cm

Find the missing dimension of the triangle described.

13. Area: 20 in.²
base: 8 in.

14. Area: 32 ft²
height: 4 ft

15. Area: 30 cm²
height: 6 cm

16. Hang Gliders Some hang glider wings are in the shape of a triangle. The base of a wing is 208 inches and the area of the wing is 16,848 square inches. Find the height of the wing.

Algebra Find the area of the figure when the given lengths, in meters, are $a = 3$, $b = 2$, and $c = 7$.

17.

18.

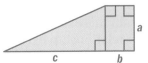

19. Writing Two triangles have the same height. The base of one triangle is twice as long as the other. How do the two areas compare?

20. Critical Thinking A triangle and a rectangle have the same area and the same base. What can you say about their heights?

21. Puerto Rico Use the flag of Puerto Rico at the right. How much of the area of the flag does the triangle cover?

22. Challenge How can you use triangles to find the area of a regular hexagon? Describe your method and include a drawing.

9 in.
14 in.
21 in.

Mixed Review

Tell whether the measure is a *mass*, *capacity*, or *length*. *(Lessons 3.2, 4.7)*

23. 4 kg   **24.** 917 cm   **25.** 14 L   **26.** 14.2 g

27. The area of a parallelogram is 135 square centimeters and the height is 15 centimeters. What is the base? *(Lesson 10.1)*

Basic Skills Find the product.

28. $(5)(4.5)$ **29.** $(3.25)(5)$ **30.** $(7.05)(6)$ **31.** $(3)(8.21)(4)$

Test-Taking Practice

32. Multiple Choice What is the area of the figure shown?

A. 12 in.^{2} **B.** 48 in.^{2}

C. 60 in.^{2} **D.** 72 in.^{2}

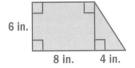

6 in.
8 in.   4 in.

33. Short Response The area of a triangle is 160 square millimeters. The height is 40 millimeters. Explain how to find the base.

Hands-on Activity

GOAL
Investigate the circumference of a circle.

MATERIALS
· metric ruler   · scissors
· compass
· string

Investigating Circumference

In this activity, you will investigate the relationship between the *diameter* of a circle and the *circumference*, the distance around the circle.

circumference   diameter

Explore   **Find the ratio of the circumference of a circle to the diameter of the circle.**

1 Use a compass to draw a circle with a diameter of 8 centimeters. You will need to set the opening of your compass to 4 centimeters.

2 Cut a piece of string so that the length equals the circumference of the circle. Then measure the string to the nearest tenth of a centimeter.

---

3 Find the ratio of the circumference to the diameter by dividing the circumference in Step 2 by the diameter given in Step 1. Round your answer to the nearest hundredth.

$$\frac{\text{Circumference in Step 2}}{\text{Diameter in Step 1}} \approx \frac{25.1}{8} \approx 3.14$$

Your turn now   **Repeat Steps 1–3 above to find the ratio of the circumference to the diameter for a circle with the given diameter.**

1. 2 centimeters   **2.** 2.5 centimeters   **3.** 3 centimeters

Stop and Think

4. Critical Thinking Is it possible for a circle to have a circumference of 20 centimeters and a diameter of 5 centimeters? Explain.

Circumference of a Circle

BEFORE	▶ Now	WHY?
You found the perimeter of a rectangle.	You'll find the circumference of a circle.	So you can estimate a crater's circumference, as in Example 4.

Word Watch

circle, p. 485
center, p. 485
radius, p. 485
diameter, p. 485
circumference, p. 485
pi (π), p. 485

Finding Circumference A **circle** is the set of all points in a plane that are the same distance from a point called the **center** . The **radius** , *r,* is the distance from the center to any point on the circle. The distance across the circle through its center is the **diameter** , *d.*

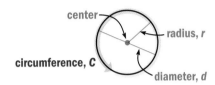

The distance around a circle is called the **circumference** , *C.*

The ratio of any circle's circumference to its diameter is always the same. This ratio is 3.14159 . . . . It is represented by the Greek letter π, or **pi** . You can use 3.14 or $\frac{22}{7}$ to approximate π.

Circumference of a Circle

Words

Circumference = pi • **diameter**

Circumference = 2 • pi • **radius**

Algebra

$C = \pi d$

$C = 2\pi r$

EXAMPLE 1 **Finding the Circumference of a Circle**

Gym Wheel The diameter of a gym wheel is 8 feet. About how far will the wheel go in one rotation? Round your answer to the nearest foot.

Solution

The distance that the gym wheel goes in one rotation is equal to the circumference of the wheel.

$C = \pi d$ Write the formula for the circumference of a circle.

$\approx (3.14)(8)$ Substitute 3.14 for π and 8 for *d.*

$= 25.12$ Simplify.

ANSWER The gym wheel will go about 25 feet in one rotation.

EXAMPLE 2 Using Radius to Find Circumference

Find the circumference of the circle shown.

The diameter of a circle is twice the radius. Use $C = 2\pi r$ to find the circumference when you know the radius of a circle.

$C = 2\pi r$ Write the formula for the circumference of a circle.

$\approx (2)(3.14)(6)$ Substitute 3.14 for π and 6 for *r*.

$= 37.68$ Simplify.

ANSWER The circumference is about 37.68 millimeters.

Your turn now   **Find the circumference of the circle.**

1.

2.

3.

EXAMPLE 3 Choosing an Approximation of Pi

Find the circumference of a circle with a diameter of 14 centimeters.

Because the diameter is a multiple of 7, use $\frac{22}{7}$ for π.

$C = \pi d$ Use the formula for the circumference of a circle.

$\approx \frac{22}{7} \cdot 14$ Substitute $\frac{22}{7}$ for π and 14 for *d*.

$= \frac{22 \cdot \overset{2}{\cancel{14}}}{\underset{1}{\cancel{7}}}$ Multiply. Divide out the common factor.

$= 44$ Simplify.

ANSWER The circumference of the circle is about 44 centimeters.

> **HELP** with **Solving**
>
> When the diameter or the radius of a circle is a multiple of 7, use $\frac{22}{7}$ for pi.

Your turn now   **Find the circumference of the circle described. Tell what value you used for π. Explain your choice.**

4. $d = 10$ ft   **5.** $d = 35$ km   **6.** $r = 42$ cm

EXAMPLE 4 **Applying Circumference**

Geology The Barringer Meteor Crater has a diameter of about 1186 meters. Find the circumference to the nearest meter.

Solution

$C = \pi d$ Write the formula for the circumference of a circle.

$\approx (3.14)(1186)$ Substitute 3.14 for π and 1186 for d.

$= 3724.04$ Simplify.

ANSWER The circumference of the crater is about 3724 meters.

10.3 Exercises

More Practice, p. 717

INTERNET
eWorkbook Plus
CLASSZONE.COM

Getting Ready to Practice

Vocabulary **Copy and complete the statement.**

1. The distance across a circle through its center is the ? .

2. The distance around a circle is the ? .

3. The distance from the center to any point on the circle is the ? .

4. The ratio of the circumference of a circle to its diameter is ? .

Find the circumference of the circle.

5.

7 cm

6.

9 ft

7.

4 in.

8.

8 m

9. **Find the Error** Your friend is finding the circumference of a circle with a radius of 3 millimeters. Describe and correct the error.

$C = \pi d$
$\approx (3.14)(3)$
$= 9.42$ mm

Find the circumference of the circle described. Tell what value you used for π. Explain your choice.

10. $d = 28$ m   11. $d = 12$ yd   12. $r = 2$ in.   13. $r = 21$ km

Practice and Problem Solving

with **Homework**

Example	Exercises
1	14, 21
2	15, 16, 22–24
3	17–20
4	21–24

Online Resources
CLASSZONE.COM

· More Examples
· eTutorial Plus

Find the circumference of the circular object. Round your answer to the nearest whole number.

14.

23 ft

15.

3 in.

16.

4 m

Find the circumference of the circle described. Tell what value you used for π. Explain your choice.

17. $r = 17$ mm   **18.** $d = 70$ yd   **19.** $d = 49$ mi   **20.** $r = 6$ in.

21. Hockey The diameter of a hockey puck is 3 inches. What is the circumference of a hockey puck?

22. Ribbon You want to wrap a ribbon around a circular candle that has a radius of 4.5 centimeters. You have 30 centimeters of ribbon. Do you have enough ribbon to fit around the candle at least one time?

23. Horse Training A horse trainer stands in the center of a circular track. A horse walks around the track. The trainer is 14 feet from the horse at all times. About how many times must the horse walk around the track in order to travel 440 feet?

14 ft

24. Astronomy The radius of the outer edge of the outermost ring of Saturn is about 480,000 kilometers. Find the circumference of the outer edge of the outermost ring to the nearest hundred thousand kilometers.

25. Critical Thinking Which is a better estimate for pi: 3.14 or $\frac{22}{7}$? Explain.

26. Explain The circumference of Earth at the equator is about 24,900 miles. Find the diameter of Earth to the nearest mile. Explain how you found the answer.

27. Challenge Find the perimeter of the figure at the right.

4 ft
3 ft
5 ft
12 ft

What do you think?

Sports

■ **Horse Training**

A *round pen* is a circular pen used for training horses. A round pen with a diameter of 50 feet has a circumference of about 157 feet. Compare this to the perimeter of your classroom.

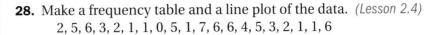

Mixed Review

28. Make a frequency table and a line plot of the data. *(Lesson 2.4)*
2, 5, 6, 3, 2, 1, 1, 0, 5, 1, 7, 6, 6, 4, 5, 3, 2, 1, 1, 6

Choose a Strategy Use a strategy from the list to solve the following problem. Explain your choice of strategy.

29. Suppose you fold a piece of paper in half. Then you fold it in half again in the other direction and draw a figure at the folded corner like the one shown. Describe the shape that will be cut out when you unfold the paper.

> **Problem Solving Strategies**
> ▪ Draw a Diagram
> ▪ Make a List
> ▪ Solve a Simpler Problem
> ▪ Make a Model

Basic Skills Evaluate the expression.

30. $6(4)^2$ **31.** $(2.5)(5)^2$ **32.** $(2.4)(3.1)^2$ **33.** $(4 \cdot 3)^2$

Test-Taking Practice

34. Multiple Choice The diameter of a bicycle tire is 22 inches. About how far will the tire go in one rotation?

    A. 35 in.   **B.** 69 in.   **C.** 139 in.   **D.** 380 in.

35. Multiple Choice What is the approximate circumference of a circle with a radius of 25 centimeters?

    F. 78.5 cm   **G.** 157 cm   **H.** 1962.5 cm   **I.** 3925 cm

BRAIN GAME

Tangrams

Tangrams is a puzzle game that was developed in China. The object of the game is to create a design using all seven tangram pieces, also known as *tans*. The tangram pieces may not overlap.

Trace the tangram pieces shown below and cut them out. Then use them to create the design shown at the right.

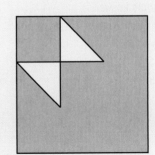

Technology Activity

Circumference of a Circle

GOAL Use a calculator to find the circumference of a circle.

Example **You can find the circumference of a circle using the pi key on a calculator.**

The *Place Charles de Gaulle*, a traffic circle which surrounds the Arc de Triomphe in Paris, has a diameter of about 306 meters. What is the circumference of the *Place Charles de Gaulle*?

Solution

Use the formula $C = \pi d$ to find the circumference of a circle. To enter π on a calculator, you can use the approximation 3.14 or you can use the pi key, $\boxed{\pi}$.

Method 1 Use 3.14 for π.

Keystrokes	Display
3 . 1 4 $\boxed{\times}$ 3 0 6 $\boxed{=}$	960.84

Method 2 Use the $\boxed{\pi}$ key.

Keystrokes	Display
$\boxed{\pi}$ $\boxed{\times}$ 3 0 6 $\boxed{=}$	961.327352

ANSWER The circumference of the *Place Charles de Gaulle* is about 961 meters.

HELP with Technology

Although both methods in the Example give approximately the same answer, using the pi key gives a slightly more accurate answer.

Your turn now **Use a calculator to find the circumference of the circle described. Round your answer to the nearest whole number.**

1. $d = 12$ ft **2.** $d = 86$ in. **3.** $d = 341$ cm **4.** $d = 7.95$ m

5. $r = 15$ km **6.** $r = 550$ in. **7.** $r = 0.8$ m **8.** $r = 30.57$ mi

9. Arctic Circle The Arctic Circle, located at 66.5° N latitude, has a radius of about 2543 kilometers. What is the circumference of the Arctic Circle to the nearest hundred kilometers?

Area of a Circle

BEFORE	▶ Now	WHY?
You found the areas of triangles and parallelograms.	You'll find the area of a circle.	So you can find the area lit by a lighthouse beam, as in Ex. 15.

In the Real World

Button Designs You are making a design for a circular button. Your design fits on a circle with a radius of 3 centimeters. How much area will be covered by your design?

The area of a circle is the amount of surface covered by the circle.

Area of a Circle

Words Area = (pi)(radius)^2

Algebra $A = \pi r^2$

EXAMPLE 1 **Finding the Area of a Circle**

To answer the question above, find the area of a circle with a radius of 3 centimeters. Round to the nearest square centimeter.

$A = \pi r^2$ Write the formula for the area of a circle.

$\approx (3.14)(3)^2$ Substitute 3.14 for π and 3 for r.

$= 28.26$ Simplify.

ANSWER The area covered by your design is about 28 square centimeters.

Your turn now **Find the area of the circle.**

1.

2 in.

2.

4 ft

3.

20 cm

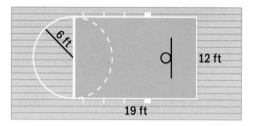

EXAMPLE 2 Finding the Area of Combined Figures

Basketball Find the area of the free throw area to the nearest square foot.

Solution

① Find the area of each shape.

Rectangle	**Half-circle**
$A = lw$	$A = \frac{1}{2}\pi r^2$
$= 19 \cdot 12$	$\approx \frac{1}{2}(3.14)(6)^2$
$= 228$	$= 56.52$

② Add the areas to find the total area: $228 + 56.52 = 284.52$.

ANSWER The area of the free throw area is about 285 square feet.

EXAMPLE 3 Comparing Areas

Pizza How many times as great as the area of an 8 inch pizza is the area of a 16 inch pizza?

Solution

① Find the area of each pizza.

8 inch pizza

$$A = \pi r^2$$
$$\approx (3.14)(4)^2$$
$$= 50.24 \text{ in.}^2$$

16 inch pizza

$$A = \pi r^2$$
$$\approx (3.14)(8)^2$$
$$= 200.96 \text{ in.}^2$$

② Divide the area of the 16 inch pizza by the area of the 8 inch pizza.

$$\frac{200.96}{50.24} = 4$$

ANSWER The area of a 16 inch pizza is 4 times the area of an 8 inch pizza.

Watch Out!

Be sure to read diagrams carefully. The diagrams in Example 3 give the diameters of the pizzas. To find the area of each pizza, you must first find its *radius*.

Your turn now Find the area of the figure to the nearest whole unit.

4.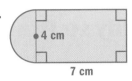
4 cm
7 cm

5.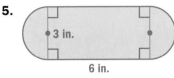
3 in.
6 in.

Making Circle Graphs A circle graph is made of *sectors* that represent portions of a data set. Each sector is formed by an angle whose vertex is the center of the circle. In a circle graph, the sum of the measures of all these angles is 360°.

EXAMPLE 4 Making a Circle Graph

Ski Trails The table shows what fraction of the trails at a ski resort are beginner, intermediate, and expert. Make a circle graph to represent the data.

Types of Ski Trails			
Trail Type	Beginner	Intermediate	Expert
Fraction of Trails	$\frac{3}{10}$	$\frac{1}{2}$	$\frac{1}{5}$

HELP with **Review**

Need help with reading and interpreting circle graphs? See p. 88.

Solution

① Find the angle measure of each sector. Each sector's angle measure is a fraction of 360°. Multiply each fraction in the table by 360° to get the angle measure for each sector.

Beginner	Intermediate	Expert
$\frac{3}{10}(360°) = 108°$	$\frac{1}{2}(360°) = 180°$	$\frac{1}{5}(360°) = 72°$

② Draw the circle graph.

Use a compass to draw a circle.

Use a protractor to draw the angle for each sector.

Label each sector and give your graph a title.

180° 108°
72°

Type of Trail
Beginner
Intermediate
Expert

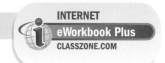
Getting Ready to Practice

1. Vocabulary You can use the expression πr^2 to find the __?__ of a circle.

Find the area of the circle described to the nearest tenth of a unit.

2. $r = 3$ mm   **3.** $r = 2$ km   **4.** $d = 17$ ft   **5.** $d = 24$ yd

6. School Orchestra Make a circle graph to represent the data in the table.

Students in the School Orchestra			
Grade	6th	7th	8th
Students	$\frac{7}{20}$	$\frac{2}{5}$	$\frac{1}{4}$

Practice and Problem Solving

HELP with Homework

Example	Exercises
1	7–11, 15–16
2	12–14
3	17
4	18–21

Online Resources
CLASSZONE.COM

· More Examples
· eTutorial Plus

In Exercises 7–11, find the area of the circle to the nearest whole unit.

7.

12 ft

8.

30 mi

9.

18 m

10. Find the area of a circle with a radius of 5 feet.

11. Find the area of a circle with a radius of 2.1 centimeters.

Find the area of the figure to the nearest tenth of a unit.

12.
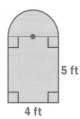
5 ft
4 ft

13.
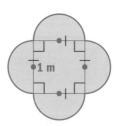
1 m

14.
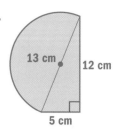
13 cm   12 cm
5 cm

15. Lighthouses A lighthouse beam makes a circle that reaches 18 miles from the lighthouse. Find the area that is lit by the lighthouse beam to the nearest square mile.

lighthouse
18 mi

16. Lawn Sprinklers A circular flower garden has an area of about 314 square feet. A sprinkler at the center of the garden covers an area that has a radius of 12 feet. Will the sprinkler water the entire garden?

17. Eyes In a dark room, the iris of your eye opens until the pupil is about 8 millimeters in diameter. In a lighted room, the pupil has a diameter of about 2 millimeters. How many times as great as the area of the pupil in the lighted room is the area of the pupil in the dark room?

In Exercises 18–21, use the table of information about animals at an animal shelter.

18. What is the total number of animals available for adoption?

19. Find the fraction of all the animals that are in each category.

20. Find the angle measures for the sectors of a circle graph.

21. Make a circle graph of the data.

Animals Available for Adoption	
Type of animal	**Number available**
Dog	10
Cat	15
Rabbit	7
Other	8

22. Weather Weather radar information is displayed on a screen with a scale of 1 in. : 2 mi. The circle on the screen has a radius of 4 inches. About how many square miles does the radar cover?

23. Challenge Use the expression πr^2 to write an expression for the area of a circle when the radius is doubled.

Mixed Review

Classify the polygon with the given number of sides. *(Lesson 9.6)*

24. 3   **25.** 4   **26.** 5   **27.** 6

Find the circumference of the circle described. *(Lesson 10.3)*

28. $d = 7$ yd   **29.** $d = 8$ in.   **30.** $r = 3$ m   **31.** $r = 6$ ft

Basic Skills **Find the mean, median, mode(s), and range.**

32. 11, 15, 22, 10, 6, 14, 12, 14   **33.** 120, 85, 61, 101, 88

Test-Taking Practice

34. Extended Response You are painting a wall that has a circular window. You have enough paint to cover 70 square feet of wall. Do you need to buy more paint? Explain how you got your answer.

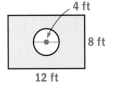

Constructions

GOAL Construct geometric figures.

📓 **Word Watch**

arc, p. 496
perpendicular
  bisector, p. 497
bisector of an angle, p. 497

Copying Figures You can use a compass and a straightedge to construct geometric figures. Use a compass to draw **arcs**, which are parts of circles. Use a straightedge to draw lines, rays, and segments.

EXAMPLE 1 **Copying a Segment**

Use a compass and a straightedge to copy a segment.

① Draw any $\overline{AB}$. Then draw a ray with endpoint C.

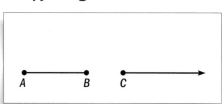

② Draw an arc with center A that passes through B. Using the same compass setting, draw an arc with center C as shown. Label D. $\overline{CD}$ and $\overline{AB}$ have the same length.

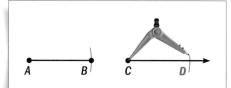

EXAMPLE 2 **Copying an Angle**

Use a compass and a straightedge to copy an angle.

① Draw any $\angle A$. Then draw a ray with endpoint D. Draw an arc with center A that intersects the sides of $\angle A$. Label B and C. Using the same compass setting, draw an arc with center D. Label E.

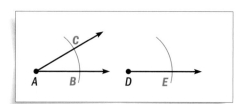

② Draw an arc with center B that passes through C. Using the same compass setting, draw an arc with center E. Label F. Draw a ray from D through F as shown. $\angle D$ and $\angle A$ have the same measure.

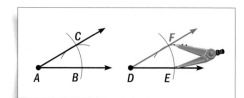

Bisecting Figures The **perpendicular bisector** of a segment is the line that divides the segment into two segments of equal length and forms four right angles. The **bisector of an angle** is the ray that divides the angle into two angles with the same measure.

EXAMPLE 3   Constructing a Perpendicular Bisector

Construct the perpendicular bisector of a segment.

① Draw any $\overline{AB}$. Using any compass setting greater than half the length of $\overline{AB}$, draw an arc with center A.

② Using the same compass setting, draw an arc with center B that intersects the first arc. Label the intersections C and D.

③ Draw $\overleftrightarrow{CD}$, the perpendicular bisector of $\overline{AB}$.

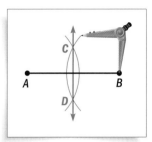

EXAMPLE 4   Constructing an Angle Bisector

Construct the bisector of an angle.

① Draw any $\angle A$. Using any compass setting, draw an arc with center A that intersects the sides of $\angle A$ as shown. Label B and C.

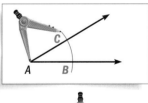

② Using any compass setting, draw an arc with center B. Using the same compass setting, draw an arc with center C that intersects the first arc as shown. Label the intersection D.

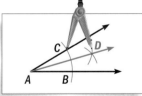

③ Draw $\overrightarrow{AD}$, the bisector of $\angle A$.

Exercises

In Exercises 1 and 2, use a compass and straightedge.

1. Draw any segment and copy it. Then construct the perpendicular bisector of the segment you constructed.

2. Draw any angle and copy it. Then construct the bisector of the angle you constructed.

Notebook Review

LESSONS 10.1 TO 10.4

Review the vocabulary definitions in your notebook.

Copy the review examples in your notebook. Then complete the exercises.

Check Your Definitions

area, p. 62

base and height of a parallelogram, p. 476

perpendicular, p. 476

base and height of a triangle, p. 480

circle, p. 485

center, p. 485

radius, p. 485

diameter, p. 485

circumference, p. 485

pi (π), p. 485

Use Your Vocabulary

1. Copy and complete: The distance from the center to any point on the circle is called the _?_.

10.1–10.2 Can you find the area of a parallelogram or triangle?

 EXAMPLE

a. Find the area of the parallelogram.

$A = bh$

$= 15 \cdot 5$

$= 75$

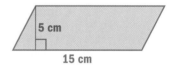

5 cm

15 cm

ANSWER The area of the parallelogram is 75 square centimeters.

b. Find the area of the triangle.

$A = \frac{1}{2}bh$

$= \frac{1}{2} \cdot 22 \cdot 7$

$= 77$

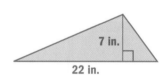

7 in.

22 in.

ANSWER The area of the triangle is 77 square inches.

✓ **Find the area of the parallelogram or the triangle.**

2.
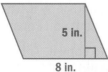

5 in.

8 in.

3.

5 m

4 m

4.
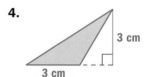

3 cm

3 cm

10.3–10.4 Can you find circumference and area of a circle?

 EXAMPLE Find the circumference and the area of the circle shown at the right.

$$C = \pi d \qquad\qquad A = \pi r^2$$
$$\approx (3.14)(10) \qquad \approx (3.14)(5)^2$$
$$= 31.4 \qquad\qquad = 78.5$$

ANSWER The circumference of the circle is about 31.4 yards. The area of the circle is about 78.5 square yards.

☑ **Find the circumference and area of the circle to the nearest whole unit.**

5. $d = 100$ cm **6.** $d = 42$ mm **7.** $r = 47$ m

Stop *and* **Think** about Lessons 10.1–10.4

8. Writing Compare the formula for the area of a parallelogram to the formula for the area of a triangle. How are they alike? different?

9. Critical Thinking Sketch two different triangles that have an area of 24 square centimeters.

Review Quiz 1

Find the area of the figure to the nearest whole unit.

1.

6 in.
3 in.

2.

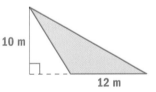
10 m
12 m

3.

7 yd

4. A parallelogram has an area of 32 square feet and a height of 4 feet. What is the base?

5. A triangle has a height of 6 meters and an area of 12 square meters. What is the base?

6. Find the circumference of a circle with a diameter of 22 feet.

7. Communication Cellular telephones send messages within a circular area called a *cell*. Suppose a cell has a radius of about 8 miles. Find the area of the cell to the nearest square mile.

Solid Figures

10.5

BEFORE	▶ Now	WHY?
You classified polygons by their sides.	You'll classify solids.	So you can name the shape of a skateboard jump, as in Ex. 18.

Word Watch

solid, p. 500
prism, p. 500
cylinder, p. 500
pyramid, p. 500
cone, p. 500
sphere, p. 500
face, p. 501
edge, p. 501
vertex, p. 501

In the Real World

Candles A **solid** is a three-dimensional figure that encloses a part of space. The candle at the right is an example of a solid. Some solids can be classified by the number and shape of their *bases*. The candle is a *triangular pyramid*.

Classifying Solids

Rectangular prism   **Triangular prism**

A **prism** is a solid with two parallel bases that are congruent polygons.

A **cylinder** is a solid with two parallel bases that are congruent circles.

A **pyramid** is a solid made up of polygons. The base can be any polygon, and the other polygons are triangles that share a common vertex.

A **cone** is a solid that has one circular base and a vertex that is not in the same plane.

A **sphere** is the set of all points that are the same distance from a point called the center.

EXAMPLE 1 **Classifying Solids**

Classify the solid.

a.

cone

b.

triangular prism

c.

cylinder

Faces, Edges, and Vertices Some solids are formed by polygons called **faces** . The segments where the faces meet are **edges** . Each point where the edges meet is called a **vertex** . The plural of vertex is *vertices*.

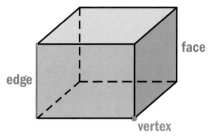

face

edge

vertex

EXAMPLE 2 **Counting Faces, Edges, and Vertices**

Count the number of faces, edges, and vertices of the square pyramid shown.

ANSWER There are 4 triangular faces and 1 square base for a total of 5 faces. There are 8 edges. There are 5 vertices.

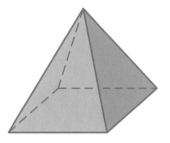

with Review

Need help with congruent figures? See p. 454.

EXAMPLE 3 **Drawing a Solid**

(1 To draw a triangular prism, first draw the congruent bases.

(2 Then connect the corresponding vertices.

(3 Partially erase hidden lines to create dashed lines.

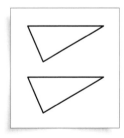

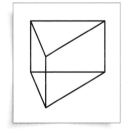

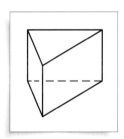

Your turn now **Classify the solid. Then count the number of faces, edges, and vertices.**

1.

2.

3.

4. A cube is a rectangular prism with square faces. Draw a cube.

Getting Ready to Practice

1. **Vocabulary** Prisms and _?_ have two bases. Pyramids and _?_ have only one base.

Classify the solid.

2.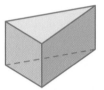

3.

4.

5. Count the number of faces, edges, and vertices of the solid in Exercise 4.

6. **Guided Problem Solving** Follow the steps below to make a sketch of a party hat.

   (1) Draw an oval on your paper to represent a circle. Draw a point outside the oval. The point should be directly above the center of the oval.

   (2) Draw segments from the right side and the left side of the oval to the point you drew. The segments will look like two sides of a triangle.

   (3) Classify the solid you drew.

Practice and Problem Solving

with Homework

Example	Exercises
1	7–12, 15–17
2	10–12, 18
3	13–14

Online Resources
CLASSZONE.COM
· More Examples
· eTutorial Plus

Tell whether the solid has a base. Then classify the solid.

7.

8.

9.

Classify the solid. Then count the number of faces, edges, and vertices.

10.

11.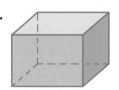

12.

Draw the solid described.

13. pyramid with a square base   **14.** cylinder

Tell whether the statement is *true* or *false*. If it is false, rewrite the statement to make it true.

15. A cone has two circles as bases.

16. A cylinder can have two triangles as bases.

17. A triangular prism has two congruent bases.

18. **Skateboarding** A skateboard jump is shown at the right. What type of solid does it resemble? How many faces, edges, and vertices does this solid have?

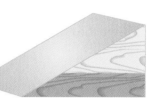

Copy and complete the statement using *faces*, *edges*, or *vertices*.

19. A square pyramid has 8 _?_.   **20.** A hexagonal pyramid has 12 _?_.

21. A hexagonal prism has 8 _?_.   **22.** An octagonal prism has 24 _?_.

23. **Challenge** Explain how to find the number of edges of any pyramid whose base is a polygon with *n* sides.

Mixed Review

Estimate the difference. *(Lesson 1.2)*

24. $502 - 209$ **25.** $482 - 396$ **26.** $256 - 89$

Copy and complete the statement. *(Lesson 4.8)*

27. $5 \text{ cm} = \underline{?} \text{ mm}$ **28.** $10 \text{ kg} = \underline{?} \text{ g}$ **29.** $35 \text{ m} = \underline{?} \text{ km}$

30. Find the area of a circle with a diameter of 10 centimeters. *(Lesson 10.4)*

Basic Skills **Evaluate using the order of operations.**

31. $2(4) + 2(5) + 2(6)$ **32.** $2(4 \times 3) + 2(4 \times 2)$ **33.** $4(6) + 3(4 + 5)$

Test-Taking Practice

34. **Multiple Choice** Which statement about a rectangular prism is false?

    A. It has 8 vertices.   **B.** Its faces are polygons.

    C. Its faces are rectangles.   **D.** It has 8 edges.

35. **Short Response** What is the minimum number of edges that a pyramid can have? that a prism can have? Explain your reasoning.

Problem Solving Strategies

Perform an Experiment

Make a List

Work Backward

Solve a Simpler Problem

Break into Parts

Make a Model

Look for a Pattern

Break into Parts

Problem You want to cover a bookend with fabric. The bookend is a triangular prism with the given dimensions. Find the total area you will be covering.

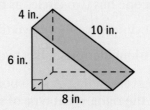

4 in.
10 in.
6 in.
8 in.

❶ Read and Understand

Read the problem twice.

You need to find the total area of all the faces of the prism.

❷ Make a Plan

Decide on a strategy to use.

One way to solve the problem is to break it into parts and find the area of each face.

❸ Solve the Problem

Reread the problem and break it into parts.

First, sketch the 5 faces of the prism: 3 rectangles and 2 triangles. Then find the area of each face.

 4 in.
6 in.

 4 in.
8 in.

 4 in.
10 in.

$A = 6 \cdot 4 = 24$ $A = 8 \cdot 4 = 32$ $A = 10 \cdot 4 = 40$

 6 in.
8 in.

 6 in.
8 in.

$A = \frac{1}{2}(8)(6) = 24$ $A = \frac{1}{2}(8)(6) = 24$

Add to find the total area: $24 + 32 + 40 + 24 + 24 = 144$

ANSWER The total area you will cover is 144 square inches.

❹ Look Back

Check to be sure that your answer has the correct units.

Use the strategy _break into parts._

1. **Neighborhood Party** Use the table below to find the total cost for 100 people to attend a 3 hour neighborhood party.

Neighborhood Party Costs	
Tent rental	$250 for 3 hours
Band	$150 per hour
Dinner	$20 per person

2. **Museum Prices** Use the table below to find the total cost for a group of 2 adults, 2 students, 1 senior citizen, and 1 pre-schooler to attend the museum.

Museum Admission Prices	
Seniors	$7
Adults	$10
Students	$5
Children under 6	$2

3. **Ramps** You want to carpet all sides of the ramp shown except the bottom. The ramp is a triangular prism. How many square feet of carpet do you need?

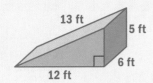

4. **Borders** You want to put metal borders on a piece of stained glass in the shape of the figure shown. How much metal will you need?

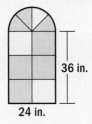

Mixed Problem Solving

Use any strategy to solve the problem.

5. **Spinners** You spin the spinner below two times and add the numbers you get. How many different sums are possible?

6. **Money** You spent $25.25 at the bookstore, $19.99 at the home electronics store, $15.75 at a restaurant, and you have $19.01 left. How much money did you start with?

7. **Find the Pattern** Describe the pattern. Then sketch the next two pictures in the pattern.

8. **Tickets** You go to a concert where the 200 tickets are numbered from 1 to 200. A prize will be given for every ticket whose number includes the digit 7. How many prizes will be given?

9. **Paper Folding** What is the minimum number of folds you have to make to create nine congruent rectangles from a rectangular piece of paper?

Surface Area of a Prism

BEFORE	▶ Now	WHY?
You found areas of polygons.	You'll find the surface area of a prism.	So you know how much paper you need for a piñata, as in Ex. 14.

Word Watch

surface area, p. 506

Activity You can break a prism into parts to find the total area.

① Mentally unfold a box into a *net,* a flat view of the faces of the box.

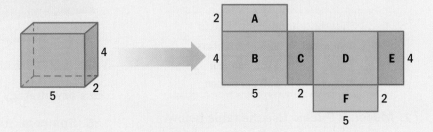

② Find the area of each rectangular face of the net. Record your results in a table like the one shown.

Face	A	B	C	D	E	F
Area	?	?	?	?	?	?

③ Add the areas of the six faces to find the total area.

In the activity, you found the *surface area* of a rectangular prism. The **surface area**, S, of a prism is the sum of the areas of its faces.

EXAMPLE 1 **Finding the Surface Area of a Prism**

Find the surface area of the rectangular prism.

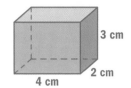

① Find the area of each face.

Area of the top or bottom face: $4 \times 2 = 8$
Area of the front or back face: $4 \times 3 = 12$
Area of the left or right face: $3 \times 2 = 6$

② Add the areas of all six faces to find the surface area.

$$S = 8 + 8 + 12 + 12 + 6 + 6$$

$$= 52$$

ANSWER The surface area is 52 square centimeters.

EXAMPLE 2 **Drawing a Diagram**

Find the surface area of a rectangular prism that is 8 inches by 2 inches by 5 inches.

(1 Draw a diagram of the prism and label the dimensions.

(2 Find the area of each face. Then add these areas to find the surface area.

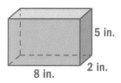

5 in.

2 in.

8 in.

$$S = (8 \times 2) + (8 \times 2) + (8 \times 5) + (8 \times 5) + (5 \times 2) + (5 \times 2)$$

$$= 16 + 16 + 40 + 40 + 10 + 10$$

$$= 132$$

ANSWER The prism has a surface area of 132 square inches.

EXAMPLE 3 **Using Surface Area**

Painting You want to paint a jewelry box that is 12 inches by 7 inches by 3 inches. The label on the bottle of paint says the paint covers a total area of 300 in.^{2} Do you have enough paint to cover the entire box?

Solution

Find the surface area of the box and compare it to the area the paint will cover.

$$S = 84 + 84 + 36 + 36 + 21 + 21$$

$$= 282$$

ANSWER The surface area of the box is 282 in.^{2} Your bottle of paint covers 300 in.^{2} You do have enough paint to cover the entire box.

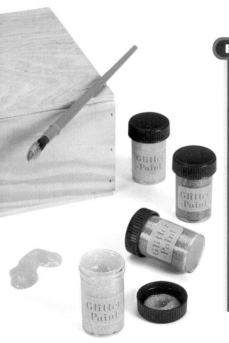

Your turn now In Exercises 2 and 3, you may want to draw a diagram.

1. Find the surface area of the rectangular prism shown at the right.

2. A rectangular prism is 3 feet by 4 feet by 6 feet. Find its surface area.

3 mm

5 mm

12 mm

3. You have 60 square stickers. Each sticker has an area of 1 square inch. Do you have enough stickers to cover a rectangular box that is 2 inches by 4 inches by 6 inches?

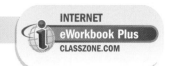

Getting Ready to Practice

1. **Vocabulary** The ? of a prism is the sum of the areas of its faces.

Find the surface area of the rectangular prism.

2.
3 m
12 m
4 m

3.
5 ft
6 ft
4 ft

4.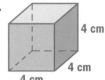
4 cm
4 cm
4 cm

5. **Guided Problem Solving** You make a rectangular cake that is 9 inches wide, 13 inches long, and 2 inches high. You remove it from the pan to frost it. How many square inches of frosting do you need?

(1) Find the area of each of the faces.

(2) Tell which face(s) do not need to be frosted.

(3) Find the surface area of the part of the cake that needs to be frosted.

Practice and Problem Solving

Find the surface area of the rectangular prism.

6.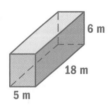
6 m
18 m
5 m

7.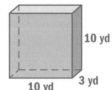
10 yd
10 yd
3 yd

8.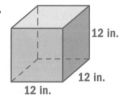
12 in.
12 in.
12 in.

9. **Find the Error** A student finds the surface area of a rectangular prism that is 5 units by 8 units by 6 units. Describe and correct the error.

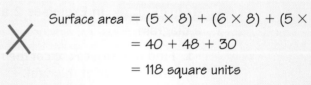

X   Surface area = $(5 \times 8) + (6 \times 8) + (5 \times 6)$

= $40 + 48 + 30$

= 118 square units

Draw a diagram of the rectangular prism described. Then find the surface area.

10. 3 in. by 12 in. by 5 in.

11. 2 m by 6 m by 7 m

12. 10 cm by 6 cm by 12 cm

13. 4 ft by 12 ft by 10 ft

14. Piñata You are making a piñata that is in the shape of a rectangular prism. The prism is 2 feet by 2 feet by 3 feet. You have enough tissue paper to cover 35 square feet of the piñata. Do you have enough tissue paper to cover the entire piñata?

15. Writing Explain how the surface area changes when all of the dimensions of a rectangular prism are doubled.

Each solid is made up of two rectangular prisms. Find the surface area of the solid.

16.

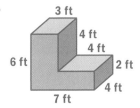

17.

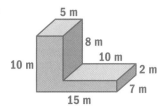

18. Challenge You need to cover the outside of a 1 foot by 1 foot by 1 foot box with paper. The paper comes in 8 inch by 11 inch sheets. How many sheets of paper will you need to cover the box? Explain.

Mixed Review

19. Find the least common multiple of 4 and 6. *(Lesson 5.4)*

Classify the solid. *(Lesson 10.5)*

20.

21.

22.

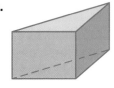

Basic Skills **Solve the equation using mental math.**

23. $15x = 45$ **24.** $60x = 180$ **25.** $25x = 250$ **26.** $120x = 600$

Test-Taking Practice

27. Multiple Choice What is the surface area of a rectangular prism that is 4 feet by 6 feet by 8 feet?

 A. 384 ft^2 **B.** 208 ft^2 **C.** 192 ft^2 **D.** 104 ft^2

28. Short Response A can of paint covers 300 square inches. You want to paint a rectangular box that is 20 inches by 10 inches by 8 inches. How many cans of paint should you buy? Explain your answer.

Volume of a Prism

LESSON 10.7

BEFORE	▶ Now	WHY?
You found the surface area of a rectangular prism.	You'll find the volume of a rectangular prism.	So you can find the length of a pool at an aquarium, as in Example 3.

In the Real World

Word Watch

volume, p. 510

Block Puzzles A manufacturer puts puzzles into cube-shaped boxes. Groups of the boxes are stacked, as shown in Example 1, and then put into a rectangular carton for shipping. How many puzzle boxes will fit in one carton?

EXAMPLE 1 **Counting Cubes in a Stack**

To find the total number of puzzle boxes that will fit in one carton, multiply the number of boxes in one layer by the number of layers. The boxes are stacked in 2 layers. Each layer is a rectangle that is 4 boxes long and 3 boxes wide.

> **Boxes in one layer × Number of layers = Number of boxes**
>
> $$3 \times 4 \times 2 = 24$$

ANSWER The manufacturer can fit 24 puzzle boxes in one carton.

The **volume** of a solid, such as the box in Example 1, is the amount of space the solid occupies. Volume is measured in cubic units. One way to find the volume of a rectangular prism is to use the formula below.

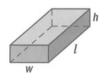

Volume of a Rectangular Prism

Words Volume = length · width · height

Algebra $V = lwh$

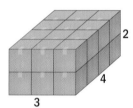

EXAMPLE 2 Finding the Volume of a Prism

Find the volume of the rectangular prism.

$V = lwh$ Write the volume formula.

$\quad = 8 \cdot 6 \cdot 4$ Substitute for *l*, *w*, and *h*.

$\quad = 192$ Simplify.

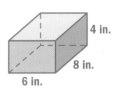

ANSWER The volume is 192 cubic inches.

Your turn now   Find the volume of the rectangular prism.

1.

2.
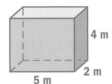

3.
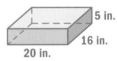

EXAMPLE 3 Using the Formula for Volume

Aquariums A pool at an aquarium is a rectangular prism that is 30 meters wide and 12 meters deep. The volume of the pool is 21,600 cubic meters. How long is the pool?

Solution

$V = lwh$ Write the volume formula.

$21,600 = l \cdot 30 \cdot 12$ Substitute for *V*, *w*, and *h*.

$21,600 = l \cdot 360$ Simplify.

$l = 21,600 \div 360$ Write a related division equation.

$l = 60$ Simplify.

ANSWER The length of the pool is 60 meters.

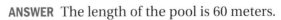

Sea Lion at Magic Mountain

Your turn now   In Exercises 4 and 5, the solids are rectangular prisms.

4. The volume of a swimming pool is 3750 cubic meters. The pool is 25 meters wide and 3 meters deep. How long is the pool?

5. The volume of a bathtub is 16 cubic feet. The bathtub is 4 feet long and 2 feet wide. How deep is the bathtub?

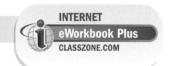

Getting Ready to Practice

1. **Vocabulary** To find the _?_ of a rectangular prism, you find the product of the length, the width, and the height.

Find the volume of the rectangular prism.

2.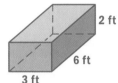
3.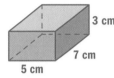

4.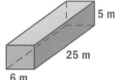

5. **Guided Problem Solving** Use the pasta box shown to find the volume of the part of the pasta box that is not filled with pasta.

   (1 Find the volume of the pasta box shown.

   (2 Find the volume of the pasta in the pasta box.

   (3 Subtract the volume of the pasta from the volume of the pasta box.

Practice and Problem Solving

HELP with Homework

Example	Exercises
1	6–10
2	6–10
3	11–13

Online Resources
CLASSZONE.COM

· More Examples
· eTutorial Plus

Find the volume of the rectangular prism.

6.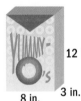
7.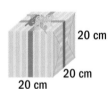
8.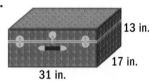

9. Find the volume of a rectangular prism that is 12 feet by 5 feet by 7 feet.

10. **Planters** A planter in the shape of a rectangular prism is 24 inches by 4 inches by 5 inches. How much dirt is needed to fill the planter?

Find the missing dimension of the rectangular prism described.

11. Volume: 60 ft³
    length: 10 ft
    width: 2 ft

12. Volume: 96 cm³
    length: 16 cm
    height: 3 cm

13. Volume: 2500 m³
    width: 25 m
    height: 5 m

■ **Landing Pits**

Some landing pits have a trampoline bed placed about halfway down the pit in order to reduce the number of foam cubes needed.
Use the information for Exercise 15 to estimate how many foam cubes are needed if a trampoline bed is placed so that the depth of the landing pit is 4 feet.

Extended Problem Solving **In Exercises 14–16, use this information.**
A gymnastics center wants to buy foam cubes for a landing pit. The landing pit is a rectangular prism that is 120 inches long by 96 inches wide. The volume is 829,440 cubic inches.

14. Find the depth of the landing pit.

15. Estimate Each foam cube has a side length of 6 inches. About how many foam cubes will fit in the landing pit?

16. A company recommends buying only enough cubes to fill 70% of the landing pit. About how many cubes should the center order?

17. Critical Thinking You find the volume of a rectangular prism using the formula $V = lwh$. Your friend finds the volume of the same prism by multiplying the area of the base by the height. Are the methods the same or are they different? Explain.

18. Writing Explain why the formula $V = s^3$ can be used to find the volume of a cube with a side length of s.

19. Challenge Find all the different whole number lengths, widths, and heights a rectangular prism can have if its volume is 375 cubic centimeters.

Mixed Review

20. Your time in a road race is 40 minutes and 32 seconds. Your friend finishes 3 minutes and 43 seconds later. What is your friend's time? *(Lesson 6.6)*

21. Find the surface area of a rectangular prism that is 22 centimeters by 4 centimeters by 15 centimeters. *(Lesson 10.6)*

Basic Skills **Copy and complete the statement with <, >, or =.**

22. $\frac{7}{10}$ _?_ $\frac{3}{10}$ **23.** $\frac{1}{8}$ _?_ $\frac{7}{8}$ **24.** $\frac{5}{12}$ _?_ $\frac{4}{9}$ **25.** $\frac{2}{3}$ _?_ $\frac{10}{15}$

Test-Taking Practice

26. Multiple Choice What is the volume of a rectangular prism that is 18 meters by 15 meters by 12 meters?

A. 45 m^3 **B.** 90 m^3 **C.** 1332 m^3 **D.** 3240 m^3

27. Multiple Choice The volume of a fish tank is 864 cubic inches. The fish tank is a rectangular prism. The length of the fish tank is 12 inches and the height is 9 inches. What is the width of the fish tank?

F. 4 inches   **G.** 8 inches   **H.** 648 inches   **I.** 843 inches

Mass, Weight, and Capacity

GOAL Determine mass, weight, and capacity by reading scales.

Metric Measuring Metric units of mass include grams (g), milligrams (mg), and kilograms (kg). Metric units of capacity include liters (L), milliliters (mL), and kiloliters (kL).

EXAMPLE 1 Measuring Mass in Metric Units

Use the spring balance to find the mass of the meteorite.

Recall that 1 kg equals 1000 g. Each 1000 g on the scale is divided into 10 equal parts,

so each mark represents $\frac{1000}{10}$, or 100 g.

The pointer on the scale is at the sixth mark.

$$\text{Mass} = 6(100)$$
$$= 600$$

ANSWER The mass of the meteorite is 600 g.

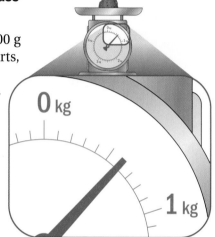

EXAMPLE 2 Measuring Capacity in Metric Units

Find the amount of liquid in the measuring cup.

Each 100 mL on the measuring cup is divided into 4 intervals, so each interval represents $\frac{100}{4}$, or 25 mL. The liquid is 3 intervals past 200 mL.

$$\text{Capacity} = 200 + 3(25)$$
$$= 275$$

ANSWER There are 275 mL of liquid in the measuring cup.

Customary Measuring Customary units of weight include ounces (oz), pounds (lb), and tons (T). Customary units of capacity include fluid ounces (fl oz), cups (c), pints (pt), quarts (qt), and gallons (gal).

EXAMPLE 3 **Measuring Weight in Customary Units**

Use the spring balance to find the weight of the watermelon.

Each pound on the scale is divided into 16 equal parts, so each mark represents $\frac{1}{16}$ lb. The pointer on the scale is 8 marks past 7 lb.

ANSWER The weight of the watermelon is $7\frac{8}{16}$ lb, or $7\frac{1}{2}$ lb.

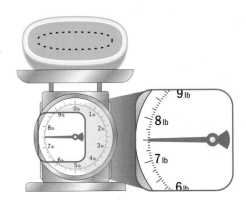

EXAMPLE 4 **Measuring Customary Capacity**

Find the amount of liquid in the measuring cup.

Each cup on the measuring cup is divided into 4 intervals, so each interval represents $\frac{1}{4}$ c. The liquid is 2 intervals past 1 c.

ANSWER The amount of liquid is $1\frac{2}{4}$ c, or $1\frac{1}{2}$ c.

Exercises

1. Find the mass of the oranges.

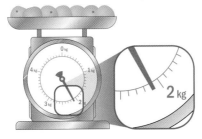

2. Find the amount of liquid in the measuring cup.

3. Estimate the total weight in pounds of the books you carried home from school today. Then use a bathroom scale to find the actual weight. Compare your estimate to the actual weight.

Notebook Review

Review the vocabulary definitions in your notebook.

Copy the review examples in your notebook. Then complete the exercises.

Check Your Definitions

solid, p. 500

prism, p. 500

cylinder, p. 500

pyramid, p. 500

cone, p. 500

sphere, p. 500

face, p. 501

edge, p. 501

vertex, p. 501

surface area, p. 506

volume, p. 510

Use Your Vocabulary

1. Copy and complete: A _?_ has one circular base.

10.5 Can you classify solid figures?

 EXAMPLE Identify the bases of the solid shown at the right. Then classify the solid.

ANSWER The two bases of the solid are circles. The solid is a cylinder.

☑ **2.** Classify the solid. Then count the number of faces, edges, and vertices.

10.6–10.7 Can you find surface area and volume of a prism?

 EXAMPLE A box measures 14 inches by 18 inches by 4 inches. What is the surface area and the volume of the box?

Surface Area

Area of the top or bottom: $14 \cdot 18 = 252$

Area of the front or back: $4 \cdot 14 = 56$

Area of the left or right: $4 \cdot 18 = 72$

Surface area: $2(252) + 2(56) + 2(72) = 760$

Volume

$V = lwh$

$= 14 \cdot 18 \cdot 4$

$= 1008$

ANSWER The surface area is 760 square inches, and the volume is 1008 cubic inches.

☑ **3.** Find the surface area and the volume of the rectangular prism shown at the right.

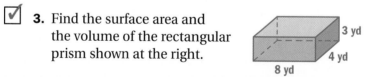

3 yd

4 yd

8 yd

4. **Writing** Explain the difference between the surface area and the volume of a rectangular prism.

5. **Critical Thinking** Explain how you can tell the difference between a prism and a pyramid.

Review Quiz 2

Classify the solid.

1.

2.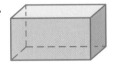

3.

4. Count the number of faces, edges, and vertices of the solid in Exercise 2.

5. **Sofa** You are covering a sofa cushion that is a rectangular prism. It measures 18 inches by 21 inches by 4 inches. About how many square inches of fabric do you need?

6. Find the surface area and the volume of the rectangular prism shown at the right.

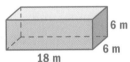

6 m
6 m
18 m

7. A rectangular prism has a width of 5 meters, a height of 3 meters, and a volume of 105 cubic meters. Find the length.

Counting Blocks

Two views of a tower of blocks are shown. Each block is a cube that measures 1 inch by 1 inch by 1 inch. Find the volume of the tower. Then find the area of the outer surface, including the base.

Front View

Back View

10 Chapter Review

📓 Vocabulary

base of a parallelogram,
   p. 476
height of a parallelogram,
   p. 476
perpendicular, p. 476
base of a triangle, p. 480
height of a triangle,
   p. 480
circle, p. 485

center, p. 485
radius, p. 485
diameter, p. 485
circumference, p. 485
pi (π), p. 485
solid, p. 500
prism, p. 500
cylinder, p. 500
pyramid, p. 500

cone, p. 500
sphere, p. 500
face, p. 501
edge, p. 501
vertex, p. 501
surface area, p. 506
volume, p. 510

Vocabulary Review

Tell whether the statement is *true* or *false*.

1. The circumference of a circle is measured in square units.

2. The surface area of a prism is measured in square units.

3. The distance from the center of a circle to any point on the circle is called the diameter.

Copy and complete the statement.

4. Two intersecting lines that meet at a right angle are _?_.

5. The base of a cone is a _?_.

6. The _?_ of a prism is the sum of the areas of its faces.

7. The _?_ of a prism is the amount of space that it occupies.

Review Questions

Find the area of the figure. *(Lessons 10.1, 10.2, 10.4)*

8.
28 mm
30 mm

9.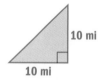
10 mi
10 mi

10.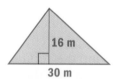
16 m
30 m

11.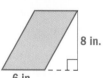
8 in.
6 in.

12.
3 cm

13.
10 yd

14. The area of a parallelogram is 68 square meters and the base is 4 meters. Find the height of the parallelogram. *(Lesson 10.1)*

15. The area of a triangle is 100 square inches and the height is 20 inches. What is the base? *(Lesson 10.2)*

Find the circumference of the circle described. *(Lesson 10.3)*

16. diameter = 5 m   **17.** diameter = 35 in.   **18.** radius = 3 yd

19. The trunk of a tree has a circumference of about 75 inches. Find the diameter of the tree to the nearest inch. *(Lesson 10.3)*

Find the area of the figure to the nearest tenth of a unit. *(Lesson 10.4)*

20.

20 cm
16 cm

21.
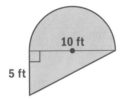
10 ft
5 ft

22.
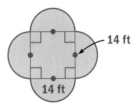
14 ft
14 ft

23. Make a circle graph to represent the karate data shown below. *(Lesson 10.4)*

Number of Karate Students at Each Level					
Black Belt	Red Belt	Blue Belt	Green Belt	Orange Belt	White Belt
3	6	15	22	13	8

Classify the solid. *(Lesson 10.5)*

24.

25.

26.

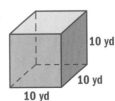

27. Count the number of faces, edges, and vertices of the solid in Exercise 25. *(Lesson 10.5)*

Find the surface area and the volume of the rectangular prism.
(Lessons 10.6, 10.7)

28.
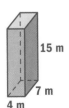
15 m
7 m
4 m

29.
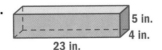
5 in.
4 in.
23 in.

30.
10 yd
10 yd
10 yd

Chapter Test

1. The base of a parallelogram is 6 inches and the height is 4 inches. Find the area of the parallelogram.

2. The base of a triangle is 10 centimeters and the height is 18 centimeters. Find the area of the triangle.

3. A parallelogram has an area of 60 square feet and a height of 5 feet. Find the base.

4. **Craters** Tycho is a crater located on the moon. Tycho has a radius of about 43.5 kilometers. Find the circumference of Tycho to the nearest kilometer.

Find the area of the figure.

5.
5 m

6.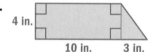
4 in.
10 in.   3 in.

7.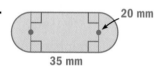
20 mm
35 mm

8. Classify the solid shown at the right.

9. Draw a triangular prism.

Find the surface area and the volume of the rectangular prism.

10.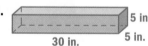
5 in.
30 in.   5 in.

11.
8 ft
6 ft   6 ft

12.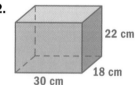
22 cm
30 cm   18 cm

13. Count the faces, edges, and vertices of the solid in Exercise 12.

14. **Painting** You are painting a rectangular box that is 5 feet by 4 feet by 2 feet. The paint can says that the paint will cover 100 square feet. Do you have enough paint to cover the entire box?

15. **Tissue Box** A tissue box measures 9 inches by 5 inches by 3 inches. Find the volume of the tissue box.

16. **Plant Sale** The number of plants sold at a plant sale is shown. Make a circle graph to represent the data.

Types of Plants Sold	
Type of plant	**Plants sold**
potted palm	70
geranium	30
African violet	50

Chapter Standardized Test

Test-Taking Strategy Concentrate on the question that you are working on rather than the time that is remaining for the test.

Multiple Choice

1. A parallelogram has an area of 35 square meters. The height of the parallelogram is 7 meters. What is the length of the base?

A. 5 m **B.** 28 m **C.** 42 m **D.** 245 m

2. What is the area of the triangle?

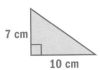

F. 17 cm^2 **G.** 35 cm^2

H. 70 cm^2 **I.** 140 cm^2

3. What is the approximate circumference of a circle that has a diameter of 6 inches?

A. 9.42 in. **B.** 18.84 in.

C. 28.26 in. **D.** 56.52 in.

4. What is the approximate area of a circle that has a radius of 8 feet?

F. 25.12 ft^2 **G.** 50.24 ft^2

H. 200.96 ft^2 **I.** 803.84 ft^2

5. What is the approximate area of the figure?

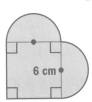

A. 54.84 cm^2 **B.** 64.26 cm^2

C. 73.68 cm^2 **D.** 92.52 cm^2

6. Classify the solid.

F. Cone

G. Sphere

H. Triangular pyramid

I. Triangular prism

7. Which of the following is *true* about the solid in Exercise 6?

A. There are 12 faces.

B. There are 8 edges.

C. There are 8 vertices.

D. There are 6 edges.

8. What is the surface area of the prism shown?

F. 20 yd^2 **G.** 129 yd^2

H. 258 yd^2 **I.** 270 yd^2

9. What is the volume of the prism shown in Exercise 8?

A. 23 yd^3 **B.** 135 yd^3

C. 225 yd^3 **D.** 270 yd^3

Short Response

10. Can you use this expression to find the area of a half-circle: $\frac{1}{2}\pi r^2$? Explain.

Extended Response

11. You want to estimate the diameter of a large tree trunk. Your only tools are a large piece of rope and a ruler. Describe the steps you would follow to get a reasonable estimate of the tree's diameter.

Strategies for Answering
Context-Based Multiple Choice Questions

Some of the information you need to solve a context-based multiple choice question may appear in a table, a diagram, or a graph.

Problem 1

A magazine ad for a car includes a scale drawing of the car. The actual width of the car is 200 centimeters. What is the actual length of the car?

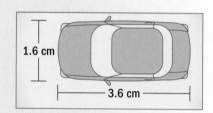

1.6 cm

3.6 cm

A. 125 cm   **B.** 203.6 cm   **C.** 450 cm   **D.** 720 cm

Solution

Read the problem carefully. Decide what information you are given and how you can use it to solve the problem.

1) From the problem and diagram, you know:

width on drawing = 1.6 centimeters   actual width = 200 centimeters

length on drawing = 3.6 centimeters   actual length = ?

You can use the width on the drawing and the actual width to find the scale of the drawing. Then use the scale to find the actual length.

Find the scale.

2) The scale of the drawing is $\dfrac{1.6 \text{ cm}}{200 \text{ cm}}$ or $\dfrac{1 \text{ cm}}{125 \text{ cm}}$.

Write and solve a proportion to find the actual length of the car. Use cross products.

3) $\dfrac{1 \text{ cm}}{125 \text{ cm}} = \dfrac{\text{Length on drawing}}{\text{Actual length}}$ Write a proportion.

$\dfrac{1 \text{ cm}}{125 \text{ cm}} = \dfrac{3.6 \text{ cm}}{x \text{ cm}}$ Substitute values.

$1 \cdot x = (125)(3.6)$ The cross products are equal.

$x = 450$ Multiply.

The actual length is 450 centimeters. The correct answer is C.

Use one of the strategies on pages 202–203.

4) Check to see that your answer is reasonable. For example, because $125 \times 3.6 \approx 100 \times 4 = 400$, the most reasonable answer is C.

Problem 2

A storage chest in the shape of a rectangular prism has the dimensions shown. What is the surface area of the chest?

Surface	Length	Width
front and back	3 ft	2 ft
top and bottom	3 ft	1.5 ft
left and right	2 ft	1.5 ft

F. 13 ft^2 **G.** 13.5 ft^2 **H.** 27 ft^2 **I.** 67.5 ft^2

Solution

Read the problem carefully. Recall that the surface area of a prism is the sum of the areas of its faces.

1) Use the table to make a sketch. Find the area of each face of the chest. Then add to find the surface area S.

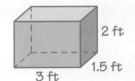

Find the surface area.

2) $S = (3 \times 2) + (3 \times 2) + (3 \times 1.5) +$
$(3 \times 1.5) + (2 \times 1.5) + (2 \times 1.5)$

$= 6 + 6 + 4.5 + 4.5 + 3 + 3$

$= 27$

The surface area is 27 square feet. The correct answer is H.

Watch Out!

It is important to be sure that you know what question you are trying to answer. Some of the choices given may be correct answers to slightly different questions.

Your turn now

1. What is the volume of the storage chest in Problem 2?

    A. 6.5 ft^3 **B.** 9 ft^3 **C.** 18 ft^3 **D.** 27 ft^3

2. How many degrees greater than the measure of $\angle A$ is the measure of $\angle B$?

    F. 23°   **G.** 41°

    H. 64°   **I.** 95°

3. You are creating a game board as shown. What is the least number of additional squares that you must shade so that the finished game board will have a diagonal line of symmetry?

    A. 1   **B.** 2   **C.** 3   **D.** 4

GO ON

Multiple Choice

1. Students voted for their favorite fruit. The results are shown in the circle graph below. What percent of the 250 students who voted chose apples?

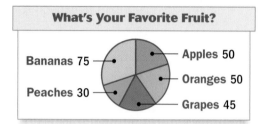

What's Your Favorite Fruit?

Bananas 75
Peaches 30
Apples 50
Oranges 50
Grapes 45

A. 20%   **B.** 25%   **C.** 50%   **D.** 100%

2. Which statement about the figure is *false*?

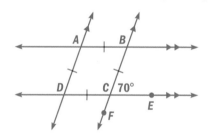

F. $\overleftrightarrow{AB}$ is parallel to $\overleftrightarrow{DC}$.

G. $\overrightarrow{AB}$ has endpoint A.

H. $\angle ECF$ is acute.

I. Quadrilateral $ABCD$ is a rhombus.

3. The table shows the total number of diagonals that can be drawn in a regular polygon with the given number of sides. How many diagonals can be drawn in a regular octagon?

Number of sides	3	4	5	6	7
Number of diagonals	0	2	5	9	14

A. 16   **B.** 18   **C.** 20   **D.** 28

In Exercises 4 and 5, use the scale drawing below. It shows the actual measures of a street sign.

4. About how much metal is needed to make the sign?

F. 97 square inches

G. 453 square inches

H. 471 square inches

I. 510 square inches

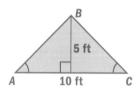

33 in.

12 in.

(1 in.:18 in.)

5. The actual width of the sign is 12 inches. What is the width of the sign on the scale drawing?

A. 0.6 inch

B. $0.\overline{6}$ inch

C. 0.7 inch

D. 1 inch

In the triangle below, $m\angle ABC = 90°$. Use the diagram in Exercises 6 and 7.

6. What is the measure of $\angle BAC$?

F. 10°   **G.** 45°   **H.** 90°   **I.** 180°

7. What is the total area of the triangle shown?

A. 25 square feet   **B.** 30 square feet

C. 35 square feet   **D.** 50 square feet

Short Response

8. Eighteen students in a class of 25 students plan to go on a hiking trip. What percent of the students plan to go on the trip? What percent do not plan to go? Explain how you found your answers.

9. Engineers tested two cars to find their fuel efficiency. Car A traveled 225 miles and used 14 gallons of gas. Car B traveled 312 miles and used 15 gallons of gas. Which car has better fuel efficiency? Explain.

10. The sales tax rate in Arbordale is 7.5%. Find the amount of sales tax on the purchase of a $19,276 car. Show your work.

11. The Vaughn family wants to spend no more than 24% of their income for their mortgage. Their annual income is $84,000. What is the greatest amount of money they can spend each month on their mortgage if they stay within their budget? Show your steps.

12. Nine apes at a zoo eat a total of 12 pounds of oranges per day. How many pounds of oranges would be needed for 12 apes? How many apes could be fed with 20 pounds of oranges? Explain how you found your answers.

Extended Response

13. A circular rug is shown. How many square feet of floor are covered by this rug? Binding ribbon is sold by the foot. How much binding ribbon is needed to bind off the blue outer edge of the rug? Explain how you found your answers.

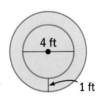

4 ft
1 ft

14. A popcorn box is shaped like a rectangular prism. It has length 10 cm, width 4.5 cm, and height 16 cm. Sketch the popcorn box. How much cardboard would be needed to make the box, assuming all faces are closed and there are no overlaps? How much popcorn could the box hold? Show how you found your answers.

15. Create a new parallelogram by multiplying the sides and height of the parallelogram shown by 3. Keep the angle measures the same. Is the new parallelogram similar to the old one? Is it congruent to the old one? Explain why or why not. Then find the perimeters and the areas of the old and the new parallelograms. Is the ratio of the areas the same as the ratio of the perimeters? Explain.

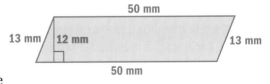

50 mm
13 mm 12 mm 13 mm
50 mm

16. The design for a pillow cover is shown. Ignoring color, tell how many lines of symmetry the design has. The measure of ∠1 is 30°. Explain how you can use the symmetry of the design to find the measures of the rest of the numbered angles.

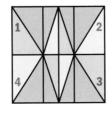

Cumulative Practice for Chapters 8–10

Chapter 8

Multiple Choice In Exercises 1–10, choose the letter of the correct answer.

1. Mr. and Mrs. Chin have 4 nephews and 2 nieces. What is the ratio of nieces to nephews? *(Lesson 8.1)*

   A. $1:3$ **B.** $1:2$ **C.** $2:1$ **D.** $3:1$

2. A car travels 3 miles in 4 minutes. At this rate, how far does the car travel in one minute? *(Lesson 8.2)*

   F. 0.75 miles   **G.** 1.33 miles

   H. 12 miles   **I.** 45 miles

3. What is the solution of the proportion $\frac{9}{36} = \frac{y}{16?}$ *(Lesson 8.3)*

   A. 4   **B.** $4\frac{1}{2}$ **C.** 108   **D.** 144

4. Henry bought 3 yards of fabric for a costume. He paid $12.60. How much would 5 yards of the fabric cost? *(Lesson 8.3)*

   F. $4.20   **G.** $7.56   **H.** $8.40   **I.** $21

5. A scale drawing of a fountain has a scale of 1 in. : 2 ft. The actual diameter of the circular fountain is 8 feet. What is the diameter on the scale drawing? *(Lesson 8.4)*

   A. 2 in.   **B.** 4 in.   **C.** 8 in.   **D.** 16 in.

6. The distance on a map between Franklin and Lincoln is about 6 inches. Use the scale 1 in. : 10 mi to estimate the actual distance between the towns. *(Lesson 8.4)*

   F. 30 mi   **G.** 40 mi   **H.** 60 mi   **I.** 180 mi

7. How can you write 0.07 as a percent? *(Lesson 8.5)*

   A. 0.07%   **B.** 7%   **C.** 70%   **D.** 700%

8. Which number is *not* equivalent to the other numbers? *(Lesson 8.6)*

   F. $\frac{73}{200}$ **G.** $\frac{3}{8}$ **H.** 0.375   **I.** 37.5%

9. What is 5% of 200? *(Lesson 8.6)*

   A. 5   **B.** 10   **C.** 40   **D.** 82.05

10. You deposit $250 into an account with an annual interest rate of 4%. How much simple interest will you earn on that money in 3 years? *(Lesson 8.7)*

   F. $10   **G.** $20   **H.** $25   **I.** $30

11. **Short Response** Your restaurant bill is $31.96. You want to leave a tip of about 20%. Estimate the amount of the tip. Then estimate your share of the total cost if you divide it into three equal parts. Explain how you found your answers. *(Lesson 8.7)*

12. **Extended Response** A gym bag that costs $35 is on sale for 30% off. You need to pay 6% sales tax on your purchase. *(Lesson 8.7)*

   a. Find the cost of the gym bag. Show your work.

   b. If you pay with two $20 bills, how much change will you receive? Explain.

Chapter 9

Multiple Choice In Exercises 13–20, choose the letter of the correct answer.

13. Which two symbols *cannot* represent the same figure? *(Lesson 9.1)*

A. $\overline{AB}$ and $\overline{BA}$ **B.** $\overleftrightarrow{CD}$ and $\overleftrightarrow{DC}$

C. $\overrightarrow{PQ}$ and $\overrightarrow{QP}$ **D.** $\overrightarrow{RS}$ and $\overrightarrow{RT}$

14. What is the closest approximation to the measure of $\angle P$? *(Lesson 9.2)*

F. 30°   **G.** 60°

H. 90°   **I.** 110°

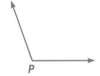

15. Classify an angle with measure 64°. *(Lesson 9.3)*

A. acute   **B.** straight

C. obtuse   **D.** right

16. Which angle measure represents an angle that is supplementary to a 37° angle? *(Lesson 9.3)*

F. 37°   **G.** 53°   **H.** 127°   **I.** 143°

17. The measures of two angles of a triangle are 46° and 42°. Classify the triangle. *(Lesson 9.4)*

A. acute   **B.** obtuse

C. equilateral   **D.** right

18. Which statement is true? *(Lesson 9.5)*

F. Every parallelogram is a rhombus.

G. Every rhombus is a square.

H. Every rectangle is a parallelogram.

I. Every quadrilateral is a rhombus.

19. Which name does *not* apply to the figure shown? *(Lessons 9.4, 9.6)*

A. equilateral triangle

B. scalene triangle

C. regular triangle

D. polygon

20. How many lines of symmetry does the figure shown have? *(Lesson 9.8)*

F. 0

G. 1

H. 2

I. 3

21. Short Response Draw two congruent right triangles, $\triangle ABC$ and $\triangle DEF$. List the corresponding parts. Explain why $\angle A$ and $\angle D$ have the same measure. *(Lessons 9.4, 9.7)*

22. Extended Response In the figure, $m\angle 2 = 50°$. *(Lesson 9.3)*

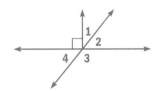

a. Name two complementary angles.

b. Name two vertical angles.

c. Name two supplementary angles.

d. Find the measures of $\angle 1$, $\angle 3$, and $\angle 4$. Explain how you found your answers.

Chapter 10

Multiple Choice In Exercises 23–32, choose the letter of the correct answer.

23. What is the area of a parallelogram with a base of 14 centimeters and a height of 8 centimeters? *(Lesson 10.1)*

A. 44 cm   **B.** 112 cm

C. 44 cm^2 **D.** 112 cm^2

24. The area of a parallelogram is 110 square inches. The height is 10 inches. What is the base? *(Lesson 10.1)*

F. 11 in.   **G.** 22 in.   **H.** 100 in.   **I.** 110 in.

25. A pennant in the shape of a triangle has an area of 50 square inches. The base is 10 inches. What is the height? *(Lesson 10.2)*

A. 5 in.   **B.** 10 in.   **C.** 25 in.   **D.** 500 in.

26. What is the area of the figure? *(Lesson 10.2)*

F. 8 m^2

G. 10 m^2

H. 12 m^2

I. 16 m^2

2 m

2 m   4 m

27. What is the approximate circumference of a CD with a radius of 4.5 centimeters? *(Lesson 10.3)*

A. 14.13 cm   **B.** 28.26 cm

C. 29.88 cm   **D.** 63.59 cm

28. What is the approximate area of a circle with a diameter of 10 feet? *(Lesson 10.4)*

F. 15.7 ft^2 **G.** 31.4 ft^2

H. 78.5 ft^2 **I.** 314 ft^2

29. Which solid has 4 faces? *(Lesson 10.5)*

A. triangular prism

B. triangular pyramid

C. rectangular prism

D. rectangular pyramid

30. How many edges does a triangular prism have? *(Lesson 10.5)*

F. 6   **G.** 8   **H.** 9   **I.** 12

31. A box in the shape of a rectangular prism is 9 centimeters by 7 centimeters by 3 centimeters. What is the surface area of the box? *(Lesson 10.6)*

A. 19 ft^2 **B.** 66 ft^2

C. 189 ft^2 **D.** 222 ft^2

32. A wading pool is 6 feet by 4 feet by 2 feet. What is its volume? *(Lesson 10.7)*

F. 12 ft^2 **G.** 12 ft^3 **H.** 48 ft^2 **I.** 48 ft^3

33. Short Response A soccer team had 12 wins, 6 losses, and 2 ties during one season. Make a circle graph of the data. Explain your steps. *(Lesson 10.4)*

34. Extended Response Kim wants to make a cushion shaped like a rectangular prism for her couch. The cushion will be 16 inches by 18 inches by 4 inches. *(Lessons 10.6, 10.7)*

a. To find how much fabric she needs to cover the cushion, should Kim find the *surface area* or the *volume?* How much fabric does she need?

b. To find how much filling Kim needs for the cushion, should she find the *surface area* or the *volume?* How much filling does she need?

UNIT 4

Integers, Algebra, and Probability

From Chapter 12, p. 605

How much bamboo does a giant panda eat?

UNIT 4	STANDARDIZED TEST PREP

Strategies and practice directly follow Chapter 13.

11 Integers

Chapter Warm-Up Games

Review skills you need for this chapter in these quick games.

BEFORE

In previous chapters you've...

- Plotted points
- Studied line symmetry

Now

In Chapter 11 you'll study...

- Comparing and ordering integers
- Adding and subtracting integers
- Multiplying and dividing integers
- Transformations in a coordinate plane

WHY?

So you can solve real-world problems about...

- scuba divers, p. 535
- Mauna Loa, pp. 544–545
- black bears, p. 552
- animation, p. 566

Internet Preview
CLASSZONE.COM

- eEdition Plus Online
- eWorkbook Plus Online
- eTutorial Plus Online
- State Test Practice
- More Examples

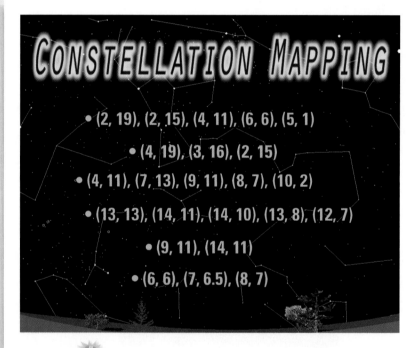

CONSTELLATION MAPPING

- (2, 19), (2, 15), (4, 11), (6, 6), (5, 1)
- (4, 19), (3, 16), (2, 15)
- (4, 11), (7, 13), (9, 11), (8, 7), (10, 2)
- (13, 13), (14, 11), (14, 10), (13, 8), (12, 7)
- (9, 11), (14, 11)
- (6, 6), (7, 6.5), (8, 7)

Key Skill:
Plotting points

Materials:
graph paper

Plot each group of points in the same coordinate plane. Then connect the points in each group in the order they are given. The resulting diagram will be a map of a famous constellation.

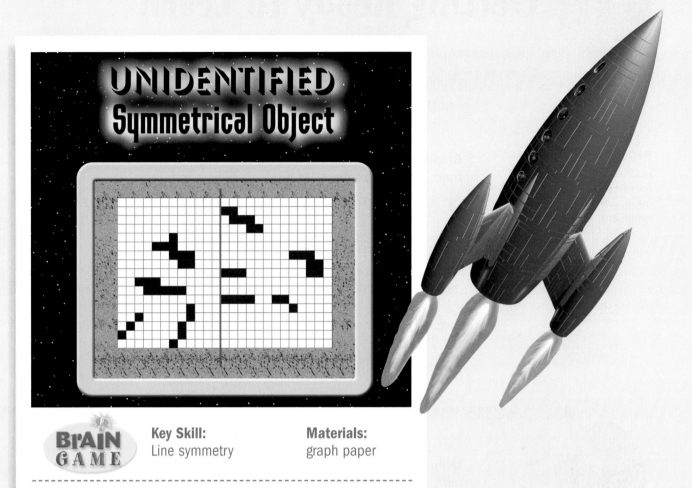

UNIDENTIFIED Symmetrical Object

BrAIN GAME

Key Skill:
Line symmetry

Materials:
graph paper

- Some of the data beamed to Earth from a distant spaceship's computer have been lost in transmission. Your goal is to reconstruct a picture sent by the ship.

- The picture sent by the ship has line symmetry. Copy the drawing and the line of symmetry shown above onto graph paper. Then reconstruct the picture.

Stop _and_ Think

1. **Extension** The constellation you plotted on page 530 is Orion. Draw a picture of another star grouping, such as the Big Dipper. Then write directions for graphing the star grouping in a coordinate plane.

2. **Writing** Describe the procedure you used to reconstruct the *Unidentified Symmetrical Object*.

CHAPTER 11 Getting Ready to Learn

Review What You Need to Know

1. Using Vocabulary Explain what it means for two figures to be congruent.

Graph the numbers on a number line. Then order the numbers from least to greatest. *(p. 685)*

2. 4, 3, 7, 8, 6, 5   **3.** 12, 2, 14, 19, 9   **4.** 16, 27, 21, 18, 23

Find the sum, difference, product, or quotient. *(p. 5)*

5. $189 + 12$ **6.** $316 - 29$ **7.** 16×43

8. $140 \div 28$ **9.** $420 + 297$ **10.** 45×34

Graph and connect the points. Then identify the resulting figure. *(pp. 83, 449)*

11. $A(2, 1)$, $B(3, 4)$, $C(0, 4)$ **12.** $D(6, 2)$, $E(8, 2)$, $F(6, 5)$, $G(8, 5)$

Word Watch

Review Words

ordered pair, p. 83
coordinates, p. 83
mean, p. 93
congruent, p. 454

Notebook

You should include material that appears on a notebook like this in your own notes.

Know How to Take Notes

Using Multiple Representations You can often record a number in different ways in your notes. In earlier chapters, you saw decimals represented in several ways as shown below.

Expanded form	1 one + 7 tenths + 3 hundredths
	1.0 + 0.7 + 0.03
Decimal form	1.73
Word form	one and seventy-three hundredths
Visual form	

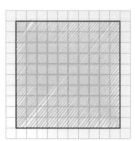

1 one (1 whole)   73 hundredths

In Chapter 11, you will use number line models with integers.

Comparing Integers

11.1

BEFORE
You compared and ordered fractions and decimals.

▶ **Now**
You'll compare and order integers.

WHY?
So you can order temperatures, as in Exercise 34.

In the Real World

Word Watch

integer, p. 533
positive integer, p. 533
negative integer, p. 533
opposites, p. 534

Space Shuttles During a countdown for a shuttle launch, "T+10 seconds" means 10 seconds after liftoff. What number represents "T−10 seconds"?

During a launch, each second can be assigned an *integer*. The following numbers are **integers** .

$$\ldots, -5, -4, -3, -2, -1, 0, 1, 2, 3, 4, 5, \ldots$$

Negative integers are integers that are less than 0. **Positive integers** are integers that are greater than 0. Zero is neither negative nor positive.

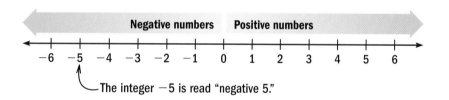

The integer −5 is read "negative 5."

Integers are often used to represent real-world quantities. Words like *profit*, *increase*, and *above* often indicate a positive integer. Words like *loss*, *decrease*, and *below* indicate a negative integer.

EXAMPLE 1 Using Integers

Write the integer that represents the situation.

a. The countdown for the space shuttle is at "T−10 seconds."

ANSWER −10 seconds

b. A withdrawal of $25

ANSWER −$25

Your turn now Write the integer that represents the situation.

1. a $15 profit   **2.** a 9 point decrease   **3.** a loss of 5 yards

Opposites Numbers increase as you move from left to right on a number line. Two numbers are **opposites** if they are the same distance from 0 on a number line, but are on opposite sides of 0.

HELP with **Reading**

The integer −3 is read as "negative 3" or as "the opposite of 3."

EXAMPLE 2 **Identifying Opposites**

Find the opposite of −3.

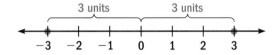

ANSWER The opposite of −3 is 3.

EXAMPLE 3 **Comparing Integers**

Compare −8 and −5.

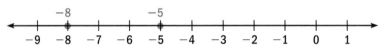

ANSWER Because −8 is to the left of −5 on the number line, $-8 < -5$.

Your turn now **Find the opposite of the integer.**

4. 8   **5.** −7   **6.** −12   **7.** 0

Copy and complete the statement using < or >.

8. −2 ? 2   **9.** 0 ? −1   **10.** 4 ? −5   **11.** −8 ? −9

EXAMPLE 4 **Ordering Integers**

Golf In a golf tournament, the player with the lowest score wins. The table shows the scores of several golfers (including the winner) in the 2001 Masters. Who won?

Golfer	Score
David Duvall	−14
Shingo Katayama	4
Jesper Parnevik	−5
Duffy Waldorf	0
Tiger Woods	−16

Solution

ANSWER Tiger Woods won the 2001 Masters with the lowest score of −16.

Exercises

More Practice, p. 718

Getting Ready to Practice

Vocabulary Find the opposite of the integer.

1. 9   **2.** -1 **3.** -15

Copy and complete the statement using < or >.

4. $-7 \underline{\ ?\ } 0$ **5.** $-2 \underline{\ ?\ } -6$ **6.** $8 \underline{\ ?\ } -9$

Graph the integers on a number line. Then order the integers from least to greatest.

7. $-3, 2, 7, -9, 0$ **8.** $-2, -5, 6, 10, -8$ **9.** $-9, 0, -2, -3, -5$

10. Scuba Divers A scuba diver is 12 feet below sea level. A second scuba diver is 25 feet below sea level. Write integers to represent the divers' positions relative to sea level.

Practice and Problem Solving

Write the integer that represents the situation.

11. 6 degrees below 0   **12.** an increase of 20 cm

13. 5 people join the Math Club   **14.** a loss of $3

15. a withdrawal of 25 dollars   **16.** 2 feet under water

17. In-line Skating In-line skates are on sale for $10 off, helmets are $5 off, and knee pads are $4 off. Use an integer to represent the change in price for each item.

Find the opposite of the integer.

18. 4   **19.** -8 **20.** -11 **21.** 0

Copy and complete the statement using < or >.

22. $-3 \underline{\ ?\ } 7$ **23.** $-6 \underline{\ ?\ } 0$ **24.** $0 \underline{\ ?\ } -4$ **25.** $5 \underline{\ ?\ } -7$

26. $-9 \underline{\ ?\ } 9$ **27.** $1 \underline{\ ?\ } -5$ **28.** $-11 \underline{\ ?\ } -12$ **29.** $-10 \underline{\ ?\ } -8$

Order the integers from least to greatest.

30. $8, -2, 6, 7, -3$ **31.** $-8, 0, 5, -1, 1$

32. $-1, 4, -4, 9, -6$ **33.** $0, -3, -9, 6, -6$

HELP with **Homework**

Example	Exercises
1	11–17
2	18–21
3	22–29
4	30–34

Online Resources
CLASSZONE.COM

· More Examples
· eTutorial Plus

34. Temperatures The table shows the average low temperature for each month in Big Delta, Alaska. Order the temperatures from least to greatest. Which month has the lowest average low temperature?

Average Low Temperatures in Big Delta, Alaska											
Month	Jan.	Feb.	Mar.	Apr.	May	June	July	Aug.	Sept.	Oct.	Nov.	Dec.
°F	−11	−6	3	21	37	47	51	46	36	18	−2	−9

Number Sense **Tell whether the statement is *true* or *false*.**

35. The opposite of five is greater than negative four.

36. Zero is greater than negative seven.

37. The opposite of negative nine is less than ten.

 38. Writing A number is sometimes less than its opposite. Use examples to explain this statement.

39. Challenge Two integers are opposites of each other. One integer is 7 units to the right of −5 on a number line. What are the two integers?

Mixed Review

Use a number line to add the numbers. *(p. 688)*

40. $5 + 4$

41. $12 + 3$

42. $8 + 2$

Classify the solid. *(Lesson 10.5)*

43.

44.

45.

Basic Skills **Evaluate the expression when *x* = 4.5 and *y* = 1.23.**

46. $6.07 - x$

47. $x + 2.58$

48. $y + 10.9$

Test-Taking Practice

49. Multiple Choice A 2-degree increase in temperature is represented by which of the following?

A. −20   **B.** −2   **C.** 2   **D.** 20

50. Multiple Choice If the integers 12, −4, 11, −12, 6, and −7 are put in order from least to greatest, which integer will be third in the list?

F. −12   **G.** −4   **H.** 6   **I.** 12

Hands-on Activity

Modeling Integer Addition

In this activity, you will use integer chips to model integer addition.

 = positive 1   ⊖ = negative 1

Explore **Model 3 + (−5) using integer chips.**

When you combine a positive integer chip and a negative integer chip, the result is zero. This pair of integer chips is called a *zero pair*.

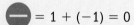 = 1 + (−1) = 0

1 Represent the expression using integer chips.

2 Group the zero pairs, if any.

3 Remove the zero pairs and write the result.

3 + (−5)

3 + (−5) = −2

Your turn now **Use the model to evaluate the expression.**

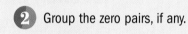

1.
2 + (−4)

2.
−2 + 5

3.
4 + (−4)

Stop and Think

4. **Critical Thinking** Use integer chips to demonstrate that the expressions 4 + (−3) and −3 + 4 are equivalent. Does the commutative property of addition appear to be true for integers?

5. **Make a Conclusion** Based on your answers to Exercises 1–3, suggest a method for finding the sum of two integers with different signs without using integer chips.

Adding Integers

BEFORE	▶ Now	WHY?
You added whole numbers, fractions, and decimals.	You'll add integers.	So you can find the change in stock value, as in Ex. 34.

In the Real World

Football During a high school football game, your team gained 6 yards on the first play, lost 8 yards on the second play, and gained 11 yards on the third play. Did your team gain the 10 yards needed for a first down?

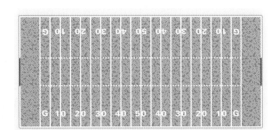

EXAMPLE 1 Modeling Integer Addition

To understand the problem above, read and organize the information.

First play: 6 means a gain of 6 yards.

Second play: −8 means a loss of 8 yards.

Third play: 11 means a gain of 11 yards.

Start at 0 on a number line. Use arrows to represent gains and losses. Move right to add a positive number and left to add a negative number.

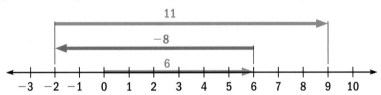

First play: $0 + 6 = 6$

Second play: $6 + (-8) = -2$

Third play: $-2 + 11 = 9$

ANSWER Your team gained only 9 yards during the three plays, which was not enough for a first down.

Your turn now Find the sum using a number line.

1. $-4 + (-4)$ **2.** $-6 + 6$ **3.** $-8 + 10$ **4.** $5 + (-9)$

Absolute Value The **absolute value** of a number is its distance from 0 on a number line. The absolute value of a number a is written $|a|$.

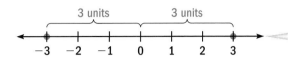

3 units   3 units

−3 −2 −1 0 1 2 3

The absolute value of −3 is 3 and the absolute value of 3 is 3.
$|-3| = |3| = 3$

You can use absolute value to add integers.

Adding Integers

Words	Numbers
Same Signs To add two integers with the same sign, add their absolute values and write their common sign.	$3 + 5 = 8$ $-3 + (-5) = -8$
Different Signs To add two integers with different signs, first subtract the lesser absolute value from the greater absolute value. Then write the sign of the number with the greater absolute value.	$-7 + 10 = 3$ $7 + (-10) = -3$

EXAMPLE 2 **Adding Integers**

HELP with Solving

When you find the sum of two numbers with different signs, you first find the number with the greater absolute value.

a. In the sum $-4 + (-7)$, both numbers have a negative sign. To find the sum, find $|-4| + |-7|$ and write a negative sign.

$$-4 + (-7) = -11$$

b. In the sum $-8 + 3$, the numbers have different signs and -8 has the greater absolute value. To find the sum, find $|-8| - |3|$ and write a negative sign.

$$-8 + 3 = -5$$

c. In the sum $-6 + 9$, the numbers have different signs and 9 has the greater absolute value. To find the sum, find $|9| - |-6|$.

$$-6 + 9 = 3$$

Your turn now **Find the absolute value of each number in the expression. Then find the sum.**

5. $-10 + (-5)$ **6.** $-9 + (-2)$ **7.** $8 + (-15)$ **8.** $25 + (-25)$

11.2 Exercises

More Practice, p. 718

INTERNET
eWorkbook Plus
CLASSZONE.COM

Getting Ready to Practice

Vocabulary Find the absolute value of the number.

1. -5 **2.** -8 **3.** 7 **4.** 0

Find the sum.

5. $5 + (-4)$ **6.** $-3 + (-6)$ **7.** $-7 + (-1)$ **8.** $2 + (-8)$

9. Find the Error Describe and correct the error in the solution.

$$\times \quad -1 + 5 = 5$$

number line showing $-3, -2, -1, 0, 1, 2, 3, 4, 5, 6, 7$

Practice and Problem Solving

HELP with **Homework**

Example	Exercises
1	10-13
2	14-33

Online Resources
CLASSZONE.COM

· More Examples
· eTutorial Plus

Find the sum using a number line.

10. $-1 + 6$ **11.** $8 + (-9)$ **12.** $-3 + (-3)$ **13.** $5 + (-5)$

Find the absolute value of the number.

14. -28 **15.** -100 **16.** 49 **17.** 35

Find the sum.

18. $2 + (-5)$ **19.** $0 + (-4)$ **20.** $-3 + (-7)$ **21.** $-10 + 3$

22. $-1 + (-9)$ **23.** $-4 + (-6)$ **24.** $-14 + 8$ **25.** $7 + (-1)$

26. $13 + (-13)$ **27.** $-10 + 10$ **28.** $-1 + 17$ **29.** $5 + (-15)$

30. $15 + (-8)$ **31.** $-19 + (-1)$ **32.** $-21 + (-2)$ **33.** $18 + (-27)$

34. Stocks The table shows the changes in value of a $58 stock in one week. Write an addition expression that describes the situation. Then find the value of the stock at the end of the week.

Change in Stock Value				
Day of the Week	Monday	Tuesday	Wednesday	Thursday	Friday
Change in Value	up $8	down $12	down $20	up $3	up $4

Copy and complete the statement using <, >, or =.

35. $3 + (-5) \; \underline{?} \; -4 + (-2)$ **36.** $-8 + (-1) \; \underline{?} \; -6 + 3$

37. $12 + (-7) + 6 \; \underline{?} \; -5 + 5 + 10$ **38.** $-9 + (-4) + (-3) \; \underline{?} \; 8 + (-9) + (-15)$

39. Game Shows In a contest, students gain or lose points by answering questions. You begin with 25 points, you lose 40 points, and then gain 10 points. Write an addition expression that represents the problem. Then find your score.

Algebra Evaluate the expression when $a = -6$ and $b = 9$.

40. $a + b$ **41.** $b + a$

42. $-11 + a + b$ **43.** $b + (-8) + a$

Tell whether the statement is *always*, *sometimes*, or *never* true.

44. The sum of two negative integers is positive.

45. The sum of two positive integers is positive.

46. The sum of a positive integer and a negative integer is zero.

47. Critical Thinking What is the sum of a number and its opposite? Give examples to support your answer.

48. Challenge The sum of 7 and another integer is -5. What is the other integer?

■ **Game Shows**

By 1940 there were 50 quiz shows on the air. By the end of the decade there were 200 shows on the air. Shows like "Dr. IQ" and "Professor Peter Puzzleworth" were popular. What was the increase in the number of game shows on the air from 1940 to the end of the decade?

Mixed Review

Find the percent of the number. *(Lesson 8.7)*

49. 2% of 50   **50.** 65% of 80   **51.** 24.5% of 200

52. Draw an obtuse angle. Use a protractor to find the measure of your angle. *(Lessons 9.2, 9.3)*

Copy and complete the statement using < or >. *(Lesson 11.1)*

53. -5 ? 5 **54.** 4 ? -1 **55.** -13 ? -19 **56.** -24 ? 0

Basic Skills Find the difference.

57. $38 - 19$ **58.** $52 - 26$ **59.** $123 - 48$ **60.** $301 - 99$

Test-Taking Practice

61. Multiple Choice Which expression does not have a sum of -7?

     A. $-4 + (-3)$ **B.** $10 + (-17)$ **C.** $-13 + 6$ **D.** $-5 + 2$

62. Short Response A football team lost 3 yards on the first play, lost 5 yards on the second play, and gained 12 yards on the third play. Did the team gain the 10 yards needed for a first down? Explain how you found your answer.

Modeling Integer Subtraction

In this activity, you will use integer chips to model integer subtraction.

 = 1   = −1   = 0 (zero pair)

Explore 1) Model −6 − (−2) using integer chips.

1 Start with 6 negative integer chips.

−6

2 To subtract −2, remove 2 negative integer chips.

−6 − (−2)

3 Count the remaining integer chips and write the result.

−6 − (−2) = −4

> **Your turn now** Use an integer chip model to evaluate the expression.
>
> **1.** −5 − (−1)   **2.** −7 − (−4)   **3.** −8 − (−6)

Explore 2) Model −3 − 1 using integer chips.

1 Start with 3 negative integer chips.

−3

2 There are no positive integer chips, so add a zero pair.

−3 = −3 + 0

3 To subtract 1, remove 1 positive integer chip.

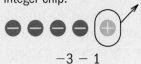

−3 − 1

4 Count the remaining integer chips and write the result.

−3 − 1 = −4

Your turn now Use an integer chip model to evaluate the expression.

4. $-5 - 2$ **5.** $-6 - 3$ **6.** $-7 - 4$

Explore 3 Model $-2 - (-4)$ using integer chips.

1 Start with 2 negative integer chips.

-2

2 There are not enough integer chips to remove 4 negative chips, so add two zero pairs.

$-2 = -2 + 0 + 0$

3 To subtract -4, remove 4 negative integer chips.

$-2 - (-4)$

4 Count the remaining integer chips and write the result.

$-2 - (-4) = 2$

Your turn now Use an integer chip model to evaluate the expression.

7. $-1 - (-3)$ **8.** $-4 - (-7)$ **9.** $-2 - (-6)$

10. $-5 - 3$ **11.** $-7 - 2$ **12.** $-10 - 6$

13. $-2 - (-2)$ **14.** $4 - (-1)$ **15.** $2 - (-3)$

Stop *and* **Think**

16. Critical Thinking Use integer chips to demonstrate that the expressions $-5 - (-8)$ and $-8 - (-5)$ are not equivalent.

17. Interpret When you subtract a positive integer from a negative integer, will you get a *negative* or a *positive* integer? Use examples to support your answer.

Subtracting Integers

BEFORE | ▶ **Now** | **WHY?**
You subtracted whole numbers, fractions, and decimals. | You'll subtract integers. | So you can calculate differences in elevation, as in Exercise 37.

(**In the Real World**)

Word Watch

Review Words

opposites, p. 534

Mauna Loa The base of the Hawaiian volcano Mauna Loa is about 13,000 meters below sea level. Its summit is 4170 meters above sea level. In Example 3, you will use integer subtraction to find the difference between the elevations of the base and summit.

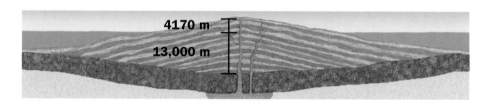

4170 m

13,000 m

EXAMPLE 1 **Modeling Integer Subtraction**

a. Find the difference 3 − 5.

When you add a positive integer, you move to the right on a number line. When you *subtract* a positive integer, you move to the left.

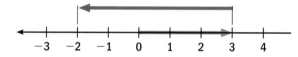

To find 3 − 5, move right 3 units then left 5 units.

ANSWER The final position is −2. So, 3 − 5 = −2.

HELP with Notetaking

In your notes on subtracting integers, you may want to include a number line model as in Example 1 and a numerical example as in Example 2.

b. Find the difference 2 − (−4).

When you add a negative integer, you move to the left on a number line. So to *subtract* a negative integer, you move to the right.

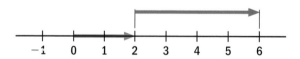

To find 2 − (−4), move right 2 units then right 4 units.

ANSWER The final position is 6. So, 2 − (−4) = 6.

Your turn now **Use a number line to find the difference.**

1. 4 − 6   **2.** 7 − 10   **3.** 3 − (−4)   **4.** 0 − (−4)

Subtracting Integers As you saw in Example 1, the direction you move to subtract an integer is the opposite of the direction you would move to add the integer. You can use opposites and rules for adding integers to subtract integers.

Subtracting Integers

Words To subtract an integer b from an integer a, add the opposite of b to a.

Algebra $a - b = a + (-b)$ **Numbers** $4 - 7 = 4 + (-7)$
$3 - (-2) = 3 + 2$

EXAMPLE 2 **Subtracting Integers**

Find the difference.

a. $-2 - (-9) = -2 + 9$ To subtract -9, add its opposite.

$= 7$ Find $|9| - |-2|$. Use the sign of 9.

b. $-5 - 7 = -5 + (-7)$ To subtract 7, add its opposite.

$= -12$ Find $|-5| + |-7|$. Use the common sign.

Your turn now **Find the difference.**

5. $3 - 7$ **6.** $-5 - 6$ **7.** $4 - (-8)$ **8.** $-2 - (-9)$

EXAMPLE 3 **Using Integers to Solve Problems**

Use the information on page 544 to find the approximate difference between the elevations of Mauna Loa's summit and base.

(1 Use integers to represent the two elevations.

summit: 4170 meters   **base:** $-13,000$ meters

(2 Subtract the lesser elevation from the greater.

$4170 - (-13,000) = 4170 + 13,000$ To subtract $-13,000$,
$= 17,170$ add its opposite.

ANSWER The difference between the elevations is 17,170 meters.

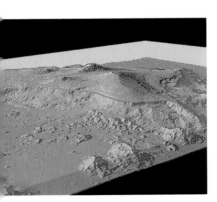

Computer-generated image of the island of Hawaii

Getting Ready to Practice

1. Vocabulary To subtract 5 from 2, add the __?__ of 5 to 2.

Use a number line to find the difference.

2. $4 - 7$ **3.** $-5 - 6$ **4.** $-2 - (-3)$ **5.** $5 - (-1)$

Find the difference.

6. $2 - 11$ **7.** $3 - (-8)$ **8.** $-8 - (-7)$ **9.** $-10 - 12$

10. Elevation The highest elevation in the United States is 20,320 feet above sea level on Mount McKinley in Alaska. The lowest elevation in the United States is 282 feet below sea level in Death Valley, California. What is the difference between the elevations of these two locations?

Practice and Problem Solving

with Homework

Example	Exercises
1	11–19
2	20–35
3	36, 37

Online Resources
CLASSZONE.COM
· More Examples
· eTutorial Plus

Use a number line to find the difference.

11. $6 - 7$ **12.** $1 - 4$ **13.** $8 - 12$ **14.** $6 - (-6)$

15. $3 - (-2)$ **16.** $9 - (-8)$ **17.** $-2 - (-5)$ **18.** $-9 - (-9)$

19. Find the Error Describe and correct the error in the solution.

$$\times \quad 4 - (-6) = -2$$

$$-3 \ -2 \ -1 \ \ 0 \ \ 1 \ \ 2 \ \ 3 \ \ 4 \ \ 5 \ \ 6 \ \ 7 \ \ 8 \ \ 9 \ \ 10$$

Find the difference.

20. $0 - 4$ **21.** $5 - 6$ **22.** $-2 - 2$ **23.** $7 - 9$

24. $-5 - 5$ **25.** $-8 - 9$ **26.** $-10 - 7$ **27.** $-2 - 12$

28. $6 - (-2)$ **29.** $4 - (-3)$ **30.** $11 - (-11)$ **31.** $13 - (-10)$

32. $-2 - (-8)$ **33.** $-5 - (-15)$ **34.** $-14 - (-6)$ **35.** $-12 - (-3)$

36. Cooking You are making frozen juice bars. You pour juice that has a temperature of 10°C into paper cups and freeze the juice to a temperature of $-2°C$. What is the change in temperature?

37. Elevator A mine elevator is 50 feet below the ground. It travels down another 75 feet. Find the elevator's elevation relative to ground level.

xy **Algebra** **Evaluate the expression when $a = -2$, $b = -5$, $c = 3$, and $d = 4$.**

38. $b - a + c$ **39.** $d - b + a$ **40.** $c - a - d$ **41.** $a - b - c$

42. Sunken Ships A diver marks the position of the bow of a sunken ship relative to the water's surface as -44 feet. The position of the stern is -53 feet. Use these integers to write a subtraction problem. What information about the ship can you find by solving the problem?

Evaluate the expression.

43. $5 + (-6) - 14 + 1(9)$

44. $-6 + 5(4) - (-7) + 3^2$

45. $7^2 - 10 + (-3) + 2(8)$

46. $9(3) + (-4) - 6 + 8^2$

Challenge **Tell whether the statement is *always*, *sometimes*, or *never* true.**

47. A negative integer minus a negative integer is negative.

48. A positive integer minus a positive integer is positive.

49. A positive integer minus a negative integer is positive.

50. A negative integer minus a positive integer is negative.

Mixed Review

Find the product. *(Lesson 7.3)*

51. $2\frac{3}{5} \cdot 3\frac{8}{9}$ **52.** $1\frac{1}{3} \cdot 4\frac{5}{6}$ **53.** $3\frac{1}{8} \cdot \frac{7}{5}$ **54.** $5\frac{1}{7} \cdot 3\frac{2}{9}$

Find the sum. *(Lesson 11.2)*

55. $6 + (-6)$ **56.** $4 + (-7)$ **57.** $-1 + 5$ **58.** $-8 + (-6)$

Basic Skills **Find the product.**

59. 2.4×3 **60.** 1.8×1.1 **61.** 0.63×0.2 **62.** 0.32×0.09

Test-Taking Practice

63. Multiple Choice What is the value of the expression $4 - (-17)$?

A. -21 **B.** -13 **C.** 13 **D.** 21

64. Short Response At noon the temperature was $8°F$. By 6 P.M. the temperature had dropped $12°$. What was the temperature at 6 P.M.? Show how to solve the problem using a number line and then using the rules for subtracting integers.

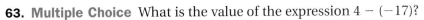

Notebook Review

Review the vocabulary definitions in your notebook.

Copy the review examples in your notebook. Then complete the exercises.

Check Your Definitions

integer, p. 533   negative integer, p. 533   absolute value, p. 539

positive integer, p. 533   opposites, p. 534

Use Your Vocabulary

1. Copy and complete: The numbers 12 and −12 are called ? .

2. Copy and complete: The ? of −5 is written |−5| and it equals 5.

11.1 Can you compare integers?

 EXAMPLE Compare −7 and −3.

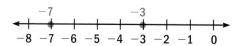

ANSWER Because −7 is to the left of −3 on a number line, −7 < −3.

✓ **Copy and complete the statement using < or >.**

   3. 5 ? −5   **4.** −3 ? −2   **5.** 1 ? −4   **6.** 0 ? −1

11.2–11.3 Can you add and subtract integers?

 EXAMPLE

   a. $-6 + (-7) = -13$ Find $|-6| + |-7|$. Use the common sign.

   b. $-8 - (-6) = -8 + 6$ To subtract −6, add its opposite.

              $= -2$ Find $|-8| - |6|$. Use the sign of −8.

✓ **Find the sum or difference.**

   7. $-9 + 9$ **8.** $-2 + (-2)$ **9.** $-13 + 8$ **10.** $11 + (-10)$

   11. $10 - 15$ **12.** $-9 - 8$ **13.** $5 - (-9)$ **14.** $-4 - (-7)$

Stop *and* Think   about Lessons 11.1–11.3

15. Writing Explain the thinking process involved in evaluating $-1 - (-2)$.

16. Critical Thinking Use examples to show what is meant by the opposite of the opposite of an integer.

Review Quiz 1

Find the opposite and the absolute value of the number.

1. 6   **2.** -4 **3.** -10 **4.** 0

Order the integers from least to greatest.

5. $-1, 8, 0, -4, 1$ **6.** $-5, 3, -7, -3, 5$

7. $12, -9, 3, -4, 8$ **8.** $-2, 1, 10, -11, -14$

Find the sum or difference.

9. $-3 + 6$ **10.** $6 + (-7)$ **11.** $11 + (-11)$ **12.** $-5 + (-15)$

13. $2 - 10$ **14.** $-14 - 4$ **15.** $-8 - (-10)$ **16.** $4 - (-12)$

17. Temperatures The coldest recorded average temperature for Cape Hatteras, North Carolina, during the month of January was about 35°F. The average temperature in Minneapolis-St. Paul, Minnesota, during January of the same year was 2°F below zero. Find the difference between these average temperatures.

Magic Square

In the magic square at the right, the sum of each row, column, and diagonal is the same. Copy and complete the magic square.

Multiplying Integers

BEFORE   ▶ **Now**   **WHY?**

You multiplied whole numbers, fractions, and decimals.

You'll multiply integers.

So you can find changes in water levels, as in Example 2.

Word Watch

Review Words

positive integer, p. 533
negative integer, p. 533

Activity   You can use addition to understand integer multiplication.

1   Copy and complete the table below.

Product	Repeated Addition	Result
4 • 2	= 2 + 2 + 2 + 2	= ?
4 • 1	= 1 + 1 + 1 + 1	= ?
4 • 0	= 0 + 0 + 0 + 0	= ?
4 • (−1)	= (−1) + (−1) + (−1) + (−1)	= ?
4 • (−2)	= (−2) + (−2) + (−2) + (−2)	= ?

2   Describe the pattern of the results. Use the pattern to find 4 • (−3).

3   Copy the table at the right. Then look for a pattern to complete it.

4   What do you observe about the product of two integers with the same sign? with different signs?

Product	Result
2 • (−4)	= ?
1 • (−4)	= ?
0 • (−4)	= ?
(−1) • (−4)	= ?
(−2) • (−4)	= ?

In the activity, you may have observed the following rules about multiplying integers.

Multiplying Integers

Words	**Numbers**
The product of two positive integers is positive.	3(5) = 15
The product of two negative integers is positive.	−4(−6) = 24
The product of a positive integer and a negative integer is negative.	2(−8) = −16

EXAMPLE 1 Multiplying Integers

a. $-7(-4) = 28$ The product of two negative integers is positive.

b. $8(-6) = -48$ The product of a positive integer and a negative integer is negative.

c. $-3(10) = -30$ The product of a positive integer and a negative integer is negative.

Your turn now Find the product.

1. $9(8)$ **2.** $-2(-11)$ **3.** $7(-7)$ **4.** $-8(4)$

What do you think?

Science

■ **Bay of Fundy**

The Bay of Fundy is located in Canada. The tides in the bay are the highest in the world. Use the information in Example 2. On average, how many high tides occur each day? each week?

EXAMPLE 2 Applying Integers

Bay of Fundy In the Bay of Fundy, there are about 6 hours between each high and low tide. Suppose that the water level decreases at a rate of about 4 feet per hour during this time. What is the change in the water level?

Bay of Fundy at high tide

Solution

$$\text{Change in water level} = \begin{array}{c}\text{Rate} \\ \text{of change}\end{array} \times \begin{array}{c}\text{Number} \\ \text{of hours}\end{array}$$

$$= -4 \times 6$$

$$= -24$$

ANSWER The water level decreases by about 24 feet between tides.

EXAMPLE 3 Evaluating Expressions

xy **Algebra** Evaluate $-5n$, when $n = -12$.

$-5n = -5(-12)$ Substitute -12 for n.

     $= 60$ The product of two negative integers is positive.

Your turn now Evaluate the expression when $x = 3$ and $y = -2$.

5. $-2x$ **6.** $6y$ **7.** $-5y$ **8.** xy

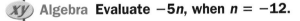

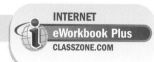

11.4 Exercises

More Practice, p. 718

Getting Ready to Practice

Vocabulary **Copy and complete the statement.**

1. The product of two negative integers is a _?_ integer.

2. The product of a negative integer and a positive integer is a _?_ integer.

Find the product.

3. 7(3)   **4.** −5(2)   **5.** 9(−4)   **6.** −8(−1)

7. Find the Error Describe and correct the error in the solution.

$$(-2)(-6) = -12$$

Practice and Problem Solving

HELP with **Homework**

Example	Exercises
1	8–26
2	27, 28
3	29–36

Online Resources
CLASSZONE.COM

· More Examples
· eTutorial Plus

Find the product.

8. 6(4)   **9.** 3(8)   **10.** 5(−7)   **11.** 2(−9)

12. −8(3)   **13.** −7(6)   **14.** −2(−9)   **15.** −10(−1)

16. 15(−3)   **17.** 1(13)   **18.** −12(−8)   **19.** −7(0)

20. 20(11)   **21.** 18(−10)   **22.** −30(30)   **23.** −12(−50)

24. Find the product of negative 3 and negative 9.

25. Find the product of positive 7 and negative 8.

26. Find the product of negative 10 and positive 5.

27. Diving Think of the surface of the ocean as zero on a number line. A sea otter can dive to −30 meters. A dolphin can dive to a point 10 times as deep. What is the dolphin's position relative to sea level?

28. Bears A female Asiatic black bear loses about 7 pounds per month during her 6 months of hibernation. What is her change in weight during hibernation? If the bear weighs 210 pounds before hibernation, what does she weigh after hibernation?

Algebra **Evaluate the expression when** $n = -6$, $p = 5$, **and** $t = -10$.

29. $7n$ **30.** $-8p$ **31.** $-6n$ **32.** np

33. pt **34.** nt **35.** $-2nt$ **36.** $-4pt$

Number Sense **Tell whether the statement is** *always*, *sometimes*, **or** *never* **true.**

37. A negative integer times a negative integer is positive.

38. A negative integer times a positive integer is negative.

39. A positive integer times a negative integer is positive.

40. Critical Thinking Evaluate $3(-5)$ and $(-5)3$. What do you notice about the results? What property holds for multiplication of integers?

Find the missing numbers in the pattern.

41. $-5, -10, \underline{?}, -40, -80, \underline{?}$ **42.** $-12, \underline{?}, -36, -48, \underline{?}, -72$

43. $3, \underline{?}, 3, -3, \underline{?}, -3$ **44.** $-4, \underline{?}, -16, 32, \underline{?}, \underline{?}$

45. Challenge Find the missing numbers: $\dfrac{3}{2}, -\dfrac{3}{4}, \underline{?}, -\dfrac{3}{16}, \underline{?}, \underline{?}$.

Mixed Review

46. Find the surface area and volume of the rectangular prism. *(Lessons 10.6, 10.7)*

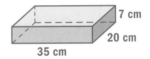
7 cm
20 cm
35 cm

Find the sum or difference. *(Lessons 11.2, 11.3)*

47. $-4 + 12$ **48.** $5 + (-8)$ **49.** $-7 + (-7)$ **50.** $-11 + 11$

51. $16 - 20$ **52.** $-31 - 9$ **53.** $-36 - (-11)$ **54.** $18 - (-25)$

Basic Skills **Find the quotient.**

55. $10.9 \div 0.5$ **56.** $21 \div 1.2$ **57.** $8.52 \div 0.16$ **58.** $28.4 \div 0.04$

Test-Taking Practice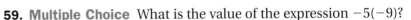

59. Multiple Choice What is the value of the expression $-5(-9)$?

     A. -45 **B.** -14 **C.** 14 **D.** 45

60. Multiple Choice Which statement is true?

     F. $3(-6) = -18$ **G.** $-2(-9) = -18$

     H. $4(-7) = 28$ **I.** $-4(-8) = -32$

Dividing Integers

BEFORE	Now	WHY?
You divided whole numbers, fractions, and decimals.	You'll divide integers.	So you can find average temperatures, as in Example 3.

Word Watch

Review Words
mean, p. 93

Activity **You can use multiplication to understand integer division.**

One way to find the quotient of two integers, such as $-32 \div 4$, is to rewrite the division problem as a multiplication problem.

① Rewrite the problem using multiplication.

$$-32 \div 4 = \underline{?} \quad\longrightarrow\quad \underline{?} \times 4 = -32$$

---

② Use mental math to solve the multiplication problem.

$$\underline{?} \times 4 = -32 \quad\longrightarrow\quad -8 \times 4 = -32$$

In Exercises 1–3, rewrite the problem using multiplication to find the quotient. Then use your results in Exercises 4–6.

1. $40 \div (-8) = \underline{?}$ **2.** $-45 \div (-9) = \underline{?}$ **3.** $-20 \div 5 = \underline{?}$

4. Is a positive integer divided by a positive integer *positive* or *negative*?

5. Is a negative integer divided by a negative integer *positive* or *negative*?

6. Is a positive integer divided by a negative integer *positive* or *negative*?

7. Is a negative integer divided by a positive integer *positive* or *negative*?

EXAMPLE 1 **Dividing Integers Using Mental Math**

Divide by solving a related multiplication equation.

  a. $-36 \div (-6) = 6$ Ask, "what number times -6 equals -36?"

  b. $27 \div (-9) = -3$ Ask, "what number times -9 equals 27?"

  c. $-42 \div 7 = -6$ Ask, "what number times 7 equals -42?"

Your turn now **Divide by solving a related multiplication equation.**

  1. $-30 \div 5$ **2.** $18 \div (-2)$ **3.** $-27 \div (-9)$ **4.** $0 \div (-5)$

Dividing Integers

Words	**Numbers**
The quotient of two positive integers is positive.	$15 \div 3 = 5$
The quotient of two negative integers is positive.	$-14 \div (-7) = 2$
The quotient of a positive integer and a negative integer is negative.	$12 \div (-4) = -3$
The quotient of a negative integer and a positive integer is negative.	$-10 \div 2 = -5$

EXAMPLE 2 **Dividing Integers**

a. $-54 \div (-6) = 9$ The quotient of two negative integers is positive.

b. $14 \div (-2) = -7$ The quotient of a positive integer and a negative integer is negative.

c. $-24 \div 3 = -8$ The quotient of a negative integer and a positive integer is negative.

EXAMPLE 3 **Finding the Mean of Integers**

Antarctica A scientist in Antarctica records the maximum temperature 3 days in a row. Find the mean of the temperatures shown on the thermometers.

$$\text{Mean} = \frac{-6 + (-4) + (-2)}{3}$$

$$= \frac{-12}{3}$$

$$= -4$$

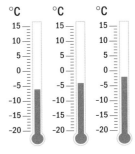

ANSWER The mean of the temperatures is $-4°C$.

What do you think?

Science

■ **Antarctica**

The U.S. has 3 stations in Antarctica: Palmer Station, South Pole Station, and McMurdo Station. The summer population of the stations are about 40, 130, and 1100 respectively. What fraction of the summer population is at McMurdo Station?

Your turn now **Find the quotient.**

5. $-63 \div 7$ **6.** $40 \div (-5)$ **7.** $5 \div (-5)$ **8.** $-22 \div (-2)$

Getting Ready to Practice

1. Vocabulary To find the mean of a group of integers, you add the integers and _?_ by the number of integers.

Divide by solving a related multiplication equation.

2. $-4 \div 2$ **3.** $6 \div (-3)$ **4.** $0 \div (-12)$ **5.** $-2 \div (-2)$

Find the quotient.

6. $9 \div (-3)$ **7.** $15 \div (-3)$ **8.** $-10 \div 5$ **9.** $-12 \div (-6)$

10. Find the mean of -8, -3, 2, and -7.

11. Find the Error Describe and correct the error in the solution.

$$X \quad -18 \div (-3) = -6$$

Practice and Problem Solving

with Homework

Example	Exercises
1	12–17
2	18–29
3	30–34

Online Resources
CLASSZONE.COM

· More Examples
· eTutorial Plus

Divide by solving a related multiplication equation.

12. $6 \div (-2)$ **13.** $4 \div (-1)$ **14.** $-21 \div (-3)$

15. $-45 \div (-5)$ **16.** $-30 \div 6$ **17.** $-14 \div 7$

Find the quotient.

18. $-12 \div (-3)$ **19.** $-18 \div (-6)$ **20.** $-24 \div 8$

21. $28 \div (-7)$ **22.** $39 \div (-13)$ **23.** $-30 \div 2$

24. $-500 \div 250$ **25.** $-90 \div 15$ **26.** $110 \div (-11)$

27. $750 \div (-50)$ **28.** $-128 \div (-32)$ **29.** $-195 \div (-15)$

30. Find the mean of -11, -15, 12, and -6.

31. Find the mean of -9, -2, -8, and 19.

32. Golf Five talented golfers play a game of golf. Their scores are shown below. Find the mean of the scores.

Golfer	Sara	Lauren	Matt	Audrey	Isaias
Score	4	5	-2	-4	-3

Global Temperatures The table shows the highest and lowest recorded temperatures for each continent.

Global Temperatures							
Continent	Africa	Antarctica	Asia	Australia	Europe	North America	South America
High Temperature (°F)	136	59	129	128	122	134	120
Low Temperature (°F)	−11	−129	−90	−9	−67	−81	−27

33. Find the mean of the low temperatures.

34. Find the mean of the high temperatures.

35. **Compare** Find the range of the high temperatures and the range of the low temperatures. Which set of data has the greater range?

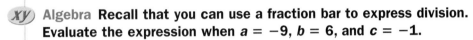 **Algebra** **Recall that you can use a fraction bar to express division. Evaluate the expression when $a = -9$, $b = 6$, and $c = -1$.**

36. $\dfrac{36}{a}$ **37.** $\dfrac{b}{-6}$ **38.** $\dfrac{a}{3}$ **39.** $\dfrac{-54}{a}$

40. $\dfrac{-81}{a}$ **41.** $\dfrac{84}{c}$ **42.** $\dfrac{66}{-b}$ **43.** $\dfrac{-72}{-c}$

Extended Problem Solving **The table shows how much money a student earned or spent each day for one week.**

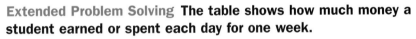

44. Copy the first two columns of the table. Use positive and negative integers to show which amounts represent earnings and which amounts represent money spent.

45. Find the mean of the data.

46. **Interpret** What can you tell about the student's earning and spending habits from the mean?

Day	Amount	Activity
Sunday	$20	Earned money weeding gardens
Monday	$5	Earned money running errands
Tuesday	$3	Bought ice cream
Wednesday	$9	Earned money mowing the lawn
Thursday	$0	No activity
Friday	$21	Bought new jeans
Saturday	$10	Went to a movie

47. **Challenge** You record the daily low temperature for seven days in a row. The mean of the seven temperatures is −2°C. Six of the temperatures are shown below. Find the seventh temperature.

$-4°C \qquad 0°C \qquad -2°C \qquad -3°C \qquad -1°C \qquad 2°C$

48. Graph the points $A(1, 2)$, $B(1, 4)$, $C(3, 6)$, $D(5, 6)$, and $E(7, 4)$ on a coordinate grid. Connect the points to form a polygon. Then classify the polygon. *(Lessons 2.6, 9.6)*

Choose a Strategy **Use a strategy from the list to solve the following problem. Explain your choice of strategy.**

Problem Solving Strategies
- Guess, Check, and Revise
- Perform an Experiment
- Solve a Simpler Problem
- Break into Parts

49. How many square inches of carpet are needed to cover the platform shown?

15 in.
13 in.   12 in.   13 in.
25 in.

Basic Skills **Copy and complete the statement.**

50. 9 and 3 hundredths centimeters = _?_ centimeters

51. 3 and 1 tenth meters = _?_ meters

Test-Taking Practice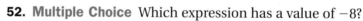

52. Multiple Choice Which expression has a value of -8?

A. $-96 \div (-12)$ **B.** $56 \div (-7)$ **C.** $-32 \div (-4)$ **D.** $56 \div (-8)$

53. Multiple Choice What is the mean of the integers below?

$-16, -13, -9, -4, 4, 8$

F. -8 **G.** -6 **H.** -5 **I.** 5

Mystery Dog

Copy and complete the equations using the numbers listed at the right. Then use the corresponding letters to spell out a type of dog.

1. _?_ $\div (-8) = -6$ **2.** $24 \div$ _?_ $= -4$

3. _?_ $\div (-4) = -9$ **4.** _?_ $\div (-4) = 3$

5. $35 \div (-7) =$ _?_   **6.** $-30 \div$ _?_ $= 2$

Numbers	Letters
48	V
36	Z
-5	L
-6	I
-12	S
-15	A

Technology Activity

Integer Operations

GOAL Use a calculator to perform operations with integers.

Example You can use the [(-)] key to enter negative temperatures.

The average monthly temperatures during the months of December through March in Caribou, Maine, are listed below, to the nearest degree. Find the mean of the temperatures.

$$-10°C \qquad -13°C \qquad -11°C \qquad -4°C$$

Solution

To find the mean of the temperatures, first find the sum of the temperatures. To enter a negative number, use the negation key, [(-)], not the subtraction key, [-].

Keystrokes   **Display**

[(-)] 10 [+] [(-)] 13 [+] [(-)] 11 [+] [(-)] 4 [=]   **−38**

Then divide the sum by the number of temperatures.

Keystrokes   **Display**

[(-)] 38 [÷] 4 [=]   **−9.5**

ANSWER The mean of the temperatures is −9.5°C.

Your turn now Use a calculator to evaluate the expression.

1. $28 - (-937)$ **2.** $402 \times (-59)$ **3.** $-45 + 63 - (-30)$

4. $-33 \times (-74)$ **5.** $810 \div (-45)$ **6.** $-72 \div (-6) + (-93)$

7. Volcanoes New Zealand has three submarine volcanoes whose elevations are −700 meters, −450 meters, and −140 meters. Find the mean of the elevations.

8. Money You have a savings account. During the week you withdraw $75, withdraw $115, deposit $100, and withdraw $55. At the end of the week, do you have more or less money in the account than you had at the beginning of the week? Describe the change in the amount of money.

Draw a Graph

Make a List

Work Backward

Solve a Simpler Problem

Make a Model

Draw a Graph

Break into Parts

Look for a Pattern

Problem You are visiting a city with streets arranged in a grid. You leave your hotel and walk 8 blocks east and 3 blocks north to get to a museum. Then you walk 2 blocks north and 5 blocks west to get to a restaurant. What is the least number of blocks you have to walk to return to your hotel?

❶ Read and Understand

Read the problem carefully.

You want to find the least number of blocks from the restaurant to the hotel.

❷ Make a Plan

Decide on a strategy to use.

One way to solve this problem is by drawing a graph of your route.

❸ Solve the Problem

Reread the problem and draw a graph.

Draw a grid on which each square represents 1 city block. Trace your route and mark key points. Then look for possible routes from the restaurant back to the hotel.

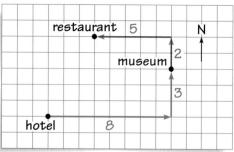

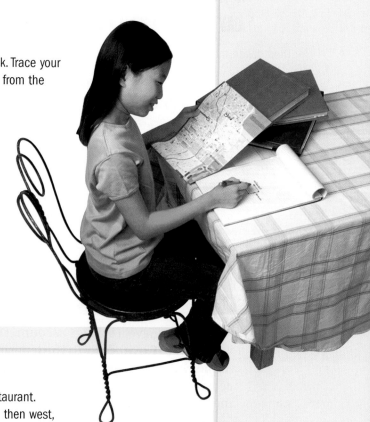

ANSWER There are many possible routes, but the shortest routes are all 8 blocks long.

❹ Look Back

The hotel is 5 blocks south and 3 blocks west of the restaurant. So, you must walk 8 blocks total whether you walk south then west, west then south, or some combination of the two.

Use the strategy *draw a graph*.

1. **Walking** In a city you walk 2 blocks west, 5 blocks north, then 2 blocks east. Will you reach the same location if you instead walk 5 blocks north?

2. **Driving** You want to drive from your house to a restaurant as shown on the map below. Write driving directions for a route that makes the least number of turns possible. You may not drive through the parks.

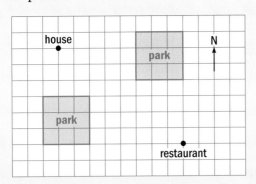

3. **Animation** You are animating Figure *ABCD* with coordinates *A*(3, 0), *B*(3, 2), *C*(0, 2), and *D*(0, 0). As part of the animation, you double each coordinate to create a new Figure *WXYZ*. Is the new figure similar to the original? Explain.

4. **Page Layout** You are placing digital photos on a page in a yearbook and you want them to be congruent. Will a photo with vertices *A*(0, 10), *B*(0, 7), *C*(2, 7), and *D*(2, 10) be congruent to a photo with vertices *W*(6, 3), *X*(6, 0), *Y*(8, 0), and *Z*(8, 6)? Why or why not?

5. **Symmetry** A figure is formed by connecting the points (5, 1), (1, 3), (3, 5), (1, 7), (5, 9), (9, 7), (7, 5), and (9, 3) in order. Identify the lines of symmetry.

Mixed Problem Solving

Use any strategy to solve the problem.

6. **Mystery Digit** If you evaluate the power 9^{20}, what will the ones' digit be?

7. **Oranges** You take an orange and cut it into two pieces. Then you cut each of those pieces in half. You continue this process 3 more times. How many pieces of the orange do you have?

8. **Mystery Number** Your friend is thinking of a number. If you double the number, subtract 5, divide by 3, and add 8, you get 11. What is your friend's number?

9. **Bowling** At an amusement park, you roll three balls up a ramp toward the target. Each ball lands in one of three regions on the target. How many different point totals are possible?

10. **Chess** At the end of each game in a chess tournament, the losing player is required to drop out. If you win the tournament after playing in four games, how many players were there at the beginning of the tournament?

Translations in a Coordinate Plane

BEFORE	▶ Now	WHY?
You graphed points with positive coordinates.	You'll graph points with negative coordinates.	So you can describe the path of a tornado, as in Ex. 26.

coordinate plane, p. 562
quadrant, p. 562
translation, p. 563
image, p. 563

The Coordinate Plane In Chapter 2 you graphed points whose coordinates were positive or zero on a coordinate grid. Now you'll graph points whose coordinates are integers on a **coordinate plane** as shown below.

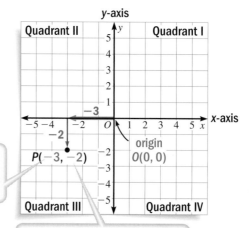

The *x*-coordinate tells you how many units to move to the left or right.

The *y*-coordinate tells you how many units to move up or down.

EXAMPLE 1 Graphing Points

Graph the point and describe its location.

a. To graph $A(-2, 0)$, start at $(0, 0)$.
Move 2 units to the left
and 0 units up.
Point A is on the x-axis.

b. To graph $B(4, -2)$, start at $(0, 0)$.
Move 4 units to the right
and 2 units down.
Point B is in Quadrant IV.

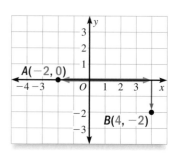

HELP with Review

Need help graphing ordered pairs with positive coordinates? See p. 83.

Your turn now Graph the point and describe its location.

1. $A(0, -3)$ **2.** $B(-2, -1)$ **3.** $C(-1, 2)$ **4.** $D(1, -4)$

Translations In a **translation** , each point of a figure slides the same distance in the same direction. The new figure is the **image** of the original figure.

For example, each point on $\triangle DEF$ has moved 6 units to the right and 3 units up from each point on $\triangle ABC$. $\triangle DEF$ is the image of $\triangle ABC$. Notice that in a translation, the image is congruent to the original figure.

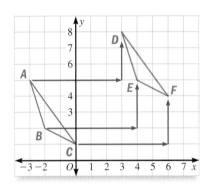

EXAMPLE 2 **Translating a Figure**

Animation In an animation, a kite will be translated 4 units to the right and 5 units down. The images of points A, B, C, and D will be points P, Q, R, and S. Draw the image and give the coordinates of points P, Q, R, and S.

Solution

To draw the image think of sliding the original figure 4 units to the right and 5 units down. You'll get the same image if you add 4 to the x-coordinates and subtract 5 from the y-coordinates.

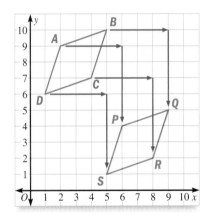

$A(2, 9) \Rightarrow (2 + 4, 9 - 5) \Rightarrow P(6, 4)$

$B(5, 10) \Rightarrow (5 + 4, 10 - 5) \Rightarrow Q(9, 5)$

$C(4, 7) \Rightarrow (4 + 4, 7 - 5) \Rightarrow R(8, 2)$

$D(1, 6) \Rightarrow (1 + 4, 6 - 5) \Rightarrow S(5, 1)$

ANSWER The coordinates are $P(6, 4)$, $Q(9, 5)$, $R(8, 2)$, and $S(5, 1)$.

Your turn now **Graph the points and connect them to form $\triangle ABC$. Then translate the triangle 3 units to the left and 2 units down to form $\triangle DEF$. Give the coordinates of the vertices of $\triangle DEF$.**

5. $A(-4, 1)$, $B(-1, -1)$, $C(2, 1)$ **6.** $A(2, -1)$, $B(-4, 2)$, $C(0, -2)$

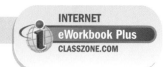
Getting Ready to Practice

Vocabulary **Tell whether the statement is _true_ or _false_.**

1. The *y*-axis is the horizontal axis on a coordinate plane.

2. A quadrant is one of three sections that make up the coordinate plane.

Graph the point and describe its location.

3. *A*(5, −1)   **4.** *B*(0, 3)   **5.** *C*(−4, −3)   **6.** *D*(−3, 3)

7. Graph the points *P*(−5, 4) and *Q*(−2, −2). Connect the points to form a segment. Then translate the segment 1 unit to the left and 2 units down to form $\overline{RS}$. Give the coordinates of the endpoints of $\overline{RS}$.

8. **Guided Problem Solving** In the diagram, the red boat is the image of the blue boat after a translation. How would you describe the translation to a friend?

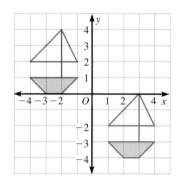

(**1** Find the *x*-coordinate change.

(**2** Find the *y*-coordinate change.

(**3** Describe the translation in words.

Practice and Problem Solving

with Homework

Example	Exercises
1	9-23
2	24-26

Online Resources
CLASSZONE.COM

· More Examples
· eTutorial Plus

Graph the point and describe its location.

9. *A*(5, 0)   **10.** *B*(3, 4)   **11.** *C*(−1, 3)   **12.** *D*(0, −7)

13. *E*(−4, −4)   **14.** *F*(−7, −5)   **15.** *G*(3, −2)   **16.** *H*(−5, 2)

In Exercises 17–22, use the map shown to give the coordinates of the location.

17. school   **18.** library

19. statue   **20.** post office

21. city hall   **22.** store

23. **Writing** Describe in words how to graph a point on a coordinate plane.

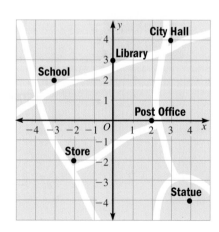

Draw the figure on a coordinate plane. Then translate the figure as described. Give the coordinates of the vertices of the image.

24. △*QRS*: *Q*(−4, −2), *R*(6, 3), *S*(3, −3)

Translation: 2 units to the right and 5 units down to form △*TUV*

25. Rectangle *JKLM*: *J*(3, 4), *K*(4, 3), *L*(−1, −2), *M*(−2, −1)

Translation: 7 units to the left and 4 units down to form rectangle *EFGH*

26. Tornados The graph shows the approximate points where a tornado touched down in South Dakota. Describe the translation between point *A* and point *B*, point *B* and point *C*, and point *A* and point *C*.

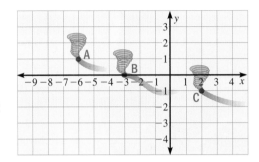

Critical Thinking Identify the quadrant that contains an ordered pair that fits the given description.

27. (positive, positive)

28. (negative, negative)

29. (negative, positive)

30. (positive, negative)

Decide Tell whether the red figure is the image of the blue figure after a translation. If it is, describe the translation. If it is not, explain why not.

31.

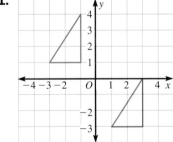

32.

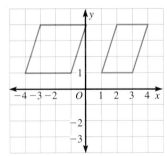

33.

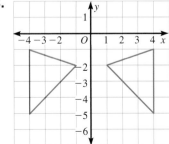

34.

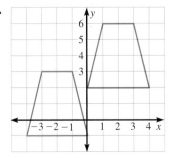

Art

35. **Animation** Translations are often used by animators to show movement. Copy the coordinate plane shown. Complete the next two translations of the musical note to continue the pattern. Then shade the notes to make it look like they are fading away into the background.

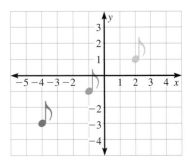

36. Create your own wallpaper border by translating a simple design. Describe your translation in words.

37. **Challenge** Translate the figure shown by subtracting 2.5 from the *x*-coordinate and adding 0.75 to the *y*-coordinate of each vertex. Graph the image and give the coordinates of its vertices.

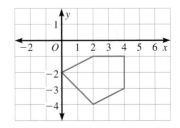

■ **Animation**

When animating music, an animator must find the number of frames needed for an entire song. If the length of a song is 3 minutes and the song uses 24 frames per second, how many frames are needed?

 38. **Algebra** Write the coordinates of the image of the point (*x*, *y*) after a translation of *a* units to the right and *b* units down.

Mixed Review

Write the number in words and as a percent. *(Lesson 8.5)*

39. 0.35   **40.** 0.02   **41.** $\frac{15}{100}$ **42.** $\frac{9.4}{100}$

43. Draw an obtuse scalene triangle. *(Lesson 9.4)*

44. Find the opposite of 6. *(Lesson 11.1)*

Basic Skills **Find the quotient.**

45. 8.4 ÷ 1.2   **46.** 49 ÷ 0.07   **47.** 1.64 ÷ 0.8   **48.** 1.65 ÷ 0.55

Test-Taking Practice

49. **Multiple Choice** In which quadrant is the point (−9, 4)?

     A. I   **B.** II   **C.** III   **D.** IV

50. **Multiple Choice** You translate a point 6 units to the left of the origin, and then 5 units down. Which ordered pair describes the point's new location?

     F. (−6, −5)   **G.** (0, 5)   **H.** (−5, −6)   **I.** (5, −6)

Reflections and Rotations

BEFORE	▶ Now	WHY?
You learned how to recognize translations.	You'll learn how to recognize reflections and rotations.	So you can identify transformations, as in Exs. 11–13.

Photography The photograph appears to show eight pelicans. In fact, there are four pelicans reflected in the line to produce a congruent image. In a **reflection**, the original figure is flipped over a line to produce a congruent mirror image. The line is called the **line of reflection**.

line of reflection

EXAMPLE 1 Identifying Reflections

Tell whether the red figure is a reflection of the blue figure. If it is a reflection, identify the line of reflection.

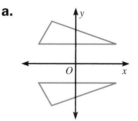

a.

b.

c.

HELP with Solving

In Example 1, you can see that a figure that is not flipped or is not congruent to the original figure cannot be a reflection.

Yes. The line of reflection is the *x*-axis.

No. The figures are not congruent.

No. The image is not flipped.

Your turn now Tell whether the red figure is a reflection of the blue figure. If it is a reflection, identify the line of reflection.

1.

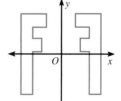

2.

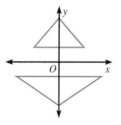

3.

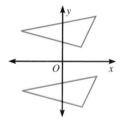

Rotations The blue figure below was turned 90° clockwise about the origin to produce the congruent red image. The diagram illustrates a rotation. In a **rotation**, a figure is rotated through a given angle about a fixed point called the **center of rotation**. The angle is called the **angle of rotation**. In this book, you'll be looking at clockwise rotations.

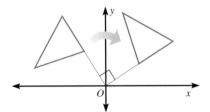

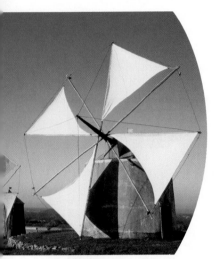

A traditional windmill in Portugal

EXAMPLE 2 **Identifying Rotations**

Tell whether the red figure is a rotation of the blue figure about the origin. If it is a rotation, state the angle of rotation.

a.

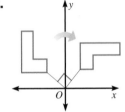

Yes. The figure is rotated 90°.

b.

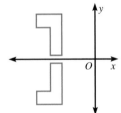

No. This is a flip, not a turn.

c.

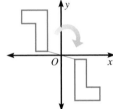

Yes. The figure is rotated 180°.

Transformations A **transformation**, such as a translation, reflection, or rotation, is a movement of a figure on a plane.

EXAMPLE 3 **Identifying Transformations**

HELP with Solving

You can use tracing paper to help you identify transformations. Trace the original figure, then try to slide, flip, or turn it to produce the image.

Tell whether the transformation is a *translation*, a *reflection*, or a *rotation*.

a.

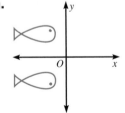

reflection

b.

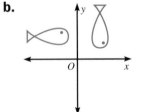

rotation

c.

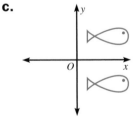

translation

Getting Ready to Practice

1. **Vocabulary** What is the difference between a reflection and a rotation?

Tell whether the transformation is a *translation*, a *reflection*, or a *rotation*.

2.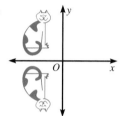

3.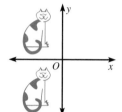

4.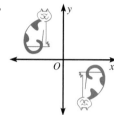

Practice and Problem Solving

Example Exercises

Example	Exercises
1	5–7, 9
2	8–10
3	11–13

Online Resources
CLASSZONE.COM
· More Examples
· eTutorial Plus

Tell whether the red figure is a reflection of the blue figure. If it is, identify the line of reflection. If it is not, explain why not.

5.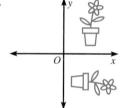

6.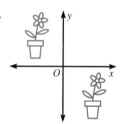

7.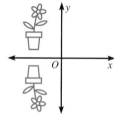

8. Use the figures in Exercises 5–7. Tell whether the red figure is a rotation of the blue figure about the origin. If it is a rotation, state the angle of rotation.

Jewelry In Exercise 9, use photographs *A* and *B*.

9. **Analyze** At a glance, which piece of jewelry has a design that appears to be based on a reflection? Which design appears to be based on a series of rotations about its center?

   A. 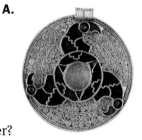   B.

10. Create your own jewelry design based on a series of rotations.

Tell whether the transformation is a *translation*, a *reflection*, or a *rotation*.

11.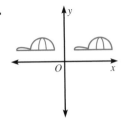

12.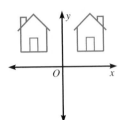

13.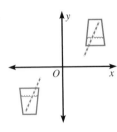

14. Find the Error The red figure at the right is supposed to be a reflection in the *y*-axis of the blue figure. Find and correct the error.

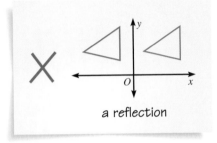

a reflection

Copy and reflect the figure in the indicated axis.

15. *y*-axis

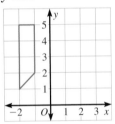

16. *x*-axis

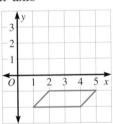

17. *x*-axis

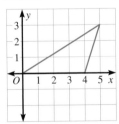

Weaving Ignoring color, tell whether the design can be formed by a reflection. Then tell whether it can be formed by a series of translations or rotations. Describe any transformations that apply.

18.

19.

20.

21.

For each figure, graph the points and connect them to form a polygon. Then tell whether the transformation from Figure 1 to Figure 2 is a *translation*, a *reflection*, or a *rotation*.

22. Figure 1: $A(2, 1)$, $B(5, 2)$, $C(4, 6)$
Figure 2: $D(-2, 1)$, $E(-5, 2)$, $F(-4, 6)$

23. Figure 1: $G(2, 1)$, $H(2, 3)$, $I(4, 4)$, $J(4, 2)$
Figure 2: $K(1, -2)$, $L(3, -2)$, $M(4, -4)$, $N(2, -4)$

24. Critical Thinking The statement $(x, y) \rightarrow (x, -y)$ is a rule for a reflection. For example, the reflection of point $(3, 2)$ is $(3, -2)$. Use the rule to plot several points and their images. What axis is the line of reflection? Write and test a rule for reflecting points in the other axis.

25. Challenge Draw a transformation on a coordinate plane that is a translation, a reflection, and a rotation.

Mixed Review

Divide. Round to the nearest tenth if necessary. *(Lesson 4.6)*

26. $49 \div 0.8$ **27.** $45.6 \div 1.5$ **28.** $21.3 \div 0.03$ **29.** $70.56 \div 2.3$

Find the product or quotient. *(Lessons 11.4, 11.5)*

30. $4(-8)$ **31.** $-6(-9)$ **32.** $-15 \div (-3)$ **33.** $-16 \div 2$

Choose a Strategy Use a strategy from the list to solve the following problem. Explain your choice of strategy.

34. Your friend treated you to lunch and left a tip of $5. How much was the bill if this was a 20% tip?

Problem Solving Strategies
- Guess, Check, and Revise
- Draw a Diagram
- Work Backward
- Break into Parts

Basic Skills **Write the decimal as a fraction or mixed number in simplest form.**

35. 0.6   **36.** 0.75   **37.** 3.08   **38.** 0.204

Test-Taking Practice

39. Extended Response One quadrant of a quilt pattern is shown. What transformation does it show? Complete the other 3 quadrants using a series of 3 reflections. Then complete the other 3 quadrants using a series of 3 rotations. Compare the results.

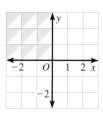

Tessellations

GOAL Identify and construct tessellations.

Word Watch

tessellation, p. 572
regular tessellation, p. 572

A **tessellation** is a repeating pattern of figures that fill a plane with no gaps or overlaps. A **regular tessellation** is made from only one type of regular polygon. For example, the kitchen floor tiles below suggest a regular tessellation.

Not all regular polygons can form regular tessellations.

EXAMPLE 1   Forming Regular Tessellations

Tell whether the polygon can form a regular tessellation.

a. regular pentagon   **b.** regular hexagon

Solution

a. Start with a regular pentagon. Make 2 copies and fit the pentagons together as shown. The gap around their common vertex cannot be filled by a fourth regular pentagon. So, regular pentagons cannot form a regular tessellation.

b. Start with a regular hexagon. Make 6 copies and fit the hexagons together as shown. The resulting pattern will fill a plane with no gaps or overlaps. So, regular hexagons can form a regular tessellation.

Other Tessellations The only regular polygons that form regular tessellations are equilateral triangles, squares, and regular hexagons. Tessellations can also be formed using more than one regular polygon, or one or more nonregular polygons. The polygons may be translated, reflected, or rotated to fill the plane.

EXAMPLE **2** **Forming Tessellations**

Draw a tessellation of the scalene triangle shown.

Solution

> 1 Locate and mark a point at the middle of one side of the triangle. Rotate the triangle 180° about the point to form a parallelogram.

> 2 Translate the parallelogram as shown so that the pattern fills the plane with no gaps or overlaps.

Exercises

1. Draw a regular tessellation of equilateral triangles. Describe any transformations you use.

In Exercises 2–4, use the given triangle and the method in Example 2 to draw a tessellation.

2.

3.

4.

5. You can use any quadrilateral to create a tessellation.

First, locate and mark a point in the middle of one side.

Then, rotate the quadrilateral 180° about the point to form a hexagon.

Finally, translate the hexagons to draw a tessellation.

Draw any quadrilateral and use this method to create a tessellation.

Notebook Review

Review the vocabulary definitions in your notebook.

Copy the review examples in your notebook. Then complete the exercises.

Check Your Definitions

coordinate plane, p. 562   reflection, p. 567   center of rotation, p. 568

quadrant, p. 562   line of reflection, p. 567   angle of rotation, p. 568

translation, p. 563   rotation, p. 568   transformation, p. 568

image, p. 563

Use Your Vocabulary

1. Copy and complete: In a ?, a figure is turned about a fixed point called the ?.

11.4–11.5 Can you multiply and divide integers?

EXAMPLE $-4(-8) = 32$ The product of two negative integers is positive.

$72 \div (-8) = -9$ The quotient of a positive integer and a negative integer is negative.

 Find the product.   **2.** $6(-6)$ **3.** $-7(8)$ **4.** $-5(-9)$

Find the quotient.   **5.** $42 \div (-7)$ **6.** $-18 \div 3$ **7.** $-20 \div (-5)$

11.6 Can you translate in a coordinate plane?

EXAMPLE Translate $\triangle ABC$ 3 units to the left and 4 units up to form $\triangle XYZ$. Give the coordinates of points X, Y, and Z.

ANSWER $A(-1, -1) \Longrightarrow X(-4, 3)$

$B(3, 0) \Longrightarrow Y(0, 4)$

$C(2, -3) \Longrightarrow Z(-1, 1)$

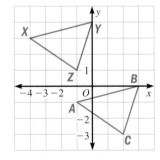

8. The vertices of rectangle $GHIJ$ are $G(-2, -1)$, $H(1, -1)$, $I(1, -3)$, and $J(-2, -3)$. Draw rectangle $GHIJ$ in a coordinate plane. Then translate it 3 units to the left and 3 units up to form rectangle $QRST$. Give the coordinates of points Q, R, S, and T.

11.7 Can you identify transformations?

EXAMPLE Tell whether the transformation is a *translation*, a *reflection*, or a *rotation*.

ANSWER The transformation is a reflection in the *y*-axis.

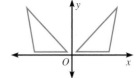

✓ **Tell whether the transformation is a *translation*, a *reflection*, or a *rotation*.**

9.

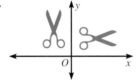

10.

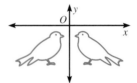

Stop and Think about Lessons 11.4–11.7

11. Writing Explain how to tell if one figure is a translation of another.

12. Critical Thinking Draw a transformation in a coordinate plane that is both a translation and a reflection.

Review Quiz 2

Find the product or quotient.

1. $7(-7)$ **2.** $-3(9)$ **3.** $-5(-8)$ **4.** $-6(0)$

5. $-140 \div 7$ **6.** $-30 \div (-6)$ **7.** $-25 \div (-5)$ **8.** $32 \div (-4)$

9. The vertices of $\triangle ABC$ are $A(-2, -3)$, $B(1, -1)$, and $C(0, 4)$. Draw $\triangle ABC$ in a coordinate plane. Then translate it 5 units to the right and 4 units up to form $\triangle DEF$. Give the coordinates of points D, E, and F.

Tell whether the transformation is a *translation*, a *reflection*, or a *rotation*.

10.

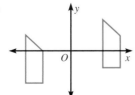

11.

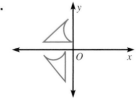

Chapter Review

 Vocabulary

integer, p. 533
positive integer, p. 533
negative integer, p. 533
opposites, p. 534
absolute value, p. 539
coordinate plane, 562

quadrant, p. 562
translation, p. 563
image, p. 563
reflection, p. 567
line of reflection, p. 567
rotation, p. 568

center of rotation,
    p. 568
angle of rotation,
    p. 568
transformation, p. 568

Vocabulary Review

Copy and complete the statement.

1. $\underline{\ ?\ }$ are integers that are less than zero.

2. The $\underline{\ ?\ }$ is divided into four quadrants.

3. The $\underline{\ ?\ }$ of 10 is -10.

4. In a $\underline{\ ?\ }$, each point of a figure slides the same distance in the same direction.

5. In a rotation, the $\underline{\ ?\ }$ is congruent to the original figure.

6. In a reflection, the original figure is flipped over the $\underline{\ ?\ }$ to form a congruent mirror image.

Review Questions

Write the integer that represents the situation. *(Lesson 11.1)*

7. a profit of $25

8. 15 degrees below zero

9. a decrease of 3 centimeters

Find the opposite of the integer. *(Lesson 11.1)*

10. 7

11. -30

12. 0

13. 2

Order the integers from least to greatest. *(Lesson 11.1)*

14. $3, -4, 10, 2, -9$

15. $-8, 0, -13, 6, -6$

16. $5, -15, 7, -5, -7$

17. $-1, 10, -100, 1000, 1$

Find the absolute value of the number. *(Lesson 11.2)*

18. -21

19. 8

20. 100

21. -10

Find the sum. *(Lesson 11.2)*

22. $2 + (-3)$

23. $7 + (-4)$

24. $-1 + 1$

25. $-12 + 2$

26. $-9 + 17$

27. $-8 + (-9)$

28. $-6 + (-11)$

29. $-10 + (-20)$

Find the difference. *(Lesson 11.3)*

30. $2 - 6$ **31.** $5 - 10$ **32.** $-8 - 3$ **33.** $-14 - 4$

34. $15 - (-9)$ **35.** $18 - (-6)$ **36.** $-13 - (-7)$ **37.** $-5 - (-25)$

Find the product. *(Lesson 11.4)*

38. $2(-2)$ **39.** $5(-6)$ **40.** $3(-11)$ **41.** $-9(7)$

42. $-10(4)$ **43.** $-3(-90)$ **44.** $-7(-8)$ **45.** $-2(-12)$

Find the quotient. *(Lesson 11.5)*

46. $-20 \div 2$ **47.** $-35 \div 5$ **48.** $150 \div (-3)$ **49.** $24 \div (-6)$

50. $81 \div (-9)$ **51.** $-12 \div (-4)$ **52.** $-48 \div (-8)$ **53.** $-50 \div (-10)$

Draw the figure in a coordinate plane. Then translate the figure as described. Give the coordinates of the vertices of the image. *(Lesson 11.6)*

54. $\triangle ABC$: $A(-3, 6)$, $B(-1, 4)$, $C(-4, 2)$

Translation: 5 units to the right and 3 units down to form $\triangle DEF$

55. $\triangle HJK$: $H(-2, 3)$, $J(2, 2)$, $K(-1, -1)$

Translation: 4 units to the right and 3 units up to form $\triangle RST$

56. Rhombus $MNPQ$: $M(0, 2)$, $N(3, 0)$, $P(0, -2)$, $Q(-3, 0)$

Translation: 2 units to the left and 2 units down to form rhombus $VXYZ$

Tell whether the transformation is a *translation*, a *reflection*, or a *rotation*. If it is a reflection, identify the line of reflection. If it is a rotation, state the angle of rotation. *(Lesson 11.7)*

57.
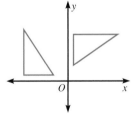

58.
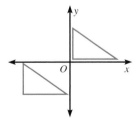

59.
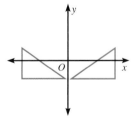

60.
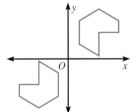

61.
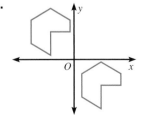

62.
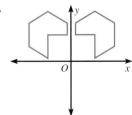

Chapter Test

Write the integer that represents the situation.

1. an increase of $20   **2.** a profit of $5   **3.** a loss of 10 meters   **4.** 15 degrees below 0

Order the integers from least to greatest.

5. $-1, 9, -6, 3, 0$ **6.** $21, -22, 13, -14, 4$ **7.** $-1, 10, -11, -111, 110$

Find the sum.

8. $3 + (-4)$ **9.** $9 + (-9)$ **10.** $15 + (-5)$ **11.** $-7 + 2$

12. $-6 + 11$ **13.** $-1 + (-1)$ **14.** $-8 + (-10)$ **15.** $-12 + (-12)$

Find the difference.

16. $8 - 9$ **17.** $2 - 12$ **18.** $-6 - 10$ **19.** $-15 - 15$

20. $8 - (-18)$ **21.** $5 - (-13)$ **22.** $-14 - (-7)$ **23.** $-10 - (-20)$

Find the product or quotient.

24. $5(-5)$ **25.** $8(-9)$ **26.** $-7(4)$ **27.** $-3(6)$

28. $44 \div (-2)$ **29.** $-54 \div 9$ **30.** $-42 \div (-6)$ **31.** $-10 \div (-10)$

32. Temperature On Monday at noon, the temperature was 23°F. By 9 P.M., the temperature was −4°F. On Tuesday at noon, the temperature was 18°F. By 9 P.M. the temperature was −11°F. On which day did the greater change in temperature occur?

33. Graph the points $A(3, 2)$, $B(4, -4)$, and $C(-2, -3)$. Then translate $\triangle ABC$ 4 units to the left and 5 units up to form $\triangle XYZ$. Give the coordinates of points X, Y, and Z.

Tell whether the transformation is a *translation*, a *reflection*, or a *rotation*. If it is a reflection, identify the line of reflection. If it is a rotation, state the angle of rotation.

34.

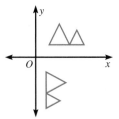

35.

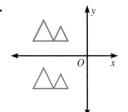

36.

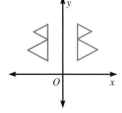

Chapter Standardized Test

Test-Taking Strategy Don't rush through easy questions. You want to avoid making careless errors.

Multiple Choice

1. What number would you use to represent a decrease of 9 in.?

   A. -12 **B.** -9

   C. 3 **D.** 9

2. Which expression has a value of -3?

   F. $9 + (-6)$ **G.** $-9 + 6$

   H. $6 + 9$ **I.** $-6 + (-9)$

3. What is the value of $-5 - 9$?

   A. -14 **B.** -4 **C.** 4 **D.** 14

4. Which expression has a value that is the opposite of 1?

   F. $-20 - 19$ **G.** $-14 + 15$

   H. $3 + (-4)$ **I.** $-9 + 10$

5. What is the value of $-16(-4)$?

   A. -64 **B.** -20 **C.** 20 **D.** 64

6. The table shows the temperatures of three of Saturn's moons. Find the mean of the temperatures.

Mimas	$-328°F$
Enceladus	$-330°F$
Tethys	$-305°F$

   F. $-330°F$ **G.** $-328°F$

   H. $-321°F$ **I.** $25°F$

7. Which of the following is true?

   A. $-19 > 24$ **B.** $-5 < -4$

   C. $45 < -45$ **D.** $-12 > -11$

8. Use the figure shown. If you add 2 to each x-coordinate and subtract 3 from each y-coordinate, what will be the coordinates of the vertices of the image?

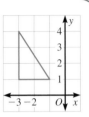

   F. $(-5, 4), (-5, 1), (-3, 1)$

   G. $(-1, 1), (-1, -2), (1, -2)$

   H. $(-1, 1), (-1, -4), (1, -4)$

   I. $(-6, 6), (-6, 3), (-4, 3)$

9. Which transformation shows a rotation?

   A.   **B.**

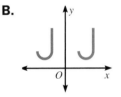

   C.   **D.**

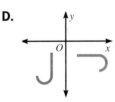

Short Response

10. The base of a 15 foot wall is at an elevation of -7 feet relative to sea level. Write and evaluate an addition expression to represent the elevation of the top of the wall.

Extended Response

11. Graph the points $A(-2, 4)$, $B(-3, 1)$, and $C(-1, 1)$ and connect them. Translate $\triangle ABC$ 4 units to the right to form $\triangle XYZ$. Give the coordinates of each vertex. Describe a different transformation of $\triangle ABC$ to $\triangle XZY$.

12

Equations and Functions

Chapter Warm-Up Game

Review skills you need for this chapter in this game. Work with a partner.

Key Skill:
Evaluating expressions

BEFORE

In previous chapters you've...

- Used geometry formulas
- Evaluated expressions

Now

In Chapter 12 you'll study...

- Writing expressions and equations
- Solving equations
- Representing functions using tables, equations, and graphs

WHY?

So you can solve real-world problems about...

- the Grand Canyon, p. 586
- shopping, p. 589
- cheerleading, p. 599
- hurricanes, p. 601
- giant pandas, p. 605

Internet Preview
CLASSZONE.COM

- eEdition Plus Online
- eWorkbook Plus Online
- eTutorial Plus Online
- State Test Practice
- More Examples

EXPRESSION RACE

MATERIALS

- *Expression Race* game board
- 1 number cube
- 1 place marker for each player

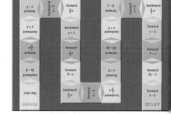

PREPARE Each player puts a place marker on the START space. Take turns. On your turn, follow the steps on page 581.

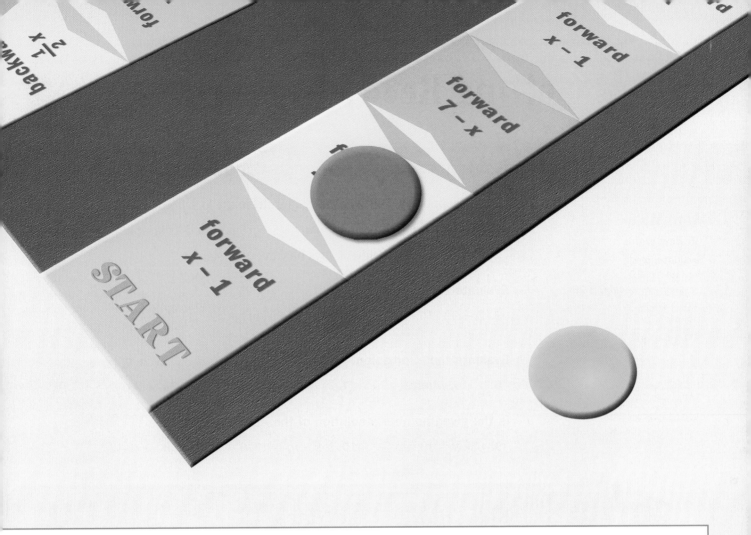

backward
$\frac{x}{2}$

forward
$x - 1$

forward
$7 - x$

forward
$x - 1$

START

forward
$x - 1$

① ROLL the number cube. The number you roll is the *x*-value for the expression on the space your marker is on.

② EVALUATE the expression on your space for the *x*-value you rolled. If the result is a fraction, round to the nearest whole number.

③ MOVE your marker forward or backward the same number of spaces as your result from Step 2.

HOW TO WIN

Be the first player to land on the FINISH space, or be closest to the FINISH space after a set period of time.

Stop *and* Think

1. **Writing** If you are on the space labeled "Forward $13 - 2x$," what is the best number to roll? Explain your thinking.

2. **Critical Thinking** If you rolled a 2 on every turn, would you ever get to the FINISH space? Explain why or why not. What if you rolled a 3 on every turn?

Getting Ready to Learn

Review What You Need to Know

Word Watch

Review Words

evaluate, p. 21
variable, p. 29
variable expression, p. 29
equation, p. 36
solution, p. 36

Using Vocabulary **Tell whether the statement is *true* or *false*.**

1. The letter a in the equation $2a + 5 = 15$ is called a variable.

2. A variable expression always has an equal sign.

Evaluate the expression. *(p. 21)*

3. $3 + 9 \times 10$ **4.** $15 \div (14 - 11) + 42$ **5.** $\dfrac{12 \times 5}{30 \div 3}$

Evaluate the expression. *(p. 29)*

6. $t + 4$, when $t = 20$ **7.** $z \div 4$, when $z = 16$ **8.** $7p$, when $p = 8$

Is the given number a solution of the equation? *(p. 36)*

9. $6 + x = 19$; 11   **10.** $24 - m = 17$; 6   **11.** $5n = 60$; 12

You should include material that appears on a notebook like this in your own notes.

Know How to Take Notes

Making a Flow Chart You can show a mathematical process in your notes using a flow chart like the one below for the order of operations.

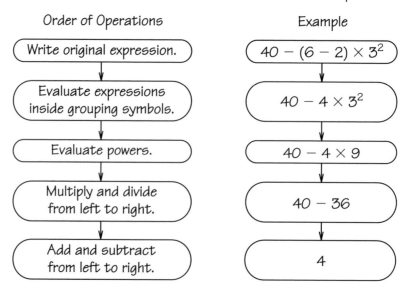

In Lesson 12.6, you can use a flow chart to remember the steps for identifying linear equations.

582

LESSON 12.1

Writing Expressions and Equations

BEFORE	▶ Now	WHY?
You evaluated numerical and variable expressions.	You'll write variable expressions and equations.	So you can find the time left on a videotape, as in Ex. 38.

In the Real World

Word Watch

Review Words
variable expression, p. 29
equation, p. 36

Art Show Your school's art show has *x* pieces in it. You expect to add 3 pieces. What will be the total number of pieces in the show? You will see a way to express the total in Example 1.

To write phrases and sentences as variable expressions or equations, look for key words that indicate addition, subtraction, multiplication, or division.

Addition	Subtraction	Multiplication	Division
plus	minus	times	divided by
the sum of	the difference of	the product of	the quotient of
increased by	decreased by	multiplied by	
total	fewer than	of	
more than	less than		
added to	subtracted from		

EXAMPLE 1 Expressions: Adding and Subtracting

Write the phrase as an expression. Let *x* represent the number.

Phrase	Expression
3 pieces **added to** *x* pieces in the show	$x + 3$
The sum of 4 and a number	$4 + x$
The difference of 12 and a number	$12 - x$
9 **less than** the number of boys	$x - 9$

Your turn now Write the phrase as a variable expression.

1. 16 decreased by a number *d*

2. The total of 10 and a number *n*

3. A number *h* increased by 15

4. 10 subtracted from a number *m*

5. Four fewer than a number *g*

6. Seven more than a number *k*

Watch Out!

Order is important with subtraction and division. "The quotient of a number and 6" means $\frac{y}{6}$, not $\frac{6}{y}$.

EXAMPLE 2 **Expressions: Multiplying and Dividing**

Write the phrase as an expression. Let y represent the number.

Phrase	Expression
The product of 5 and the number of girls	$5 \cdot y$, or $5y$
8 multiplied by a number	$y \cdot 8$, or $8y$
The quotient of a number and 6	$\frac{y}{6}$
24 divided by the number of hours	$\frac{24}{y}$

Writing Equations To translate a sentence into an equation, look for key words like *is* or *equals* to find the place for the equal sign.

EXAMPLE 3 **Writing Simple Equations**

Write the sentence as an equation.

Sentence	Equation
A number x minus 5 **is** 12.	$x - 5 = 12$
15 times a number y **is** 75.	$15y = 75$

EXAMPLE 4 **Modeling a Situation**

Restaurant Three friends share the cost of a dinner equally. The cost of the dinner is $27. Write a multiplication equation that you could use to find the amount a that each friend pays.

Solution

Number of friends • **Amount each pays** = Total cost

$$3a = 27$$

Your turn now In Exercises 7–10, write the sentence as an equation.

7. A number n added to 4 is 11.   **8.** The quotient of x and 96 is 8.

9. A number p times 3 is 36.   **10.** Twelve minus a number q is 2.

11. Today's high temperature of 59°F is 3°F less than yesterday's high temperature t. Write a subtraction equation you could use to find t.

Getting Ready to Practice

1. Vocabulary The phrase *decreased by* represents the operation of __?__.

Write the phrase as an expression. Let *x* represent the number.

2. 13 more than a number

3. A number times 7

4. A number divided by 16

5. 21 minus a number

In Exercises 6–9, write the sentence as an equation.

6. A number y added to 4 is 7.

7. A number h divided by 6 is 2.

8. 6 times a number t is 42.

9. The difference of s and 32 is 6.

10. Test Scores You have 29 correct answers on a test, which is four more correct answers than Sara has. Write an equation you could use to find s, the number of correct answers Sara has.

Practice and Problem Solving

Write the phrase as an expression. Let *x* represent the number.

11. A number divided by 9

12. A number decreased by 4

13. 16 subtracted from a number

14. The total of 17 and a number

15. 20 multiplied by a number

16. The quotient of a number and 2

17. A number increased by 18

18. 10 minus a number

19. 27 less than a number

20. The product of 6 and a number

21. Writing Explain how the phrases representing the expressions $y - 2$ and $2 - y$ are different.

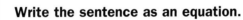

Write the sentence as an equation.

22. 11 fewer than a number k is 3.

23. A number n plus 6 is 30.

24. A number c times 15 is 90.

25. 32 divided by a number r is 2.

26. The sum of 9 and q is 15.

27. The product of x and 3 is 123.

28. The quotient of 50 and w is 10.

29. A number t decreased by 4 is 26.

Write a phrase for the variable expression.

30. $n + 4$ **31.** $y - 7$ **32.** $8r$ **33.** $\dfrac{d}{3}$

HELP with **Homework**

Example	Exercises
1	11–21
2	11–20
3	22–29
4	34–38

Online Resources
CLASSZONE.COM

· More Examples
· eTutorial Plus

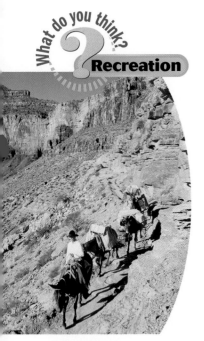

Recreation

Grand Canyon

In the Grand Canyon, the temperature increases as you go down. When it is 75°F at the top of the canyon, it might be 110°F at the bottom. What is the change in the temperature?

Interpret **In Exercises 34–37, match the situation with the equation that describes it.**

A. $x - 8 = 24$ **B.** $8x = 24$ **C.** $8 + x = 24$ **D.** $\dfrac{x}{8} = 24$

34. You have $8. How much more do you need to make a $24 purchase?

35. You pay $24 for shoes after an $8 discount. What was the original price?

36. The total cost of tickets for a concert is split equally among 8 friends, with each paying $24. What is the total cost of the tickets?

37. You earn $24 for eight hours of work. How much do you earn per hour?

38. **Videotape** You record 95 minutes of material on a videotape. The tape can fit 120 minutes of material. Write an addition equation you could use to find m, the number of minutes left on the tape.

39. **Grand Canyon** In Grand Canyon National Park, the elevation of the North Kaibab trailhead is 8241 feet. The elevation of Bright Angel Camp is 2400 feet. Write two equations you could use to find c, the difference in elevation between the trailhead and Bright Angel Camp.

Challenge **Write a sentence about a real-world situation that could be represented by the equation.**

40. $6 + y = 20$ **41.** $k - 25 = 60$ **42.** $4m = 32$ **43.** $\dfrac{r}{5} = 25$

Mixed Review

44. Graph each figure. Then tell whether Figure 2 is a reflection of Figure 1. If it is a reflection, identify the line of reflection. *(Lesson 11.7)*

Figure 1: $A(-1, 1)$, $B(-3, 0)$, $C(-3, 4)$ **Figure 2:** $P(1, 1)$, $Q(3, 0)$, $R(3, 4)$

Basic Skills **Solve the equation using mental math.**

45. $d + 6 = 15$ **46.** $45 - f = 10$ **47.** $8g = 88$ **48.** $48 \div x = 6$

Test-Taking Practice

49. **Multiple Choice** Which of the following can represent "twelve more than seventeen bicycles"?

   A. $17 - 12$ **B.** $17 + 12$ **C.** $12 > 17$ **D.** $17 \div 12$

50. **Multiple Choice** Nathan has 12 video games. He receives more for his birthday. He now has 28 video games. Which equation could you use to find v, the number of video games he receives for his birthday?

   F. $12 + v = 28$ **G.** $12 - v = 28$ **H.** $12v = 28$ **I.** $\dfrac{28}{v} = 12$

GOAL

Use algebra tiles to solve addition equations.

MATERIALS

• algebra tiles

Algebra Tiles

You can solve some simple equations using these two types of algebra tiles.

x-tile

Represents the variable *x*.

1-tile

Represents positive 1.

Explore **Use algebra tiles to solve the equation *x* + 3 = 7.**

1 Represent the equation using an *x*-tile and ten 1-tiles.

2 To solve the equation, you must get the *x*-tile by itself on one side. You can take away three 1-tiles from each side. By taking away the same amount on each side, you keep the two sides equal.

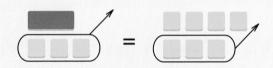

3 Notice that one *x*-tile remains on the left side and four 1-tiles remain on the right side. So, *x* = 4.

Your turn now **Use algebra tiles to solve the equation.**

1. $x + 2 = 3$ **2.** $x + 3 = 6$ **3.** $x + 1 = 4$ **4.** $x + 4 = 8$

5. $1 + x = 7$ **6.** $4 + x = 7$ **7.** $2 + x = 9$ **8.** $3 + x = 5$

Stop *and* **Think**

9. Writing Describe how you could solve equations like those in Exercises 1–8 without using algebra tiles.

Solving Addition Equations

BEFORE	▶ Now	WHY?
You solved equations using mental math.	You'll solve one-step addition equations.	So you can find the cost of time on a parking meter, as in Ex. 25.

Word Watch

Review Words

variable, p. 29
solution, p. 36
solve, p. 37

Algebra Tiles One way to solve addition equations is to use algebra tiles.

An x-tile represents the variable x.   **A 1-tile represents positive 1.**

You can model an equation by imagining that tiles are placed on a balance scale, as shown below.

$$x + 2 = 4$$

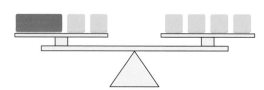

You can solve the equation by removing tiles until the x-tile is by itself on one side. If you remove tiles from one side, you must remove the same number of tiles from the other side to keep the scale balanced.

EXAMPLE 1 **Solving Equations Using Algebra Tiles**

Use algebra tiles to solve x + 2 = 4.

① Represent the equation using algebra tiles.

② Take away two 1-tiles from each side.

③ The remaining tiles show that the value of x is 2.

ANSWER The solution is 2.

Your turn now Use algebra tiles to solve the equation.

1. $x + 1 = 5$ **2.** $x + 3 = 9$ **3.** $4 + x = 4$ **4.** $7 + x = 8$

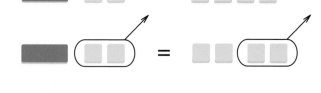

The idea behind the algebra tile method can be used to solve equations with numbers that are hard to model with tiles.

Solving Addition Equations

To solve an addition equation, subtract the same number from each side so that the variable is by itself on one side.

EXAMPLE 2 Solving an Addition Equation

Solve the equation $y + 25 = 140$.

$$
\begin{array}{rl}
y + 25 = \ 140 & \text{Write the original equation.} \\
\underline{-\ 25 \quad -\ 25} & \text{Subtract 25 from each side.} \\
y \quad\ = \ 115 & \text{Simplify.}
\end{array}
$$

HELP with **Solving**

After solving an equation, you should always check your solution.

$$
\begin{array}{rl}
\checkmark \ \textbf{Check} \ \ y + 25 = 140 & \text{Write the original equation.} \\
115 + 25 \stackrel{?}{=} 140 & \text{Substitute 115 for } y. \\
140 = 140\checkmark & \text{Solution checks.}
\end{array}
$$

EXAMPLE 3 Using an Addition Equation

Shopping You buy some clothing that costs $17.45. What is the amount of change c that the clerk should give you if you pay with a $20 bill?

Solution

$$
\begin{array}{ll}
\text{Cost + \textbf{Change} = Amount paid} & \text{Write a verbal model.} \\
\begin{array}{rl}
17.45 + c = & 20.00 \\
\underline{-\ 17.45 \qquad\ -\ 17.45} \\
c = & 2.55
\end{array} &
\begin{array}{l}
\text{Write an equation.} \\
\text{Subtract 17.45 from each side.} \\
\text{Simplify.}
\end{array}
\end{array}
$$

ANSWER The clerk should give you $2.55 in change.

Your turn now Solve the equation. Then check the solution.

5. $p + 24 = 88$ **6.** $15 + q = 105$ **7.** $r + 39 = 76$

8. $s + 2.5 = 10.7$ **9.** $8.35 + t = 10.55$ **10.** $u + 1.85 = 50$

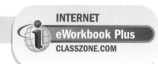
Getting Ready to Practice

Vocabulary **Tell whether the given number is a solution of the equation.**

1. $x + 3 = 8; 5$ **2.** $x + 1.1 = 3.7; 2.6$ **3.** $3.5 + x = 3.5; 3.5$

Solve the equation. Then check the solution.

4. $x + 5 = 7$ **5.** $m + 9 = 15$ **6.** $6 + y = 6$ **7.** $15 + p = 50$

8. Guided Problem Solving A video game has 16 levels. You have reached level 5. Write and solve an addition equation to find the number of levels you have left.

   (1 What is the unknown value? Choose a variable to represent it.

   (2 Write an equation using the information in the problem.

   (3 Solve the equation. Check your solution.

Practice and Problem Solving

Solve the equation.

9. $x + 1 = 8$ **10.** $x + 5 = 11$ **11.** $x + 2 = 2$ **12.** $4 + x = 9$

13. $10 + x = 15$ **14.** $6 + x = 13$ **15.** $4 + x = 20$ **16.** $x + 3 = 18$

17. $a + 13 = 26$ **18.** $b + 22 = 40$ **19.** $d + 27 = 34$ **20.** $c + 35 = 35$

21. $42 + g = 70$ **22.** $17 + h = 66$ **23.** $j + 68 = 100$ **24.** $k + 8 = 73$

25. Parking Meter You have 10 minutes left at a parking meter. After you put in a quarter, you have 25 minutes left. Write and solve an addition equation to find q, the number of minutes a quarter is worth.

26. Find the Error Describe and correct the error in the solution of the equation $b + 6 = 18$.

$$
\begin{array}{rcl}
b + 6 &=& 18 \\
+ 6 &=& + 6 \\
\hline
b &=& 24
\end{array}
$$

The solution is 24.

HELP with **Homework**

Example	Exercises
1	9–16
2	9–24, 26
3	25

Online Resources
CLASSZONE.COM

· More Examples
· eTutorial Plus

Estimation **Estimate the solution of the equation.**

27. $x + 3\frac{6}{7} = 27\frac{24}{25}$ **28.** $y + 10\frac{1}{12} = 24\frac{13}{15}$

Choose a Method Solve the equation. Tell whether you used *algebra tiles*, *mental math*, or *paper and pencil*.

29. $x + 3 = 9$ **30.** $y + 25 = 80$ **31.** $z + 5.6 = 8.3$

32. $q + 8 = 12$ **33.** $20 + p = 37$ **34.** $0.08 + r = 1.28$

35. $m + 3.7 = 9.9$ **36.** $n + 0.8 = 1.5$ **37.** $9.5 + d = 14.3$

38. $1.4 + a = 2.2$ **39.** $0.3 + b = 2$ **40.** $4 + c = 4$

 41. Geometry The perimeter of the triangle shown is 11.1 kilometers. Write and solve an addition equation to find the length of the third side.

Extended Problem Solving Lois is training for a marathon. Her goal is to travel 28 miles for the week.

42. Mental Math Lois travels 6 miles on Monday, 8 miles on Wednesday, and 6 miles on Thursday. How many miles has she traveled so far?

43. Use Exercise 42 to write an addition equation you could use to find the number of miles Lois has left to travel to meet her goal.

44. Explain Solve the equation you wrote in Exercise 43. Explain how to check your solution.

Challenge Solve the equation.

45. $x + 5 = 4$ **46.** $10 + x = -4$ **47.** $3 + x = -7$ **48.** $-3 + x = 9$

Mixed Review

49. Tell whether 97 is *prime* or *composite*. Explain. *(Lesson 5.1)*

50. Write the sentence as an equation: The difference of 26 and a number c is 19. *(Lesson 12.1)*

Basic Skills Find the sum.

51. $12.4 + 5.6$ **52.** $4.7 + 9.9$ **53.** $0.25 + 2.09$ **54.** $2.4 + 23.05$

Test-Taking Practice

55. Multiple Choice What is the solution of $12 + x = 21$?

    A. 6   **B.** 9   **C.** 11   **D.** 33

56. Short Response Write and solve an equation for the sentence: A number x added to 33 is 50. Explain how you found your solution.

Solving Subtraction Equations

12.3

BEFORE

You solved one-step addition equations.

▶ **Now**

You'll solve one-step subtraction equations.

WHY?

So you can find the number of berries in a carton, as in Ex. 24.

In the Real World

Word Watch

Review Words
variable, p. 29
solution, p. 36
solve, p. 37

Collecting You gave away 2 scallop shells from your collection and now you have 5 scallop shells left. How many scallop shells did you have at the start?

An equation that represents this situation is $x - 2 = 5$, where x is the number of scallop shells you had in your collection at the start.

EXAMPLE 1 **Working Backward**

One way to solve the equation above to find the number of scallop shells you had in your collection at the start is to work backward.

After giving away 2 scallop shells, you have 5 scallop shells. $x - 2 = 5$

To find the value x you had before subtracting 2, you can add 2 to *undo* the subtraction. $5 + 2 = x$

ANSWER You had 7 scallop shells in your collection at the start.

✓**Check** $x - 2 = 5$ Write the original equation.

$7 - 2 \stackrel{?}{=} 5$ Substitute 7 for x.

$5 = 5$✓   Solution checks.

Isolating the Variable You can also solve the equation in Example 1 by getting the variable by itself as you did in Lesson 12.2. You would write the following steps.

$$\begin{array}{rcr} x - 2 &=& 5 \\ +2 & & +2 \\ \hline x &=& 7 \end{array}$$

By adding 2 to each side of the equation, you undo the subtraction while keeping the two sides of the equation equal to each other.

Solving Subtraction Equations

To solve a subtraction equation, add the same number to each side so that the variable is by itself on one side.

EXAMPLE 2 **Solving Subtraction Equations**

Solve the equation.

a. $14 = n - 6$ **b.** $m - 3.1 = 11.95$

Solution

a. In this equation, the variable is on the right side of the equation.

$$14 = n - 6 \qquad \text{Write the original equation.}$$
$$\underline{+ 6 \qquad + 6} \qquad \text{Add 6 to each side.}$$
$$20 = n \qquad \text{Simplify.}$$

b.
$$m - 3.1 = 11.95 \qquad \text{Write the original equation.}$$
$$\underline{+ 3.1 \qquad + 3.1} \qquad \text{Add 3.1 to each side.}$$
$$m \quad = \quad 15.05 \qquad \text{Simplify.}$$

Watch Out!

Line up decimal points correctly before adding decimals.

WRONG	RIGHT
11.95	11.95
+ 3.1	+ 3.1
12.26	15.05

EXAMPLE 3 **Using a Subtraction Equation**

Elevator You are riding an elevator. You go down 14 floors and exit on the 23rd floor. On what floor did you enter the elevator?

Solution

Let f represent the number of the floor on which you entered the elevator.

$$f - 14 = 23 \qquad \text{Write an equation.}$$
$$\underline{+ 14 \qquad + 14} \qquad \text{Add 14 to each side.}$$
$$f \quad = \quad 37 \qquad \text{Simplify.}$$

ANSWER You entered the elevator on the 37th floor.

Your turn now **Solve the equation. Then check the solution.**

1. $q - 7 = 2$ **2.** $25 = s - 17$ **3.** $3.2 = r - 2.1$

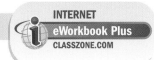

Getting Ready to Practice

1. **Vocabulary** When solving an addition or a subtraction equation, you should get the ? by itself on one side of the equation.

Tell whether the given number is a solution of the equation.

2. $x - 3 = 9$; 6

3. $x - 8 = 8$; 0

4. $x - 7.1 = 10.4$; 17.5

Solve the equation. Then check the solution.

5. $p - 2 = 7$

6. $z - 1 = 4$

7. $16 = m - 6$

8. **Guided Problem Solving** Your class is planting trees in parks. After planting 17 trees, the class has 14 trees left to plant. Write and solve a subtraction equation to find the number of trees the class started with.

(1 What is the unknown value? Choose a variable to represent it.

(2 Write a subtraction equation using the information in the problem.

(3 Solve the equation. Check your solution.

Practice and Problem Solving

Solve the equation.

9. $w - 7 = 6$

10. $y - 8 = 5$

11. $z - 2 = 1$

12. $p - 3 = 0$

13. $q - 5 = 10$

14. $r - 9 = 7$

15. $b - 4 = 19$

16. $d - 6 = 12$

17. $c - 0 = 11$

18. $3 = m - 15$

19. $7 = n - 8$

20. $22 = p - 12$

21. $20 = g - 13$

22. $25 = h - 19$

23. $39 = j - 14$

24. **Berries** You eat 9 strawberries from a carton. There are 12 strawberries remaining in the carton. How many strawberries were in the full carton? Write and solve a subtraction equation for the situation.

25. **Writing** Compare solving a subtraction equation to solving an addition equation. How are the steps alike? How are they different?

Number Sense **Without solving the equations, tell which equation has a greater solution. Explain.**

26. $x - 50 = 3271$ or $x - 500 = 3271$

27. $x - 368 = 532$ or $x - 368 = 475$

HELP with Homework

Example	Exercises
1	9–17
2	9–23, 25, 30–35
3	24

Online Resources
CLASSZONE.COM
· More Examples
· eTutorial Plus

Compare In Exercises 28 and 29, write and solve two different subtraction equations for the situation. Compare the solutions.

28. **Paper Route** You are delivering newspapers on your paper route. You have to deliver to 8 more houses. You have already delivered to 21 houses. How many houses are on your route?

29. **Sports** You have lost track of how many softball games your team played this season. You know your team won 12 games. Your friend reminds you that your team lost 9 games. How many games did your team play?

Solve the equation.

30. $x - 4.2 = 7.1$

31. $x - 2.8 = 6.5$

32. $13.4 = x - 1.8$

33. $x - 17.06 = 13$

34. $x - 5.97 = 3.86$

35. $6.02 = x - 9.3$

36. $a - 1\frac{1}{3} = 2\frac{1}{6}$

37. $b - \frac{5}{8} = 3\frac{1}{4}$

38. $c - 2\frac{2}{3} = 3\frac{3}{4}$

Challenge **Solve the equation.**

39. $x - 15 = -2$

40. $x - 10 = -20$

41. $x - (-9) = -17$

Mixed Review

Plot the point. Name the quadrant that contains the point. (Lesson 11.6)

42. $A(4, -5)$

43. $B(-3, 2)$

44. $C(-6, -1)$

Solve the equation. (Lesson 12.2)

45. $x + 4 = 6$

46. $b + 5 = 8$

47. $9 + p = 17$

Basic Skills **Find the quotient.**

48. $456 \div 57$

49. $252 \div 28$

50. $64.6 \div 9.5$

Test-Taking Practice

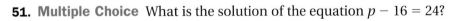

51. **Multiple Choice** What is the solution of the equation $p - 16 = 24$?

   A. 8   **B.** 12   **C.** 32   **D.** 40

52. **Multiple Choice** Which equation does *not* have 8 as a solution?

   F. $t - 1 = 7$ **G.** $t - 5 = 3$ **H.** $t - 6 = 14$ **I.** $0 = t - 8$

Notebook Review

Review the vocabulary definitions in your notebook.

Copy the review examples in your notebook. Then complete the exercises.

Check Your Definitions

variable expression, p. 29

equation, p. 36
solution, p. 36

solve, p. 37

Use Your Vocabulary

1. Explain the difference between a variable expression and an equation.

12.1 Can you write variable expressions and equations?

 EXAMPLE

Words	Algebra
A number y increased by 8	$y + 8$
The difference of 2 and a number y	$2 - y$
The product of 10 and a number y is 30.	$10y = 30$

☑ **Write the phrase as an expression. Let x represent the number.**

2. A number divided by 7
3. A number times 6
4. 80 less than a number
5. 25 plus a number
6. Write the sentence as an equation: Forty more than a number p is 62.

12.2–12.3 Can you solve addition and subtraction equations?

 EXAMPLE

a.
$$13 = f + 8$$
$$\underline{-8 \quad\quad -8}$$
$$5 = f$$

b.
$$g - 4 = 11$$
$$\underline{+4 \quad\quad +4}$$
$$g = 15$$

☑ **Solve the equation.**

7. $x + 8 = 15$
8. $10 + y = 30$
9. $32 = a + 17$
10. $b + 0.7 = 1.9$
11. $23.2 + c = 40$
12. $15 = q - 5$
13. $r - 10 = 11$
14. $s - 25 = 18$
15. $5.7 = t - 24$

16. **Writing** Explain how writing an equation to model a situation is similar to translating one language into another language.

17. **Critical Thinking** Write two different addition or subtraction equations that have the same solution.

Review Quiz 1

Write the phrase as an expression. Let *x* represent the number.

1. A number decreased by 5
2. The total of 14 and a number
3. A number multiplied by 9
4. The quotient of a number and 10

Write the sentence as an equation. Let *y* represent the number.

5. 8 more than a number is 35.
6. 48 divided by a number is 6.
7. 3 times a number is 0.
8. 10 less than a number is 10.

Solve the equation.

9. $x + 15 = 29$
10. $3 + y = 14$
11. $24 = f + 17$
12. $d - 5 = 9$
13. $z - 14 = 2$
14. $12 = a - 12$

15. **Lizards** A Komodo dragon can grow to be 120 inches long. Suppose one of these lizards is 92 inches long. Write and solve an addition equation to find *x*, the number of inches it still needs to grow to be 120 inches long.

Symbologic

Use the first two symbol equations to complete the third equation.

$$\square + \bullet + \bullet = \triangle + \bullet$$
$$\square + \triangle + \square = \bullet + \bullet$$
$$\square + \square + \square = \underline{\ ?\ }$$

Solving Multiplication and Division Equations

BEFORE

You solved one-step addition and subtraction equations.

▶ **Now**

You'll solve multiplication and division equations.

WHY?

So you can make predictions about a hurricane's travel time, as in Ex. 33.

Word Watch

Review Words

variable, p. 29
solution, p. 36
solve, p. 37

Activity You can use algebra tiles to solve a multiplication equation.

① Use algebra tiles to represent the equation $2x = 6$.

② Divide the x-tiles into two equal groups. Divide the 1-tiles into the same number of equal groups.

③ Match a group on the left with a group on the right. Explain how this tells you the solution of the equation.

Use algebra tiles to solve the equation.

1. $2x = 8$ **2.** $3x = 9$ **3.** $4x = 12$

The activity shows how you can solve a multiplication equation using algebra tiles. You can also use division to solve a multiplication equation.

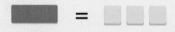 **EXAMPLE 1** **Solving a Multiplication Equation**

Solve the equation $5x = 20$.

$5x = 20$	Write the original equation.
$\dfrac{5x}{5} = \dfrac{20}{5}$	Divide each side by 5.
$x = 4$	Simplify.

HELP with **Review**

As you saw on page 253, the fraction bar is a way to express division. You will write division using a fraction bar when you solve multiplication and division equations.

Your turn now Solve the equation. Then check the solution.

1. $4n = 20$ **2.** $3m = 15$ **3.** $24 = 2p$ **4.** $65 = 5q$

Solving Multiplication and Division Equations

You can use multiplication and division to undo each other when trying to get the variable by itself on one side of an equation.

Multiplication Equations To solve a multiplication equation, *divide* each side by the number the variable is multiplied by.

Division Equations To solve a division equation, *multiply* each side by the divisor.

EXAMPLE 2 Solving a Division Equation

Solve the equation $\frac{x}{7} = 3$.

$\frac{x}{7} = 3$ Write the original equation.

$7 \cdot \frac{x}{7} = 7 \cdot 3$ Multiply each side by 7.

$x = 21$ Simplify.

EXAMPLE 3 Using an Equation

Cheerleading In cheerleader tryouts, 27 students are placed in groups of 3 to make human pyramids. Write and solve a multiplication equation to find *n*, the number of pyramids the 27 students form.

Solution

$27 = 3n$ Write an equation.

$\frac{27}{3} = \frac{3n}{3}$ Divide each side by 3.

$9 = n$ Simplify.

ANSWER The 27 students will form 9 pyramids.

Your turn now Solve the equation. Then check the solution.

5. $\frac{a}{2} = 7$ **6.** $\frac{b}{5} = 6$ **7.** $45 = \frac{c}{3}$ **8.** $12 = \frac{d}{8}$

INTERNET
eWorkbook Plus
CLASSZONE.COM

Getting Ready to Practice

1. Vocabulary You can solve a multiplication equation by _?_. You can solve a division equation by _?_.

Solve the equation. Then check the solution.

2. $5x = 35$ **3.** $14 = 7y$ **4.** $14 = \dfrac{a}{2}$ **5.** $\dfrac{c}{6} = 2$

In Exercises 6 and 7, write the sentence as an equation. Then solve the equation.

6. Five times a number x is 105. **7.** 24 is a number c divided by 2.

8. Pretzels You purchase 8 soft pretzels for your friends. You pay $14. Write a multiplication equation you can use to find the cost of a soft pretzel. Then solve the equation.

Practice and Problem Solving

Copy and complete the solution.

9. $5x = 10$

$$\dfrac{5x}{?} = \dfrac{10}{?}$$

$$x = \underline{?}$$

10. $27 = 9x$

$$\dfrac{27}{?} = \dfrac{9x}{?}$$

$$\underline{?} = x$$

11. $\dfrac{x}{9} = 4$

$$\underline{?} \cdot \dfrac{x}{9} = \underline{?} \cdot 4$$

$$x = \underline{?}$$

Solve the equation.

12. $4m = 32$ **13.** $3n = 60$ **14.** $5p = 0$ **15.** $7q = 63$

16. $35 = 7g$ **17.** $42 = 3h$ **18.** $72 = 6j$ **19.** $51 = 17k$

20. $\dfrac{t}{10} = 12$ **21.** $\dfrac{u}{5} = 10$ **22.** $\dfrac{w}{6} = 15$ **23.** $\dfrac{x}{21} = 4$

24. $5 = \dfrac{a}{4}$ **25.** $12 = \dfrac{b}{7}$ **26.** $9 = \dfrac{c}{30}$ **27.** $7 = \dfrac{d}{14}$

In Exercises 28–31, write the sentence as an equation. Then solve the equation.

28. 112 is 8 times a number y. **29.** Eleven times a number b is 44.

30. A number f divided by 6 is 9. **31.** 27 is a number n divided by 3.

32. Pens Four friends share a box of pens. Each receives 3 pens. Write and solve a division equation to find the number of pens in the box.

HELP with **Homework**

Example Exercises

1   9, 10, 12-19
2   11, 20-27
3   28-34

Online Resources
CLASSZONE.COM

· More Examples
· eTutorial Plus

33. Hurricanes A hurricane is traveling at an average speed of 24 miles per hour. Write and solve a multiplication equation to predict how many hours it will take to travel 1728 miles if it continues at this speed.

34. Sports A team won 45% of its games this year. The team won 9 games. Write and solve a multiplication equation to find the number of games the team played.

35. Critical Thinking Explain why you can multiply each side of the equation $\frac{1}{4}x = 20$ by the reciprocal of $\frac{1}{4}$ to solve the equation.

Solve the equation.

36. $5m = 28$ **37.** $40 = 9p$ **38.** $\frac{x}{4} = 2.7$

39. $8q = -56$ **40.** $-450 = -10s$ **41.** $\frac{w}{5} = -4$

42. Challenge An *acre* covers 43,560 square feet. The unit is based on early farmers' fields that were 10 times as long as they were wide. Find $10x$ and x, the length and width, in feet, of such a field.

$A = 43{,}560 \text{ ft}^2$ x

$10x$

■ **Hurricanes**

The product of a hurricane's speed (in miles per hour) and its rainfall (in inches) is about 100. What rainfall can you expect from a storm traveling 5 miles per hour?

Mixed Review

Evaluate the expression when $x = 3$. *(Lesson 1.5)*

43. $5x + 4$ **44.** $8 + 7x$ **45.** $30 - 3x$

Solve the equation. *(Lesson 12.3)*

46. $b - 8 = 17$ **47.** $x - 12 = 5$ **48.** $41 = m - 19$

Basic Skills **Copy and complete the statement using <, >, or =.**

49. $\frac{3}{8}$ $\underline{\ ?\ }$ $\frac{3}{4}$ **50.** $\frac{7}{9}$ $\underline{\ ?\ }$ $\frac{2}{3}$ **51.** $\frac{1}{2}$ $\underline{\ ?\ }$ $\frac{8}{16}$

Test-Taking Practice

52. Multiple Choice Solve the equation $12x = 120$.

     A. 10   **B.** 108   **C.** 132   **D.** 1440

53. Multiple Choice Solve the equation $\frac{z}{8} = 7$.

     F. $\frac{7}{8}$ **G.** 8   **H.** 15   **I.** 56

Solving Inequalities

GOAL Solve one-step inequalities.

Word Watch

inequality, p. 602
solve an inequality, p. 602
solution of an inequality,
   p. 602
graph of an inequality,
   p. 603

An **inequality** is a statement formed by placing an inequality symbol between two expressions. To translate sentences into inequalities, look for the following phrases.

Phrase	Symbol
is less than	$<$
is less than or equal to	$\leq$
is greater than	$>$
is greater than or equal to	$\geq$

HELP with **Review**

Need help writing
expressions? See
pages 583–584.

EXAMPLE 1 **Writing Simple Inequalities**

Write the sentence as an inequality. Let *x* represent the number.

Sentence	Inequality
A number is less than 5.	$x < 5$
Twice a number is greater than or equal to 8.	$2x \geq 8$
A number minus 7 is less than or equal to 5.	$x - 7 \leq 5$

EXAMPLE 2 **Modeling a Situation**

Restaurant A restaurant can seat 54 people. If a party of 12 joins the number of people already seated, the restaurant will still not be full. Write an inequality you could use to find the number of people *n* that are already seated in the restaurant.

Solution

$$\underset{\text{seated}}{\text{Number already}} \quad + \quad \underset{\text{join}}{\text{Number who}} \quad < \quad \underset{\text{can seat}}{\text{Number restaurant}}$$

$$n + 12 < 54$$

Solving Inequalities You **solve** an inequality by finding the *solution*. The **solution** of an inequality is the set of all values of the variable that make the inequality true. Solving an inequality is similar to solving an equation. You perform the same operation on each side of the inequality in order to get the variable by itself.

HELP with **Reading**

In Example 3, the solution is $x \geq 1$. This means that the solution is the set of all numbers that are greater than or equal to 1. So, for example, 1 and 8 are solutions, but 0 and -5 are not solutions.

EXAMPLE 3 Solving an Inequality

Solve the inequality $x + 2 \geq 3$.

$x + 2 \geq 3$	Write the original inequality.
$x + 2 - 2 \geq 3 - 2$	Subtract 2 from each side.
$x \geq 1$	Simplify.

Graphing Solutions The **graph** of an inequality is all the points on a number line that represent the solution of the inequality. An open dot on a graph indicates a number that is not part of the solution.

EXAMPLE 4 Graphing Solutions of an Inequality

Solve the inequality $3x < 21$. Then graph the solution.

$3x < 21$	Write the original inequality.
$\dfrac{3x}{3} < \dfrac{21}{3}$	Divide each side by 3.
$x < 7$	Simplify.

7 is not part of the solution, so use an open dot at 7 on the graph.

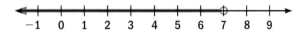

Exercises

1. **Saving** A bicycle costs $275. If you double the amount you've saved, you will have more than enough to buy the bicycle. Write an inequality you could use to find how much you have saved.

Solve the inequality. Then graph the solution.

2. $x + 1 > 3$ 3. $x + 2 \leq 2$ 4. $x - 4 < 0$ 5. $x - 2 \geq 5$

6. $3x \leq 9$ 7. $2x > 12$ 8. $\dfrac{x}{2} \geq 1$ 9. $\dfrac{x}{3} < 4$

10. **Modeling Inequalities** Label 11 cards with the integers -5 through 5. Arrange the cards face up in order from least to greatest. If the integer on a card is a solution of the inequality $3x \leq 6$, leave the card face up. If not, turn the card over. Use your results to solve the inequality $3x \leq 6$.

GOAL
Find an expression for
an input-output table.

MATERIALS
• paper
• pencil

Input-Output Tables

Imagine a machine that evaluates expressions. The value of the
variable is the *input* and the value of the expression is the *output*.

9 → $x - 6$ → 3

Explore **Find an expression for an input-output table.**

1 Look for a relationship between the first input
and the first output. Write an expression that
gives the value of the output when the input is x.
The first output is twice the first input, so try $2x$.

Input	Output
2	4
3	5
4	6
5	7

2 → $2x$ → 4

2 Check whether the expression works for the
next input-output pair.

3 → $2x$ → 6

The output
should be 5.

3 If the expression doesn't work, try another expression using a different operation.
The first output is 2 more than the first input, so try $x + 2$.

2 → $x + 2$ → 4   3 → $x + 2$ → 5   4 → $x + 2$ → 6   5 → $x + 2$ → 7

Your turn now **Find an expression for the input-output table.**

1.

Input	12	11	10	9
Output	10	9	8	7

2.

Input	3	7	10	12
Output	9	21	30	36

Stop and Think

3. Critical Thinking A machine performs one of the four basic operations.
Can a given input value produce more than one output value?

Functions

BEFORE	▶ Now	WHY?
You evaluated variable expressions.	You'll evaluate functions and write function rules.	So you can find miles driven on a road trip, as in Ex. 29.

In the Real World

Word Watch

function, p. 605
input, p. 605
output, p. 605

Giant Pandas Giant pandas eat about 30 pounds of bamboo every day. About how many pounds of bamboo will a giant panda eat in 2 days? in 3 days? in 4 days?

The *function rule* below relates the pounds of bamboo a panda eats to the number of days.

$$\text{Pounds of bamboo} = 30 \times \text{Number of days}$$

A **function** is a pairing of each number in one set with a number in a second set. Starting with a number in the first set, called an **input**, the function pairs it with exactly one number in the second set, called an **output**.

EXAMPLE 1 Evaluating a Function

To solve the problem above about giant pandas, you can make an *input-output table*. Use the function rule $p = 30d$, where d is the number of days (input) and p is the pounds of bamboo eaten (output).

Input Days, d	Substitute in the function $p = 30d$	Output Pounds eaten, p
1	$p = 30(1)$	30
2	$p = 30(2)$	60
3	$p = 30(3)$	90
4	$p = 30(4)$	120

ANSWER A giant panda will eat about 60 pounds of bamboo in 2 days, about 90 pounds in 3 days, and about 120 pounds in 4 days.

Your turn now Make an input-output table using the function rule and the input values $x = 5, 6, 7, 8,$ and 9.

1. $y = x - 1$ **2.** $y = 10 - x$ **3.** $y = 5x$ **4.** $y = 2x + 3$

with **Reading**

A function rule is written so that it tells you what to do to the input to get the output. In Example 2, the rule $y = x - 4$ tells you to subtract 4 from the input to get the output.

EXAMPLE 2 **Using a Table to Write a Rule**

Write a function rule for the input-output table.

a.

Input, x	Output, y
10	6
11	7
12	8
13	9

b.

Input, m	Output, n
0	0
3	1
6	2
9	3

Solution

  a. Each output y is 4 less than the input x. A function rule is $y = x - 4$.

  b. Each output n is the input m divided by 3. A function rule is $n = \frac{m}{3}$.

EXAMPLE 3 **Making a Table to Write a Rule**

Pattern Make an input-output table using the number of squares s as the input and the number of triangles t as the output. Then write a function rule that relates s and t.

with **Solving**

It can be helpful to choose letters that remind you of what the variables stand for. Example 3 uses s and t, the first letters of the words *squares* and *triangles*.

Solution

Each output value is 2 times the input value. There are 2 triangles for every square.

ANSWER A function rule for this pattern is $t = 2s$.

Squares, s	Triangles, t
1	2
2	4
3	6
4	8

Your turn now Write a function rule for the relationship.

  5. First make an input-output table. Use the number of dots in the bottom row n as the input and the total number of dots t as the output.

  6. Use the input-output table at the right.

Input, x	9	18	27	36
Output, y	1	2	3	4

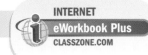
12.5 Exercises

More Practice, p. 719

Getting Ready to Practice

1. **Vocabulary** In a function, each _?_ has exactly one _?_.

Make an input-output table using the function rule and the input values x = 2, 4, 6, 8, and 10.

2. $y = x + 8$ 3. $y = 2x$ 4. $y = \dfrac{x}{2}$ 5. $y = 3x - 2$

6. **School Dance** The table shows the amount c your class charges for t tickets to the school dance. Write a function rule that relates the input t and the output c.

Tickets, t	Cost, c
2	$12
3	$18
4	$24
5	$30

Practice and Problem Solving

Make an input-output table using the function rule and the input values x = 3, 6, 9, 12, and 15.

7. $y = 6x$ 8. $y = x + 10$ 9. $y = 15 - x$ 10. $y = \dfrac{x}{3}$

11. $y = 4x + 1$ 12. $y = 8x - 5$ 13. $y = 2x - 4$ 14. $y = 20 - x$

15. **Measurement** A function rule to convert inches to centimeters is $c = 2.54i$, where c is the number of centimeters and i is the number of inches. Make an input-output table using the input values of 3 inches, 6 inches, 9 inches, 12 inches, and 36 inches. Round to the nearest tenth of a centimeter.

Write a function rule for the input-output table.

16.

Original price, p	Sale price, s
$50	$45
$60	$55
$70	$65
$80	$75

17.

Age now, n	Age in 15 years, t
10	25
11	26
12	27
13	28

18.

Boxes, b	1	2	3	4
Muffins, m	12	24	36	48

19.

Invited guests, g	80	100	120	140
Banquet tables, t	8	10	12	14

HELP with Homework

Example	Exercises
1	7–15
2	16–19
3	20–24

Online Resources
CLASSZONE.COM

· More Examples
· eTutorial Plus

Make an input-output table. Then write a function rule for the relationship.

20. input: cats
output: paws

21. input: hours
output: minutes

22. input: feet
output: yards

Geometry **Make an input-output table. Then write a function rule that relates the input n and the output p.**

23. Each figure is made up of equilateral triangles. Let n represent the number of triangles and let p represent the perimeter of the figure.

1   2   3   4   5

24. Each figure is made up of 5-pointed stars. Let n represent the number of stars and let p represent the number of points.

1   2   3   4

25. Writing Create your own visual pattern that can be represented with a function rule, as in Exercises 23 and 24. Make an input-output table and write the function rule.

26. Temperature To convert degrees Celsius C to degrees Fahrenheit F, you can use the function rule $F = 1.8C + 32$. Make an input-output table using the input values of $0°C$, $5°C$, $10°C$, $15°C$, $20°C$, and $25°C$.

Copy and complete the table using the function rule given.

27. $k = j + 25$

j	0	3	8	?	?
k	?	?	?	40	100

28. $q = 1.6p$

p	10	15	?	?	?
q	?	?	32	40	56

29. Road Trip While on a road trip, you record the following times and miles driven. Assume you travel at a constant rate. Copy and complete the table. Then write a function rule that relates the input t and the output d.

Time	9:00	10:30	11:00	1:00	2:00	?
Time elapsed, t	0	90	120	240	?	?
Miles driven, d	0	75	100	200	?	450

30. Challenge Make an input-output table using $x = y^2$ and the values $y = -4, -2, 0, 2,$ and 4. Does the equation represent a function if x is considered the input and y is considered the output?

Mixed Review

31. Find the time that has elapsed from 11:59 A.M. to 4:43 P.M. *(Lesson 6.6)*

Solve the equation. *(Lesson 12.4)*

32. $9t = 81$ **33.** $2x = 26$ **34.** $\dfrac{n}{6} = 7$ **35.** $\dfrac{f}{4} = 12$

Choose a Strategy Use a strategy from the list to solve the following problem. Explain your choice of strategy.

> **Problem Solving Strategies**
> - Perform an Experiment
> - Make a List or Table
> - Solve a Simpler Problem
> - Draw a Graph

36. In a city, you walk 3 blocks north, 5 blocks east, 2 blocks north, 6 blocks west, and 6 blocks south. Describe the shortest walking route to get back to your starting point.

Basic Skills   **Graph the points on the same coordinate grid.**

37. (0, 5)   **38.** (2, 0)   **39.** (1, 3)   **40.** (4, 2)

Test-Taking Practice

41. Extended Response Make input-output tables for converting from dollars to quarters and from quarters to nickels. Write function rules for the conversions. Then use your results to write a function rule for converting from dollars directly to nickels.

Function Assembly Line

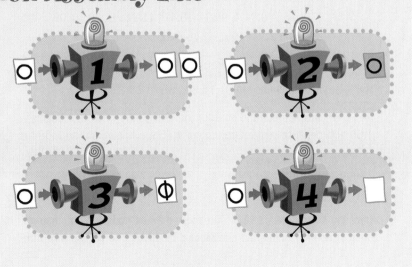

Each machine takes input and gives output as shown. What is the final output if the machines are used in the given order? The starting input is ⬜ and the output of each machine becomes the input of the next machine.

1. Machine 1, Machine 3

2. Machine 4, Machine 2

3. Machine 2, Machine 3, Machine 1

Problem Solving Strategies

Draw a Diagram

Work Backward

Solve a Simpler Problem

Make a Model

Look for a Pattern

Break into Parts

Draw a Graph

Look for a Pattern

Problem You need to leave school at 1:15 P.M. for a short appointment and you expect to return a half hour later. You know that the first three class periods start at 8:15 A.M., 9:04 A.M., and 9:53 A.M. and that all eight periods are the same length. Will you return in time for your 8th period class?

❶ Read and Understand

Read the problem carefully.

You want to find when 8th period begins and the time you'll return.

❷ Make a Plan

Decide on a strategy to use.

One way to solve the problem is to look for a pattern in the class starting times.

❸ Solve the Problem

Reread the problem and look for a pattern.

First, figure out how you get from one starting time to the next. Do you add, subtract, multiply, or divide?

$$8:15 \quad 9:04 \quad 9:53$$
$$+49 \quad +49$$

You *add* 49 minutes to find the starting time for the next period.

Continue the pattern by adding 49 minutes to each starting time until you reach 8th period.

Period	1st	2nd	3rd	4th	5th	6th	7th	8th
Starting time	8:15	9:04	9:53	10:42	11:31	12:20	1:09	1:58

$$+49 \quad +49 \quad +49 \quad +49 \quad +49 \quad +49 \quad +49$$

You'll return 30 minutes after 1:15 P.M., which is at 1:45 P.M.

ANSWER You will return in time for your 8th period class that begins at 1:58 P.M., because your return time of 1:45 P.M. is earlier than 1:58 P.M.

❹ Look Back

Because 49 minutes is 11 minutes less than an hour, you can instead think of adding 1 hour and subtracting 11 minutes to get the next time.

Use the strategy *look for a pattern*.

1. **Bus Travel** A bus left at 4:55 P.M., 5:07 P.M., 5:19 P.M., and 5:31 P.M. Assume the bus schedule continues to follow a pattern. Describe the pattern and predict when the next bus will leave if it is now 6:20 P.M.

2. **Train Travel** A train schedule lists departures at 8:03 A.M., 8:34 A.M., 9:05 A.M., and 9:36 A.M. Assume the departure times continue to follow a pattern. Predict the departure times for the next three trains.

3. **Number Patterns** Describe the pattern. Then find the next three numbers.

    13, 8, 3, −2, ?, ?, ?

4. **Letter Patterns** Describe the pattern. Then find the next two letters.

    A, E, I, M, ?, ?

5. **Necklace** A friend asks you to finish stringing beads on a necklace. Describe the pattern the friend used and find the next five beads to continue the pattern.

6. **Auto Repair** You buy a set of socket wrenches that come in $\frac{15}{16}$, 1, $1\frac{1}{16}$, and $1\frac{1}{8}$ inch sizes. Predict the next two sizes.

7. **Secret Code** A number from 1–26 was assigned to each letter of the alphabet. Decode the secret message.

    6   3–12–15–4–12–17

    10–22   9–18–11–26–5.

Mixed Problem Solving

Use any strategy to solve the problem.

8. **Coordinate Graphing** Begin at (3, 4). Move up 6 units. Then move to the right 2 units and then down 12 units. What are the coordinates of your new position?

9. **Money** You spend $4.25 on lunch, lend a friend $2.50, find a quarter, buy a snack for $1.35, and then have $2.35 left. How much money did you have before lunch?

10. **Street Numbers** You paint house numbers on curbs for homeowners. You have number stencils, but you are missing the number 3. How many numbers between 1 and 200 are you unable to paint?

11. **Playhouse** You are building a playhouse. Calculate the surface area of the exterior surfaces. Do not include the door or the floor.

    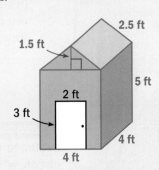

Graphing Functions

BEFORE	▶ Now	WHY?
You graphed ordered pairs in a coordinate plane.	You'll graph linear functions in a coordinate plane.	So you can predict time spent making signs, as in Ex. 28.

In the Real World

Word Watch

linear function, p. 613

Walking You are training for a long distance walking race. In your practice walks, you maintain a steady rate of about 15 minutes per mile. How can you use a graph to represent this relationship?

The number of miles you walk x and the number of minutes it takes y are related by the rule $y = 15x$. So, the distances and times for practice walks are represented by points on the graph of the function $y = 15x$.

EXAMPLE 1 **Graphing a Function**

To graph the function $y = 15x$ mentioned above, follow the steps below.

1 Make an input-output table for the function $y = 15x$.

Input, x	Output, y
0	0
1	15
2	30
3	45

2 Write the input and output values as ordered pairs: (input, output).

(0, 0), (1, 15), (2, 30), (3, 45)

3 Graph the ordered pairs. Notice that the points all lie along a straight line. If you chose other input values for your table, the points you would graph would also lie along that same line.

4 Draw a line through the points. That line represents the complete graph of the function $y = 15x$.

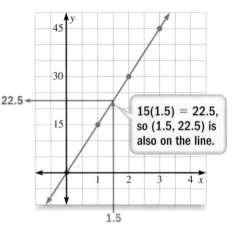

$15(1.5) = 22.5$, so (1.5, 22.5) is also on the line.

Your turn now Copy the table and graph from Example 1. Then evaluate the function for the given input. Graph the ordered pair to check whether the point is on the line.

1. $x = 6$ **2.** $x = 2.5$ **3.** $x = \dfrac{1}{2}$

Representing Functions

There are many ways to represent the same function.

Words A number is the sum of another number and one.

Algebra $y = x + 1$

Ordered Pairs $(-2, -1), (-1, 0), (0, 1), (1, 2), (2, 3)$

Input-Output Table

Input, x	Output, y
-2	-1
-1	0
0	1
1	2
2	3

Graph

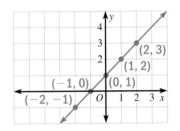

Types of Functions A **linear function** is a function whose graph is a straight line. Not all functions are linear functions.

EXAMPLE 2 Identifying Linear Functions

with Notetaking

It may be helpful to include a flow chart in your notes on identifying linear functions. Your flow chart should include steps for graphing ordered pairs, as in Example 1, and a step for deciding whether you can draw a line through the points.

Tell whether the function is *linear* or *not linear*. Explain.

a.

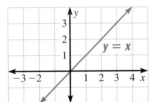

The function is linear, because the graph is a straight line.

b.

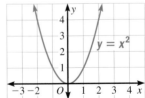

The function is not linear, because the graph is not a straight line.

Your turn now Graph the function using the input values $x = 1, 2, 3, 4,$ and 5. Tell whether the function is *linear* or *not linear*. Explain.

4. $y = x - 1$ **5.** $y = 3 - x$ **6.** $y = 2x + 1$

7. Can a graph in the shape of a V represent a linear function? Explain.

You can use the graph of a linear function to help make predictions.

EXAMPLE 3 **Looking for a Pattern**

Pools The graph shows the time it takes to fill a wading pool to various depths. Predict how long it takes to fill the pool to a depth of 15 inches.

Solution

1. Write some ordered pairs from the graph.

   (2, 6), (4, 12), (6, 18), (8, 24)

2. Write a function rule.

   $t = 3d$, where d is depth in inches and t is time in minutes

3. Evaluate the function when $d = 15$.

   $t = 3(15) = 45$

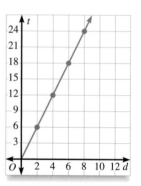

ANSWER The water will be 15 inches deep in about 45 minutes.

HELP with **Solving**

In many situations, including those in Examples 1 and 3, it does not make sense to have values less than 0. In Example 3, it also does not make sense for *d*-values to be greater than the height of the pool.

12.6 Exercises

More Practice, p. 719

INTERNET
eWorkbook Plus
CLASSZONE.COM

Getting Ready to Practice

1. **Vocabulary** A function whose graph is a straight line is a ? function.

Make an input-output table using the function rule and the input values *x* = 0, 1, 2, 3, and 4. Graph the function.

2. $y = 5 + x$

3. $y = 2x - 3$

Lunch The table shows the cost of a salad with a cup of soup for lunch.

Ounces of salad, *s*	Total cost of lunch, *t*
2	$2.50
4	$3.00
6	$3.50
8	$4.00

4. Write the values in the table as ordered pairs (ounces, total cost).

5. Use the ordered pairs from Exercise 4 to graph the function. Is the function linear?

6. Use the graph to find the cost of a 7 ounce salad with a cup of soup.

Practice and Problem Solving

with Homework

Example	Exercises
1	7–19, 23
2	20–22
3	24–27

Online Resources
CLASSZONE.COM

· More Examples
· eTutorial Plus

Graph the ordered pairs. Draw a line through the points.

7. $(-3, -1), (0, 0), (3, 1), (6, 2)$

8. $(-1, 2), (1, 2), (3, 2), (5, 2)$

9. $(0, -1), (2, 2), (4, 5), (6, 8)$

10. $(0, 6), (1.5, 4.5), (3, 3) (4.5, 1.5)$

Make an input-output table using the function rule and the input values $x = 0, 1, 2, 3,$ and 4. Graph the function.

11. $y = x + 4$

12. $y = 3x$

13. $y = 7 - x$

14. $y = 5x + 1$

15. $y = x + 2.5$

16. $y = \frac{1}{2}x$

17. $y = \frac{1}{2}x + 2$

18. $y = x - 3$

19. $y = 10 - 3x$

Decide Tell whether the function is *linear* or *not linear*. Explain.

20. $y = 2x - 3$

21. $y = 5 - x$

22. $y = x^2 - 1$

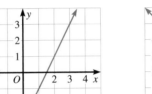
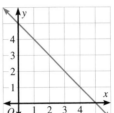
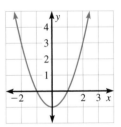

23. **Writing** The number of skiers a ski lift carries is estimated by the function rule $y = 2x$, where x is the number of hours and y is the number of skiers in thousands. How can you use a graph of the function to find the number of skiers carried in 8.5 hours? How can you find the number of skiers carried in 8.5 hours without making a graph?

Look for a Pattern Graph the ordered pairs and draw a line through the points. Write a function rule for the ordered pairs.

24. $(0, 1), (1, 2), (2, 3), (3, 4), (4, 5)$

25. $(-1, 3), (0, 4), (1, 5), (2, 6), (3, 7)$

26. $(0, 0), \left(\frac{1}{2}, 1\right), (1, 2), \left(1\frac{1}{2}, 3\right), (2, 4)$

27. $(0, 5), (1, 4), (2, 3), (3, 2), (4, 1)$

28. **Signs** You are making signs for your school's art festival. The table shows the amount of time it takes you to make signs. Use ordered pairs from the table to graph the function. Then predict how many signs you can make in 5 hours (300 minutes).

Number of signs	Time (min)
2	40
4	80
6	120
8	160

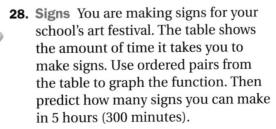

Extended Problem Solving In Exercises 29–31, use the function $V = s^3$ to find the volume of a cube, where s is the side length of the cube.

HELP with **Solving**

You don't always use x and y to label the axes of your graphs. In Ex. 30, the horizontal axis should be labeled s and the vertical axis should be labeled V.

29. **Evaluate** Make an input-output table using the input values 1, 2, 4, 8, and 16.

30. **Graph** Graph the ordered pairs from the table. Is the function linear?

31. **Compare** How does the volume of a cube change when its side length doubles?

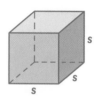

32. **Challenge** The function for finding the area of a circle is $A = \pi r^2$, where r is the radius of the circle. Make an input-output table for the function. Graph the function. How does the area change if the input value is doubled? tripled? quadrupled?

Mixed Review

Write the fraction or mixed number as a decimal. Use bar notation to show a repeating decimal. *(Lesson 5.8)*

33. $\frac{3}{10}$

34. $\frac{11}{6}$

35. $1\frac{4}{11}$

36. $6\frac{3}{8}$

Copy and complete the statement. *(Lesson 8.1)*

37. $\frac{2}{3} = \frac{8}{?}$

38. $\frac{20}{?} = \frac{4}{5}$

39. $\frac{?}{11} = \frac{18}{22}$

40. $\frac{40}{100} = \frac{?}{25}$

41. Write a function rule for the input-output table. *(Lesson 12.5)*

Input, x	7	8	9	10
Output, y	15	16	17	18

Basic Skills You have $21. Determine how many packs of trading cards you can buy for the given price.

42. $3 per pack

43. $1.50 per pack

44. $1.75 per pack

Test-Taking Practice

INTERNET

State Test Practice

CLASSZONE.COM

45. **Multiple Choice** What ordered pairs are part of the graph of the function $y = 5x + 7$?

   A. (5, 7), (10, 14), (15, 21)

   B. (0, 7), (1, 2), (2, −3)

   C. (0, 5), (1, 12), (2, 19)

   D. (1, 12), (2, 17), (4, 27)

46. **Short Response** On the same coordinate plane, graph the functions $y = 3x + 4$, $y = 3x$, and $y = 3x − 4$. Use the input values $x = 0, 1, 2, 3,$ and 4. What do you notice about the graphs?

CALCULATOR

Graphing Linear Functions

GOAL Use a graphing calculator to graph linear functions.

Example **You can graph linear functions using a graphing calculator.**

At a local bank, a money order costs the amount of the money order plus a $1 fee. A function rule for the money order is $y = x + 1$, where x is the amount of the money order and y is the total cost. Graph this function.

Solution

1 To enter the function rule into a graphing calculator, press $\boxed{\text{Y=}}$. With the cursor next to $Y_1 =$, enter the function rule by pressing $\boxed{x}$ $\boxed{+}$ 1.

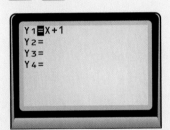

2 To display the graph, press $\boxed{\text{GRAPH}}$. If you use the standard viewing window, the graph shows values from -10 through 10 along the x- and y-axes.

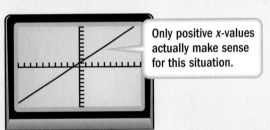

Only positive x-values actually make sense for this situation.

Your turn now **Use a graphing calculator to graph the function. In Exercises 11 and 12, also tell what x-values make sense.**

1. $y = x + 2$ **2.** $y = x - 4$ **3.** $y = 3x$ **4.** $y = \dfrac{x}{3}$ **5.** $y = \dfrac{1}{5}x$

6. $y = 3 - x$ **7.** $y = 3x - 5$ **8.** $y = 2x + 1$ **9.** $y = 1 - 4x$ **10.** $y = -x$

11. Geometry The function rule $y = 3.14x$ can be used to estimate the circumference of a circle, where x is the diameter of the circle.

12. Snow Under certain weather conditions, the function rule $y = 0.1x$ can be used to estimate the number of inches of water y contained in x inches of snow.

Notebook Review

Review the vocabulary definitions in your notebook.

Copy the review examples in your notebook. Then complete the exercises.

Check Your Definitions

function, p. 605   input, output, p. 605   linear function, p. 613

Use Your Vocabulary

1. Copy and complete: You can use a table of _?_ and _?_ values to graph a function.

2. How can you tell from its graph whether a function is linear?

12.4 Can you solve multiplication and division equations?

 EXAMPLE

a. $2x = 10$

$\dfrac{2x}{2} = \dfrac{10}{2}$

$x = 5$

b. $7 = \dfrac{z}{3}$

$3 \cdot 7 = 3 \cdot \dfrac{z}{3}$

$21 = z$

 Solve the equation.

3. $6p = 18$ **4.** $68 = 4q$ **5.** $15 = \dfrac{w}{8}$ **6.** $\dfrac{x}{2} = 10$

12.5–12.6 Can you evaluate and graph functions?

EXAMPLE Graph the function $y = x - 2$.

Table

Input, x	$y = x - 2$	Output, y
0	$y = 0 - 2$	-2
1	$y = 1 - 2$	-1
2	$y = 2 - 2$	0
3	$y = 3 - 2$	1

Ordered Pairs

$(0, -2)$
$(1, -1)$
$(2, 0)$
$(3, 1)$

Graph

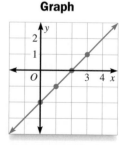

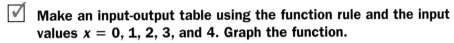

☑ **Make an input-output table using the function rule and the input values $x = 0, 1, 2, 3,$ and 4. Graph the function.**

7. $y = x + 5$ **8.** $y = 17 - x$ **9.** $y = 4x - 5$ **10.** $y = \frac{1}{2}x + 4$

11. Write a function rule for the input-output table.

Days, d	7	14	21	28
Weeks, w	1	2	3	4

Stop and Think about Lessons 12.4–12.6

12. Explain The formula for the area of a rectangle is $A = lw$, where w is the width and l is the length. Explain how to solve for the length of a rectangle if you are given the area and the width.

Review Quiz 2

Solve the equation.

1. $10w = 20$ **2.** $13x = 78$ **3.** $72 = 2z$ **4.** $77 = 7y$

5. $\frac{a}{5} = 8$ **6.** $\frac{b}{13} = 4$ **7.** $24 = \frac{c}{2}$ **8.** $6 = \frac{d}{30}$

Write the sentence as an equation. Then solve the equation.

9. Five times a number r is 75.   **10.** A number d divided by 7 is 8.

11. Wages You earn $5 per hour raking. Write and solve a multiplication equation to find t, the number of hours you must work to earn $35.

Write a function rule for the input-output table.

12.

Tickets, t	Cost, c
2	$8
4	$16
6	$24
8	$32

13.

Sale price, s	Original price, p
$70	$80
$63	$73
$85	$95
$56	$66

Make an input-output table using the function rule and the input values $x = 3, 6, 9,$ and 12. Graph the function.

14. $y = x$ **15.** $y = 5x - 10$ **16.** $y = 14 - x$ **17.** $y = \frac{1}{3}x + 3$

Chapter Review

 **Vocabulary**

function, p. 605   input, output, p. 605   linear function, p. 613

Vocabulary Review

1. In the function $y = 3x + 1$, what variable represents the input? the output?

2. In a function, what is special about the relationship of inputs and outputs?

3. Sketch an example of a linear function.

4. Sketch an example of a function that is not linear.

Review Questions

Write the phrase as an expression. Let x represent the number.
(Lesson 12.1)

5. The difference of 7 and a number

6. A number times 16

7. 15 more than a number

8. The quotient of a number and 2

Write the sentence as an equation. *(Lesson 12.1)*

9. A number n divided by 3 is 15.

10. Five less than a number p is 7.

11. The product of 2 and a number q is 10.

12. 100 is 40 increased by a number r.

Solve the equation. *(Lessons 12.2, 12.3)*

13. $a + 8 = 12$
14. $3 + b = 21$
15. $32 = 12 + c$
16. $22 = d + 18$

17. $69 = f + 17$
18. $32 + e = 51$
19. $g + 2.7 = 4.6$
20. $12.5 = 1.9 + h$

21. $x - 7 = 9$
22. $p - 8 = 21$
23. $q - 31 = 13$
24. $2 = r - 29$

25. $19 = s - 19$
26. $57 = t - 24$
27. $18 = w - 3.8$
28. $z - 4.02 = 1.86$

29. Sports Your friend hits a golf ball 250 yards. Your ball lands 35 yards short of it. Write and solve an addition equation to find the distance your ball traveled. *(Lesson 12.2)*

30. Employees Eleven employees of a company are out of the office. There are 98 employees currently in the office. Write and solve a subtraction equation to find the total number of employees. *(Lesson 12.3)*

Solve the equation. *(Lesson 12.4)*

31. $4p = 36$

32. $5q = 105$

33. $58 = 2r$

34. $140 = 7s$

35. $3t = 132$

36. $10u = 1000$

37. $135 = 9w$

38. $0 = 12x$

39. $\dfrac{a}{5} = 4$

40. $\dfrac{b}{2} = 25$

41. $10 = \dfrac{c}{3}$

42. $12 = \dfrac{d}{10}$

43. $\dfrac{h}{7} = 5$

44. $\dfrac{k}{6} = 12$

45. $\dfrac{m}{20} = 4$

46. $\dfrac{n}{11} = 15$

47. Geometry A rectangle has a width of 3 feet and an area of 57 square feet. Write and solve a multiplication equation to find the length of the rectangle. *(Lesson 12.4)*

Make an input-output table using the function rule and the input values *x* = 0, 5, 10, 15, and 20. *(Lesson 12.5)*

48. $y = 10x$

49. $y = 2x + 15$

50. $y = 100 - x$

51. $y = \dfrac{x}{5}$

Write a function rule for the input-output table. *(Lesson 12.5)*

52.

Words, *w*	Pages, *p*
250	1
500	2
750	3
1000	4

53.

Sale, *s*	Regular, *r*
$5.00	$7.50
$10.00	$12.50
$15.00	$17.50
$20.00	$22.50

54.

Gallons, *g*	Cups, *c*
1	16
2	32
3	48
4	64

Make an input-output table. Then write a function rule for the relationship. *(Lesson 12.5)*

55. input: months; output: years

56. input: age now; output: age in 20 years

Make an input-output table using the function rule and the input values *x* = 0, 2, 4, 6, and 8. Graph the function. *(Lesson 12.6)*

57. $y = 12 - x$

58. $y = 3x - 4$

59. $y = \dfrac{1}{2}x + 3$

Graph the ordered pairs. Write a function rule for the ordered pairs. *(Lesson 12.6)*

60. $(0, 0), (2, 1), (4, 2), (6, 3), (8, 4)$

61. $(1, 8), (2, 7), (3, 6), (4, 5), (5, 4)$

62. Tell whether the function at the right is *linear* or *not linear*. Explain. *(Lesson 12.6)*

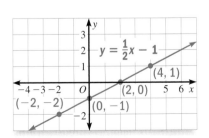

12 Chapter Test

Write the sentence as an equation.

1. Five times a number b is 30.

2. 15 is a number c divided by 3.

3. A number d decreased by 5 is 22.

4. The sum of e and 25 is 100.

Solve the equation.

5. $x + 4 = 15$

6. $7 + y = 13$

7. $z + 9 = 18$

8. $25 = w + 3$

9. $a - 8 = 24$

10. $b - 17 = 15$

11. $44 = c - 12$

12. $d - 52 = 9$

13. Pottery A pottery class has 26 students. Seventeen of the students are girls. Write and solve an addition equation to find the number of boys in the class.

Solve the equation.

14. $15p = 60$

15. $9q = 99$

16. $198 = 6r$

17. $52 = 2s$

18. $\frac{m}{7} = 7$

19. $\frac{n}{13} = 4$

20. $9 = \frac{w}{20}$

21. $16 = \frac{x}{3}$

22. Music Jorge practiced his trumpet three times as long as Randy did. Jorge practiced for 105 minutes. Write and solve a multiplication equation to find how long Randy practiced.

Make an input-output table using the function rule and the input values x = 0, 3, 6, 9, and 12.

23. $y = 5x$

24. $y = 4x + 6$

25. $y = 60 - 2x$

26. $y = \frac{x}{3}$

Make an input-output table. Then write a function rule for the relationship.

27. input: kilometers
output: meters

28. input: age as freshman
output: age as senior

29. input: side length of square
output: area of square

Make an input-output table using the function rule and the input values x = 2, 4, 6, 8, and 10. Graph the function.

30. $y = 12 - x$

31. $y = 3x - 4$

32. $y = \frac{1}{2}x + 1$

33. Graph the ordered pairs (7, 3), (8, 4), (9, 5), (10, 6), and (11, 7). Write a function rule for the ordered pairs.

Chapter Standardized Test

Test-Taking Strategy If you find yourself becoming tense and worried, stop and take some deep breaths. This can help you to feel calmer and more relaxed.

Multiple Choice

1. What equation represents "25 less than a number k is 17"?

   A. $k - 25 = 17$ **B.** $25 - k = 17$

   C. $17 - k = 25$ **D.** $25 + k = 17$

2. Your friend has done one fourth the number of math puzzles you have done. If z is the number of puzzles you have done, what is an expression for the number your friend has done?

   F. $z - \frac{1}{4}$ **G.** $z + \frac{1}{4}$ **H.** $\frac{z}{4}$ **I.** $4z$

3. What is the solution of the equation $x + 12 = 24$?

   A. 2   **B.** 12   **C.** 18   **D.** 40

4. What is the solution of the equation $11 = n - 5$?

   F. -6 **G.** 6   **H.** 16   **I.** 55

5. Which whole number is closest to the solution of the equation $t - 15.2 = 23.9$?

   A. 8   **B.** 9   **C.** 38   **D.** 39

6. You buy a pair of soccer shin guards for d dollars. If you give the clerk $20 and receive $2.05 in change, which equation can you use to find d?

   F. $d + 20 = 2.05$ **G.** $2.05d = 20$

   H. $d - 2.05 = 20$ **I.** $20 = d + 2.05$

7. What is the solution of the equation $9p = 108$?

   A. 2   **B.** 12   **C.** 99   **D.** 972

8. What is the solution of the equation $\frac{b}{5} = 18$?

   F. $\frac{18}{5}$ **G.** 13   **H.** 90   **I.** 95

9. What is the solution of the equation $20 = \frac{d}{20}$?

   A. $\frac{1}{20}$ **B.** 1   **C.** 40   **D.** 400

10. What is the output y of the function $y = 3x - 5$ when the input x is 5?

   F. 0   **G.** 3   **H.** 5   **I.** 10

11. Which function rule has the following graph?

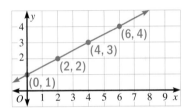

   A. $y = 2x + 1$ **B.** $y = x + 2$

   C. $x = 2y + 1$ **D.** $y = \frac{1}{2}x + 1$

Short Response

12. Graph the function $y = 5 - x$. Use the input values $x = 0, 1, 2, 3,$ and 4. Show your steps.

Extended Response

13. A triangle has a base of 10 centimeters. Choose various heights h as inputs. For each input, find the area A of the triangle as the output. Record your results in an input-output table. Graph the ordered pairs (h, A). Write a function rule relating h and A.

Investigating

Measuring Elephants

Scientists who study elephants often need to know the sizes of the animals they observe. However, it can be very difficult to get a wild elephant to stand still while a human measures it.

Instead, scientists have found a method of estimating the shoulder height of an elephant by using the circumference of the elephant's forefoot. Scientists can find the circumference of the forefoot easily by measuring the tracks left by an elephant passing through the mud.

The table below contains measurements of 16 elephants from Africa.

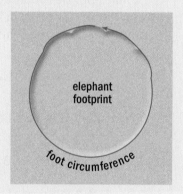

Elephant Measurements								
Forefoot circumference (cm)	110	112	145	130	120	120	107	117
Shoulder height (cm)	252	204	309	284	272	267	239	237
Forefoot circumference (cm)	105	115	117	140	117	110	120	110
Shoulder height (cm)	229	239	252	304	249	244	224	249

1. Use the data in the table to make a graph. Put foot circumference on the *x*-axis, numbering from 100 to 150 and using increments of 5. Put shoulder height on the *y*-axis, numbering from 200 to 310 and using increments of 10.

2. **Critical Thinking** What patterns do you notice in your graph? In general, what happens to an elephant's shoulder height as the foot circumference increases?

Testing a Formula

Scientists in the field use a rule of thumb to estimate elephant heights. According to this rule of thumb, an elephant's shoulder height is about twice the circumference of the elephant's forefoot.

3. Express the scientists' rule of thumb as a formula. Let x be the forefoot circumference. Let y be the shoulder height.

4. Use your formula from Exercise 3. Copy and complete the input-output table. Then plot the information from the table on your graph from Exercise 1. Draw a line through the new points. This line represents the scientists' prediction of an elephant's height, based on its foot circumference.

Input, x	Output, y
110	?
120	?
140	?

5. Compare the data points you plotted in Exercise 1 with the line you drew in Exercise 4. Do most of the data points fall above or below the line? Do any of the points fall on the line?

6. **Critical Thinking** Do you think that the scientists' rule of thumb is a good one? If you use the rule of thumb, are you likely to overestimate or underestimate the height of an elephant? Explain your thinking.

Project IDEAS

- **Experiment** Measure the foot length and the height of each student in your class. Make a graph of the data. What patterns do you notice in your graph?

- **Report** Find out about the sizes, weights, and life spans of a particular type of elephant. Use a poster to present your information.

- **Research** Scientists who study animals in the wild use a variety of methods to observe and understand their subjects. Learn more about the methods scientists use to study a particular animal and present your findings to the class.

- **Career** People who study data and look for patterns are called statisticians. Learn more about the different kinds of work statisticians do. Present your findings to the class.

INTERNET
Project Support
CLASSZONE.COM

13

Probability and Statistics

Chapter Warm-Up Games

Review skills you need for this chapter in these quick games.

BEFORE

In previous chapters you've...

- Solved proportions
- Compared percents, decimals, and fractions

Now

In Chapter 13 you'll study...

- Probability
- Misleading statistics
- Stem-and-leaf plots
- Box-and-whisker plots
- Choosing a data display

WHY?

So you can solve real-world problems about...

- football, p. 630
- pottery, p. 636
- storms, p. 651
- communication, p. 665

Internet Preview
CLASSZONE.COM

- eEdition Plus Online
- eWorkbook Plus Online
- eTutorial Plus Online
- State Test Practice
- More Examples

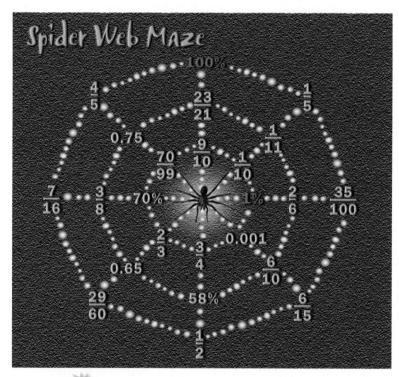

Spider Web Maze

BRAIN GAME

Key Skill:
Comparing percents, decimals, and fractions

- Copy the spider web maze. Start at 1% near the center of the web. Your goal is to escape to 100% at the top of the web.

- Move along the threads of the web. You may only move to a number that is greater than the number you are on. You may not pass through the spider at the center of the web.

Butterfly Challenge

Texan-Crescent

$\dfrac{3}{10} = \dfrac{?}{40}$

Indian

$\dfrac{2}{5} = \dfrac{?}{20}$

Nymph

$\dfrac{4}{7} = \dfrac{?}{35}$

Buckeye

$\dfrac{2}{9} = \dfrac{?}{18}$

Empress

$\dfrac{7}{8} = \dfrac{?}{24}$

Silverspot

$\dfrac{2}{3} = \dfrac{?}{15}$

Red-Rim

$\dfrac{3}{7} = \dfrac{?}{14}$

Morpho

$\dfrac{3}{8} = \dfrac{?}{24}$

Orion

$\dfrac{1}{6} = \dfrac{?}{108}$

BRAIN GAME

Key Skill:
Solving proportions

- Copy and solve the proportions. Order your answers from least to greatest. Write the butterfly names associated with your answers in the same order.

- The first letters of the names will spell out the name of a butterfly whose name is also a word that means "sulfur."

Stop *and* Think

1. **Critical Thinking** Give an example from *Spider Web Maze* in which simplifying helped you compare two fractions. Give an example in which you changed a fraction to a decimal in order to compare two numbers.

2. **Extension** For each proportion in *Butterfly Challenge*, find one of the cross products. Order these products from least to greatest. Write the butterfly names associated with the products in the same order. The last letters of the names will spell out the lifespan of the butterfly whose name you spelled in the puzzle.

Getting Ready to Learn

Review What You Need to Know

Using Vocabulary **Copy and complete using a review word.**

1. If a value occurs the most often in a data set, then it is called the ? .

2. The ? is the sum of the data values divided by the number of values.

Find the mean, median, mode(s), and range of the data. *(p. 93)*

3. 13, 2, 23, 12, 2, 3, 8

4. 8, 9, 3, 4, 8, 6, 9, 8, 9, 6

Write the fraction as a decimal and as a percent. *(p. 399)*

5. $\frac{1}{4}$ **6.** $\frac{5}{5}$ **7.** $\frac{2}{3}$ **8.** $\frac{1}{8}$

The table shows the results of a survey asking 100 students their favorite after-school activity. *(p. 491)*

9. Make a circle graph of the data.

10. Which activity is preferred by slightly less than one fourth of the students?

Activity	Students
sports	28
music lessons	24
clubs	35
other	13

Word Watch

Review Words

circle graph, p. 88
mean, p. 93
median, p. 93
mode, p. 93
range, p. 94
decimal, p. 108
fraction, p. 228
percent, p. 395

Notebook

You should include material that appears on a notebook like this in your own notes.

Know How to Take Notes

Summarizing Material At the end of the year, write a summary of key ideas from different lessons that are related to each other. Include definitions and examples of the key ideas.

Simplifying
Fractions

$$\frac{10}{80} = \frac{1 \times 10}{8 \times 10}$$

$$= \frac{1 \times \cancel{10}^{1}}{8 \times \cancel{10}_{1}}$$

$$= \frac{1}{8}$$

Fractions
to Decimals

$$\frac{1}{8} \rightarrow 8\overline{)1.000}$$

$$\begin{array}{r} .125 \\ \underline{8} \\ 20 \\ \underline{16} \\ 40 \\ \underline{40} \\ 0 \end{array}$$

Decimals
to Percents

$$0.125 = \frac{125}{1000}$$

$$= \frac{12.5}{100}$$

$$= 12.5\%$$

You can use this tool to connect Chapter 13 with other chapters.

Hands-on Activity

Conducting an Experiment

You can predict the results of rolling a number cube and use an experiment to test your predictions.

Explore **Make and test predictions about rolling a number cube.**

1 Predict whether a number *less than 2*, *equal to 2*, or *greater than 2* will occur most often when you roll a number cube 30 times. Explain your answer.

2 Make a frequency table like the one at the right. Then roll a number cube 30 times and record your results in the frequency table.

Number on cube	Tally	Frequency
1	?	?
2	?	?
3	?	?
4	?	?
5	?	?
6	?	?

3 What fraction of the results is less than 2? equal to 2? greater than 2? Do your results match your predictions?

Your turn now

1. Predict whether a number *less than 4, equal to 4,* or *greater than 4* will occur most often when you roll a number cube 30 times. Then repeat the experiment above to test your prediction.

Stop *and* Think

2. Critical Thinking When you roll a number cube, do you think that any one of the numbers is more likely to occur than each of the other numbers? Use the data in the two frequency tables you made above to support your answer.

Introduction to Probability

BEFORE	**Now**	**WHY?**
You wrote ratios.	You'll write probabilities.	So you can find the likelihood of winning a raffle, as in Ex. 27.

In the Real World

Word Watch

outcome, p. 630
event, p. 630
favorable outcomes, p. 630
probability, p. 630
complementary events,
    p. 632

Football A coin toss determines starting plays in a football game. A team captain calls "heads." How likely is it that the captain's team will win the toss?

Tossing a coin is an example of an *experiment*. An **outcome**, such as "heads," is a possible result of an experiment. An **event** is a collection of outcomes. Once you specify an event, the outcomes for that event are called **favorable outcomes**. You can find *probabilities* by counting favorable outcomes.

Finding Probabilities

The **probability** that an event will occur when all outcomes of an experiment are equally likely is as follows.

$$\text{Probability of event} = \frac{\text{Number of favorable outcomes}}{\text{Number of possible outcomes}}$$

EXAMPLE 1 Finding a Probability

In the coin toss problem above, there is 1 favorable outcome, which is "heads." The 2 possible outcomes are "heads" and "tails."

$$\text{Probability of winning the toss} = \frac{\text{Number of favorable outcomes}}{\text{Number of possible outcomes}} = \frac{1}{2}$$

ANSWER The captain's team is as likely to win the toss as to lose it.

Probabilities As shown in Example 1, an event that has a probability of $\frac{1}{2}$ is likely to occur half the time. The probability P of an event is a measure of the likelihood that the event will occur. You can write probabilities as fractions, decimals, and percents.

$P = 0$	$P = 0.25$	$P = 0.50$	$P = 0.75$	$P = 1$
Impossible	Unlikely	Likely to occur half the time	Likely	Certain

EXAMPLE 2 **Describing Probabilities**

HELP with Solving

When you flip a coin, roll a number cube, or randomly choose objects from a bag, you are assuming that all the outcomes are equally likely to occur.

You roll a number cube. Find and describe the probability of the event.

a. You roll an odd number.

Because there are 3 odd outcomes,

$P = \frac{3}{6} = 0.5 = 50\%$.

ANSWER You are likely to roll an odd number half the time.

b. You roll a whole number.

Because all 6 outcomes are whole numbers, $P = \frac{6}{6} = 1 = 100\%$.

ANSWER You are certain to roll a whole number.

c. You roll a 7.

Because 7 is not one of the outcomes, $P = \frac{0}{6} = 0 = 0\%$.

ANSWER It is impossible to roll a 7.

d. You roll a number less than 3.

Because there are 2 outcomes less than 3, $P = \frac{2}{6} = 0.\overline{3} = 33\frac{1}{3}\%$.

ANSWER You are unlikely to roll a number less than 3.

Your turn now **Find the probability of the event.**

1. You roll a number greater than 3 on a number cube.

2. You randomly choose a red marble from a bag of 4 green, 2 blue, and 7 red marbles.

Complementary Events Two events are **complementary events**, or *complements* of each other, if they have no outcomes in common and if together they contain all the outcomes of the experiment.

EXAMPLE 3 Complementary Events

The outcomes on the spinner are equally likely. You spin the spinner.

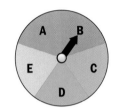

a. Find the probability of spinning a vowel.

b. Describe the complement of the event in part (a) and find its probability.

Solution

a. Because 2 of the 5 letters are vowels, $P = \frac{2}{5}$.

b. The complement of spinning a vowel is spinning a consonant. Because 3 of the 5 letters are consonants, $P = \frac{3}{5}$.

13.1 Exercises

More Practice, p. 720

INTERNET
eWorkbook Plus
CLASSZONE.COM

Getting Ready to Practice

Vocabulary List all the favorable outcomes for the given event.

1. Spinning a vowel on the spinner

2. Rolling an integer on a number cube

3. Randomly choosing a red marble

4. Socks A drawer contains 6 blue and 4 red socks. You randomly choose one sock. Find the probability that you choose a red sock.

A hat holds 10 tiles labeled A, C, R, U, 1, 4, 5, 7, 8, and 9.

5. You randomly choose one tile. Find the probability that it is a letter.

6. Describe the complement of the event in Exercise 5 and find its probability.

HELP with **Homework**

Example	Exercises
1	7–10, 19–21
2	11–18
3	22–24

Online Resources
CLASSZONE.COM
· More Examples
· eTutorial Plus

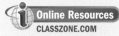

Weather

Groundhogs

The groundhog Punxsutawney Phil saw his shadow 10 times from 1988 to 2002. You randomly choose one year from 1988 to 2002. Find the probability that you select a year in which Phil did not predict six more weeks of winter.

Practice and Problem Solving

You roll a number cube. Find the probability of the event.

7. You roll a 1.   **8.** You roll a prime number.

9. You roll an 8.   **10.** You roll a multiple of 3.

Tell whether the event is *impossible, unlikely, likely,* or *certain.*

11. A student randomly chosen from a class is right-handed.

12. It will be Monday in one of the next 10 days.

13. June will have 31 days this year.

14. A person bowls a perfect score.

You spin the spinner, which is divided into equal parts. Find the probability of the event. Then tell whether the event is *impossible, unlikely, likely,* or *certain.*

15. You spin a 5.   **16.** You spin an integer.

17. You spin an 8.   **18.** You spin a factor of 12.

19. Find the Error Describe and correct the error in finding the probability of rolling a 5 on a number cube.

$$\times \quad \text{Probability of rolling 5} = \frac{1}{5}$$

20. Video Games You randomly choose a level from 12 different levels in a video game. You don't know which 4 levels have secret warp zones. Find the probability that you choose a level that has a secret warp zone.

21. Alphabet A bag holds 26 letter tiles. Each tile has a different letter of the alphabet. You randomly choose one tile. Find the probability that it is a consonant.

Describe the complement of the event. Then find its probability.

22. You roll an odd number on a number cube.

23. You randomly choose a consonant from the letters in MATH.

24. You randomly choose a red tile from a box of 4 red and 8 blue tiles.

25. Groundhogs The groundhog Punxsutawney Phil is said to predict six more weeks of winter if he sees his shadow on February 2. From 1901 to 2000, Phil saw his shadow 87 of the 100 recorded years. You randomly choose one year from 1901 to 2000. Find the probability that you select a year in which Phil saw his shadow.

26. **Piano Keys** A piano has 52 white keys and 36 black keys. Eight keys produce a C note. You randomly play one key. Find the probability that it produces a C note.

27. **Raffles** The probability of losing a raffle is 98%. Describe the complement of losing a raffle and find its probability.

28. **CD Changer** A CD changer holds 3 CDs. Each CD has 12 songs. You let the CD changer randomly select which song to play first. Find the probability that your favorite song is played first.

29. **Critical Thinking** Can the probability of an event be greater than 1? Can the probability of an event be less than 0? Explain.

Odds The *odds in favor* of an event is the ratio of favorable outcomes to unfavorable outcomes. You want to roll a 6 on a number cube.

30. List all the favorable outcomes. Then list all the unfavorable outcomes.

31. Find the odds in favor of rolling a 6. Explain your answer.

32. **Challenge** An experiment is *fair* if each event is equally likely to occur. You roll a number cube to find out which of two players goes first in a game. Describe two ways that you can fairly decide who goes first.

Mixed Review

33. Find the volume of a rectangular prism that is 12 inches by 3 inches by 6 inches. *(Lesson 10.7)*

Graph the function using the input values x = 0, 3, 6, and 9. *(Lesson 12.6)*

34. $y = x + 7$ 35. $y = x - 4$ 36. $y = 2x$

Basic Skills **Order the numbers from least to greatest.**

37. 6.23, 62.3, 623, 0.623, 6230   38. 1441, 1.441, 144.1, 0.1441, 14.41

Test-Taking Practice

39. **Multiple Choice** The outcomes on the spinner are equally likely. You spin the spinner. Find the probability of spinning a multiple of 4.

  A. $\frac{1}{2}$ **B.** $\frac{3}{4}$ **C.** $\frac{7}{8}$ **D.** 1

40. **Multiple Choice** A bag holds 6 red, 8 yellow, and 6 green marbles. You randomly choose one marble. Find the probability that it is red.

  F. $\frac{3}{20}$ **G.** $\frac{3}{10}$ **H.** $\frac{1}{3}$ **I.** $\frac{3}{5}$

Technology Activity

Testing Probabilities

GOAL Use a calculator to generate a random set of data so you can test probabilities.

Example You can use the random integer feature **RANDI** to generate a random set of integers.

Generate a random set of data to show the results of 10 rolls on a number cube. Then compare your results with the probability of rolling an odd number.

HELP with **Technology**

The display **RANDI(1, 6)** tells you that the integers 1 through 6 are the only possible outcomes of the simulation.

Solution

To simulate rolling a number cube, use the random integer feature **RANDI**.

Keystrokes   **Display**

   **RANDI(1, 6)**

Press ⬜**=** 10 times to generate the results of rolling a number cube 10 times. Record your results as you generate them. Suppose you generate the following numbers:

    2, 4, 5, 6, 3, 1, 3, 4, 3, and 5.

In the simulation, 6 of the 10 results are odd numbers.

ANSWER You generated an odd number $\frac{6}{10}$, or $\frac{3}{5}$, of the time. This is slightly greater than the probability of rolling an odd number, $\frac{1}{2}$.

Your turn now Use a calculator to solve the problems below.

1. Let 1 represent heads and 2 represent tails. Generate a random set of data to show the results of 15 coin tosses. Then compare your results with the probability of getting heads.

2. A spinner is divided into three equal sections. Let 1 and 2 represent red and 3 represent green. Generate a random set of data to show the results of 24 spins. Then compare your results with the probability of spinning green.

13.2

Finding Outcomes

BEFORE	▶ Now	WHY?
You identified outcomes.	You'll use diagrams, tables, and lists to find outcomes.	So you can arrange a movie schedule, as in Ex. 11.

In the Real World

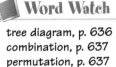

Word Watch

tree diagram, p. 636
combination, p. 637
permutation, p. 637

Pottery Your art class is painting pottery for an art fair. You can choose a small or a large size, and you can paint a vase, a jar, or a plate. What are the different kinds of pottery you can paint?

A **tree diagram** can help you organize a list of possible outcomes by placing different choices on different branches of the "tree."

EXAMPLE 1 Using Tree Diagrams

To find all possible outcomes in the problem above, use a tree diagram.

① List the sizes.	② For each size list the items.	③ Find the outcomes.
small	**vase**	**small vase**
	jar	**small jar**
	plate	**small plate**
large	**vase**	**large vase**
	jar	**large jar**
	plate	**large plate**

Your turn now **Use a tree diagram to find all the possible outcomes.**

1. You can order a tuna, ham, roast beef, or egg sandwich. You can choose rye, white, wheat, or oatmeal bread. Find all the possible sandwiches.

2. A roller hockey team is choosing jerseys. The body can be red, white, purple, green, or blue. The sleeves can be black, red, or blue. Find all the possible jerseys that the team can choose from.

Combinations and Permutations To choose outcomes, you need to decide whether the order of the objects matters. A **combination** is a grouping of objects in which order is not important. A **permutation** is an arrangement of objects in which order is important.

EXAMPLE 2 Finding Combinations

Sundaes You can choose 2 toppings for a sundae from nuts, sprinkles, caramel, and marshmallows. Find all the possible pairs of toppings.

Solution

Each outcome is a combination because it doesn't matter which topping you choose first. Use a table to show all the possible pairs of toppings.

Nuts	Sprinkles	Caramel	Marshmallows	Outcomes
X	X			nuts, sprinkles
X		X		nuts, caramel
X			X	nuts, marshmallows
	X	X		sprinkles, caramel
	X		X	sprinkles, marshmallows
		X	X	caramel, marshmallows

EXAMPLE 3 Finding Permutations

Find all the two-digit numbers that can be formed using two different digits from 1, 4, 7, and 9.

Solution

Each outcome is a permutation because the order of the digits matters. You can use an organized list to arrange all the possible outcomes.

Starts with 1:	Starts with 4:	Starts with 7:	Starts with 9:
14 17 19	41 47 49	71 74 79	91 94 97

Your turn now **Find all the possible outcomes.**

3. You can choose two toppings for a pizza from pepperoni, olives, mushrooms, and onions. Find all the possible pairs of toppings.

4. You are placing a math book, a novel, and a dictionary on a shelf. Find all the possible ways you can order the books on the shelf.

INTERNET
eWorkbook Plus
CLASSZONE.COM

Getting Ready to Practice

1. **Vocabulary** Choosing any 2 DVDs from 5 DVDs describes a ?.
   Arranging 4 letters to make a word describes a ?.

2. **Outfits** You pack a solid shirt, a striped shirt, a plaid shirt, tan shorts, and jeans for a weekend trip. Find all the different outfits you can wear.

3. **Car Ride** You are taking a car ride with your aunt and uncle. Only your aunt and uncle can drive. Copy and complete the tree diagram at the right. Then find all the possible ways that two people can sit in front.

Driver	Front passenger
?	?
	?
?	?
	?

Practice and Problem Solving

HELP with Homework

Example	Exercises
1	4–7
2	8–10
3	8–10

Online Resources
CLASSZONE.COM
· More Examples
· eTutorial Plus

In Exercises 4–7, use a tree diagram to find all the possible outcomes.

4. Wrapping paper: gold, silver
   Bow: red, blue, white, green

5. Room: kitchen, bathroom
   Paint color: white, beige, gray

6. Pet: dog, cat, horse, gerbil, bird
   Gender: male, female

7. City: Dallas, New York, Miami
   Month of travel: June, July, August

8. **Phones** A phone company offers 5 phone plan options: call waiting, call forwarding, voice mail, three-way calling, and caller ID. You can choose 3 options. Use a table to find all the possible sets of 3 options.

9. **Sculptures** You have 5 different colors of clay: blue, green, yellow, red, and purple. Each clay sculpture you can make uses exactly 2 different colors. Use a table to find all the different sculptures you can make.

10. **Numbers** Copy and complete the cards below to list all the two-digit numbers that can be formed using two different digits from 3, 4, 5, and 6.

Starts with 3:
Starts with 4:
Starts with 5:
Starts with 6:

11. **Movies** You rent 4 movies for a party: a comedy, a drama, a science fiction movie, and an adventure movie. Find all the possible orders in which to show two of the movies.

12. Writing Write a problem that can be solved using the tree diagram at the right.

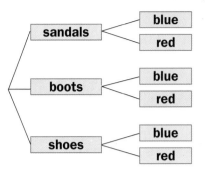

13. Eating Out For the first course, you can order soup or salad. For the main course, you can order pasta, seafood, or beef. For dessert, you can order pie, cake, or ice cream. Find all the possible meals.

14. Ice Skating Jenna, Karen, Angela, and Terry draw numbers from a hat to determine the order in an ice skating competition. Find all the ways that the skaters can be arranged if Jenna skates first.

15. Critical Thinking The sixth-grade class is electing 4 class officers: president, vice-president, secretary, and treasurer. The class is also choosing a 5-person fundraising committee. Tell which situation is a combination and which is a permutation. Explain your reasoning.

16. Challenge The rides at a fair are a Ferris wheel, a carousel, a log ride, and bumper cars. Find all the different ways you can go on the rides.

Mixed Review

17. A circular garden has a radius of 6 meters. Find its area. *(Lesson 10.4)*

A bag has 6 tiles labeled A, B, E, L, R, and U. You randomly choose one tile. Find the probability of the event. *(Lesson 13.1)*

18. You choose an R. **19.** You choose a vowel. **20.** You choose an S.

Basic Skills **Write the fraction in simplest form.**

21. $\frac{4}{10}$ **22.** $\frac{6}{9}$ **23.** $\frac{10}{12}$ **24.** $\frac{12}{20}$

Test-Taking Practice

25. Multiple Choice Tom, Gerald, and John are competing as a team in a speedskating relay race. In how many different ways can they arrange themselves for the race?

A. 3 **B.** 6 **C.** 9 **D.** 12

26. Short Response Juggling balls come in blue, green, red, orange, and purple. A juggler wants to choose exactly 3 of these colors at once. How many different groups of colors can the juggler choose from? Explain how you got your answer.

Guess, Check, and Revise
Solve a Simpler Problem
Make a Model
Break into Parts
Act it Out
Draw a Graph
Look for a Pattern

Act It Out

Problem Holly, Paul, Anne, and Jim are rehearsing a dance routine. How many different ways can you arrange the four dancers in a line if Anne must be first or second?

① Read and Understand

Read the problem carefully.

You need to place four people in a line. Anne must be either first or second in line.

② Make a Plan

Decide on a strategy to use.

You can solve the problem by acting it out. You need four people to act out the roles of Holly, Paul, Anne, and Jim.

③ Solve the Problem

Reread the problem and act it out.

Work in a group of four students playing the roles of Holly, Paul, Anne, and Jim. Arrange yourselves in as many ways as possible. List the arrangements.

If Anne is first, then the possible arrangements are as follows.

Anne, Holly, Paul, Jim   Anne, Holly, Jim, Paul
Anne, Paul, Holly, Jim   Anne, Paul, Jim, Holly
Anne, Jim, Paul, Holly   Anne, Jim, Holly, Paul

If Anne is second, then the possible arrangements are as follows.

Holly, Anne, Paul, Jim   Holly, Anne, Jim, Paul
Paul, Anne, Holly, Jim   Paul, Anne, Jim, Holly
Jim, Anne, Paul, Holly   Jim, Anne, Holly, Paul

ANSWER There are 12 ways to arrange the dancers in a line if Anne is the first or second person in line.

④ Look Back

You can solve the problem a different way. Use a tree diagram to find all the possible ways to arrange the four dancers. Then count all the outcomes in which Anne is either first or second.

Use the strategy *act it out*.

1. **Tug-of-War** Lauren, Luis, Carol, and Nia are a team playing tug-of-war. How many different ways can you arrange them if Luis cannot be the person in front?

2. **Trading Cards** You have $4. You sell a trading card for $1 and then buy 2 more trading cards for $2 each. Then you sell both of those cards for $3 each. How much money do you have now?

3. **Socks** A bag has 4 socks of different colors: blue, red, white, and black. How many different ways can you choose two socks?

4. **Seating** Betty, Louis, Carl, Mary, Phil, and Kate are sitting in seats 1 through 6 shown below. Phil is sitting in seat 3. Betty is sitting across from Phil. Carl is sitting between Betty and Kate. Mary is sitting across from Carl. In which seat is Louis sitting?

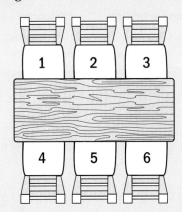

5. **Games** A game starts with 6 tokens on a table. Two players take turns removing 1, 2, or 3 tokens. The player who removes the last token on his or her turn wins. If you go first, how many tokens should you remove to guarantee that you win the game?

Mixed Problem Solving

Use any strategy to solve the problem.

6. **Graphing** Starting at $(-2, -4)$, go up 4 units, then to the left 2 units, then down 3 units, and then to the right 7 units. What are the coordinates of your new position?

7. **Talent Show** You sold 35 tickets to a community talent show. Tickets cost $3 per adult and $2 per child. You raised $84 for the show. How many adult tickets did you sell?

8. **Counting Off** There are 20 people seated in a room. They count off by 2's starting with the number 2. All the people with numbers that are divisible by 4 stand up. Then the people with numbers that are divisible by 8 sit down. How many people are now seated?

9. **Cubes** The rectangular prism below is made up of cubes. The cubes in the top and bottom rows are blue. The cubes in the middle two rows are red. How many more blue faces than red faces are showing on the six sides of the prism?

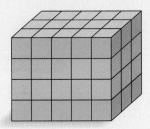

Probability of Independent Events

BEFORE

You found the probability of a single event.

▶ **Now**

You'll find the probability of two independent events.

WHY?

So you can analyze a game, as in Example 3.

Word Watch

independent events, p. 642

(**In the Real World**

Recreation You and your friend each randomly choose to go swimming or play basketball on Saturday. What is the probability that both of you choose basketball?

Two events are **independent** if the occurrence of one event does not affect the likelihood that the other event will occur.

EXAMPLE 1 **Two Independent Events**

To answer the question above, make a tree diagram of the possible outcomes. Note that your choice does not affect your friend's choice.

Your choice	Friend's choice	Outcome
swimming (S)	S	S S
	B	S B
basketball (B)	S	B S
	B	B B

1 of the 4 outcomes is favorable.

ANSWER The probability that both of you choose basketball is $\frac{1}{4}$.

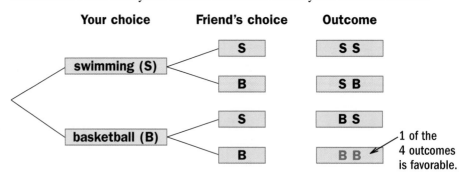
Your turn now **Use the situation in Example 1.**

1. Find the probability that both of you choose the same activity.

2. Find the probability that at least one of you chooses swimming.

EXAMPLE 2 Probability of a Sum

The spinners at the right are each divided into equal parts. You spin the spinners. Find the probability that the sum is at least 4.

You can use a table of sums to list all the possible outcomes.

	1	2	3	4	5	6
1	2	3	4	5	6	7
2	3	4	5	6	7	8

9 of the 12 sums are at least 4.

ANSWER The probability that the sum is at least 4 is $\frac{9}{12} = \frac{3}{4}$.

EXAMPLE 3 Three Independent Events

Games You are playing a game in which 3 canes are tossed. One side of each cane is flat, and the other side is round. Find the probability that all 3 canes land the same side up.

Solution

You can use a tree diagram to find all the possible outcomes.

First cane	Second cane	Third cane	Outcome
		R	R R R
	R	F	R R F
round (R)		R	R F R
	F	F	R F F
		R	F R R
	R	F	F R F
flat (F)		R	F F R
	F	F	F F F

2 canes round side up
1 cane flat side up

ANSWER The probability that all 3 canes land the same side up is $\frac{2}{8} = \frac{1}{4}$.

Your turn now Find the probability of the event.

3. The sum in Example 2 is at most 4.

4. Exactly 1 cane in Example 3 lands flat side up.

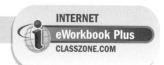

Getting Ready to Practice

Vocabulary **You randomly choose two marbles from a bag of 6 red and 4 blue marbles. Tell whether the two events are independent. Explain.**

1. You choose a red marble and put it back in the bag. Then you choose a blue marble.

2. You choose a blue marble but don't put it back in the bag. Then you choose a red marble.

Each spinner is divided into equal parts. You spin the spinners. Find the probability of the event.

3. You spin green on both spinners.

4. You spin red on at least 1 spinner.

5. **Carnival** You and a friend each randomly choose among the dunk tank, face painting, and the balloon throw for your first carnival activity. Find the probability that you both choose the same activity.

Practice and Problem Solving

with Homework

Example	Exercises
1	6–11, 18
2	12–17
3	19–22

Online Resources
CLASSZONE.COM

· More Examples
· eTutorial Plus

The spinner is divided into equal parts. You spin it twice. Find the probability of the event.

6. You spin two odd numbers.

7. You spin at least one even number.

You toss a coin twice. Find the probability of the event.

8. You get heads both times.

9. You get heads 0 times.

10. You get tails at least 1 time.

11. You get tails exactly 1 time.

A bag contains three tiles numbered 1, 2, and 3. Another bag contains four tiles numbered 1, 3, 5, and 7. You randomly draw one tile from each bag. Find the probability of the event.

12. The sum is 8.

13. The sum is 9.

14. The sum is odd.

15. The sum is prime.

16. The sum is 11.

17. The sum is even.

18. **Hidden Coin** You are guessing which of 2 hands is holding a coin. Find all the possible results of playing the game twice. Then find the probability that you guess correctly both times.

You toss a coin three times. Find the probability of the event.

19. You get heads 3 times.

20. You get tails exactly 1 time.

21. You get tails at least 2 times.

22. You get heads at most 2 times.

23. Order the events in Exercises 19–22 from least likely to occur to most likely to occur.

24. Acting It Out You have 3 shirts: solid, striped, and floral. You have 2 pairs of shorts: khaki and plaid. You have 3 sweaters: orange, green, and blue. You randomly choose one of each type of clothing. Find the probability that you choose a floral shirt, plaid shorts, and a green sweater.

25. Critical Thinking A bag contains only blue and red tiles. You draw a blue tile but do not put it back in the bag. Does this *increase*, *decrease*, or *not change* the probability that the next tile chosen is red? Explain.

26. Challenge You forgot the last 2 digits of your user ID for a games website. You know that both digits are odd. Find the probability that you type the correct last digits by randomly typing 2 odd numbers.

Mixed Review

Find the mean, median, and mode(s) of the data. *(Lesson 2.8)*

27. 14, 16, 12, 11, 14, 15, 13, 20

28. 15, 28, 21, 17, 28, 20, 21

Solve the proportion. *(Lesson 8.3)*

29. $\frac{4}{3} = \frac{x}{12}$

30. $\frac{5}{25} = \frac{s}{15}$

31. $\frac{10}{30} = \frac{6}{c}$

32. $\frac{24}{9} = \frac{8}{n}$

Basic Skills **Find the total amount spent.**

33. 6 bottles of water for $.95 each

34. 2 boxes of cereal for $3.45 each

Test-Taking Practice

35. Multiple Choice You are guessing on 2 multiple-choice questions. Each question has answer choices A, B, and C. Find the probability that you answer both questions correctly.

A. $\frac{1}{9}$

B. $\frac{1}{6}$

C. $\frac{1}{2}$

D. $\frac{2}{3}$

36. Multiple Choice A token is red on one side and yellow on the other side. You toss it twice. Find the probability that you get red both times.

F. $\frac{1}{8}$

G. $\frac{1}{4}$

H. $\frac{1}{2}$

I. $\frac{2}{3}$

Notebook Review

Review the vocabulary definitions in your notebook.

Copy the review examples in your notebook. Then complete the exercises.

Check Your Definitions

outcome, p. 630

event, p. 630

favorable outcomes, p. 630

probability, p. 630

complementary events, p. 632

tree diagram, p. 636

combination, p. 637

permutation, p. 637

independent events, p. 642

Use Your Vocabulary

1. Describe the complement of rolling an even number on a number cube.

2. **Writing** Explain how a combination and a permutation are different.

13.1 Can you find probabilities of single events?

Review **EXAMPLE** The probability of rolling an even number on a number cube is as follows.

$$\frac{\text{Number of favorable outcomes}}{\text{Number of possible outcomes}} = \frac{3}{6} = \frac{1}{2}$$

✓ **You roll a number cube. Find the probability of the event.**

3. You roll a 5.　　**4.** You roll an 8.　　**5.** You roll a factor of 24.

13.2–13.3 Can you find outcomes and probabilities?

 EXAMPLE You toss a coin twice. Find the probability that you get tails both times.

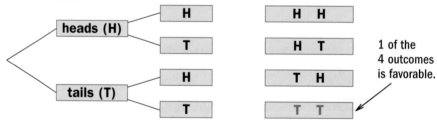

1 of the 4 outcomes is favorable.

ANSWER The probability that you get tails both times is $\frac{1}{4}$.

✓ **6.** Find all the different ways you can arrange the letters of the word ACT. Then find the probability that you randomly choose an arrangement in which the letter C is not the first letter.

Stop *and* **Think**   about Lessons 13.1–13.3

7. **Writing** Explain whether a percent greater than 100% can represent a probability.

8. **Critical Thinking** How are the probabilities of two complementary events related? Explain your answer.

Review Quiz 1

A bag contains twelve tiles numbered 1 through 12. You randomly choose one tile from the bag. Find the probability of the event.

1. You choose a 7.

2. You choose an even number.

3. You choose a multiple of 3.

4. You choose a 15.

5. **Posters** A poster comes in 3 sizes: 1 foot by 2 feet, 2 feet by 4 feet, and 3 feet by 6 feet. You can choose a black-and-white or a colored poster. List all the different kinds of posters you can choose from.

6. Find all the two-digit numbers that can be formed using two different digits from 1, 2, 4, and 6.

7. **Phone Numbers** You forgot the first two digits of your friend's phone number. You know that each of the digits is 7 or 8. Find the probability that you get the correct first two digits by randomly choosing 7 or 8.

Create a Spinner

Create a spinner that has 6 equal parts. Use the clues below to find out which numbers to put on the spinner.

- The probability of spinning a 4 is $\frac{1}{3}$.

- The probability of spinning a 2 is $\frac{1}{6}$.

- The probability of spinning a factor of 15 is $\frac{1}{2}$.

- The sum of the odd numbers on the spinner is 13.

Misleading Statistics

BEFORE	Now	WHY?
You made conclusions based on graphs of data.	You'll recognize how statistics can be misleading.	So you can interpret a graph of storms, as in Exs. 7–9.

Word Watch

Review Words

scale, p. 68
bar graph, p. 79
line graph, p. 84
mean, p. 93
median, p. 93
mode, p. 93

Activity You can use graphs to influence the way people interpret data.

The table at the right shows the results of a survey asking 100 students their favorite drink.

Drink	Students
Milk	25
Juice	21
Soda	31
Water	23

(1) Draw a bar graph of the data with a scale from 0 to 35 in increments of 5.

(2) Draw a bar graph of the data with a scale from 0 to 50 in increments of 10.

(3) Which graph is more likely to persuade someone that students drink too much soda? Explain your choice.

Misleading Graphs How someone draws a graph can affect how the information is interpreted. Bar and line graphs could be misleading if the scale appears to distort the data in some way.

EXAMPLE 1 **Potentially Misleading Graphs**

Movies The bar graph shows the number of admissions to movie theaters in the United States in 3 different years. Without using the scale, compare admissions in 1990 and 2000. Then compare the admissions using the scale.

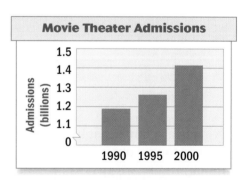

Movie Theater Admissions

Solution

Admissions in 1990 appear to have been about half the number in 2000, because the 1990 bar is half as high as the 2000 bar.

Admissions in 1990 were actually about 86% of admissions in 2000, because $1.2 \div 1.4 \approx 86\%$. The break in the scale distorts the relative heights of the bars.

1. Tell which line graph makes the average price of a movie ticket in the United States appear to increase more dramatically. Explain.

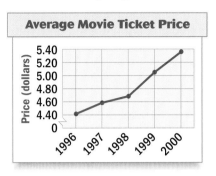

HELP with **Review**

Need help with finding the mean, median, and mode? See p. 93.

Misleading Averages An *average* can be represented by the mean, the median, or the mode. You may get a misleading impression of a data set if the average that is used does not represent the data well.

EXAMPLE 2 **Misleading Averages**

Cameras A store owner says that the average price of a digital camera at the store is $65. The prices of the 10 digital cameras sold at the store are:

$65, $65, $80, $90, $95, $100, $112, $120, $168, and $215.

Does $65 describe the prices well? Why might a store owner use this number?

Solution

The mode, $65, does not describe the data well because it is less than most of the prices. A store owner might use $65 as the average price to convince people that the store sells very inexpensive digital cameras.

HELP with **Solving**

If one data value is very small or very large compared to the other data, then the mean could be distorted.

Your turn now The numbers of monthly book donations to a library are listed below. Use these data in Exercises 2 and 3.

23, 28, 36, 45, 25, 31, 39, 47, 28, 32, 40, 226

2. Does 50 describe the numbers of donations well? Why or why not?

3. Why might a library use 50 as the average number of donated books?

Getting Ready to Practice

1. **Vocabulary** Describe how the scale affects a graph's appearance.

Jumping **The bar graph shows various long jump records.**

2. Without looking at the scale, about how many times greater does the record for kangaroos appear to be than the record for humans? for frogs?

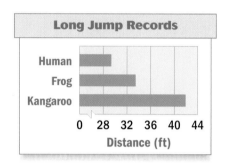

3. Using the scale, is the record for kangaroos *less than* or *greater than* two times the record for humans? for frogs?

4. **Guided Problem Solving** Jill says that her average score on a game is 500. Do the scores below support this? Why would Jill say this?

   350, 305, 300, 200, 500, 325, 375, 225, 275, 500

   (**1** Find the mean, median, and mode(s) of the scores.

   (**2** Does 500 describe Jill's scores well? Why or why not?

   (**3** Why would Jill use 500 as her average score?

Practice and Problem Solving

5. **Dogs** Which line graph would a dog walker use to persuade you to get your dog walked for 60 minutes? Explain.

HELP with Homework

Example	Exercises
1	5, 7–9
2	6, 10–11

Online Resources
CLASSZONE.COM

· More Examples
· eTutorial Plus

6. **Skateboarding** A reporter says that the average age of the athletes in a skateboarding competition is 18 years. All the ages are listed below. Why do you think this average was used? Is there a better one?

   15, 17, 29, 17, 15, 16, 15, 20

■ **Storms**

Hurricanes are rated on a scale of 1 to 5, with 5 being the most intense. From 1900 to 1996, the United States mainland had 57 hurricanes rated 1, 37 hurricanes rated 2, 47 hurricanes rated 3, 15 hurricanes rated 4, and 2 hurricanes rated 5. What fraction of the hurricanes were rated 3 or higher?

Storms The bar graph shows how many hurricanes and tropical storms started in various months from 1995 to 2001 in the Eastern Pacific.

7. Without looking at the scale or the data values, about how many times more storms appeared to start from July to September than from April to June?

8. Using the data values, about how many times more storms actually started from July to September than from April to June?

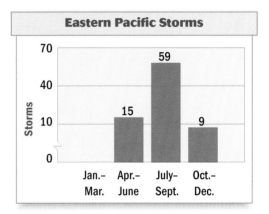

9. Would a travel agent use *the data values* or *the bars on the graph* to convince someone not to travel to the Eastern Pacific in the summer?

Baseball The numbers of games won by a baseball team in 10 seasons are listed below.

82, 94, 97, 88, 88, 71, 69, 55, 59, 72

10. A sports report states that the average number of wins by the team is 88. Does 88 describe the numbers of wins well? Why or why not?

11. Why might a report use 88 as the average number of wins?

Electives The circle graph shows the results of a survey asking students their favorite elective.

12. Without looking at the percents, which elective appears to have the most responses? Explain.

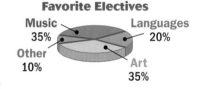

13. Draw a circle graph that more accurately shows the actual percent for each elective.

Houses The list below shows the prices of several houses in a region.

$115,000, $115,000, $130,000, $140,000, $145,000, $150,000, $152,000, $190,000, $198,000, $215,000

14. A real estate agent says that the average cost of a home in the region is $115,000. Does $115,000 describe the prices well? Why or why not?

15. Why might a real estate agent use $115,000 as the average price?

 16. Which average provides you with the information you would most want to know when buying a house? Why?

17. Bears The table shows the number of grizzly bears that were born in Yellowstone from 1992 to 1998. Draw a bar graph that makes the number of newborns in 1998 appear to be twice the number in 1992.

Year	1992	1993	1994	1995	1996	1997	1998
Newborns	60	41	47	37	72	62	70

Challenge The graph below shows the numbers, in millions, of CD shipments in the United States in 1998 and 1999.

18. About how many times greater in area is the picture for 1999 than the picture for 1998? Explain how this may distort the data.

19. Was the actual number of shipments in 1999 *less than* or *greater than* twice the number of shipments in 1998?

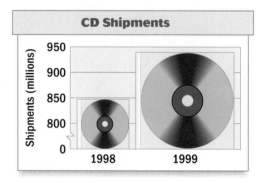

Mixed Review

20. Write *6 more than a number* as a variable expression. *(Lesson 12.1)*

21. You toss a coin twice. Find the probability that you get heads at least one time. *(Lesson 13.3)*

Basic Skills **Find the range of the data.**

22. 14, 16, 11, 10, 13, 15, 21, 18   **23.** 532, 416, 501, 543, 580, 499

Test-Taking Practice

24. Short Response The bar graph shows the heights of two buildings. Without looking at the scale, tell how many times taller Building B appears than Building A. Does your answer represent the actual relationship? Explain.

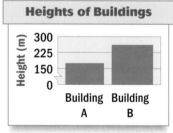

25. Multiple Choice The list below shows the number of cars at a car wash each day last week. You want it to seem as successful as possible. Which value would you use as the average number of cars washed per day?

   73, 80, 106, 73, 73, 85, 98

   A. mean   **B.** median   **C.** mode   **D.** range

Stem-and-Leaf Plots

BEFORE	▶ Now	WHY?
You organized data using line plots and frequency tables.	You'll organize data using stem-and-leaf plots.	So you can organize scores in bowling games, as in Ex. 12.

 **Word Watch**

stem-and-leaf plot, p. 653
leaf, p. 653
stem, p. 653

In the Real World

Internet The table lists how long, in minutes, you were online each day for the past 21 days. How can you display the data so you can see them grouped in an orderly way?

You can use a *stem-and-leaf plot* to organize a large set of data. In a **stem-and-leaf plot**, each data value has two parts, a *stem* and a *leaf*. The **leaf** is the last digit on the right. The **stem** is the remaining digits. For example, the leaf of the data value 37 is 7. The stem is 3.

Daily Internet Use (minutes)			
SUNDAY	22	27	42
MONDAY	41	23	19
TUESDAY	15	35	29
WEDNESDAY	28	54	53
THURSDAY	50	70	31
FRIDAY	19	40	31
SATURDAY	44	37	35

EXAMPLE 1 Making a Stem-and-Leaf Plot

To organize the minutes online in the table above, you can make a stem-and-leaf plot. The numbers range from 15 to 70. So, the least stem is 1 and the greatest stem is 7.

Watch Out!

Be sure to include all of the stems between the least and the greatest. In Example 1, 6 is a stem even though none of the data values have a 6 in the tens' place.

(1) **Order the stems from least to greatest.**

```
1 |
2 |
3 |
4 |
5 |
6 |
7 |
```

(2) **Write the leaves next to their stems.**

```
1 | 9 5 9
2 | 2 7 3 9 8
3 | 5 1 1 7 5
4 | 2 1 0 4
5 | 4 3 0
6 |
7 | 0
```
↖ This stands for 53.

(3) **Order the leaves from least to greatest.**

```
1 | 5 9 9
2 | 2 3 7 8 9
3 | 1 1 5 5 7
4 | 0 1 2 4
5 | 0 3 4
6 |
7 | 0      Key: 5│3 = 53
```

Your turn now Make a stem-and-leaf plot of the data.

1. 31, 14, 22, 51, 33, 16, 21, 24, 22, 15, 30, 28, 39

EXAMPLE 2 **Interpreting Stem-and-Leaf Plots**

Diners The stem-and-leaf plot shows the ages of people at a diner.

a. What is the range of the ages?

b. Describe the age group with the most people.

```
0 | 4  6  7  9
1 | 0  1  1  2  2  2  4  9
2 | 2  5  8
3 | 0  1  4      Key: 3 | 1 = 31
```

Solution

a. The youngest person at the diner is 4 years old, because the least data value is 0 | 4. The oldest person is 34 years old, because the greatest data value is 3 | 4. The range is 30 years, because 34 − 4 = 30.

b. The stem of 1 has more leaves than any other, so the age group with the most people is 10–19 years.

EXAMPLE 3 **Finding the Mean, Median, and Mode**

Use the stem-and-leaf plot.

a. Find the mean.

b. Find the median.

c. Find the mode.

```
5 | 7  7
6 | 1  2  7
7 | 0  4      Key: 5 | 7 = 5.7
```

Solution

Make an ordered list of the 7 values in the stem-and-leaf plot.

5.7, 5.7, 6.1, 6.2, 6.7, 7.0, 7.4

a. Mean $= \dfrac{5.7 + 5.7 + 6.1 + 6.2 + 6.7 + 7.0 + 7.4}{7} = \dfrac{44.8}{7} = 6.4$

b. The median is 6.2, because the middle value is 6.2.

c. The mode is 5.7, because it occurs the most times.

Your turn now **Use the stem-and-leaf plot in Example 2.**

2. Describe the ages of the people at the diner who are not in the most common age group.

3. Find the mean, median, and mode(s) of the data.

13.5 Exercises

More Practice, p. 720

Getting Ready to Practice

1. **Vocabulary** Identify the stems and the leaves in the stem-and-leaf plot.

   ```
   1 | 2 4 7
   2 | 1 9
   3 | 5 6 8 9    Key: 1│4 = 14
   ```

Pets **The list below shows the weights, in pounds, of pets owned by students.**

   25, 7, 8, 10, 13, 22, 10, 15, 12, 13, 9, 40, 15, 21, 14

2. Find the least stem and the greatest stem for the data.

3. Make a stem-and-leaf plot of the data.

4. Which stem has the most leaves? Explain what this means.

Practice and Problem Solving

Make a stem-and-leaf plot of the data.

5. 15, 18, 24, 32, 28, 18, 21, 16, 32, 41, 25, 31, 18, 25

6. 67, 55, 61, 69, 50, 51, 67, 62, 39, 50, 35, 62, 58, 60

7. 15, 38, 9, 33, 16, 7, 5, 35, 30, 35, 55, 49, 41, 52, 51

8. **Find the Error** Describe and correct the error in making the stem-and-leaf plot.

   ```
      1 | 5 9
   ✗  2 | 0 2
      4 | 3 3 7    Key: 4│3 = 43
   ```

Tennis **The stem-and-leaf plot shows the lengths, in minutes, of mixed doubles finals matches in Wimbledon tennis for a period of years.**

9. Find the mean, median, mode(s), and range.

10. Which stem has the most leaves? Explain what this means.

11. Describe the relationship between the shortest and longest matches in two different ways.

   ```
    5 | 9
    6 | 6 9
    7 | 1 1 3 3 3 5
    8 | 5 5
    9 | 3 7
   10 | 0
   11 |
   12 | 1    Key: 12│1 = 121
   ```

HELP with **Homework**

Example	Exercises
1	5–8
2	9–11
3	9–11

Online Resources
CLASSZONE.COM

· More Examples
· eTutorial Plus

Bowling The table shows your bowling scores in several games.

12. Make a stem-and-leaf plot of the scores. Use the key 19 | 6 = 196.

13. Suppose your goal was to score at least 230 in 10 of the games. By how many games did you miss your goal?

Bowling Scores				
181	222	196	210	217
195	199	204	215	190
202	251	222	230	235

Cell Phones In Exercises 14 and 15, use the stem-and-leaf plot. It shows the weights, in ounces, of 15 cell phones at a store.

14. Find the mean, median, and mode(s).

15. **Writing** Which number would you use as the average weight? Explain.

16. **Challenge** The least value of a data set is 12.3. The greatest value is 90.7. Is it appropriate to make a stem-and-leaf plot of the data? Explain.

```
4 | 0 3 8 8
5 | 0 4 9
6 | 0 1 2
7 | 1 2 9
8 | 2 6    Key: 8 | 6 = 8.6
```

Mixed Review

Graph the integer on a number line. *(Lesson 11.1)*

17. −6
18. 5
19. 0
20. −2

21. Your score on a cooking contest is 7. All the scores of the 10 contestants are listed below. What average can you use so you can say that your score is above average? Explain. *(Lesson 13.4)*

7, 10, 10, 6, 9, 5, 8, 7, 5, 5

Basic Skills Copy and complete the statement with <, >, or =.

22. 35.89 ? 35.889
23. 2.162 ? 2.1005
24. 6.017 ? 6.01700

Test-Taking Practice

25. **Multiple Choice** Use the stem-and-leaf plot to find the median of the data.

```
0 | 9 9
1 | 5 5 6 7 9
2 | 0 0 0 1 2    Key: 2 | 0 = 20
```

A. 8   **B.** 18   **C.** 20   **D.** 22

26. **Short Response** Make a stem-and-leaf plot of Gary's test scores below. Did Gary get mostly 90s, 80s, or 70s? Explain.

78, 96, 96, 83, 94, 88, 93, 79, 99, 86, 86

Box-and-Whisker Plots

BEFORE

You represented data using stem-and-leaf plots.

▶ **Now**

You'll represent data using box-and-whisker plots.

WHY?

So you can compare durations of solar eclipses, as in Ex. 11.

Word Watch

box-and-whisker plot, p. 657
lower quartile, p. 657
upper quartile, p. 657
lower extreme, p. 657
upper extreme, p. 657

(**In the Real World**

Ticket Prices The notebook shows the ticket prices for different concerts that you attended. How can you display the data so you can see how spread out they are?

A **box-and-whisker plot** divides a data set into four parts, two below the median and two above it. The **lower quartile** is the median of the lower half of the data. The **upper quartile** is the median of the upper half. The **lower extreme** is the least data value. The **upper extreme** is the greatest data value.

EXAMPLE 1 Making a Box-and-Whisker Plot

To display the ticket prices above, make a box-and-whisker plot.

① Order the data to find the median, the quartiles, and the extremes.

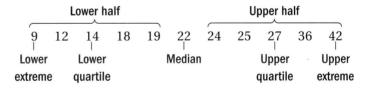

② Plot the five values below a number line.

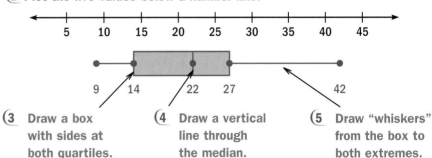

 **with Solving**

As shown in Example 1, if a data set has an odd number of data values, then the median is not included in either half of the data.

③ Draw a box with sides at both quartiles.

④ Draw a vertical line through the median.

⑤ Draw "whiskers" from the box to both extremes.

Your turn now Make a box-and-whisker plot of the data.

1. 5, 9, 16, 8, 6, 15, 14, 5, 15, 12   **2.** 35, 19, 63, 48, 67, 50, 44, 58, 53

EXAMPLE **2** **Reading a Box-and-Whisker Plot**

Identify the median, the lower and upper quartiles, and the lower and upper extremes in the box-and-whisker plot below.

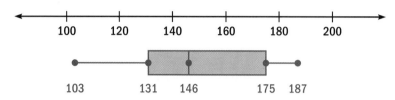

ANSWER The median is 146. The lower quartile is 131. The upper quartile is 175. The lower extreme is 103. The upper extreme is 187.

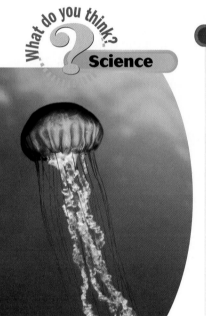

What do you think?

Science

■ **Jellyfish**

A moon jellyfish is shown in the photo above. The largest jellyfish can grow up to 90 inches in body width. How does this width compare to the body widths of the moon jellyfish samples in Example 3?

EXAMPLE **3** **Interpreting Box-and-Whisker Plots**

Jellyfish The box-and-whisker plots below represent the body widths, in inches, of a sample of jellyfish from two different species.

a. Find the range of the body widths.

b. Compare the body widths in the two samples.

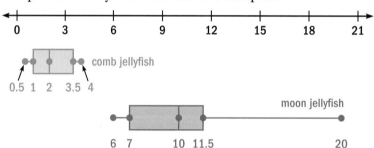

Solution

a. The range is the difference between the extremes.
The range for comb jellyfish is 3.5 inches, because $4 - 0.5 = 3.5$.
The range for moon jellyfish is 14 inches, because $20 - 6 = 14$.

b. All of the moon jellyfish in the sample have a greater body width than any of the comb jellyfish.

Your turn now Use the box-and-whisker plots above.

3. Find the range of the data in Example 2.

4. Identify the median, the lower and upper quartiles, and the lower and upper extremes for the body widths of the moon jellyfish in Example 3.

Getting Ready to Practice

1. **Vocabulary** Identify the median, the lower quartile, the upper quartile, the lower extreme, and the upper extreme in the box-and-whisker plot.

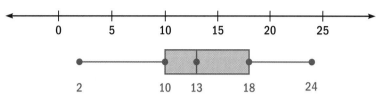

2. **Find the Error** Describe and correct the error in finding the upper quartile.

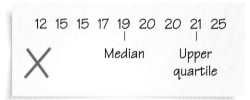

3. **Recycling** The list below shows the numbers of recyclable cans collected by ten classes. Make a box-and-whisker plot of the data.

   36, 42, 12, 39, 34, 71, 33, 32, 40, 32

Practice and Problem Solving

DVD Players **The box-and-whisker plot below shows the prices, in dollars, of various DVD players offered at a store. Identify the value.**

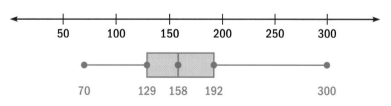

4. lower extreme   5. upper quartile   6. median

Make a box-and-whisker plot of the data.

7. 9, 11, 15, 8, 6, 18, 13, 14, 10   8. 22, 7, 4, 29, 15, 30, 8, 9, 11

9. 37, 14, 30, 24, 32, 16, 20, 13   10. 17, 3, 42, 39, 10, 12, 33, 25

11. **Solar Eclipses** In a total solar eclipse, the moon is between Earth and the Sun. The list below shows the lengths, in seconds, of 13 total solar eclipses from 1981 to 2000. Make a box-and-whisker plot of the data.

    122, 311, 120, 119, 226, 153, 413, 321, 263, 129, 170, 249, 143

with **Homework**

Example	Exercises
1	7–12
2	4–6, 13
3	14–17

Online Resources
CLASSZONE.COM
· More Examples
· eTutorial Plus

Extended Problem Solving Use the table shown for Exercises 12–14. The table shows the running times, in minutes, of the movies that won the award for Best Picture from 1970 to 1999.

12. Graph Make a box-and-whisker plot of each set of data using the same number line.

13. Interpret Identify the median and the range of the running times for each decade.

14. Compare Compare and contrast the running times of the Best Pictures in the 1970s, the 1980s, and the 1990s.

Running Times of Best Pictures (minutes)		
1970s	**1980s**	**1990s**
170	124	183
104	123	118
175	188	131
129	132	197
200	158	142
133	150	177
119	120	160
93	160	194
183	133	122
105	99	121

Bobsleds The box-and-whisker plots show the differences, in seconds, between the gold and silver medalists' times in men's Olympic bobsled events from 1928 to 2002.

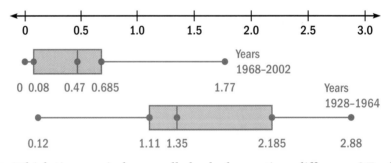

15. Which time period generally had a lesser time difference? Explain.

16. Which time period had a wider range of time differences? Explain.

17. In a box-and-whisker plot, the box represents about 50% of the data. The whiskers each represent about 25% of the data. About what percent of the time differences from 1928 to 1964 were between 1.11 seconds and 2.88 seconds?

18. Critical Thinking Explain why the medians of the lower half and the upper half of a set of data are called quartiles.

19. Challenge Make a data set of 10 values that meets these conditions:
    median = 123
    lower quartile = 92
    upper extreme = 170
    range = 87

Choose a Strategy Use a strategy from the list to solve the following problem. Explain your choice of strategy.

> **Problem Solving Strategies**
> ▪ Guess, Check, and Revise
> ▪ Draw a Diagram
> ▪ Make a Table
> ▪ Look for a Pattern

20. A ferry arrives at 11:07 A.M., 11:21 A.M., 11:35 A.M., and 11:49 A.M. Predict when the next two ferries will arrive.

Basic Skills Find the sum or difference.

21. $10.3 + 1.7$ **22.** $2.6 + 94.8$ **23.** $3.07 - 0.589$ **24.** $21.9 - 6.7$

Test-Taking Practice

INTERNET
State Test Practice
CLASSZONE.COM

25. Multiple Choice Find the range in the box-and-whisker plot.

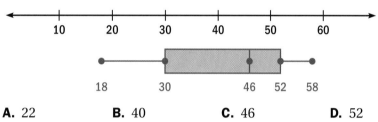

A. 22   **B.** 40   **C.** 46   **D.** 52

26. Short Response Make a box-and-whisker plot of the data. Explain your steps.

13, 14, 22, 25, 30, 29, 27, 18, 19, 14, 18, 19

BRAIN GAME

Solve the Riddle

Who earns a living by driving customers away?

Each data value has a letter underneath it.

16	19	18	15	20	10	27	14	30	8	13	12	8	7	23
(A)	(S)	(F)	(V)	(X)	(E)	(U)	(O)	(D)	(I)	(L)	(B)	(I)	(T)	(R)

Replace each **?** with the letter of the correct data value.

?		?	?	?	?		?	?	?	?	?	?
mean		lower extreme	mean	upper quartile	mode		upper extreme	range	mode	median	lower quartile	range

Choosing an Appropriate Data Display

LESSON 13.7

BEFORE	▶ Now	WHY?
You created different data displays.	You'll choose appropriate data displays.	So you can graph the results of a competition, as in Ex. 10.

Word Watch

Review Words

line plot, p. 73
bar graph, p. 79
line graph, p. 84
circle graph, p. 88
stem-and-leaf plot, p. 653
box-and-whisker plot, p. 657

Data Displays Below is a summary of the different ways you can display data and how each display is often used.

Appropriate Data Displays	
A **line plot** shows how often each number occurs.	× × × × × ×
A **bar graph** shows how different categories of data compare.	(bar graph)
A **line graph** represents data that change over time.	(line graph)
A **circle graph** represents data as parts of a whole.	(circle graph)
A **stem-and-leaf plot** displays all the data values and orders the data from least to greatest.	1 | 0 1 2 2 2 | 4 8 8 3 | 9
A **box-and-whisker plot** shows the spread of data using the median, the quartiles, and the extremes.	(box-and-whisker plot)

EXAMPLE 1 Choosing Between Two Displays

Stamps Which graph makes it easier to compare the number of people who prefer sports stamps to the total number of people?

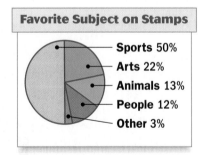

Favorite Subject on Stamps

- **Sports** 50%
- **Arts** 22%
- **Animals** 13%
- **People** 12%
- **Other** 3%

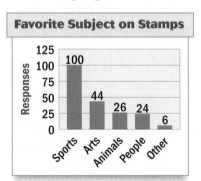

Favorite Subject on Stamps

ANSWER The circle graph shows the whole, so it makes it easier to see that 50% of the people chose sports as their favorite stamp subject.

EXAMPLE 2 Making an Appropriate Display

Sunglasses You ask 20 people at a beach how many pairs of sunglasses they own. The list below shows their responses. Make a data display that shows the spread of data.

0, 1, 1, 1, 2, 2, 2, 2, 2, 3, 3, 3, 3, 3, 4, 4, 4, 6, 6, 10

Solution

You can use a box-and-whisker plot to show the spread of data. The box tells you that about half of the people own 2 to 4 pairs of sunglasses.

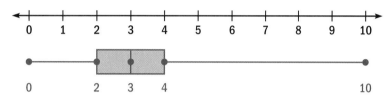

EXAMPLE 3 Choosing the Appropriate Display

Weather The data displays organize the daily high temperatures, in degrees Fahrenheit, during a recent month in Boston, Massachusetts. Which display is appropriate for finding the median high temperature?

```
3 | 6
4 | 0 1 4 5 7 8 9 9 9
5 | 3 3 3 4 6 6 6 8 8
6 | 0 0 2 3 5 5 7
7 | 2 3
8 | 4 5
```
Key: 3 | 6 = 36°F

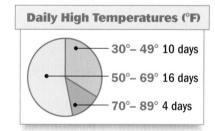

Daily High Temperatures (°F)

30°– 49° 10 days
50°– 69° 16 days
70°– 89° 4 days

Solution

The stem-and-leaf plot is appropriate for finding the median high temperature, 56°F, because it displays the data in order. The circle graph is not appropriate because it does not display the temperatures.

HELP with Notetaking

For each type of data display you studied in this book, you may want to include an example in your notebook along with a summary of the information that you can read from the display.

Your turn now Choose an appropriate display for the given situation.

1. You record the temperature, in degrees Fahrenheit, at noon for seven days in a row. The data are listed below. Which data display would you use to show how the temperature changed during that time?

50°F   42°F   30°F   32°F   45°F   55°F   50°F

Getting Ready to Practice

Vocabulary **Match the data display with its description.**

1. line plot
2. circle graph
3. line graph
4. stem-and-leaf plot
5. bar graph

A. shows all values and orders data

B. displays data changing over time

C. uses X's to show how often a number occurs

D. shows how data in various categories compare

E. represents data as parts of a whole

6. **Soccer** Which data displays make it possible to compare the number of soccer players in each age group in the table?

Age	11	12	13
Players	1	9	3

Practice and Problem Solving

HELP with Homework

Example	Exercises
1	7
2	8–10
3	11, 12

Online Resources
CLASSZONE.COM

· More Examples
· eTutorial Plus

7. Tell which data display makes it easier to see the number of students who read 5 books last month.

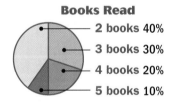

Books Read

Books Read
- 2 books 40%
- 3 books 30%
- 4 books 20%
- 5 books 10%

8. **Stocks** The closing prices of a company stock on Monday through Friday are listed in order below. Make a data display that shows the change in price over the week.

$26.20, $25.50, $25.00, $24.80, $24.65

9. **Concerts** The list below shows the ages of the first twelve people who enter a concert hall. Make a data display that orders the ages from least to greatest. Then use the display to find the median of the ages.

34, 19, 60, 45, 42, 38, 49, 58, 70, 41, 39, 31

10. **Bicycle Stunts** The list shows the scores of 10 athletes at a bicycle stunt competition. Make a data display that shows the median and the spread of the scores.

Bicycle Stunt Scores				
91.4	91.0	90.3	90.0	89.7
89.4	87.5	86.7	84.3	84.1

Communication **In Exercises 11 and 12, use the table below. It shows the results of a survey asking 100 students their favorite way to get in touch with friends.**

11. Tell whether a *line graph* or a *bar graph* is appropriate for displaying the data. Then use your choice to make a display of the results of the survey.

12. Make a data display that is appropriate for comparing the results for each category to the overall results of the survey.

Form of communication	Responses
instant messaging	33
e-mail	20
telephone	28
letter writing	11
other	8

13. Critical Thinking Name two data displays that you can use to find the mode of a set of data. Explain your reasoning.

14. Challenge Describe how you might use the following data displays to show where most of the data belong: bar graph, line plot, circle graph, and stem-and-leaf plot.

Mixed Review

15. Make a stem-and-leaf plot of the data. *(Lesson 13.5)*

32, 34, 14, 8, 18, 32, 36, 35, 9, 15, 12, 41, 37, 12, 16, 12, 10

16. Make a box-and-whisker plot of the data. *(Lesson 13.6)*

23, 62, 32, 32, 10, 24, 35, 27, 22, 21, 19, 16

Basic Skills **Evaluate the expression.**

17. $24 - 3^3 \div 9$　　　**18.** $61 - 5 \times 2^3$　　　**19.** $7 \times 6 + 68 \div 4$

Test-Taking Practice

20. Extended Response The table shows the cost to mail a post card in the United States in different years. Tell which data display you would use to show the changing cost to mail a post card over the years. Explain your choice. Then make the data display.

Year	Cost of post card
1960	$.03
1970	$.05
1980	$.10
1990	$.15
2000	$.20

Notebook Review

Review the vocabulary definitions in your notebook.

Copy the review examples in your notebook. Then complete the exercises.

Check Your Definitions

stem-and-leaf plot, p. 653

leaf, p. 653

stem, p. 653

box-and-whisker plot, p. 657

lower quartile, p. 657

upper quartile, p. 657

lower extreme, p. 657

upper extreme, p. 657

Use Your Vocabulary

1. Identify the stem and the leaf in the number 36.

2. Identify the lower quartile in the set of data:
15, 17, 17, 18, 20, 21, 22, 26, 29.

13.4 Can you recognize misleading statistics?

 EXAMPLE Explain why the bar graph could be misleading.

Value A appears to be one fourth of Value B. However, using the scale, Value A is about 63% of Value B, because $100 \div 160 \approx 63\%$.

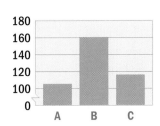

3. Use the graph in the Example above. What fraction of Value B does Value C appear to be without using the scale? using the scale?

13.5 Can you make stem-and-leaf plots?

 EXAMPLE Make a stem-and-leaf plot of the data.

15, 11, 9, 7, 32, 21, 16, 9, 13, 17, 15, 8, 30, 20, 23

(1 Order the stems from least to greatest.

```
0 |
1 |
2 |
3 |
```

(2 Write the leaves next to their stems.

```
0 | 9 7 9 8
1 | 5 1 6 3 7 5
2 | 1 0 3
3 | 2 0
```

(3 Order the leaves from least to greatest.

```
0 | 7 8 9 9
1 | 1 3 5 5 6 7
2 | 0 1 3
3 | 0 2     Key: 2|3 = 23
```

4. Make a stem-and-leaf plot of the data.
5, 10, 12, 31, 28, 50, 8, 7, 15, 19, 24, 36

13.6–13.7 Can you make appropriate data displays?

Review **EXAMPLE** Make a box-and-whisker plot to show the spread of data.

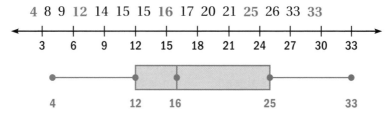

4 8 9 12 14 15 15 16 17 20 21 25 26 33 33

☑ **5.** Make a box-and-whisker plot of the data.
13, 16, 21, 31, 50, 18, 24, 19, 27, 22

6. The low temperature in a city was 52°F on Sunday, 49°F on Monday, 45°F on Tuesday, and 48°F on Wednesday. Make a data display that shows the change in temperature over the four days.

Stop and Think about Lessons 13.4–13.7

7. Writing Describe how the scale can affect your impression of the data in a line graph and in a bar graph.

Review Quiz 2

1. Which line graph might a travel agent use to convince people that train travel is becoming too expensive? Explain your choice.

2. Make a stem-and-leaf plot of the data: 36, 33, 21, 8, 39, 24, 26, 50, 4, 16.

3. Make a box-and-whisker plot of the data: 80, 81, 90, 83, 74, 73, 91, 84, 86.

4. Survey In a survey of 100 people, 64 people liked a new movie, 20 people didn't like the movie, and the rest have not seen it. Make a data display that compares the results for each response to all the responses.

Chapter Review

Vocabulary

outcome, p. 630
event, p. 630
favorable outcomes,
    p. 630
probability, p. 630
complementary events,
    p. 632
tree diagram, p. 636

combination, p. 637
permutation, p. 637
independent events,
    p. 642
stem-and-leaf plot,
    p. 653
leaf, p. 653

stem, p. 653
box-and-whisker plot,
    p. 657
lower quartile, p. 657
upper quartile, p. 657
lower extreme, p. 657
upper extreme, p. 657

Vocabulary Review

Copy and complete the statement.

1. Two events are _?_ if they have no outcomes in common and if together they contain all the outcomes of the experiment.

2. Two events are _?_ if the occurrence of one event does not affect the likelihood that the other event will occur.

3. An arrangement of objects in which order is important is called a _?_.

4. In a stem-and-leaf plot, the _?_ is the last digit on the right, and the _?_ is the remaining digits.

5. In a box-and-whisker plot, the _?_ is the least data value, and the _?_ is the greatest data value.

6. Outcomes for which an event occurs are called _?_ outcomes.

Review Questions

You roll a number cube. Find the probability of the event. *(Lesson 13.1)*

7. You roll a number less than 4.

8. You roll a number greater than 6.

9. You roll a factor of 60.

10. You don't roll a multiple of 3.

11. **Birthdays** You randomly choose a birthday in July. Find the probability that it is not an even date. *(Lesson 13.1)*

Use a tree diagram to find all the possible outcomes. *(Lesson 13.2)*

12. Dish: taco, burrito, enchilada
Sauce: mild, hot, extra hot

13. City: Pittsburgh, Dallas, Miami, Los Angeles
Souvenir: hat, T-shirt, poster

14. **Computers** You can choose 2 free accessories from among a printer, a camera, and a scanner when you buy a computer. Find all the possible pairs of accessories you can choose from. *(Lesson 13.2)*

15. Diving Leah, Sarah, Jenny, and Michelle are competing in a diving competition. Find all the possible top two placements. *(Lesson 13.2)*

The spinners at the right are each divided into equal parts. You spin the spinners. Find the probability of the event. *(Lesson 13.3)*

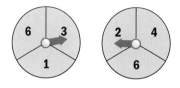

16. You spin a sum of 5.   **17.** You spin two sixes.

18. You spin an odd sum.   **19.** You spin two prime numbers.

20. Your friend is thinking of a two-digit number. You know that the first digit is 6 or 7, and the second digit is 1 or 2. Find the probability that you randomly choose the correct number. *(Lesson 13.3)*

21. What fraction of Value A does Value B appear to be without using the scale? If you use the scale, what fraction of Value A is Value B? *(Lesson 13.4)*

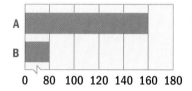

Basketball The list below shows the total points earned by a basketball team during each finals match. *(Lesson 13.4)*

98, 78, 100, 98, 82, 79, 88

22. A local sports reporter states that the average points per game is 98. Does 98 describe the total points well? Why or why not?

Make a stem-and-leaf plot of the data. *(Lesson 13.5)*

23. 45, 52, 59, 32, 48, 55, 41, 60

24. 18, 24, 27, 14, 33, 28, 45, 72, 49, 12, 25

Use the stem-and-leaf plot below to find the quantity. *(Lesson 13.5)*

25. mean

26. median

27. mode

```
3 | 4  6  7  7
4 |
5 | 0  0  0  1  6
6 | 2  5          Key: 3 | 7 = 37
```

Make a box-and-whisker plot of the data. *(Lesson 13.6)*

28. 13, 5, 10, 6, 17, 8, 5, 7, 13, 9, 11

29. 65, 70, 76, 59, 41, 23, 77, 58, 71, 63, 59, 54

30. Music After playing 3 new songs, a disc jockey records that 186 callers prefer the first song, 79 callers prefer the second song, and 310 callers prefer the third song. Which data display would you use to compare the responses for the first song to all the responses? *(Lesson 13.7)*

Chapter Test

A bag contains 10 tiles labeled 1, 4, 7, 8, L, T, M, O, U, and Z. You randomly choose one tile. Find the probability of the event.

1. You choose a letter.

2. You choose an odd number.

3. You choose a factor of 16.

4. You don't choose a consonant.

5. Clothing You have 4 shirts: solid, striped, checkered, and plaid. You have 2 pairs of pants: overalls and jeans. Use a tree diagram to find all the possible outfits you can wear.

6. Vacation You want to go to a museum, an aquarium, a circus, and an amusement park during your vacation. You have time for only 2 places. Find all the combinations of 2 places that you can choose from.

7. Photos You are arranging your brother, sister, and cousin for a photo. Find all the possible ways you can arrange them in a row.

Each spinner is divided into equal parts. You spin the spinners. Find the probability of the event.

8. You spin green on both spinners.

9. You spin blue on at least 1 spinner.

10. You spin yellow on exactly 1 spinner.

11. You don't spin orange on either spinner.

12. Fuel Prices Which line graph would someone use to convince people that the price per gallon of gasoline in a state was stable over seven months? Explain.

13. In-line Skates An advertiser says that the average price of inline skates at a store is $130. The list below shows the prices of inline skates offered at the store. Why do you think this average was used?

$150, $250, $200, $190, $150, $100, $130, $130, $130, $190

14. Make a stem-and-leaf plot of the data.
90, 81, 93, 95, 68, 63, 97, 88, 59, 39, 54

15. Make a box-and-whisker plot of the data.
98, 117, 129, 154, 160, 145, 120, 135, 172

16. License Plates You record the states of the first 200 license plates of vehicles you see enter a highway. You find 134 Oklahoma plates, 35 Texas plates, and 31 Louisiana plates. Which data display would you use to compare the number of Texas plates to total plates?

Chapter Standardized Test

Test-Taking Strategy Work at your own pace. Do not think about how fast other students complete the test.

Multiple Choice

1. A bag holds 9 red and 3 blue marbles. If you randomly choose one marble from the bag, find the probability that it is blue.

   A. $\frac{1}{4}$ **B.** $\frac{1}{3}$ **C.** $\frac{5}{12}$ **D.** $\frac{7}{12}$

2. Find the mode in the stem-and-leaf plot below.

   ```
   4 | 3 5 8
   5 | 2 5 5 9
   6 | 0 0 0 6
   7 | 2          Key: 5 | 9 = 59
   ```

   F. 55   **G.** 57   **H.** 60   **I.** 72

3. You toss a coin twice. Find the probability of getting heads at least one time.

   A. $\frac{1}{4}$ **B.** $\frac{1}{2}$ **C.** $\frac{3}{4}$ **D.** 1

4. You can choose 2 kinds of flowers for a garden from lilies, daisies, roses, carnations, and irises. How many pairs of flowers are possible?

   F. 3   **G.** 7   **H.** 10   **I.** 14

5. You roll a number cube. Which event is most likely to occur?

   A. You roll a 9.   **B.** You roll an integer.

   C. You roll a 5.   **D.** Your roll is even.

6. How many different ways can you arrange two letters from the word MATH?

   F. 4   **G.** 6   **H.** 8   **I.** 12

7. Find the range in the box-and-whisker plot.

   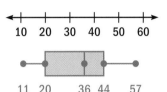

   A. 22   **B.** 36   **C.** 46   **D.** 57

8. You are guessing on 1 true-and-false question and 1 multiple-choice question with answer choices A, B, C, and D. Find the probability that you answer both questions correctly.

   F. $\frac{1}{8}$ **G.** $\frac{1}{6}$ **H.** $\frac{1}{4}$ **I.** $\frac{1}{3}$

9. Which data display would you use to show the value of a baseball card over 50 years?

   A. bar graph   **B.** stem-and-leaf plot

   C. line plot   **D.** line graph

Short Response

10. Bob's scores in a board game are 430, 290, 330, 330, 610, and 380. Bob says that his average score is 395. Explain whether 395 describes the scores well. Then tell why Bob would use 395 as his average score.

Extended Response

11. In a survey of 425 students, 254 liked a science museum, 102 didn't like the museum, and the rest did not have an opinion. Describe a strategy to draw a bar graph that makes it appear that one third as many students didn't like the museum as students who did. Then draw the graph.

Strategies for Answering
Extended Response Questions

Problem

Salad ingredients cost $.25 per ounce at a salad bar. You plan to buy a salad and a $1.00 bottle of juice. Make a function table to show the total cost of the juice and salad for 0, 1, 2, 3, 4, 5, and 6 ounces of salad. Graph the function. Find the cost of juice and a 10 ounce salad, and explain how you found your answer.

Full credit solution

The function table is correct and reflects an understanding of the relationship between the number of ounces of salad and the total cost of the juice and the salad.

Let x represent the number of ounces of salad. Let y represent the cost in dollars of the juice and salad.

Ounces of salad, x	0	1	2	3	4	5	6
Total cost, y	$1.00	$1.25	$1.50	$1.75	$2.00	$2.25	$2.50

The graph correctly represents the data in the table.

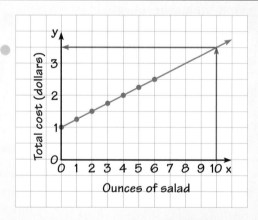

The answer is correct. The explanation is clear and reflects correct mathematical thinking.

The total cost of juice and a 10 ounce salad is $3.50.

To find my answer, I drew a line through the plotted points. I found 10 ounces on the x-axis. Then I drew lines up to the graph and across to the y-axis, meeting the y-axis at $3.50.

Partial credit solution

The function table is correct
and reflects an understanding
of the relationship between
the number of ounces of
salad and the total cost of
the juice and the salad.

Ounces of salad, x	Total cost, y
0	$1.00
1	$1.25
2	$1.50
3	$1.75
4	$2.00
5	$2.25
6	$2.50

The graph correctly represents
the data in the table.

The answer is incorrect. — The total cost is $4.50.

The explanation does
not reflect correct
mathematical reasoning.

To find my answer, I used
the table. Five ounces cost
$2.25, so 10 ounces cost twice that, or $4.50.

Watch Out!

Scoring is often
based on how clearly you
explain your reasoning.

Your turn now

1. One student's answer to the problem on page 672 is given below.
   Score the solution as *full credit, partial credit,* or *no credit.* Explain
   your choice. If you choose *partial credit* or *no credit,* explain how
   you would change the answer to earn a score of *full credit.*

Ounces of salad, x	Total cost, y
0	$0
1	$.25
2	$.50
3	$.75
4	$1.00
5	$1.25
6	$1.50

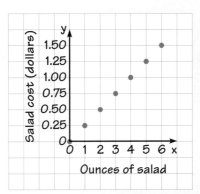

The total cost of juice and a 10 ounce salad is $3.50.

To find my answer, I multiplied the salad cost per ounce by the number
of ounces and added the juice cost. Salad costs $.25 per ounce, so
10 ounces cost $2.50. So, the total cost is $2.50 + $1.00, or $3.50.

Extended Response

1. The temperature was 17°F at 4:00 P.M. By 10:00 P.M. the temperature had dropped to −7°F. The temperature decreased by the same amount each hour. Use a number line to show how many degrees the temperature decreased each hour. Explain your work.

2. The first ten letters of the Braille alphabet are shown below. These ten letters are formed by arranging 1 to 4 dots in a 2 by 2 grid as shown. Which of these Braille letters are reflections of each other? Which are rotations of each other? Explain how you found your answers.

    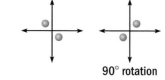

    For example:

    90° rotation

    A   B   C   D   E   F   G   H   I   J

3. The lowest daily temperatures for one week are listed below. Find the mean, median, mode, and range of the data. Show your work. Which average does not represent the data well? Why?

    −5°F   0°F   1°F   2°F   −4°F   −3°F   2°F

4. Brad has $10 to spend. He will buy a sticker book. How much money will he have left after he buys the sticker book? With the money that Brad has left, what is the greatest number of stickers n he can buy? Write and solve a multiplication equation to answer this question. Show your work.

Item	Price
sticker book	$6.00
stamp book	$4.95
stamps	$.35
stickers	$.40

5. A CD player costs $185. Nathan has already saved $65. Nathan will save $40 a week from a baby-sitting job. Write a function rule to represent the amount of money Nathan will have after n weeks. Then use an input-output table to find how many weeks Nathan needs to baby-sit to have enough money to buy the CD player.

6. The spinner at the right is divided into four equal sections. Make a tree diagram to show all the possible outcomes when you spin the spinner two times. Use the tree diagram to find the probability that the sum of the numbers from two spins is 5. Show your work.

7. The data below show the sizes of classes at North Junior High School. Make a stem-and-leaf plot of the data. Then make a box-and-whisker plot of the data. Compare the information you can get from each data display.

    15, 23, 38, 12, 24, 26, 14, 23, 34, 34, 23, 17, 30, 23, 24, 28,
    32, 26, 28, 17, 21, 29, 31, 26, 21

Multiple Choice

8. A test has 20 questions that are each worth 5 points. The teacher marked −2 next to four of the questions on Maura's test. What was Maura's score on the test?

   A. −8   **B.** 8   **C.** 90   **D.** 92

9. Suppose *s* represents the number of cups of sugar in a recipe. The amount of flour is twice the amount of sugar. Which expression represents the number of cups of flour?

   F. $s - 2$ **G.** $s + 2$ **H.** $2s$ **I.** $\dfrac{s}{2}$

10. After Julie gave Cara $7, Cara had a total of $40. Which equation could you use to find the amount of money *m* that Cara originally had?

   A. $m - 7 = 40$ **B.** $m + 7 = 40$

   C. $7m = 40$ **D.** $\dfrac{m}{7} = 40$

11. Carl has $3. How many different lunches of one sandwich and one drink can he order?

   F. 3
   G. 4
   H. 6
   I. 9

Item	Cost
tuna	$2.50
hot dog	$1.75
chicken	$2.95
milk	$.60
juice	$.50
lemonade	$1.00

12. A survey asks students to name their favorite type of music. Which type of graph would be the best for displaying the data?

   A. line graph

   B. bar graph

   C. stem-and-leaf plot

   D. box-and-whisker plot

Short Response

13. Tim is a contestant in a game show. He has a score of −$250. He correctly answers a question worth $500, but then misses a question worth $150 to end the game. If the other player has a final score of $25, does Tim win? Explain.

14. Make a bar graph of the company profit data shown that makes it appear that the profits have increased much more steeply than they actually have. Explain why your graph gives this impression.

Year	1999	2000	2001	2002
Profits	$28,000	$32,000	$39,000	$48,000

15. Find all the possible orders in which a salesperson can visit Boston, Chicago, and New York. If the order is chosen randomly, what is the probability that the salesperson will visit Chicago first? Explain.

16. The graph shows the relationship between time traveled, *t*, and distance, *D*, for a car driven at a constant rate. Write a rule for the function. Use the rule to predict the number of hours it takes to drive 240 miles at this rate. Explain.

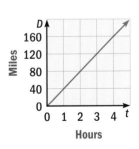

Cumulative Practice for Chapters 11–13

Chapter 11

Multiple Choice In Exercises 1–10, choose the letter of the correct answer.

1. The peak of a mountain is 10,016 feet above sea level. Which number would you use to represent the height of the peak? *(Lesson 11.1)*

   A. −10,016 feet   **B.** −5008 feet

   C. 5008 feet   **D.** 10,016 feet

2. Which list of integers is in order from greatest to least? *(Lesson 11.1)*

   F. $0, 2, -27, -28$ **G.** $2, 0, -28, -27$

   H. $2, 0, -27, -28$ **I.** $-28, -27, 0, 2$

3. Which expression does not have the same value as the other three expressions? *(Lessons 11.1, 11.2)*

   A. the absolute value of 7

   B. the absolute value of −7

   C. the opposite of 7

   D. the opposite of −7

4. Find the sum $-12 + 6$. *(Lesson 11.2)*

   F. -18 **G.** -6 **H.** 6   **I.** 18

5. What is the value of the expression $-6 - (-9)$? *(Lesson 11.3)*

   A. -15 **B.** -3 **C.** 3   **D.** 15

6. A record high temperature is 134°F. A record low is −80°F. What is the difference in these temperatures? *(Lesson 11.3)*

   F. $-54°F$ **G.** $54°F$ **H.** $214°F$ **I.** $224°F$

7. Which statement is true? *(Lesson 11.4)*

   A. $4(-4) = 16$ **B.** $-8(4) = 32$

   C. $4(3) = -12$ **D.** $-9(-9) = 81$

8. Find the quotient $-54 \div (-9)$. *(Lesson 11.5)*

   F. -7 **G.** -6 **H.** 6   **I.** 7

9. The yards gained and lost during a football game were $-3, 2, 4, -2, -7,$ and 0. Find the mean of the data. *(Lesson 11.5)*

   A. -1.2 **B.** -1 **C.** 1   **D.** 1.2

10. Use the figure shown. You translate the figure 1 unit to the right and 2 units down. Which point is not a vertex of the translated figure? *(Lesson 11.6)*

    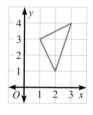

    F. $(2, 1)$ **G.** $(3, -1)$ **H.** $(4, 2)$ **I.** $(5, 3)$

11. **Short Response** Graph the point $(-2, -3)$. Then graph the image when the point is translated 2 units to the left and 5 units up. State the quadrants in which the point and its image are located. Explain how you found your answers. *(Lesson 11.6)*

12. **Extended Response** *(Lesson 11.7)*

    a. Graph $\triangle ABC$ with vertices $A(1, -2)$, $B(4, -1)$, and $C(1, 3)$. Graph $\triangle DEF$ with vertices $D(-1, -2)$, $E(-4, -1)$, and $F(-1, 3)$.

    b. Tell whether the transformation from $\triangle ABC$ to $\triangle DEF$ is a *translation*, a *reflection*, or a *rotation*. Then describe the transformation.

Chapter 12

Multiple Choice In Exercises 13–22, choose the letter of the correct answer.

13. Write the phrase as an expression: 16 decreased by f. *(Lesson 12.1)*

A. $f - 16$ **B.** $16 \div f$

C. $16 \cdot f$ **D.** $16 - f$

14. Karen had 32 CDs. She was given c more CDs. She now has 41 CDs. Which equation can you use to find c? *(Lesson 12.1)*

F. $32 + c = 41$ **G.** $32 - c = 41$

H. $32c = 41$ **I.** $32 \div c = 41$

15. What would you do to both sides of the equation $24 + x = 39$ to solve it? *(Lesson 12.2)*

A. add 24   **B.** add 39

C. subtract 24   **D.** subtract 39

16. What is the solution of the equation $x + 13 = 20$? *(Lesson 12.2)*

F. -7 **G.** 7   **H.** 17   **I.** 33

17. Which equation does *not* have 12 as a solution? *(Lesson 12.3)*

A. $t - 4 = 8$ **B.** $t - 6 = 6$

C. $t - 7 = 5$ **D.** $t - 1 = 13$

18. What is the solution of the equation $9p = 81$? *(Lesson 12.4)*

F. -9 **G.** 9   **H.** 72   **I.** 729

19. What is the solution of the equation $\frac{x}{3} = 27$? *(Lesson 12.4)*

A. 9   **B.** 24   **C.** 30   **D.** 81

20. When the input x is 8, what is the output of the function $y = 4x - 10$? *(Lesson 12.5)*

F. 4.5   **G.** 22   **H.** 32   **I.** 38

21. Which equation is a function rule for the input-output table shown? *(Lesson 12.5)*

Input, x	0	2	4	6	8
Output, y	3	5	7	9	11

A. $y = \frac{x}{3}$ **B.** $y = 3x$

C. $y = x - 3$ **D.** $y = x + 3$

22. Which function rule has the graph shown? *(Lesson 12.6)*

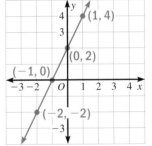

F. $y = x + 2$

G. $y = 2x + 2$

H. $y = \frac{1}{2}x + 2$

I. $y = 2x - 2$

23. Short Response Each angelfish in an aquarium needs 2 gallons of water. Write and solve a multiplication equation to find the number of angelfish a that you can put in a 20 gallon tank. Explain how you found your answer. *(Lesson 12.2)*

24. Extended Response Your brother is planning a car trip. He expects to drive at an average speed of 50 miles per hour. *(Lessons 12.5, 12.6)*

a. Make an input-output table that represents the relationship between the time t and the distance d he drives. Use the input values $t = 1, 2, 3,$ and 4.

b. Write a function rule that relates t and d.

c. Graph the function.

GO ON

Chapter 13

Multiple Choice In Exercises 25–32, choose the letter of the correct answer.

25. There are nine cards in a bag, numbered 1 through 9. You randomly choose one card. What is the probability that it is an even number? *(Lesson 13.1)*

   A. $\frac{4}{9}$ B. $\frac{1}{2}$ C. $\frac{5}{9}$ D. 1

26. Find the probability of the complement of rolling a 4 on a number cube. *(Lesson 13.1)*

   F. 0   G. $\frac{1}{6}$ H. $\frac{1}{4}$ I. $\frac{5}{6}$

27. Alberto, Chris, Edgar, and Manny are running in a relay race. How many ways can you order the first two runners? *(Lesson 13.2)*

   A. 2   B. 6   C. 8   D. 12

28. The spinner is divided into equal parts. You spin the spinner twice. Find the probability that you get an even number at least one time. *(Lesson 13.3)*

   F. 0   G. $\frac{1}{4}$ H. $\frac{1}{2}$ I. $\frac{3}{4}$

29. Which is least likely to affect how the information in a bar graph is interpreted? *(Lesson 13.4)*

   A. Using very small increments in the scale

   B. Drawing the bars horizontally

   C. Putting a vertical break in the scale

   D. Using very large increments in the scale

30. What is the median of the data shown in the stem-and-leaf plot? *(Lesson 13.5)*

1	3 7 8
2	1 1 6 8
3	0
4	0 8 9 Key: 3	0 = 30

   F. 13   G. 21   H. 26   I. 49

31. Use the box-and-whisker plot shown to find the difference between the upper quartile and the lower quartile. *(Lesson 13.6)*

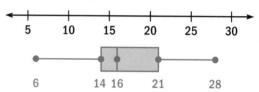

   A. 7   B. 14   C. 21   D. 22

32. Which display would best show increases in parking fees over time? *(Lesson 13.7)*

   F. stem-and-leaf plot   G. line plot

   H. line graph   I. circle graph

33. **Short Response** Choices at Casa Burrito are: vegetarian, chicken, or beef; regular-size or large; with mild salsa or hot salsa. Use a tree diagram to find all the different burrito orders possible. *(Lesson 13.2)*

34. **Extended Response** A model train club says that the average age of its members is 15. The ages of all the members are listed below. *(Lessons 13.4, 13.5, 13.6)*

   27, 40, 14, 59, 28, 29, 15, 13, 29, 37, 53, 15, 67, 36, 15

   a. Make a stem-and-leaf plot of the ages. Which age group has the most people?

   b. Make a box-and-whisker plot of the data.

   c. Does 15 describe the ages well? Explain.

End-of-Course Test

Number Sense, Measurement, and Decimals

Find the sum, difference, product, or quotient.

1. $839 + 296$

2. $156 - 39$

3. 18×36

4. $424 \div 8$

5. $6.468 + 4.22$

6. $5.174 - 2.01$

7. $8 - 3.21$

8. 0.826×3

9. 3.4×5.06

10. 3.4×0.001

11. $128 \div 0.4$

12. $9.186 \div 1000$

13. Write your answers to Exercises 8 and 9 in words.

Estimate the sum, difference, product, or quotient using the given method.

14. 49×89 (rounding)

15. $537 - 22$ (rounding)

16. $353 \div 39$ (compatible numbers)

17. $3.13 + 4.45 + 2.92$ (front-end estimation)

18. The data show the ages of students enrolled in a diving class. Make a frequency table and a bar graph of the data. Then find the mean, median, mode(s), and range of the data. Choose the best average(s) to represent the data. Explain your choice.

　　12, 13, 16, 12, 15, 12, 11, 15, 12, 12

Evaluate the expression.

19. $30 - 4 \times 6$

20. $6 \times (8 - 2) \div 4$

21. 2×5^2

22. $\frac{x}{7}$, when $x = 84$

23. $6 + 3n$, when $n = 5$

24. y^3, when $y = 2$

Order the numbers from least to greatest.

25. 18.14, 18.04, 18.41, 18.4, 18.401

26. 5.6, 5.59, 5.505, 5.575, 5.063

Choose an appropriate unit in the given system(s) to measure the item.

27. height of a tree (metric, customary)

28. length of a highway (metric, customary)

29. capacity of a fish tank (metric)

30. mass of a pencil (metric)

Solve.

31. Jill bought a pen for $2.39 and a pad of graph paper for $3.98. How much change should she get from a $20 bill?

32. Find the area and perimeter of a square with side length 4.7 meters.

Fraction Concepts and Operations

Write the prime factorization of the number.

33. 40   **34.** 72   **35.** 56   **36.** 120

Find the GCF and LCM of the numbers.

37. 16, 24   **38.** 12, 40   **39.** 7, 18

Order the fractions from least to greatest.

40. $\dfrac{1}{3}, \dfrac{1}{9}, \dfrac{1}{12}, \dfrac{1}{4}$ **41.** $\dfrac{3}{8}, \dfrac{2}{5}, \dfrac{1}{2}, \dfrac{7}{20}$ **42.** $\dfrac{2}{3}, \dfrac{9}{10}, \dfrac{3}{4}, \dfrac{4}{5}$

Write the decimals as fractions or mixed numbers in simplest form and write the fractions or mixed numbers as decimals.

43. 0.26   **44.** 5.6   **45.** 3.06   **46.** 0.175

47. $\dfrac{19}{25}$ **48.** $2\dfrac{3}{8}$ **49.** $\dfrac{1}{6}$ **50.** $\dfrac{17}{1000}$

Estimate and then find the sum, difference, product, or quotient.

51. $\dfrac{5}{8} + \dfrac{7}{8}$ **52.** $7\dfrac{1}{5} + 3\dfrac{2}{3}$ **53.** $6 - 2\dfrac{3}{7}$ **54.** $9\dfrac{1}{2} - 4\dfrac{5}{6}$

55. $\dfrac{3}{5} \times \dfrac{2}{3}$ **56.** $3\dfrac{1}{4} \times 6\dfrac{2}{3}$ **57.** $\dfrac{4}{9} \div 3$ **58.** $2\dfrac{5}{6} \div 1\dfrac{3}{5}$

Add or subtract.

59.   7 h 41 min 45 sec
     + 8 h 34 min 18 sec

60.   8 h 12 min
     − 3 h 58 min

61.   2 yd 2 ft
     + 3 yd 2 ft

In Exercises 62–64, choose an appropriate customary unit of measure.

62. weight of an orange   **63.** capacity of a bathtub   **64.** capacity of a teaspoon

65. Atiba was $53\dfrac{7}{8}$ inches tall last year. This year, he is $56\dfrac{1}{4}$ inches tall. How many inches did he grow over the past year?

66. Nick jogged $4\dfrac{1}{10}$ miles on Sunday and $2\dfrac{2}{5}$ miles on Tuesday. How many more miles did he jog on Sunday than on Tuesday?

Proportions, Percent, and Geometry

Solve the proportion.

67. $\dfrac{12}{x} = \dfrac{4}{7}$
68. $\dfrac{9}{12} = \dfrac{x}{48}$
69. $\dfrac{4}{18} = \dfrac{6}{x}$
70. $\dfrac{x}{42} = \dfrac{5}{6}$

Write the number as a fraction, a decimal, and a percent.

71. $\dfrac{2}{5}$
72. $\dfrac{3}{8}$
73. 54%
74. 6%
75. 0.125

Find the percent of the number.

76. 7% of 83
77. 85% of 500
78. $66\frac{2}{3}$% of 90
79. 14.5% of 8

In Exercises 80–83, use the diagram shown.

80. Name two rays that form a right angle.

81. Name a pair of supplementary angles.

82. Name a pair of vertical angles.

83. Use a protractor to draw an angle that has the same measure as $\angle CAE$.

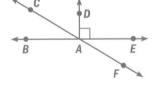

Classify the figure in as many ways as possible. Then find the area.

84.
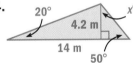

85.
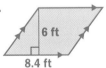

86.

87. In Exercise 84, find the value of x.

88. In Exercise 86, find the circumference.

89. Draw a rectangle and show its lines of symmetry.

In Exercises 90–92, name the solid that matches the description.

90. Its one base is a circle.
91. Its two bases are circles.
92. Its one base can be a triangle.

93. A jewelry box is 3 in. by 4 in. by 5 in. Find its surface area and volume.

94. The regular price of a sweatshirt is $22.50. Find the cost after a discount of 20%.

95. Two cities are 60 miles apart. How many centimeters apart are the cities on a map with a scale of 1 cm : 80 mi?

Integers, Algebra, and Probability

Order the integers from least to greatest.

96. $6, -16, 0, -6, 8$

97. $0, -8, 5, -10, -5, 8$

Find the sum, difference, product, or quotient.

98. $16 + (-10)$ **99.** $-5 + (-7)$ **100.** $-9 - 2$ **101.** $-4 - (-7)$

102. $-8 \div (-2)$ **103.** $-6(5)$ **104.** $(-7)(-4)$ **105.** $30 \div (-6)$

Graph the points and connect them to form △ABC. Then translate △ABC 4 units to the right and 2 units down to form △DEF. Give the coordinates of the vertices of △DEF.

106. $A(-4, 8), B(0, 6), C(2, 3)$

107. $A(0, -3), B(-5, -2), C(4, -2)$

Tell whether the transformation is a *translation*, a *reflection*, or a *rotation*.

108.
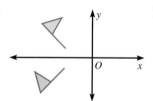

109.
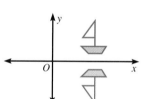

110.
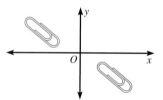

Write the equation.

111. 16 more than a number is 28.

112. 6 less than a number is 8.

Solve the equation.

113. $89 = x + 18$ **114.** $m - 24 = 56$ **115.** $6q = -42$ **116.** $\frac{w}{12} = 6$

You roll a number cube. Find the probability of the event.

117. You roll a number less than 7.

118. You roll a factor of 40.

119. Use a tree diagram to find all the possible sandwiches you can make using either ham, turkey, or bologna and either mustard, mayonnaise, or ketchup.

120. The data show Pam's Spanish test grades. Make a stem-and-leaf plot and a box-and-whisker plot of the data. Then write a paragraph explaining each plot.

87, 75, 90, 65, 98, 75, 85, 70, 60, 88, 92, 50, 95

Contents of Student Resources

Skills Review Handbook

Whole Number Place Value

The **whole numbers** are the numbers 0, 1, 2, 3, ... A **digit** is any of the numbers 0, 1, 2, 3, 4, 5, 6, 7, 8, or 9. The value of each digit in a whole number depends on its position within the number. For example, in the whole number 127,891, the 8 has a value of 800 because it is in the hundreds' place and $8 \times 100 = 800$.

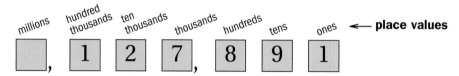

←— **place values**

EXAMPLE Write the number 4062 in expanded form and in words.

Expanded form: $4062 = 4000 + 60 + 2$

The zero in the hundreds' place is a placeholder.

$= (4 \times 1000) + (6 \times 10) + (2 \times 1)$

Words: four thousand, sixty-two

EXAMPLE Write the number in standard form.

a. $(6 \times 100,000) + (4 \times 1000) + (2 \times 100) + (3 \times 1) = 600,000 + 4000 + 200 + 3$
$$= 604,203$$

b. seventy-three thousand, five hundred six

Write 7 in the ten thousands' place, 3 in the thousands' place, 5 in the hundreds' place, and 6 in the ones' place. Write a zero as a placeholder in the tens' place. The answer is 73,506.

● Practice

Identify the place value of the red digit. Then write the number in expanded form and in words.

1. 5890   **2.** 50,208   **3.** 906,201   **4.** 1,350,601

Write the number in standard form.

5. $(1 \times 100,000) + (5 \times 1000) + (3 \times 100)$ **6.** $(7 \times 10,000) + (9 \times 10) + (3 \times 1)$

7. forty-two thousand, six hundred   **8.** six hundred fifty-one thousand, forty-one

Ordering Whole Numbers

A **number line** is a line whose points are associated with numbers. The numbers from left to right are in order from least to greatest. You can graph whole numbers on a number line to compare and order them. You can also compare the digits in each place from left to right.

The symbol < means *is less than* and the symbol > means *is greater than*.

EXAMPLE Use a number line to order 18, 9, 21, and 12.

Graph all the numbers on the same number line.

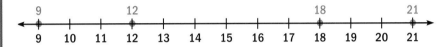

ANSWER From the number line, you can see that the order from least to greatest is 9, 12, 18, 21 and from greatest to least is 21, 18, 12, 9.

EXAMPLE Compare the numbers.

a. 3496 and 3469

Compare each place from left to right.

3496   The thousands' and hundreds' digits are the same.

3469   The tens' digits are different. 9 is greater than 6.

ANSWER 3496 is greater than 3469. Write 3496 > 3469.

b. 9801 and 10,981

Compare each place from left to right.

9,801   No ten-thousands' digit means 0 ten-thousands.

10,981   The ten-thousands' digit is 1. 1 is greater than 0.

ANSWER 9801 is less than 10,981. Write 9801 < 10,981.

● Practice

Use a number line to order the numbers from least to greatest.

1. 11, 0, 8, 3, 10

2. 21, 17, 7, 11, 20

3. 87, 78, 90, 85, 79

4. 101, 110, 107, 97, 111

5. 521, 518, 508, 512, 510

6. 1010, 998, 1001, 1011

Compare the numbers.

7. 207 and 148

8. 2095 and 2905

9. 3465 and 3492

10. 873 and 1073

11. 21,539 and 9847

12. 103,264 and 13,264

Rounding Whole Numbers

To **round** a whole number means to approximate the number to a given place value. For example, 84 rounded to the nearest ten is 80, because 84 is closer to 80 than to 90. When rounding to a specified place value, look at the digit to the right of that place value.

If the digit to the right is less than 5 (0, 1, 2, 3, or 4), round down.

If the digit to the right is 5 or greater (5, 6, 7, 8, or 9), round up.

EXAMPLE **Round the number to the place value of the red digit.**

   a. 479   **b.** 35,174

Solution

  a. Because the 4 is in the hundreds' place, round 479 to the nearest hundred. Notice that 479 is between 400 and 500, so it will round to one of these two numbers.

479 is closer to 500 than to 400.

     The digit to the right of the 4 is a 7. Because 7 is greater than 5, you round up.

     ANSWER 479 rounded to the nearest hundred is 500.

  b. Because the 5 is in the thousands' place, round 35,174 to the nearest thousand. Notice that 35,174 is between 35,000 and 36,000, so it will round to one of these two numbers.

35,174 is closer to 35,000 than to 36,000.

     The digit to the right of the 5 is a 1. Because 1 is less than 5, you round down.

     ANSWER 35,174 rounded to the nearest thousand is 35,000.

● Practice

Round the number to the place value of the red digit.

  1. 86   **2.** 21   **3.** 247   **4.** 558   **5.** 4283

  6. 9561   **7.** 10,954   **8.** 36,982   **9.** 143,543   **10.** 593,121

Number Fact Families

Inverse operations are operations that "undo" each other, such as addition and subtraction or multiplication and division. A **number fact family** consists of three numbers related by inverse operations. For example, the facts $6 \times 2 = 12$, $2 \times 6 = 12$, $12 \div 6 = 2$, and $12 \div 2 = 6$ are in the same fact family.

EXAMPLE Copy and complete the number fact family.

$$4 + 2 = 6 \qquad 2 + \underline{?} = 6 \qquad 6 - \underline{?} = 2 \qquad 6 - \underline{?} = 4$$

Solution

The numbers in this fact family are 4, 2, and 6. Identify which of the three numbers is missing in each of the last three equations.

The 4 is missing in $2 + \underline{?} = 6$ and in $6 - \underline{?} = 2$.
The 2 is missing in $6 - \underline{?} = 4$.

ANSWER The complete number fact family is:
$4 + 2 = 6$; $2 + 4 = 6$; $6 - 4 = 2$; $6 - 2 = 4$.

EXAMPLE Write a related division equation for $4 \times 7 = 28$.

Think of the number fact family that contains the multiplication fact $4 \times 7 = 28$. The three numbers in this fact family are 4, 7, and 28, so the two related division equations are $28 \div 4 = 7$ and $28 \div 7 = 4$.

You can also think about "undoing" the multiplication. You multiply 4 and 7 to get 28, so divide 28 by 4 to get 7 or divide 28 by 7 to get 4.

● Practice

In Exercises 1–4, copy and complete the number fact family.

1. $14 - 9 = 5 \qquad 14 - \underline{?} = 9 \qquad \underline{?} + 9 = 14 \qquad 9 + \underline{?} = \underline{?}$

2. $2 \times 8 = 16 \qquad 8 \times \underline{?} = 16 \qquad 16 \div \underline{?} = 8 \qquad \underline{?} \div \underline{?} = 2$

3. $32 \div \underline{?} = 4 \qquad 32 \div \underline{?} = 8 \qquad 8 \times \underline{?} = 32 \qquad \underline{?} \times \underline{?} = 32$

4. $\underline{?} + 5 = 11 \qquad \underline{?} + 6 = 11 \qquad 11 - \underline{?} = 5 \qquad \underline{?} - \underline{?} = 6$

5. Write a related subtraction equation for $7 + 8 = 15$.

6. Write a related multiplication equation for $54 \div 6 = 9$.

Addition and Subtraction on a Number Line

To **add** two whole numbers on a number line:

(1) Start at 0. Move to the *right* as far as the first number.

(2) To add the second number, continue from the location of the first number and move to the *right* the number of units indicated by the second number. The final location is the answer.

EXAMPLE Use a number line to add 4 + 5.

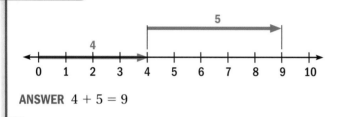

Start at 0.
Move 4 units to the *right*.
Then move 5 more units to the *right*.

ANSWER $4 + 5 = 9$

To **subtract** two whole numbers on a number line:

(1) Start at 0. Move to the *right* as far as the first number.

(2) To subtract the second number, continue from the location of the first number and move to the *left* the number of units indicated by the second number. The final location is the answer.

EXAMPLE Use a number line to subtract 11 − 7.

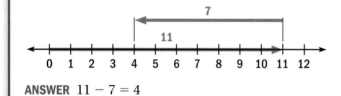

Start at 0.
Move 11 units to the *right*.
Then move 7 units to the *left*.

ANSWER $11 - 7 = 4$

● Practice

Use a number line to add or subtract the numbers.

1. $8 + 5$ **2.** $7 + 8$ **3.** $4 + 7$ **4.** $3 + 9$

5. $10 + 3$ **6.** $12 + 12$ **7.** $8 + 12$ **8.** $15 + 8$

9. $10 - 4$ **10.** $12 - 6$ **11.** $14 - 6$ **12.** $15 - 7$

13. $17 - 9$ **14.** $22 - 8$ **15.** $19 - 3$ **16.** $18 - 5$

Addition and Subtraction of Whole Numbers

A **sum** is the result when you add two or more numbers. A **difference** is the result when you subtract two numbers. To add and subtract whole numbers, write the numbers in columns by place value. Start computing with the digits in the ones' place. Moving to the left, add or subtract the digits one place value at a time, regrouping as needed.

EXAMPLE Find the sum 287 + 36.

(1 Add the ones. Then regroup the 13 ones as 1 ten and 3 ones.

```
    1
  287
+  36
    3
```

(2 Add the tens. Then regroup the 12 tens as 1 hundred and 2 tens.

```
   1 1
  287
+  36
   23
```

(3 Add the hundreds.

```
   1 1
  287
+  36
  323
```

EXAMPLE Find the difference 305 − 86.

(1 Start with the ones. There are not enough ones in 305 to subtract 6. You will need to regroup. There are no tens, so go to the hundreds' place.

```
  305
−  86
```

(2 Regroup the 3 hundreds as 2 hundreds and 10 tens. Then regroup the 10 tens as 9 tens and 10 ones. Now subtract one place value at a time.

```
      9
  2  10  15  ◄── 5 ones plus
  3   0   5      10 ones from
−      8   6     regrouping makes
  2   1   9      15 ones.
```

✓ **Check** Because addition and subtraction are *inverse operations*, you can check your answer by adding: 219 + 86 = 305.

Practice

Find the sum or difference.

1. 43 + 28

2. 81 + 59

3. 192 + 48

4. 85 + 357

5. 235 + 165

6. 586 + 287

7. 283 + 1129

8. 3547 + 385

9. 75 − 58

10. 62 − 17

11. 245 − 26

12. 574 − 67

13. 326 − 177

14. 402 − 258

15. 1461 − 282

16. 4340 − 173

Multiplication of Whole Numbers

A **product** is the result when you multiply two or more numbers. To **multiply** two whole numbers, multiply the entire top number by the digit in each place value of the bottom number to obtain partial products. Then add the partial products.

EXAMPLE Find the product 263 × 54.

(1 Multiply 263 by the ones' digit in 54.

$$
\begin{array}{r}
21 \\
263 \\
\times\ 54 \\
\hline
1052
\end{array}
$$

(2 Multiply by the tens' digit. Start the partial product in the tens' place.

$$
\begin{array}{r}
31 \\
263 \\
\times\ 54 \\
\hline
1052 \\
1315
\end{array}
$$

(3 Add the partial products.

$$
\begin{array}{r}
263 \\
\times\ 54 \\
\hline
1052 \\
1315 \\
\hline
14{,}202
\end{array}
$$

To multiply a whole number by a *power of 10*, such as 10, 100 or 1000, write the number followed by the number of zeros in the power. Because multiplying by such powers of 10 shifts each digit of the number to a higher place value, the zeros are needed as placeholders.

EXAMPLE Find the product.

a. 74×100

b. 234×1000

Solution

a. 100 is a power of 10 with 2 zeros, so write 2 zeros after 74.

ANSWER $74 \times 100 = 7400$

b. 1000 is a power of 10 with 3 zeros, so write 3 zeros after 234. — Place commas as necessary.

ANSWER $234 \times 1000 = 234{,}000$

● Practice

Find the product.

1. 41×80 **2.** 73×34 **3.** 26×37 **4.** 68×42

5. 217×28 **6.** 483×53 **7.** 975×62 **8.** 371×88

9. 1987×74 **10.** 6581×25 **11.** 4657×10 **12.** 9876×100

13. 123×100 **14.** 2568×1000 **15.** $2319 \times 10{,}000$ **16.** $7923 \times 100{,}000$

Division of Whole Numbers

In a division problem, the number being divided is called the **dividend** and the number it is being divided by is called the **divisor**. The result of the division is called the **quotient**. To **divide** two whole numbers, you use the following pattern: divide, multiply, subtract, bring down. Continue this pattern until there are no more digits to bring down. If the divisor does not divide the dividend evenly, then there is a **remainder**.

EXAMPLE Find the quotient 236 ÷ 4.

(1 Decide where to write the first digit of the quotient. Because 4 is between 2 and 23, place the first digit above the 3.

(2 Because 23 ÷ 4 is between 5 and 6, multiply 4 by **5**. Then subtract **20** from 23. Be sure the difference is less than the divisor.

(3 Bring down the next digit, **6**. Divide 36 by 4. Because 36 ÷ 4 = **9**, multiply 4 by **9**. Subtract **36**. The remainder is 0.

divisor → 4)236 ← first digit of quotient
└ dividend

$$\begin{array}{r} 5 \\ 4)\overline{236} \\ 20 \\ \hline 3 \end{array}$$

$$\begin{array}{r} 59 \\ 4)\overline{236} \\ 20 \\ \hline 36 \\ 36 \\ \hline 0 \end{array}$$

EXAMPLE Find the quotient 7346 ÷ 24.

(1 □ ← first digit of quotient
24)7346

(2
$$\begin{array}{r} 30 \\ 24)\overline{7346} \\ 72 \\ \hline 14 \end{array}$$
← Bring down the **4**. But 24 < 14, so write a **0**.

(3
$$\begin{array}{r} 306 \text{ R2} \\ 24)\overline{7346} \\ 72 \\ \hline 146 \\ 144 \\ \hline 2 \end{array}$$
← remainder

Then bring down the **6** to continue dividing.

✓ **Check** (24 × 306) + 2 = 7346, so the answer 306 R2 is correct.

● Practice

Find the quotient.

1. 6)852   **2.** 5)650   **3.** 7)378   **4.** 7)126

5. 3645 ÷ 9   **6.** 2388 ÷ 4   **7.** 580 ÷ 10   **8.** 783 ÷ 12

9. 436 ÷ 33   **10.** 2100 ÷ 100   **11.** 1617 ÷ 65   **12.** 1488 ÷ 72

Estimating Sums

To **estimate** the solution of a problem means to find an approximate answer. One way to estimate a sum when all the numbers have the same number of digits is to use **front-end estimation**. First add the digits in the *greatest* place to get a low estimate. Then use the remaining digits to adjust the sum and get a closer estimate.

EXAMPLE Estimate the sum 465 + 342 + 198.

(1 Add the digits in the greatest place: the hundreds' place.

$$
\begin{array}{r}
465 \\
342 \\
+\ 198 \\
\hline
800
\end{array}
$$

(2 Estimate the sum of the remaining digits. Look for more hundreds.

$$
\begin{array}{r}
465 \searrow \\
342 \rightarrow \text{about } 100 \\
+\ 198 \rightarrow \text{about } 100 \\
\hline
\text{about } 200 \text{ more}
\end{array}
$$

(3 Add the two sums.

$$
\begin{array}{r}
800 \\
+\ 200 \\
\hline
1000
\end{array}
$$

ANSWER The sum 465 + 342 + 198 is *about* 1000.

When numbers being added have about the same value, you can use *clustering* to estimate their sum.

EXAMPLE Estimate the sum 72 + 68 + 65.

The numbers all cluster around the value 70.

$$
\begin{array}{r}
72 \\
68 \\
+\ 65
\end{array}
\longrightarrow
\begin{array}{r}
70 \\
70 \\
+\ 70
\end{array}
\qquad 3 \times 70 = 210
$$

ANSWER The sum 72 + 68 + 65 is *about* 210.

Practice

Estimate the sum.

1. 290 + 419 + 578

2. 549 + 127 + 328

3. 643 + 294 + 861

4. 328 + 560 + 781 + 533

5. 1289 + 2716 + 5952

6. 6429 + 5381 + 7232

7. 42 + 43 + 36 + 37

8. 99 + 100 + 95 + 107

9. 274 + 292 + 307 + 315

Estimating Differences

One way to estimate a difference is to find a low estimate and a high estimate.

EXAMPLE Find a low and high estimate for the difference 534 − 278.

(1) For the **low estimate**, round the greater number down and the lesser number up to decrease the difference.

$$
\begin{array}{r}
534 \\
- 278
\end{array}
\quad\longrightarrow\quad
\begin{array}{r}
500 \\
- 300 \\
\hline
200
\end{array}
$$

(2) For the **high estimate**, round the greater number up and the lesser number down to increase the difference.

$$
\begin{array}{r}
534 \\
- 278
\end{array}
\quad\longrightarrow\quad
\begin{array}{r}
600 \\
- 200 \\
\hline
400
\end{array}
$$

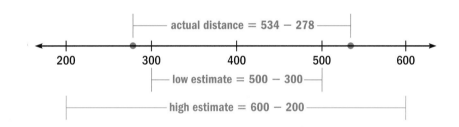

ANSWER The difference 534 − 278 is between 200 and 400.

Practice

Find a low and high estimate for the difference.

1. 924
− 105

2. 876
− 328

3. 724
− 286

4. 639
− 427

5. 642
− 268

6. 745
− 197

7. 839
− 381

8. 593
− 402

9. 2768
− 1319

10. 2913
− 1245

11. 7943
− 3872

12. 5639
− 2088

13. 6543
− 1739

14. 7561
− 2972

15. 8421
− 6384

16. 5129
− 2876

Estimating Products

One way to estimate a product is to find a low estimate and
a high estimate.

EXAMPLE Find a low and high estimate for the product 253 × 15.

For the **low estimate**,
round both factors *down*.

For the **high estimate**,
round both factors *up*.

$$\begin{array}{r} 200 \\ \times\ 10 \\ \hline 2000 \end{array}$$

$$\begin{array}{r} 300 \\ \times\ 20 \\ \hline 6000 \end{array}$$

ANSWER The product 253 × 15 is between 2000 and 6000.

Another way is to use compatible numbers. **Compatible numbers** are
numbers that are easy to use in computations .

EXAMPLE Use compatible numbers to estimate the product 147 × 12.

Replace 147 and 12 with two numbers
that are easy to multiply.

$$\begin{array}{r} 147 \\ \times\ 12 \\ \end{array} \longrightarrow \begin{array}{r} 150 \\ \times\ 10 \\ \hline 1500 \end{array}$$

ANSWER The product 147 × 12 is *about* 1500.

Practice

Find a low and high estimate for the product.

1. 42 × 21   **2.** 63 × 59   **3.** 74 × 38   **4.** 92 × 29

5. 129 × 34   **6.** 563 × 48   **7.** 67 × 215   **8.** 26 × 749

9. 4786 × 73   **10.** 1793 × 41   **11.** 13 × 6721   **12.** 64 × 8516

Use compatible numbers to estimate the product.

13. 213 × 53   **14.** 395 × 43   **15.** 528 × 98   **16.** 821 × 78

17. 22 × 742   **18.** 14 × 683   **19.** 52 × 932   **20.** 62 × 287

21. 865 × 712   **22.** 912 × 233   **23.** 268 × 543   **24.** 387 × 603

25. 2751 × 32   **26.** 8613 × 44   **27.** 98 × 7361   **28.** 67 × 1322

Estimating Quotients

One way to estimate a quotient is to find a low estimate and a high estimate by using numbers that divide with no remainder.

EXAMPLE **Find a low and high estimate for the quotient 2692 ÷ 8.**

Replace 2692 with numbers that are easily divisible by 8.

For the **low estimate**, use a number less than 2692.

$$\begin{array}{r} 300 \\ 8)\overline{2400} \end{array}$$

For the **high estimate**, use a number greater than 2692.

$$\begin{array}{r} 400 \\ 8)\overline{3200} \end{array}$$

ANSWER The quotient 2692 ÷ 8 is between 300 and 400.

Another way to estimate a quotient is to use compatible numbers.

EXAMPLE **Use compatible numbers to estimate the quotient 99 ÷ 23.**

Look for numbers close to 99 and 23 that divide evenly.

$$23)\overline{99} \quad \longrightarrow \quad \begin{array}{r} 4 \\ 25)\overline{100} \end{array}$$

ANSWER The quotient 99 ÷ 23 is *about* 4.

Practice

Find a low and high estimate for the quotient.

1. 211 ÷ 4   **2.** 423 ÷ 5   **3.** 394 ÷ 6   **4.** 449 ÷ 8

5. 198 ÷ 6   **6.** 347 ÷ 9   **7.** 1946 ÷ 7   **8.** 2124 ÷ 4

9. 2198 ÷ 6   **10.** 2476 ÷ 9   **11.** 3601 ÷ 8   **12.** 1396 ÷ 3

13. 5989 ÷ 5   **14.** 7431 ÷ 4   **15.** 6172 ÷ 7   **16.** 4382 ÷ 9

Use compatible numbers to estimate the quotient.

17. 125 ÷ 62   **18.** 239 ÷ 38   **19.** 489 ÷ 48   **20.** 342 ÷ 81

21. 973 ÷ 87   **22.** 391 ÷ 42   **23.** 632 ÷ 87   **24.** 439 ÷ 58

25. 4201 ÷ 43   **26.** 2702 ÷ 73   **27.** 7378 ÷ 92   **28.** 1024 ÷ 28

Solving Problems Using Addition and Subtraction

You can use the following guidelines to tell whether to use addition or subtraction to solve a word problem.

Use *addition* when you need to combine, add on, or find a total.

Use *subtraction* when you need to compare, take away, find how many are left, or find how many more you need.

EXAMPLE **You paid $15 for a T-shirt and $35 for a pair of jeans. How much did you pay in all?**

You need to find a total, so you need to add.

$15 + $35 = $50

ANSWER You paid $50 in all.

EXAMPLE **You need to make 40 muffins for a bake sale. You already made 24 muffins. How many more do you need to make?**

You need to find how many more you need, so you need to subtract.

40 − 24 = 16

ANSWER You need to make 16 more muffins.

● Practice

1. You have $13 to spend. You buy a poster for $4. How much money do you have left?

2. You spend $19 for a movie on DVD and $8 for a movie on video tape. How much more did you spend for the DVD movie?

3. You buy 18 pencils and 8 pens. How many items did you buy in all?

4. You have 27 stamps in your stamp collection. Your friend gives you 8 stamps. How many stamps do you have in your collection now?

5. You need $25 for school supplies. You have $18. How much more money do you need for school supplies?

6. You have to sell 31 tickets for the dance. You have already sold 14 of them. How many more do you have to sell?

Solving Problems Using Multiplication and Division

You can use the following guidelines to tell whether to use multiplication or division to solve a word problem.

Use *multiplication* when you need to combine or join together the total number of objects in groups of equal size.

Use *division* when you need to find the number of equal groups or find the number in each equal group.

EXAMPLE **You buy 4 packages of markers. Each package contains 8 markers. How many markers did you buy?**

You need to combine groups of equal size, so you need to multiply.

$4 \times 8 = 32$

ANSWER You bought 32 markers.

EXAMPLE **You have 20 beads. You put an equal number of beads on 5 bracelets. How many beads do you put on each bracelet?**

You need to find the number in each equal group, so you need to divide.

$20 \div 5 = 4$

ANSWER You put 4 beads on each bracelet.

● Practice

1. You order 6 packages of folders for the school store. Each package contains 10 folders. How many folders do you get?

2. You have 30 plants. You split the plants evenly among 5 pots. How many plants do you put in each pot?

3. You buy 32 bottles of water in boxes of 8. How many boxes did you buy?

4. You have 4 boxes of straws. Each box contains 12 straws. How many straws do you have?

5. You buy 5 CDs at a yard sale for $4 each. How much did you spend?

6. You need to make 96 cookies. One batch of cookies makes 24. How many batches do you need to make?

Operations with Money

You can use the following guidelines to tell whether to use subtraction or addition to solve a money problem.

Use *addition* when finding the total cost of several items.

Use *subtraction* when finding how much change you should receive.

EXAMPLE **You buy a book for $4.89. You give the clerk $10.00. How much change do you receive?**

You are finding the amount of change, so you need to subtract.

Subtract as you would with whole numbers.

$$
\begin{array}{r}
9 \\
9 \; \cancel{10} \; 10 \\
\cancel{10} . \cancel{0} \; \cancel{0} \\
- \quad 4 . 8 \; 9 \\
\hline
5 . 1 \; 1
\end{array}
$$

> Place the decimal point in the answer so that it lines up with the other decimal points.

ANSWER Your change is $5.11.

EXAMPLE **You buy shoes for $28.99, a backpack for $32.50, and jeans for $29.95. How much do you spend in all?**

You are finding the total cost of several items, so you need to add.

Add as you would with whole numbers.

$$
\begin{array}{r}
2 \; 2 \; 1 \\
28.99 \\
32.50 \\
+ \quad 29.95 \\
\hline
91.44
\end{array}
$$

> Place the decimal point in the answer so that it lines up with the other decimal points.

ANSWER You spent $91.44 in all.

● Practice

1. You buy a carton of juice for $2.98. You give the clerk $5. How much change do you receive?

2. You buy a calendar for $12.48. You give the clerk $13.03. How much change do you receive?

3. You buy a package of CDs for $18.98, a printer cartridge for $21.35, and a box of printer paper for $17.75. How much do you spend in all?

Adding and Subtracting Decimals

You add and subtract decimals one place value at a time from right to left in the same way you add and subtract whole numbers. Line up the decimal points in your calculation and place a decimal point in your answer.

EXAMPLE Find the sum 16.8 + 29.5.

1 Line up the decimal points. Add the tenths. Regroup the 13 tenths as **1** one and **3** tenths.

$$
\begin{array}{r}
1 \\
16.8 \\
+\,29.5 \\
\hline
3
\end{array}
$$

2 Add the ones. Regroup the 16 ones as **1** ten and **6** ones. Then add the tens. Write the decimal point.

$$
\begin{array}{r}
1\ \ 1 \\
16.8 \\
+\,29.5 \\
\hline
46.3
\end{array}
$$

Line up the decimal point in the sum with the other decimal points.

EXAMPLE Find the difference 18.25 − 6.79.

1 Line up the decimal points. Regroup to be able to subtract the hundredths. The 2 tenths become **1** tenth and **10** hundredths. Then subtract the hundredths.

$$
\begin{array}{r}
1\,15 \\
18.2\cancel{5} \\
-\ \ 6.79 \\
\hline
6
\end{array}
$$

5 hundredths plus 10 hundredths from regrouping makes 15 hundredths.

2 Regroup to be able to subtract the tenths. The 8 ones become **7** ones and **10** tenths. Now subtract the tenths. Then subtract the ones and the tens. Write the decimal point.

$$
\begin{array}{r}
11 \\
7\ \ \cancel{1}\,15 \\
1\cancel{8}.2\cancel{5} \\
-\ \ 6.79 \\
\hline
11.46
\end{array}
$$

Line up the decimal point in the difference with the other decimal points.

Practice

Find the sum or difference.

1. 17.9 + 23.5

2. 25.8 + 17.3

3. 56.3 + 86.7

4. 2.76 + 8.54

5. 6.91 + 4.38

6. 7.35 + 8.96

7. 10.65 + 9.48

8. 24.76 + 8.08

9. 48.55 + 8.67

10. 18.2 − 10.8

11. 36.4 − 19.9

12. 64.3 − 25.6

13. 9.75 − 2.87

14. 7.14 − 2.94

15. 8.75 − 2.99

16. 45.78 − 6.89

17. 28.93 − 9.06

18. 72.17 − 8.28

Modeling Fractions

A **fraction** is used to describe one or more parts of a whole or a set. The top part of a fraction is called the **numerator**. It tells how many parts of the whole or how many objects from the set to consider. The bottom part of a fraction is called the **denominator**. It tells how many equal sized parts make up the whole or how many objects make up the set.

EXAMPLE Write a fraction to represent the shaded region or part of a set.

a.

b.

Solution

a. The region is divided into 3 equal parts and 2 of the parts are shaded. The fraction that represents the shaded part of the set is $\frac{2}{3}$.

b. There are 8 objects in this set and five of the objects are shaded. The fraction that represents the shaded part of the set is $\frac{5}{8}$.

● Practice

Write a fraction to represent the shaded region or part of a set.

1.

2.

3.

4.

5.

6.

7.

8.

9.

10.

11.

12.

Units of Time

Use the equivalent units of time given at the right to change one unit of time to another.

Divide to change from a smaller unit to a larger unit.
Multiply to change from a larger unit to a smaller unit.

> 1 week = 7 days
> 1 day = 24 hours
> 1 hour = 60 minutes
> 1 minute = 60 seconds

EXAMPLE **Copy and complete.**

a. 28 days = $\underline{?}$ weeks

b. 3 hours 15 minutes = $\underline{?}$ minutes

c. 67 seconds = $\underline{?}$ minutes $\underline{?}$ seconds

Solution

a. You are changing days to weeks, a smaller unit to a larger unit. There are 7 days in one week, so divide by 7.

$$28 \text{ days} = (28 \div 7) \text{ weeks}$$
$$= 4 \text{ weeks}$$

b. You are changing hours to minutes, a larger unit to a smaller unit. There are 60 minutes in one hour, so multiply by 60. Then add the extra minutes.

$$3 \text{ hours } 15 \text{ minutes} = [(3 \times 60) + 15] \text{ minutes}$$
$$= (180 + 15) \text{ minutes}$$
$$= 195 \text{ minutes}$$

c. You are changing seconds to minutes, a smaller unit to a larger unit. There are 60 seconds in one minute, so divide by 60. If there is a remainder, write it as seconds.

$$\begin{array}{r} 1 \longleftarrow \text{minutes} \\ 60\overline{)67} \\ \underline{60} \\ 7 \longleftarrow \text{extra seconds} \end{array}$$

1 minute 7 seconds

Practice

Copy and complete.

1. 4 hours = $\underline{?}$ minutes

2. 3 weeks = $\underline{?}$ days

3. 96 hours = $\underline{?}$ days

4. 420 seconds = $\underline{?}$ minutes

5. 1 week 5 days = $\underline{?}$ days

6. 2 hours 25 minutes = $\underline{?}$ minutes

7. 2 days 4 hours = $\underline{?}$ hours

8. 3 minutes 10 seconds = $\underline{?}$ seconds

9. 16 days = $\underline{?}$ weeks $\underline{?}$ days

10. 90 minutes = $\underline{?}$ hours $\underline{?}$ minutes

11. 40 hours = $\underline{?}$ days $\underline{?}$ hours

12. 200 seconds = $\underline{?}$ minutes $\underline{?}$ seconds

Perimeter and Area

Perimeter is the distance around a figure measured in linear units.

Area is the amount of surface covered by a figure measured in square units.

EXAMPLE Find the perimeter of the rectangle below.

To find the perimeter, add the side lengths.
3 in. + 6 in. + 3 in. + 6 in. = 18 in.

ANSWER The perimeter is 18 inches.

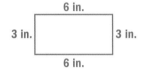

EXAMPLE Find the area.

a.

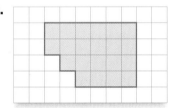

Find the area by counting the number of squares inside the figure. There are 21 squares. So the area is 21 square units.

b.

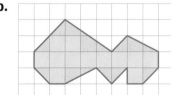

Count the **whole squares**. Estimate how many more whole squares can be made by the **partial squares**. The total area is about 12 + 8 = 20 square units.

● Practice

Find the perimeter.

1.

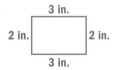
3 in.
2 in. · 2 in.
3 in.

2.

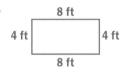
8 ft
4 ft · 4 ft
8 ft

3.

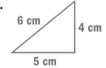
6 cm
4 cm
5 cm

Find the area.

4.

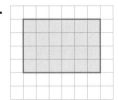

5.

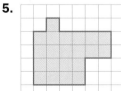

6.

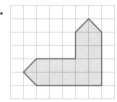

Venn Diagrams and Logical Reasoning

A **Venn diagram** uses shapes to show how sets are related.

EXAMPLE **Draw and use a Venn diagram.**

a. Draw a Venn diagram of the whole numbers between 0 and 10 where set A consists of even whole numbers and set B consists of multiples of 3.

b. If an even whole number is between 0 and 10, then is it *always*, *sometimes*, or *never* a multiple of 3?

c. If a number is in set B, then is it *always*, *sometimes*, or *never* in set A?

Solution

a.

Whole numbers greater than 0 and less than 10

A   B
2   6
1   4   8   3   9
5   7

All whole numbers between 0 and 10 are placed somewhere in the rectangle.

b. This statement is *sometimes* true because 6 is an even whole number that is a multiple of 3, but 2, 4, and 8, the other even whole numbers between 0 and 10, are not multiples of 3.

c. This statement is *sometimes* true because 3 and 9 are in set B only, but 6 is in sets B and A.

Practice

Draw a Venn diagram of the sets described.

1. Use the set of whole numbers less than 15. Set A consists of multiples of 3 and set B consists of multiples of 4.

2. Use the set of whole numbers between 10 and 20. Set C consists of numbers less than 15 and set D consists of numbers greater than 12.

Use the Venn diagrams from Exercises 1 and 2 to tell whether the statement is *always*, *sometimes*, or *never* true. Explain your reasoning.

3. If a number is in set A, then it is in set B.

4. If a number is between 12 and 15, then it is in both set C and set D.

5. If a number is greater than 15, then it is in set C.

Reading Bar Graphs

Data are numbers or facts. One way to display data is in **bar graphs**, which use bars to show how quantities compare.

EXAMPLE A group of students collected data on the number of students in each sixth grade math period at their school. The bar graph below displays the data they collected.

a. Which class has the most students?

b. Which class has 15 students?

Solution

a. The longest bar in the bar graph represents period 3, which shows a class with 25 students. So period 3 has the most students.

b. Look at the vertical scale and locate 15. Then find the bar that ends at 15. The bar that shows 15 students represents period 5.

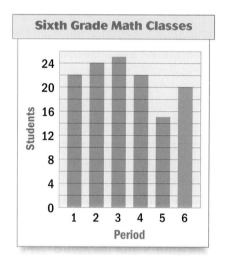

Sixth Grade Math Classes

● Practice

Use the bar graph above.

1. How many students are in period 6?

2. Which two periods have the same number of students?

3. Which period has 24 students?

4. Which period has the fewest students?

5. How many more students are in period 1 than in period 5?

6. Which period has two more students than period 4?

7. Which two periods have a difference of 1 in the number of students they have?

Reading Line Graphs

You can use a line graph to display data. A **line graph** uses line segments to show how quantities change over time.

EXAMPLE The line graph below shows the data you collected on the depth of a creek behind your house each day for one week.

a. Did the depth of the creek *increase* or *decrease* from Monday to Tuesday?

b. On which day was the creek 6 inches deep when you measured it?

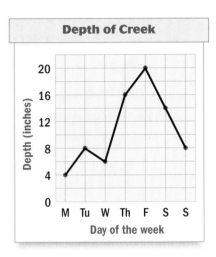

Depth of Creek

Solution

a. If the line rises from left to right, the data increase. If the line falls from left to right, the data decrease. Because the line from Monday to Tuesday rises, the depth of the creek increased.

b. Look at the vertical scale and locate 6. Then find the bullet on the horizontal line with the value of 6. The creek was 6 inches deep when you measured it on Wednesday.

● Practice

Use the line graph above.

1. On which day was the creek 16 inches deep when you measured it?

2. Between which two days did the depth of the creek decrease by 2 inches?

3. How deep was the creek on Sunday?

4. On which day was the creek the deepest?

5. Did the depth of the creek *increase* or *decrease* from Friday to Saturday?

6. On which two days was the depth of the creek the same when you measured it?

7. On which day was the creek the shallowest?

8. Between which two days did the depth of the creek increase the most? How much was the increase?

Reading a Pictograph

A **pictograph** is a way to display data using pictures. To read a pictograph, find the key and read the amount that each symbol represents. Multiply that amount by the number of whole symbols shown for the category. Then find and add on the value of any partial symbols.

EXAMPLE The pictograph shows data on the eye colors of students in a history class. How many students have green eyes?

Solution

Each symbol represents 2 students.

The 3 whole symbols represent $3 \times 2 = 6$ students.

Because $\frac{1}{2}$ of 2 is 1, the half symbol represents 1 student.

ANSWER $6 + 1 = 7$, so there are 7 students with green eyes.

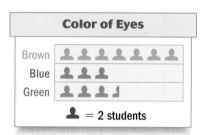

Practice

Use the pictograph above.

1. Which eye color do most students have? How many students have this eye color?

2. Which eye color do the fewest students have? How many students have this eye color?

Use the pictograph at the right.

3. How many pictures were taken on Tuesday?

4. On which day were the most pictures taken? How many pictures were taken?

5. About how many fewer pictures were taken on Thursday than on Monday?

6. How many pictures were taken on Wednesday?

7. On which day was the number of pictures taken twice the number taken on Tuesday?

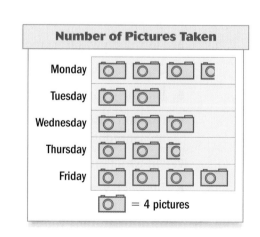

Making a Pictograph

To make a pictograph, first choose a symbol and find an appropriate amount for that symbol to represent. Then draw the graph.

EXAMPLE You collected data on the types of bagels sold in one hour at a bagel shop. Make a pictograph of the data.

Bagels Sold in One Hour	
Type of bagel	**Number sold**
plain	12
sesame	7
rye	4
cinnamon raisin	10
egg	11

Solution

Choose a symbol to represent 2 bagels. Half of a symbol represents 1 bagel. Write the types of bagels along the left hand side of the graph. Then draw symbols to represent the number of bagels of each type sold that hour.

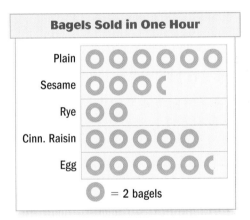

Practice

Make a pictograph of the data.

1.

CDs Sold in One Day	
Type of CD	**Number sold**
country	15
rock	25
pop	35

2.

Pets Owned by Students	
Pet	**Number of students**
dog	24
cat	18
turtle	6
rabbit	3
hamster	21

Extra Practice

Chapter 1

1.1 **Find the sum, difference, product, or quotient.**

1. $262 - 59$ **2.** $47 + 158$ **3.** $306 \div 6$ **4.** 34×21

5. 34×5 **6.** $348 - 72$ **7.** $156 \div 4$ **8.** $13 + 19$

1.1 **Describe the pattern. Then find the next two numbers.**

9. 5, 9, 13, 17, ? , ?   **10.** 50, 43, 36, 29, ? , ?   **11.** 1600, 800, 400, 200, ? , ?

1.2 **Estimate the sum, difference, product, or quotient.**

12. $257 + 91$ **13.** $435 - 69$ **14.** 173×29 **15.** $381 \div 52$

16. $680 + 134$ **17.** $805 - 37$ **18.** $583 \div 61$ **19.** 48×32

1.2 **20.** You are buying spring water for use by runners at a road race. The water comes in cases of 36 bottles each. You buy 12 cases. Estimate the number of bottles you buy.

1.3 **Find the value of the power.**

21. 7^3 **22.** 6^4 **23.** 2 cubed   **24.** 12 squared

1.4 **Evaluate the expression.**

25. $27 - 17 + 4$ **26.** $5 \times 12 \div 20$ **27.** $18 + 9 \div 3$ **28.** $4 + 3^3$

29. $9 \times (2 + 6) \div 12$ **30.** $100 \div 5^2 + 5$ **31.** $10 - 2 \times 3 + 7$ **32.** $\dfrac{8^2}{9 - 5}$

1.5 **Evaluate the expression when $x = 9$ and $y = 4$.**

33. $3x$ **34.** $4x + y$ **35.** $92 - x^2$ **36.** $2x \div 3 + 5$

37. $y + x + 1$ **38.** $6 - y$ **39.** $x - y \div 2$ **40.** $x + y^2$

1.5 **41.** Let a represent your age in years. Your cousin is 9 years older. You can use the expression $a + 9$ to represent your cousin's age. Use the expression to find how old your cousin is if you are 13 years old.

1.6 **Solve the equation using mental math.**

42. $2b = 8$ **43.** $8 + z = 11$ **44.** $x - 2 = 21$ **45.** $18 \div x = 9$

46. $1 + x = 4$ **47.** $13 - q = 9$ **48.** $70 \div t = 10$ **49.** $4 \cdot c = 0$

1.7 **50.** The product of two whole numbers is 56. Their difference is 10. Find the two numbers. Begin by making a list of all the pairs of numbers whose product is 56.

Chapter 2

2.1 **1.** Find the length of the line segment to the nearest centimeter.

_____

2.1 **Choose an appropriate customary unit and metric unit for the length.**

2. your height   **3.** distance between towns   **4.** thickness of a ruler

2.2 **Find the perimeter and the area of the rectangle or square.**

5. a rectangle that is 6 in. by 3 in.   **6.** a square that is 12 mi by 12 mi

2.3 **The scale on a map is 1 cm : 120 km. Find the actual distance, in kilometers, for the given length on the map.**

7. 2 cm   **8.** 5 cm   **9.** 7 cm   **10.** 18 cm

2.4 **The following data show the heights, in inches, of flowers in a flower box.**

4, 6, 5, 5, 5, 6, 8, 4, 6, 5, 5, 6, 5

11. Make a frequency table of the data.   **12.** Make a line plot of the data.

2.5 **13.** Make a bar graph of the fish swimming speed data at the right.

Fish	Carp	Cod	Mackerel	Pike
Speed (km/h)	6	8	11	6

2.6 **Graph the points on the same coordinate grid.**

14. (0, 0)   **15.** (7, 1)   **16.** (2, 3)   **17.** (5, 4)   **18.** (1, 0)

2.6 **19.** Make a line graph of the running data at the right.

Time spent running (seconds)	0	10	20	30	40
Distance from start (meters)	0	25	40	45	45

2.7 **The circle graph shows the number of bagels sold at a bakery in one day.**

20. What type of bagel was most popular?

21. Suppose 300 bagels were sold at the bakery. Predict how many sesame bagels would be sold.

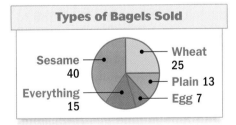

Types of Bagels Sold

Sesame 40
Wheat 25
Plain 13
Everything 15
Egg 7

2.8 **Find the mean, median, mode(s), and range. Then choose the best average(s) to represent a typical data value. Explain your choice.**

22. Number of telephones in students' homes: 3, 4, 3, 4, 1, 2, 4, 2, 3, 4

23. Temperatures at 6 A.M. (°F): 22, 25, 30, 31, 34, 40, 49

Chapter 3

3.1 **Write the number as a decimal.**

    1. fifty and forty-two hundredths   **2.** seventy-two thousandths

3.1 **Write the decimal in words.**

    3. 0.008   **4.** 2.09   **5.** 1.11   **6.** 12.721   **7.** 7.0275

3.2   **8.** Find the length of the word *mathematics* to the nearest tenth of a centimeter.

3.2   **9.** A pencil is 15 centimeters long. Write the length of the pencil to the nearest hundredth of a meter.

3.3 **Copy and complete the statement with <, >, or =.**

    10. 5.7 _?_ 7.5   **11.** 13.76 _?_ 13.81   **12.** 6.05 _?_ 6.50

    13. 17.98 _?_ 17.89   **14.** 0.03 _?_ 0.003   **15.** 0.84 _?_ 0.840

3.3 **Order the numbers from least to greatest.**

    16. 0.90, 0.09, 0.99   **17.** 2.3, 2.12, 2.01   **18.** 4.5, 4.05, 4.55

3.4 **Round the decimal as specified.**

    19. 13.2709 (nearest tenth)   **20.** 0.090909 (nearest hundredth)

3.4 **Round the decimal to the place value of the leading digit.**

    21. 0.7004   **22.** 0.06111   **23.** 0.0089   **24.** 0.000192

3.5 **Use rounding to estimate the sum or difference.**

    25. 3.9 − 2.1   **26.** 4.7 + 5.2   **27.** 6.7 + 12.4   **28.** 19.73 − 5.82

3.5 **Use front-end estimation to estimate the sum.**

    29. 13.89 + 8.72 + 9.45   **30.** 6.25 + 8.33 + 9.40   **31.** 7.30 + 2.50 + 3.80

3.6 **Find the sum or difference.**

    32. 3.8 + 9.2   **33.** 2.11 + 8.7   **34.** 13.2 − 4.7   **35.** 8.24 − 6.1

3.6 **Evaluate the expression when $x = 0.35$ and $y = 2.19$.**

    36. $x + 0.062$ **37.** $2.1 + x$ **38.** $8.5 - y$ **39.** $y - x$

3.6   **40.** Tell which property is being illustrated: $1.8 + 6.3 = 6.3 + 1.8$.

Chapter 4

4.1   **Find the product. Use estimation to check your answer.**

1. 4×8.13 **2.** 27.5×6 **3.** 22×5.69 **4.** 3.897×14

4.2   **Use the distributive property to find the product.**

5. $6(8.2 + 3)$ **6.** $6(20 - 3)$ **7.** $7(29)$ **8.** $8(4.8)$

4.3   **Multiply. Use estimation to check that the product is reasonable.**

9. 0.8×2.6 **10.** 9.2×0.36 **11.** 4.09×1.23 **12.** 0.005×2.1

4.4   **Copy the answer and place the decimal point in the correct location.**

13. $35.2 \div 11 = \textbf{32}$ **14.** $492.17 \div 7 = \textbf{7031}$ **15.** $29 \div 8 = \textbf{3625}$

4.4   **Divide. Round to the nearest tenth if necessary.**

16. $9.9 \div 11$ **17.** $13.5 \div 9$ **18.** $21 \div 8$ **19.** $4.2 \div 4$

4.5   **Find the product or quotient using mental math.**

20. 16.9×1000 **21.** 2.05×100 **22.** 40×0.01 **23.** 17.98×0.1
24. $0.008 \div 10$ **25.** $935 \div 1000$ **26.** $8.3 \div 0.01$ **27.** $9.38 \div 0.1$

4.6   **Divide. Round to the nearest tenth if necessary.**

28. $0.9 \div 0.3$ **29.** $4.2 \div 3.5$ **30.** $50 \div 1.5$ **31.** $39 \div 7.8$
32. $9.25 \div 0.4$ **33.** $9.9 \div 0.03$ **34.** $8.3 \div 0.41$ **35.** $6.32 \div 7.4$

4.7   **Choose an appropriate metric unit to measure the item.**

36. mass of a marble   **37.** mass of a cat

38. capacity of a soup spoon   **39.** capacity of a water tank

40. mass of a facial tissue   **41.** capacity of a large can of paint

4.8   **Copy and complete the statement.**

42. $188 \text{ mg} = \underline{?} \text{ g}$ **43.** $480 \text{ L} = \underline{?} \text{ mL}$ **44.** $3.8 \text{ km} = \underline{?} \text{ m}$
45. $67.4 \text{ kg} = \underline{?} \text{ g}$ **46.** $25 \text{ mL} = \underline{?} \text{ L}$ **47.** $100 \text{ cm} = \underline{?} \text{ mm}$

4.8   **Copy and complete the statement with** $<$**,** $>$**, or** $=$**.**

48. $212 \text{ m} \underline{?} 0.1 \text{ km}$ **49.** $4.9 \text{ mm} \underline{?} 5 \text{ cm}$ **50.** $0.025 \text{ L} \underline{?} 249 \text{ mL}$
51. $1.6 \text{ kL} \underline{?} 160{,}000 \text{ mL}$ **52.** $980 \text{ g} \underline{?} 0.98 \text{ kg}$ **53.** $3800 \text{ mg} \underline{?} 4.9 \text{ g}$

Chapter 5

5.1 **Test the number for divisibility by 2, 3, 5, 6, 9, and 10.**

1. 406 **2.** 721 **3.** 534 **4.** 1557 **5.** 510

5.1 **Tell whether the number is *prime*, *composite*, or *neither*.**

6. 13 **7.** 8 **8.** 25 **9.** 1 **10.** 71

5.1 **Write the prime factorization of the number.**

11. 95 **12.** 330 **13.** 76 **14.** 400 **15.** 175

5.2 **Find the GCF of the numbers.**

16. 15, 21 **17.** 8, 20 **18.** 16, 24 **19.** 25, 50, 70

5.3 **Write two fractions that are equivalent to the given fraction.**

20. $\frac{1}{4}$ **21.** $\frac{2}{5}$ **22.** $\frac{5}{6}$ **23.** $\frac{3}{10}$ **24.** $\frac{4}{7}$

5.3 **Tell whether the fraction is in simplest form. If not, simplify it.**

25. $\frac{5}{9}$ **26.** $\frac{18}{27}$ **27.** $\frac{3}{42}$ **28.** $\frac{17}{20}$ **29.** $\frac{12}{15}$

5.4 **Find the LCM of the numbers.**

30. 3, 9 **31.** 8, 12 **32.** 20, 30 **33.** 4, 8, 10

5.5 **Order the fractions from least to greatest.**

34. $\frac{1}{2}, \frac{2}{5}, \frac{3}{8}$ **35.** $\frac{13}{15}, \frac{9}{10}, \frac{4}{5}$ **36.** $\frac{7}{12}, \frac{2}{3}, \frac{5}{9}, \frac{11}{18}$ **37.** $\frac{2}{5}, \frac{4}{15}, \frac{3}{20}, \frac{2}{9}$

5.6 **Rewrite the number as an improper fraction or mixed number.**

38. $1\frac{3}{4}$ **39.** $3\frac{8}{9}$ **40.** $5\frac{3}{10}$ **41.** $2\frac{3}{7}$ **42.** $1\frac{6}{11}$

43. $\frac{13}{6}$ **44.** $\frac{21}{4}$ **45.** $\frac{17}{5}$ **46.** $\frac{20}{3}$ **47.** $\frac{19}{12}$

5.6 **Order the numbers from least to greatest.**

48. $2\frac{1}{2}, \frac{19}{16}, \frac{35}{12}$ **49.** $2\frac{1}{4}, \frac{17}{8}, 2\frac{1}{3}, \frac{55}{24}$ **50.** $\frac{13}{8}, 1\frac{2}{5}, \frac{7}{4}, 2$

5.7 **Write the decimal as a fraction or mixed number in simplest form.**

51. 0.95 **52.** 3.8 **53.** 2.08 **54.** 6.09 **55.** 0.645

5.8 **Write the fraction or mixed number as a decimal.**

56. $\frac{5}{8}$ **57.** $\frac{7}{4}$ **58.** $\frac{8}{15}$ **59.** $5\frac{1}{6}$ **60.** $\frac{57}{40}$

Chapter 6

6.1 Estimate the sum or difference.

1. $\frac{15}{16} - \frac{5}{8}$

2. $\frac{1}{8} + \frac{5}{6}$

3. $\frac{7}{12} - \frac{8}{15}$

4. $\frac{5}{12} + \frac{3}{5}$

5. $7\frac{1}{8} - 2\frac{5}{6}$

6. $1\frac{2}{3} + 2\frac{7}{9}$

7. $5\frac{8}{15} + 3\frac{5}{12}$

8. $6\frac{2}{9} - 1\frac{6}{7}$

Find the sum or difference.

6.2

9. $\frac{5}{8} + \frac{1}{8}$

10. $\frac{7}{12} + \frac{5}{12}$

11. $\frac{8}{15} - \frac{4}{15}$

12. $\frac{5}{9} - \frac{4}{9}$

13. $\frac{17}{20} - \frac{9}{20}$

14. $\frac{2}{11} + \frac{7}{11}$

15. $\frac{7}{10} - \frac{3}{10}$

16. $\frac{5}{14} + \frac{3}{14}$

6.3

17. $\frac{5}{9} - \frac{1}{6}$

18. $\frac{2}{3} - \frac{1}{2}$

19. $\frac{11}{16} + \frac{1}{4}$

20. $\frac{2}{7} + \frac{2}{3}$

21. $\frac{11}{15} - \frac{1}{10}$

22. $\frac{6}{13} + \frac{1}{3}$

23. $\frac{7}{20} + \frac{3}{5}$

24. $\frac{9}{16} - \frac{1}{8}$

6.4

25. $6\frac{5}{6} - 4\frac{1}{6}$

26. $2\frac{5}{12} + 4\frac{2}{3}$

27. $3\frac{1}{2} + 12\frac{3}{4}$

28. $9\frac{2}{3} - 1\frac{3}{8}$

29. $1\frac{5}{14} + 6\frac{3}{14}$

30. $12\frac{1}{2} - 3\frac{1}{5}$

31. $3\frac{7}{8} - 3\frac{3}{4}$

32. $2\frac{5}{9} + 4\frac{1}{6}$

6.5

33. $3\frac{2}{13} - 1\frac{9}{13}$

34. $8\frac{3}{4} - 6\frac{4}{5}$

35. $2\frac{3}{8} - \frac{5}{8}$

36. $4 - 2\frac{3}{4}$

37. $4\frac{1}{10} - 3\frac{1}{2}$

38. $4\frac{1}{6} - 1\frac{2}{3}$

39. $9 - 6\frac{4}{5}$

40. $5\frac{2}{3} - 4\frac{3}{4}$

6.6 Add or subtract the measures of time.

41.
```
  6 h 15 min
− 2 h 40 min
```

42.
```
       45 min
+ 4 h 25 min
```

43.
```
  1 h 24 min 38 sec
+      56 min 12 sec
```

44.
```
  4 h 17 min
−      38 min
```

45.
```
  5 h 28 min
+ 1 h 47 min
```

46.
```
  3 h  4 min 12 sec
+ 2 h 17 min 35 sec
```

6.6 Find the elapsed time.

47. 6:00 A.M. to 8:30 A.M.

48. 9:00 A.M. to 3:15 P.M.

49. 6:30 P.M. to 12:15 A.M.

50. 7:30 A.M. to 9:10 P.M.

51. 3:40 P.M. to 5:15 P.M.

52. 11:40 P.M. to 2:30 A.M.

6.6

53. You went on a hike with a group of friends from 8:15 A.M. to 4:30 P.M. How long were you hiking?

Chapter 7

7.1 **Use compatible numbers to estimate the product.**

1. $25 \times \frac{3}{8}$ **2.** $10 \times \frac{1}{3}$ **3.** $\frac{9}{10} \times 32$ **4.** $\frac{5}{7} \times 34$

Find the product.

7.1 **5.** $8 \times \frac{3}{4}$ **6.** $6 \times \frac{5}{8}$ **7.** $\frac{4}{7} \times 28$ **8.** $\frac{2}{3} \times 7$

7.2 **9.** $\frac{5}{3} \times \frac{3}{4}$ **10.** $\frac{7}{12} \times \frac{8}{9}$ **11.** $\frac{1}{3} \times \frac{2}{9}$ **12.** $\frac{4}{9} \times \frac{3}{8} \times \frac{2}{3}$

7.3 **13.** $4 \times 1\frac{5}{6}$ **14.** $\frac{2}{5} \times 3\frac{2}{5}$ **15.** $1\frac{3}{4} \times \frac{2}{3}$ **16.** $2\frac{1}{4} \times 1\frac{1}{3}$

Find the quotient.

7.4 **17.** $\frac{5}{6} \div 4$ **18.** $1 \div \frac{5}{12}$ **19.** $\frac{1}{5} \div \frac{5}{4}$ **20.** $\frac{2}{3} \div \frac{1}{9}$

7.5 **21.** $2\frac{1}{4} \div \frac{3}{4}$ **22.** $\frac{7}{8} \div 1\frac{1}{2}$ **23.** $1\frac{4}{5} \div 4$ **24.** $12 \div 1\frac{1}{2}$

25. $3\frac{1}{2} \div 1\frac{1}{5}$ **26.** $5\frac{2}{5} \div 1\frac{1}{8}$ **27.** $6 \div 2\frac{2}{5}$ **28.** $3\frac{3}{4} \div 6\frac{1}{2}$

7.5 **Solve the problem. Explain why you chose the operation you used.**

29. You buy 10 yards of fabric to make some costumes. If each costume needs $3\frac{5}{8}$ yards of fabric, do you have enough fabric to make 3 costumes?

30. Amy is $1\frac{1}{3}$ feet taller than Frank. Frank is $4\frac{1}{4}$ feet tall. How tall is Amy?

7.6 **Copy and complete the statement using an appropriate customary unit.**

31. weight of a horse = 850 ? **32.** capacity of a washing machine = 19 ?

33. weight of a jar of jam = 10 ? **34.** capacity of a can of soup = 12 ?

7.7 **Copy and complete the statement.**

35. 3 gal 2 qt = ? qt **36.** 2 yd 6 in. = ? in. **37.** 25 oz = ? lb ? oz, or ? lb

7.7 **Change the measurement to the specified unit.**

38. $3\frac{1}{4}$ cups to fluid ounces **39.** $1\frac{1}{8}$ tons to pounds **40.** 9 pints to gallons

7.7 **Find the sum or difference.**

41. 3 lb 6 oz + 2 lb 10 oz **42.** 3 ft 5 in. − 1 ft 9 in. **43.** 1 yd 2 ft + 2 yd 2 ft

Chapter 8

8.1 **Write the ratio in simplest form.**

1. $12 : 18$ **2.** 6 to 3   **3.** $2 : 10$ **4.** 5 to 20   **5.** $16 : 12$

Copy and complete the statement.

8.1   **6.** $\dfrac{3}{8} = \dfrac{9}{?}$ **7.** $\dfrac{10}{?} = \dfrac{1}{2}$ **8.** $\dfrac{?}{12} = \dfrac{7}{6}$ **9.** $\dfrac{3}{5} = \dfrac{?}{15}$

8.2   **10.** $\dfrac{\$5}{2 \text{ items}} = \dfrac{?}{12 \text{ items}}$ **11.** $\dfrac{38 \text{ cm}}{30 \text{ min}} = \dfrac{?}{15 \text{ min}}$ **12.** $\dfrac{?}{3 \text{ classes}} = \dfrac{25 \text{ students}}{1 \text{ class}}$

8.2 **Write the unit rate.**

13. $\dfrac{2750 \text{ visitors}}{10 \text{ hours}}$ **14.** $\dfrac{90 \text{ meters}}{18 \text{ seconds}}$ **15.** $\dfrac{5000 \text{ words}}{25 \text{ pages}}$ **16.** $\dfrac{40,000 \text{ bits}}{5 \text{ minutes}}$

8.3 **Solve the proportion.**

17. $\dfrac{81}{6} = \dfrac{27}{r}$ **18.** $\dfrac{16}{x} = \dfrac{40}{25}$ **19.** $\dfrac{8}{20} = \dfrac{b}{28}$ **20.** $\dfrac{a}{51} = \dfrac{10}{15}$

8.4 **A scale drawing of a room has a scale of 1 in. : 8 ft. In the drawing, the floor of the room is 2.5 inches long by 2 inches wide.**

21. What are the actual dimensions of the floor of the room?

22. What is the ratio of the floor area of the room in the drawing to the floor area of the actual room?

8.5 **Write the percent as a decimal and a fraction.**

23. 18%   **24.** 69%   **25.** 2.5%   **26.** 45%

8.6 **Write the fraction or decimal as a percent.**

27. $\dfrac{17}{20}$ **28.** $\dfrac{3}{8}$ **29.** 0.83   **30.** 0.9   **31.** 0.005

8.6 **Order the numbers from least to greatest.**

32. $0.24, \dfrac{7}{25}, \dfrac{1}{4}, 23\%$ **33.** $67\%, \dfrac{5}{6}, 0.76, \dfrac{2}{3}$ **34.** $0.2, \dfrac{3}{20}, 14\%, 0.018$

8.7 **Find the percent of the number.**

35. 20% of 90   **36.** 8% of 4   **37.** 16% of 350   **38.** $33\dfrac{1}{3}\%$ of 150

8.7 **39.** A bank account pays 4% annual interest. How much simple interest will $2000 earn in 6 years?

8.7 **40.** You want to buy a sweater that costs $18.50. The sales tax is 5%. You realize that you have only $20 with you. Can you buy the sweater?

Chapter 9

Use the diagram at the right.

9.1 **1.** Name two rays and two segments with endpoint *B*.

2. Name two parallel lines.

3. Name two lines that intersect at *D*.

9.2 **4.** Name three angles with vertex *B*.

5. Name an angle in the diagram whose measure is 50°.

9.2 **6.** Use a protractor to draw an angle that has a measure of 108°.

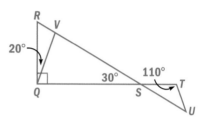

Use the diagram at the right.

9.3 **7.** Classify each angle as *acute, right, obtuse,* or *straight*: ∠*RQS,* ∠*QSU,* ∠*QSR,* ∠*QST.*

8. Find the measures of ∠*TSU,* ∠*VQS,* and ∠*RST.*

9.4 **9.** Find the measures of ∠*QRS,* ∠*QVR,* and ∠*QVS.*

10. Classify each triangle by its angles as *acute, right,* or *obtuse*: △*STU,* △*SVQ,* △*QRV,* △*QRS.*

9.5 **Copy and complete the statement using *All, Some,* or *No.***

11. _?_ squares are parallelograms.   **12.** _?_ rhombuses are squares.

13. _?_ rectangles are rhombuses.   **14.** _?_ quadrilaterals have four right angles.

9.6 **Classify the polygon and tell whether it is regular.**

15.    **16.**   **17.**    **18.**

9.7 **△*XYZ* and △*DEF* are congruent.**

19. List the corresponding parts.

20. How long is $\overline{EF}$? Explain.

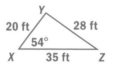

9.8 **Tell whether the figure has line symmetry. If so, copy the figure and draw all lines of symmetry.**

21.   **22.**   **23.**   **24.**

Chapter 10

10.1 **Find the unknown measure of the parallelogram described.**

1. base = 12 ft, height = 30 ft, Area = ___?___   **2.** base = 5 m, Area = 20 m², height = ___?___

10.2 **Find the area of the triangle.**

3.

4.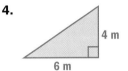

5.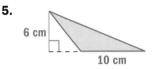

10.3 **Find the circumference of the circle described. Tell what value you used for π. Explain your choice.**

6. $r = 80$ m   **7.** $d = 35$ cm   **8.** $d = 9$ mm   **9.** $r = 7$ in.

10.4 **Find the area of the circle described. Round to the nearest tenth of a unit.**

10. $r = 42$ m   **11.** $d = 8$ cm   **12.** $d = 200$ mm   **13.** $r = 15$ ft

10.4 **Find the area of the figure to the nearest whole unit.**

14.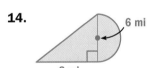

15.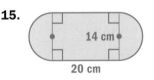

16.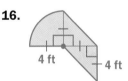

10.4 **17.** The table shows how many of the 40 volunteers will be assigned to each of the three types of jobs. Make a circle graph of the data.

Spring Fundraiser Volunteers			
Job	tickets	snacks	booths
Number of volunteers	8	6	26

10.5 **Draw the solid described.**

18. cone   **19.** pyramid with a rectangular base

10.5 **20.** Count the number of faces, edges, and vertices of the solid you drew in Exercise 19.

10.6 **Draw a diagram of the rectangular prism described. Then find the surface area.**

21. 5 cm by 5 cm by 3 cm   **22.** 6 in. by 4 in. by 10 in.

10.7 **23.** Find the volumes of the prisms described in Exercises 21 and 22.

Chapter 11

11.1 **1.** Find the opposites of the integers 4, −18, and 0.

11.1 **Copy and complete the statement using < or >.**

    2. −4 ? 0   **3.** 2 ? −5   **4.** −10 ? −11   **5.** −8 ? 13

11.1 **Order the integers from least to greatest.**

    6. 3, −4, 7, 2, −1   **7.** 0, 2, −3, 5, 3   **8.** −5, 6, −1, −4, −3   **9.** −7, 9, −9, 8, −6

    Find the sum or difference.

11.2 **10.** 8 + (−22)   **11.** −6 + 10   **12.** 6 + (−12)   **13.** −5 + (−5)

    14. 2 + (−15)   **15.** −14 + 14   **16.** −20 + 16   **17.** −9 + (−5)

11.3 **18.** 2 − 7   **19.** 13 − (−3)   **20.** −7 − 9   **21.** −24 − (−7)

    22. 16 − (−17)   **23.** −10 − 18   **24.** −9 − (−11)   **25.** 8 − 17

    Find the product or quotient.

11.4 **26.** 13(4)   **27.** −8(5)   **28.** −6(10)   **29.** −7(−20)

    30. 0(−12)   **31.** −4(−8)   **32.** 14(−5)   **33.** −11(−9)

11.5 **34.** −9 ÷ (−1)   **35.** −200 ÷ 25   **36.** 42 ÷ (−6)   **37.** −70 ÷ (−14)

    38. 110 ÷ (−5)   **39.** −45 ÷ 15   **40.** −51 ÷ (−17)   **41.** 300 ÷ (−12)

11.6 **Graph the point and describe its location.**

    42. $P(3, -7)$ **43.** $Q(4, 4)$ **44.** $R(-2, -6)$ **45.** $S(-8, 4)$ **46.** $T(-5, 0)$

11.6 **Draw the figure on a coordinate plane. Then translate the figure as described. Give the coordinates of the vertices of the image.**

    47. $\triangle ABC$: $A(0, 4)$, $B(-2, 2)$, $C(1, -1)$
        Translation: 3 units to the left and 4 units up to form $\triangle DEF$

    48. $\triangle ABC$: $A(-5, 3)$, $B(1, 4)$, $C(-2, -3)$
        Translation: 5 units to the right and 2 units down to form $\triangle DEF$

11.7 **Tell whether the transformation is a *translation*, a *reflection*, or a *rotation*.**

  49. 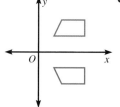   **50.** 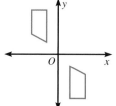   **51.** 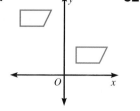   **52.**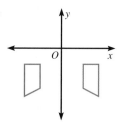

Extra Practice

Chapter 12

12.1 Write the phrase as an expression. Let _n_ represent the number.

1. A number increased by 7

2. 30 multiplied by a number

3. A number subtracted from 20

4. The quotient of a number and 50

12.1 Write the sentence as an equation.

5. The product of 8 and a number _n_ is 32.

6. The sum of 7 and a number _x_ is 19.

7. A number _y_ divided by 6 is 5.

8. 15 less than a number _k_ is 6.

Solve the equation.

12.2   **9.** $9 + p = 38$ **10.** $x + 17 = 50$ **11.** $16 + z = 30$ **12.** $q + 2.8 = 4.7$

12.3 **13.** $8 = z - 8$ **14.** $x - 31 = 41$ **15.** $1 = n - 24$ **16.** $w - 4.8 = 2.5$

12.4 **17.** $30 = 3n$ **18.** $20c = 100$ **19.** $8n = 72$ **20.** $68 = 4x$

     21. $\dfrac{x}{12} = 5$ **22.** $10 = \dfrac{b}{8}$ **23.** $\dfrac{x}{7} = 3$ **24.** $\dfrac{n}{5} = 13$

12.5 Make an input-output table using the function rule and the input values _x_ = 4, 8, 12, 16, and 20.

25. $y = x - 3$ **26.** $y = 5x$ **27.** $y = 2x + 5$ **28.** $y = \dfrac{x}{4}$

12.5 29. Write a function rule for the input-output table.

Price of each item, _p_	$10	$20	$30	$40	$50
Total cost of items, _c_	$60	$120	$180	$240	$300

12.5 Make an input-output table. Then write a function rule for the relationship.

30. input: dollars
     output: cents

31. input: quarts
     output: gallons

12.6 Make an input-output table using the function rule and the input values _x_ = 0, 1, 2, 3, and 4. Graph the function.

32. $y = 10 - x$ **33.** $y = x - 2$ **34.** $y = 2x + 1$ **35.** $y = \dfrac{1}{2}x + 3$

12.6 Graph the ordered pairs and draw a line through the points. Write a function rule for the ordered pairs.

36. $(-2, 1), (-1, 2), (0, 3), (1, 4), (2, 5)$

37. $(-6, -2), (-3, -1), (0, 0), (3, 1), (6, 2)$

Chapter 13

13.1 **A box contains seven tiles numbered 1 through 7. You randomly choose a tile. Find the probability of the event.**

1. You choose an odd number.　　**2.** You choose a multiple of 3.

3. You choose a number less than 10.　　**4.** You choose the number 18.

13.1 **5.** Describe the complement of the event in Exercise 2. Then find its probability.

13.2 **6.** The cover of a yearbook can be white, red, or gold. The printing on the cover can be black or blue. Use a tree diagram to find all the possible covers.

13.2 **7.** An electronic lock has four buttons, labeled 1, 2, 3, and 4. List all possible two-digit numbers that can be formed using these four buttons. Include repeated digits, such as 11.

13.3 **You toss a coin and then you roll a number cube. Find the probability of the event.**

8. You get tails and then roll a 2.

9. You get heads and then roll an even number.

13.4 **10.** A family, using the data below, claims that the average water bill on their street is $147. Does $147 describe the average water bill well? Why or why not?

$98, $105, $105, $106, $110, $118, $125, $125, $130, $448

In Exercises 11–13, use the list of data below. The data show the number of students using the library's study room each day.

9, 4, 8, 11, 24, 8, 20, 15, 29, 7, 6, 7, 8, 16, 20, 19, 24, 21, 12, 18

13.5 **11.** Make a stem-and-leaf plot of the data.　　**12.** Find the mean, median, and mode(s).

13.6 **13.** Make a box-and-whisker plot of the data. Find the range.

13.7 **Choose an appropriate data display for the given situation. Explain your choice.**

14. Each student in a math class gives the number of pets in his or her family. You want to find the most common number of pets.

15. You have data on the average rainfall in your town each year for the past 50 years and want to see how the average has changed over time.

16. You want to compare the number of votes each candidate for class president received to the total number of votes cast.

Table of Symbols

Symbol	Meaning	Page
$+$	plus	5
$=$	equals, is equal to	5, 36
$-$	minus	6
$\times$	times	6
$\div$	divided by	6
R	remainder	6
$\approx$	is about equal to	13
4^3	4 to the 3rd power	17
( )	parentheses—a grouping symbol	21
$\dfrac{14}{2}$	14 divided by 2	22
$3 \cdot x$ $3(x)$ $3x$	3 times x	30
$\overset{?}{=}$	is equal to?	36
$\neq$	is not equal to	36
(4, 3)	ordered pair of numbers	83
28.6	decimal point	108
$<$	is less than	118, 602
$>$	is greater than	118, 602
...	continues on	235
$1.1\overline{6}$	repeating decimal 1.16666...	254
$a:b, \dfrac{a}{b}$	ratio of a to b	374

Symbol	Meaning	Page
%	percent	395
$\overleftrightarrow{AB}$	line AB	421
$\overrightarrow{AB}$	ray AB	421
$\overline{AB}$	segment AB	421
⇉	parallel lines	422
$\angle PQR$	angle PQR	425
$\circ$	degree(s)	426
$m\angle B$	measure of angle B	426
⦜	right angle	430
$\triangle ABC$	triangle with vertices A, B, and C	436
π	pi—a number approximately equal to 3.14	485
-3	negative 3	533
-3	the opposite of 3	534
$|a|$	the absolute value of a number a	539
$\leq$	is less than or equal to	602
$\geq$	is greater than or equal to	602

Table of Measures

Time

60 seconds (sec) = 1 minute (min)
60 minutes = 1 hour (h)
24 hours = 1 day
7 days = 1 week
4 weeks (approx.) = 1 month

$\left.\begin{matrix} 365 \text{ days} \\ 52 \text{ weeks (approx.)} \\ 12 \text{ months} \end{matrix}\right\}$ = 1 year

10 years = 1 decade
100 years = 1 century

METRIC

Length

10 millimeters (mm) = 1 centimeter (cm)
$\left.\begin{matrix} 100 \text{ cm} \\ 1000 \text{ mm} \end{matrix}\right\}$ = 1 meter (m)
1000 m = 1 kilometer (km)

Area

100 square millimeters = 1 square centimeter
(mm^2)   (cm^2)
10,000 cm^2 = 1 square meter (m^2)
10,000 m^2 = 1 hectare (ha)

Volume

1000 cubic millimeters = 1 cubic centimeter
(mm^3)   (cm^3)
1,000,000 cm^3 = 1 cubic meter (m^3)

Liquid Capacity

$\left.\begin{matrix} 1000 \text{ milliliters (mL)} \\ 1000 \text{ cubic centimeters } (cm^3) \end{matrix}\right\}$ = 1 liter (L)
1000 L = 1 kiloliter (kL)

Mass

1000 milligrams (mg) = 1 gram (g)
1000 g = 1 kilogram (kg)
1000 kg = 1 metric ton (t)

Temperature   Degrees Celsius (°C)

0°C = freezing point of water
37°C = normal body temperature
100°C = boiling point of water

UNITED STATES CUSTOMARY

Length

12 inches (in.) = 1 foot (ft)
$\left.\begin{matrix} 36 \text{ in.} \\ 3 \text{ ft} \end{matrix}\right\}$ = 1 yard (yd)
$\left.\begin{matrix} 5280 \text{ ft} \\ 1760 \text{ yd} \end{matrix}\right\}$ = 1 mile (mi)

Area

144 square inches ($in.^2$) = 1 square foot (ft^2)
9 ft^2 = 1 square yard (yd^2)
$\left.\begin{matrix} 43,560 \text{ } ft^2 \\ 4840 \text{ } yd^2 \end{matrix}\right\}$ = 1 acre (A)

Volume

1728 cubic inches ($in.^3$) = 1 cubic foot (ft^3)
27 ft^3 = 1 cubic yard (yd^3)

Liquid Capacity

8 fluid ounces (fl oz) = 1 cup (c)
2 c = 1 pint (pt)
2 pt = 1 quart (qt)
4 qt = 1 gallon (gal)

Weight

16 ounces (oz) = 1 pound (lb)
2000 lb = 1 ton

Temperature   Degrees Fahrenheit (°F)

32°F = freezing point of water
98.6°F = normal body temperature
212°F = boiling point of water

Table of Measures

Table of Formulas

Geometric Formulas

Rectangle

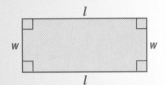

Area (p. 62)
A = length · width
$A = lw$

Perimeter (p. 61)
$P = 2$ · length $+ 2$ · width
$P = 2l + 2w$

Square

Area (p. 62)
A = (side length)^2
$A = s^2$

Perimeter (p. 62)
$P = 4$ · side length
$P = 4s$

Parallelogram

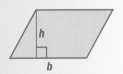

Area (p. 476)
A = base · height
$A = bh$

Triangle

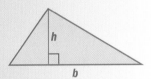

Area (p. 480)
$A = \frac{1}{2}$ · base · height
$A = \frac{1}{2}bh$

Circle

Area (p. 491)
A = (pi)(radius)$^2 = \pi r^2$

Circumference (p. 485)
C = pi · diameter $= \pi d$
$C = 2$ · pi · radius $= 2\pi r$

Rectangular Prism

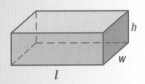

Surface Area (p. 506)
S = sum of areas of faces

Volume (p. 510)
V = length · width · height
$V = lwh$

Other Formulas

Distance traveled	(p. 154)	$d = rt$ where d = distance, r = rate, and t = time
Simple interest	(p. 408)	$I = Prt$ where I = simple interest, P = principal, r = annual interest rate, and t = time in years
Temperature	(p. 317)	$F = \frac{9}{5}C + 32$ and $C = \frac{5}{9}(F - 32)$ where F = degrees Fahrenheit and C = degrees Celsius

Table of Formulas

Table of Properties

Number Properties

Addition Property of 0 (p. 37) The sum of any number and 0 is that number.	**Numbers** **Algebra**	$7 + 0 = 7$ $a + 0 = a$
Multiplication Property of 0 (p. 37) The product of any number and 0 is 0.	**Numbers** **Algebra**	$4 \times 0 = 0$ $a \times 0 = 0$
Multiplication Property of 1 (p. 37) The product of any number and 1 is that number.	**Numbers** **Algebra**	$3 \times 1 = 3$ $a \times 1 = a$
Commutative Property of Addition (p. 137) You can add numbers in any order.	**Numbers** **Algebra**	$2 + 5 = 5 + 2$ $a + b = b + a$
Associative Property of Addition (p. 137) The value of a sum does not depend on how the numbers are grouped.	**Numbers** **Algebra**	$(2 + 4) + 6 = 2 + (4 + 6)$ $(a + b) + c = a + (b + c)$
Commutative Property of Multiplication (p. 155) You can multiply numbers in any order.	**Numbers** **Algebra**	$2 \times 6.5 = 6.5 \times 2$ $a \cdot b = b \cdot a$
Associative Property of Multiplication (p. 155) The value of a product does not depend on how the numbers are grouped.	**Numbers** **Algebra**	$(6 \times 2.5) \times 4 = 6 \times (2.5 \times 4)$ $(a \cdot b) \cdot c = a \cdot (b \cdot c)$
Distributive Property (p. 159) You can multiply a number and a sum by multiplying the number by each part of the sum and then adding these products. The same property applies with subtraction.	**Numbers** **Algebra**	$3(4 + 6) = 3(4) + 3(6)$ $2(8 - 5) = 2(8) - 2(5)$ $a(b + c) = ab + ac$ $a(b - c) = ab - ac$
Cross Products Property (p. 383) In a proportion, the cross products are equal.	**Numbers** **Algebra**	If $\frac{3}{4} = \frac{6}{8}$, then $3 \cdot 8 = 4 \cdot 6$. If $\frac{a}{b} = \frac{c}{d}$ and b and d do not equal 0, then $ad = bc$.

The following pages provide extra practice with three types of questions that you might encounter on standardized tests. All of the exercises provide practice with problem solving skills.

For the Short Response and Extended Response exercises, you will be expected to explain your reasoning. Strategies for answering these types of questions appear on the following pages:

• Building Test-Taking Skills: Short Response, pages 362–363
• Building Test-Taking Skills: Extended Response, pages 672–673

Contents

Gridded Response

1. At Tony's Pizza Place, you get a free pizza after you buy 10 pizzas. Mr. Ridell gets 60 pizzas for a party at the middle school. If a pizza costs $9, how much, in dollars, did Mr. Ridell pay?

2. Sarah bought 2 adult movie tickets and 3 children's movie tickets for a total of $34. If each adult ticket costs $8, what is the cost, in dollars, of one children's ticket?

3. During a basketball game, a coach tells the team that the ball must be passed among three different players before anyone can shoot. As shown below, Amy has the ball. In how many different ways can the ball be passed from Amy to two other teammates?

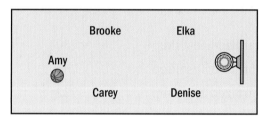

Short Response

4. A cookbook has the following guidelines for cooking slices of bacon in a microwave oven. For how long should 9 slices of bacon be cooked? Explain how you found your answer.

Slices	Cooking time
2	2 min
4	3 min 30 sec
6	5 min
8	6 min 30 sec

5. Mark paid $70 for a shirt and two pairs of the same style jeans. If one pair of the jeans cost $17 more than the shirt, what was the price of the shirt? Explain how you found your answer.

6. Four friends are standing in line for lunch. Tate is ahead of Anton in line. Beth is not first or last in line. Craig is directly in front of Tate. In what order from first to last are the four friends standing? Explain your reasoning.

Extended Response

7. Consider the expression $2^2 \cdot 2^3$. Rewrite the expression as a product of twos. Now rewrite this expression as a single power. How is the exponent in this new expression related to the exponents in the original expression? Write a rule for finding the product of two powers with the same base.

8. You start an e-mail chain by sending an e-mail to 3 friends. This is the first link in the chain. Those 3 friends then forward the e-mail to 3 more friends. This is the second link in the chain. How many links would it take for the e-mail to reach a total of 1000 people? Explain how you found your answer.

9. **Open-Ended** You can use addition, subtraction, multiplication, and division to define new operations. For example, suppose the operation "*" is defined as $a * b = a \div b + ab$. Find $12 * 3$. Define the operation "#" so that $8 \# 6 = 7$. Explain how you wrote your definition.

Gridded Response

1. Ann evenly distributed 2 pounds of fertilizer over the 23-foot-by-20-foot garden on one side of her house. She also wants to fertilize the 46-foot-by-30-foot garden on the other side of her house. If Ann wants to use the same amount of fertilizer per square foot for both gardens, how many pounds of fertilizer will Ann need for the 46-foot-by-30-foot garden?

2. A scale drawing of David's bedroom is shown. David wants to put up a wallpaper border along the top edge of the walls of his room. How many *yards* of border does David need?

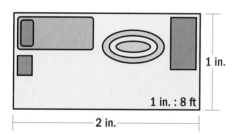

Short Response

3. Paula is selling 12 flower wreaths at a craft fair. The line plot below shows the prices of the wreaths. Find the mean, median, and mode of the prices. Explain your answers.

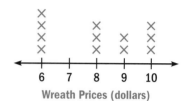

Wreath Prices (dollars)

4. **Open-Ended** A town requires a corral for one horse to have an area of at least 1000 square feet. For each additional horse, the corral must have an additional 300 square feet. Give the dimensions of a rectangular corral that would meet the minimum space requirements for 5 horses. Explain your answer.

5. The median height of the students in Mrs. Jones' class is 65 inches. The heights have a range of 6 inches. Is it possible that a student in the class has a height of 71 inches? Explain your answer.

Extended Response

6. Mr. Frank's and Ms. McCarty's classes each recorded the total numbers of hours all students in the class spent doing homework each week for four weeks. The results are shown in the double bar graph.

a. Which class spent more hours doing homework in Week 3?

b. During which week was the difference in homework hours between the two classes the greatest? Explain your answer.

c. Without doing any calculations, tell which class spent more total hours doing homework over the four weeks. Explain how you know.

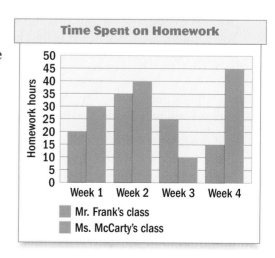

Gridded Response

1. If the boxes in the expression below are filled with the digits 0, 0, 8, 5, 9, and 3, what is the greatest value the expression can have?

$$\boxed{?} . \boxed{?} \boxed{?} - \boxed{?} . \boxed{?} \boxed{?}$$

2. Beth's hourly salary for each of several years is shown in the table. If the pattern continues, in what year will Beth make $10.50 an hour?

Year	Hourly salary
2001	$8.05
2002	$8.40
2003	$8.75
2004	$9.10

3. What decimal is halfway between 0.99 and 1.00 on a number line?

Short Response

4. A scale drawing of Farm Pond is shown below. What is a reasonable estimate of the area of Farm Pond? Explain your method.

Farm Pond

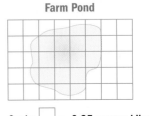

Scale: $\boxed{}$ = 0.25 square kilometer

5. **Open-Ended** You have a piece of paper that measures 8.5 inches by 11 inches. How could you use the paper to draw a length of 5 inches? Explain.

6. Derek and Reggie measure each other's height to the nearest inch. Derek is 70 inches tall and Reggie is 68 inches tall. Is it possible that Derek is actually 3 inches taller than Reggie? Explain.

Extended Response

7. The boys' track team at Kennedy Middle School has enough runners to enter two teams of 4 runners in the 4 x 100 meter relay. The runners' best individual times, in seconds, are shown in the table. Assume that all 8 runners will match their best times in the race.

Team 1	Team 2
10.99	10.90
11.50	11.15
11.54	11.25
11.09	11.05

a. Without performing any calculations, determine which relay team will win. Explain your reasoning.

b. If the fastest 4 runners all ran on the same relay team, by how many seconds would they beat the relay team made up of the 4 remaining runners? Show your work.

c. The track coach decides that the fastest person on a relay team should always run last. In how many different ways can the other 3 runners be ordered? Explain.

Gridded Response

1. A toy racecar crosses the starting line of a racetrack traveling at a constant speed of 20 feet per second. If the car completes 3 laps of the racetrack in 9.75 seconds, how many feet long is the racetrack?

2. Kasey writes down her race times in the 50 meter freestyle for each of her 6 swim meets. The times, in seconds, are shown below. However, one of the times got wet and can no longer be read. If Kasey knows that her mean time is 26.86 seconds, what is the missing race time, in seconds?

25.95	26.58
28.03	27.19
27.24	

3. What is the unknown number in the following pattern?

   0.115, _?_ , 0.46, 0.92, 1.84

Short Response

4. When will the product of a whole number and a decimal be greater than the whole number? When will it be less than the whole number? Give examples to support your answers.

5. The table below shows the deer population in a 10,000 acre park for a four year period.

Year	1999	2000	2001	2002
Total population	38	69	100	131

   a. If the pattern continues, what will the total population of deer be in the year 2008? Explain your answer.

   b. Population density is found by dividing the total population by the area. What will the deer population density be in the year 2008 if the pattern continues?

Extended Response

6. Irene is designing a rectangular flowerbed that will have a fence surrounding it. The length of the flowerbed will be three times as long as the width.

   a. The width of the flowerbed is 8.2 feet. Estimate the perimeter, in feet, of the flowerbed. Show your work.

   b. Irene wants to spread bark mulch on the flowerbed. Estimate the area, in square yards, of the flowerbed. Explain your answer.

7. **Open-Ended** You have a balance scale and the weights shown. How can you use the weights to measure the following amounts of sand: 1 g, 2 g, 3 g, 4 g, 5 g, 6 g, 7 g, 8 g, 9 g, and 10 g? For example, to measure 5 grams of sand, you could put the 2 gram weight and 3 gram weight on one side of the scale and add sand to the other side of the scale until the two sides balance.

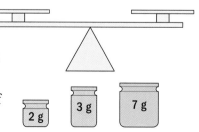

Gridded Response

1. Sheri ran a mile in 6.15 minutes. Previously, her best time was 6.25 minutes. By how many *seconds* did Sheri's time improve?

2. Seth and Steve both work as security guards for a software company. Seth works the night shift every 6 days, and Steve works the night shift every 8 days. Seth and Steve both worked the night shift on July 1. On what date in July will Seth and Steve next work the night shift together?

Short Response

3. **Open-Ended** Name two fractions that are greater than $\frac{5}{7}$ and less than $\frac{6}{7}$. Explain your method.

4. Tom is building a deck. He has nails that are $1\frac{3}{4}$ inches long and $1\frac{1}{2}$ inches long. He wants to use the nails to make a design in the wood, and he does not want the tips of the nails to come through the wood. If the deck is $\frac{13}{8}$ inches thick, does it matter which size nail Tom uses? Explain.

$\frac{13}{8}$ in.

5. You are waiting in line to ride a roller coaster. The roller coaster holds a total of 16 people, and the first 2 people in line get to sit in the front row. If there are 193 people ahead of you in line and the roller coaster is always fully loaded, will you get to sit in the front row? Explain.

Extended Response

6. Dana and Leo noticed that the divisibility rule for 6 combines the divisibility rules for 2 and 3. They decide to write some new rules of divisibility by combining two or more of the divisibility rules.

   a. What rules could Leo combine to determine if a number is divisible by 15? Explain your answer.

   b. Use your new rule to determine which of the following numbers are divisible by 15: 350, 510, 585, 665.

   c. Without doing any calculations, determine which of the numbers in Part B are divisible by 30. Explain your answer.

7. Marci rounds a decimal to the nearest whole number and gets 6. Bill rounds another decimal to the nearest whole number and gets 5.

   a. What is the least value that Marci's decimal can have?

   b. What is the greatest value that Bill's decimal can have if you round to the nearest hundreths place?

   c. Use your answers to Parts A and B to find the least possible difference between the two decimals. Show your work.

Gridded Response

1. The weights, in pounds, of 6 pineapples at a fruit stand are shown below. What is the range, in pounds, of the pineapples' weights?

   $4, 3\frac{3}{4}, 4\frac{1}{4}, 4\frac{1}{8}, 4\frac{5}{8}, 4\frac{7}{16}$

2. Harry is taking an English test that has a multiple choice section and an essay section. He looked at the clock at the beginning and at the end of the test. If Harry spent 3 times as long on the essay section as on the multiple choice section, how many minutes did he spend on the essay section?

   Beginning of test   End of test

Short Response

3. **Open-Ended** Wood manufacturers allow plywood to be slightly less thick or slightly more thick than intended. The amount less than or greater than the intended thickness is called the *tolerance*.

   a. The tolerance for a piece of $\frac{3}{4}$ inch plywood is $\frac{1}{32}$ inch. Besides $\frac{3}{4}$ inch, what are three different thicknesses that the plywood could have?

   b. If you were manufacturing wood posts that are supposed to be 4 inches thick, what would you make the tolerance? Explain your reasoning.

4. You set your watch to chime every 15 minutes. Your friend sets her watch to chime every 25 minutes. If both watches chime at 1:22 P.M., what is the next time that they will both chime simultaneously? Show your work.

Extended Response

5. Using the Calories listed for each ingredient, Thalia estimated that there were approximately 2985 Calories in the entire pie. She placed a piece of the pie on the plate shown and had it analyzed by a lab to determine the number of Calories in the piece of pie. The lab got Thalia's results mixed up with those from three other samples. A technician told Thalia that her results were one of the following, but he couldn't tell her which one: 314 Calories, 604 Calories, 894 Calories, 952 Calories. Decide which lab result is Thalia's. Explain your answer.

6. An ice-skating rink is open from 6:30 A.M. to 4:45 P.M. every day. On Saturday, Shawna teaches 45-minute ice-skating lessons at the rink. How many lessons can Shawna teach on Saturday if she starts 30 minutes after the rink opens and takes a 10 minute break between lessons? If she makes $25 an hour for the time she spends teaching lessons, what is the greatest amount Shawna can make on Saturday? Explain your answers.

Gridded Response

1. Ralph makes $2\frac{1}{2}$ batches of oatmeal cookies. Each batch makes 24 cookies. Ralph gives away $\frac{1}{4}$ of the cookies to his class at school and $\frac{2}{5}$ of the remaining cookies to his bus driver. How many cookies does Ralph have left?

2. The sixth grade students at Jackson Middle School voted on where to go for their class trip. The circle graph shows the results. If 144 students voted, how many more votes were for the science museum than for the amusement park?

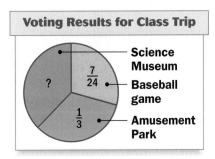

Voting Results for Class Trip

Science Museum

$\frac{7}{24}$ — Baseball game

$\frac{1}{3}$ — Amusement Park

?

3. A rectangular cake is $12\frac{1}{2}$ inches by 15 inches. You want to cut the cake into square pieces that are $2\frac{1}{2}$ inches by $2\frac{1}{2}$ inches. How many pieces can you cut?

Short Response

4. A slice of bread weighs about one ounce. Will two plain quarter-pound hamburgers on rolls weigh more or less than a pound? Explain.

5. A company sells 1-quart containers and 4-gallon containers of a pre-prepared smoothie base that can be used to make smoothies. A certain smoothie recipe calls for 4 fluid ounces of smoothie base for each smoothie. How many more smoothies can be made with the 4-gallon container of smoothie base than with the 1-quart container of smoothie base? Show your work.

Extended Response

6. Of all the animals on a farm, $\frac{1}{4}$ are chickens, $\frac{1}{3}$ are cows, $\frac{3}{8}$ are pigs, and the rest are horses.

   a. Can the total number of animals on the farm be 12? Explain your reasoning.

   b. What is the least possible number of animals on the farm? Show how you found your answer.

7. Open-Ended You are making a bookcase with two shelves to hold a 32-volume set of encyclopedias. The wood you are using to make the bookcase is $\frac{3}{4}$ inch thick. Each volume of the encyclopedia is $1\frac{1}{2}$ inches thick, 9 inches wide, and 11 inches tall. What width and what height do you think the bookcase should have? Explain your reasoning.

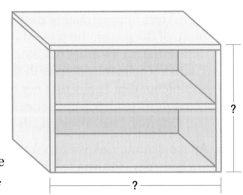

Gridded Response

1. The bar graph shows the results of a survey in which randomly selected students at Hopedale Middle School were asked whether they wanted a bald eagle, a cougar, a hornet, or a buffalo for the school mascot. If there are 500 students at Hopedale Middle School, how many students would you expect to want a cougar as mascot?

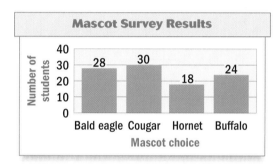

Mascot Survey Results

2. Michelle owns jazz, rap, and rock CDs. The ratio of jazz CDs to rap CDs is equal to the ratio of rap CDs to rock CDs. If Michelle owns 4 jazz CDs and 16 rock CDs, how many rap CDs does she own?

Short Response

3. Bart wants to buy a shirt that costs $30 and a belt that costs $22. He has a coupon for 20% off the price of any one item. To save the most money, should Bart apply the coupon to the shirt or the belt? Explain.

4. Property taxes are based on the assessed value of the property and on the tax rate. Find the property tax on a house having a market value of $180,000. The assessment rate is 40%, and the tax rate is $3.50 per $100. Explain how you found your answer.

Extended Response

5. The owners of Bird World know that more people prefer parakeets than canaries. Therefore, they stock 6 parakeets for every 1 canary.

a. Use the rule of stocking 6 parakeets for every 1 canary to find the number of parakeets in stock when the total number of parakeets and canaries is 21. Explain your method.

b. If there are 30 parakeets in stock, how many canaries are in stock?

c. If there are 7 canaries in stock, what is the total number of parakeets and canaries in the store? Explain.

6. **Open-Ended** A coin-sorting machine sorts your coins for you so that you can get back as many bills as possible for your money. For this service, you get only 90% of the money you put in, and the machine keeps the rest. Jared puts a jar of coins into the machine and gets $18. What was the total value of the coins in the jar? If Jared put in at least one penny, one nickel, one dime, and one quarter, what is one example of the number of each type of coin that Jared could have put into the machine? Explain your answers.

Gridded Response

1. A stained-glass window is made up of small equilateral triangles, as shown below. How many equilateral triangles of all sizes can be found in the window?

2. What is the value of x in the parallelogram?

$$(2x - 42)° \quad x°$$
$$x° \quad (2x - 42)°$$

3. The complement of $\angle ABC$ is equal to the supplement of an angle measuring 150°. What is the measure, in degrees, of $\angle ABC$?

Short Response

4. Figure $ABCDEF$ is a regular hexagon with three diagonals drawn between opposite vertices. If the area of $\triangle AHB$ is 5 square meters, what is the area of hexagon $ABCDEF$? If the perimeter of $\triangle AHB$ is 10.2 meters, what is the perimeter of hexagon $ABCDEF$? Explain.

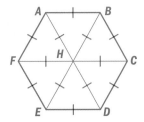

5. **Open-Ended** What are possible values of x, y, w, and z in the figure at the right? Explain your reasoning.

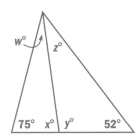

Extended Response

6. An unfinished furniture company sells a coffee table, an end table, and a snack table as a set. The table tops are all similar rectangles. It takes Yoanna 36 minutes to sand the top of the coffee table.

   a. How does the area of the snack table top compare to the area of the coffee table top?

   b. Assuming Yoanna works at the same rate on all three tables, how long does it take her to sand the top of the snack table?

   c. How long does it take Yoanna to sand the top of the end table? Explain your answer.

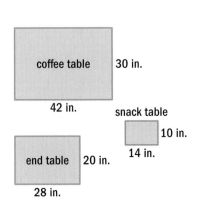

7. **Open-Ended** Draw a design that has exactly 2 lines of symmetry and uses at least 3 different geometric figures. Explain how you created your design.

Gridded Response

1. Susan drew a diagram of her patio on a sheet of grid paper. Each square in the diagram below represents an area of 1 square yard. What is the area, in square yards, of the patio?

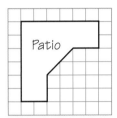

2. A dunk tank at a carnival is in the shape of a cube with a side length of 10 feet. If 75% of the tank is filled with water, how many feet high is the water level?

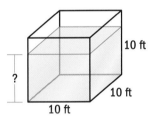

Short Response

3. If the net below is folded along the dashed lines, and the solid lines are joined together, what solid will be formed? Explain how you know.

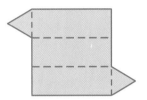

4. A circle has a radius of 6 centimeters. A square has a side length of 12 centimeters. Without doing any calculations, determine whether the circle or the square has the greater area. Explain your reasoning.

5. A diagram of a set of concrete steps is shown below. Each cube in the diagram represents a volume of 1 cubic foot. What volume of concrete is needed for the set of steps? Show your work.

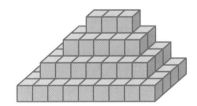

Extended Response

6. Deborah's bicycle wheel has a diameter of 26 inches. Deborah rides her bicycle so that the front wheel makes 120 complete rotations. To the nearest ten feet, how many feet has she traveled? Explain.

7. **Open-Ended** John is designing a gift box that he can fill with jelly beans. He estimates that because of the amount of jelly beans that he has, the box has to have a volume of 1800 cubic centimeters. John also wants to wrap the box, but he has only 900 square centimeters of gift wrap. What length, width, and height could John make the gift box? Explain how you found your answer.

Gridded Response

In Exercises 1 and 2, use the bar graph of the daily high temperatures in a city in Alaska during one week in January.

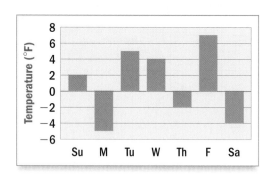

1. What is the range of the temperatures, in degrees?

2. What is the mean of the temperatures, in degrees?

3. Darren took a math quiz. On his paper, his teacher wrote the points she took off for incorrect answers: $-3, -3, -1$. If Darren got a total of 58 points on the quiz, how many points was it possible to receive?

Short Response

4. Samantha is tiling her kitchen floor. She places tiles together to form the design shown. Describe how tile 2 is related to tile 1, how tile 3 is related to tile 2, and how tile 4 is related to tile 3. Then describe how the group of tiles 5 through 8 is related to the group of tiles 1 through 4.

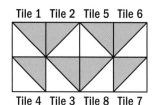

Tile 1   Tile 2   Tile 5   Tile 6

Tile 4   Tile 3   Tile 8   Tile 7

5. What is the next figure in the pattern below? Explain your reasoning?

Extended Response

6. **a.** Draw a triangle with vertices $A(-5, -5)$, $B(-5, -2)$, and $C(-3, -2)$.

   b. Translate $\triangle ABC$ 5 units up and then reflect it in the y-axis. Draw the new triangle. Reflect original $\triangle ABC$ in the y-axis and then translate 5 units up. Draw the new triangle.

   c. Did it matter in what order you performed the transformations in Parts A and B? Is this true for *any* reflection and translation? Explain.

7. **Open-Ended** Describe a series of transformations that will transform pentagon *ABCDE* to pentagon *RSTUV*. Make a sketch of each transformation. How did you decide what transformations to use?

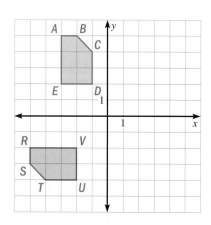

UNIT 4

Chapters 11 and 12

Gridded Response

1. The graph shows the cost of one round of miniature golf for various numbers of children and adults. How many more dollars does a round of miniature golf cost for a group of 5 adults than for a group of 5 children?

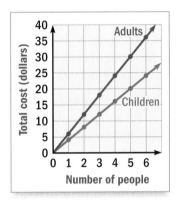

2. A scuba diver is 15 feet below the surface of the water and is rising at a rate of 30 feet per minute. How many seconds will it take for the diver to be just 5 feet below the surface of the water?

Short Response

3. If (x, y) represents the coordinates of a point in the blue figure, what are the coordinates of the corresponding point in the red figure? Explain your reasoning.

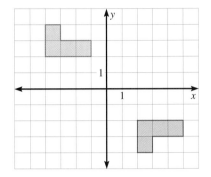

4. A shoe store is having a clearance sale. The table below gives the original price x and the sale price y for several different shoes. Write a function rule that relates x and y. By what percent are the shoes marked down? Explain your reasoning.

Original price, x	$20	$25	$30	$35
Sale price, y	$16	$20	$24	$28

Extended Response

5. The figures below form a pattern. Let the input x be the number below a figure, and let the output y be the number of squares in a figure. Write a function rule that relates x and y. Explain how you wrote the rule. Then find the number of squares in the fourteenth figure. Show your work.

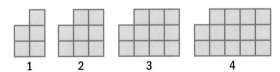

6. Open-Ended Zoe is trying to earn money by knitting and selling scarves. She pays $120 for knitting needles and enough yarn to make 20 scarves. Assuming that Zoe can sell all 20 scarves, the function rule $p = 20c - 120$ relates Zoe's profit p and the amount she charges per scarf c. Decide what Zoe should charge for each scarf. Explain.

Gridded Response

1. Gwen wants to buy two of the items shown below. How many combinations of two different items can Gwen buy if she has only $5 to spend?

2. The stem-and-leaf plot shows Tim's bowling scores for the past 6 games. After the next game, Tim wants his mean score for the 7 games to be at least 125. What is the lowest score that Tim can get and still reach his goal?

```
10 | 5
11 | 0 6
12 |
13 | 7 7 9    Key: 13 | 7 = 137
```

Short Response

3. Based on last year's record, the probability that the boys' soccer team will win a game is $\frac{3}{4}$. If the probability that the boys' soccer team will tie a game is $\frac{1}{6}$, what is the probability that they will lose a game? Explain your reasoning.

4. You roll two number cubes. What is the probability that the sum of the numbers you roll will be 8? Show your work.

5. The bar graph shows the number of boxes of two types of cereal sold in a store in one day. How could the bar graph be misleading? Redraw the bar graph so that it is not misleading.

Extended Response

6. **Open-Ended** A school has two academic trivia teams that compete in local competitions. In the competitions, the highest score wins. The scores for each team in the last six competitions are given in the table. Only one team can be sent to the state academic trivia competition to represent the school. Decide which team should be sent to the state competition and explain why you think so. Include one type of average and one type of graph in your explanation.

Competition number	Team A's score	Team B's score
1	91	118
2	120	115
3	102	126
4	130	124
5	139	126
6	138	125

Glossary

	Example
a	
absolute value (p. 539) The absolute value of a number is its distance from 0 on a number line. The absolute value of a is written $|a|$.	$$|2| = |-2| = 2$$
acute angle (p. 430) An angle whose measure is less than 90°.	
acute triangle (p. 436) A triangle with three acute angles.	
angle (p. 425) A figure formed by two rays with the same endpoint.	$\angle DEF$, or $\angle E$, or $\angle FED$
angle of rotation (p. 568) *See* rotation.	
annual interest rate (p. 408) The percent of the principal you earn or pay per year.	If you deposit $100 in a bank account that pays 4% per year, then 4% is the *annual interest rate*.
area (pp. 62, 702) The amount of surface covered by a figure. Area is measured in square units such as square feet (ft^2) or square meters (m^2).	*Area* = 12 square units
associative property of addition (p. 137) The value of a sum does not depend on how the numbers are grouped.	$(a + b) + c = a + (b + c)$ $(2 + 5) + 4 = 2 + (5 + 4)$
associative property of multiplication (p. 155) The value of a product does not depend on how the numbers are grouped.	$(a \cdot b) \cdot c = a \cdot (b \cdot c)$ $(2 \times 6.5) \times 4 = 2 \times (6.5 \times 4)$
average (p. 649) A single number used to describe what is typical of a set of data. *See* mean, median, *and* mode.	

Example

axes **(pp. 83, 562)** A horizontal number line, the *horizontal axis*, and a vertical number line, the *vertical axis*, that meet at (0, 0).

See coordinate plane.

b

bar graph **(pp. 79, 704)** A graph in which the lengths of bars are used to represent and compare data.

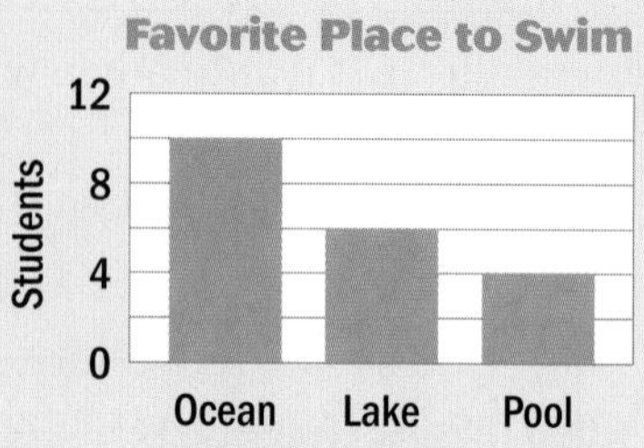
Favorite Place to Swim
Students
12
8
4
0
Ocean
Lake
Pool

base of a parallelogram **(p. 476)** The base of a parallelogram is the length of any of its sides.

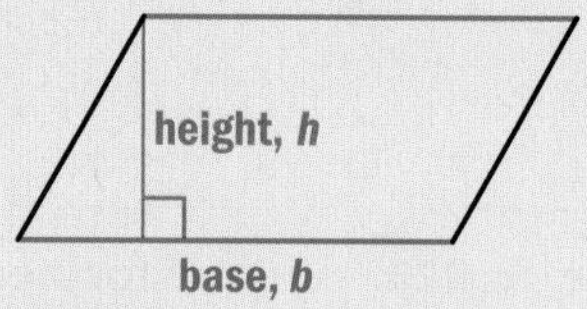
height, h
base, b

base of a power **(p. 16)** The base of a power is the repeated factor.

The *base* of the power 2^3 is 2.

base of a solid **(p. 500)** *See* prism, cylinder, pyramid, *and* cone.

base of a triangle **(p. 480)** The length of any of its sides.

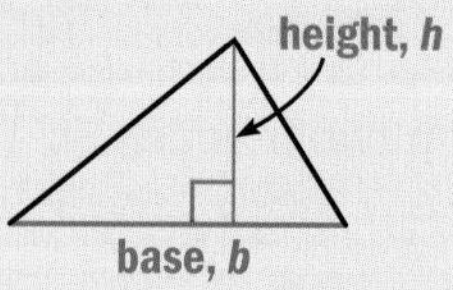
height, h
base, b

benchmark **(p. 57)** A familiar object that can be used to approximate the size of a unit.

The length of a small paper clip is about one inch.

box-and-whisker plot **(p. 657)** A display that divides a data set into four parts, two below the median and two above it.

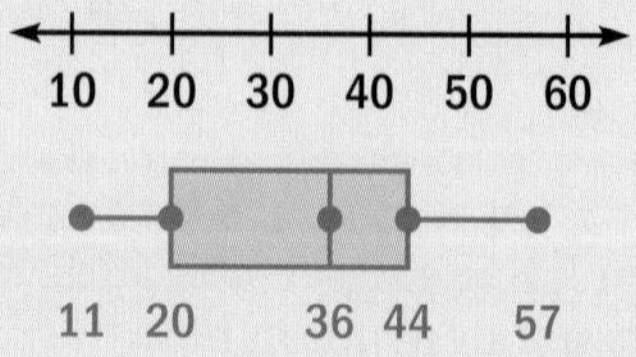
10 20 30 40 50 60
11 20 36 44 57

c

capacity **(p. 188)** Capacity measures the amount that a container can hold.

	Example
center of a circle (p. 485) The point inside a circle that is the same distance from all points on the circle.	*See* circle.
center of rotation (p. 568) *See* rotation.	
circle (p. 485) The set of all points in a plane that are the same distance from a point called the *center*.	
circle graph (p. 88) A graph that represents data as parts of a circle. The entire circle represents all of the data.	**Opinions of Roller Coasters**
circumference (p. 485) The distance around a circle.	
clustering (p. 692) A method of estimating a sum when numbers being added have about the same value.	You can estimate the sum $72 + 69 + 65$ as $3(70) = 210$.
combination (p. 637) A grouping of objects in which order is not important.	Counting the ways to choose two essays to write from eight possibilities involves a *combination*.
common factor (p. 222) A whole number that is a factor of two or more nonzero whole numbers.	The *common factors* of 64 and 120 are 1, 2, 4, and 8.
common multiple (p. 235) A whole number that is a multiple of two or more nonzero whole numbers.	The *common multiples* of 6 and 8 are 24, 48, 72, 96, ...
commutative property of addition (p. 137) In a sum, you can add numbers in any order.	$a + b = b + a$ $2 + 5 = 5 + 2$

	Example
commutative property of multiplication (p. 155) In a product, you can multiply numbers in any order.	$a \cdot b = b \cdot a$ $2 \times 6.5 = 6.5 \times 2$
compatible numbers (pp. 13, 694) Numbers that are easy to use in computations.	You can estimate the quotient $2605 \div 7$ by using the *compatible numbers* 2800 and 7. Because $2800 \div 7 = 400$, $2605 \div 7 \approx 400$.
complementary angles (p. 431) Two angles whose measures have a sum of 90°.	
complementary events (p. 632) Events that have no outcomes in common and that together contain all the outcomes of the experiment.	Rolling an odd number on a number cube and rolling an even number on a number cube are *complementary events*, or *complements*.
composite number (p. 215) A whole number greater than 1 that has factors other than itself and 1.	6 is a *composite number* because its factors are 1, 2, 3, and 6.
cone (p. 500) A solid that has one circular base and a vertex that is not in the same plane.	
congruent figures (p. 454) Figures with the same size and shape.	
coordinate grid (p. 83) *See* coordinate plane.	
coordinate plane (p. 562) A plane divided into four *quadrants* by a horizontal number line called the *x*-axis and a vertical number line called the *y*-axis.	

coordinates (pp. 83, 562) The numbers in an ordered pair that locate a point on a coordinate grid. *See also* x-coordinate *and* y-coordinate.	The numbers 4 and 3 in the *ordered pair* (4, 3) are the *coordinates* of the graph of (4, 3), which is located 4 units to the right and 3 units up from (0, 0).
corresponding parts (p. 455) The matching sides and angles of two figures.	Corresponding parts: $\angle U$ and $\angle X$, $\angle V$ and $\angle Y$, $\angle W$ and $\angle Z$, $\overline{UV}$ and $\overline{XY}$, $\overline{VW}$ and $\overline{YZ}$, $\overline{UW}$ and $\overline{XZ}$.
cross products (p. 383) For the proportion $\frac{a}{b} = \frac{c}{d}$, where $b \neq 0$ and $d \neq 0$, the cross products are ad and bc.	In the proportion $\frac{2}{3} = \frac{8}{12}$, the *cross products* are $2 \cdot 12$ and $3 \cdot 8$.
cube (pp. 459, 501) A rectangular prism with 6 congruent square faces.	*See* solid.
cubed (p. 17) A number cubed is the third power of the number.	4 *cubed* indicates 4^3, or 64.
cylinder (p. 500) A solid with two parallel bases that are congruent circles.	

data (pp. 72, 704) Information, often given in the form of numbers or facts.	
decimal (p. 108) A number that is written using the base-ten place value system. Each place value is ten times the place value to the right.	The *decimal* 3.12 represents 3 ones plus 1 tenth plus 2 hundredths, or three and twelve hundredths.
degree (°) (p. 426) A unit used to measure angles. There are 180° on a *protractor*, a semicircular tool used to measure degrees.	**The measure of the angle is 90°.**

Glossary

	Example
denominator (pp. 228, 700) The number below the fraction bar in a fraction. It represents the number of equal parts into which the whole is divided or the number of objects that make up the set.	In the fraction $\frac{3}{4}$, the *denominator* is 4.
diagonal (p. 450) A segment, other than a side, that connects two vertices of a polygon.	diagonals
diameter of a circle (p. 485) The distance across the circle through its center.	*See* circumference.
difference (pp. 6, 689) The result when one number is subtracted from another.	The *difference* of 7 and 3 is $7 - 3$, or 4.
digit (p. 684) Any of the numbers 0, 1, 2, 3, 4, 5, 6, 7, 8, or 9.	In the whole number 127,891, the *digit* 8 has a value of 800, or 8×100, because it is in the hundreds' place.
discount (p. 407) An amount subtracted from the regular price of an item to get the sale price.	When $40 sneakers are on sale at 25% off, the *discount* is 25% of $40, or $10.
distributive property (p. 159) You can multiply a number and a sum by multiplying the number by each part of the sum and then adding these products. The same property applies with subtraction.	$a(b + c) = ab + ac$ $3(4 + 6) = 3(4) + 3(6)$ $a(b - c) = ab - ac$ $2(8 - 5) = 2(8) - 2(5)$
dividend (pp. 6, 691) A number that is divided by another number.	In $18 \div 6 = 3$, the *dividend* is 18.
divisible (p. 214) A number is divisible by another number if that other number is a factor of the first.	Because $3 \times 4 = 12$, 12 is *divisible* by 3 and by 4.
divisor (pp. 6, 691) The number by which another number is divided.	In $18 \div 6 = 3$, the *divisor* is 6.

	Example

double bar graph (p. 80) A bar graph that shows two sets of data on the same graph.

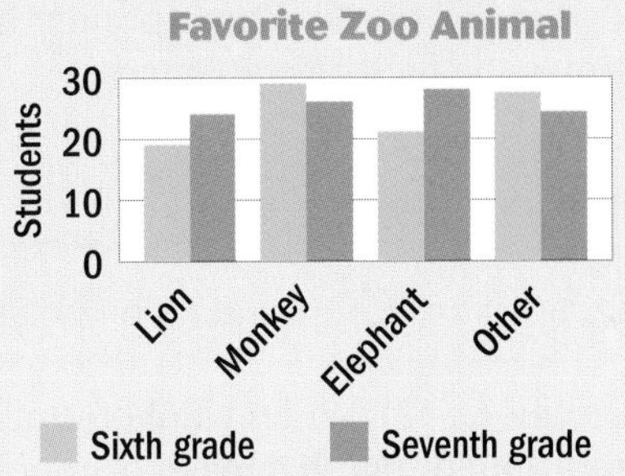

Favorite Zoo Animal

e

edges of a solid (p. 501) The segments where the faces meet.

See vertex of a solid.

elapsed time (p. 299) The amount of time between a start time and an end time.

The *elapsed time* from 7:15 A.M. to 12 P.M. is 4 hours and 45 minutes.

endpoint (p. 421) *See* segment *and* ray.

equation (p. 36) A mathematical sentence formed by placing an equal sign (=) between two expressions.

$3y = 21$ and $x - 3 = 7$ are *equations*.

equilateral triangle (p. 437) A triangle with three sides of the same length.

equivalent fractions (p. 228) Fractions that represent the same number.

$\frac{5}{15}$ and $\frac{20}{60}$ are *equivalent fractions* that both represent $\frac{1}{3}$.

equivalent ratios (p. 375) Ratios that can be written as equivalent fractions.

See equivalent fractions.

estimate (p. 692) To find an approximate solution to a problem.

You can *estimate* the sum $88 + 51$ as $90 + 50$, or 140.

evaluate (pp. 21, 29) To find the value of an expression.

To *evaluate* $2t - 1$ when $t = 3$, substitute 3 for t and find the value of $2 \times 3 - 1$. So, $2t - 1 = 5$ when $t = 3$.

event (p. 630) A collection of outcomes of an experiment.

The *event* "getting an odd number" on a number cube consists of the outcomes 1, 3, and 5.

	Example
exponent (p. 16) The exponent of a power is the number of times the factor is repeated.	The *exponent* of the power 2^3 is 3.

(f)

	Example
faces of a solid (p. 501) The polygons that form the solid figure.	*See* vertex of a solid.
factor (p. 16) When whole numbers other than zero are multiplied together, each number is a factor of the product.	Because $2 \times 3 \times 7 = 42$, 2, 3, and 7 are *factors* of 42.
factor tree (p. 216) A diagram that can be used to write the prime factorization of a number.	90 9 × 10 3 × 3 × 2 × 5
favorable outcomes (p. 630) Once you specify an event, the outcomes for that event are *favorable outcomes*.	If you toss a number cube, the *favorable outcomes* for getting an odd number are 1, 3, and 5.
fraction (p. 228, 700) A number of the form $\frac{a}{b}$ ($b \neq 0$) used to describe parts of a whole or a set.	$\frac{3}{8}$
frequency table (p. 72) A table that displays the number of times each item or category occurs in a data set.	Art Project | Tally | Frequency painting | 卌 I | 6 sculpture | IIII | 4 drawing | II | 2
front-end estimation (p. 131, 692) A method of estimating a sum by adding the front-end digits and using the remaining digits to adjust the sum.	To estimate the sum $3.75 + 1.28 + 6.93$, first add the ones: $3 + 1 + 6 = 10$. Then estimate the sum of the remaining digits: $0.75 + 0.28 + 0.93 \approx 2$. The sum is about $10 + 2$, or 12.
function (p. 605) A pairing of two values, called an *input* and an *output*. In a function, each input has exactly one output.	see table below

Input, x	Output, y
-2	-1
-1	0
0	1
1	2
2	3

	Example

g

graph of an inequality (p. 603) All the points on a number line that represent the solution of the inequality.

The number line shows the solution of $x < 2$. The open dot at 2 shows that 2 is not part of the solution.

greatest common factor (GCF) (p. 222) The largest of the common factors of two or more nonzero whole numbers.

The *greatest common factor* of 64 and 120 is the greatest of the common factors 1, 2, 4, and 8, which is 8.

grouping symbols (p. 21) Symbols such as parentheses, brackets, or fraction bars that group parts of an expression.

The parentheses in $12 \div (4 - 1)$ are *grouping symbols* that indicate that the subtraction is done first.

h

height of a parallelogram (p. 476) The perpendicular distance between the side whose length is the base and the opposite side.

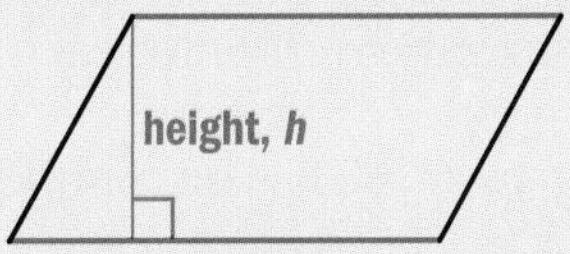

height of a triangle (p. 480) The perpendicular distance between the side whose length is the base and the vertex opposite that side.

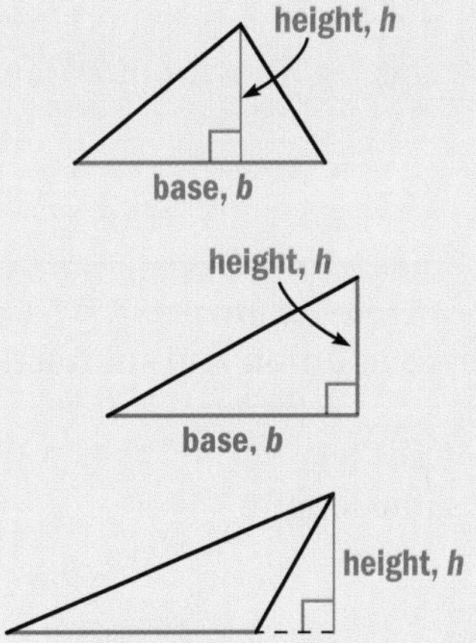

hexagon (p. 449) A polygon with six sides.

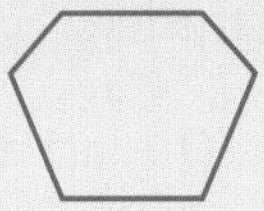

i	**Example**
image (pp. 562, 567, 568) The new figure that results from the translation, reflection, or rotation of a figure in a coordinate plane.	*See* translation, rotation, *and* reflection.
improper fraction (p. 244) Any fraction in which the numerator is greater than or equal to the denominator.	$\frac{21}{8}$ and $\frac{6}{6}$ are *improper fractions*.
independent events (p. 642) Events for which the occurrence of one event does not affect the likelihood that the other event will occur.	If you roll a number cube and then flip a coin, getting a 6 and getting heads are *independent events*.
inequality (p. 602) A statement formed by placing an inequality symbol such as < (is less than) or > (is greater than) between two expressions.	$2 > x$, $n + 12 < 54$, and $x - 7 \leq 5$ are *inequalities*.
input (p. 605) *See* function.	
input-output table (p. 605) A table used to represent a function by listing the *output* for each of several different *inputs*.	*See* function.
integers (p. 533) The numbers . . . , $-5, -4, -3, -2, -1, 0, 1, 2, 3, 4, 5, ...$	*See* number line.
interest (p. 408) An amount of money paid for the use of money.	*See* simple interest.
intersecting lines (p. 422) Lines in a plane that meet at a point.	
inverse operations (p. 687) Operations that "undo" each other, such as addition and subtraction or multiplication and division.	
isosceles triangle (p. 437) A triangle with at least two sides of the same length.	

l	
leading digit (p. 13) The leading digit of a whole number is the first digit at the left.	The *leading digit* of 59 is 5.
leaf (p. 653) The last digit on the right of a number displayed in a stem-and-leaf plot.	*See* stem-and-leaf plot.

	Example
least common denominator (LCD) (p. 239) The least common multiple of the denominators of two or more fractions.	The *least common denominator* of $\frac{5}{6}$ and $\frac{7}{9}$ is the least common multiple of 6 and 9, or 18.
least common multiple (LCM) (p. 236) The smallest of the common multiples of two or more nonzero whole numbers.	The *least common multiple* of 9 and 12 is the smallest of the common multiples 36, 72, 108, . . . , or 36.
line (p. 421) A set of points that extends without end in two opposite directions.	
line graph (pp. 84, 705) A graph that represents data using points connected by line segments to show how quantities change over time.	
line of reflection (p. 527) *See* reflection.	
line of symmetry (p. 460) *See* line symmetry.	
line plot (p. 73) A number line diagram that uses X marks to show the frequencies of items or categories being tallied.	
line symmetry (p. 460) A figure has line symmetry if a line can be drawn that divides the figure into two congruent parts that are mirror images of each other. The line is the *line of symmetry*.	

linear function (p. 613) A function whose graph is a straight line.

lower extreme (p. 657) The least value of a data set.

See box-and-whisker plot.

lower quartile (p. 657) The median of the lower half of a data set.

See box-and-whisker plot.

m

mean (p. 93) The sum of the data values divided by the number of values.

The *mean* of the values 7, 10, 9, and 6 is

$$\frac{7 + 10 + 9 + 6}{4} = \frac{32}{4} = 8.$$

median (p. 93) The middle data value when the values are written in numerical order. If a data set has an even number of values, the median is the mean of the two middle values.

The *median* of the ages

36, 36, 37, 37, 39, 40, 41

is 37, because 37 is the middle number.

mixed number (p. 244) The sum of a whole number and a fraction less than 1.

$2\frac{5}{8}$ is a *mixed number*.

mode (p. 93) The data value that occurs most often. A data set can have one mode, more than one mode, or no mode.

In the data set

36, 36, 37, 37, 39, 40, 41,

both 36 and 37 occur twice, so there are two *modes*, 36 and 37.

multiple (p. 235) A multiple of a whole number is the product of the number and any nonzero whole number.

The *multiples* of 2 are 2, 4, 6, 8, 10, ...

n

negative integers (p. 533) Integers that are less than 0.

The *negative integers* are $-1, -2, -3, -4, ...$

	Example
net (p. 506) A two-dimensional figure that can be folded to form a solid.	**Net** **Solid**
number fact family (p. 687) Four number facts consisting of three numbers related by inverse operations.	The facts $8 + 2 = 10$, $10 - 2 = 8$, $2 + 8 = 10$, and $10 - 8 = 2$ are in the same *number fact family*.
number line (pp. 118, 685) A line whose points are associated with numbers. You can use a number line to compare and order numbers. The numbers on a number line increase from left to right.	
numerator (pp. 228, 700) The number above the fraction bar in a fraction. It represents the number of equal parts out of the whole or the number of objects from the set that are being considered.	In the fraction $\frac{3}{4}$, the *numerator* is 3.
numerical expression (p. 21) An expression, consisting of numbers and operations to be performed, that represents a particular value.	The *numerical expression* $2 \times 3 - 1$ represents 5.

O

obtuse angle (p. 430) An angle whose measure is between 90° and 180°.	
obtuse triangle (p. 436) A triangle with one obtuse angle.	

	Example
octagon (p. 449) A polygon with eight sides.	
opposites (p. 534) Numbers that are the same distance from 0 on a number line, but are on opposite sides of 0.	3 and -3 are *opposites*.
order of operations (p. 21) The order in which to perform operations when evaluating expressions with more than one operation.	$1 + 3^2(5 - 1) = 1 + 3^2(4) =$ $1 + 9(4) = 1 + 36 = 37$
ordered pair (pp. 83, 562) *See* coordinates.	*See* coordinate plane.
origin (pp. 83, 562) The point (0, 0) on a coordinate plane.	*See* coordinate plane.
outcome (p. 630) A possible result of an experiment.	When you toss a coin, the *outcomes* are heads and tails.
output (p. 605) *See* function.	

P

parallel lines (p. 422) Lines in the same plane that never meet.	
parallelogram (p. 445) A quadrilateral with two pairs of parallel sides.	
pentagon (p. 449) A polygon with five sides.	
percent (p. 395) A ratio that compares a number to 100. *Percent* means "per hundred."	$43\% = \dfrac{43}{100} = 0.43$
perimeter (pp. 61, 702) The distance around a figure, measured in linear units such as feet, inches, or meters.	
	Perimeter = 5 + 7 + 8, or 20 cm

	Example
permutation (p. 637) An arrangement of objects in which order is important.	Counting the ways to list the members of the student council in a program involves a *permutation*.
perpendicular lines (p. 476) Two lines are perpendicular if they meet at a right angle.	
pi (π) (p. 485) The ratio of the circumference of a circle to its diameter.	You can use 3.14 or $\frac{22}{7}$ to approximate π.
pictograph (p. 706) A graph that uses pictures or symbols to display data.	**Color of Eyes** ♟ = 2 students
place value (pp. 108, 684) The place value of each digit in a number depends on its position within the number.	In 723, the 2 is in the tens' place and it has a value of 20.
plane (p. 422) A flat surface that extends without end in all directions.	
point (p. 421) A position in space represented with a dot.	•*P*
polygon (p. 449) A closed plane figure that is formed by three or more segments called sides. Each side intersects exactly two other sides at a *vertex*.	 vertex
positive integers (p. 533) Integers that are greater than 0.	The *positive integers* are 1, 2, 3, 4, ...
power (p. 16) An expression, such as 2^3, that represents a product with a repeated factor.	The third *power* of 2 is $2^3 = 2 \times 2 \times 2$, which represents the product of three factors of 2.

	Example
prime factorization (p. 216) A whole number written as the product of prime factors.	The *prime factorization* of 20 is $2^2 \times 5$.
prime number (p. 215) A whole number greater than 1 whose only factors are 1 and itself.	59 is a *prime number*, because its only factors are 1 and itself.
principal (p. 408) An amount of money that is saved or borrowed.	If you deposit $100 in a bank account that pays 4% annual interest, then the *principal* is $100.
prism (p. 500) A solid with two parallel bases that are congruent polygons.	 **Rectangular Prism** **Triangular Prism**
probability of an event (p. 630) A measure of the likelihood that the event will occur, computed as $\dfrac{\text{number of favorable outcomes}}{\text{number of possible outcomes}}$ when all the outcomes are equally likely.	If you toss a number cube, the *probability* that you roll an odd number is $\dfrac{3}{6} = 0.5 = 50\%$.
product (pp. 6, 690) The result when two or more numbers are multiplied.	The *product* of 3 and 4 is 3×4, or 12.
proper fraction (p. 245) A fraction in which the numerator is less than the denominator.	$\dfrac{2}{3}$ is a *proper fraction*.
proportion (p. 383) An equation you write to show that two ratios are equivalent.	The equation $\dfrac{2}{3} = \dfrac{8}{12}$ is a *proportion*.
pyramid (p. 500) A solid made up of polygons. The base can be any polygon, and the other polygons are triangles that share a common vertex.	
q	
quadrants (p. 562) The four regions into which a coordinate plane is divided by the *x*-axis and the *y*-axis. *See also* coordinate plane.	*See* coordinate plane.
quadrilateral (p. 445) A plane figure formed by four segments called sides. Each side intersects exactly two other sides, one at each endpoint, and no two sides are part of the same line.	

Glossary

	Example
quotient (pp. 6, 691) The result of a division.	The *quotient* of 18 and 6 is 18 ÷ 6, or 3.

r

radius of a circle (p. 485) The distance from the center to any point on the circle. The plural of radius is *radii*.	*See* circumference.
range (p. 94) The difference between the greatest data value and the least data value.	In the data set 36, 36, 37, 37, 39, 40, 41, the *range* is $41 - 36 = 5$.
rate (p. 379) A ratio of two measures that have different units.	The International Space Station orbits Earth at an average *rate* of 15 miles every 3 seconds, or 5 miles per second.
ratio (p. 374) The ratio of a number a to a nonzero number b is the quotient when a is divided by b.	The *ratio* of a to b can be written as $\frac{a}{b}$, as $a : b$, or as "a to b."
ray (p. 421) A part of a line that has one *endpoint* and extends without end in one direction.	 $\overrightarrow{AB}$ **with endpoint A.**
reciprocals (p. 334) Two numbers whose product is 1.	Because $\frac{3}{5} \times \frac{5}{3} = 1$, $\frac{3}{5}$ and $\frac{5}{3}$ are *reciprocals*.
rectangle (p. 445) A parallelogram with four right angles.	
rectangular prism (p. 500) A prism with rectangular bases.	*See* prism.
reflection (p. 567) An operation that flips a figure over a line called the *line of reflection* to produce a congruent mirror image.	 The *x*-axis is the *line of reflection*.

	Example
regular polygon (p. 450) A polygon with equal side lengths and equal angle measures.	 **Regular**　　**Not Regular**
remainder (pp. 6, 691) If a divisor does not divide a dividend evenly, the remainder is the whole number left over after the division.	$\begin{array}{r} 8\ \text{R4} \longleftarrow remainder \\ 7\overline{)60} \\ \underline{56} \\ 4 \end{array}$
repeating decimal (p. 254) A decimal that has one or more digits that repeat forever.	$0.3333...$ and $2.\overline{01}$ are *repeating decimals*.
rhombus (p. 445) A parallelogram with four sides of equal length.	
right angle (p. 430) An angle whose measure is exactly 90°.	
right triangle (p. 436) A triangle with one right angle.	
rotation (p. 568) An operation that rotates a figure through a given *angle of rotation* about a fixed point, the *center of rotation*, to produce a congruent image.	The origin is the center of rotation and the angle of rotation is 90°.

	Example
round (pp. 124, 686) To approximate a number to a given place value.	518 *rounded* to the nearest ten is 520, and 518 *rounded* to the nearest hundred is 500.

S

scale (p. 68) In a scale drawing, a key that tells how the drawing's dimensions and the actual dimensions are related.	If the scale on a scale drawing is 1 in. : 10 ft, then each inch on the drawing represents 10 feet on the scale drawing.
scale drawing (p. 68) A drawing of an object with the same shape as the original object, but not the same size.	
scalene triangle (p. 437) A triangle with three sides of different lengths.	
segment (p. 421) A part of a line that consists of two *endpoints* and all the points between them.	 **$\overline{AB}$ or $\overline{BA}$ with *endpoints* A and B.**
similar figures (p. 454) Figures with the same shape but not necessarily the same size.	
simple interest (p. 408) Interest paid only on the principal.	If you deposit $100 in a bank account that pays 4% annual interest, you will earn $100(0.04), or $4, *simple interest* in one year.
simplest form of a fraction (p. 229) A fraction is in simplest form if its numerator and denominator have a greatest common factor of 1.	The *simplest form* of the fraction $\frac{4}{12}$ is $\frac{1}{3}$.
solid (p. 500) A three-dimensional figure that encloses a part of space.	

	Example
solution of an equation (p. 36) A number that, when substituted for a variable, makes the equation true.	10 is the *solution of the equation* $x - 3 = 7$.
solution of an inequality (p. 602) The group of all values of the variable that make the inequality true.	The *solution of the inequality* $x + 2 \geq 3$ is $x \geq 1$, or all numbers that are greater than or equal to 1.
solve an equation (p. 37) To find all the solutions of an equation by finding all the values of the variable that make the equation true.	To *solve the equation* $n \div 4 = 7$, find the number that can be divided by 4 to equal 7; $28 \div 4 = 7$, so the solution is 28.
solve an inequality (p. 602) Find all values of the variable that make the inequality true.	To *solve* $x + 2 \geq 3$, subtract 2 from each side to get $x \geq 1$.
sphere (p. 500) The set of points in space that are a given distance from a given point.	
square (p. 445) A parallelogram with four right angles and four sides of equal length.	
squared (p. 17) A number squared is the second power of the number.	3 *squared* indicates 3^2, or 9.
stem (p. 653) All the digits except the last digit on the right of a number displayed in a stem-and-leaf plot.	*See* stem-and-leaf plot.
stem-and-leaf plot (p. 653) A data display that can be used to organize a large set of data.	0 | 7 8 9 9 1 | 1 3 5 5 6 7 2 | 0 1 3 3 | 0 2 Key: 2|3 = 23 stem↗ ↖leaf
straight angle (p. 430) An angle whose measure is exactly 180°.	
sum (pp. 5, 689) The result when two or more numbers are added.	The *sum* of 2 and 5 is $2 + 5$, or 7.

	Example
supplementary angles (p. 431) Two angles whose measures have a sum of 180°.	
surface area of a prism (p. 506) The sum of the areas of the faces of the prism. Surface area is measured in square units.	 *Surface Area* $= 2(8 \times 6) + 2(8 \times 4) + 2(6 \times 4) =$ 208 square inches

t

terminating decimal (p. 254) A decimal that has a final digit.	0.084 and 0.6 are *terminating decimals*.
transformation (p. 568) A movement of a figure in a coordinate plane. Three types of transformations are *translations*, *reflections*, and *rotations*.	*See* translation, rotation, *and* reflection.
translation (p. 562) An operation that slides each point of a figure the same distance in the same direction to produce a figure that is congruent to the original figure.	
tree diagram (p. 636) A diagram that shows all the possible outcomes as choices on different branches of the "tree."	
triangle (p. 436) A closed plane figure with three straight sides that connect three points.	

	Example
triangular prism (p. 500) A prism with triangular bases.	*See* prism.

u

	Example
unit rate (p. 379) A rate with a denominator of 1.	55 miles per hour and $.25 per ounce are *unit rates*.
upper extreme (p. 657) The greatest value of a data set.	*See* box-and-whisker plot.
upper quartile (p. 657) The median of the upper half of a data set.	*See* box-and-whisker plot.

v

	Example
variable (p. 29) A symbol, usually a letter, that represents one or more numbers.	x is a *variable* in $4x - 3$ and in $x + 3 = 5$.
variable expression (p. 29) An expression consisting of one or more numbers, variables, and operations to be performed.	$4x - 3$ and $2t^2$ are *variable expressions*.
Venn diagram (p. 703) A diagram that uses shapes to show how sets are related.	
verbal model (p. 41) Words that describe how real-life values are related. Verbal models can be expressed using math symbols.	You pay $50 for a gym membership and $3 per visit. Find your total cost for 20 visits. *Verbal model:* $\dfrac{\text{Total}}{\text{cost}} = \dfrac{\text{Membership}}{\text{cost}} + \dfrac{\text{Visits}}{\text{cost}}$
vertex of a polygon (p. 449) A point at which two sides of a polygon meet. The plural of vertex is *vertices*.	*See* polygon.
vertex of a solid (p. 501) A point where the edges meet. The plural of vertex is *vertices*.	

	Example

vertex of an angle (p. 425) The endpoint of the rays that form the angle.

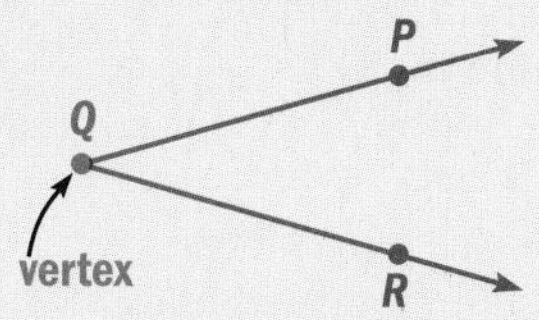

vertical angles (p. 431) When two lines intersect, the angles opposite each other are vertical angles.

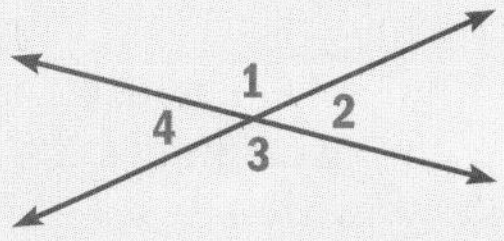

∠1 and ∠3 are vertical angles;
∠2 and ∠4 are also vertical angles.

volume of a solid (p. 510) The amount of space that the solid occupies. Volume is measured in cubic units.

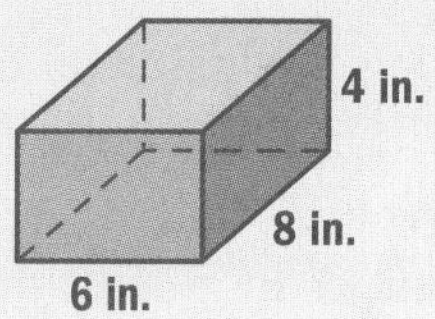

Volume $= lwh = 6 \cdot 8 \cdot 4 =$
192 cubic inches

W

whole numbers (p. 684) The numbers 0, 1, 2, 3 . . . .

X

***x*-axis** (p. 562) The horizontal axis in a coordinate plane. *See also* coordinate plane.

See coordinate plane.

***x*-coordinate** (p. 562) The first coordinate in an ordered pair, which tells you how many units to move to the left or right.

In the ordered pair $(-3, -2)$, the *x*-coordinate, -3, tells you to move 3 units to the left. *See also* coordinate plane.

y

***y*-axis** (p. 562) The vertical axis in a coordinate plane. *See also* coordinate plane.

See coordinate plane.

***y*-coordinate** (p. 562) The second coordinate in an ordered pair, which tells you how many units to move up or down.

In the ordered pair $(-3, -2)$, the *y*-coordinate, -2, tells you to move 2 units down. *See also* coordinate plane.

Index

Index

Index

dividing, 180–184
  by powers of ten, 177–179
  using mental math, 160
  by a whole number, 169–173
estimating
  products, 154, 165
  quotients, 181
  sums and differences, 130–133
expanded form, 108
fractions and, 249–257, 395–403
metric lengths and, 112–117
mixed numbers and, 250–252,
  254–257
modeling, 107, 136, 153, 163, 164,
  249
multiplying, 153–168
  by powers of ten, 176–179
  using mental math, 160
  using a model, 153, 163, 164
ordering, 118–121
percent and, 395–403
place value, 107–111
probability and, 631
ratios and, 375
repeating, 254
rounding, 124–128
subtracting, 136–141, 699
terminating, 254
Decimal point, 107
Decision making, *See also* Choose a
  method; Choose a strategy
  decide, 8, 168, 194, 218, 301, 337,
    341, 347, 382, 424, 565
Degree, 426
Denominator, 228, 700
Deductive reasoning, *See* Activities;
  Critical thinking; Reasoning
Diagonal, 450
Diagram
  concept map, 372
  tree, 216–219, 222, 636, 638, 639,
    642, 643, 646
  Venn, 420, 445, 703
Diameter, of a circle, 484, 485
Difference, definition of, 689
Discount, percent, 407
Discrete math, 8, 19, 348–349, 420,
  501, 630–632, 637
Distance formula, 154, 160
Distributive property, 159–162
Dividend, definition of, 691
Divisibility, 214–215
Divisibility rules, 213–219

Division
  for changing customary units,
    350–355
  for changing metric units, 191–195
  by decimals, 180–184
  of a decimal by a whole number,
    169–173
  equations, 36–40, 334
    solving, 599–603
    writing, 583–586
  estimating quotients, 13–15, 181
  expressions, 29–33, 582–586
  fact families, 3, 687
  fraction, 333–343
    modeling, 333
  integer, 554–559
  inverse operation for, 687
  mental math, 177
  mixed number, 339–343
    modeling, 339, 341
  by powers of ten, 177–179
  for simplifying fractions, 229
  whole number, 6–9, 691
Divisor, definition of, 691
Double bar graph, 80–82, 87
Draw a diagram, problem solving
    strategy, xxxv, 43, 66–67, 70,
    507
Draw a graph, problem solving
    strategy, 560–561
Drawing
  angles, 426
  constructions, 496–497
  flow charts, 582
  scale, 68–71, 388–391
  a solid, 501
  Venn diagrams, 420, 703

e

Edge(s), of a solid, 501
Elapsed time, 299–301, 308–309
Eliminate possibilities, *See* Problem
    solving
Endpoint, 421
Equation(s)
  addition, 37–40, 437, 438, 587–591
  checking solutions, 36
  definition of, 36
  division, 36–40, 334, 599–601, 687
  mental math and, 36–40
  modeling, 587–588, 598
  multiplication, 37–40, 313, 321,

  598–603, 687
  related, 63, 385, 477, 481, 511, 687
  solving, 37–40
    addition, 587–591
    division, 599–601
    multiplication, 598–601
    subtraction, 592–595
  subtraction, 36–40, 272, 545,
    592–595
  writing, 583–586
Equilateral triangle, 437
Equivalent fractions, 226–232
  modeling, 226–227
  writing to compare fractions,
    239–242
Equivalent rate, 379
Equivalent ratios, 375
Error analysis, 8, 18, 24, 31, 32, 39,
    45, 59, 64, 70, 95, 109, 116,
    127, 132, 156, 161, 167, 183,
    217, 224, 237, 251, 274, 279,
    287, 292, 323, 329, 336, 342,
    353, 376, 409, 428, 487, 508,
    540, 546, 552, 556, 569, 590,
    633, 655, 659
Estimation
  activity, 10–11
  angle measure, 427, 428
  to answer multiple choice
    questions, 202
  area, 477
  using benchmarks
    capacity, 188, 189, 345, 346
    length, 57, 59
    mass, 187, 188, 189
    weight, 344–346
  to calculate tip, 407
  to check answers, 138, 141, 154,
    165, 166, 167, 181, 198, 327,
    340, 341, 356, 411
  using clustering, 692
  using compatible numbers, 13,
    165, 315, 316, 340, 694, 695
  decimal
    products, 154, 165, 166
    quotients, 181
    sums and differences, 130–133
  exercises, 26–27, 52, 59, 65, 86,
    116, 139, 143, 156, 157, 183,
    283, 316, 325, 328, 332, 342,
    343, 354, 359, 405, 409, 433,
    479, 503, 513, 515, 590
  with fractions
    products, 315–317

Index

Index

Open-ended, exercises, 19 (Ex. 42),
65 (Ex. 29), 116 (Exs. 21–24),
183 (Ex. 49), 270 (Ex. 35), 274
(Ex. 38), 280 (Ex. 42), 287 (Ex.
46), 337 (Ex. 40), 571 (Ex. 25),
586 (Exs. 40–43), 660 (Ex. 19)
Opposites, 534–536
Optical illusions, 60
Ordered pair, 83
Ordering
decimals, 118–121
fractions, 239–242
integers, 534–536
whole numbers, 685
Order of operations, 21–25
Origin, on a coordinate plane, 83
Ounce, 344
Outcome(s)
combinations and, 637–641
favorable, 630
finding, using tree diagrams, 636,
638, 639
independent events, 642–645
permutations and, 637–641
possible, 630, 636–645
Outlier, 649
Output, 604, 605–609

Parallel lines, 422
Parallelogram(s), 445–448
area of, 475–479
base, 476
classifying, 446
height, 476
Parentheses, 21, 137, 159
Pattern(s)
crystal, 470–471
equivalent fractions, 226–227
geometric, 19, 348, 349, 405
graph, 53, 148–149, 308–309,
624–625
linear functions and, 614
numeric, 7, 256, 333, 342, 357, 404,
405, 550, 553, 608, 610, 611
tessellations, 572–573
Pentagon, 449
Percent, 394–413
circle graphs and, 396, 398
decimals and, 395–403
discount, 407
fractions and, 395–403

mental math, 407
modeling, 394, 395
of a number, 406–411
sales tax, 407
Perform an experiment, problem
solving strategy, 185–186
Perimeter
comparing, 389
definition of, 61, 702
ratios of, 389
of a rectangle, 61, 63–67, 162, 702
of a square, 62–65
of a triangle, 702
Permutation, 637–641
Perpendicular bisector, 497
constructing, 497
Perpendicular lines, 476
Pi, 484, 485
on a calculator, 490
choosing an approximation for,
486
Pictograph
definition of, 706
examples, 177, 179, 184
making, 707
reading, 706
Pint, 345
Place value
decimal, 107–111
chart, 108
comparing, 119
in measurement, 113, 114
modeling, 107
whole number, 684
Plane, 422
coordinate, 562
Plane figures, *See* Geometry
Points, 421
graphing on the coordinate plane,
83, 562
of intersection, 422
naming, 421
on a number line, 118, 244, 248,
534, 685, 686
Polygon(s), 449–453
classifying, 449–453
diagonal of, 450
regular, 450
tessellations, 572–573
Positive integer, 533
Possible outcome(s), 630, 636–645
complementary events and, 632
tree diagrams and, 636, 638, 639,
642, 643, 646

Pound, 344
Powers, 16–20
base, 16
cubed, 17
exponents, 16
order of operations and, 21–24
of ten, multiplying and dividing
by, 176–179
squared, 17
Prediction
using bar graphs, 148–149
using circle graphs, 89–91, 99
using line graphs, 308–309
using patterns, 148–149, 256, 614
using probability, 629
Price, unit, 380
Prime factorization, 216–219,
222–223
for finding least common
multiple, 236
Prime number(s), 215–219
Principal, interest and, 408
Prism, 500
as a crystal form, 470–471
surface area of, 504–509, 523
volume of, 510–513
Probability
complementary events, 632–635
determining, 630–635
event, 630
experimental, 629, 635
formula, 630
game, 647
of independent events, 642–645
likelihood and, 631
odds, 634
outcome, 630
predicting with, 629
random numbers and, 635
simulation, 635
theoretical, 630–635
tree diagrams and, 636, 638, 642,
643, 646
Problem solving, *See also* Error
analysis
choose a method, 287, 354, 386,
402, 591
choose an operation, 340, 342
addition or subtraction, 696
multiplication or division, 697
choose a strategy, 33, 35, 60, 67,
97, 111, 117, 135, 157, 186,
221, 232, 252, 281, 294, 297,
330, 349, 378, 403, 405, 453,

Rectangular prism, 500
  surface area, 506–509
  volume, 510–513
Recursive patterns, 7–8, 342,
  348–349, 553, 610–611
Reflection, 567–571
  line of, 567
  tessellation and, 572–573
Regular polygon, 450
Regular tessellations, 572–573
Remainder, in division, 691
Renaming
  units of measure, 298–299,
    352–355
  whole numbers as fractions,
    290–291
Repeating decimal, 254
Report, project, 149, 309, 471, 625
Representation, *See also* Modeling;
    Number line
  of decimals, fractions, and
    percents, 107, 108, 136, 153,
    163, 164, 177, 180, 226, 227,
    228, 239, 243, 244, 249, 253,
    271, 276, 289, 290, 313, 314,
    318, 319, 320, 321, 326, 333,
    334, 339, 532
  of functions, 612–616
  of geometric patterns, 19, 606, 608
  of statistical graphs, 73, 79–80, 84,
    662–663
Research, project, 149, 309, 471, 625
Review, *See also* Assessment;
    Internet; Notebook Review;
    Skills Review Handbook
  basic skills, 4, 9, 19, 33, 40, 45, 60,
    65, 71, 75, 82, 86, 91, 97, 111,
    117, 121, 128, 133, 140, 157,
    162, 168, 173, 179, 184, 190,
    195, 219, 225, 232, 238, 242,
    248, 252, 256, 270, 275, 281,
    288, 294, 301, 317, 325, 330,
    338, 343, 347, 354, 378, 382,
    387, 391, 398, 403, 424, 429,
    434, 440, 448, 457, 463, 479,
    483, 489, 495, 503, 509, 513,
    536, 541, 547, 553, 558, 566,
    571, 586, 591, 595, 601, 609,
    616, 634, 639, 645, 652, 656,
    661, 665
  Chapter Review, 48–49, 100–101,
    144–145, 198–199, 260–261,
    304–305, 358–359, 414–415,
    466–467, 518–519, 576–577,

    620–621, 668–669
  Extra Practice, 708–720
  Mixed Review, 9, 15, 19, 25, 33, 40,
    45, 60, 65, 71, 75, 82, 86, 91,
    97, 111, 117, 121, 128, 133,
    140, 157, 162, 168, 173, 179,
    184, 190, 195, 219, 225, 232,
    238, 242, 248, 252, 256, 270,
    275, 281, 288, 294, 301, 317,
    325, 330, 338, 343, 347, 354,
    378, 382, 387, 391, 398, 403,
    410, 424, 429, 434, 440, 448,
    457, 463, 479, 483, 489, 495,
    503, 509, 513, 536, 541, 547,
    553, 558, 566, 571, 586, 591,
    595, 601, 609, 616, 634, 639,
    645, 652, 656, 661, 665
  student help with, 5, 63, 73, 79,
    114, 159, 272, 277, 375, 385,
    389, 454, 493, 501, 562, 598,
    602, 649
Rhombohedron, 470
Rhombus, 445–448, 470
Right angle, 430–434
Right triangle, 436
Rotation, 568–571
  angle of, 568
  center of, 568
  tessellation and, 572–573
Rounding
  to check answers, 138, 141
  decimals, 124–128
  to estimate differences
    decimal, 130–131
    fraction, 268–270
    whole number, 12, 693
  to estimate products, 13, 154, 166,
    694
  to estimate quotients, 13, 181, 695
  to estimate sums
    decimal, 130–131
    fraction, 268–270
    whole number, 12, 692
  fractions, 267–270
  whole numbers, 686

S

Sales tax, 407
Sample space, 636–639, 642–645
Scaffolding, *See* Problem solving
Scale
  for a bar graph, 79–82

  for a box-and-whisker plot,
    657–661
  for a drawing, 68, 388
  for a graph, selecting, 79–82,
    84–87, 657–661
  for a line graph, 84–87
  on a map, 68, 70–71, 390–391
Scale drawing, 68–71, 388–391, 522
Scalene triangle, 437
Scalenohedron, 470
Scatter plot, 87
Second, unit of time, 298
Sector, of a circle graph, 493
Segment, 421–422
  bisecting, 497
  copying, 496
Sequences, *See* Pattern
Short Response questions, 15, 33,
    51, 65, 82, 97, 128, 140, 147,
    157, 168, 184, 201, 205, 206,
    207, 208, 219, 225, 238, 263,
    270, 281, 307, 325, 330, 343,
    347, 361, 362–363, 364, 366,
    367, 368, 398, 410, 417, 448,
    469, 483, 509, 521, 541, 547,
    579, 591, 616, 623, 639, 652,
    656, 671, 675, 676, 677, 678,
    726–738
  strategies for answering, 362–363
Similar figures, 454–457
Simple interest, 168, 408
Simplest form
  fraction, 229
  ratio, 374
Simulation, 635
Skills Review Handbook, 684–707
  estimation
    differences, 693
    products, 694
    quotients, 695
    sums, 692
  fractions, 700
  graphs
    bar, 704
    line, 705
    pictograph, 706–707
  logical reasoning, 703
    Venn diagrams, 703
  measurement
    area, 702
    perimeter, 702
    time, 701

number sense
  comparing and ordering whole
    numbers, 685
  fact families, 687
  rounding whole numbers, 686
  whole number place value, 684
operations
  addition, 688, 689, 698, 699
  division, 691
  multiplication, 690
  subtraction, 688, 689, 698, 699
problem solving, 696, 697
Solid(s), 500–521
  classifying, 470, 500–503
  definition of, 500
  drawing, 501
  prism
    surface area of, 504–509
    volume of, 510–513
Solution
  of an equation, 36
    checking, 36
  of an inequality, 602
Solve a related problem, problem
    solving strategy, 348–349
Solve a simpler problem, problem
    solving strategy, xli, 404–405,
    407
Solving equations, *See* Equations
Spatial reasoning, 458–459, 470–471,
    489, 504–505, 506–509, 517,
    572–573
Sphere, 500
Spreadsheet(s), 87, 158, 441
Spring balance, 514, 515
Square, 445–448
  area of, 62–65, 166
  definition of, 62, 445
  perimeter of, 62–65
Square units, 62
Stacked bar graph, 82
Standard form
  of a decimal number, 108
  of a whole number, 684
Standardized test practice, *See*
    Assessment; Test-taking skills;
    Test-Taking Strategies
Statistics
  bar graph, 79–80
  box-and-whisker plot, 657–658
  line graph, 84
  line plot, 73
  lower extreme, 657
  lower quartile, 657

mean, 93–97, 555–559, 654–656
median, 93–97, 654–661
misleading, 648–652
mode, 93–97, 654–656
range, 94–97, 654–656
stem-and-leaf plot, 653–654
upper extreme, 657
upper quartile, 657
Stem, stem-and-leaf plot, 653
Stem-and-leaf plot, 653–656
  choosing a data display, 662–665
  key, 653
  leaf, 653
  making, 653
  reading and interpreting, 654
  stem, 653
Stop and Think, exercises, *See*
    Thinking skills
Straight angle, 430–434
Strategies, *See* Problem Solving
    Strategies; Test-Taking
    Strategies
Student help, *See also* Internet
  with homework, 8, 14, 18, 23, 31,
    39, 44, 58, 64, 70, 74, 81, 85,
    90, 95, 109, 115, 120, 127, 132,
    139, 156, 161, 167, 171, 178,
    182, 189, 193, 217, 224, 231,
    237, 241, 247, 251, 255, 269,
    273, 279, 287, 292, 300, 316,
    323, 328, 336, 341, 346, 353,
    376, 381, 386, 390, 397, 402,
    409, 423, 428, 433, 439, 447,
    451, 456, 462, 478, 482, 488,
    494, 502, 508, 512, 535, 540,
    546, 552, 556, 564, 569, 585,
    590, 594, 600, 607, 615, 633,
    638, 644, 650, 655, 659, 664
  with note taking, 30, 37, 94, 107,
    126, 187, 228, 278, 313, 395,
    406, 445, 476, 544, 613, 663
  with reading, 13, 69, 89, 118, 138,
    379, 383, 422, 426, 450, 534,
    606
  with review, 5, 63, 73, 79, 114, 159,
    272, 277, 375, 385, 389, 452,
    454, 493, 501, 562, 598, 602,
    649
  with solving, 6, 13, 43, 57, 114, 136,
    153, 165, 170, 176, 180, 192,
    215, 216, 236, 239, 249, 254,
    267, 314, 321, 322, 326, 351,
    400, 422, 461, 480, 486, 539,
    567, 568, 589, 606, 616, 631, 649

with technology, 20, 257, 295, 355,
    411, 490, 635
with vocabulary, 56, 345, 431
Subtraction
  checking, 6, 689
  of decimals, 136–141, 699
  equations, 36–40, 272, 545
    solving, 592–595
    writing, 583–586
  estimating differences
    decimal, 130–133
    fraction, 268–270
    whole number, 12–15, 693
  expressions, 29–33, 583, 585
  fact families, 3, 687
  of fractions, 272–275, 277–281,
    284–295
    modeling, 289
  integer, 542–547
    modeling, 542–543
  inverse operation for, 687
  of measurements, 298–301,
    352–355
  of mixed numbers, 284, 286–295
  modeling, 289
  with money, 698
  whole number, 6–9, 687–689
Sum, definition of, 689
Supplementary angles, 431–434
Surface area
  definition of, 506
  of a prism, 504–509, 523
Survey, graphing results of, 79–82, 87,
    665
Symbolic notation, *See* Algebra;
    Geometry
Symbols, table of, 721
Symmetry, line, 460–463

t

Table
  of data, 72, 79, 84, 87, 493, 653
  of formulas, 723
  for a function, 604–608, 612–616
  of measures, 722
  of properties, 724
  of symbols, 721
Table, making a, problem solving
    strategy, 220–221, 637
Tally charts, *See* Frequency table
Tangram, 479, 489
Tax, percent and, 407

Technology, *See also* Calculator; Graphing calculator; Technology Activities
    student help with, 20, 257, 295, 355, 411, 490, 635
    uses of, 87, 125

Technology Activities
    calculator
      Adding and Subtracting Decimals, 141
      Changing Units, 355
      Circumference of a Circle, 490
      Decimals and Fractions, 257
      Finding a Percent of a Number, 411
      Finding Values of Powers, 20
      Integer Operations, 559
      Testing Probabilities, 635
    computer
      Angle Measures of Triangles, 441
      Creating Data Displays, 87
      Multiplying Decimals by Whole Numbers, 158
      Using the Internet, 295
    graphing calculator, Graphing Linear Functions, 617

Temperature, 317
Terminating decimal, 254
Tessellations, 572–573
Test practice, *See* Assessment; Test-taking skills; Test-Taking Strategies
Test-taking skills, *See also* Assessment; Problem solving
    practicing, 204–205, 364–365, 524–525, 674–675, 726–738
    strategies for extended response questions, 672–673
    strategies for multiple choice questions, 202–203
      context-based, 522–523
    strategies for short response questions, 362–363
Test-Taking Strategies, 51, 103, 147, 201, 263, 307, 361, 417, 469, 521, 579, 623, 671, *See also* Problem Solving Strategies
Theoretical probability, *See* Probability
Thinking skills, 3, 11, 27, 28, 47, 53, 77, 78, 92, 105, 112, 113, 129, 143, 151, 163, 175, 197, 211, 213, 227, 234, 243, 259, 265,

276, 283, 289, 303, 311, 319, 332, 333, 357, 371, 373, 393, 394, 413, 419, 435, 443, 444, 465, 473, 475, 484, 499, 517, 531, 537, 543, 549, 575, 581, 587, 597, 604, 619, 627, 629, 647, 667, *See also* Critical thinking; Error analysis

Three-dimensional figures, *See* Geometry; Solid
Tiling patterns, *See* Tessellations
Time
    adding and subtracting measures of, 298–301, 610
    changing among units of, 701
    elapsed, 299–301, 308–309
    solstice, 308
Tips, 407–409, 413, 415–417
Ton, 344
Transformation(s), 568
    reflection, 567–571
    rotation, 568–571
    tessellations, 572–573
    translation, 563–566
Translation, 563–566
    tessellation and, 572–573
Tree diagram
    factor tree, 216–219, 222
    possible outcomes, 636, 638, 639, 642, 643, 646
Triangle(s)
    acute, 436
    angle measures, sum of, 435, 437–438
    area of, 480–483
    base, 480
    classifying, 436–440
    congruent, 454–457
    definition of, 436, 449
    equilateral, 437
    height, 480
    isosceles, 437
    obtuse, 436
    right, 436
    scalene, 437
    similar, 454–457
Triangular prism, 500
Two-dimensional figures, *See* Geometry

U

Unit price, 380

Unit rate(s), 379–382
    comparing, 380
Unknown, representing, 28
Unlike denominators, 277, 285–286
Upper extreme, 657
Upper quartile, 657
Use a Venn diagram, problem solving strategy, xlii

V

Variable(s)
    expressions and, 28–33, 582–586
    expressions with two, 30–33
Variable expression, 29–33, 582–586
Venn diagram, xlii, 420, 445, 703
Verbal model
    definition of, 41
    examples, 42, 138, 159, 192, 271, 272, 313, 321, 334, 383, 408, 437, 476, 480, 485, 491, 510, 539, 545, 550, 555, 589, 613
    writing to solve problems, 138, 192, 384, 386, 584, 589
Vertex (vertices)
    angle, 425
    of a cone, 500
    polygon, 449
    of a pyramid, 500
    of a solid, 501
    triangle, 436
Vertical angles, 431–434
Vertical axis, 83
Volume(s)
    comparing, 185–186
    definition of, 510
    of a rectangular prism, 185–186, 510–513

W

Weight
    adding and subtracting measures of, 352–354
    benchmarks for, 344
      estimating with, 344–346
    changing units, 350–355
    choosing appropriate units of, 344
    customary units, 344–347, 514–515
What do you think? questions, 9, 15, 22, 32, 59, 64, 71, 84, 94, 110, 116, 121, 125, 128, 133, 139,

Credits

Cover Photography

Ralph Mercer

Photography

ii *top* Meridian Creative Group, *bottom* RMIP/Richard Haynes; **iii** *top* Sharon Hoogstraten, *bottom* Jerry Head Jr.; **vi** Jeff Rotman/Getty Images; **vii** Rubberball Productions; **viii** PhotoDisc/Getty Images; **ix** Bob Tringali/Sportschrome; **x** Adrian Peacock/ImageState; **xi** PhotoDisc/Getty Images; **xii** AFP/Jeff Kowalsky/Corbis; **xiii** Rubberball Productions; **xiv** PhotoDisc/Getty Images; **xv** Jeff Hunter/Getty Images; **xvi** Jacob Taposchaner/Getty Images; **xvii** PhotoDisc/Getty Images; **xviii** John Giustina/Getty Images; **xix** Frank Siteman; **xxi** *top* Royalty-Free/Corbis, *center* Comstock Images, *bottom* Mary Kate Denny/PhotoEdit; **xxxiv** Cathy Melloan/PhotoEdit; **xxxvi** Comstock Images; **xxxvii** School Division/Houghton Mifflin; **xxxviii** Frank Siteman; **xl** *left* Oscar Palmquist/LightWave, *right* C-Squared Studios/PhotoDisc/Getty Images; **xlii** Jack Affleck/Index Stock Imagery/Picturequest; **1** *bl* John Terence Turner/ Getty Images; **2** *cr* Kelly/Mooney Photography/Corbis; **3** Nick Koudis/ PhotoDisc #10, *tl* Joe McBride/Getty Images; **6** *cl* Frank Siteman, *cr* C-Squared Studios/Artville: Musical Instruments; **7** *tl* Mike Blake/Corbis; **9** *tl* Getty Images/Anup Shah; **12** *bl* © Karl Weatherly/Corbis; **14** *cl* Tim Hawley/FoodPix; Comstock RF; **15** *tl* BG Photography Inc.; **16** *tr* Adam Block/NOAO/AURA/NSF; **18** *bl* Frank Siteman; **19** *tr, tl* School Division, Houghton Mifflin Co.; **22** *cl* © Konrad Wothe/Look; **23** *br* School Division, Houghton Mifflin Co.; **24** *bl* Paul A. Soulders/Corbis; **29** *tr* Photonica, Comstock: Pets & Vets; **31** *br* Corbis: Storm Chaser (vol. 107); **32** *cl* Matthias Breiter/Accent Alaska, *br* Joe Atlas/Brand X Pictures: Summer Fun; **34** *cr* Frank Siteman; **35** *tr* Stanley Brown/Getty Images; **36** *bl* Steven Simpson/Getty Images, *tr* Joe Atlas/Brand X Pictures: Summer Fun; **38** *tl* Matthais Breiter/Accent Alaska, *tr* Daniel J Cox/Getty Images; **39** *bl, cl* Frank Siteman; **40** *tl* David Young-Wolff/PhotoEdit, *tr* Corbis: Sports Objects (vol. 174); **41** *cl* David Young-Wolff/PhotoEdit; **41** *cr* PhotoDisc; **42** *tl, tc* School Division, Houghton Mifflin Co., *cl* PhotoDisc; **44** *tl* John Lund/Getty Images; **49** *br* Joseph Sohm/Corbis; **50** *br* Javier Pierini/PhotoDisc, Inc.; **52, 53** *b* John Shaw/Panoramic Images; **55** *bc* Kendra Knight/AGE; **56** *tc* PhotoDisc; **56** *cl* Mark E. Gibson/Corbis; **58** *c* David A. Northcott/Corbis, *cr* Burke/Triolo/Artville: Bugs and Insects; **59** *tc* PhotoDisc, *cl* Galen Rowell/Corbis; **60** *c* School Division/Houghton Mifflin; **61** *bl* PhotoDisc; **64** *bl* Mug Shots/Corbis/Stock Market; **65** *tl* Picture Desk, *cl* CinemaPhoto/Corbis; **66** *cr* Frank Siteman; **67** *tr* Tim Wright/Corbis; **68** *bl* Carson Ganci/Corbis; **69** *bl* Melcher Media, Inc./photo by McDougal Littell School Division. Bark canoe boat from "Amazing Book of Paper Boats" copyright 2001 by Melcher Media, Inc.; **70** *cl* Jamie Harron/Corbis, *cr* Peggy Heard/Corbis; **71** *tl* Tony Arruza/Corbis; **72** *cl* David Young-Wolff/Getty Images, *br* PhotoDisc; **74** *tl* Ken Redding/Corbis; **75** *tl* Corbis Images/PictureQuest; **79** *bl* Nigel J. Dennis, Gallo Images/Corbis, *tr* Becky & Jay Dickman/Corbis; **80** *cl* PhotoDisc: Nature, Wildlife, Environment CD#44; **81** *tl* Tony Freeman/PhotoEdit; **82** *tl* Richard Hamilton Smith/Corbis; **83** *cl* Nick Dolding/Getty Images; **84** *tl* Westlight Stock — OZ Productions/Corbis; **85** *bl* PhotoDisc; **86** *tl* Ariel Skelley/Corbis/Stock Market; **88** *cl* Kwame Zikomo/SuperStock; **90** *bl* PhotoDisc; **93** *tr* Franz Walther/Artville: Air and Space, *bl* Franz Walther/Artville: Air and Space; **94** *tl* NASA Johnson Space Center, *cr* Central Stock; **96** *tl* Ralph A. Clevenger/Corbis, *tr* Susan Wilder Crane; **100** *bl, br* School Division/Houghton Mifflin; **104** *cr* PhotoDisc: Backgrounds & Objects CD#8; **105** *tl* PhotoDisc: Backgrounds & Objects CD#8, Eyewire, *c* PhotoDisc: Family & Friends CD#121; **108** *bl* Pierce Williams/FPW Photo; **110** *cl* Pierce Williams/FPW Photo, *br inset* Copyright © Vaughan Fleming/ Science Photo Library/Photo Researchers, *br* PhotoDisc, Inc.; **111** *tl* Sportschrome; **113** *tr* Michael S. Yamashita/Corbis, *bl* ©1996 Hans Larsson/Matrix; **115** *tr* Valerie Giles/Photo Researchers, Inc., *br* Joseph T. Collins/Photo Researchers, Inc.; **116** *tl, tr* Ken O'Donoghue, *cl* Richard Bucich; **119** *bl* Pets International, LTD.- Super Pet; **121** *tl* Science Source/Photo Researchers, Inc.; **125** *bl* Dustin W. Carr/Harold G. Craighead/Cornell University; **127** *bl* J. Grant Brittain/Transworld Skateboarding; **128** *tl* Peter Menzel/Stock Boston; **130** *bl* A. Ramey/Stock Boston, *tr* PhotoDisc; **132** *tl* Image 100 LTD/Corbis/Stock Market; **133** *tl* Galen Rowell/Corbis; **134** *cr* Frank Siteman; **135** *tr* James Muldowney/Stone; **138** *bl* Cosmo Condina/Getty Images; **139** *bl* John Thompson, *br* PhotoDisc; **140** *tl* NASA; **145** *cr* Philip Gould/Corbis; **146** *cr* EIT Consortium/NASA; **148** *l* Paul McCormick/Getty Images; **149** *right* Paul Sauders/Getty Images; **150, 151,** *top* Ken O'Donoghue; **151** *cr* Ken O'Donoghue; **154** *tl* Jeff Schultz/Alaska Stock Images; **157** *tl* Bob Krist/Corbis; **159** *tr* Paul Barton/Corbis; **160** *cl* NASA; **161** *tl* Robert Frerck/Woodfin Camp and Associates; **162** *tl* Bettmann/Corbis; **164** *tr* Patricia Fogden/Corbis, *bl* Kevin Schafer/Getty Images; **166** *tl* Bureau of Reclamation; **168** *tl* Tim Hawley/FoodPix; **169** *tr* Stephen Simpson/Getty Images, *bl* John Terence Turner/Getty Images, *tr* Stephen Simpson/Getty Images; **170** *cl* Michel Tcherevkoff Ltd./Getty Images; **171** *tl* Kai Pfaffenbach/Corbis; **172** *tl* Gunter Marx/Corbis; **177** *tl* Tom Paiva/Getty Images; **178** *cr* Christie's Images/Corbis; **179** *tl* Reuters NewMedia Inc./Corbis; **180** *tr* Gerry Penny/Corbis; **181** *cl* Stephen Rose; **183** *cl* Harold Blank; **184** *tl* Bob Krist/eStock Photography/Picturequest; **185** *br* Frank Siteman; **186** *tr* PhotoDisc, Inc.; **187** *tr, cr* Frank Siteman; **188** *bl* School Division/Houghton Mifflin; **189** *br* Paul Souders/Getty Images; **192** *bl* CSA Plastock/Photonica; **193** *cl* FoodPix/Getty Images; **194** *cl* Ryan McVay/ PhotoDisc, *cr* ball - LightWave, pin - C Squared Studios/PhotoDisc: Sports Goods CD#25; **198** *cr* Bob Krist/Getty Images; **200** *br* Brandon D. Cole/Corbis; **209** *bl* Ken O'Donoghue; **210** *cr* PhotoSpin/Powerphotos, C Squared Studios/PhotoDisc; **211** *cr* Joshua Ets-Hokin/PhotoDisc: Object Series- In Character CD#20; **214** *tr, bl* Julie Lemberger/Corbis; **215** *bl* Ed Crockett; **218** Stockbyte: Education (cd 137- set of 5); **220** *cr* Frank Siteman; **221** *cl* Photospin-PowerPhotos: Money & Finance Vol. 29, *tr* Michael Newman/PhotoEdit; **222** *bl* Bonnie Kamin/Index Stock Imagery/Picturequest, *tr* Joe Atlas/Brand X Pictures: Summer Fun; **223** *bl* Michael S. Yamashita/Corbis; **224** *tl* courtesy of Taymark; **225** *tl* Richard Nowitz/Photo Researchers, Inc.; **229** *bl* © RNT Productions/Corbis; **230** *bl* Frank Siteman; **231** *cl* Kelly/Mooney Photography/Corbis; **235** *bl* Schepler's Ferry Service; **237** *tl* Michael Newman/PhotoEdit; **240** *bl* Steve Skjold/Skjold Stock Photography; **241** *tl* Richard Bradbury/Getty Images; **242** *tl* NASA; **244** *tl* David Young-Wolff/PhotoEdit; **246** *tl* William Strode/SuperStock; **247** *bl* Lisette Le Bon/SuperStock, *tr* Ken O'Donoghue; **250** *tl* Powerphotos/PhotoSpin; **251** *tl* Peter Cade/Getty Images; **252** *tl* PhotoSpin; **256** *tl* Blair Seitz/Stock Connection/Picturequest; **261** *cr* Theodore Lillie and courtesy of Branders.com; **262** *br* Frank Siteman/Stock, Boston Inc./Picturequest; **264, 265** *top* Stuart Westmorland/Getty Images; **267** *cl* © S. Blair Hedges; **268** *cl* Steven Needham/Envision; **269** *tl* Jeff Greenberg/PhotoEdit; **270** *tl* Robert Koropp, *tr* Copyright 2002 Action Products International, Inc. www.apii.com; **273** *tl* Tony Freeman/PhotoEdit; **278** *cl* Gail Shumway/Getty Images; **279** *tl* Steve Skjold/Skjold Stock Photography; **280** *cl* Raymond Gehman/Corbis; **284** *bl* © Richard Hutchings/Corbis; **285** *cl* Dave G. Houser/Corbis; **286** *tr, tl* John Marshall; **287** *cl* Jeff Kowalsky/Corbis; **288** *tl* Darrell Gulin/Getty Images; **291** *cl* Domenico Ruzza/Envision; **292** *tl* Stephen Frisch/Picturequest; **293** *tl* Andrew J. Martinez/Photo Researchers, Inc., *br* School Division, Houghton Mifflin Co.; **294** *tl, tr* JimMcElholm/Single Source Inc.; **296** *br* Frank Siteman; **297** *tr* Kevin R. Morris/Corbis; **298** *bl, tr* Getty Images; **300** *tl* Jeff Rotman/Getty Images; **308** *tl* Greg Martin/SuperStock; **309** *tr* Courtesy of Earth Image © 2002 The Living Earth; **310** *cr* Brett/Cartwright/Getty; **311** *tl* Jake Martin/Allsport/Getty Images, *cr* Jean-Yves Ruszniewski/Corbis; **315** *tl* Ken O'Donoghue; **314** *bl* Rubberball Prod.: Teens & Young Adults 2; **316** *cl* Charles E. Rotkin/Corbis; **317** *tc* Michele Burgess/Corbis, *tl* Johanna Kriesel/Corbis, *cl* Lake County Museum/Corbis; **320** *tr* Scooter image courtesy of Razor USA; **320** *bl* Myrleen Ferguson Cate/PhotoEdit; **324** *tl* RMIP/Richard Haynes, *br* Richard During/Getty Images; **325** *tr* Mike Powell/Allsport, *tl* PhotoDisc; **327** *bl* Sportschrome/Bongarts; **328** *tl* Adrian Peacock/Pictor; **329** *cl* Courtesy of MIT; **335** *tl* Courtesy of Howe Caverns, Inc.; **336** *tl* School Division/Houghton Mifflin; **337** *cl, cr* LightWave; **338** *tl* PhotoDisc; **340** *br* LightWave, *bl* Scott Speakes/Corbis; **342** *cl* Stephen Frink/Corbis; **344** *cl* PhotoDisc; *bl* Steve Skjold/Skjold Stock Photography; *c* Photospin-

PowerPhotos: Sports and Recreation Vol. 5; *cr* Courtesy of American Honda Motors Co., Inc; **346** *cl* Howard Berman/Getty Images; **347** *tl* Kevin Fleming/Corbis *tr* School Division/Houghton Mifflin; **348** *br* Frank Siteman; **349** *tr* Spencer Grant/PhotoEdit; **350** *tl* Burke/Triolo/Brand X Pictures: Home Improvements; *tc* Corbis: Home & Family (vol. 108); *tr* C Squared Studios/PhotoDisc: Market Fresh/Object Series CD#49; **351** *bl* Nik Wheeler/Corbis; **352** *tl* Courtesy of Marklin, Inc. Train Model: Marklin German Federal Railroad class 18.4 Steam Locomotive. Length: 40-1/8", Gauge: 1, Scale: 1:32.; **353** *bl* DanFornari©WHOI, *cr* James Marshall/Corbis; **354** *tl* Bettmann/Corbis; **359** *tr* John Warden/Index Stock Imagery/Picturequest; **360** *cr* LightWave, *br* Artville: Musical Instruments; **369** *bl* PhotoDisc: Supporting Cast: Teens/Objects Series CD#39; **370, 371** *tr* Ken O'Donoghue; **374** *bl* PhotoDisc: Supporting Cast: Teens/Objects Series CD#39; **375** *cl* PhotoDisc; **376** *bc* EyeWire: CD/Instrumental Objects; **377** *tl* Medford Taylor/National Geographic Image Collection; **381** *tl* Charles W. Melton, *cr* Jeremy Barker; **382** *tl* Buddy Mays/Words & Pictures/Picturequest; **384** *cl* Stephen Studd/Getty Images; **387** *tl* Tim Flach/Getty Images; **388** *cl* Seitzinger/Derbymania; **389** *tl* Ralf-Finn Hestoft/Index Stock Imagery/Picturequest; **390** *cr* CSA Plastock/Photonica; **395** *tr* Lawrence Manning/Corbis; **396** *cl* Comstock: CD Pets & Vets; **398** *cl* PhotoDisc: Backgrounds & Objects CD #8, PhotoDisc: Tools of the Trade CD #48, *tl* PhotoSpin/PowerPhotos: Africa Vol 16, PhotoDisc: Tools of the Trade CD #48; **399** *bl* David Young-Wolff/PhotoEdit; **400** *bl* Burgess Blevins/Getty Images; **401** *bl* PhotoDisc; **402** *cl* James J. Bissell/SuperStock; **404** *cr* Frank Siteman; **405** *tr* Ryan McVay/Getty Images; **407** *cl* Kevin Horan/Getty; **409** *cl* Frank Siteman; **410** *tl* PhotoDisc; **415** *br* Bruce Burkhardt/Corbis; **416** *br* PhotoDisc; **419** *c* PhotoDisc: InfoMedia 2/Objects CD#26; **422** *tr* USGS; **423** *bc* LightWave, *br* Geoff du Feu/Getty Images; **425** *bl* Chuck Savage/Corbis; **428** *cl* Jeff Hunter/Getty Images; **430** *tr* Bob Krist/Corbis/Stock Market; **432** *tl* Hideo Kurihara/Getty; **434** *tl* Jim Karageorg/Masterfile; **436** *tr* Pete Saloutos/Corbis; **438** *br* U.S. Postal Service; **440** *tl* Barnabas Bosshart/Corbis; **447** *tl* Cathy Melloan/PhotoEdit; **449** *tr* Gary Holscher/Getty Images; **451** *cl, c, cr* Masterfile, *bl* Cathy Melloan/PhotoEdit, *bc* PhotoSpin, *br* Christine Osborne/Corbis; **452** *br* Tuthill, David W., *bl* Tony Freeman/Photoedit/Picturequest; **455** *cr* Michael Cerone/SuperStock, *cl* Raymond Gehman/Corbis; **458** *br* Frank Siteman; **459** *tr* Corbis Images/PictureQuest; **460** *cl* The Fusions Collection/Stockbyte: Music (cd 36), *cr* The Fusions Collection/Stockbyte: Music (cd 36); **462** *tl* Comstock: Whimsical Pop-Ins, *tr* Photospin-PowerPhotos: Frames Vol. 14, *tc* haitianartwork.com, *cr* PhotoDisc: Sports Goods CD#25, *cl* Corbis: Sports Objects (vol. 174), *c* Artville: Bugs and Insects; **463** *tl* Peter Grumann/Getty Images; **470** *l* Jose Manuel Sanchis Calvete/Corbis; **471** *right* Photo Disk/Objects of Nature CD #38, *c* Eduardo Fuss; **472, 473** Jay Syverson/Corbis; **477** *cl* Roger Ressmeyer/Corbis; **478** *bc* Michael Freeman/Corbis, *br* Digital Art/Corbis; **479** *tl* Arthur Bickerstaffe, *tr* Ken O'Donoghue; **481** *cl* PhotoDisc; **482** *tl* Mike Zens/Corbis, *bl* Corbis Images/Picturequest, *bc* PhotoDisc: Government and Social Issues CD#25, *br* Lawrence Manning/Corbis; **483** *tl* Kevin Fleming/Corbis, *cr* Stockbyte: Flags-The Americas (cd 68); **485** *bl* Michael Lamarra; **487** *tl* PhotoDisc; **488** *tl* Dave Bartruff/Corbis, *tc* C Squared Studios/Artville: Musical Instruments, *tr* William Sallaz/Duomo/Corbis, *cl* LightWave; **491** *tr* © Rubberball Productions/Rubberball Production/Picturequest ; **492** *tl* Bob Daemmrich/Stock Market/Picturequest ; **493** *cr* Jack Affleck/Index Stock Imagery/Picturequest; **494** *bl* John Lund/Getty Images; **497** *cl* Stockbyte CD 29 HouseholdObjects (cd 29); **500** *tr, bl* Ken O'Donoghue; **502** *cr* Ken O'Donoghue, *c* PhotoDisc: Sports Goods CD#25, *cl* EyeWire: Instrumental Objects; **503** *tl* Jacob Taposchaner/Getty Images; **504** *cr* Frank Siteman; **505** *tr* Frank Wartenberg/Corbis; **507** *cl* Ken O' Donoghue; **509** *tl* Richard Cummins/Corbis; **510** *tr, cl, bl* Ken O'Donoghue, toy cube courtesy of Regan Universal Press/Andrews McMeel Publishing, **511** *cl* Joseph Sohm/Corbis; **513** *tl* Marvin Sharp/Sharp's Images Photography; **515** *tl* PhotoSpin PowerPhotos: Food Basics Vol. 2; **519** *cr* Stockbyte: Busy Kids 1 (cd 55); **520** *br* PhotoDisc, Inc.; **529** *bl* Keren Su/Corbis; **530** *cr* Copyright © 2002 SPACE.com, Inc. All rights reserved; **531** *tr* Rick Fischer/Masterfile; **533** *bl* Corbis: Space and Spaceflight (vol. 56), *tr* EAC Images/NASA/Aurora & Quanta Productions; **534** *bl* Chris Trotman/Corbis; **535** *tl* PhotoDisc; **538** *bl* Comstock: Sportsview 1; **541** *tl* Bettmann/Corbis; **545** *bl* Oregon State University/University of Hawaii School of Ocean and Earth Science and Technology/USGS; **546** *bl* Stockbyte: Food Cutouts 3 (cd 61); **547** *tl* Stephen Frink/Getty Images; **551** *cr* Francois Gohier/Photo Researchers, Inc., *cl* Francois Gohier/Photo Researchers, Inc.; **552** *br* Alexis Nees/Animals Animals; **555** *bl* Jose Azel/Aurora & Quanta Productions; **557** *tr* NASA/USGS/Stockli, Nelson, Hasler/Laboratory for Atmospheres/Goddard Space Flight Center, *bl* Bob Daemmrich/Stock, Boston Inc./Picturequest ; **560** *br* Frank Siteman; **561** *tr* Mantha Granger/Edge productions, Cognoscenti Map Guides; **565** *tl* Corbis: Storm Chaser (vol. 107); **566** *tl* Michael Newman/PhotoEdit/Photo Researchers, Inc.; **567** *tr* Steve Bloom/Getty Images; **568** *tl* George Hunter/Getty Images; **569** *br* Mary Louise Brimberg/National Geographic Image Collection, *bl* Bridgeman Art Library; **570** *bl* Coco McCoy/Rainbow/PictureQuest, *c* Bill Gillette/Stock Boston Inc./Picturequest, *cr* Neil Beer/Photodisk, *bc* The Design Library/photostogo.com/Index Stock Photography, Inc, *br* © Danny Lehman/Corbis; **572** *tc; bl* Philadelphia Museum of Art/Corbis; **573** *tl* Priscilla Connell/Photostogo/Index Stock Photography, Inc.; **576** *cr* George D. Lepp/Corbis; **578** *br* Sergei Ilnitsky/Corbis; **583** *bl, tr* Ken O'Donoghue; **584** *bl* Tom Stewart/Corbis Stock Market; **586** *tl* Tom Bean/Corbis; **589** *bl* Ryan McVay/PhotoDisc: Shopping Spree VL 05; **591** *cl* Jim Cummins/Getty; **592** *tr, bl* Ken O'Donoghue; **594** *tl* Stephen McBrady/PhotoEdit/Picturequest; **595** *tl* Rubberball Prod: CD Silhouettes of Occupations; **599** *bl* Tony Anderson/Getty; **601** *tl* AFP Photo/RobertSullivan/Corbis; **603** *bl* Dana White/PhotoEdit; **605** *tr* Keren Su/Corbis, *bl* John Giustina/Getty; **607** *tl* Brad Hitz/Getty; **608** *bl* Mark E. Gibson; **610** *br* Frank Siteman; **611** *tr* Tim Macpherson/Getty; **612** *bl* Maxime Laurent/Digitalvision: Urban Leisure; **615** *bl* Charles Gupton/Corbis Stock Market; **620** *br* C-Squared Studios/PhotoDisc/Getty Images; **622** *cr* EyeWire: Instrumental Objects; **624** *l* Ian Murphy/Getty Images, *tc* Stan Osolinski/Getty Images; **625** *r* Stan Osolinski/Getty Images, *br* Nicholas Parfitt/Getty Images; **627** *cr, tl* PhotoDisc: Nature, Wildlife, Environment CD#44; **630** *bl* Ron Avery/SuperStock, *tr* Steve Skjold/Skjold Stock Photography; **631** *bl* Ken O'Donoghue; **633** *cl* Jason Cohn/Corbis; **636** *tr, cl* Steve Skjold/Skjold Stock Photography; **637** *cl* Comstock: Food Icons; **639** *tl* Chris Trotman/Corbis; **640** *r* Frank Siteman; **641** *tr* David Young-Wolff/PhotoEdit; **643** *cl* Ken O'Donoghue, *tr* Anne-Marie Weber/Getty Images; **651** *tl* NASA; **654** *tl* Richard Cummins/Corbis, *cr* PhotoDisc; **655** *tl* Chris Whitehead/Getty Images; **656** *tl* Alistair Berg/Getty; **658** *cl* Atlantech,Inc: SeaLifeStyles; **659** *tl* David Young-Wolff/Getty; **660** *cl* Wally McNamee/Corbis; **663** *tl* Stephanie Rausser/Getty Images; **664** *bl* Rubberball Prod.: Silhouettes of Sports 2; **669** *br* Michelle D. Bridwell/PhotoEdit; **725** Mary Kate Denny/PhotoEdit.

Illustration

Rob Dunlavey
52, 150, 151, 264, 265, 370, 371, 473, 580, 581

Laurie O'Keefe
116, 118, 267, 291

School Division, Houghton Mifflin Co.
347, 422

Sam Ward
xxv, 17, 24, 25, 45, 47, 62, 73, 97, 120, 123, 131, 156, 167, 173, 182, 190, 195, 219, 238, 248, 255, 274, 275, 303, 330, 332, 343, 378, 385, 397, 403, 438, 453, 457, 495, 508, 536, 590, 600, 609, 634, 645, 661

Chapter 1

1.1 Getting Ready to Practice (p. 7) 5. 81
7. 432   9. 783   11. 55 R2   13. subtract 10; 20, 10
15. $156

1.1 Practice and Problem Solving (pp. 8–9)
17. 16   19. 19 R1   21. 236   23. 600   25. 687
27. 57 R7   29. 613   31. 7719   33. subtract 2; 22, 20
35. add 8; 36, 44   37. 13   39. 14 days   41. false;
product   43. true   45. 1   47. 6   49. 47 litters
51. Add 67 five times.   57. 90   59. 300   61. 1000
63. 5000   65. 4   67. 11   69. 27   71. 5

1.2 Getting Ready to Practice (p. 14) 1. yes
3. no; 7200   5. 600, 100; 500   7. 4000, 6000; 10,000

1.2 Practice and Problem Solving
(pp. 14–15) 9–31. Estimates may vary.   9. 100
11. 100   13. 400   15. 300   17. 500   19. 1500
21. 80   23. 10   25. 100   27. 900   29. 4800   31. 20
33. about 200 students   35. yes   37. no   39. no
41. *Sample answer:* about 130 mi   43. Low. *Sample
answer:* You want to be sure you have enough
paint.   47. 2064   49. 714   51. 64   53. 121

1.3 Getting Ready to Practice (p. 18)
1. base; 27   3. exponent; 1

1.3 Practice and Problem Solving (pp. 18–19)
7. 8^2 9. 9^4 11. 7^4 13. *Sample answer:* 4^3 means
$4 \times 4 \times 4$, not 4×3; $4 \times 4 \times 4 = 64$.   15. 144
17. 10,000   19. 32   21. 1   23. 64   25. 1000
27. 1,000,000   29. 1, 1, 1; the value is 1.   31. 4^3
33. 10^3 35. 5^3 37. 25^5 39. 64 tiles   41. 84 people
43. 8, 5   45. 200   47. 350   49. tens   51. hundreds

1.3 Technology Activity (p. 20) 1. 390,625
3. 1,048,576   5. 2,825,761   7. 191,102,976
9. 42,144,192   11. 442,050,625   13. 19,683
15. 2,476,099   17. 1,048,576

1.4 Getting Ready to Practice (p. 23)
1. grouping symbols   3. 8   5. 8   7. 2

1.4 Practice and Problem Solving
(pp. 23–25) 9. 3   11. 6   13. 1   15. 24   17. 2   19. 3
21. 13   23. 4   25. 8   27. $18; multiply $4 by 3.

Subtract the product from $30.   29. *Sample
answer:* in order from left to right; The same rule
applies: multiply and divide in order from left to
right.   31. false; 13   33. true   35. true   41. 177
43. 14   45. 114   47. 188 seats   55. $7   57. $4 \times 4 \times
4 \times 4 = 256$ 59. $1 \times 1 \times 1 \times 1 \times 1 = 1$ 61. 4, 41,
404, 414

1.1–1.4 Notebook Review (pp. 26–27)
1. divide; subtract   2. base: 9; exponent: 5
3. 1135   4. 454   5. 1495   6. 64 R3
7–10. Estimates may vary.   7. 190   8. 470   9. 900
10. 68   11. 25   12. 64   13. 19   14. 8   15. High;
low; if both numbers are rounded up, the estimate
will be greater than the actual sum. If both
numbers are rounded down, the estimate will be
less than the actual sum.

1.5 Getting Ready to Practice (p. 31) 1. *a*
3. *Sample answer:* 3(2) means to multiply 3 and 2.
$3t = 3(2) = 6$ 5. 63   7. 11   9. 12   11. 15

1.5 Practice and Problem Solving
(pp. 31–33) 13. 16   15. 6   17. 5   19. 45   21. 7   23. 7
25. 3   27. 4 mi   29. 12 ft   31. 14 ft   33. 9   35. 2
37. 21   39. 15   41. 36   43. 4   45. 18 mi. *Sample
answer:* The speed, *r*, is 6 miles per hour and the
time, *t*, is 3 hours. Substitute these values into the
expression $r \cdot t$ and multiply.   47. my friend; me
49. 9   51. 20   53. 33   55. 28   59. 26   61. 3   63. $\times$;
+; $\times$. *Sample answer:* Guess, Check, and Revise;
it is the best choice of the strategies listed.
65. true   67. true   69. false; 6   71. true

1.6 Problem Solving Strategies (p. 35)
1. 7 pots of tulips and 5 pots of daffodils
3. 8 questions worth 5 points and 5 questions worth
12 points   5. 18 ft   7. 3 months   9. $A - 6 = B$

1.6 Getting Ready to Practice (p. 38)
1. solution   3. 5 is a solution.   5. 5 is a solution.
7. 3   9. 10   11. 13   13. 9

1.6 Practice and Problem Solving
(pp. 39–40) 15. 3 is a solution.   17. 2 is not a
solution.   19. 9 is not a solution.   21. 7 is not a
solution.   23. 8 is a solution.   29. 14   31. 8   33. 3

35. 9 **37.** 13 **39.** 11 **41.** 0 **43.** The 0 in the second line should be 1. $5x = 5$; $5(1) = 5$; So, 1 is the solution. **45–53.** Methods will vary. **45.** 12 is not a solution. **47.** 8 is not a solution. **49.** 18 is not a solution. **51.** 7 is a solution. **53.** 26 is not a solution. **55.** 60 h **61.** about 1200 people **63.** 24 **65.** 6 **67.** $20 \div 2$

1.7 Getting Ready to Practice (p. 44)

1. Step 1: Read and Understand: Read the problem carefully. Identify the question and any important information. Step 2: Make a Plan: Decide on a problem solving strategy. Step 3: Solve the Problem: Use the problem solving strategy to answer the question. Step 4: Look Back: Check that your answer is reasonable.

1.7 Practice and Problem Solving

(pp. 44–45) **3.** 7 posts **5.** $277 **7.** 6 and 4 **9.** *Sample answer:* Have 6 people represent adults. Give each of these people $12. Have 4 people represent children. Give each of these people $7. Put all of the money together and count it to find the total cost. **11.** 6 tickets **13.** 8 people; 10 people **15.** 17^2 **17.** 8^4 **19.** 8 **21.** 10 **23.** 20,000 **25.** 900,000

1.5–1.7 Notebook Review (pp. 46–47)

1. variable **2.** Yes; because $3 \cdot 5 = 15$. **3.** 25 **4.** 2 **5.** 6 **6.** 6 **7.** 1 **8.** 8 **9.** $140 **10.** No; any number times 0 is always 0. **11.** *Sample answer:* It helps you to make sure your answer is reasonable.

Chapter Review (pp. 48–49) **1.** order of operations **3.** base **5.** equation **7.** 1113 **9.** 525 **11.** 78 R3 **13.** 413 **15.** add 9; 45, 54 **17.** subtract 10; 27, 17 **19–25.** Estimates may vary. **19.** 400 **21.** 20 **23.** 1800 **25.** 400 **27.** 343 **29.** 625 **31.** 169 **33.** 2500 **35.** 5 **37.** 6 **39.** 80,000 **41.** 3 **43.** 3 **45.** 4 **47.** 10 **49.** 9 **51.** 7 **53.** 15 **55.** 25 **57.** 66 in. **59.** 5 **61.** 0 **63.** 60 **65.** 4 **67.** $3.20

Chapter 2

2.1 Getting Ready to Practice (p. 58) **1.** ft
3. cm **5.** Answers may vary. **7.** miles; kilometers

2.1 Practice and Problem Solving

(pp. 58–60) **9.** 2 in. **11.** 38 mm; 4 cm **17.** miles; kilometers **19.** feet or yards; meters **21.** inches; centimeters **23.** feet; meters **25–29.** Sample answers are given. **25.** 3 elbow to knuckle units; 3 ft **27.** 26 paper clips; 26 in. **29.** 45 little fingers; 45 cm **31.** *Sample answer:* The left end of the eraser is not lined up at the mark for 0. The length of the eraser is about 2 inches. **33.** reasonable **35.** not reasonable; millimeters **41.** *Sample answer:* It will depend on how close the width of the table and the width of the doorway are to each other. If they are very close, then an actual measurement is needed. If they are not close, then an estimate is sufficient. **43.** A good answer should mention a benchmark that is familiar to students and about 1 mile long. *Sample answer:* Imagine how long the distance is in the chosen benchmark. **45.** 16 **47.** 14 **49.** 12 in., 12 in., and 8 in. *Sample answer:* I used Guess, Check, and Revise because I thought guessing the lengths of the sides and then checking to see if they worked was the easiest strategy to use.

2.2 Getting Ready to Practice (p. 63)

1. perimeter; area **3.** $P = 18$ ft; $A = 14$ ft^2 **5.** Step 1: perimeter; Step 2: $64 = 4s$; Step 3: 16 ft

2.2 Practice and Problem Solving

(pp. 64–65) **7.** area **9.** $P = 20$ in; $A = 21$ in.^{2} **11.** $P = 32$ yd; $A = 64$ yd^2 **13.** $P = 72$ ft; $A = 323$ ft^2 **15.** area **17.** perimeter **19.** 1600 ft^2 **21.** $42 = l \cdot 3$; 14 in. **23.** $100 = 4s$; 25 ft **25.** The square has an area of 64 square inches and the rectangle has an area of 128 square inches. The area of the rectangle is twice the area of the square. **27.** No; a low estimate for the area of the lawn is $30 \cdot 50 = 1500$ square feet, which is exactly the area the fertilizer will cover. **29.** *Sample answer:* One rectangle has sides of length 3 and 5, while the second rectangle has sides of length 2 and 6. **31.** 48 ft^2 **33.** 64 **35.** 1000 **37.** 3 cm **39.** *Sample answer:* 1500

2.3 Problem Solving Strategies (p. 67)

1. 7 yd by 1 yd, 6 yd by 2 yd, 5 yd by 3 yd, 4 yd by 4 yd **3.** *Sample answer:* Place the 5 centimeter rod end to end with the 7 centimeter rod to make a 12 centimeter rod. Use the difference between this combination and the 13 centimeter rod to measure 1 centimeter. **5.** 1 mi **7.** 6 **9.** any animal name that has three letters in it, such as "cat"

2.3 Getting Ready to Practice (p. 70)
1. Each inch on the scale drawing represents 40 miles on the actual object. **3.** 3 cm **5.** 10 cm

2.3 Practice and Problem Solving

(pp. 70–71) **7.** 300 mi **9.** 750 mi **11.** 6 cm **13.** 2 in. **15.** 7 in. **17.** *Sample answer:* The actual length of 20 feet corresponds to 5 feet in the scale. So you should multiply 2 inches by 4, and the length of the model is 8 inches.

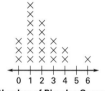

The length of the model is 8 inches.
19. 5 cm **21.** 4500 m **23.** 20; 120 times taller **25.** reasonable **27.** 0, 1, 3, 4, 8, 16 **29.** 11, 14, 22, 23, 25

2.4 Getting Ready to Practice (p. 74)
1. frequency **3.**

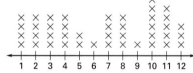

Number of Bicycles Owned

2.4 Practice and Problem Solving

(pp. 74–75)

5.

Type of call	Tally	Frequency
building fires	卌 I	6
other fires	卌 卌 II	12
hazardous materials	卌 II	7
rescues	III	3
false alarms	卌 II	7
mutual aid	IIII	4

7. 39 calls

9.

Point values of shots	Tally	Frequency
1	卌 II	7
2	卌 卌 I	11
3	III	3

2 occurs most often and 3 occurs least often.

Number of Shots with Given Value

11. *Sample answer:* The frequency table is easier to use to find the number of occurrences. The line plot is easier to use to see the items that occurred most or least often. **13.** 4 days **15.** No. *Sample answer:* The items being tallied are not numbers, so a line plot cannot be used to display the data. **17.** Check line plots of birth months of classmates.

Birth Months of United States Presidents

19. 2 more students **21.** 0, 7, 14, 21, 28, 35 **23.** 0, 20, 40, 60, 80, 100

2.1–2.4 Notebook Review (pp. 76–77)
1. The area of a figure is the amount of surface the figure covers. The perimeter of a figure is the distance around the figure. **2.** $P = 28$ in.; $A = 49$ in.^{2} **3.** 4 in.; 4 in. **4.** 64 m **5.** 96 m **6.** 64 m **7.** 192 m

8.

Number	Tally	Frequency
10	II	2
11	III	3
12	III	3
13	III	3
14	I	1
15	III	3

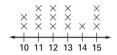

9. A good situation for an estimate will be one in which an exact measurement is not needed, such as the distance between a city in California and a city in New York. **10.** Frequency tables and line plots are similar in that they both tell how frequent a number occurs. They are different in that the frequency table makes it easier to see the number of occurrences, whereas the line plot makes it easier to see which item occurred most or least often.

2.5 Getting Ready to Practice (p. 81)

1. *Sample answer:* Start the scale at 0 and end at a value greater than the greatest data value. Use equal increments along the scale.

3.
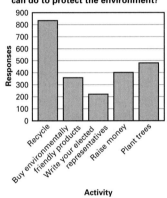

2.5 Practice and Problem Solving
(pp. 81–82) **5.**
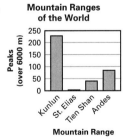

7.
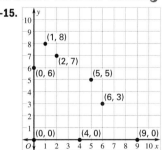

9. ice cream   **11.** *Sample answer:* If the greatest data value in the scale is much greater than the actual greatest data value and the increments are too large, the differences in the bars will seem to be less than they really are.   **15.** 4   **17.** 8
19. \$4.75   **21.** \$2.25

2.6 Getting Ready to Practice (p. 85) **1.** *C*
3. *E*   **5.** 160; 200   **7.** No. *Sample answer:* They watched less television from 1992 to 1996, and then more television from 1996 to 2000.

2.6 Practice and Problem Solving
(pp. 85–86) **8–15.**
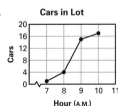

17.
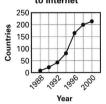

19.
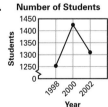

21. Countries Connected to Internet   about 125 countries

23. 127 beats per minute **25.** 2 inches on the map represents 15 miles on the ground. **27.** 18 **29.** 75

2.6 Technology Activity (p. 87)
1.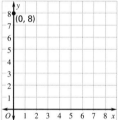

2.7 Getting Ready to Practice (p. 89)
5. Look at the sections for ages from 0 to 34. They make up about half of the circle, which means they make up about half of the population.

2.7 Practice and Problem Solving
(pp. 90-91) **7.** A **9.** Arctic Ocean **11.** 335 million km^2 **13.** 148 doubles **15.** 108 home runs **17.** $160,000 **19.** about $1900 **21.** fall; bar graph **23.** 276 people **27.** 6 **29.**

31. 156 **33.** 225

2.8 Getting Ready to Practice (p. 95)
1. range; median **3.** mean = 8, median = 8, mode = 8, range = 5 **5.** Step 1: mean = 26, median = 23, mode = 21; Step 2: The mean is a little higher than the typical age; the median represents the data well; the mode is a little lower than the typical age. Step 3: median

2.8 Practice and Problem Solving
(pp. 95-97) **7.** mean = 11, median = 9, mode = 5, range = 20 **9.** mean = 31, median = 33, modes = 25 and 37, range = 24 **11.** mean = 40, median = 30, mode = 30, range = 70 **13.** mean = 155, median = 175, mode = 180; *Sample answer:* The median or the mode is the best average to represent a typical score because either is closer to the middle of the set. **15.** mean = 73, median = 73, mode = 77, range = 10 **17.** green **19.** No;

no; the data sets are not numerical. **21.** 832 **23.** No; 8; the mean given is too close to the least data value. **25.** No; 16; the mean given is too close to the greatest data value. **27.** true **29.** false **31.** A good answer should include these two points for each of the three averages. • The data set listed should actually have the average given. • The context should make it very clear that the given average is most descriptive of the data set. **35.** 25 people **37.** thirty-five **39.** six hundred seven

2.5–2.8 Notebook Review (pp. 98–99)
1. ordered pair **2.** Add the values and divide by the number of values. **3.** *Sample answer:* Start the scale at 0 and end the scale at 16, using equal increments of 2.

4. 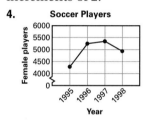 **5.**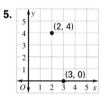

6. Lake Ontario **7.** mean = 50, median = 45, modes = 39 and 45, range = 43 **8.** *Sample answer:* Start the scale at 0 and end the scale at a value greater than the greatest data value, using equal increments along the scale. **9.** *Sample answer:* Data values that are much less or much greater than most of the other data values can make the mean less or greater than the average that best represents the data.

Chapter Review (pp. 100–101)
1. The answer should include any three of the following: inch, foot, yard, mile. **3.** false **5.** coordinate **7.** median; median; mean **9.** feet or yards; meters **11.** miles; kilometers **13.** paper clip; 3 in. **15.** *Sample answer:* 3 little fingers; 35 mm; 4 cm **17.** $P = 36$ yd; $A = 81$ yd^2 **19.** 256 in. **21.**

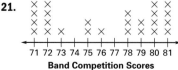

23–26.

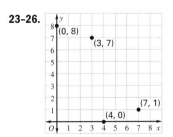

27.

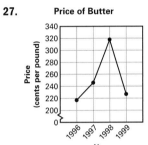

29. 20 more wins   **31.** mean = 120, median = 100, mode = 100, range = 130   **33.** Median. *Sample answer:* It is the closest to most of the data.

Chapter 3

3.1 Getting Ready to Practice (p. 109)
1. hundredths   **3.** hundred-thousandths
5. *Sample answer:* There is no *and* after "hundred," so the number should have a zero to the left of the decimal point. The answer should be 0.412.   **7.** 6.009   **9.** eight and fourteen ten-thousandths   **11.** twenty-four and six thousandths

3.1 Practice and Problem Solving
(pp. 109–111) **13.** 7   **15.** 15; 150   **21.** 30.15
23. 0.705   **25.** 86.0143   **27.** four and sixteen hundredths   **29.** seventeen and twenty-two thousandths   **31.** ten and two hundred fifty-five ten-thousandths   **33.** 1.99 km   **35.** $.20
37. $.70   **39.** 0.09; 0.002   **41.** 0.007; 0.0002
43. one and five hundredths carats

45.

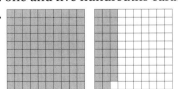

47. 14.76

49. 85.30   **51.** Russia   **55.** 5. *Sample answer:* I chose Draw a Diagram because it was easy to draw and label booths and spaces until the length is about 50 feet.   **57.** four million, twenty-seven thousand

3.2 Getting Ready to Practice (p. 115)
1. 0.01   **3.** 100   **5.** Step 1: 4 mm; Step 2: 0.4; Step 3: 2.4 cm

3.2 Practice and Problem Solving
(pp. 115–117) **7.** 5.02   **9.** 12.004   **11.** 0.88 m
13. *A*; 1.3 cm; *B*; 3.9 cm; *C*; 4.5 cm; *D*; 7.4 cm; *E*; 9.0 cm   **15.** 3.4 cm   **17.** 0.96 cm   **19.** 1.14 m
21. Answers may vary.   **23.** Answers may vary.
25. 1.372 m   **27.** 2 cm   **29.** greater than
31. equal to

3.3 Getting Ready to Practice (p. 120)
1. 7.55   **3.** 7.38   **5.** $2.79, $3.07, $3.29, $3.70, $3.79, $3.92

3.3 Practice and Problem Solving
(pp. 120–121) **7.** >   **9.** >   **11.** >   **13.** =   **15.** Yes; since 27.36 < 27.4, the book will stand upright.
17. 9.06, 9.07, 9.1   **19.** 0.1, 0.9, 1.1, 1.5   **21.** 0.98, 1.05, 1.15, 1.2   **23.** 0.055, 0.065, 0.55, 0.555, 0.56
25. Mauna Kea, Haleakala, West Maui, West Molokai   **27.** *Sample answer:* 8.7   **29.** *Sample answer:* 3.65   **33.** 28.0016   **35.** 107,000

3.1–3.3 Notebook Review (pp. 122–123)
1. hundredths   **2.** *Sample answer:* It separates the whole number part from the decimal part.
3. eleven and two tenths centimeters; 11.2 cm
4. twenty-six hundredths meter; 0.26 m   **5.** >   **6.** <
7. =   **8.** 0.082, 0.09, 0.75, 0.91, 0.94   **9.** *Sample answer:* Five hundred ten-thousandths means the last digit in the decimal is in the ten-thousandths' place. Five hundred ten thousandths means the last digit in the decimal is in the thousandths' place.   **10.** *Sample answer:* The last 0 in 0.50 represents 0 hundredths. Since 50 hundredths and 5 tenths represent the same part of one whole, they are equal.

3.4 Getting Ready to Practice (p. 126)
1. 2; 0.02   **3.** 1; 0.001   **5.** 8.2   **7.** 10.629
9. 8,400,000; 8.4 million

3.4 Practice and Problem Solving

(pp. 127–128) **11.** 10 **13.** 1.4 **15.** 3 **17.** 9.0
19. 3.90 **21.** 7.296 **23.** 0.03 **25.** 0.009 **27.** 0.0002
29. 0.00010 **31.** *Sample answer:* because many of
the scores would round to 81 **33.** 15,900,000;
15.9 million **35.** 10,000,000; 10.0 million
37. 1.29 **39.** 1.71 **41.** California: 76,700,000,
76.7 million; Illinois: 41,900,000, 41.9 million;
New York: 62,000,000, 62.0 million; Ohio:
60,200,000, 60.2 million; Washington: 48,100,000,
48.1 million **43.** *Sample answer:* 3.9, 4.2, 4.45
45. *Sample answer:* 3.35, 3.42, 3.44 **49.** *Sample
answer:* 800 **51.** *Sample answer:* 310 **53.** =
55. 1926 **57.** 115

3.5 Getting Ready to Practice (p. 132)

1. 1 and 5 **3.** 18 **5.** Step 1: Check drawings. Step
2: 150 cm; Step 3: 150 centimeters is less than
157.16 centimeters, so they will fit beneath the
shelf.

3.5 Practice and Problem Solving

(pp. 132–133) **7.** 12 **9.** 2 **11.** 3 **13.** 8 **15.** 25
17. 0 **19.** $4.00; high; $1.15 was rounded down.
21. 15 **23.** 12 **25.** 11 **27.** Mount Kosciusko: 1.38,
Vinson Massif: 3.04, Mount Elbrus: 3.5, Mount
Kilimanjaro: 3.7, Mount McKinley: 3.85, Mount
Aconcagua: 4.33, Mount Everest: 5.50; 3.7 mi
29. *Sample answer:* The median; it is closer to
more of the heights than the mean is. **31.** 16
33. 5 **35.** 17.802 **37.** $12.00 **39.** $1.50

3.6 Problem Solving Strategies (p. 135)

1. 7 medals **3.** 3 buses **5.** no **7.** 652, 265, 256,
526, 562 **9.** $30

3.6 Getting Ready to Practice (p. 138)

1. commutative **3.** 18.64 **5.** 3.75 **7.** associative
property

3.6 Practice and Problem Solving

(pp. 139–140) **9.** 9.26 **11.** 24.54 **13.** 9.961 **15.** 3.26
17. 4.47 **19.** 2.76 **21.** 6.92 **23.** 5.74 **25.** 11.15
27. associative property; 19.5 **29.** commutative
property; 6.74 **31.** $4.76 **33.** 28.25 **35.** 21 cm
37. 12.3 m **39.** whistle

41.

Number	Tally	Frequency
0	I	1
1	IIII	4
2	II	2
3	IIII	4
4	III	3
5	IIII I	5
6	II	2
7	I	1
8	I	1
9	II	2

43. 168 **45.** 864

3.6 Technology Activity (p. 141) **1.** 7.385

3. 8.653 **5.** 4.852 **7.** 20.1 in. **9.** 7.514 mi

3.4–3.6 Notebook Review (pp. 142–143)

1. low **2.** commutative property **3.** 5.6
4. 3.047 **5.** 11 **6.** 7 **7.** 17 **8.** 16.298 **9.** 8.288
10. It increases the estimate and makes it more
accurate. **11.** *Sample answer:* With the decimal
points lined up, you add or subtract digits with
the same place value.

Chapter Review (pp. 144–145) **1.** fifteen

and three hundred sixty-eight thousandths
3. commutative property **5.** 12.2 **7.** 6.011 **9.** 4.4
11. 3.5 cm **13.** 17.02, 17.12, 17.20, 17.21 **15.** >
17. < **19.** = **21.** < **23.** 0.007 **25.** 1.61 **27.** 12
29. 4 **31.** 12 **33.** 9 **35.** 27 **37.** 18 **39.** 0.2 mi
41. $.68, $1.13, $1.49, $1.50, $1.62, $1.85; Paris;
London **43.** 5.98 **45.** 7.27 **47.** 8.143 **49.** 4.805
51. 5.63 **53.** 7.36 **55.** 12.657 **57.** 1.656

Chapter 4

4.1 Getting Ready to Practice (p. 155)

1. associative property of multiplication **3.** 15.60
5. 0.6; 6 tenths. **7.** 15.82; 15 and 82 hundredths.

4.1 Practice and Problem Solving

(pp. 156–157) **9.** 0.8; 8 tenths. **11.** 0.06; 6
hundredths. **13.** 7.857 **15.** *Sample answer:* There
should be four decimal places in the answer and

there are only three. The decimal point is in the wrong place. The correct product is 0.0112.
17. 19.53   **19.** 95.58   **21.** 17.6   **23.** 24.576
25. 31.875   **27.** 0.09   **29.** 83; associative
31. $338.45   **33.** $41.69   **35.** *Sample answer:* 24×1 is 24, which is less than the actual product.
37. *Sample answer:* It does not change the answer in any way or have any effect on the value of the number; if there is a digit in the tenths' place, there must be a digit in the hundredths' place to represent cents.   **39.** 15   **43.** 60   **45.** *Sample answer:* 14   **47.** *Sample answer:* 11   **49.** hundred
51. ten thousand

4.1 Technology Activity (p. 158)
1. $1474.48; $76,672.96   **3.** $1408.40; $73,236.80

4.2 Getting Ready to Practice (p. 161)
1. $2(3.1) + 2(7.4)$ **3.** 50, 7   **5.** 3.2, 8

4.2 Practice and Problem Solving
(pp. 161–162)   **7.** 332   **9.** 58   **11.** 67.2   **13.** 75
15. 271.8   **17.** 90.86   **19.** The 2 was distributed to the 32 and not to the 6. The solution should be $2(32 + 6) = 2(32) + 2(6) = 64 + 12 = 76.$
21. 7, 7   **23.** 60   **25.** 686   **27.** 369   **29.** 46
31. 48.3   **33.** $14.75   **35.** 5¢   **37.** 66 in.
39. $5x + 26$ **45.** 7.06, 7.6, 7.61, 7.63   **47.** 5.93
49. 2.528   **51.** 30,000

4.3 Getting Ready to Practice (p. 166)
1. sum   **3.** 0.8   **5.** 15.708   **7.** 17.325 ft^2

4.3 Practice and Problem Solving
(pp. 167–168)   **9.** 0.27   **11.** *Sample answer:* The original problem has two decimal places, so the answer should also have two decimal places. The solution should be

$$\begin{array}{r} 7.5 \\ \times\ 3.8 \\ \hline 6\ 00 \\ 22\ 5\ \\ \hline 28.50 \end{array}$$

13. 60.532   **15.** 0.18   **17.** 2.976   **19.** 14.3444
21. 14.95   **23.** 0.09008   **25.** 84.4262   **27.** 2.89 ft^2
29. 2.25 in.   **31.** >   **33.** <   **35.** no; 3.78   **37.** yes
39. ham: $4.12; cheese: $2.40; turkey: $5.31; total: $11.83   **41.** *Sample answer:* Use zero as a

placeholder when the number of decimal places needed is greater than the number of digits in the product. For example, $0.2 \times 0.036 = 0.0072$, where the two zeros before the 7 were added to create four decimal places.   **43.** Less than. *Sample answer:* A model can be used to show that the number of squares shaded for the product is less than the number of squares shaded for either of the two numbers.

45–48.

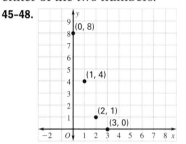

49. fifteen and two hundredths miles
51. 335   **53.** 15

4.4 Getting Ready to Practice (p. 171)
1. quotient   **3.** divisor   **5.** 4.4   **7.** 1.2

4.4 Practice and Problem Solving
(pp. 171–173)   **9.** 8.25   **11.** 1.75   **13.** 7.4   **15.** 0.7
17. 3.5   **19.** 4.8   **21.** 4.0   **23.** 6.7   **25.** 9.5   **27.** 1.9
29. 3.7 min   **31.** $9.80   **33.** $11.50   **35.** 0.308
37. 0.310   **39.** 0.4   **41.** 3.6   **43.** =   **45.** 8 tram cars
47. 11.25 mL. *Sample answer:* Exact; the experiment may not work if one has too much or too little.   **49.** 10   **51.** 0.01   **53.** 9   **55.** 2
57. 34.146   **59.** 8.3889   **61.** *Sample answer:* 790
63. *Sample answer:* 1000

4.1–4.4 Notebook Review (pp. 174–175)
1. distributive property   **2.** 5.226   **3.** 0.6   **4.** 12.48
5. 290   **6.** 184   **7.** 417   **8.** 153   **9.** 0.42   **10.** 40.392
11. 0.0852   **12.** 7.3   **13.** 6.5   **14.** 3.3   **15.** 0.2
16. *Sample answer:* Write 5.1 as $5 + 0.1$ and use the distributive property. So, $7(5 + 0.1) = 35 + 0.7 = 35.7$.   **17.** Add the number of decimal places in each of the two factors to find the number of decimal places in the product. Because $2 + 1 = 3$, the product has 3 decimal places.

4.5 Getting Ready to Practice (p. 178)
1. 10, 100   **3.** 75.8   **5.** 0.1635   **7.** 1.34   **9.** 521
11. 5670 in.^{2}

4.5 Practice and Problem Solving

(pp. 178–179) **17.** 743.4 **19.** 5020 **21.** 10
23. 0.03457 **25.** 1257 **27.** 317.25
29. 87,200 microns **31.** 375 **33.** 634 **35.** 9.1
37. 81,000 **39.** > **43.** 20.89 **45.** 1.27 **47.** 0.0896
49. 48.3042 **51.** $.09 **53.** $8.68

4.6 Getting Ready to Practice (p. 182)

1. dividend: 8.49, divisor: 0.3 **3.** 28)̄476 **5.** 21)̄0.4
7. 500 **9.** 2.05

4.6 Practice and Problem Solving

(pp. 182–184) **11.** 91 ÷ 43 **13.** 700 ÷ 38
15. 132 ÷ 55 **17.** 1390 ÷ 32 **19.** 80 **21.** 8.6
23. 3.1 **25.** 1.5 **27.** 75.7 **29.** 2.3 **31.** 365.76 cm.
Sample answer: Multiplication will show how long
the pictures are. **33.** 4.6 cm. *Sample answer:*
Division will give the width of the rectangle.
35. $1.11 **37.** $2.59 **39.** 0.03 **41.** 800 **43.** 108
45. 304.3 **47.** 32.5 mi/gal **49.** *Sample answer:*
1.8 + 1.7 = 3.5, 7.1 − 3.6 = 3.5, 1.75 × 2 = 3.5,
10.5 ÷ 3 = 3.5 **51.** 1.65 **53.** 13.18 **55.** 5.0 times
greater **57.** = **59.** < **63.** 6 **65.** 28 **67.** 3
69. 32.148 **71.** banana; 30 students
73. 95 students

4.7 Problem Solving Strategies (p. 186)

1. *Sample answer:* Jump rope 10 times.
3. 5 toothpicks **5.** 1 ft by 100 ft, 2 ft by 50 ft, 4 ft
by 25 ft, 5 ft by 20 ft, 10 ft by 10 ft **7.** 23 and 25

4.7 Getting Ready to Practice (p. 189)

1. capacity **3.** length **5.** kilogram **7.** capacity

4.7 Practice and Problem Solving

(pp. 189–190) **9.** mass **11.** capacity **13.** length
15. length **17.** nickel **19.** Grams. *Sample answer:*
It is closest to the mass of a paper clip. **21.** liter
23. kilogram **25.** milliliter **27.** Liters. *Sample
answer:* The amounts used would be closest
to the capacity of a large bottle of water.
29. 2886.8 L; 2.8868 kL **31.** 1000 **33.** 6000
35. 0.004 **39.** 0.093 **41.** 0.057 **43.** 0.374
45. *Sample answer:* 5 **47.** *Sample answer:* 100

4.8 Getting Ready to Practice (p. 193)

1. meter, gram, liter **3.** 0.52 **5.** 800

4.8 Practice and Problem Solving

(pp. 193–195) **7.** divide **9.** multiply **11.** 10
13. 1000 **15.** 0.8 **17.** 0.255 **19.** 4000 **21.** 800
23. 8100 **25.** 0.75 L **27.** 0.64 m **29.** < **31.** <
33. > **35.** arm span **37.** 7.26 kg; 5.98 kg; 2.72 kg;
6.79 kg **39.** mean = 4.998 kg, median = 5.25 kg,
mode = 2.72 kg. *Sample answer:* Mean; it is closer
to the middle of all the data. **41.** 1.44 km^2
43. The answer in square meters will be 1,000,000
times the answer in square kilometers. **45.** yes
49. 64 **51.** 64 **53.** 2.4 **55.** 32.618 **57.** 4.587
59. 3160 **61.** 101, 105, 110, 150

4.5–4.8 Notebook Review (pp. 196–197)

1. mass, capacity **2.** *Sample answer:* Multiply
both the divisor and the dividend by a power of 10
that will make the divisor a whole number.
3. 380.6 **4.** 4.591 **5.** 62.137 **6.** 97,800 **7.** 1069.0
8. 43.7 **9.** 23.8 **10.** 606.4 **11.** gram **12.** milliliter
13. 0.0245 **14.** 21,200 **15.** 2 **16.** divide; multiply

Chapter Review (pp. 198–199) **1.** distributive

property **3.** milliliter, liter, kiloliter **5.** multiply
7. 20.9 **9.** 144.532 **11.** 102 **13.** 1304.96
15. $130.50 **17.** 231 **19.** 16 **21.** 44.5 **23.** 235
25. 2.96 **27.** 0.5202 **29.** 0.0427 **31.** 2.6256
33. 12.645 **35.** 3.9483 **37.** 2.4 **39.** 6.9 **41.** 9.7
43. 4.1 **45.** 19.8 **47.** 1.6 **49.** 90 **51.** 12.5
53. $1.35 **55.** 24 **57.** 0.6569 **59.** 0.08147
61. 3.2 mm **63.** milligram **65.** milliliter
67. gram **69.** 0.729 **71.** 54,900 **73.** 17
75. 30,000 **77.** 2.7 mg, 0.027 kg, 270 g
79. 8 cm, 0.8 m, 8000 mm

Chapter 5

5.1 Getting Ready to Practice (p. 216)

1. *Sample answer:* All even numbers are divisible
by 2. **3.** *Sample answer:* A number is divisible by
5 if it ends in a 5 or a 0. **5.** composite **7.** prime
9. **11.**

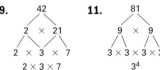

5.1 Practice and Problem Solving

(pp. 217–219) **13.** 1, 2, 7, 14 **15.** 1, 19 **17.** 1, 2, 4, 5,
10, 20, 25, 50, 100 **19.** 1, 11, 121 **21.** 140 is

divisible by 2, 5, and 10, but not by 3, 6, or 9.
23. 282 is divisible by 2, 3, and 6, but not by 5, 9, or 10.   **25.** 1578 is divisible by 2, 3, and 6, but not by 5, 9, or 10.   **27.** 8745 is divisible by 3 and 5, but not by 2, 6, 9, or 10.   **29.** prime   **31.** composite
33. prime   **35.** composite   **37.** Yes. *Sample answer:* 117 is divisible by 3.   **39.** 3×13 **41.** $3^2 \times 7$
43. 2×3^3 **45.** $2 \times 3 \times 5^2$ **49.** true   **51.** false
53. 2, 3, 4, or 6; 24, 16, 12, or 8   **55.** 2; *Sample answer:* if there are 2 students per team, there will be 24 teams in races of 6 teams. The winners of the 4 races will be in the runoff.   **57.** 30   **59.** 90
61. 53×67 **65.** 296   **67.** 216   **69.** 32.1   **71.** 3.0
73. 103 stickers

5.2 Problem Solving Strategies (p. 221)
1. 4 possibilities   **3.** 5 ways   **5.** 6 code words
7. 12 tacks   **9.** No; the cars will only hold 20 people and they need to hold 21 people.

5.2 Getting Ready to Practice (p. 224)
1. 2   **3.** 15

5.2 Practice and Problem Solving
(pp. 224–225) **5.** The factor of 14 is not included in the factors of 28. So the GCF is 14.   **7.** 12
9. 11   **11.** 8   **13.** 18   **15.** 4   **17.** 1   **19.** 8   **21.** 13
23. 16 people   **25.** sometimes   **27.** always
33. 0.0005   **35.** 900   **37.** $\frac{3}{8}$

5.3 Getting Ready to Practice (p. 230) **1.** yes
3. no; $\frac{1}{3}$ **9.** blue: $\frac{5}{18}$; orange: $\frac{1}{2}$; green: $\frac{2}{9}$

5.3 Practice and Problem Solving
(pp. 231–232) **11–17.** Answers may vary.
11. $\frac{2}{20}, \frac{3}{30}$ **13.** $\frac{6}{10}, \frac{9}{15}$ **15.** $\frac{18}{40}, \frac{27}{60}$ **17.** $\frac{6}{200}, \frac{9}{300}$
19. 45   **21.** 4   **23.** 54   **25.** 7   **27.** no; $\frac{1}{3}$ **29.** yes
31. no; $\frac{8}{9}$ **33.** no; $\frac{2}{7}$ **35.** $\frac{1}{2}$ **37.** 5   **39.** 54
41. $\frac{1}{16}$ **43.** sometimes   **49.** 2   **51.** 4   **53.** $\frac{4}{12}$.
Sample answer: I used Make a Table to solve the problem so I could keep track of the numerators and denominators and their relationships.
55. 1200   **57.** 120,000

5.1–5.3 Notebook Review (pp. 233–234)
1. prime number   **2.** 3, 9, composite number
3. 49 is not divisible by 2, 3, 5, 6, 9, or 10.   **4.** 252 is divisible by 2, 3, 6, and 9, but not by 5 or 10.
5. 396 is divisible by 2, 3, 6, and 9, but not by 5 or 10.   **6.** 1402 is divisible by 2, but not by 3, 5, 6, 9, or 10.   **7.** 12   **8.** 27   **9.** $\frac{1}{7}$ **10.** $\frac{2}{3}$ **11.** $\frac{5}{16}$ **12.** $\frac{4}{9}$
13. *Sample answer:* You can use the rules to quickly determine a factor of a number.
14. *Sample answer:* 8 and 16; multiplied 8 by two different numbers.

5.4 Getting Ready to Practice (p. 237)
1. 7, 14, 21   **3.** 11, 22, 33   **5.** 96   **7.** Step 1: 6, 12, 18, 24, 30, 36, . . .; 3, 6, 9, 12, 15, 18, 21, . . .; Step 2: 6, 12, 18; Step 3: game 6; 3 times

5.4 Practice and Problem Solving
(pp. 237–238) **9.** 40   **11.** 60   **13.** 16   **15.** 72   **17.** 84
19. 396   **21.** 135   **23.** 360   **25.** 300th customer; find the LCM of 20 and 75.   **27.** 3 and 17   **29.** 4 and 16
31. 2.056   **33.** 54.5   **35.** 0.25   **37.** *Sample answer:* $\frac{6}{20}, \frac{9}{30}$ **39.** *Sample answer:* $\frac{24}{34}, \frac{36}{51}$ **41.** >   **43.** <

5.5 Getting Ready to Practice (p. 241)
1. the least common multiple of the denominators
3. 6; >   **5.** 20; <

5.5 Practice and Problem Solving
(pp. 241–242) **7.** >   **9.** >   **11.** >   **13.** <   **15.** =   **17.** >
19. $\frac{7}{8}$ in. album   **21.** $\frac{5}{8}, \frac{2}{3}, \frac{3}{4}$ **23.** $\frac{4}{5}, \frac{17}{20}, \frac{9}{10}$
25. $\frac{5}{9}, \frac{7}{12}, \frac{3}{4}$ **27.** $\frac{3}{8}, \frac{4}{9}, \frac{11}{24}$ **29.** The bracelet containing $\frac{2}{3}$ gold.   **31.** Africa   **33.** South America
37. 12,000   **39.** $\frac{1}{4}$ **41.** $\frac{2}{5}$ **43.** 137   **45.** 1402

5.6 Getting Ready to Practice (p. 246)
1. A fraction is improper if its numerator is greater than or equal to its denominator.   **3.** 13   **5.** 3
7. =   **9.** <

5.6 Practice and Problem Solving
(pp. 247–248) **11.** $2\frac{1}{8}$ in.; $\frac{17}{8}$ in.   **13.** $\frac{9}{2}$ **15.** $\frac{17}{5}$
17. $\frac{23}{3}$ **19.** $\frac{21}{2}$ **21.** $2\frac{2}{3}$ **23.** $3\frac{3}{5}$ **25.** $6\frac{1}{2}$ **27.** $1\frac{5}{7}$

29. $2\frac{3}{4}, 3, \frac{7}{2}$　**31.** $5, \frac{41}{8}, 5\frac{1}{6}, \frac{17}{3}$　**33.** $\frac{6}{6}$　**35.** $\frac{14}{14}$

37. *Sample answer:* $1\frac{4}{5}$　**39.** *Sample answer:* $3\frac{1}{4}$

43. 19　**45.** 18　**47.** twenty-three and five tenths

49. seventy-eight and fifteen hundredths

51. 10,000　**53.** 4390

5.7 Getting Ready to Practice (p. 251)

1. When the GCF of the numerator and denominator is 1.　**3.** 27　**5.** 2　**7.** Write a mixed number with the whole number being 128 and the fraction $\frac{4}{10}$ which simplifies to $\frac{2}{5}$.

5.7 Practice and Problem Solving

(pp. 251–252) 9. $0.53; \frac{53}{100}$　**11.** $3.11; 3\frac{11}{100}$　**13.** $\frac{18}{25}$

15. $9\frac{3}{10}$　**17.** $3\frac{1}{100}$　**19.** $\frac{403}{500}$　**21.** $\frac{1}{40}$　**23.** $9\frac{401}{1000}$

25. clothing, food, gifts, electronics, furniture

27. $\frac{1177}{2500}$ in.　**33.** 0.7　**35.** 0.6　**37.** $\frac{11}{36}, \frac{1}{2}, \frac{13}{18}, \frac{5}{6}$

39. 300

5.8 Getting Ready to Practice (p. 255)

1. terminating　**3.** repeating　**5.** $0.\overline{1}$　**7.** $8.\overline{04}$

9. 0.4　**11.** 2.75　**13.** 0.67 lb

5.8 Practice and Problem Solving

(pp. 255–256) 15. 0.388888 . . .　**17.** 0.49159159 . . .

19. 0.8　**21.** 2.84　**23.** 3.75　**25.** $0.2\overline{7}$　**27.** $5.\overline{8}$

29. $0.58\overline{3}$　**31.** $1\frac{3}{4}; 1.75$　**33.** 0.92; 0.08　**35.** true

37. $0.\overline{09}, 0.\overline{18}, 0.\overline{27}; 0.\overline{36}, 0.\overline{45}$　**39.** 0.5　**41.** 2.000

43. grams　**45.** milligrams　**47.** $2^2 \times 17$

49. $2^3 \times 3^2 \times 7$　**51.** *Sample answer:* 10,000

5.8 Technology Activity (p. 257) 1. 0.83

3. 0.31　**5.** 5.38　**7.** 13.39　**9.** 29.19　**11.** 50.82

13. $13.38

5.4–5.8 Notebook Review (pp. 258–259)

1. Multiples of 6: 6, 12, 18, 24, 30, 36, 42, 48, 54, 60, 66, 72, 78, 84, 90, 96; multiples of 8: 8, 16, 24, 32, 40, 48, 56, 64, 72, 80, 88, 96; no; the LCM of 6 and 8 is 24, not 48.　**2.** repeating decimal

3. $\frac{7}{25}, \frac{3}{10}, \frac{2}{5}, \frac{7}{10}$　**4.** $1\frac{1}{4} < \frac{5}{3}$　**5.** $\frac{7}{2} > 3\frac{1}{8}$　**6.** $\frac{13}{20}$

7. 2.65　**8.** Find the smallest of all of the common multiples; use the prime factorization and multiply together the prime factors, using each the greatest number of times it is a factor of any of the numbers. *Sample answer:* Use prime factorization if the numbers are large and list multiples if the numbers are small.　**9.** Yes. *Sample answer:* It is hard to compare them in different forms.

Chapter Review (pp. 260–261) 1. a multiple

shared by two or more numbers　**3.** *Sample answer:* 2, 3, 5; their only factors are 1 and itself.

5. equivalent　**7.** proper fraction　**9.** 150 is divisible by 2, 3, 5, 6, and 10, but not by 9.　**11.** 430 is divisible by 2, 5, and 10, but not by 3, 6, or 9.

13. 1464 is divisible by 2, 3, and 6, but not by 5, 9, or 10.　**15.** 2970 is divisible by 2, 3, 5, 6, 9, and 10.

17. $2^4 \times 5$　**19.** $2^2 \times 3^3$　**21.** $3^2 \times 23$　**23.** $3^2 \times 7^2$

25. 4　**27.** 5　**29.** 9　**31.** 13　**33.** no; $\frac{3}{8}$　**35.** no; $\frac{11}{31}$

37. 20　**39.** 76　**41.** 104　**43.** 40　**45.** 60 min　**47.** >

49. <　**51.** $\frac{5}{28}, \frac{3}{14}, \frac{1}{4}$　**53.** $\frac{1}{72}, \frac{1}{24}, \frac{1}{18}, \frac{1}{12}$　**55.** $\frac{21}{5}$

57. $2\frac{5}{9}$　**59.** $4\frac{4}{5}$　**61.** $\frac{121}{200}$　**63.** 3.4　**65.** 2.125

Chapter 6

6.1 Getting Ready to Practice (p. 269)

1. Fractions; whole number　**3.** 0　**5.** 4

7. *Sample answer:* 7　**9.** *Sample answer:* $\frac{1}{2}$

6.1 Practice and Problem Solving

(pp. 269–270) 11. 1　**13.** 4　**15–25.** Estimates may vary.　**15.** 0　**17.** 0　**19.** 1　**21.** 5　**23.** 5　**25.** 3

27. 5 c　**29.** high estimate; so that you will not run out of paint　**31.** high　**33.** low　**37.** 5　**39.** 6

41. $\frac{8}{3}$　**43.** $\frac{33}{4}$　**45.** 1012　**47.** 577

6.2 Getting Ready to Practice (p. 273)

1. numerators; common denominator　**3.** $1\frac{1}{5}$

5. $\frac{3}{4}$

6.2 Practice and Problem Solving

(pp. 273–275) 7. $\frac{2}{3}$　**9.** $\frac{7}{9}$　**11.** $\frac{1}{2}$　**13.** $\frac{1}{2}$　**15.** $1\frac{1}{7}$

17. $\frac{5}{8}$　**19.** $1\frac{4}{7}$　**21.** $\frac{4}{5}$　**23.** $\frac{1}{2}$ of the drawing

25. $1\frac{1}{2}$ ft   **27.** 1 mi   **29.** $\frac{1}{4}$ **31.** $\frac{1}{2}$ **33.** 1   **35.** $\frac{21}{25}$
37. $\frac{3}{100}$ **41.** 10   **43.** 36   **45.** 195   **47.** 2430

6.3 Getting Ready to Practice (p. 279)
1. LCD   **3.** $1\frac{1}{18}$ **5.** $\frac{1}{2}$

6.3 Practice and Problem Solving
(pp. 279–281) **7.** $\frac{5}{9}$ **9.** $\frac{11}{30}$ **11.** $1\frac{5}{14}$ **13.** $\frac{5}{12}$ **15.** $\frac{11}{12}$
17. $\frac{23}{40}$ **19.** $\frac{2}{3}$ **21.** $\frac{13}{28}$ **23.** $\frac{1}{5}$ in.   **25.** $\frac{5}{6}$ **27.** $\frac{1}{6}$ **29.** $\frac{1}{9}$
31. $1\frac{1}{12}$ **33.** $1\frac{7}{8}$ in.   **35.** $1\frac{3}{14}$ yd   **37.** $\frac{1}{12}$ **39.** $\frac{8}{15}$
41. central and southern regions   **43.** *Sample answer:* Yes, as long as he or she adds the fractions $\frac{6}{8}$ and $\frac{4}{8}$ and then simplifies the answer of $\frac{10}{8}$ to $1\frac{1}{4}$.
45. $1\frac{5}{12}$ **51.** $1\frac{1}{5}$ **53.** $1\frac{1}{2}$ **55.** 450, 455, 504, 540, 545

6.1–6.3 Notebook Review (pp. 282–283)
1. *Sample answer:* Since $\frac{1}{2}$ is halfway between 3 and 4, round up to 4.   **2.** 24   **3–6.** Estimates may vary.   **3.** 1   **4.** $\frac{1}{2}$ **5.** 1   **6.** 6   **7.** $\frac{2}{3}$ **8.** $1\frac{1}{2}$
9. $\frac{2}{5}$ **10.** $\frac{1}{4}$ **11.** $\frac{9}{10}$ **12.** $1\frac{1}{8}$ **13.** $\frac{13}{28}$ **14.** $\frac{1}{18}$
15. Half. *Sample answer:* Each estimate will be within $\frac{1}{4}$ of the actual value, rather than $\frac{1}{2}$.
16. No. As long as you use a common denominator, you can get the correct answer.

6.4 Getting Ready to Practice (p. 286)   **1.** $2\frac{3}{4}$
3. $4\frac{3}{4}$ **5.** $3\frac{5}{7}$ **7.** $6\frac{1}{4}$ **9.** $1\frac{2}{5}$ **11.** $3\frac{3}{4}$ **13.** $1\frac{5}{12}$ ft

6.4 Practice and Problem Solving
(pp. 287–288) **15.** $10\frac{1}{3}$ **17.** $7\frac{9}{10}$ **19.** $10\frac{5}{12}$
21. $16\frac{1}{9}$ **23.** $3\frac{7}{12}$ **25.** $2\frac{7}{12}$ **27.** $1\frac{5}{8}$ in.
29. $11\frac{14}{15}$; pencil and paper   **31.** $9\frac{5}{6}$; mental math

33. 8; mental math   **35.** 4; mental math   **37.** $7\frac{1}{3}$
39. $\frac{1}{2}$ **41.** $3\frac{1}{2}$ **43.** $1\frac{1}{4}$ **45.** $37\frac{1}{2}$ cents   **47.** $6\frac{1}{12}$; answers may vary.   **49.** $10\frac{1}{2}$ ft   **51.** <   **53.** <   **55.** $\frac{1}{2}$
57. $\frac{1}{24}$ **59.** 190,000   **61.** 8,900,000

6.5 Getting Ready to Practice (p. 292)
1. 7   **3.** 4   **5.** $1\frac{1}{3}$ **7.** $1\frac{3}{4}$ **9.** $9\frac{3}{4}$ mi

6.5 Practice and Problem Solving
(pp. 292–294) **11.** $2\frac{1}{2}$ **13.** $4\frac{5}{7}$ **15.** $2\frac{1}{8}$ **17.** $9\frac{7}{15}$
19. $1\frac{9}{14}$ **21.** $\frac{3}{4}$ **23.** $1\frac{3}{4}$ mi   **25.** *Sample answer:* $4\frac{2}{5}$
should be renamed as $3\frac{7}{5}$; the solution should be
$4\frac{2}{5} - 1\frac{4}{5} = 3\frac{7}{5} - 1\frac{4}{5} = 2\frac{3}{5}$.   **27.** Yes; you cannot
subtract $\frac{5}{6}$ from $\frac{1}{2}$.   **29.** Yes; you cannot subtract $\frac{5}{7}$
from $\frac{4}{7}$.   **31.** No; you can subtract 0 from $\frac{2}{5}$.
33. Yes; you cannot subtract $\frac{3}{4}$ from $\frac{2}{3}$.   **35.** $\frac{1}{4}$
37. $\frac{1}{8}$ **39.** $\frac{1}{3}$ ft   **41.** $1\frac{1}{3}$ **43.** $1\frac{19}{20}$ **45.** $4\frac{1}{6}$ **47.** $\frac{3}{4}$
49. $21\frac{3}{4}$ in.   **51.** $19\frac{1}{2}$ in.   **55.** $5\frac{1}{9}$ **57.** $3\frac{3}{4}$ **59.** 3.3 m.
Sample answer: I used Draw a Diagram because the picture helped me see what I needed to find.
61. 4; 50   **63.** 660

6.5 Technology Activity (p. 295) **1.** The A4 size
is $2\frac{3}{8}$ inches wider and $3\frac{5}{12}$ inches longer.
3. The two sizes are the same width, and the U.S. legal size is 3 inches longer.

6.6 Problem Solving Strategies (p. 297)
1. 79 points   **3.** 60   **5.** Wednesday   **7.** Row 1: remove 8; Row 2: remove 3; Row 3: remove 6
9. 32 yd^2

6.6 Getting Ready to Practice (p. 300)
1. 2   **3.** 5   **5.** 1 h 36 min   **7.** 6 h 31 min 22 sec
9. 5 h 15 min

6.6 Practice and Problem Solving

(pp. 300–301) **11.** 3 h 25 min **13.** 5 h 33 min 35 sec
15. 2 h 15 min **17.** 2 h **19.** 4 h 35 min
21. 7 h 50 min **23.** 6 h 20 min **25.** 1 h 35 min
27. yes **29.** 10:05 P.M. **31.** yes **33.** no **35.** $\frac{3}{4}$
37. $1\frac{11}{18}$ **39.** 320 **41.** 1800

6.4–6.6 Notebook Review (pp. 302–303)

1. *Sample answer:* 3 can be rewritten as $2\frac{3}{3}$, so $3\frac{1}{3}$
is equal to $2\frac{4}{3}$. **2.** elapsed time **3.** $8\frac{5}{7}$ **4.** $9\frac{7}{24}$
5. $5\frac{5}{14}$ **6.** $5\frac{2}{3}$ **7.** $2\frac{7}{12}$ **8.** $2\frac{13}{15}$ **9.** $1\frac{3}{8}$ **10.** $1\frac{2}{5}$
11. 6 h 15 min **12.** 8 h 15 min **13.** *Sample
answer:* Sometimes you have to rename.

Chapter Review (pp. 304–305) **1.** half, mixed
numbers **3.** elapsed time **5-13.** Estimates may
vary. **5.** $1\frac{1}{2}$ **7.** 1 **9.** 12 **11.** 3 **13.** 5 h **15.** $1\frac{2}{3}$
17. $\frac{3}{5}$ **19.** $\frac{3}{5}$ **21.** $\frac{1}{10}$ **23.** $\frac{1}{12}$ in. **25.** $8\frac{1}{7}$ **27.** $3\frac{17}{21}$
29. $11\frac{1}{2}$ **31.** $4\frac{13}{30}$ **33.** $2\frac{8}{9}$ **35.** $5\frac{7}{10}$ **37.** $1\frac{5}{16}$ lb
39. 4 h 40 min 7 sec **41.** 2 h **43.** 6 h 15 min
45. 6 h 4 min

Chapter 7

7.1 Getting Ready to Practice (p. 315) **1.** yes
3. $3\frac{1}{2}$ **5.** 15 **7.** 4 **9.** 6

7.1 Practice and Problem Solving

(pp. 316–317) **11.** $2\frac{4}{7}$ **13.** $7\frac{1}{2}$ **15.** $\frac{5}{6}$ **17.** $2\frac{1}{2}$ **19.** 6
21. 40 **23.** 40 min **25.** $2\frac{1}{2}$ mi **27.** 20; 5 **29.** 30; 12
31. 48; 42 **33.** 33; 22 **35.** Parks: 48 million acres;
Preserves: 21 million acres; Recreation areas:
3 million acres; Monuments and other: 3 million
acres **37.** High; yes. *Sample answer:* If the rack is
too large, it will still hold all of the CDs; however,
if it is too small, it will not hold all of them.
39. 100 **41.** 44 **43.** 95°F **49.** 1.3413 **51.** 0.04366
53. $\frac{1}{2}$ **55.** 0 **57.** $\frac{2}{3}$

7.2 Getting Ready to Practice (p. 323) **1.** if
the GCF of the numerator and denominator is 1

3. $\frac{3}{10}$ **5.** $\frac{7}{10}$ **7.** $\frac{2}{3}$ **9.** The GCF of 3 and 9 is 3, and
9 divided by 3 is 3, not 2. The solution is $\frac{5}{12}$.

7.2 Practice and Problem Solving

(pp. 323–325) **11.** $\frac{4}{21}$ **13.** $\frac{3}{16}$ **15.** $\frac{3}{20}$ **17.** $\frac{4}{45}$ **19.** $\frac{1}{35}$
21. $\frac{6}{55}$ **23.** $\frac{2}{15}$ **25.** $\frac{1}{4}$ **27.** $\frac{1}{2}$ **29.** $\frac{3}{5}$ **31.** $\frac{5}{16}$ **33.** $\frac{1}{7}$
35. $\frac{3}{8}$ mi **37.** < **39.** = **41.** < **43.** $\frac{11}{12}$ **45.** $\frac{9}{50}$
47. $\frac{4}{13}$ **49.** $\frac{5}{28}$ **53.** 3 **55.** 4 **57.** 10 **59.** 18
61. *Sample answer:* 1000

7.3 Getting Ready to Practice (p. 328)

1. *Sample answer:* $2\frac{1}{2}$; $\frac{5}{4}$ **3.** no **5.** Yes; divide 9
into 18 and 9, and divide 5 into 25 and 10. **7.** 34
9. $2\frac{11}{12}$

7.3 Practice and Problem Solving

(pp. 328–330) **11.** $\frac{11}{12}$ **13.** $11\frac{1}{3}$ **15.** $2\frac{11}{12}$ **17.** $3\frac{4}{15}$
19. $9\frac{1}{3}$ **21.** 2 **23.** $1\frac{1}{8}$ **25.** $22\frac{1}{2}$ **27.** 15 **29.** 16
31. $1\frac{1}{32}$ yd² **33.** 70 min **35.** $5\frac{3}{4}$ must be changed
to an improper fraction and then multiplied by 3.
The solution should be $3 \times \frac{23}{4} = \frac{69}{4} = 17\frac{1}{4}$.
37. $9\frac{1}{24}$ **39.** $14\frac{7}{12}$ **41.** 5 × 3. *Sample answer:*
With 5 × 3, one factor is rounded up and one is
rounded down, so the estimate will be better.
43. $5\frac{8}{25}$ in.² **45.** 24 ft **49.** 6 h 27 min
51. the number of groups

7.1–7.3 Notebook Review (pp. 331–332)

1. improper fractions **2.** 3; $3\frac{1}{6}$ **3.** 9; $8\frac{1}{4}$
4. 6; $5\frac{5}{8}$ **5.** 8; $8\frac{4}{7}$ **6.** $\frac{2}{7}$ **7.** $4\frac{2}{3}$ **8.** $5\frac{1}{4}$ **9.** $22\frac{1}{2}$
10. The product will be less than the whole
number if the fraction is less than 1, and greater
than the whole number if the fraction is greater
then 1 (an improper fraction).

7.4 Getting Ready to Practice (p. 336)

1. no **3.** yes **5.** $\frac{9}{2} \times \frac{4}{3} = 6$ **7.** $\frac{2}{3} \times \frac{1}{4} = \frac{1}{6}$

9. Step 1: $12 \div \frac{5}{8}$; Step 2: $19\frac{1}{5}$; Step 3: *Sample answer:* You can only make 19 magnets because you cannot make $\frac{1}{5}$ of a magnet.

7.4 Practice and Problem Solving

(pp. 336–338) **11.** $\frac{7}{3}$ **13.** $\frac{3}{1}$ or 3 **15.** $\frac{1}{10}$ **17.** $\frac{2}{7}$ **19.** $\frac{5}{8}$ **21.** 1 **23.** 5, 30 **25.** The dividend must be multiplied by the reciprocal of the divisor. The solution should be $\frac{3}{4} \div \frac{1}{8} = \frac{3}{4} \times \frac{8}{1} = 6$. **27.** $1\frac{11}{24}$ **29.** 14 **31.** $\frac{2}{5}$ **33.** $\frac{5}{9}$ **35.** $\frac{1}{20}$ **37.** $2\frac{7}{10}$ **39.** 45 mi/h **41.** 8 teacups; 5 mugs **43.** More teacups; it takes less clay to make a teacup. **45.** <; you are dividing $\frac{3}{5}$ into smaller parts. **47.** <; you are dividing 6 by a fraction greater than 1. **49.** $1\frac{2}{3}$ **51.** $1\frac{4}{5}$ **53.** $12 per hour **55.** 12 lots; cut in half **59.** *Sample answer:* 7 **61.** *Sample answer:* 5 **63.** 3 **65.** $4\frac{8}{9}$ **67.** $5.22 **69.** $7.61

7.5 Getting Ready to Practice (p. 341)

1. $\frac{8}{19}$ **3.** $\frac{7}{30}$; $\frac{7}{36}$ **5.** $\frac{3}{8}$; $5\frac{1}{4}$

7.5 Practice and Problem Solving

(pp. 341–343) **7.** $3\frac{3}{4} \div \frac{3}{4}$; 5 **9.** No. *Sample answer:* Mixed numbers must be converted to improper fractions before the reciprocal can be found. **11.** 39 **13.** $\frac{7}{10}$ **15.** $\frac{2}{15}$ **17.** $1\frac{3}{5}$ **19.** 7 **21.** $\frac{17}{31}$ **23.** 9 books **25.** *Sample answer:* 6 **27.** *Sample answer:* 7 **29.** $1\frac{3}{16}$ lb. *Sample answer:* Use subtraction to find the difference in weights. **31.** $5\frac{7}{8}$ ft. *Sample answer:* Use multiplication by one half to find half *of* the total length. **33.** divide by 2; $\frac{1}{32}$, $\frac{1}{64}$ **35.** greater than 1; 8 **37.** less than 1; $\frac{9}{10}$ **39.** $5\frac{1}{2}$ yd **41.** $2\frac{7}{40}$ **43.** $3\frac{3}{4} \div 31$ **45.** about 7 min **47.** $5\frac{7}{10}$ **51.** $9\frac{2}{7}$ **53.** $3\frac{5}{9}$ **55.** 38

7.6 Getting Ready to Practice (p. 346)

1. fluid ounces, cups, pints, quarts, gallons **3.** pounds **5.** cups or ounces

7.6 Practice and Problem Solving

(pp. 346–347) **11.** gallons **13.** cups **15.** gallons **17.** pints **19.** weight **21.** capacity **23.** capacity **25.** More than. *Sample answer:* A bathroom sink is larger than a quart of milk. **27.** Less than. *Sample answer:* An ice cube tray holds only about half a quart of water. **29.** *Sample answer:* 1 ounce: 5 quarters; 1 pound: loaf of bread; 1 ton: ten 200 lb men; 1 fluid ounce: 2 tablespoons; 1 cup: small glass; 1 pint: tall glass; 1 quart: large mayonnaise jar; 1 gallon: 2 rectangular cartons of ice cream **31.** 760 **33.** 0.175 **35.** 0.075 **37.** $0.\overline{2}$ **39.** no

7.7 Problem Solving Strategies

(p. 349) **1.** *Sample answer:* You can use 10 hot dogs : 6 students as a scale; 50 hot dogs. **3.** 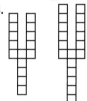 **5.** 8 vocabulary questions and 3 short answer questions

7. 20 **9.** $9\frac{1}{2}$ in. by 12 in.

7.7 Getting Ready to Practice (p. 352) **1.** 1

3. 16 **5.** 720 **7.** 4300 **9.** 51 ft **11.** 11 lb 2 oz; 1 lb 4 oz

7.7 Practice and Problem Solving

(pp. 353–354) **13.** 13 **15.** 5, 4 **17.** $7\frac{1}{2}$ **19.** 12,000 lb **21.** 5 qt **23.** $3\frac{3}{4}$ ft **25.** 10 oz **27.** $4\frac{1}{4}$ pt **29.** 7 c **31.** $1\frac{1}{2}$ qt **33.** 12 ft 3 in. **35.** 7 gal **37.** 6 T 1919 lb **39.** $17\frac{3}{5}$ T **41.** about 50 mi **43.** <. *Sample answer:* I chose paper and pencil because it is hard to find $\frac{7}{8}$ times 5280 mentally. **45.** =. *Sample answer:* I chose paper and pencil because it is hard to multiply $1\frac{2}{3}$ by 8 mentally. **47.** >. *Sample answer:* I chose paper and pencil because it is hard to divide 280 by 16 mentally. **51.** 9, 3 **53.** $\frac{28}{45}$ **55.** $\frac{1}{76}$ **57.** 6 **59.** 9

7.7 Technology Activity (p. 355) **1.** 79; 55; 862 **3.** 26; 110; 35

7.4–7.7 Notebook Review (pp. 356–357)
1. reciprocal **2.** $1\frac{4}{21}$ **3.** $\frac{4}{35}$ **4.** $\frac{5}{32}$ **5.** $3\frac{6}{7}$ **6.** 750 **7.** $\frac{7}{16}$ **8.** 58 **9.** 8 yd; 2 yd 2 ft **10.** pounds **11.** *Sample answer:* To use division, divide 30 by 4 and simplify. To multiply by a form of 1, multiply 30 quarts by $\frac{1\text{ gallon}}{4\text{ quarts}}$ and simplify. The methods are similar in that you end up dividing by 4 in both.

Chapter Review (pp. 358–359) **1.** true **3.** false **5.** false **7.** true **9.** true **11.** 7 **13.** 35 **15.** $5\frac{1}{4}$ h **17.** $\frac{1}{5}$ **19.** $\frac{9}{23}$ **21.** $\frac{1}{18}$ **23.** $\frac{7}{30}$ **25.** $1\frac{1}{5}$ **27.** $15\frac{1}{3}$ **29.** 8 **31.** 6 **33.** $\frac{1}{3}$ **35.** 16 **37.** $1\frac{1}{10}$ **39.** $\frac{9}{25}$ **41.** 13; yes; 60 divided by $4\frac{1}{2}$ is $13\frac{1}{3}$, so there is $\frac{1}{3}$ of a sandwich left over. **43.** pounds **45.** ounces **47.** 44 **49.** $1\frac{1}{2}$ **51.** 3750 lb **53.** 12 qt **55.** 4 lb 11 oz

Chapter 8

8.1 Getting Ready to Practice (p. 376)
1. 5 : 12, 5 to 12 **3.** $\frac{2}{5}$ **5.** $\frac{4}{1}$ **7.** 8 **9.** 18

8.1 Practice and Problem Solving
(pp. 376–378) **11.** $\frac{13}{20}$, 13 : 20 **13.** 9 **15.** 3 **17.** $\frac{31}{76}$, 31 : 76, 31 to 76 **19.** $\frac{1}{2}$ **21.** $\frac{2}{3}$ **23.** Joel **25.** John **27.** 34. *Sample answer:* Subtract the number of altos, basses, and tenors from the total number of singers. **29.** $\frac{1}{8}$ **31.** Rewrite both fractions with the least common denominator. The fraction with the greater numerator is the larger fraction. **35.** 16,000
37.

Sample answer: I used the strategy Solve a Related Problem to continue the related number pattern.
39. 50 **41.** 0.07

8.2 Getting Ready to Practice (p. 381)
1. unit rate **3.** equivalent **5.** 180,000 L

8.2 Practice and Problem Solving
(pp. 381–382) **7.** 12 oz **9.** 18 mi **11.** $\frac{3\text{ m}}{1\text{ sec}}$ **13.** not equivalent **15.** $\frac{20\text{ words}}{5\text{ min}}$; $\frac{4\text{ words}}{1\text{ min}}$ **17.** $\frac{160\text{ mi}}{4\text{ h}}$; $\frac{40\text{ mi}}{1\text{ h}}$ **19.** 21,000,000 gal **21.** $\frac{2.21\text{ lb}}{1\text{ kg}}$ **23.** $\frac{2.54\text{ cm}}{1\text{ in.}}$ **25.** 18 oz box; the unit price for the 18 ounce box is about \$.22 and the unit price for the 12 ounce box is \$.25. **27.** No; the unit rate for both rates is $\frac{5\text{ mi}}{1\text{ sec}}$. **29.** 6 m **31.** 8 **33.** 18

8.3 Getting Ready to Practice
(p. 385) **1.** 3x, 72 **3.** yes **5.** no **7.** 30 **9.** 8 **11.** 72 in.

8.3 Practice and Problem Solving
(pp. 386–387) **13.** yes **15.** no **17.** 1 **19.** 3 **21.** 10 **23.** 100 **25.** 30 **27.** 10 **29.** 350 gal **31.** 9 questions **33.** *Sample answer:* mental math; 6 **35.** *Sample answer:* related equation; 33 **37.** 12; 20 **39.** yes **41.** *Sample answer:* Since multiplying 12 by $1\frac{1}{2}$ gives 18, multiply 30 by $1\frac{1}{2}$ to find the unknown value, 45. **43.** *Sample answer:* 3.52 lb **45.** 34 cm; 42 cm^2

8.4 Getting Ready to Practice (p. 390)
1. 1 in. to 5 ft; $\frac{1\text{ in.}}{5\text{ ft}}$ **3.** about 300 ft

8.4 Practice and Problem Solving
(pp. 390–391) **5.** 10 cm **7.** 400 mi **9.** 225 mi **11.** A good answer should include the use of the ratio $\frac{1}{2}$ in proportions to find the width and length of the enlarged rectangle. For Rectangle 1, the enlarged rectangle will be 8 cm × 4 cm. For Rectangle 2, the enlarged rectangle will be 6 cm × 10 cm. For Rectangle 3, the enlarged rectangle will be 12 cm × 12 cm. **13.** For all rectangles, the ratio of the perimeters is $\frac{1\text{ cm}}{2\text{ cm}}$ and the ratio of the areas is $\frac{1\text{ cm}^2}{4\text{ cm}^2}$. The ratio of the perimeters is the same as the scale, and the ratio of the areas is the

square of the scale. **15.** $\dfrac{1 \text{ cm}}{5 \text{ m}}$ **17.** No; no. *Sample answer:* Since 12 inches = 1 foot, the number 12 should be squared to find the number of square inches in 1 square foot. Similarly, since 3 feet = 1 yard, the number 3 should be squared to find the number of square feet in 1 square yard. **19.** pounds **21.** 33 **23.** 16 **25.** 7.1 **27.** 0.68

8.1–8.4 Notebook Review (pp. 392–393)
1. rate **2.** ratios, equivalent **3.** 12 and $4x$ **4.** 45 sec **5.** <; $0.\overline{6} < 0.\overline{7}$ **6.** $2.50 per pound **7.** 12 **8.** 125 ft **9.** *Sample answer:* They both are ratios of measures that have different units. A rate can have a denominator other than 1, but a unit rate must have a denominator of 1.

8.5 Getting Ready to Practice (p. 397)
1. 100 **3.** eighty-one hundredths, 81% **5.** sixty-three hundredths, 63% **7.** 20% of the students

8.5 Practice and Problem Solving
(pp. 397–398) **9.** 68%, 0.68, $\dfrac{68}{100} = \dfrac{17}{25}$ **11.** forty-two hundredths, 42% **13.** fifty-seven hundredths, 57% **15.** twenty-eight hundredths, 28% **17.** two-hundred hundredths, 200% **23.** 36%, 0.36, $\dfrac{36}{100} = \dfrac{9}{25}$ **25.** 43%; add 22% for 4 or 5 days to 21% for 6 or 7 days to get 43%. **27.** 1 day or less: 0.19, $\dfrac{19}{100}$; 2 or 3 days: 0.38, $\dfrac{38}{100} = \dfrac{19}{50}$; 4 or 5 days: 0.22, $\dfrac{22}{100} = \dfrac{11}{50}$; 6 or 7 days: 0.21, $\dfrac{21}{100}$ **29.** > **35.** 2 h 15 min **37.** 1.57, 3.8, 4.1 **39.** 9, 9.2, 9.4

8.6 Getting Ready to Practice (p. 401)
1. 60% **7.** 64% do not sew

8.6 Practice and Problem Solving
(pp. 402–403) **9.** 65% **11.** 28% **13.** 20% **15.** 8.4% **17.** 58.7% **19.** 1.5% **21.** 90% **23.** 15%, 0.16, $\dfrac{1}{4}$ **25.** 50%, $\dfrac{2}{3}$, $\dfrac{7}{10}$, 0.77 **27.** 0.3, 33%, $\dfrac{1}{3}$, 34% **29.** 27.5% **31.** 56% **33.** *Sample answer:* mental math; 36% **35.** *Sample answer:* calculator; 44% **37.** 350% **39.** 0.4% **41.** John; Vince **43.** 29 **45.** $\dfrac{3000 \text{ ants}}{1 \text{ h}}$ **47.** 0.37, $\dfrac{37}{100}$ **49.** 0.96, $\dfrac{24}{25}$ **51.** 150 **53.** 1.875

8.7 Problem Solving Strategies (p. 405)
1. 14; 33 **3.** 10,000 **5.** 6 **7.** 2 packages of pencils and 6 packages of pens, or 7 packages of pencils and 3 packages of pens **9.** 18 different meals

8.7 Getting Ready to Practice (p. 408)
1. I = simple interest; P = principal; r = annual interest rate; t = time in years **3.** 9 **5.** 60

8.7 Practice and Problem Solving
(pp. 409–410) **7.** 42 **9.** 10 **11.** 54 **13.** 8.1 **15.** 37.2 **17.** 21 **19.** 1% is $\dfrac{1}{100}$. The answer should be $\dfrac{1}{100} \times 400 = \dfrac{400}{100} = 4$. **21.** $52.50 **23.** $55 **25.** $5.04 **27.** $3.20 **29.** $12.80 **31–35.** Estimates may vary. **31.** 600 **33.** 40 **35.** 72 **37.** double the answer; triple the answer **39.** $244; $258.64 **41.** buying the package **43.** 10; 8; 10; 22 **45.** 700 m **47.** 9.25 **49.** 12.7

8.7 Technology Activity (p. 411)
1. 7.2 **3.** 7.809 **5.** 24.057 **7.** $19.50 **9.** $32.18

8.5–8.7 Notebook Review (pp. 412–413)
1. principal **2.** 0.16, $\dfrac{16}{100} = \dfrac{4}{25}$ **3.** 70% **4.** 24% **5.** 24% **6.** 87.5% **7.** 100 **8.** 63 **9.** 2.4 **10.** 110.5 **11.** $9 **12.** *Sample answer:* Change the percent to either a fraction or a decimal and multiply. Consider if it is easier to change the percent to a fraction or to a decimal, and whether the number is easy to divide by the denominator of the fraction.

Chapter Review (pp. 414–415)
1. false **3.** true **5.** cross products **7.** 9 **9.** 4 **11.** $\dfrac{1}{2}$ **13.** $\dfrac{1}{4}$ **15.** $\dfrac{60 \text{ mi}}{1 \text{ h}}$ **17.** 9 **19.** 30 **21.** 175 ft $\times$ 75 ft **23.** thirty-four hundredths, 34% **25.** five hundredths, 5% **27.** 0.64, $\dfrac{64}{100} = \dfrac{16}{25}$ **29.** 0.90, $\dfrac{90}{100} = \dfrac{9}{10}$ **31.** 40% **33.** 62.5% **35.** 0.2, 25%, $\dfrac{1}{3}$, 0.35, 40%, $\dfrac{3}{5}$ **37.** 12 **39.** 400 **41.** $17.25

Chapter 9

9.1 Getting Ready to Practice (p. 423)
5. *Sample answer:* $\overrightarrow{LQ}$ 7. $\overleftrightarrow{ML}$ and $\overleftrightarrow{PQ}$

9.1 Practice and Problem Solving
(pp. 423–424) 9. segment, $\overline{JK}$ 11. *Sample answer:*
A, B, C 13. *Sample answer:* $\overleftrightarrow{AB}$, $\overleftrightarrow{DE}$ 15. $\overline{EA}$
17. intersecting   19. $\overrightarrow{SV}$, $\overrightarrow{VS}$, $\overrightarrow{VO}$, $\overrightarrow{OP}$, or $\overrightarrow{PO}$
21. $\overline{SV}$, $\overline{VO}$, or $\overline{PO}$ 23. ray   25. $\overset{\bullet}{W}\text{———}\overset{\bullet}{V}$
27. $\overset{\bullet}{Q}\text{———}\overset{\bullet}{P}$ 29. False; $\overrightarrow{AB}$ is a ray and $\overleftrightarrow{AB}$
is a line.   31. True; the letters are interchangeable.
33. Answers may vary.   35. <   37. >

9.2 Getting Ready to Practice (p. 427)
1. E; $\overrightarrow{ED}$ and $\overrightarrow{EF}$ 3. $\angle U$, $\angle TUV$, $\angle VUT$
5. *Sample:*

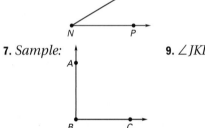

7. *Sample:*   9. $\angle JKL$ 11. $\angle TUV$

9.2 Practice and Problem Solving
(pp. 428–429) 13. $60°$ 15. $60°$ 17. $130°$
19. *Sample:*

21. *Sample:* $\overset{\bullet}{L}\text{———}\overset{\bullet}{M}\text{———}\overset{\bullet}{N}$
27. *Sample answer:* Between 90° and 135°; 120°
29. $\dfrac{13}{11}$ or $1\dfrac{2}{11}$ 31. $\dfrac{4}{5}$ 33. 6   35. 10   37. thirty-one
ten-thousandths   39. fifty-two and one hundred
forty-one thousandths

9.3 Getting Ready to Practice (p. 432)
5. *Sample answer:* $\angle CAB$ and $\angle FAE$ 7. *Sample
answer:* $\angle DAC$ and $\angle FAD$ 9. complementary
11. supplementary   13. $60°$

9.3 Practice and Problem Solving
(pp. 433–434) 15. right   17. obtuse   19. $\angle BAD$ is
obtuse; $\angle CAD$ is right; $\angle BAC$ is acute.   21. $\angle PTN$
and $\angle RTS$; $\angle PTR$ and $\angle NTS$ 23. $m\angle 1 = 90°$,
$m\angle 2 = 90°$, $m\angle 3 = 90°$ 25. complementary
27. neither   29. 49   31. *Sample:*

33. *Sample:*   35. perpendicular

37. neither   39. $80°$ 43. 168   45.

47. 47.29

9.4 Getting Ready to Practice (p. 438)
7. right, isosceles   9. 25

9.4 Practice and Problem Solving
(pp. 439–440) 11. obtuse   13. acute   15. equilateral
17. scalene   19. 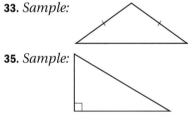   21. 86

23. not a triangle   25. is a triangle; obtuse
27. is a triangle; acute   29. always   31. never
33. *Sample:*

35. *Sample:*

37. acute isosceles triangle   41. *Sample answer:*
$\angle 1$ and $\angle 2$, $\angle 2$ and $\angle 3$ 43. $\dfrac{7}{20}$ 45. $6\dfrac{21}{50}$

9.4 Technology Activity (p. 441) 1. 50   3. 34
5. 106.9   7. $65°$

9.1–9.4 Notebook Review (pp. 442–443)
1. angle   2. supplementary   3. *Sample answer:*
$\overrightarrow{EA}$ 4. *Sample answer:* $\overleftrightarrow{FC}$ 5. obtuse   6. straight
7. 45; right, isosceles   8. 60; acute, equilateral

9. Subtract the measure from 90°; subtract the measure from 180°. **10.** A triangle has 3 angles whose sum is 180°. If there were 2 right angles, then there could only be 2 angles because 90° and 90° add up to 180°.

9.5 Getting Ready to Practice (p. 447)

1. parallelogram **3.** True; a rhombus and a square both have 4 sides of equal length. **5.** parallelogram
7. parallelogram, rhombus

9.5 Practice and Problem Solving

(pp. 447–448) **9.** All **11.** Some **13.** rectangle, rhombus, square **15.**

17. rectangle, square **19.** 1: square; 2: rectangle; 3: rhombus **21.** 4 **23.** 77 **25.** Squares are always rectangles, so the rhombus must be a rectangle.

27. $\frac{2}{5}$, 42%, 0.45 **29.** is a triangle; acute

31. is a triangle; right **33.** $11.00

9.6 Getting Ready to Practice (p. 451) **5.** yes
7. *Sample answer:* There are only 5 diagonals, not 7. Two of the segments drawn from the vertex are sides of the octagon and therefore not diagonals.

9.6 Practice and Problem Solving

(pp. 451–453) **9.** pentagon; not regular **11.** 2
13. square **15.** 72 **17.** triangle

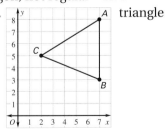

19.

Number of sides in polygon	4	5	6
Number of diagonals from one vertex	1	2	3

21. 6 **23.** 135° **25.** 32 m **27.** *Sample:*

29. 125,250; I used Solve a Simpler Problem and found the sum of the first 10 numbers, the second 10 numbers, and when I observed the pattern, used that pattern to find the entire sum. **31.** 6

9.7 Getting Ready to Practice (p. 456)
1. false **3.** false **5.** $x = 4$ yd, $y = 5$ yd

9.7 Practice and Problem Solving

(pp. 456–457) **7.** congruent **9.** $\angle A$ and $\angle D$, $\angle C$ and $\angle F$, $\angle B$ and $\angle E$, $\overline{AC}$ and $\overline{DF}$, $\overline{BC}$ and $\overline{EF}$, $\overline{AB}$ and $\overline{DE}$ **11.** $x = 90$; $y = 13$ ft **13.** Yes; no; the images are the same shape but larger than the actual photos. **15.** Congruent. *Sample answer:* The earrings are the same shape and size.
17. Neither. *Sample answer:* The batteries are neither the same shape nor the same size.
19. $\angle Y$ and $\angle B$, $\angle X$ and $\angle A$, $\angle Z$ and $\angle C$; $\overline{YX}$ and $\overline{BA}$, $\overline{YZ}$ and $\overline{BC}$, $\overline{XZ}$ and $\overline{AC}$
23. **25.** 6.076

9.8 Problem Solving Strategies (p. 459)
1. 4; 1 **5.** Yes. *Sample answer:* If the long side of the bed is placed against the 12 foot wall, then 6 feet of space along that wall remains for the desk. **7.** $40.85

9.8 Getting Ready to Practice (p. 462)
1. line symmetry **3.** 0

9.8 Practice and Problem Solving

(pp. 462–463) **5.** no **7.** yes **9.**

11. **13.**

15. 1 **17.** yes; an isosceles triangle that is not an equilateral triangle **19.** 12 **21.** 9 **23.** $\frac{1}{2}$ **25.** $\frac{1}{12}$ **27.** *Sample answer:* 240 **29.** *Sample answer:* 2100

9.5–9.8 Notebook Review (pp. 464–465)

1. parallelogram **2.** No; all angles do not have to have the same measure. **3.** rhombus, quadrilateral, parallelogram **4.** regular pentagon **5.** congruent; $\angle C$ and $\angle F$, $\angle E$ and $\angle H$, $\angle D$ and $\angle G$, $\overline{DE}$ and $\overline{GH}$, $\overline{CE}$ and $\overline{FH}$, $\overline{CD}$ and $\overline{FG}$ **6.** no **7.** no **8.** yes **9.** No; a parallelogram is a quadrilateral with 2 pairs of parallel sides and a regular hexagon has 6 sides with 3 pairs of parallel sides.

Chapter Review (pp. 466–467)
1. When two lines intersect, the angles opposite each other are called vertical angles. **3.** 3 **5.** The sum of their measures is 180°. **7.** 180° **9.** equal; equal **11.** $\overleftrightarrow{VW}$ **13.** $\overleftrightarrow{ST}$ **15.** 45° **17.** complementary **19.** *Sample:*

21. $m\angle 1 = 152°$; $m\angle 2 = 28°$; $m\angle 3 = 152°$
23. 73; acute **25.** quadrilateral **27.** quadrilateral, parallelogram **29.** similar; $\angle A$ and $\angle J$, $\angle B$ and $\angle K$, $\angle C$ and $\angle L$; $\overline{AB}$ and $\overline{JK}$; $\overline{BC}$ and $\overline{KL}$; $\overline{AC}$ and $\overline{JL}$

31. **33.**

Chapter 10

10.1 Getting Ready to Practice (p. 478)
1. base, height **3.** 200 yd^2

10.1 Practice and Problem Solving
(pp. 478–479) **5.** 84 m^2 **7.** 30 in.^{2} **9.** 63 m^2
11. 10 yd **13.** Check drawings. *Sample answer:* 1 cm by 12 cm, 2 cm by 6 cm, or 3 cm by 4 cm **15.** 14,400 km^2; high estimate; the parallelogram covers more than just the island of Puerto Rico.

17. 7 **19.** 8 **21.** *Sample:* **23.** 6 **25.** 48

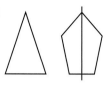

10.2 Getting Ready to Practice (p. 482)
1. height, base **3.** 8 mi^2 **5.** 6 ft^2

10.2 Practice and Problem Solving
(pp. 482–483) **7.** 20 ft^2 **9.** 24 cm^2 **11.** 675 in.^{2} **13.** 5 in. **15.** 10 cm **17.** 13 m^2 **19.** The area of the triangle with the longer base is twice as great as the area of the other triangle. **21.** $\frac{3}{14} \approx 21\%$ **23.** mass **25.** capacity **27.** 9 cm **29.** 16.25 **31.** 98.52

10.3 Getting Ready to Practice (p. 487)
1. diameter **3.** radius **5.** 22 cm **7.** 25.12 in. **9.** The radius is given, so the formula $C = 2\pi r$ should be used. The circumference is $2(3.14)(3) = 18.84$ mm. **11.** 37.68 yd; 3.14 because 12 is not a multiple of 7. **13.** 132 km; $\frac{22}{7}$ because 21 is a multiple of 7.

10.3 Practice and Problem Solving
(pp. 488–489) **15.** 19 in. **17.** 106.76 mm; 3.14 because 17 is not a multiple of 7. **19.** 154 mi; $\frac{22}{7}$ because 49 is a multiple of 7. **21.** about 9.42 in. **23.** about 5 times **25.** $\frac{22}{7}$; its value is closer to the actual value of pi. **29.** The shape will be the letter "X". *Sample answer:* I chose Make a Model so I could see the shape. **31.** 62.5 **33.** 144

10.3 Technology Activity (p. 490) **1.** 38 feet
3. 1071 cm **5.** 94 km **7.** 5 m **9.** about 16,000 km

10.4 Getting Ready to Practice (p. 494)
1. area **3.** 12.6 km^2 **5.** 452.2 yd^2

10.4 Practice and Problem Solving
(pp. 494–495) **7.** 452 ft^2 **9.** 254 m^2 **11.** 14 cm^2 **13.** 2.6 m^2 **15.** 1017 mi^2 **17.** 16 times **19.** Dog: $\frac{1}{4}$, Cat: $\frac{3}{8}$, Rabbit: $\frac{7}{40}$, Other: $\frac{1}{5}$

21.

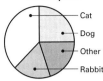

Animals Available for Adoption

- Cat
- Dog
- Other
- Rabbit

25. quadrilateral   **27.** hexagon   **29.** 25.12 in.
31. 37.68 ft   **33.** 91; 88; no mode; 59

Special Topic Exercises (p. 497)   **1.** Check drawing. A good drawing will include all necessary arcs and labels.

10.1–10.4 Notebook Review (pp. 498–499)
1. radius   **2.** 40 in.^{2} **3.** 20 m^2 **4.** 4.5 cm^2
5. 314 cm; 7850 cm^2 **6.** 132 mm; 1385 mm^2
7. 295 m; 6936 m^2 **8.** They are alike because they both involve a base and a height. They are different in that the formula for the triangle is $\frac{1}{2}$ the formula for the parallelogram.   **9.** Check drawings. *Sample bases and heights:*
1 centimeter and 48 centimeters, 2 centimeters and 24 centimeters, 3 centimeters and 16 centimeters, 4 centimeters and 12 centimeters, or 6 centimeters and 8 centimeters

10.5 Getting Ready to Practice (p. 502)
1. cylinders; cones   **3.** sphere   **5.** 5 faces, 9 edges, 6 vertices

10.5 Practice and Problem Solving
(pp. 502–503)   **7.** yes; cylinder   **9.** yes; cone
11. rectangular prism; 6 faces, 12 edges, 8 vertices
13.

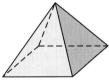

15. False. *Sample answer:* A cylinder has two circles as bases.   **17.** true   **19.** edges   **21.** faces
25. *Sample answer:* 100   **27.** 50   **29.** 0.035
31. 30   **33.** 51

10.6 Problem Solving Strategies (p. 505)
1. $2700   **3.** 168 ft^2 **5.** 7 sums   **7.** Add one dot to each row on the same side of the figure.

• • • •   • • • • •
• • • • •   • • • • •   **9.** 4 folds

10.6 Getting Ready to Practice (p. 508)
1. surface area   **3.** 148 ft^2 **5.** Step 1: top and bottom: 117 in.^{2}; long sides: 26 in.^{2}; short sides: 18 in.^{2}; Step 2: bottom; Step 3: 205 in.^{2}

10.6 Practice and Problem Solving
(pp. 508–509)   **7.** 320 yd^2 **9.** Each of the areas needs to be multiplied by 2. Surface area = $2(5 \times 8) + 2(6 \times 8) + 2(5 \times 6) = 2(40) + 2(48) + 2(30) = 236$ square units.   **11.** 136 m^2 **13.** 416 ft^2
15. The surface area of the larger prism is 4 times the surface area of the smaller prism.   **17.** 490 m^2
19. 12   **21.** sphere   **23.** 3   **25.** 10

10.7 Getting Ready to Practice (p. 512)
1. volume   **3.** 36 ft^3 **5.** Step 1: 1040 cm^3; Step 2: 455 cm^3; Step 3: 585 cm^3

10.7 Practice and Problem Solving
(pp. 512–513)   **7.** 8000 cm^3 **9.** 420 ft^3 **11.** 3 ft
13. 20 m   **15.** about 3840 cubes   **17.** Same; the *lw* part of the volume formula is the area of the base.
21. 956 cm^2 **23.** <   **25.** <

Special Topic Exercises (p. 515)   **1.** 2.1 kg
3. A good answer will include an estimate and an actual weight.

10.5–10.7 Notebook Review (pp. 516–517)
1. cone   **2.** triangular prism; 5 faces, 9 edges, 6 vertices   **3.** 136 yd^2, 96 yd^3 **4.** The surface area of a rectangular prism is the sum of the areas of its faces, while the volume is the amount of space the prism occupies.   **5.** A prism has two bases, while a pyramid has only one.

Chapter Review (pp. 518–519)   **1.** false   **3.** false
5. circle   **7.** volume   **9.** 50 mi^2 **11.** 48 in.^{2}
13. 78.5 yd^2 **15.** 10 in.   **17.** 110 in.   **19.** 24 in.
21. 64.3 ft^2 **23.**

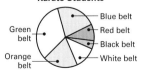

Number of Karate Students

- Blue belt
- Red belt
- Black belt
- White belt
- Orange belt
- Green belt

25. triangular prism   **27.** 5 faces, 9 edges, 6 vertices   **29.** 454 in.^{2}, 460 in.^{3}

Chapter 11

11.1 Getting Ready to Practice (p. 535)

1. -9 **3.** 15 **5.** $>$

7. $-9, -3, 0, 2, 7$

9. $-9, -5, -3, -2, 0$

11.1 Practice and Problem Solving

(pp. 535–536) **11.** -6 degrees **13.** 5 people
15. $-\$25$ **17.** in-line skates $= -\$10$;
helmets $= -\$5$; knee pads $= -\$4$ **19.** 8 **21.** 0
23. $<$ **25.** $>$ **27.** $>$ **29.** $<$ **31.** $-8, -1, 0, 1, 5$
33. $-9, -6, -3, 0, 6$ **35.** false **37.** true **41.** 15
43. cylinder **45.** rectangular prism **47.** 7.08

11.2 Getting Ready to Practice (p. 540)

1. 5 **3.** 7 **5.** 1 **7.** -8 **9.** Start at 0, move 1 unit to
the left for -1, then move 5 units to the right of
-1 to add 5. The correct sum is $-1 + 5 = 4$.

11.2 Practice and Problem Solving

(pp. 540–541) **11.** -1 **13.** 0 **15.** 100 **17.** 35
19. -4 **21.** -7 **23.** -10 **25.** 6 **27.** 0
29. -10 **31.** -20 **33.** -9 **35.** $>$ **37.** $>$
39. $25 + (-40) + 10$; -5 points **41.** 3 **43.** -5
45. always **47.** 0. *Sample answer:* $4 + (-4) = 0$,
$-7 + 7 = 0$. **49.** 1 **51.** 49 **53.** $<$ **55.** $>$ **57.** 19
59. 75

11.3 Getting Ready to Practice (p. 546)

1. opposite **3.** -11 **5.** 6 **7.** 11 **9.** -22

11.3 Practice and Problem Solving

(pp. 546–547) **11.** -1 **13.** -4 **15.** 5 **17.** 3
19. When you subtract a negative integer, you
move to the right on the number line. The
solution should be $4 - (-6) = 10$. **21.** -1
23. -2 **25.** -17 **27.** -14 **29.** 7 **31.** 23 **33.** 10
35. -9 **37.** -125 ft **39.** 7 **41.** 0 **43.** -6 **45.** 52
51. $10\frac{1}{9}$ **53.** $4\frac{3}{8}$ **55.** 0 **57.** 4 **59.** 7.2 **61.** 0.126

11.1–11.3 Notebook Review (pp. 548–549)

1. opposites **2.** absolute value **3.** $>$ **4.** $<$ **5.** $>$
6. $>$ **7.** 0 **8.** -4 **9.** -5 **10.** 1 **11.** -5 **12.** -17
13. 14 **14.** 3 **15.** *Sample answer:* Add the

opposite of -2. Then find $\left|2\right| - \left|-1\right| = 1$.
16. *Sample answer:* $-(-(3)) = (-(-3)) = 3$;
$-(-(-2)) = -(2) = -2$.

11.4 Getting Ready to Practice (p. 552)

1. positive **3.** 21 **5.** -36 **7.** The product of two
negative integers is positive. The correct solution
is $(-2)(-6) = 12$.

11.4 Practice and Problem Solving

(pp. 552–553) **9.** 24 **11.** -18 **13.** -42 **15.** 10
17. 13 **19.** 0 **21.** -180 **23.** 600 **25.** -56
27. -300 m **29.** -42 **31.** 36 **33.** -50 **35.** -120
37. always **39.** always **41.** $-20, -160$ **43.** $-3, 3$
47. 8 **49.** -14 **51.** -4 **53.** -25 **55.** 21.8
57. 53.25

11.5 Getting Ready to Practice (p. 556)

1. divide **3.** -2 **5.** 1 **7.** -5 **9.** 2 **11.** A negative
integer divided by a negative integer is positive.
The solution should be $-18 \div (-3) = 6$.

11.5 Practice and Problem Solving

(pp. 556–558) **13.** -4 **15.** 9 **17.** -2 **19.** 3 **21.** -4
23. -15 **25.** -6 **27.** -15 **29.** 13 **31.** 0 **33.** about
$-59°F$ **35.** $77°F$; $120°F$; the low temperatures
37. -1 **39.** 6 **41.** -84 **43.** -72 **45.** 0
49. 240 in.^{2}; I used Break into Parts because I could
find the area of the parallelogram and the area of
the triangle and then add to find the area of the
platform. **51.** 3.1

11.5 Technology Activity (p. 559) **1.** 965 **3.** 48

5. -18 **7.** -430 m

11.6 Problem Solving Strategies (p. 561)

1. yes **3.** Yes; *WXYZ* is the same shape as *ABCD*
but its sides are twice as long. **5.** a vertical line
through $x = 5$, a horizontal line through $y = 5$
7. 32 pieces **9.** 9 different totals

11.6 Getting Ready to Practice (p. 564)

1. false **3.** Point *A* is in
Quadrant IV.

5. Point *C* is in Quadrant III.

7. 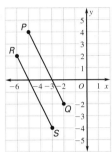 *R*(−6, 2), *S*(−3, −4)

11.6 Practice and Problem Solving

(pp. 564–566) **9.** 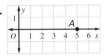 Point *A* is on the *x*-axis.

11. Point *C* is in Quadrant II.

13. Point *E* is in Quadrant III.

15. Point *G* is in Quadrant IV.

17. (−3, 2)   **19.** (4, −4)   **21.** (3, 4)   **23.** *Sample answer:* Start at (0, 0). Move to the right or left the number of units given by the *x*-coordinate. Then move up or down the number of units given by the *y*-coordinate.

25. 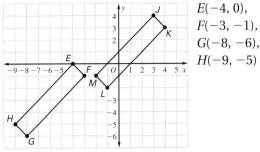 *E*(−4, 0), *F*(−3, −1), *G*(−8, −6), *H*(−9, −5)

27. I   **29.** II   **31.** Yes; slide the figure 4 units to the right and 4 units down.   **33.** No; each point did not slide the same distance.

35.

39. thirty-five hundredths; 35%   **41.** fifteen hundredths; 15%   **43.**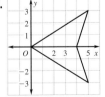
45. 7   **47.** 2.05

11.7 Getting Ready to Practice (p. 569)

1. In a reflection, the original figure is flipped over a line to produce a congruent mirror image. In a rotation, the original figure is rotated through a given angle about a fixed point.   **3.** translation

11.7 Practice and Problem Solving

(pp. 569–571) **5.** No; the image is not flipped.
7. Yes; the line of reflection is the *x*-axis.
9. A appears to be a rotation; B appears to be a reflection.   **11.** translation   **13.** rotation

15. 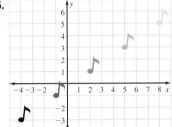   **17.**

19. Cannot be formed by a reflection; can be formed by a series of translations and by a rotation. *Sample answer:* The design can be formed by translating the columns or rows of beads up and to the right.

21. Can be formed by a reflection; cannot be formed by a translation, but can be formed by a rotation. *Sample answer:* The design can be formed by rotating a portion of the design about its center.

23. 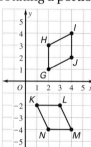 rotation **27.** 30.4 **29.** 30.7

31. 54 **33.** −8

35. $\frac{3}{5}$ **37.** $3\frac{2}{25}$

Special Topic Exercises (p. 573)

1.  *Sample answer:* Rotate the triangle 180° about the point at the middle of one side of the triangle to form a parallelogram. Then translate the parallelogram to fill the plane.

3. 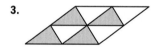 **5.** Check drawing.

11.4–11.7 Notebook Review (pp. 574–575)

1. rotation; center of rotation **2.** −36 **3.** −56
4. 45 **5.** −6 **6.** −6 **7.** 4

8. 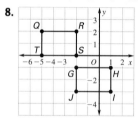 $Q(-5, 2)$, $R(-2, 2)$, $S(-2, 0)$, $T(-5, 0)$

9. rotation **10.** reflection **11.** Each point of one figure is slid the same distance in the same direction. **12.** *Sample:*

Chapter Review (pp. 576–577) **1.** Negative integers **3.** opposite **5.** image **7.** $25 **9.** −3 cm
11. 30 **13.** −2 **15.** −13, −8, −6, 0, 6 **17.** −100, −1, 1 10, 1000 **19.** 8 **21.** 10 **23.** 3 **25.** −10
27. −17 **29.** −30 **31.** −5 **33.** −18 **35.** 24

37. 20 **39.** −30 **41.** −63 **43.** 270 **45.** 24
47. −7 **49.** −4 **51.** 3 **53.** 5
55. 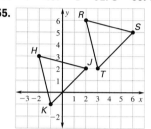 $R(2, 6)$, $S(6, 5)$, $T(3, 2)$
57. rotation; 90°
59. reflection; *y*-axis
61. translation

Chapter 12

12.1 Getting Ready to Practice (p. 585)

1. subtraction **3.** $7x$ **5.** $21 - x$ **7.** $\frac{h}{6} = 2$
9. $s - 32 = 6$

12.1 Practice and Problem Solving

(pp. 585–586) **11.** $\frac{x}{9}$ **13.** $x - 16$ **15.** $20x$ **17.** $x + 18$
19. $x - 27$ **21.** *Sample answer:* $y - 2$ means 2 less than y, while $2 - y$ means y less than 2.
23. $n + 6 = 30$ **25.** $\frac{32}{r} = 2$ **27.** $3x = 123$
29. $t - 4 = 26$ **31.** *Sample answer:* 7 less than a number y **33.** *Sample answer:* A number d divided by 3 **39.** $2400 + c = 8241$; $8241 - c = 2400$
45. 9 **47.** 11

12.2 Getting Ready to Practice (p. 590)

1. yes **3.** no **5.** 6 **7.** 35

12.2 Practice and Problem Solving

(pp. 590–591) **9.** 7 **11.** 0 **13.** 5 **15.** 16 **17.** 13
19. 7 **21.** 28 **23.** 32 **25.** $10 + q = 25$; 15 min
27. *Sample answer:* 24 **29–39.** Methods may vary.
29. 6 **31.** 2.7 **33.** 17 **35.** 6.2 **37.** 4.8 **39.** 1.7
41. $3.6 + 2.55 + x = 4.95$ km **43.** $20 + m = 28$
49. Prime; its only factors are 1 and itself. **51.** 18
53. 2.34

12.3 Getting Ready to Practice (p. 594)

1. variable **3.** no **5.** 9 **7.** 22

12.3 Practice and Problem Solving

(pp. 594–595) **9.** 13 **11.** 3 **13.** 15 **15.** 23 **17.** 11
19. 15 **21.** 33 **23.** 53 **25.** You do the same thing to both sides to solve either an addition equation or a subtraction equation; to solve an addition equation, you subtract; to solve a subtraction

equation, you add.   **27.** $x - 368 = 532$; the sum of 368 and 532 is greater than the sum of 368 and 475.   **29.** $x - 12 = 9$; $x - 9 = 12$; 21 games; the solutions are the same.   **31.** 9.3   **33.** 30.06

35. 15.32   **37.** $3\frac{7}{8}$ **43.**   Quadrant II

45. 2   **47.** 8   **49.** 9

12.1–12.3 Notebook Review (pp. 596–597)

1. A variable expression contains variables and numbers, but no equal sign. An equation contains variables, numbers, and an equal sign.   **2.** $\frac{x}{7}$

3. $6x$ **4.** $x - 80$ **5.** $25 + x$ **6.** $40 + p = 62$ **7.** 7
8. 20   **9.** 15   **10.** 1.2   **11.** 16.8   **12.** 20   **13.** 21
14. 43   **15.** 29.7   **16.** *Sample answer:* Each word is translated into a special symbol.   **17.** *Sample answer:* $3 + x = 4$; $5 + x = 6$

12.4 Getting Ready to Practice (p. 600)

1. division; multiplication   **3.** 2   **5.** 12

7. $24 = \frac{c}{2}$; 48

12.4 Practice and Problem Solving

(pp. 600–601)   **9.** 5; 5; 2   **11.** 9; 9; 36   **13.** 20   **15.** 9
17. 14   **19.** 3   **21.** 50   **23.** 84   **25.** 84   **27.** 98

29. $11b = 44$; 4   **31.** $27 = \frac{n}{3}$; 81   **33.** $24h = 1728$;

72 h   **35.** Multiplying by 4, the reciprocal of $\frac{1}{4}$, is

the same as dividing by $\frac{1}{4}$.   **37.** $4\frac{4}{9}$ **39.** -7

41. -20 **43.** 19   **45.** 21   **47.** 17   **49.** $<$ **51.** $=$

Special Topic Exercises (p. 603)   **1.** $2x > 275$

3. $x \le 0$ (number line from −5 to 4, closed circle at 0, arrow left)

5. $x \ge 7$ (number line from −1 to 9, closed circle at 7, arrow right)

7. $x > 6$ (number line from −1 to 8, open circle at 6, arrow right)

9. $x < 12$ (number line from 0 to 14, open circle at 12, arrow left)

12.5 Getting Ready to Practice (p. 607)

1. input; output

3.

Input, x	$y = 2x$	Output, y
2	$y = 2(2)$	4
4	$y = 2(4)$	8
6	$y = 2(6)$	12
8	$y = 2(8)$	16
10	$y = 2(10)$	20

5.

Input, x	$y = 3x - 2$	Output, y
2	$y = 3(2) - 2$	4
4	$y = 3(4) - 2$	10
6	$y = 3(6) - 2$	16
8	$y = 3(8) - 2$	22
10	$y = 3(10) - 2$	28

12.5 Practice and Problem Solving

(pp. 607–609)   **7.**

Input, x	$y = 6x$	Output, y
3	$y = 6(3)$	18
6	$y = 6(6)$	36
9	$y = 6(9)$	54
12	$y = 6(12)$	72
15	$y = 6(15)$	90

9.

Input, x	$y = 15 - x$	Output, y
3	$y = 15 - 3$	12
6	$y = 15 - 6$	9
9	$y = 15 - 9$	6
12	$y = 15 - 12$	3
15	$y = 15 - 15$	0

11.

Input, x	$y = 4x + 1$	Output, y
3	$y = 4(3) + 1$	13
6	$y = 4(6) + 1$	25
9	$y = 4(9) + 1$	37
12	$y = 4(12) + 1$	49
15	$y = 4(15) + 1$	61

13.

Input, x	$y = 2x - 4$	Output, y
3	$y = 2(3) - 4$	2
6	$y = 2(6) - 4$	8
9	$y = 2(9) - 4$	14
12	$y = 2(12) - 4$	20
15	$y = 2(15) - 4$	26

15.

Inches, i	$c = 2.54i$	Centimeters, c
3	$c = 2.54(3)$	7.62
6	$c = 2.54(6)$	15.24
9	$c = 2.54(9)$	22.86
12	$c = 2.54(12)$	30.48
36	$c = 2.54(36)$	91.44

17. $t = n + 15$ **19.** $t = \dfrac{g}{10}$

21.

Hours, h	Minutes, m
1	60
2	120
3	180
4	240

$m = 60h$

23.

Triangles, t	Perimeter, p
1	3
2	4
3	5
4	6
5	7

$p = t + 2$

25. A good answer will include an obvious pattern and a clear input-output table and rule. **27.** Row 1: 15, 75; Row 2: 25, 28, 33   **29.** Row 1: 6:00; Row 2: 300, 540; Row 3: 250; $d = \dfrac{5}{6}t$

31. 4 h 44 min   **33.** 13   **35.** 48

37–40.

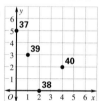

12.6 Problem Solving Strategies (p. 611)

1. add 12 min; 6:31 P.M.   **3.** subtract 5; -7, -12, -17 **5.** The pattern is: large blue bead, small yellow bead, two small green beads, small yellow bead. This pattern of five beads repeats, so the next five beads are: small yellow bead, two small green beads, small yellow bead, large blue bead. **7.** Message: I forgot my lunch. Note that the pattern used is: I = 6, J = 7, K = 8, …, Y = 22, Z = 23, A = 24, B = 25, C = 26, D = 1, E = 2, F = 3, G = 4, H = 5.   **9.** $10.20   **11.** 100 ft^2

12.6 Getting Ready to Practice (p. 614)

1. linear   **3.**

Input, x	Output, y
0	-3
1	-1
2	1
3	3
4	5

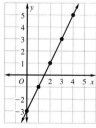

5.

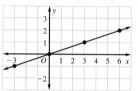

yes

12.6 Practice and Problem Solving

(pp. 615–616) **7.**

9.

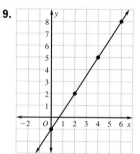

11.

Input, x	Output, y
0	4
1	5
2	6
3	7
4	8

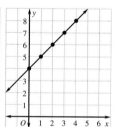

13.

Input, x	Output, y
0	7
1	6
2	5
3	4
4	3

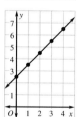

15.

Input, x	Output, y
0	2.5
1	3.5
2	4.5
3	5.5
4	6.5

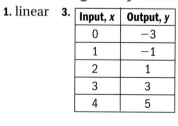

17.

Input, x	Output, y
0	2
1	$2\frac{1}{2}$
2	3
3	$3\frac{1}{2}$
4	4

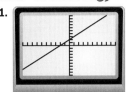

19.

Input, x	Output, y
0	10
1	7
2	4
3	1
4	−2

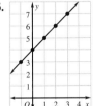

21. Linear; the graph is a straight line.

23. Extend the line so it passes through the point with x-coordinate 8.5 and determine the y-coordinate to find the number of skiers; use the function rule and substitute 8.5 for x.

25. $y = x + 4$

27. $y = 5 - x$

29.

Side, s	Volume, V
1	1
2	8
4	64
8	512
16	4096

31. 8 times as large   **33.** 0.3   **35.** $1.\overline{36}$

37. 12   **39.** 9   **41.** $y = x + 8$ **43.** 14 packs

12.6 Technology Activity (p. 617)

1.   **3.**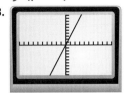

5. 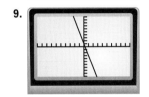   **7.**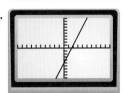

9.    **11.**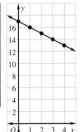

Only positive numbers make sense since you cannot have a zero or negative diameter.

12.4–12.6 Notebook Review (pp. 618–619)

1. input; output   **2.** The graph is a straight line.

3. 3   **4.** 17   **5.** 120   **6.** 20

7.

Input, x	Output, y
0	5
1	6
2	7
3	8
4	9

8.

Input, x	Output, y
0	17
1	16
2	15
3	14
4	13

9.

Input, x	Output, y
0	−5
1	−1
2	3
3	7
4	11

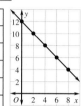

10

Input, x	Output, y
0	4
1	$4\frac{1}{2}$
2	5
3	$5\frac{1}{2}$
4	6

11. $w = \dfrac{d}{7}$ **12.** Substitute the given values for A and w and solve the equation for l.

Chapter Review (pp. 620–621)   **1.** x; y
3. *Sample:*   **5.** $7 - x$

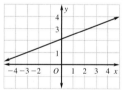

7. $15 + x$ **9.** $\dfrac{n}{3} = 15$ **11.** $2q = 10$ **13.** 4

15. 20   **17.** 52   **19.** 1.9   **21.** 16   **23.** 44   **25.** 38
27. 21.8   **29.** $x + 35 = 250$; 215 yd   **31.** 9
33. 29   **35.** 44   **37.** 15   **39.** 20   **41.** 30   **43.** 35
45. 80   **47.** $3l = 57$; 19 ft

49.

Input, x	Output, y
0	15
5	25
10	35
15	45
20	55

51.

Input, x	Output, y
0	0
5	1
10	2
15	3
20	4

53. $r = s + 2.50$

55.

Months, m	Years, y
12	1
24	2
36	3
48	4

$y = \dfrac{m}{12}$

57.

Input, x	Output, y
0	12
2	10
4	8
6	6
8	4

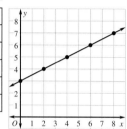

59.

Input, x	Output, y
0	3
2	4
4	5
6	6
8	7

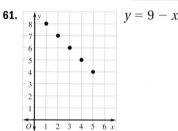

61.

$y = 9 - x$

Chapter 13

13.1 Getting Ready to Practice (p. 632)
1. spinning an A, E, or O   **3.** choosing marble 1, 2, 3, or 6   **5.** $\dfrac{2}{5}$

13.1 Practice and Problem Solving

(pp. 633–634)   **7.** $\dfrac{1}{6}$ **9.** 0   **11.** likely   **13.** impossible

15. $\dfrac{1}{8}$; unlikely   **17.** $\dfrac{1}{8}$; unlikely   **19.** The probability of rolling a 5 is one out of six numbers, so the probability is $\dfrac{1}{6}$.   **21.** $\dfrac{21}{26}$ **23.** choosing a vowel; $\dfrac{1}{4}$

25. $\dfrac{46}{53}$ **27.** winning a raffle; 2%   **29.** No; no; there cannot be more than the number of possible outcomes, nor can there be fewer than 0 outcomes.

31. $\dfrac{1}{5}$; there is one favorable outcome and there are

5 unfavorable outcomes.   **33.** 216 in.^{3}

35. 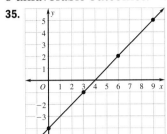   **37.** 0.623, 6.23, 62.3, 623, 6230

13.1 Technology Activity (p. 635)   **1.** A good answer should be close to $\frac{1}{2}$.

13.2 Getting Ready to Practice (p. 638)
1. combination; permutation

3. 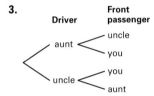   aunt and uncle, aunt and you, uncle and you, uncle and aunt

13.2 Practice and Problem Solving
(pp. 638–639)   **5.** white paint in kitchen, white paint in bathroom, beige paint in kitchen, beige paint in bathroom, gray paint in kitchen, gray paint in bathroom   **7.** Dallas in June, Dallas in July, Dallas in August, New York in June, New York in July, New York in August, Miami in June, Miami in July, Miami in August   **9.** blue and green, blue and yellow, blue and red, blue and purple, green and yellow, green and red, green and purple, yellow and red, yellow and purple, red and purple
11. comedy and drama, comedy and science fiction, comedy and adventure, drama and comedy, drama and science fiction, drama and adventure, science fiction and comedy, science fiction and drama, science fiction and adventure, adventure and comedy, adventure and drama, adventure and science fiction   **13.** soup, pasta, and pie; soup, seafood, and pie; soup, beef, and pie; salad, pasta, and pie; salad, seafood, and pie; salad, beef, and pie; soup, pasta, and cake; soup, seafood, and cake; soup, beef, and cake; salad, pasta, and cake; salad, seafood, and cake; salad, beef, and cake; soup, pasta, and ice cream; soup,

seafood, and ice cream; soup, beef, and ice cream; salad, pasta, and ice cream; salad, seafood, and ice cream; salad, beef, and ice cream
15. Choosing a 5-person fundraising committee would be a combination because the order of the persons being chosen is not important; electing 4 class officers would be a permutation because the order is important.   **17.** 113.04 m^2
19. $\frac{1}{2}$ **21.** $\frac{2}{5}$ **23.** $\frac{5}{6}$

13.3 Problem Solving Strategies (p. 641)
1. 18 ways   **3.** 6 ways   **5.** 2 tokens   **7.** 14 adult tickets   **9.** 30 more blue faces

13.3 Getting Ready to Practice (p. 644)
1. Independent; the first event does not affect the second event because you put the first marble back in the bag.   **3.** $\frac{1}{6}$ **5.** $\frac{1}{3}$

13.3 Practice and Problem Solving
(pp. 644–645)   **7.** $\frac{3}{4}$ **9.** $\frac{1}{4}$ **11.** $\frac{1}{2}$ **13.** $\frac{1}{12}$ **15.** $\frac{1}{3}$ **17.** $\frac{2}{3}$
19. $\frac{1}{8}$ **21.** $\frac{1}{2}$ **23.** heads 3 times, tails exactly 1 time, tails at least 2 times, heads at most 2 times
25. Increase; there are now fewer total tiles but the same number of red tiles.   **27.** 14.375; 14; 14
29. 16   **31.** 18   **33.** $5.70

13.1–13.3 Notebook Review (pp. 646–647)
1. rolling an odd number   **2.** A combination is a grouping of objects in which order is not important. A permutation is an arrangement of objects in which order is important.   **3.** $\frac{1}{6}$ **4.** 0
5. $\frac{5}{6}$ **6.** ACT, ATC, CAT, CTA, TAC, TCA; $\frac{2}{3}$ **7.** No, a percent greater than 100% is always greater than 1 and probabilities cannot be greater than 1.
8. The sum of their probabilities is 1. *Sample answer:* They have no outcomes in common and contain all the outcomes of the experiment.

13.4 Getting Ready to Practice (p. 650)
1. It can distort the data.   **3.** less than; less than

13.4 Practice and Problem Solving
(pp. 650–652)   **5.** B; the line in graph B is not as steep as than the line in graph A.   **7.** 2 times more

9. the data values   **11.** To make it appear that the team usually wins a lot of games.

13.

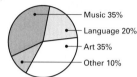

Favorite Electives

- Music 35%
- Language 20%
- Art 35%
- Other 10%

15. *Sample answer:* To show that the houses in the region are not that expensive.

17. *Sample:*

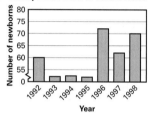

Grizzly Bears Born in Yellowstone

21. $\frac{3}{4}$ **23.** 164

13.5 Getting Ready to Practice (p. 655)

1. stems: 1, 2, 3; leaves: 2, 4, 7, 1, 9, 5, 6, 8, 9

3.
```
0 | 7 8 9
1 | 0 0 2 3 3 4 5 5
2 | 1 2 5
3 |
4 | 0
    Key: 2 | 1 = 21
```

13.5 Practice and Problem Solving
(pp. 655–656)

5.
```
1 | 5 6 8 8 8
2 | 1 4 5 5 8
3 | 1 2 2
4 | 1
    Key: 3 | 2 = 32
```

7.
```
0 | 5 7 9
1 | 5 6
2 |
3 | 0 3 5 5 8
4 | 1 9
5 | 1 2 5
    Key: 3 | 5 = 35
```

9. about 80.7; 73; 73; 62   **11.** *Sample answer:* The longest match lasted 62 minutes longer than the shortest match; the shortest match lasted more than an hour less than the longest match.

13. 7 games   **15.** *Sample answer:* Mode; a lighter phone would be preferable over a heavier phone.

17–20.

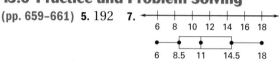

21. Mode; the mode is 5, so you could say your score of 7 is above average.   **23.** >

13.6 Getting Ready to Practice (p. 659)

1. median = 13, lower quartile = 10, upper quartile = 18, lower extreme = 2, upper extreme = 24   **3.**

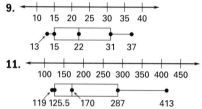

13.6 Practice and Problem Solving
(pp. 659–661) **5.** 192   **7.**

9.

11.

13. 1970s: median = 131, range = 107; 1980s: median = 132.5, range = 89; 1990s: median = 151, range = 79   **15.** 1968–2002; the median and upper and lower quartiles for 1968–2002 are all less than the median and upper and lower quartiles for 1928–1964.   **17.** 75%   **21.** 12
23. 2.481

13.7 Practice and Problem Solving
(pp. 664–665) **7.** line plot

9.
```
1 | 9
2 |
3 | 1 4 8 9
4 | 1 2 5 9
5 | 8
6 | 0
7 | 0
    Key: 3 | 4 = 34   median = 41.5
```

11. bar graph

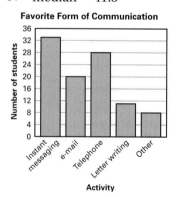

Favorite Form of Communication

13. Line plot and stem-and-leaf plot; a line plot shows how often each piece of data occurs and a stem-and-leaf plot shows each piece of data.

15.

```
0 | 8 9
1 | 0 2 2 2 4 5 6 8
2 |
3 | 2 2 4 5 6 7
4 | 1
    Key: 3 | 2 = 32
```

17. 21   **19.** 59

13.4–13.7 Notebook Review (pp. 666–667)

1. stem: 3, leaf: 6   **2.** 17   **3.** about $\frac{1}{2}$; about 72%

4.

```
0 | 5 7 8
1 | 0 2 5 9
2 | 4 8
3 | 1 6
4 |
5 | 0
    Key: 3 | 1 = 31
```

5.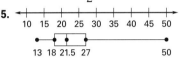

6.
Low Temperatures

7. The scale can appear to distort the data.

Chapter Review (pp. 668–669)

1. complementary   **3.** permutation   **5.** lower extreme, upper extreme   **7.** $\frac{1}{2}$ **9.** 1   **11.** $\frac{16}{31}$

13. Pittsburgh hat, Pittsburgh T-shirt, Pittsburgh poster, Dallas hat, Dallas T-shirt, Dallas poster, Miami hat, Miami T-shirt, Miami poster, Los Angeles hat, Los Angeles T-shirt, Los Angeles poster   **15.** Leah and Sarah, Leah and Jenny, Leah and Michelle, Sarah and Leah, Sarah and Jenny, Sarah and Michelle, Jenny and Leah, Jenny and Sarah, Jenny and Michelle, Michelle and Leah, Michelle and Sarah, Michelle and Jenny

17. $\frac{1}{9}$ **19.** $\frac{1}{9}$ **21.** $\frac{1}{5}$; $\frac{1}{2}$ **23.**

```
3 | 2
4 | 1 5 8
5 | 2 5 9
6 | 0
    Key: 4 | 8 = 48
```

25. 48   **27.** 50   **29.**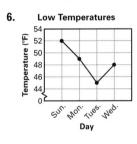

Skills Review Handbook

Whole Number Place Value (p. 684)
1. tens' place; $(5 \times 1000) + (8 \times 100) + (9 \times 10)$; five thousand eight hundred ninety   **3.** ones' place; $(9 \times 100,000) + (6 \times 1000) + (2 \times 100) + (1 \times 1)$; nine hundred six thousand, two hundred one   **5.** 105,300   **7.** 42,600

Comparing and Ordering Whole Numbers (p. 685)   **1.** 0, 3, 8, 10, 11   **3.** 78, 79, 85, 87, 90   **5.** 508, 510, 512, 518, 521   **7.** 207 > 148   **9.** 3465 < 3492   **11.** 21,539 > 9847

Rounding Whole Numbers (p. 686)   **1.** tens' place; 90   **3.** ones' place; 200   **5.** 4280   **7.** 11,000   **9.** 144,000

Fact Families (p. 687)   **1.** 5; 5; 5; 14   **3.** 8; 4; 4; 4; 8   **5.** 15 − 8 = 7 or 15 − 7 = 8

Addition and Subtraction on a Number Line (p. 688)   **1.** 13   **3.** 11   **5.** 13   **7.** 20   **9.** 6   **11.** 8   **13.** 8   **15.** 16

Addition and Subtraction of Whole Numbers (p. 689)   **1.** 71   **3.** 240   **5.** 400   **7.** 1412   **9.** 17   **11.** 219   **13.** 149   **15.** 1179

Multiplication of Whole Numbers (p. 690)   **1.** 3280   **3.** 962   **5.** 6076   **7.** 60,450   **9.** 147,038   **11.** 46,570   **13.** 12,300   **15.** 23,190,000

Division of Whole Numbers (p. 691)   **1.** 142   **3.** 54   **5.** 405   **7.** 58   **9.** 13 R7   **11.** 24 R57

Estimating Sums (p. 692)   **1–9.** Estimates may vary.   **1.** 1300   **3.** 1800   **5.** 10,000   **7.** 160   **9.** 1200

Estimating Differences (p. 693)   **1.** 700; 900   **3.** 400; 600   **5.** 300; 500   **7.** 400; 600   **9.** 0; 2000   **11.** 3000; 5000   **13.** 4000; 6000   **15.** 1000; 3000

Estimating Products (p. 694)   **1.** 800; 1500   **3.** 2100; 3200   **5.** 3000; 8000   **7.** 12,000; 21,000   **9.** 280,000; 400,000   **11.** 60,000; 140,000   **13–27.** Estimates may vary.   **13.** 10,500   **15.** 52,800   **17.** 14,000   **19.** 45,000   **21.** 630,000   **23.** 150,000   **25.** 90,000   **27.** 736,100

Estimating Quotients (p. 695) **1.** 50; 60
3. 60; 70 **5.** 30; 40 **7.** 200; 300 **9.** 300; 400
11. 400; 500 **13.** 1100; 1200 **15.** 800; 900
17-27. Estimates may vary. **17.** 2 **19.** 10 **21.** 11
23. 7 **25.** 100 **27.** 80

Solving Problems Using Addition and Subtraction (p. 696) **1.** $9 **3.** 26 items **5.** $7

Solving Problems Using Multiplication and Division (p. 697) **1.** 60 folders **3.** 4 boxes
5. $20

Operations with Money (p. 698) **1.** $2.02
3. $58.08

Adding and Subtracting Decimals (p. 699)
1. 41.4 **3.** 143 **5.** 11.29 **7.** 20.13 **9.** 57.22
11. 16.5 **13.** 6.88 **15.** 5.76 **17.** 19.87

Modeling Fractions (p. 700) **1.** $\frac{3}{4}$ **3.** $\frac{1}{2}$ **5.** $\frac{5}{14}$
7. $\frac{4}{9}$ **9.** $\frac{5}{9}$ **11.** $\frac{3}{10}$

Units of Time (p. 701) **1.** 240 **3.** 4 **5.** 12 **7.** 52
9. 2; 2 **11.** 1; 16

Perimeter and Area (p. 702) **1.** 10 in. **3.** 15 cm
5. 21 square units

Venn Diagrams and Logical Reasoning
(p. 703) **1.**

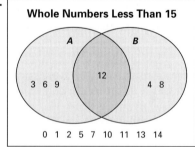

Whole Numbers Less Than 15

3. Sometimes. *Sample answer:* 12 is in both set *A*
and set *B*, but 6, for example, is only in set *A*.
5. Never. *Sample answer:* Set *C* consists of
numbers less than 15.

Reading Bar Graphs (p. 704) **1.** 20 students
3. period 2 **5.** 7 more students **7.** periods 2 and 3

Reading Line Graphs (p. 705) **1.** Thursday
3. 8 in. **5.** decrease **7.** Monday

Reading a Pictograph (p. 706) **1.** brown;
14 students **3.** 8 pictures **5.** about 4 pictures
7. Friday

Making a Pictograph (p. 707)
1. *Sample:*

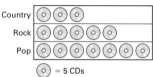

CDs Sold in One Day

Extra Practice

Chapter 1 (p. 708) **1.** 203 **3.** 51 **5.** 170 **7.** 39
9. add 4 to the previous number; 21, 25
11. divide the previous number by 2; 100, 50
13-19. Estimates may vary. **13.** 370 **15.** 8 **17.** 760
19. 1500 **21.** 343 **23.** 8 **25.** 14 **27.** 21 **29.** 6
31. 11 **33.** 27 **35.** 11 **37.** 14 **39.** 7 **41.** 22 years
old **43.** 3 **45.** 2 **47.** 4 **49.** 0

Chapter 2 (p. 709) **1.** 6 cm **3.** miles, kilometers
5. 18 in.; 18 in.^{2} **7.** 240 km **9.** 840 km
11.

Heights	Tally	Frequency
4	II	2
5	JHT I	6
6	IIII	4
7		0
8	I	1

13.

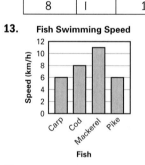

Fish Swimming Speed

14-18.

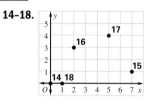

19.

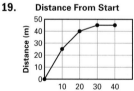

Distance From Start

21. 120 sesame bagels

23. 33, 31, no mode, 27; mean; it is in the middle
of all the data.

Chapter 3 (p. 710) **1.** 50.42 **3.** eight thousandths
5. one and eleven hundredths **7.** seven and two
hundred seventy-five ten-thousandths **9.** 0.15 m
11. < **13.** > **15.** = **17.** 2.01, 2.12, 2.3 **19.** 13.3
21. 0.7 **23.** 0.009 **25.** 2 **27.** 19 **29.** 32 **31.** 14
33. 10.81 **35.** 2.14 **37.** 2.45 **39.** 1.84

Chapter 4 (p. 711) **1.** 32.52 **3.** 125.18 **5.** 67.2
7. 203 **9.** 2.08 **11.** 5.0307 **13.** 3.2 **15.** 3.625
17. 1.5 **19.** 1.1 **21.** 205 **23.** 1.798 **25.** 0.935
27. 93.8 **29.** 1.2 **31.** 5 **33.** 330 **35.** 0.9
37. kilograms **39.** kiloliters **41.** liters **43.** 480,000
45. 67,400 **47.** 1000 **49.** < **51.** > **53.** <

Chapter 5 (p. 712) **1.** 406 is divisible by 2, but
not by 3, 5, 6, 9 or 10. **3.** 534 is divisible by 2, 3,
and 6, but not by 5, 9, or 10. **5.** 510 is divisible by
2, 3, 5, 6, and 10, but not by 9. **7.** composite
9. neither **11.** 5×19 **13.** $2^2 \times 19$ **15.** $5^2 \times 7$
17. 4 **19.** 5 **21.** Sample answer: $\frac{4}{10}, \frac{6}{15}$
23. Sample answer: $\frac{6}{20}, \frac{9}{30}$ **25.** yes **27.** no; $\frac{1}{14}$
29. no; $\frac{4}{5}$ **31.** 24 **33.** 40 **35.** $\frac{4}{5}, \frac{13}{15}, \frac{9}{10}$ **37.** $\frac{3}{20}, \frac{2}{9},$
$\frac{4}{15}, \frac{2}{5}$ **39.** $\frac{35}{9}$ **41.** $\frac{17}{7}$ **43.** $2\frac{1}{6}$ **45.** $3\frac{2}{5}$ **47.** $1\frac{7}{12}$
49. $\frac{17}{8}, 2\frac{1}{4}, \frac{55}{24}, 2\frac{1}{3}$ **51.** $\frac{19}{20}$ **53.** $2\frac{2}{25}$ **55.** $\frac{129}{200}$
57. 1.75 **59.** $5.1\overline{6}$

Chapter 6 (p. 713) **1.** $\frac{1}{2}$ **3.** 0 **5.** 4 **7.** 9 **9.** $\frac{3}{4}$
11. $\frac{4}{15}$ **13.** $\frac{2}{5}$ **15.** $\frac{2}{5}$ **17.** $\frac{7}{18}$ **19.** $\frac{15}{16}$ **21.** $\frac{19}{30}$ **23.** $\frac{19}{20}$
25. $2\frac{2}{3}$ **27.** $16\frac{1}{4}$ **29.** $7\frac{4}{7}$ **31.** $\frac{1}{8}$ **33.** $1\frac{6}{13}$ **35.** $1\frac{3}{4}$
37. $\frac{3}{5}$ **39.** $2\frac{1}{5}$ **41.** 3 h 35 min **43.** 2 h 20 min 50 sec
45. 7 h 15 min **47.** 2 h 30 min **49.** 5 h 45 min
51. 1 h 35 min **53.** 8 h 15 min

Chapter 7 (p. 714) **1.** 9 **3.** 27 **5.** 6 **7.** 16 **9.** $1\frac{1}{4}$
11. $\frac{2}{27}$ **13.** $7\frac{1}{3}$ **15.** $1\frac{1}{6}$ **17.** $\frac{5}{24}$ **19.** $\frac{4}{25}$ **21.** 3
23. $\frac{9}{20}$ **25.** $2\frac{11}{12}$ **27.** $2\frac{1}{2}$ **29.** No. Sample answer:
Use multiplication to find the total amount of
fabric needed. **31.** pounds **33.** ounces **35.** 14
37. 1; 9; $1\frac{9}{16}$ **39.** 2250 lb **41.** 6 lb **43.** 4 yd 1 ft

Chapter 8 (p. 715) **1.** 2 : 3 **3.** 1 : 5 **5.** 4 : 3 **7.** 20
9. 9 **11.** 19 cm **13.** $\frac{275 \text{ visitors}}{1 \text{ hour}}$ **15.** $\frac{200 \text{ words}}{1 \text{ page}}$
17. 2 **19.** $11\frac{1}{5}$ **21.** 20 ft by 16 ft **23.** 0.18, $\frac{9}{50}$
25. 0.025, $\frac{1}{40}$ **27.** 85% **29.** 83% **31.** 0.5%
33. $\frac{2}{3}$, 67%, 0.76, $\frac{5}{6}$ **35.** 18 **37.** 56 **39.** $480

Chapter 9 (p. 716) **1.** *Sample answer:* $\overrightarrow{BC}$ and
$\overrightarrow{BF}$; $\overline{BD}$ and $\overline{BA}$ **3.** $\overleftrightarrow{ED}$ and $\overleftrightarrow{DF}$ **5.** $\angle AED$
7. right; obtuse; acute; straight **9.** 60°; 100°; 80°
11. All **13.** Some **15.** triangle; no **17.** hexagon;
no **19.** $\overline{XY}$ and $\overline{DE}$, $\overline{YZ}$ and $\overline{EF}$, $\overline{ZX}$ and $\overline{FD}$; $\angle X$
and $\angle D$, $\angle Y$ and $\angle E$, $\angle Z$ and $\angle F$

21. yes **23.** yes

Chapter 10 (p. 717) **1.** 360 ft^2 **3.** 13.5 mm^2
5. 30 cm^2 **7.** 110 cm; $\frac{22}{7}$; 35 is a multiple of 7.
9. 44 in.; $\frac{22}{7}$; 7 is a multiple of 7. **11.** 50.2 cm^2
13. 706.5 ft^2 **15.** 434 cm^2
17. Spring Fundraiser Volunteers **19.**

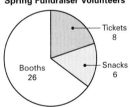
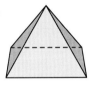

21.

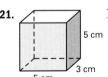

110 cm² **23.** 75 cm³; 240 in.³

Chapter 11 (p. 718) **1.** -4, 18, 0 **3.** > **5.** <
7. -3, 0, 2, 3, 5 **9.** $-9, -7, -6, 8, 9$ **11.** 4
13. -10 **15.** 0 **17.** -14 **19.** 16 **21.** -17
23. -28 **25.** -9 **27.** -40 **29.** 140 **31.** 32
33. 99 **35.** -8 **37.** 5 **39.** -3 **41.** -25

43. Quadrant I

45. 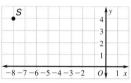 Quadrant II

47. 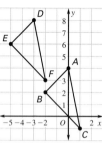 $D(-3, 8), E(-5, 6), F(-2, 3)$

49. reflection   **51.** translation

Chapter 12 (p. 719) **1.** $n + 7$ **3.** $20 - n$
5. $8n = 32$ **7.** $\frac{y}{6} = 5$ **9.** 29   **11.** 14   **13.** 16
15. 25   **17.** 10   **19.** 9   **21.** 60   **23.** 21

25.

Input, x	Output, y
4	1
8	5
12	9
16	13
20	17

27.

Input, x	Output, y
4	13
8	21
12	29
16	37
20	45

29. $c = 6p$

31. *Sample answer:* $g = \frac{q}{4}$

Quarts, q	Gallons, g
2	$\frac{1}{2}$
4	1
6	$1\frac{1}{2}$
8	2

33.

Input, x	Output, y
0	-2
1	-1
2	0
3	1
4	2

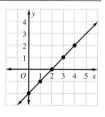

35.

Input, x	Output, y
0	3
1	$3\frac{1}{2}$
2	4
3	$4\frac{1}{2}$
4	5

37. 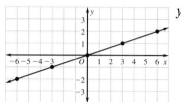 $y = \frac{x}{3}$

Chapter 13 (p. 720) **1.** $\frac{4}{7}$ **3.** 1   **5.** You do not choose a multiple of 3; $\frac{5}{7}$.   **7.** 11, 12, 13, 14, 21, 22, 23, 24, 31, 32, 33, 34, 41, 42, 43, 44   **9.** $\frac{1}{4}$

11.

```
0 | 4 6 7 7 8 8 8 9
1 | 1 2 5 6 8 9
2 | 0 0 1 4 4 9

Key: 1 | 5 = 15
```

13. 25

15. Line graph; it shows change over time.